Contributions to Finance and Accounting

The book series 'Contributions to Finance and Accounting' features the latest research from research areas like financial management, investment, capital markets, financial institutions, FinTech and financial innovation, accounting methods and standards, reporting, and corporate governance, among others. Books published in this series are primarily monographs and edited volumes that present new research results, both theoretical and empirical, on a clearly defined topic. All books are published in print and digital formats and disseminated globally.

This book series is indexed in Scopus.

Peter Brusov · Tatiana Filatova

Taxes and Taxation

Innovative Approaches in Corporate Finance, Investments, and Dividend Policy

Springer

Peter Brusov
Department of Accounting and Information Technology
National Chung Cheng University
Chia-Yi, Taiwan

Tatiana Filatova
Financial University under the Government of Russian Federation
Moscow, Russia

ISSN 2730-6038 ISSN 2730-6046 (electronic)
Contributions to Finance and Accounting
ISBN 978-3-032-11076-3 ISBN 978-3-032-11077-0 (eBook)
https://doi.org/10.1007/978-3-032-11077-0

This Springer imprint is published by the registered company Springer Nature Switzerland AG
The registered company address is: Gewerbestrasse 11, 6330 Cham, Switzerland

Dedicated to the eternal love
that touched us with its wing
and made us happy,
and without which life is meaningless.

Preface

An innovative approach in the field of *taxes and taxation* has been developed, within the framework of the Brusov – Filatova – Orekhova (BFO) theory and in its perpetuity limit — Modigliani–Miller (MM) theory under taking into account the conditions of the actual functioning of companies (frequency and method of paying taxes advanced or at the ends of periods), variable income of the company, etc.).

The analysis examines the impact of the above conditions on the current value of taxes received, which could lead to improvements in tax legislation, as well as the impact of taxes under these conditions on the key financial indicators of the company and its investment projects.

Based on the results obtained, recommendations were developed for the Regulator on the amount, frequency and procedure for paying income tax, as well as the possibility of differentiating tax payments depending on the company's debt burden and other factors. Recommendations were also developed for companies on choosing the method and frequency of tax payment in accordance with tax legislation.

The impact of the tax burden on the company's dividend policy is analyzed. A number of innovative effects are identified that can significantly affect the tax policy of regulators and management decisions of the company's management, in particular in the area of dividend policy.

Kronburg, Moscow, Russia
September 2025

Peter Brusov
Tatiana Filatova

Competing Interests The authors have no competing interests to declare that are relevant to the content of this manuscript.

About This Book

An innovative approach in the field of *taxes and taxation* has been developed, within the framework of the Brusov—Filatova—Orekhova (BFO) theory and in its perpetuity limit—Modigliani–Miller (MM) theory under taking into account the conditions of the actual functioning of companies (frequency and method of paying taxes advanced or at the ends of periods), variable income of the company, etc.).

The analysis examines the impact of the above conditions on the current value of taxes received, which could lead to improvements in tax legislation, as well as the impact of taxes under these conditions on the key financial indicators of the company and its investment projects.

Based on the results obtained, recommendations were developed for the Regulator on the amount, frequency and procedure for paying income tax, as well as the possibility of differentiating tax payments depending on the company's debt burden and other factors. Recommendations were also developed for companies on choosing the method and frequency of tax payment in accordance with tax legislation.

The impact of the tax burden on the company's dividend policy is analyzed. A number of innovative effects are identified that can significantly affect the tax policy of regulators and management decisions of the company's management, in particular in the area of dividend policy.

Contents

About the Authors

Peter Brusov is professor at the Financial University under the Government of the Russian Federation in Moscow (Russia). He is an expert in financial management, corporate finance, investments, ratings, taxation, business valuation. He is a co-author of the famous Brusov-Filatova-Orekhova theory, which replaced the well-known Modigliani-Miller theory, created by Nobel Prize Laureates. As well he is a co-author of the CAPM 2.0 model, which generalized the famous CAPM model for accounting the financial risk along with business risk. Peter Brusov is the author of the qualitatively new approach to business valuation. He has been a visiting Professor of Northwestern University (USA), Cornell University (USA), Osaka City University (Japan) and National Chung Cheng University (Taiwan) among other places. He is the author of over 550 research publications including nine monographs, numerous textbooks and articles.

Tatiana Filatova is professor at the Financial University under the Government of the Russian Federation in Moscow (Russia). She is an expert in financial management, corporate finance, investments, ratings, taxation, business valuation. Tatiana Filatova is a co-author of the famous Brusov-Filatova-Orekhova theory, which replaced the well-known Modigliani-Miller theory, created by Nobel Prize Laureates. As well she is a co-author of the CAPM 2.0 model, which generalized the famous CAPM model for accounting the financial risk along with business risk. Tatiana Filatova is the author of the qualitatively new approach to business valuation. In the past 20 years, she has been Dean of the faculties of financial management, state and municipal government at the Financial University. Tatiana Filatova is the author of over 300 research publications including eight monographs, numerous textbooks and articles.

Part I
Introduction

Chapter 1
Taxes Functions

1.1 Historical Remarks

Economists of the eighteenth and nineteenth centuries, studying the effects of taxes at the microeconomic level, noted their negative impact on production, consumption and investment. Thus, A. Smith believed that unreasonable taxes are more burdensome for society than useful for the state. According to D. Ricardo, each tax has an oppressive effect on entrepreneurs in its own way, and the "great evil" of taxation lies in their general effect. A. Marshall identified a pattern according to which the pressure of a tax on some factors is partially transferred to others, for example, from consumers to producers and back. A well-known model shows how the introduction of an excise tax leads to a decrease in equilibrium demand and supply and an increase in the equilibrium price, i.e. the tax has a depressing effect on the economy.

In the twentieth century, the works of D. Keynes, P. Samuelson and other economists described the effect of taxes at the macroeconomic level and showed that taxes reduce disposable income, consumption, business activity and production. Based on Keynesian theory and the multiplier model, in many countries at different periods, the policy of increasing government spending was successfully applied, as well as the policy of reducing the tax burden, which was considered less effective, since the tax multiplier is less than the expenditure multiplier.

It is generally believed that increasing the tax burden does not promote economic growth. However, at the macroeconomic level, it can be shown that under certain conditions, increasing the tax burden not only does not reduce the rate of economic growth, but also increases it.

At the macroeconomic level, the tax burden can be used to optimize budget policy, achieving an increase in the rate of GDP growth. At the microeconomic level, it is possible to positively influence economic activity by making changes in the taxation of individual taxes.

P. Brusov and T. Filatova, *Taxes and Taxation*, Contributions to Finance and Accounting, https://doi.org/10.1007/978-3-032-11077-0_1

The macroeconomic model allows one to find the optimal tax burden at the macroeconomic level, but at the same time does not guarantee adequate implementation of individual taxes at the microeconomic level, each of which burdens taxpayers in its own way.

Tax legislation may deviate significantly from the theoretical recommendations of economic theory.

The basis of modern tax systems is the corporate profit tax, income tax (individual income tax), social tax (contributions to state extra-budgetary funds), sales tax (value added tax), and property tax of organizations.

In monograph the impact of corporate income tax rates on the key financial indicators of the company and on the effectiveness of investment projects is investigated. The impact of the tax burden on the company's dividend policy is analyzed. A number of innovative effects are identified that can significantly affect the tax policy of regulators and management decisions of the company's management, in particular in the area of dividend policy.

1.2 Taxes and Their Functions

Taxes serve several crucial functions in modern societies, going far beyond simply funding the government. Here are the primary functions:

1.2.1 Revenue Generation (Fiscal Function)

- Core Purpose: This is the most fundamental function. Taxes provide the government with the necessary financial resources to operate and fulfill its responsibilities.
- Funds Public Goods & Services: Pays for essential services that benefit society as a whole and wouldn't be efficiently provided by the private market, such as:
  - National defense, public safety (police, fire services)
  - Infrastructure (roads, bridges, public transportation, water/sewer systems)
  - Public education
  - Healthcare systems (public hospitals, subsidies, research)
  - Social security, unemployment benefits, welfare programs
  - Judicial system, regulatory agencies
  - Parks, libraries, museums

1.2.2 Redistribution of Income and Wealth

- Promoting Equity: Taxes (especially progressive income taxes and inheritance taxes) are used to reduce economic inequality.
- Social Safety Net: Revenue funds social programs (welfare, food stamps, housing assistance, pensions) that support low-income individuals, the elderly, the disabled, and the unemployed.
- Progressive Systems: Higher tax rates on higher incomes aim to take a larger share from those with greater ability to pay, redistributing resources to fund services that benefit lower-income groups.

1.2.3 Economic Stabilization and Management (Macroeconomic Function)

- Managing the Economy: Governments use tax policy as a tool to influence the overall economy:
- Stimulating Growth: Cutting taxes (especially for lower/middle-income earners or businesses) can boost consumer spending and business investment, stimulating economic activity during recessions.
- Cooling Inflation: Raising taxes can reduce disposable income and dampen demand, helping to control inflation during economic booms.
- Influencing Investment: Tax credits, deductions, and depreciation rules can incentivize specific types of investment (e.g., R&D, green energy, small businesses).

1.2.4 Resource Allocation (Correcting Market Failures - Microeconomic Function)

- "Sin Taxes" and Pigouvian Taxes: Taxes on goods with negative externalities (costs imposed on society, like pollution or health problems) aim to reduce consumption and make producers/consumers bear the true social cost. Examples include taxes on tobacco, alcohol, carbon emissions, and sugary drinks.
- Subsidies via Tax Breaks: Tax deductions, credits, and exemptions act as subsidies to encourage desirable activities (e.g., home ownership via mortgage interest deductions, charitable giving, education savings, energy efficiency).

1.2.5 Repricing Goods and Influencing Behavior (Social Engineering)

- Promoting Social Goals: Taxes can be designed to discourage harmful activities (like smoking or excessive fuel consumption) or encourage beneficial ones (like using renewable energy, saving for retirement, or having children - via child tax credits).
- Health & Environment: Taxes directly target behaviors impacting public health and the environment.

1.2.6 Representation and State-Building

- Historical Principle: The concept of "no taxation without representation" highlights the link between taxation and citizens' demands for accountable government. Paying taxes fosters an expectation of responsive governance.
- Building State Capacity: A functioning tax system is essential for a strong, capable state that can provide services and enforce laws.
- Civic Duty: Paying taxes is often seen as a fundamental civic responsibility, contributing to the collective good.

In essence, taxes are the primary mechanism through which:

- A government funds its operations and provides essential public services.
- Society collectively pays for shared needs and infrastructure.
- Economic inequality is addressed and a social safety net is maintained.
- The government steers economic activity and corrects market inefficiencies.
- Social goals and public health/environmental concerns are promoted.

The specific balance and emphasis on these functions vary significantly depending on a country's political philosophy, economic system, and social priorities.

Part II
Capital Structure Theories

Chapter 2
Capital Structure

2.1 Introduction

Under the capital structure, one understands the relationship between equity and debt capital of the company. Does capital structure affect the company's main settings, such as the cost of capital, profit, value of the company, and the others, and, if affects, how? Choice of an optimal capital structure, i.e., a capital structure, which minimizes the weighted average cost of capital, WACC, and maximizes the value of the company, *V*, is one of the most important tasks solved by financial manager and by the management of a company. The first serious study (and first quantitative study) of influence of capital structure of the company on its indicators of activities was the work by Modigliani and Miller (1958). Until this study, the approach existed (let us call it traditional), which was based on empirical data analysis.

2.2 Basic Theories of Capital Structure

2.2.1 A Historical Point of View

From a historical point of view, **five stages** in the development of the capital structure theory can be distinguished: **First** (before 1958)—the traditional approach, based on practical experience and existed before the appearance of the first quantitative theory by Modigliani and Miller (**the second stage**) (1958–1963) (Asquith and Mullins 1986; Baumol et al. 1982; Berk and De Marzo 2007). **The third stage** (1964–2008) is the numerous attempts of scientists to modify the Modigliani–Miller theory. **The fourth stage** (2008–2019) is the appearance of Brusov–Filatova–Orekhova (BFO) theory, which removed the main restriction of the Modigliani–Miller (MM) theory associated with the infinite life–time of the company (Bhattacharya 1978). And,

P. Brusov and T. Filatova, *Taxes and Taxation*, Contributions to Finance and Accounting, https://doi.org/10.1007/978-3-032-11077-0_2

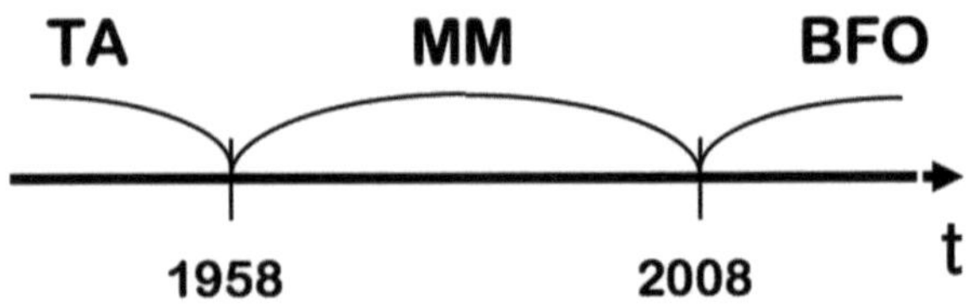

Fig. 2.1 The historical development of the theory of capital structure from the empirical traditional approach (TA) to the general theory of capital structure, BFO (Brusov–Filatova–Orekhova), through the perpetuity Modigliani–Miller theory

finally, **the fifth stage** (2019 up to now), which began a couple years ago and is associated with the adaptation of the two main theories of the capital structure (Brusov–Filatova–Orekhova and Modigliani–Miller) to the established financial practice of the company's functioning by taking into account the real conditions of their work (Brusov and Filatova 2021, 2022a, b; Brusov et al. 2021a, b, 2022a, b). (See also recently published monographs by the authors at Springer Nature Publishing (Brusov et al. 2021, 2022, 2023; Brusov and Filatova 2025a, b).

One of the most important assumptions of the Modigliani–Miller theory is that all financial flows and all companies are perpetuity. This limitation was lift out by Brusov–Filatova–Orekhova in 2008 (Filatova et al. 2008), who have created BFO (Brusov–Filatova–Orekhova) theory—modern theory of capital cost and capital structure for companies of arbitrary age (BFO-1 theory) and for companies of arbitrary life time (BFO-2 theory) (Brusov et al. 2018). Figure 2.1 shows the historical development of the theory of capital structure from the empirical traditional approach to the general theory of capital structure, BFO, through the perpetuity Modigliani–Miller theory.

One year companies were studied by Steve Myers in 2001, who showed that the weighted average cost of capital WACC is greater in this case than in the perpetual Modigliani–Miller case, and the value of company V is therefore less. Only two results for capital structure of the company were known up to 2008, when BFO theory has appeared: Modigliani–Miller for perpetuity companies and Myers for one-year company (see Fig. 2.2). The created BFO theory filled the entire interval between $t = 1$ and $t = \infty$. This expands capital structure theory for the companies of arbitrary ages and/or arbitrary life-time. Many new meaningful effects have been discovered in the BFO theory.

2.2.2 *The Empirical (Traditional) Approach*

In the traditional approach, based on practical experience and existing before the advent of the first quantitative theory of Modigliani and Miller, the weighted average cost of capital WACC and the associated capitalization of the company, $V = \text{CF}/\text{WACC}$, depend on the capital structure, the level of debt load, L. The cost

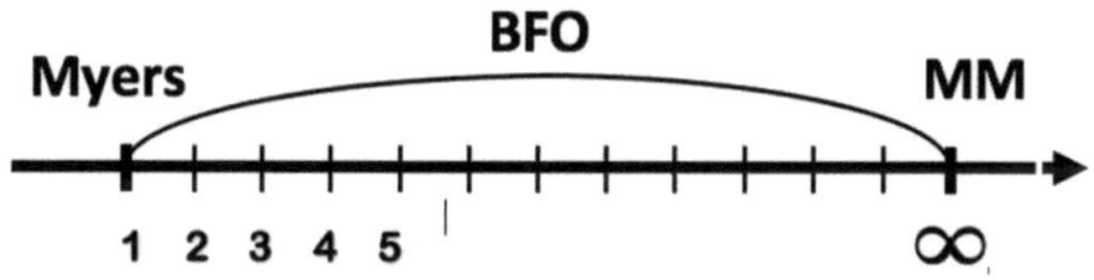

Fig. 2.2 Only two results for capital structure of the company were known before BFO theory: Modigliani–Miller (MM) for perpetuity companies and Myers for one-year company, while the created BFO theory filled the entire interval between n = 1 and $n = \infty$

of debt is always lower than the cost of equity, because the former has less risk due to the fact that the claims of creditors are satisfied before the claims of shareholders in the event of bankruptcy. As a result, an increase in the share of cheaper borrowed capital in the total capital structure to the limit that does not cause a violation of financial stability and an increase in the risk of bankruptcy leads to a decrease in the weighted average cost of capital WACC.

The return required by investors (equal to the cost of equity) is growing; however, its growth did not offset the benefits of using cheaper borrowed capital. Therefore, the traditional approach welcomes the increase in leverage $L = D/S$ and the associated increase in the value of the company $V = \mathrm{CF/WACC}$. The empirical traditional approach existed until the appearance of the first quantitative theory by Modigliani and Miller (1958).

Within the based on existing practical experience traditional approach the competition between the advantages of debt financing at a low leverage level and its disadvantages at a high leverage level forms the optimal capital structure, defined as the leverage level, at which WACC is minimal and company value, V, is maximum.

2.2.3 *The Modigliani–Miller Theory*

The Modigliani–Miller Theory with Taxes

There are two versions of the Modigliani–Miller theory: without taxes and with taxes. Without taxes the following expressions for *V*, *WACC* and k_e.

$$V = V_0 = \frac{EBIT}{k_0}, \tag{2.1}$$

were V_0 stands for the unlevered company value, EBIT stands for earnings before interest and taxes and k_0 stands for the equity cost at zero leverage level L.

From (2.1) one gets for the weighted average cost of capital WACC:

$$WACC = k_0. \tag{2.2}$$

From the expression for WACC

$$\text{WACC} = k_0 = k_e w_e + k_d w_d. \tag{2.3}$$

and accounting (2.1), one get for the equity cost, k_e,

$$\begin{aligned} k_e &= \frac{k_0}{w_e} - k_d \frac{w_d}{w_e} = \frac{k_0 (S + D)}{S} - k_d \frac{D}{S} \\ &= k_0 + (k_0 - k_d) \frac{D}{S} = k_0 + (k_0 - k_d) L \end{aligned} \tag{2.4}$$

Here, D stands for debt capital value; S stands for equity capital value; k_d and w_d stand for the cost and share of the company's debt capital; k_e and w_e stand for the equity capital cost and share. It is seen from (3.4), that the equity increases linearly with the leverage level.

The Modigliani–Miller Theory with Taxes

Within the framework of the Modigliani–Miller theory with taxes (Berk and De Marzo 2007), the following expression was postulated for the value of a company using borrowed funds, V,

$$V = V_0 + D \cdot t. \tag{2.5}$$

The expression for WACC immediately follows from (2.5)

$$WACC = k_0 \cdot (1 - w_d t) \tag{2.6}$$

The following formula for the cost of equity k_e can be obtained from (2.6) within the framework of the Modigliani–Miller theory with taxes

$$k_e = k_0 + L \cdot (k_0 - k_d)(1 - t) \tag{2.7}$$

Two formulas (2.7) (MM with taxes) and (2.4) (MM without taxes) differs by the multiplier (1–t), called the tax corrector. It is less than unit, thus the k_e (L) curve slope decreases with accounting the taxes.

2.2.4 *Modifications of Modigliani–Miller Theory*

Since the creation of Modigliani–Miller theory, numerous attempts have been made to improve and develop this theory. We will discuss some of these modifications below. One of them is Hamada model.

Hamada Model

The Modigliani–Miller theory, with accounting taxes has been united with CAPM (Capital Asset Pricing Model) in 1961 by Hamada. For the cost of equity of leveraged company the below formula has been derived

$$k_e = k_F + (k_M - k_F)b_U + (k_M - k_F)b_U\frac{D}{S}(1 - T), \qquad (2.8)$$

Here b_U is the β–coefficient of the unlevered company. First term represents risk–free profitability k_F, second term—business risk premium, $(k_M - k_F)b_U$, and third term—financial risk premium $(k_M - k_F)b_U\frac{D}{S}(1 - T)$.

In the case of a unlevered company ($D = 0$), the financial risk (the third term) is zero, and its shareholders receive only a business risk premium.

Equating CAPM formula to right side of (2.8), one gets:

$$k_F + (k_M - k_F)b_U = k_F + (k_M - k_F)b_U + (k_M - k_F)b_U\frac{D}{S}(1 - T) \qquad (2.9)$$

or

$$b = b_U\left(1 + \frac{D}{S}(1 - T)\right). \qquad (2.10)$$

Note, that Hamada's empirical result regarding the inclusion of financial risk alongside business risk, as described by the classical CAPM model, was shown by Brusov et al. (2024) to be inaccurate. Brusov et al. created an innovative model, CAPM 2.0, which correctly describes financial risk alongside business risk (Brusov et al. 2024). It was shown that along with the renormalization of the beta coefficient to the level of leverage described by the Hamada model, an additional term appears in the model, that depends on leverage level, L, debt cost, k_d, risk free profitability, k_F, and tax corrector, (1-T). This term is absent in Hamada's model and can be noticeable at high leverage levels L and large differences between debt cost, k_d and risk free profitability, k_F.

Below are the formulas for the equity cost, k_e, debt cost, k_d and WACC in the CAPM model and (in parenthesis) in the the Modigliani–Miller theory (Modigliani and Miller 1958, 1963; Miller and Modigliani 1966).

The equity cost for unlevered company:

$$k_e = k_F + \left(\overline{k}_M - k_F\right)\beta_U, \ (k_e = k_0). \qquad (2.11)$$

The equity cost for levered company:

$$k_e = k_F + \left(\overline{k}_M - k_F\right)\beta_e, \ (k_e = k_0 + (1 - T)(k_0 - k_d)L). \qquad (2.12)$$

The debt cost:

$$k_{\mathrm{d}} = k_{\mathrm{F}} + \left(\bar{k}_{\mathrm{M}} - k_{\mathrm{F}}\right)\beta_{\mathrm{d}},\ (k_{\mathrm{d}} = k_{\mathrm{F}};\ \beta_{\mathrm{d}} = 0).$$

The weighted average cost of capital WACC

$$\mathrm{WACC} = k_{\mathrm{e}}w_{\mathrm{e}} + k_{\mathrm{d}}w_{\mathrm{d}}(1 - T), \quad (\mathrm{WACC} = k_0(1 - Tw_{\mathrm{d}})). \tag{2.13}$$

The Cost of Capital Under Risky Debt

In the Modigliani–Miller theory there are two assets types: risky equity and risk-free debt). But assuming about the risk of bankruptcy of company and the ability to nonpayment of debt may change the situation with debt. It has been shown by Stiglitz (1969) and Rubinstein (1973) that the assumption concerning risky debt does not change the company value with respect to the Modigliani and Miller results under free of risk debt (Modigliani and Miller 1958, 1963; Miller and Modigliani 1966). However, the debt cost is changed from a constant value $k_{\mathrm{d}} = k_{\mathrm{F}}$ to variable one. As Hsia (1981), based on the models of pricing options, Modigliani–Miller and CAPM, has shown in the formula for the net discount profit, a term, reflecting tax shield should be discounted at the rate

$$k'_{\mathrm{d}} = k_{\mathrm{F}} + (k_0 - k_{\mathrm{F}})N(-d_1)\frac{1}{w_{\mathrm{d}}}, \tag{2.14}$$

where

$$d_1 = \frac{-\ln w_{\mathrm{d}} + k_{\mathrm{F}}t}{\sigma\sqrt{t}}k_{\mathrm{F}} + \frac{1}{2}\sigma\sqrt{t}, \tag{2.15}$$

$N(-d_1)$—cumulative normal distribution of probability of random value d_1 and t—a moment of payment a credit.

The Account of Corporate and Individual Taxes (Miller Model)

Modigliani and Miller (1963) have considered only corporate taxes, but they did not take into account the individual taxes of investors.

Miller (1977) has developed the model with account of the corporate and individual taxes and has studied the impact of leverage on the company value.

The model is described by the following formula for levered company value

$$V_{\mathrm{L}} = V_{\mathrm{U}} + \frac{I(1 - T_{\mathrm{d}})}{k_{\mathrm{d}}}\left[1 - \frac{(1 - T_{\mathrm{C}})(1 - T_{\mathrm{S}})}{(1 - T_{\mathrm{d}})}\right]. \tag{2.16}$$

Here first term means the unlevered company value

$$V_{\mathrm{U}} = \frac{\mathrm{EBIT}(1 - T_{\mathrm{C}})(1 - T_{\mathrm{S}})}{k_0}. \tag{2.17}$$

where, T_S stands for the tax on income of an individual investor from his ownership by corporation stock rate, T_C stands for the tax rate on corporate income, T_D stands for the tax rate on interest income from the provision of investor–individuals of credits to other investors and companies.

The Miller model estimates the value of levered company, accounting the corporate tax, as well as tax on individuals. Second term of sum in the Miller formula

$$\left[1 - \frac{(1 - T_{\mathrm{C}})(1 - T_{\mathrm{S}})}{(1 - T_{\mathrm{d}})}\right]D, \tag{2.18}$$

represents the gains from use of debt capital. This term replaces the tax shield in the Modigliani–Miller model with corporate taxes:

$$V_{\mathrm{L}} = V_{\mathrm{U}} + TD. \tag{2.19}$$

Alternative expression for WACC

Alternative formula for the WACC, different from Modigliani–Miller one has been derived in (Farber et al. 2006; Fernandez 2006; Berk and De Marzo 2007; Harris and Pringle 1985) from the WACC definition and the balance identity (see as well Berk and De Marzo 2007):

$$WACC = k_0(1 - w_d T) - k_d t w_d + k_{TS} t w_d, \tag{2.20}$$

where k_0, k_d and k_{TS} are the expected returns respectively on the unlevered company, the debt and the tax shield.

Some additional conditions are required Eq. (2.20) practical applicability. If the WACC is constant over time, as it stated in (Farber et al. 2006) the levered company capitalization is found by discounting with the WACC of the unlevered company.

In textbooks (Berk and De Marzo 2007; Harris and Pringle 1985) formulas for the special cases, where the WACC is constant, could be found.

In 1963 Modigliani and Miller assume that the debt value D is constant. Then, as the expected after-tax cash-flow of the unlevered firm is fixed, V_0 is constant as well. By assumption, $k_{TS} = k_D$ and the value of the tax shield is TS = tD. Thus, the capitalization of the company V is a constant and the alternative formula (2.20) becomes a formula for a constant WACC:

$$WACC = k_0(1 - w_d T) \tag{2.21}$$

Because the debt k_d and the tax shield k_{TS} have debt nature it seems reasonable that the expected returns on they are equals as suggested by "classical" Modigliani–Miller (MM) theory, which has been modified by Brusov et al. for cases of practical meanings.

The Miles–Ezzell Model Versus the Modigliani–Miller Theory

Denis M. Becker (2021) discussed the differences between the Modigliani–Miller theory (1958, 1963) and the Miles–Ezzell model (1980), which deal with the stochasticity of free cash flows. The Modigliani–Miller theory considers a stationary process, while in the Miles–Ezzell model the process is stochastic. The author conducts a numerical experiment that allows you to determine the values and discount rates using a risk–neutral approach. He analyzes three formulas.

Modigliani–Miller theory (1958, 1963)

$$WACC = k_0 \cdot (1 - w_d t) \tag{2.22}$$

Miles–Ezzell model (1980),

$$WACC = k_0 - t \cdot w_d \cdot k_f \cdot \frac{1 + k_0}{1 + k_f} \tag{2.23}$$

Cooper and Nyborg (2006)

$$WACC = k_0 - k_f \cdot w_d t \tag{2.24}$$

where k_f stands for the risk–free rate, which equals the required return of the debt holders.

The author shows that in the Miles–Ezzell model, all cash flows and the values depend on the path, in contrast to the Modigliani–Miller theory. Also, in the Miles–Ezzell model, all discount rates are time independent, with the exception of the discount rate used to discount tax shields, which depends on the duration of the cash flows. Conversely, in the Modigliani–Miller theory, all discount rates change over time, except for the constant tax shield discount rate. This affects the applicability of the well–known formula for annuities and the development of models for estimating both finite and perpetual cash flows.

In this paper Becker (2021) raises the issue of paying the debt body together with payment of interest on the debt. Regarding this issue we would like to note that in both classical MM and BFO theories, the body of the debt is not paid. In the framework of the Modigliani–Miller theory, such an account is fundamentally impossible, while in the BFO theory it can be done and was done in the framework of the BFO-2 theory, where the amount of debt D decreases with time. This decrease in the value of debt D results in a decrease in the tax shield (see BFO-2 theory).

2.3 Trade-off Theory

During decades one of the main theory of capital structure was the trade-off theory. There are two modifications of trade-off theory: the static and dynamic (Brennan et al. 1978; Leland et al. 1994; Brennan et al. 1984; Kane et al. 1984).

2.3.1 *Static Theory*

The static trade-off theory accounts the income tax and cost of bankruptcy. Within this theory the optimal capital structure is formed by the balancing act between the benefits of debt financing at low leverage level (from the tax shield from interest deduction) and the disadvantage of debt financing at high leverage level (from the increased financial distress and expected bankruptcy costs). The tax shield benefit is equal to the product of corporate income tax rate and the market value of debt and the expected bankruptcy costs are equal to the product of probability of bankruptcy and the estimated bankruptcy costs.

The static version of the trade-off theory does not take into account the costs of the adapting of the capital structure to the optimal one, economic behavior of managers, owners, and other participants of economical process, as well as a number of other factors.

2.3.2 *Dynamic Theory*

The dynamic version of trade–off theory suggests that the costs of adjusting the capital structure are high, and therefore companies will only change their capital structure if the benefits outweigh the costs. Therefore, there is an optimal range that varies on the outside of each lever but remains the same on the inside. Companies try to adjust their leverage when it reaches the edge of the optimal range. Depending on the type of adaptation costs, companies reach the target ratio faster or slower. Proportional changes involve a small adjustment, while fixed changes imply significant costs.

In the dynamic version of the trade–off theory, company capital structure decision in current period depends on the waiting company income in the next period.

As it has been shown within BFO theory (Brusov et al. 2013b, a), under increased financial distress costs and bankruptcy risk, the optimal capital structure is absent. This means that the trade-off theory does NOT work in either the static or dynamic version.

2.3.3 Proof of the Bankruptcy of the trade-off Theory

Brusov et al. (2013a) tested whether assumptions about risky debt financing (and about rising lending rates in the run–up to bankruptcy) do not lead to an increase in the weighted average cost of capital, WACC. They used the following model

$$k_0 = 24\ \%;\quad \overline{k}_{\mathrm{d}} = \left\{ \begin{array}{c} 0.07;\quad \text{at } L \leq 2 \\ 0.07 + 0.1(L-2);\quad \text{at } L > 2 \end{array} \right\}. \tag{2.25}$$

and showed that under the above conditions, WACC still decreases with leverage (Fig. 2.3).

This means there is no minimum for WACC with leverage change, and no maximum for company capitalization with leverage change. Thus, this means that there is no optimal capital structure in the famous theory of trade–offs. This fact has been explained by Brusov et al. (2013a, 2018). The explanation to this fact has been done within the Brusov–Filatova–Orekhova theory by studying the dependence of the equity cost k_e on leverage. The explanation for this fact is as follows. The dependence of the cost of equity k_e on the level of leverage undergoes significant changes when the growth in the cost of debt capital k_d with the level of leverage is included. The linear growth of the cost of equity k_e at a low level of leverage is replaced by its fall, starting from a certain value L_0. The value of L_0 sometimes correlates exactly with the initial growth point k_d with leverage level, but sometimes it takes values much higher.

The rate of decline in the cost of equity k_e with leverage increases with an increase in the growth rate of the cost of debt k_d, as well as when moving from linear to quadratic growth and exponential growth. So, we come to the conclusion that the increase in the cost of debt capital k_d with leverage leads to the decrease of equity cost k_e with leverage, starting with some value L_0. **This is the cause of the absence of weighted average capital cost growth with leverage at all its values.**

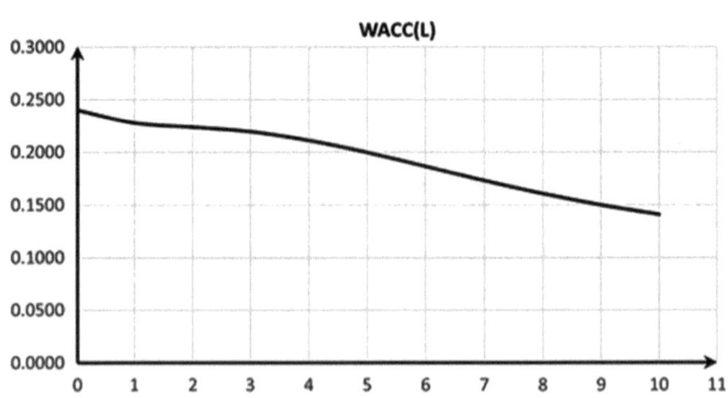

Fig. 2.3 Dependence of WACC on L

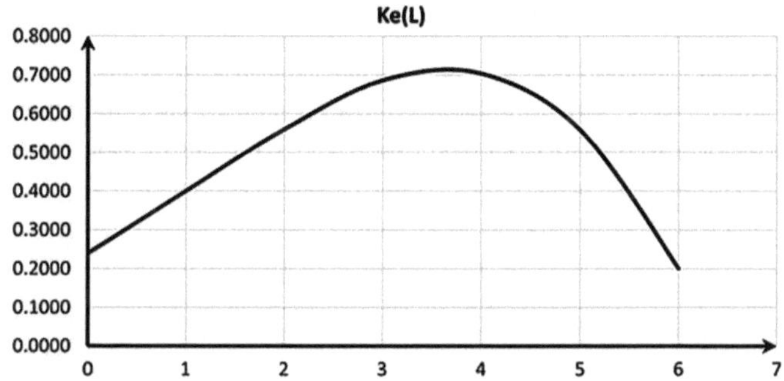

Fig. 2.4 Dependence of equity cost k_e on L

Fig. 2.5 Dependence of equity cost k_e, debt cost k_d, and WACC on leverage L

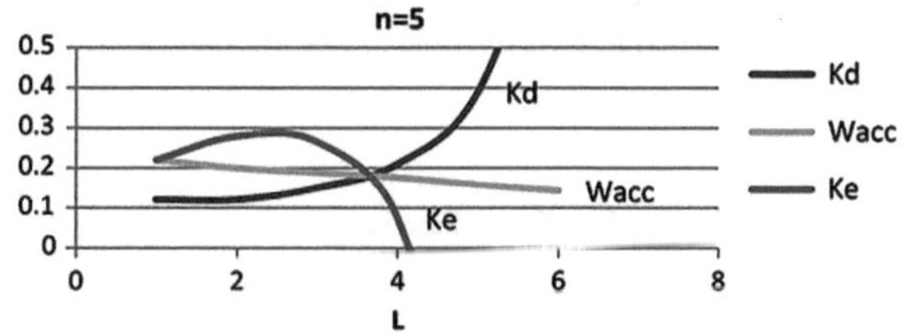

The conclusions made are independent of rate of growth of k_d with leverage (Figs. 2.4, 2.5).

Thus, this means that there is no optimal capital structure in the famous theory of trade–offs. This paradoxical conclusion explains the absence of an optimal capital structure in the famous trade–off theory. This means that the competition between the benefits of leverage and the cost of financial hardship (or the cost of bankruptcy) is NOT balanced, and the hope that trade–off theory gives us an optimal capital structure is unfortunately not realized. Mechanism of formation of the company optimal capital structure, different from suggested by trade off theory has been developed by Brusov et al. (2014a).

2.4 Accounting of Transaction Cost

If the cost of changing the capital structure to its optimal value is high, the company may decide not to change the capital structure and maintain the current capital structure.

The company may decide that it is more cost effective not to change the capital structure, even if it is not optimal, for a certain period of time. Because of this, the actual and target capital structure may differ.

2.5 Accounting of Asymmetry of Information

In real financial markets, information is asymmetric (company managers have more reliable information than investors and creditors), and the rationality of economic entities is limited.

2.6 Signaling Theory

Information asymmetry can be reduced based on certain signals for lenders and investors related to the behavior of managers in the capital market. It should take into account the previous company development and the current and projected profitability of the activity (Myers et al. 1984).

2.7 Pecking Order Theory

The pecking order theory (Myers 1984a, b; Hovakimian et al. 2001, Fama and French, 2005) describes a preferred sequence of funding types for raising capital. That is, companies first use financing from retained earnings (internal equity), the second source is debt, and the last source is the issuance of new shares of common stock (external equity). Empirical data on the leverage level of non-financial companies, combined with the decision-making process of top management and the board of directors, indicate a greater commitment to pecking order theory. Note that this theory contradicts both MM and BFO theory, which underline the quite importance of debt financing.

2.8 Behavioral Theories

Behavioral theories have been developed by Filbeck et al. (1996), Jenter (2005), Baker et al. (2002), Graham et al. (2001).

2.8.1 Manager Investment Autonomy

Company managers implement those decisions that, from their point of view, will be positively perceived by investors and, accordingly, will positively affect the market value of companies: when the market value of the company's shares and the degree of consensus between the expectations of managers and investors is high, the company conducts an additional share issue, and in the opposite situation uses debt instruments. Thus, the company capital structure is more influenced by investors, whose expectations are taken into account by company managers (Dittmar et al. 2007).

2.8.2 The Equity Market Timing Theory

The level of leverage is determined by market dynamics. Equity market timing theory means that a company should issue shares at a high price and repurchase them at a low price. The idea is to take advantage of the temporary fluctuations in the value of equity relative to the value of other forms of capital.

2.8.3 Information Cascades

To save costs and avoid mistakes, the company's capital structure can be formed not on the basis of calculations of the optimal capital structure (this is a non-trivial task and its correct solution could be found within the framework of the BFO theory) or depending on the available sources of financing of the company, but borrowed from other companies, having successful, proven managers (heads of companies), as well as using (following the majority) the most popular methods of managing the capital structure, or even simply by copying of the capital structure of successful companies in a similar industry (Bikhchandani et al. 1998).

2.9 Theories of Conflict of Interests

2.9.1 Theory of Agency Costs

The company management may make decisions that are contrary to the interests of shareholders or creditors, respectively; expenses are necessary to control its actions. For solving the agency problem the correct choice of the compensation package (the agent's share in the property, bonus, stock options) is needed, which allows you to link the managers profit with the dynamics of equity capital and ensure the motivation of managers for preservation and growth of equity capital (Jensen et al. 1973).

2.9.2 Theory of Corporate Control and Costs Monitoring

In the presence of information asymmetry, creditors providing capital are interested in the possibility of self–control of the effectiveness of its use and return. Monitoring costs are usually passed on to company owners by being included in the loan rate. The level of monitoring costs depends on the scale of the business; therefore, with the increase in the scale of the business, the company weighted average capital cost increases, and the company market value decreases.

2.9.3 Theory of Stakeholders

Stakeholder theory (Post et al. 2002) is a theory that defines and models the groups that are the stakeholders of a company. The diversity and intersection of interests of stakeholders, their different assessment of acceptable risk give rise to conditions for a conflict of their interests, that is, they make adjustments to the process of the capital structure optimizing.

2.10 BFO Theory

The restriction associated with the infinite life of companies and the eternity of cash flows within the framework of the MM theory was removed in 2008 by Brusov, Filatova and Orekhova (Filatova et al. 2008), who created the modern theory of the cost of capital and capital structure—the BFO theory, which is valid both for companies of arbitrary age, as well as for companies with an arbitrary lifetime. A generalization of the assessment of the tax shield TS and the value of the company: without leverage V0 and with leverage V was required to modify the theory of MM (see the formulas below):

$$\mathrm{TS} = k_{\mathrm{d}} DT \sum_{t=1}^{n} (1 + k_{\mathrm{d}})^{-t} = DT\left[1 - (1 + k_{\mathrm{d}})^{-n}\right]. \tag{2.26}$$

$$V_0 = \mathrm{CF}\left[1 - (1 + k_0)^{-n}\right]/k_0; \quad V = \mathrm{CF}\left[1 - (1 + \mathrm{WACC})^{-n}\right]/\mathrm{WACC}. \tag{2.27}$$

$$\frac{1 - (1 + \mathrm{WACC})^{-n}}{\mathrm{WACC}} = \frac{1 - (1 + k_0)^{-n}}{k_0\left[1 - \omega_{\mathrm{d}} T\left(1 - (1 + k_{\mathrm{d}})^{-n}\right)\right]}. \tag{2.28}$$

Here, S stands for the equity capital value, $w_{\mathrm{d}} = \frac{D}{D+S}$ stands for the debt capital share, $k_{\mathrm{e}}, w_{\mathrm{e}} = \frac{S}{D+S}$ stands for the equity cost and the equity capital share, and $L = D/S$ stands for the value of financial leverage, D stands for the debt capital value.

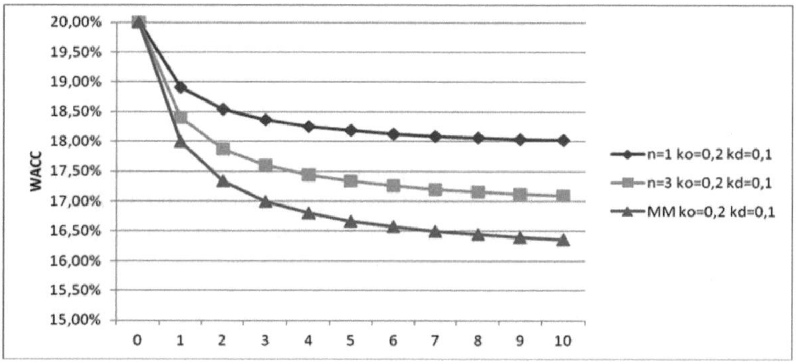

Fig. 2.6 Dependence of WACC on leverage level for $n = 1$, $n = 3$ and $n = \infty$

For a one–year company Steve Myers in 2001 has derived formula, which could be obtained easily from formula (2.28) by substituting n = 1.

$$\mathrm{WACC} = k_0 - \frac{(1 + k_0)k_\mathrm{d}}{1 + k_\mathrm{d}} w_\mathrm{d} T$$

and by substituting $n = \infty$ we arrive to the Modigliani–Miller formula for WACC (Modigliani and Miller 1963):

$$WACC = k_0 \cdot (1 - w_d t)$$

The methods and the conclusions of the Brusov–Filatova–Orekhova (BFO) theory are well–known in the scientific literature (for example, see references). In a number of works the BFO theory is used in practical calculations (Fig. 2.6).

2.10.1 Brusov–Filatova–Orekhova Theorem

Case of Absence of Corporate Taxes

Modigliani–Miller theory in case of absence of corporate taxes gives the following results for dependence of WACC and equity cost k_e on leverage:

$$V_0 = V_\mathrm{L}; \quad \mathrm{CF}/k_0 = \mathrm{CF}/\mathrm{WACC}, \quad \text{and thus } \mathrm{WACC} = k_0. \tag{2.29}$$

$$\mathrm{WACC} = w_\mathrm{e} \cdot k_\mathrm{e} + w_\mathrm{d} \cdot k_\mathrm{d}; \tag{2.30}$$

and thus

$$k_{\mathrm{e}} = \frac{\mathrm{WACC} - w_{\mathrm{d}} \cdot k_{\mathrm{d}}}{w_{\mathrm{e}}} = \frac{k_0 - \frac{L}{1+L} k_{\mathrm{d}}}{\frac{1}{1+L}}$$
$$= k_0 + L(k_0 - k_{\mathrm{d}}). \tag{2.31}$$

For the finite life–time (finite age) companies, Modigliani–Miller theorem about equality of value of financially independent and financially dependent companies ($V_0 = V_{\mathrm{L}}$) has the following view (Brusov and Filatova 2011; Brusov et al. 2011a, b, c, 2012a, b, 2013a, b, 2014a, b):

$$V_0 = V_{\mathrm{L}};$$

$$\mathrm{CF} \cdot \frac{\left[1 - (1 + k_0)^{-n}\right]}{k_0} = \mathrm{CF} \cdot \frac{\left[1 - (1 + \mathrm{WACC})^{-n}\right]}{\mathrm{WACC}}. \tag{2.32}$$

Using this relation, we prove an important Brusov–Filatova–Orekhova theorem:

Under the absence of corporate taxes, the equity cost of the company, k_{e}, as well as its weighted average cost of capital, WACC, does not depend on the life–time (age) of the company and is equal, respectively, to

$$k_{\mathrm{e}} = k_0 + L(k_0 - k_{\mathrm{d}}); \quad \mathrm{WACC} = k_0. \tag{2.33}$$

2.11 BFO Theory and Modigliani–Miller Theory Under Inflation

The influence of inflation on cost of raising capital and the company value has been studied within modern theory of capital cost and capital structure–Brusov–Filatova–Orekhova theory (BFO theory) (Brusov and Filatova 2011; Brusov et al. 2011a, b, c, 2012a, b, 2013a, b, 2014a, b; Filatova et al. 2008; Brusova 2011) and within its perpetuity limit–Modigliani–Miller theory (Modigliani and Miller 1958, 1963, Miller and Modigliani 1966). For the first time it was shown (Brusov et al. 2014b) by the direct incorporation of inflation into both theories that inflation not only increases the cost of raising capital (the equity cost and the weighted average cost of capital), but as well it changes their dependence on leverage. In particular, it increases the growth rate of equity cost with leverage. The company value is decreased under inflation (Fig. 2.7).

Formula (2.34) is the generalized Brusov–Filatova–Orekhova formula under inflation.

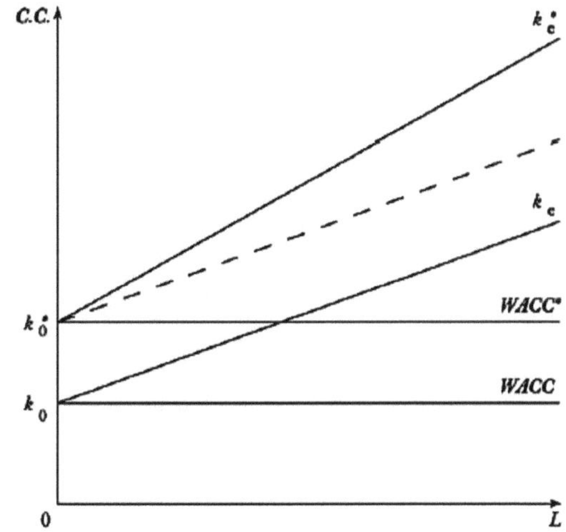

Fig. 2.7 Dependence of the equity cost and the weighted average cost of capital on leverage in the Modigliani–Miller theory without taxing under inflation. It is seen that growing rate of equity cost increases with leverage. Axis *y* means capital costs–CC

$$\frac{1-(1+\text{WACC}^*)^{-n}}{\text{WACC}^*}=\frac{1-[(1+k_0)(1+\alpha)]^{-n}}{(k_0(1+\alpha)+\alpha)\cdot\left[1-\omega_d T\left(1-((1+k_d)(1+\alpha))^{-n}\right)\right]}. \tag{2.34}$$

Here, $\text{WACC}^*=\text{WACC}\cdot(1+\alpha)+\alpha$.

In the Modigliani–Miller theory

$$WACC^*=(k_0(1+\alpha)+\alpha)\cdot(1-w_d t)$$

$$\begin{aligned}k_e^* &= k_0^*+L(1-T)\left(k_0^*-k_d^*\right)\\ &=[k_0(1+\alpha)+\alpha]+L(1-T)(k_0-k_d)(1+\alpha).\end{aligned} \tag{2.35}$$

The modified equation for the weighted average cost of capital WACC (Fig. 2.8), applicable to companies of arbitrary age under inflation, was derived in the framework of the modern theory of cost and capital structure—the theory of Brusov–Filatova–Orekhova (BFO theory). The modified BFO equation allows investigate the dependence of the weighted average cost of capital, WACC, and the cost of equity, k_e, on the level of financial leverage, L, on income tax rate, t, on the age of the company, n, on the cost of equity, k0, and the cost of debt, k_d, for various inflation rates α.

Using the modified BFO equation, authors analyzed the dependence of the weighted average cost of capital WACC on the share of debt w_d at various income taxes t, as well as the inflation rate α.

It was shown that WACC decreases with an increase leverage level L (or the share of debt, w_d), and the faster, the higher the income tax rate t. The distance between the lines, corresponding to different values of the income tax rate at the same step (10%), increases with the growth of the inflation rate α. The area of change (with

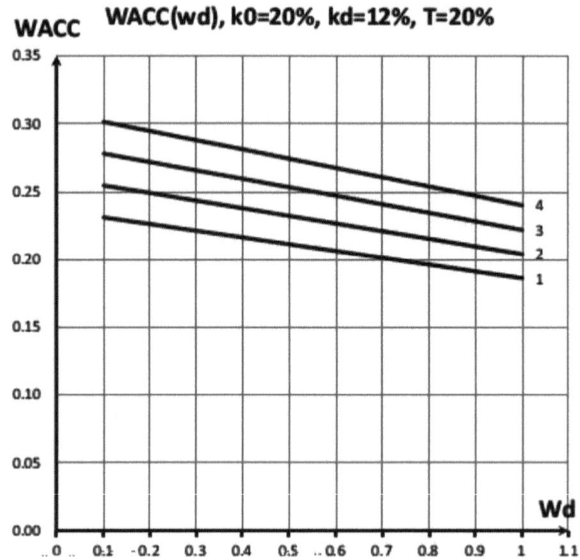

Fig. 2.8 Dependence of the weighted average cost of capital WACC on debt fraction w_d at different inflation rate α (1, $\alpha = 3\%$; 2, $\alpha = 5\%$; 3, $\alpha = 7\%$; and 4, $\alpha = 9\%$) for 5–year company

a change in the income tax rate t) of the weighted average cost of capital WACC increases with the inflation rate α, as well as with the age of the company n.

2.12 BFO Theory for the Companies Ceased to Exist at the Time Moment N (BFO–2 Theory)

The MM theory is only applicable to perpetual companies. As follows from the derivation of the BFO formula, the developed methodology is applied to companies of arbitrary age n (which have reached the age of n–years and continue to operate in the market). In other words, the BFO is applicable to the most interesting practical cases and allows you to analyze the financial condition of operating companies. However, the BFO theory also allows us to consider the financial condition of companies that have ceased to exist, i.e. those for which n means not age, but life-time, i.e. the time of existence. There can be many schemes for terminating a company: bankruptcy, merger, takeover, etc. Below we will consider one of these schemes, when the value of debt capital D becomes equal to zero at the time of the termination of the company n: in this case, the BFO theory requires minimal updates, as shown below (Brusov et al. 2018).

From the formula for the company's capitalization, it is easy to obtain an estimate of the "residual capitalization" of the company, discounted to the time moment *k:*

$$V_k = \sum_{t=k+1}^{n} \frac{\mathrm{CF}}{(1+\mathrm{WACC})^t} = \frac{\mathrm{CF}}{\mathrm{WACC}}\left[1-(1+\mathrm{WACC})^{-(n-k)}\right]. \tag{2.36}$$

Substituting

$$V_k = w_d D, \tag{2.37}$$

one gets the expression for the tax shield for n years, subject to the termination of the company's activities at time moment n:

$$\begin{aligned} TS_n &= tk_d w_d \sum_{k=1}^{n} \frac{V_{k-1}}{(1+k_d)^k} = \frac{tk_d w_d CF}{\text{WACC}} \sum_{k=1}^{n} \frac{1-(1+\text{WACC})^{-(n-k+1)}}{(1+k_d)^k} \\ &= \frac{tk_d w_d}{\text{WACC}} \left[\frac{1-(1+k_d)^{-n}}{k_d} - \frac{(1+k_d)^{-n} - (1+\text{WACC})^{-n}}{\text{WACC}-k_d} \right] \end{aligned} \tag{2.38}$$

Substituting this formula into equation

$$V_L = V_0 + (TS)_n \tag{2.39}$$

we arrive to the following equation (which is determines **the BFO-2 theory**)

$$\begin{aligned} \frac{1-(1+\text{WACC})^{-n}}{\text{WACC}} &= \frac{1-(1+k_0)^{-n}}{k_0} \\ &+ \frac{tk_d w_d}{\text{WACC}} \left[\frac{1-(1+k_d)^{-n}}{k_d} - \frac{(1+k_d)^{-n} - (1+\text{WACC})^{-n}}{\text{WACC}-k_d} \right], \end{aligned} \tag{2.40}$$

whence it is possible to find WACC for companies with an arbitrary life-time n, under condition, that the company ceases to operate at time moment *n*.

2.13 The Modigliani–Miller Theory with Advance Payments of Tax on Profit

The first serious study (and first quantitative study) of influence of capital structure of the company on its indicators of activities was the work by Nobel Prize Winners Modigliani and Miller. Their theory has a lot of limitations. One of the most important and serious assumptions of the Modigliani–Miller theory is that all financial flows as well as all companies are perpetuity. This limitation was lift out by Brusov–Filatova–Orekhova in 2008 (Filatova et al. 2008), who have created BFO theory—modern theory of capital cost and capital structure for companies of arbitrary age. Despite the fact that the Modigliani–Miller theory is currently a particular case of the general theory of capital cost and capital structure—Brusov–Filatova–Orekhova (BFO) theory—it is still widely used at the West.

Brusov et al. (2020a) discuss another limitation of the Modigliani–Miller theory: the method of paying income tax. The Modigliani–Miller theory accounts for these payments as immediate annuities, while in practice these payments are often made in advance and therefore must be accounted for as annuity-due. The authors generalized the Modigliani–Miller theory to the case of advance payments on income tax, which is widely used in practice. This generalization leads to a serious change in all the main provisions of Modigliani and Miller. These changes are as follows: WACC begins to depend on the cost of debt k_d, WACC turns out to be lower than in the case of the classical Modigliani–Miller theory, and the value of the company becomes higher. The formula for WACC has the following form

$$WACC = k_0(1 - w_d t(1 + k_d)) \tag{2.41}$$

Although the dependence of the cost of equity k_e on the level of leverage L remains linear, the angle of inclination relative to the L axis turns out to be smaller: this may lead to a modification of the company's dividend policy. Correct accounting for the method of paying income tax shows that the shortcomings of the Modigliani–Miller theory are more serious than everyone expected: the underestimation of WACC is indeed greater, as is the overestimation of the company's capitalization. This means that the systematic risks arising from the use of the modified Modigliani–Miller theory (the MMM theory) (more correct than the "classical" theory) are in practice higher than it was supposed by the "classical" version of this theory.

2.14 The Modigliani–Miller Theory with Arbitrary Frequency of Payment of Tax on Profit

One of the conditions for the real functioning of companies is the payment of income tax with an arbitrary frequency (monthly, quarterly, every six months or annually). The return is not required more than once a year, but companies may be required to file estimated taxes based on profits earned. The authors of (Acharya et al. 2011) generalized the Modigliani–Miller theory to the case of paying income tax with arbitrary periodicity. The formula for WACC has the following form Brusov and Filatova (2021)

$$WACC = k_0 \cdot \left(1 - \frac{k_d w_d t}{p} \frac{1}{(1 + k_d)^{1/p} - 1}\right) \tag{2.42}$$

and for company value

$$V = \frac{WACC}{k_0 \cdot \left(1 - \frac{k_d w_d t}{p} \frac{1}{\frac{1}{(1+k_d)}^{1/p} - 1}\right)} \tag{2.43}$$

They showed that the frequency of income tax payment affects all the main financial indicators of the company and leads to a number of important consequences. Theoretically, the authors derived all the main formulas of the modified Modigliani–Miller theory and used them to obtain all the main financial indicators of the company at arbitrary frequencies of income tax payment. They showed that: (1) all Modigliani–Miller theorems, assertions, and formulas have been changed; (2) all major financial indicators, such as the weighted average cost of capital (WACC), the value of the company, V and the cost of equity, k_e, depend on the frequency of income tax payments; (3) in the case of paying tax on profit more than once a year (with $p \neq 1$), as is the case in practice, WACC, company value, V and equity value, as well as equity cost k_e start depend on the cost of debt, k_d, and in the usual (classical) Modigliani–Miller theory, all these quantities do not depend on k_d; (4) the results obtained allow the company to choose the number of tax on profit payments per year (of course, within the framework of the current tax legislation): more frequent tax on profit payments are beneficial to both parties, the company and the tax regulator.

2.15 Generalization of the Modigliani–Miller Theory for the Case of Variable Profit

In (Brusov et al. 2021b), for the first time, the world–famous theory of Nobel laureates Modigliani and Miller was generalized to the case of variable income, which significantly expands the applicability of the theory in practice, in particular, in corporate finance, business valuation, investments, ratings etc. The following formulas for WACC and company value have been obtained

$$WACC - g = (k_0 - g) \cdot (1 - w_d t) \tag{2.44}$$

$$V = \frac{CF}{WACC - g} = \frac{CF}{(k_0 - g) \cdot (1 - w_d t)} \tag{2.45}$$

It was shown that all the theorems, assertions and formulas of Modigliani and Miller have been essentially changed. The authors obtained the following results: (1) WACC and k_0 are no longer the discount rates as it takes place in case of classical Modigliani–Miller theory with constant profit. The role of discount rate for leverage company pass from the weighted average cost of capital, WACC, to WACC–g (where g is growing rate), for a financially independent company from k_0 to k_0–g. The real discount rates WACC–g and k_0–g decrease with g, while WACC grows with g. This decrease leads to an increase of company value with g. (2) The slope of the equity cost k_e (L) grows with g. Via the fact, that the economically justified value of dividends is equal to equity cost this will modify the company's dividend policy. (3) It has been discovered the qualitatively new effect in corporate finance: the slope of the curve k_e (L) at rate $g < g^*$ turns out to be negative. This effect significantly alter the company's dividend policy principles.

2.16 The Generalization of the Brusov–Filatova–Orekhova Theory for the Case of Payments of Tax on Profit with Arbitrary Frequency

The Brusov–Filatova–Orekhova (BFO) theory and its limit of eternity, the Modigliani–Miller theory—both the main theories of the cost of capital and capital structure—consider income tax payments once a year. These payments in the real economy are made more frequently (every six months, quarter, month, etc.). In (Brusov et al. 2021b) the Modigliani–Miller theory was generalized by Brusov et al. for the case of paying income tax with arbitrary periodicity. In (Brusov and Filatova 2022b), for the first time, authors generalized the theory of Brusov–Filatova–Orekhova (BFO) to this case. Taking into account one of the features of the real functioning of companies—frequent payments of income tax—the authors brought the BFO theory closer to economic practice. Authors derived modified BFO formula

$$\frac{1-(1+WACC)^{-n}}{WACC}=\frac{1-(1+k_0)^{-n}}{k_0\cdot\left(1-\frac{k_d w_d t}{p}\frac{\left[1-(1+k_d)^{-n}\right]}{(1+k_d)^{1/p}-1}\right)} \tag{2.46}$$

and showed that:

(1) All BFO formulas change; (2) all major financial parameters of a company, such as company capitalization, V, weighted average cost of capital, WACC, cost of equity, k_e, etc. depend on the frequency of tax on profit payments. The cost of raising capital WACC decreases with the frequency of tax on profit payments and the company value, V increases with the frequency of tax on profit payments. A qualitatively new anomalous effect takes place at some age of the company, n, and at some frequency of income tax payments p: the cost of equity k_e (L) decreases with leverage level L.

Since the economically justified amount of dividends is equal to the cost of equity, this fundamentally changes the company's dividend policy. More frequent income tax payments are beneficial to both parties—the company and the tax regulator: the company, because it increases the value of the company, and the tax regulator, because it benefits from earlier payments due to the time value of money.

2.17 Benefits of Advance Payments of Tax on Profit: Consideration Within the Brusov–Filatova–Orekhova (BFO) Theory

Both theories of capital structure—the Brusov–Filatova–Orekhova (BFO) and its limit of eternity, the theory of Modigliani–Miller–consider the case of paying tax on profit at the end of the year. However, in practice, companies could make these payments in advance. In (Brusov et al. 2020a) the Modigliani–Miller theory was modified for the case of advance payments of tax on profit, and the results turned out to be completely different from the results of the usual Modigliani–Miller theory. In (Brusov et al. 2022a), the Brusov–Filatova–Orekhova (BFO) theory was modified for the first time for advance payments on income tax. The impact of such a transition to advance payments is much more significant than in the theory of MM, and even leads to a qualitatively new effect in the cost of equity dependence on leverage. Authors derived modified BFO formula for WACC

$$\frac{1-(1+WACC)^{-n}}{WACC}=\frac{1-(1+k_0)^{-n}}{k_0\cdot\left(1-w_dt\left[1-(1+k_d)^{-n}\right](1+k_d)^{1/p}\right)} \tag{2.47}$$

It is concluded that the tax shield and the way it is formed (payments at the end of the year or in advance) leads to very important consequences, changing all the company's financial indicators, such as the company's value and capital raising costs, and also significantly changing the company's dividend policy.

2.18 Influence of Method and Frequency of Profit Tax Payments on Company Financial Indicators

In practice, income tax payments may (1) be made in advance and (2) more frequently than once a year. In (Brusov et al. 2022a), the simultaneous influence of these two factors on the company's financial performance was studied. To this end, the Brusov–Filatova–Orekhova (BFO) theory was first generalized to the case of advance payments of income tax with arbitrary periodicity. Authors derived the following modified BFO formula for WACC

$$\frac{1-(1+WACC)^{-n}}{WACC}=\frac{1-(1+k_0)^{-n}}{k_0\cdot\left(1-\frac{k_dw_dt}{p}\frac{\left[1-(1+k_d)^{-n}\right]}{\left((1+k_d)^{1/p}-1\right)}(1+k_d)^{1/p}\right)} \tag{2.48}$$

It is concluded that all financial indicators of the company, such as the weighted average cost of capital (WACC) and the cost of equity (k_e), the value of the company (V) depend on the frequency of income tax payment. WACC increased with the frequency of payments, and the value of the company decreased. This meant that infrequent payments could be beneficial to the company in the case of advance income tax payments. The slope of the cost of equity, k_e (L), increased with the frequency of payments. Depending on the age of the company, k_e (L) either increased for some payment frequencies or decreased with L for all payment frequencies. The authors compared these results with their results for income tax payments at the end of the periods (see formula (1.47)) and found a huge difference: while in the latter case, WACC decreased with payment frequency, and the company capitalization increased with payment frequency, the value of WACC in this case remains bigger, and the company capitalization remains less than in the case of advance income tax payments of any frequency. The importance of advance income tax payments has been underlined by this fact. Authors developed the recommendations to regulator to increase the practice of advance payments of income tax due to the benefits of this for both parties: the companies and the state. A new effect—the decrease in equity cost with the level of leverage (L)—has been discovered.

2.19 The Brusov–Filatova–Orekhova (BFO) Theory with Variable Income

Two main theories of capital structure—Brusov–Filatova–Orekhova (BFO) and Modigliani–Miller consider the case of constant profit. But in practice, the company's income, of course, is variable. Both theories have recently been generalized to the case of variable income (Brusov et al. 2021b; Brusov and Filatova 2022b), which significantly expands the applicability of both theories of capital structure in practice. The following generalized BFO formula for WACC has been discovered

$$\frac{1-\left(\frac{1+g}{1+WACC}\right)^n}{WACC-g}=\frac{1-\left(\frac{1+g}{1+k_0}\right)^n}{(k_0-g)\cdot\left(1-w_d t\left[1-(1+k_d)^{-n}\right]\right)} \tag{2.49}$$

In the theory of Brusov–Filatova–Orekhova (BFO) (Brusov and Filatova 2022b), generalized to the case of variable income, income tax payments are made at the end of periods, while in practice these payments can also be made in advance. In (Brusov et al. 2022b) the authors considered two modifications of the Brusov–Filatova–Orekhova (BFO) theory with variable income: (1) with the payment of income tax at the end of periods and (2) with advance payments of income tax.

For these two cases, BFO formulas were derived for the weighted average cost of capital, WACC, for the value of the company, V, and within these formulas, a comprehensive analysis of the dependence of WACC, of the discount rate, WACC–g (here g is the growth rate), company capitalization, V, cost of equity, k_e, on debt financing at different values of the growth rate, g, at different values of the cost of debt capital, k_d, and at different values of the age of the company, n. The results for cases (1) and (2) are compared, which allows us to conclude that case (2) is always preferable for both the company and the regulator. This makes it possible to develop recommendations for both parties to expand the practice of advance income tax payments in the framework of real economic practice.

Brusov et al. emphasized an important observation. If in the classical versions of the Brusov–Filatova–Orekhova (BFO) theory and its perpetual limit—the theory of Nobel laureates Modigliani and Miller, where the case of constant profit was considered, and where the gap between these two theories is huge (many qualitative effects that take place in the first theory, missing in the second), when taking into account the variable profit, some effects of the BFO theory also take place in the Modigliani–Miller theory. This means that taking into account some effects that are present in economic practice (for example, variable income) brings both theories closer, and even the Modigliani–Miller theory, with all its many limitations, becomes more applicable in economic practice. However, it should be remembered that the Modigliani–Miller theory is only true for perpetual companies, while the BFO theory is valid for companies of any age and from this point of view they never coincide.

2.20 Qualitatively New Effects in the Theory of Capital Structure

Two Qualitatively new effects in the theory of capital structure.

Among the many new effects discovered in the framework of the BFO Theory, we will describe only two qualitatively new ones:

1. Golden and silver ages of the company.
2. Anomalous dependence of the cost of equity on the leverage level.

2.20.1 Golden and Silver Ages of the Company

To determine the minimum cost of raising capital depending on the age of the company, Brusov et al. In 2015, studied the dependence of the cost of raising capital on the age of the company, n, at different levels of leverage, L, at different values of capital costs. The authors used the Brusov–Filatov–Orekhova theory (Brusov and Filatova 2011; Brusov et al. 2011a, b, c, 2012a, b, 2013a, b, 2014a, b; Filatova et al. 2008; Brusova 2011).

It was shown for the first time that the value of WACC in the Modigliani–Miller theory (Modigliani and Miller 1958, 1963; Miller and Modigliani 1966) is not minimal, and the value of the company is not maximal, contrary to the opinion of all financiers: it turned out that at a certain age of the company, the value of WACC is lower than in the eternal Modigliani–Miller theory, and the value of company V is greater than the value of company V in the Modigliani–Miller theory.

Authors discovered two types of WACC dependences on the age of company n: monotonic decreasing with n and WACC decreasing with passage through minimum, followed by a limited growth (Brusov et al. 2015). The latter type of dependence of WACC on the age of company n allows the companies take advantage of the benefits given at a certain stage of their development.

Moreover, since capital costs, k_e and k_d, affect the company's golden age by changing it (for example, changing the value of dividend payments reflecting the cost of equity, etc.), the company can postpone or extend its golden age at which the cost of raising capital is minimal (and less than its perpetual limit), and the value of companies is maximum (above their perpetual value) (Fig. 2.9).

It has been shown that existence of the company "golden age" depends not on the capital costs values, but on the difference between equity k_0 and debt k_d costs. The effect of the company "golden age" takes place at small enough difference between k_0 and k_d costs, while at this difference high value this effect is absent: curve WACC(n) monotonic decreases with company age n. Curve WACC(L) for perpetuity limit ($n = \infty$) lies between curves WACC(L) for one year ($n = 1$) and three years ($n = 3$) companies (Fig. 2.10) for the companies with the "golden age", while curve WACC(L) for perpetuity limit is the lowest one for the companies without the "golden age" (Fig. 2.11).

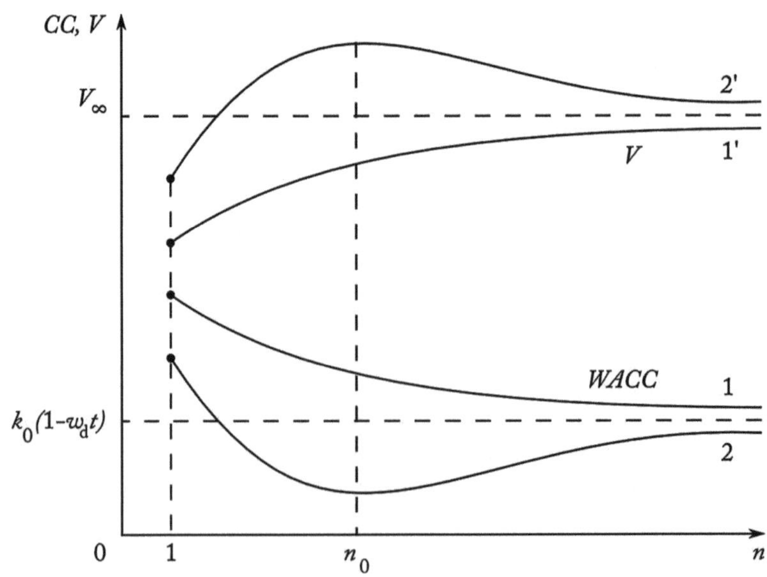

Fig. 2.9 Two types of dependences of WACC, and company value, V, on the company age *n*: 1–1′—monotonic decreasing of WACC, and company value, V, increasing with the company age *n*; 2–2'—WACC decreasing with n, passage through minimum (at n_0), followed by a limited growth and increase of V with the passage through a maximum (at n_0) and then a limited decreasing

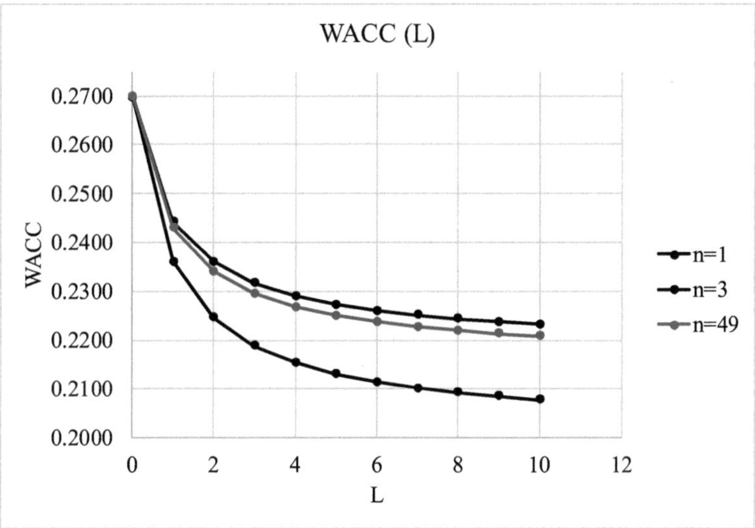

Fig. 2.10 The dependence of WACC on leverage level L at different the company age *n* (*n* = 1, 3, 49)

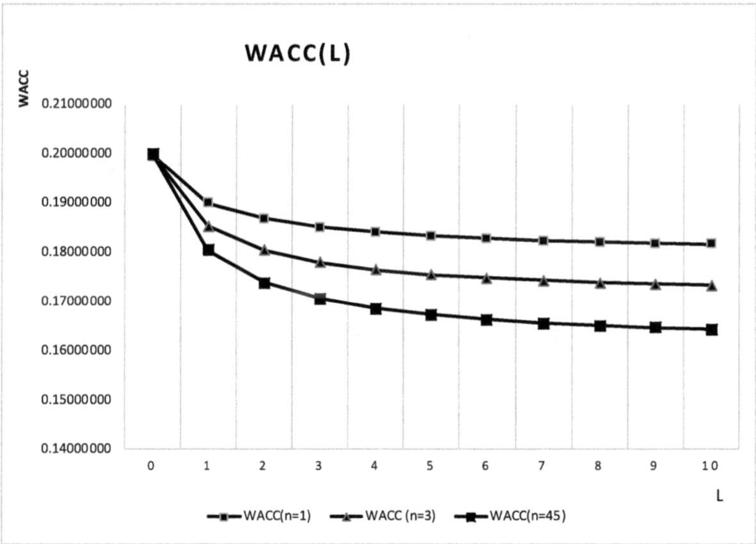

Fig. 2.11 The dependence of WACC on the leverage level, L, at different company age *n* (n = 1, 3, 45)

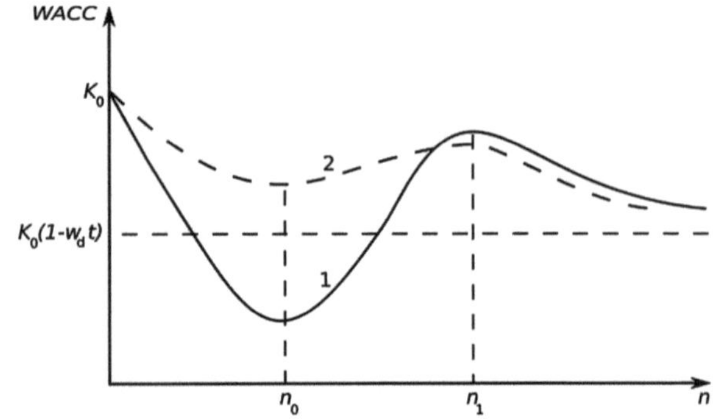

Fig. 2.12 Dependence of WACC on company age n: company "golden age" (curve 1) and company "silver age" (curve 2) under existence of "Kulik" effect, where n_0 is company "golden (silver) age" and n_1 is the company age of local maximum in the dependence of WACC(n)

2.20.2 Silver Age of the Company

2.20.3 Anomalous Dependence of the Company's Equity Value on Leverage

Brusov et al. (2013b) found a qualitatively new effect in the capital structure: a decrease in the cost of equity at a leverage level L. This effect is absent in the perpetual Modigliani–Miller limit, but appears in companies of finite age at an income tax rate exceeding a certain value T*.

For some values of the cost of equity and the cost of debt, this effect exists at the tax on income values existing in financial practice. This ensures the practical significance of the discovered effect. Accounting for this effect is important when changing tax legislation and can significantly change the company's dividend policy (Figs. 2.12, 2.13).

2.21 A Stochastic Extension the Modigliani–Miller Theory

A Stochastic Extension of the Modigliani–Miller theory has been done in a few papers.

De Marzo (1988) showed that the Modigliani–Miller theory is correct in a multi-period stochastic economy with incomplete markets. In the model author developed, companies can trade securities, and stock prices and dividends become completely interdependent. Several corporate control mechanisms were considered, including maximizing the value of the company and shareholder voting. It is shown that in equilibrium companies have no incentive to trade securities, and the set of equilibrium distributions does not change as a result of such trading.

Sethi et al. (1991) study the company value valuation problem under a partial equilibrium, a time-dependent discount rate and a general stochastic environment

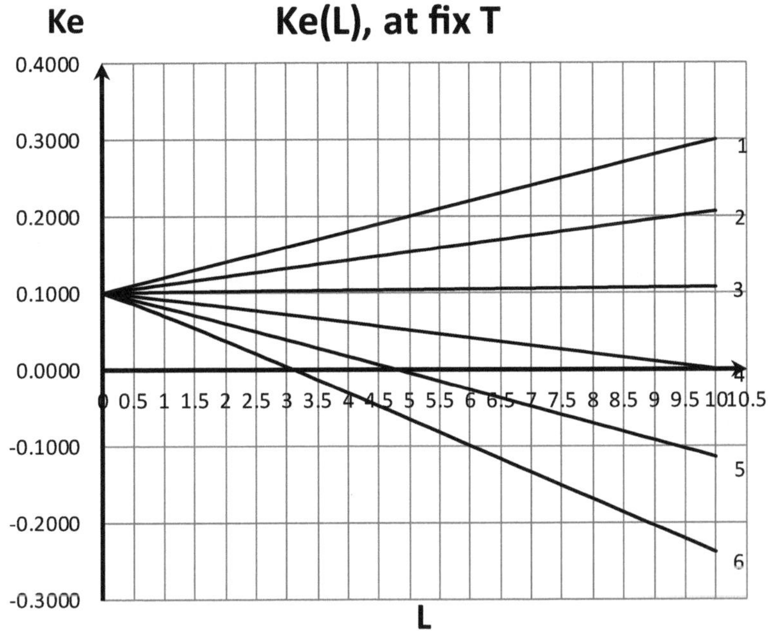

Fig. 2.13 Dependence of equity cost, k_e, on leverage level L at different tax on income rate T ($n = 5, k_0 = 10\%, k_d = 8\%$) (1—$T = 0$; 2—$T = 0.2$; 3—$T = 0.4$; 4—$T = 0.6$; 5—$T = 0.8$; 6—$T = 1$)

in a discrete-time setting. The time path of share price and the company value are obtained upon the assumption of risk neutrality.

2.22 Conclusions

This Chapter analyzes all the main existing theories of capital structure, including Modigliani–Miller and BFO. Various modifications of these two and other theories, including the latest ones, related to the conditions of the real functioning of companies and developed in recent years are discussed in detail.

The generalization of Modigliani–Miller theory for the cases of practical interest lead to a much more significant change in Modigliani–Miller theory than all previous modifications, studied over the previous decades. Obtained results showed that under such a generalization there is some convergence of Modigliani–Miller theory and BFO theory: the former theory begins to have some new properties similar to those of BFO theory, which was not there in the classical Modigliani–Miller theory, between the properties of which and of the BFO theory was a huge gap. Most of the innovative effects existing in the BFO theory are absent in the classical Modigliani–Miller theory.

All of the above means that the considered effects, such as the variable income of the company, frequent paying income tax, advance payment of income tax, the combinations of this conditions and others, are more important than the effects studied earlier and having much less influence on the Modigliani–Miller theory. Taking into account these effects leads to some convergence between Modigliani–Miller theory and the BFO theory. At the same time, one must understand that Modigliani–Miller theory remains perpetual and will never describe a company of arbitrary age, which is extremely important for the practical application of the theory.

References

Acharya V, Myers SC, Rajan R (2011) The internal governance of firms. J Financ 66(3):689–720
Arrow KJ (1963) The role of securities in the optimal allocation of risk-bearing. Rev Econ Stud 31(2):91–96
Asquith P, Mullins DW (1986) Equity issues and offering dilution. J Financ Econ 15(1–2):61–89
Baumol W, Panzar JG, Willig RD (1982) Contestable markets and the theory of industry structure. New York
Berk J, De Marzo P (2007) Corporate Finance. Pearson-Addison Wesley, Boston
Bhattacharya S (1978) Project valuation with mean–reacting cash flows. J Financ 33:1317–1331
Bikhchandani et al. (1998) Learning from the behavior of others: Conformity, fads, and informational cascades. J Econ Perspect, 12(3):151–170
Brealey RA, Myers SC, Allen F (2013) Principles of corporate finance, 11th ed. McGraw–Hill, New York
Brealey RA, Myers SC (1981) Principles of corporate finance, 1st ed. McGraw–Hill, New York
Brennan M, Schwartz E (1978) Corporate income taxes, valuation, and the problem of optimal capital structure. J Bus 51:103–114
Brennan M, Schwartz E (1984) Optimal financial policy and firm valuation. J Financ 39:593–607
Brusov P, Filatova P, Orekhova N (2013a) Absence of an optimal capital structure in the famous tradeoff theory! J Rev Glob Econ 2:94–116
Brusov P, Filatova P, Orekhova N (2014a) Mechanism of formation of the company optimal capital structure, different from suggested by trade off theory. Cogent Econ Financ 2:1–13. https://doi.org/10.1080/23322039.2013.946150
Brusov P, Filatova T (2022a) Influence of method and frequency of profit tax payments on company financial indicators. Mathematics 10(14):2479. https://doi.org/10.3390/math10142479
Brusov P, Filatova T (2022b) Generalization of the Brusov–Filatova–Orekhova theory for the case of variable income. Mathematics 10(19):3661. https://doi.org/10.3390/math10193661
Brusov PN, Filatova TV (2025a) Business valuation and company value: New qualitative approaches considering business and financial risks. Springer Nature Publishing. 1–654
Brusov PN, Filatova TV (2025b) Efficiency of investment projects: Modern investment models and their applications. Springer Nature Publishing. 1–843
Brusov P, Filatova T, Eskindarov M, Orehova N (2012b) Hidden global causes of the global financial crisis. J Rev Glob Econ 1:106–111
Brusov P, Filatova T, Kulik V (2022a) Benefits of advance payments of tax on profit: consideration within the Brusov–Filatova–Orekhova (BFO) theory. Mathematics 10(12):2013. https://doi.org/10.3390/math10122013
Brusov P, Filatova T, Orehova N (2013b) A qualitatively new effect in corporative finance: abnormal dependence of cost of equity of company on leverage. J Rev Glob Econ 2:183–193

Brusov P, Filatova T, Orehova N (2014b) Inflation in Brusov–Filatova–Orekhova theory and in its perpetuity limit–Modigliani–Miller theory. J Rev Glob Econ 3:175–185

Brusov PN, Filatova TV, Orekhova NP (2021) Ratings: critical analysis and new approaches of quantitative and qualitative methodology. Springer Nature Publishing. 1–369

Brusov PN, Filatova TV, Orekhova NP (2022) Generalized modigliani–miller theory: Applications in corporate finance, investments, taxation and ratings. Springer Nature Publishing. 1–362

Brusov PN, Filatova TV, Orekhova NP (2023) The Brusov–Filatova–Orekhova theory of capital structure: Applications in corporate finance, investments, taxation and ratings. Springer Nature Publishing. 1–769

Brusov P, Filatova T, Orekhova N, Kulik V, Chang S–I, Lin G (2022b) The generalization of the Brusov–Filatova–Orekhova theory for the case of payments of tax on profit with arbitrary frequency. Mathematics 10(8):1343. https://doi.org/10.3390/math10081343

Brusov P, Filatova T (2021) The Modigliani–Miller theory with arbitrary frequency of payment of tax on profit. Mathematics 9(11):1198

Brusov P, Filatova T, Chang S-I, Lin G (2021a) Innovative investment models with frequent payments of tax on income and of interest on debt. Mathematics 9(13):1491

Brusov PN, Filatova TV, Kulik VL (2024) Capital asset pricing model (CAPM) 2.0: Account of business and financial risk. Finance: Theory and Practice. 28(2):128–142. https://doi.org/10.26794/2587-5671-2024-28-2-128-142

Brusov P, Filatova T, Orekhova N, Kulik V, Chang S-I, Lin G (2021b) Generalization of the Modigliani–Miller theory for the case of variable profit. Mathematics 9(11):1286

Brusov P, Filatova T, Orehova N, Eskindarov M (2018) Modern corporate finance, investments, taxation and ratings, 2nd ed. Springer Nature Publishing, Cham, Switzerland, pp 1–571

Brusov PN, Filatova TV, Orekhova NP, Kulik VL, Chang SI, Lin YCG (2020a) Modification of the Modigliani–Miller theory for the case of advance payments of tax on profit. J Rev Glob Econ 9:257–267

Brusov PN, Filatova TV, Orekhova NP, Kulik VL, Chang S-I, Lin YCG (2020b) Application of the Modigliani–Miller theory, modified for the case of advance payments of tax on profit, in rating methodologies. J Rev Glob Econ 9:282–292

Brusov PN, Filatova TV, Orekhova NP, Kulik VL, Chang S-I, Lin YCG (2020c) Modification of the Modigliani–Miller theory for the case of advance payments of tax on profit. J Rev Glob Econ 9:257–267

Brusova A (2011) A comparison of the three methods of estimation of weighted average cost of capital and equity cost of company. Financ Anal Prob Sol 34(76):36–42

Baker et al. (2002) The difference between Modigliani–Miller and Miles–Ezzell and its consequences for the valuation of annuities. Cogent Econ Financ, 9:1

Becker DM (2021) The difference between Modigliani–Miller and Miles–Ezzell and its consequences for the valuation of annuities. Cogent Econ Financ 9:1. https://doi.org/10.1080/23322039.2020.1862446

Cooper IA, Nyborg KG (2006) The value of tax shields is equal to the present value of tax shields. J Financ Econ 81(1), https://ssrn.com/abstract=925390

De Marzo PM (1988) An extension of the Modigliani–Miller theorem to stochastic economies with incomplete markets and fully interdependent securities. J Econ Theory 45:353–369

Derrig R (1993) Theoretical considerations of the effect of federal income taxes on investment income in property-liability ratemaking. J Risk Insur 61:691–709

Diamond DA, He Z (2013) A theory of debt maturity: the long and short of debt overhang. J Financ 69(2):719–762

Dittmar A, Mahrt-Smith J (2007) Corporate governance and the value of cash holdings. J Financ Econ

Donaldson G (1961) Debt capacity: a study of corporate debt policy and the determination of debt capacity. Div. Res. Harvard Grad. Stud. Bus. Admin, Boston, MA

Erel I, Myers SC, Read JA Jr (2015) A theory of risk capital. J Financ Econ. https://doi.org/10.1016/j.jfineco.2013.10.006

Fairley WB (1979) Investment income and profit margins in property-liability insurance. Bell J Econ 10:191–210
Fama EF, French K (2005) Financing decisions: who issues stock? J Financ Econ 76(3):549–582. Federal Power Commission et al. v. Hope Natural Gas Co., 320 U.S. 591 (1944)
Fama EF (1977) Risk adjusted discount rates and capital budgeting under uncertainty. J Financ Econ 5(1):3–24
Fama EF (1996) Discounting under uncertainty. J Bus 69(4):415–429
Farber A, Gillet R, Szafarz A (2006) A general formula for the WACC. Int J Bus 11(2):211–218
Fernandez P (2006) A general formula for the WACC: a comment. Int J Bus 11(2):219
Filatova T, Brusov P, Orekhova N (2022) Impact of advance payments of tax on profit on effectiveness of investments. Mathematics 10(4):666. https://doi.org/10.3390/math10040666
Filatova T, Orehova N, Brusova A (2008) Weighted average cost of capital in the theory of Modigliani–Miller, modified for a finite life-time company. Bull FU 48:68–77
Filbeck G, Gorman RF, Preece DC (1996) Behavioral aspects of the intra-industry capital structure decision. J Financ Strat Dec
Fisher FM, McGowan JJ (1983) On the misuse of accounting rates of return to infer monopoly profits. Am Econ Rev 73:82–97
Frank MZ, Goyal VK (2003) Testing the pecking order theory of capital structure. J Financ Econ 67:217–248
Fulghieri P, Garcia D, Hackbarth D (2013) Asymmetric information and the pecking (dis-)order. Work. Pap., Boston Univ., Univ. N.C.
Gordon MJ, Shapiro E (1956) Capital equipment analysis: the required rate of profit. Manag Sci 3:102–110
Graham et al. (2001) A review of empirical capital structure research and directions for the future. Annu Rev Financ Econ 3:309–345
Graham JR, Leary MT (2011) A review of empirical capital structure research and directions for the future. Annu Rev Financ Econ 3:309–345
Hamada R (1969) Portfolio analysis, market equilibrium, and corporate finance. J Financ 24:13–31
Harcourt Brace Jovanovich Black F. (1986). Noise. J Financ 41(3):529–543
Harris R, Pringle J (1985) Risk-adjusted discount rates—extension form the average-risk case. J Finan Res 8(3):237–243
Hausman J, Myers SC (2002) Regulating U.S. railroads: the effects of sunk costs and asymmetric risk. J Regul Econ 22(3):287–310
Healy P, Howe C, Myers SC (2002) R&D accounting and the tradeoff between relevance and objectivity: a pharmaceutical industry simulation. J Account Res 40(3):677–710
Hirshleifer J (1965) Investment decision under uncertainty: choice—theoretic approaches. Q J Econ 79(4):509–536
Hirshleifer J (1966) Investment decision under certainty: applications of the state-preference approach. Q J Econ 80(2):252–277
Hsia (1981) Coherence of the modern theories of finance. Financ Rev 16(1):27–42
Jensen et al. (1973) Agency costs of free cash flow, corporate finance and takeovers. Am Econ Rev. 76:323–329
Jensen MC (1986) Agency costs of free cash flow, corporate finance and takeovers. Am Econ Rev 76(2):323–329
Jenter D (2005) Market timing and managerial portfolio decisions. J Financ 60(4):1903–1949, https://doi.org/10.1111/j.1540-6261.2005.00783.x
Jin L, Myers SC (2006) R2 around the world: new theory and new tests. J Financ Econ 79(2):257–292
Kane A, Marcus A, McDonald R (1984) How big is the tax advantage to debt? J Financ 39:841–853
Kaplan S, Ruback R (1995) The valuation of cash flow forecasts: an empirical analysis. J Financ 50(4):1059–1093
Keynes JM (1936) The general theory of employment, interest and money. Macmillan, New York
Kolbe AL, Tye WB, Myers SC (1993) Regulatory risk: economic principles and applications to natural gas pipelines and other industries. Springer, New York

Lambrecht B, Myers SC (2007) A theory of takeovers and disinvestment. J Financ 62(2):809–845
Lambrecht B, Myers SC (2008) Debt and managerial rents in a real-options model of the firm. J Financ Econ 89(2):209–231
Lambrecht B, Myers SC (2012) A Lintner model of dividends and managerial rents. J Financ 67(5):1761–1810
Lambrecht B, Myers SC (2015) The dynamics of investment, payout and debt. Work. Pap., Mass. Inst. Technol.
Leland H (1994) Corporate debt value, bond covenants, and optimal capital structure. J Financ, 49:1213–1252
Lemmon ML, Roberts MR, Zender J (2008) Back to the beginning: persistence and the cross-section of corporate capital structure. J Financ 63(4):1575–1608
Lemmon ML, Zender J (2010) Debt capacity and tests of capital structure theories. J Financ Quant Anal 45:1161–1187
Lintner J (1956) Distribution of incomes of corporations between dividends, retained earnings and taxes. Am Econ Rev 46:97–113
Lintner J (1965) Optimal dividends and corporate growth under uncertainty. Q J Econ 77:59–95
Majd S, Myers SC (1987) Tax asymmetries and corporate income tax reform. In: Feldstein M (ed) The effects of taxation on capital accumulation. Univ. Chic. Press, Chicago, IL, pp 343–373
Majluf NS (1978) Study on mergers: a rationale for conglomerate mergers. PhD Thesis, Mass. Inst. Technol., Cambridge
Merton RC, Perold AF (1993) Theory of risk capital in financial firms. J Appl Corp Financ 6:16–32
Miles J, Ezzell R (1980) The weighted average cost of capital, perfect capital markets and project life: a clarification. J Financ Quant Anal 15(3):719–730
Miller MH, Modigliani F (1961) Dividend policy, growth and the valuation of shares. J Bus 34:411–433
Miller MH, Modigliani F (1966) Some estimates of the cost of capital to the electric utility industry, 1954–1957. Am Econ Rev 56:333–391
Miller MH (1977) Debt and taxes. J Financ 32:261–276
Modigliani F, Miller MH (1958) The cost of capital, corporation finance and the theory of investment. Am Econ Rev 48(3):261–296
Modigliani F, Miller MH (1963) Corporate income taxes and the cost of capital: a correction. Am Econ Rev 53:433–443
Morck R, Yeung BY, Yu W (2000) The information content on stock markets: why do emerging markets have synchronous stock price movements? J Financ Econ 58:215–260
Mullins DW Jr (1976) Communications satellite corp. case study 276195. Harvard Bus. Sch., Cambridge, MA
Myers Annu (2015) Rev Financ Econ 7:1–33. Downloaded from www.annualreviews.orgAccess provided by University of California–Los Angeles UCLA on 12/11/18. For personal use only
Myers SC, Cohn R (1987) A discounted cash flow approach to property-liability insurance rate regulation. In: Cummings JD, Harrington S (eds) Fair rate of return in property liability insurance. Kluwer–Nijhoff, Dordrecht, Neth., pp 55–78
Myers SC, Dill DA, Bautista AJ (1976) Valuation of financial lease contracts. J Financ 31(3):799–819
Myers SC, Howe C (1997) A life cycle model of pharmaceutical R&D. Work. Pap., Progr. Pharm. Ind., Mass. Inst. Technol.
Myers SC, Kolbe AL, Tye WB (1983) Regulation and capital formation in the oil pipeline industry. Transp J 23(4):25–49
Myers SC, Kolbe AL, Tye WB (1985) Inflation and rate of return regulation. Res Transp Econ 2:83–119
Myers SC, Majluf NS (1984) Corporate financing and investment decisions when firms have information that investors do not have. J Financ Econ 13(2):187–221
Myers SC, Pogue GA (1973) A programming approach to corporate financial management. J Financ 29(2):579–599

Myers SC, Rajan R (1998) The paradox of liquidity. Q J Econ 113(3):733–771
Myers SC, Read JA Jr (2001) Capital allocation for insurance companies. J Risk Insur 68(4):545–580
Myers SC, Read JA Jr (2013) Real options, taxes and leverage. Work. Pap., Mass. Inst. Technol.
Myers SC, Shyam-Sunder L (1996) Measuring pharmaceutical industry risk and the cost of capital. In: Helms RB (ed) Competitive strategies in the pharmaceutical industry. Am. Enterp. Inst, Washington, DC, pp 208–237
Myers SC, Turnbull SM (1977) Capital budgeting and the capital asset pricing model: good news and bad news. J Financ 32(2):321–333
Myers SC (1967) Effects of uncertainty on the valuation of securities and the financial decisions of the firm. Ph.D. Thesis, Stanford Univ., Stanford, CA
Myers SC (1968a) A time-state-preference model of security valuation. J Financ Quant Anal 3:1–33
Myers SC (1968b) Procedures for capital budgeting under uncertainty. Ind Manag Rev 9(3):1–20
Myers SC (1972) Application of finance theory to public utility rates cases. Bell J Econ 3:58–97
Myers SC (1973a) Interactions of corporate financing and investment decisions: implications for capital budgeting. J Financ 29:1–25
Myers SC (1973b) A simple model of firm behavior under regulation and uncertainty. Bell J Econ 4:304–315
Myers SC (1973c) On public utility regulation under uncertainty. In Howard RH (ed) Risk and regulated firms. East Lansing: Div. Res. Grad. Sch. Bus., Mich. State Univ., pp 32–46
Myers SC (1977) Determinants of corporate borrowing. J Financ Econ 5(2):147–175
Myers SC (1984a) Finance theory and financial strategy. Interfaces 14:126–137
Myers SC (1984b) The capital structure puzzle. J Financ 39(3):575–592
Myers SC (1988) Fuzzy efficiency. Inst Invest 1988(Dec.):8–9
Myers SC (1989) Still searching for optimal capital structure. In: Kopke RW, Rosengren ES (eds) Are the distinctions between debt and equity disappearing? Fed. Reserve Bank, Boston, pp 80–95
Myers SC (1999) Financial architecture. Eur Financ Manag 5(2):133–141
Myers SC (2000) Outside equity. J Financ 55(3):1005–1037
Myers SC, Majd S (1990) Abandonment value and project life. In: Fabozzi F (ed) Advances in futures and options research, vol 4. JAI, Greenwich, CT, pp 1–21
Post et al. (2002) Managing the extended enterprise: The new stakeholder view, California Manage Rev 45(1):6–28, https://doi.org/10.2307/41166151
Robichek AA, Myers SC (1965) Optimal financing decisions. Prentice-Hall, Upper Saddle River, NJ
Robichek AA, Myers SC (1966a) Conceptual problems in the use of risk-adjusted discount rates. J Financ 21(4):727–730
Robichek AA, Myers SC (1966b) Problems in the theory of optimal capital structure. J Financ Quant Anal 1(2):1–35
Robichek AA, Myers SC (1966c) Valuation of the firm: effects of uncertainty in a market context. J Financ 21(2):215–227
Rosenbaum J, Pearl J (2013) Investment banking, 2nd ed. Wiley, New York
Rubinstein M (1973) A mean–variance synthesis of corporate financial theory. J Financ 28:167–181
Schwartz E (1959) The theory of the capital structure of the firm. J Financ 14:18–39
Sethi S, Derzko N, Lehoczky J (1991, October) A Stochastic extension of the Miller–Modigliani framework. Math Financ 1(4):57–76. SSRN: https://ssrn.com/abstract=1082940
Sharpe WF (1965) Capital asset prices: a theory of market equilibrium under conditions of risk. J Financ 19(3):425–442
Shleifer A, Summers LH (1988) Breach of trust in hostile takeovers. In: Auerbach AJ (ed) Corporate takeovers: causes and consequences. Univ. Chic. Press, Chicago, IL, pp 33–56
Shyam-Sunder L, Myers SC (1999) Testing static tradeoff against pecking order models of capital structure. J Financ Econ 51(2):219–244
Skinner DJ (2008) The evolving relation between earnings, dividends and stock repurchases. J Financ Econ 87:582–609

Solomon E, Laya J (1967) Measurement of company profitability: some systematic errors in the accounting rate of return. In: Robichek AA (ed) Financial research and management decisions. Wiley, New York, pp 152–183
Stiglitz J (1969) A re–examination of the Modigliani–Miller Theorem. Am Econ Rev 59:784–793
Van Horne J (1966) Capital budgeting decisions involving combinations of risky assets. Manag Sci 19:B84–92
Williams JB (1938) The theory of investment value. Harvard. Univ. Press, Cambridge, MA

Chapter 3
Capital Structure: Modigliani–Miller Theory

3.1 Introduction

One of two main theories of capital cost and capital structure is the theory of Nobel Prize winners Modigliani and Miller (1958, 1963, 1966). In this Chapter we describe the main results of this theory. Under the capital structure, one understands the relationship between equity and debt capital of the company. Does capital structure affect the company's main settings, such as the cost of capital, profit, value of the company, and the others, and, if affects, how? Choice of an optimal capital structure, i.e., a capital structure, which minimizes the weighted average cost of capital, WACC, and maximizes the value of the company, *V*, is one of the most important tasks solved by financial manager and by the management of a company. The first serious study (and first quantitative study) of influence of capital structure of the company on its indicators of activities was the work by Modigliani and Miller (1958). Until this study, the approach existed (let us call it traditional), which was based on empirical data analysis.

One of the most important assumptions of the Modigliani–Miller theory is that all financial flows are perpetuity. This limitation was lift out by Brusov–Filatova–Orekhova in 2008 (Filatova et al. 2008), who have created BFO theory—modern theory of capital cost and capital structure for companies of arbitrary age (BFO-1 theory) and for companies of arbitrary life time (BFO-2 theory) (Brusov et al. 2015). (See also recently published monographs by the authors at Springer Nature Publishing (Brusov et al. 2021, 2022, 2023; Brusov and Filatova 2025a, b). In Fig. 3.1 the historical development of capital structure theory from the traditional (empirical) approach, through perpetuity Modigliani–Miller approach to general capital structure theory–Brusov–Filatova–Orekhova (BFO) theory is shown.

In 2001 Steve Myers has considered the case of one-year company and show that in this case the weighted average cost of capital, WACC, is higher than in Modigliani–Miller case, and the capitalization of the company, *V*, is less than in Modigliani–Miller case.

P. Brusov and T. Filatova, *Taxes and Taxation*, Contributions to Finance and Accounting, https://doi.org/10.1007/978-3-032-11077-0_3

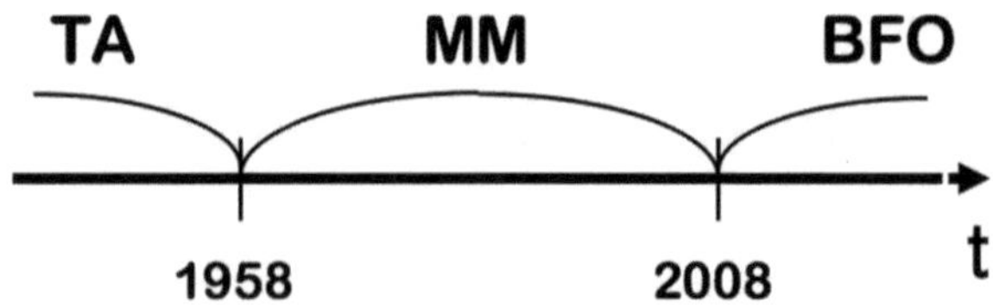

Fig. 3.1 Historical development of capital structure theory (here TA—traditional (empirical) approach, MM—Modigliani–Miller approach, BFO—Brusov–Filatova–Orekhova theory)

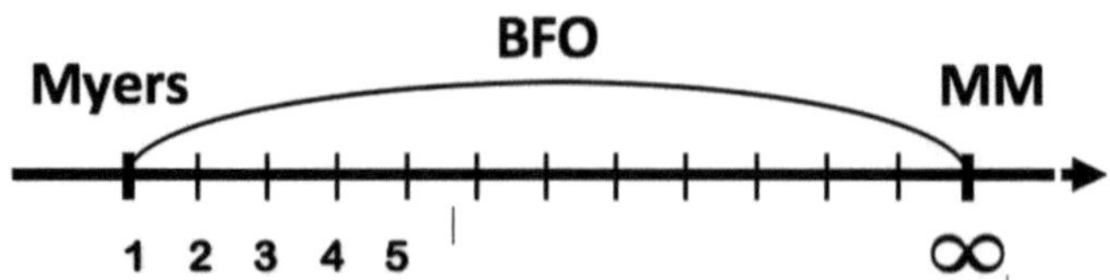

Fig. 3.2 MM theory describes perpetuity limit, Myers paper describes one-year company while BFO theory fills the whole numeric axis (from n = 1 up to perpetuity limit $n = \infty$)

So, before 2008 only two results for capital structure of the company were available: Modigliani–Miller for perpetuity company and Myers for one-year company (see Fig. 3.2). BFO theory has filled out whole interval between t = 1 and t = ∞. It gives the possibility to calculate the capitalization V, the weighted average cost of capital, $WACC$, equity cost k_e and other financial parameters for companies of arbitrary age and for companies of arbitrary life-time. BFO theory has lead to a lot of new meaningful effects in modern capital structure theory, discussed in this monograph.

3.2 The Traditional Approach

The traditional (empirical) approach told that weighted average cost of capital, WACC, and the associated company capitalization, $V = \text{CF/WACC}$, depend on the capital structure, the level of leverage, L. Debt cost always turns out to be lower than equity cost because first one has lower risk, via the fact, that in the event of bankruptcy creditor claims are met prior to shareholders claims.

As a result, an increase in the proportion of lower-cost debt capital in the overall capital structure up to the limit which does not cause violation of financial sustainability and growth of risk of bankruptcy leads to lower weighted average cost of capital, WACC.

The profitability required by investors (the equity cost) is growing; however, its growth has not led to compensation of benefits from use of lower-cost debt capital. Therefore, the traditional approach welcomes the increased leverage $L = D/S$ and the associated increase of company capitalization. The traditional (empirical) approach has existed up to appearance of the first quantitative theory by Modigliani and Miller (1958).

3.3 Modigliani–Miller Theory

3.3.1 *Modigliani–Miller Theory Without Taxes*

Modigliani and Miller (MM) in their first paper (Modigliani and Miller 1958) have come to the conclusions which were fundamentally different from the conclusions of traditional approach. Under assumptions (see Sect. 3.3.3 for details) that there are no taxes, no transaction costs, no bankruptcy costs, perfect financial markets exist with symmetry information, equivalence in borrowing costs for both companies and investors, etc., they have showed that choosing of the ratio between the debt and equity capital does not affect company value as well as capital costs (Fig. 3.3).

Under above assumptions, Modigliani and Miller have analyzed the impact of financial leverage, supposing the absence of any taxes (on corporate profit as well as individual one). They have formulated and proven two following statements.

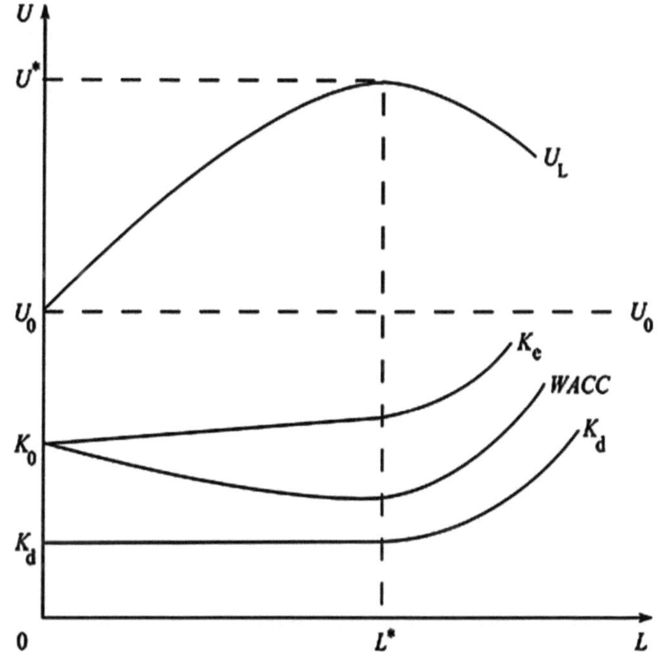

Fig. 3.3 Dependence of company capitalization, U_L, equity cost, k_e, debt cost, k_d, and weighted average cost of capital, WACC, in traditional (empirical) approach

Without taxes, the total cost of any company is determined by the value of its EBIT–Earnings Before Interest and Taxes, discounted with fixed rate k_0, ***corresponding to group of business risk of this company:***

$$V_L = V_U = \frac{\text{EBIT}}{k_0}. \tag{3.1}$$

Index L means financially dependent company (using debt financing), while index U means a financially independent company.

Authors supposed that both companies belong to the same group of business risk, and k_0 corresponds to required profitability of financially independent company, having the same business risk.

Because, as it follows from the formula (Eq. 3.1), value of the company does not depend on the value of debt, than according to Modigliani–Miller theorem (Modigliani and Miller 1958), in the absence of taxes, value of the company is independent of the method of its funding. This means as well that weighted average cost of capital, WACC, of this company does not depend on its capital structure and is equal to the capital cost, which this company will have under the funding by equity capital only.

$$V_0 = V_L; \quad \text{CF}/k_0 = \text{CF}/\text{WACC}, \quad \text{and thus WACC} = k_0.$$

Note that first Modigliani–Miller theorem is based on suggestion about independence of weighted average cost of capital and debt cost on leverage level.

From the first Modigliani–Miller theorem (Modigliani and Miller 1958), it is easy to derive an expression for the equity capital cost

$$\text{WACC} = k_0 = k_e w_e + k_d w_d. \tag{3.2}$$

Finding from here k_e, one gets

$$\begin{aligned} k_e &= \frac{k_0}{w_e} - k_d \frac{w_d}{w_e} = \frac{k_0(S+D)}{S} - k_d \frac{D}{S} \\ &= k_0 + (k_0 - k_d)\frac{D}{S} = k_0 + (k_0 - k_d)L \end{aligned} \tag{3.3}$$

Here,

D	value of debt capital of the company
S	value of equity capital of the company
$k_d, w_d = \frac{D}{D+S}$	cost and fraction of debt capital of the company
$k_e, w_e = \frac{S}{D+S}$	cost and fraction of equity capital of the company
$L = D/S$	financial leverage

Thus, we come to second statement (theorem) of Modigliani–Miller theory about the equity cost of financially dependent (leverage) company (Modigliani and Miller 1958).

Equity cost of leverage company k_e could be found as equity cost of financially independent company k_0 of the same group of risk, plus premium for risk, the value which is equal to production of difference $(k_0 - k_d)$ on leverage level L:

$$k_e = k_0 + (k_0 - k_d)L. \tag{3.4}$$

Formula (Eq. 3.4) shows that equity cost of the company increases linearly with leverage level (Fig. 3.3).

The combination of these two Modigliani–Miller statements implies that the increasing of level of debt in the capital structure of the company does not lead to increased value of firms, because the benefits gained from the use of more low-cost debt capital markets will be exactly offset by an increase in risk (we are speaking about the financial risk, the risk of bankruptcy) and, therefore, by an increase in cost of equity capital of firms: investors will increase the required level of profitability under increased risk, by which a higher level of debt in the capital structure is accompanied.

In this way, the Modigliani–Miller theorem argues that in the absence of the taxes, the capital structure of the company does not affect the value of the company and its weighted average cost of capital, WACC, and equity cost increases linearly with the increase of financial leverage.

Explanations, given by Modigliani and Miller under receiving of their conclusions, are the following (Modigliani and Miller 1958). Value of the company depends on profitability and risk only and does not depend on the capital structure. Based on the principle of preservation of the value, they postulated that the value of the company, which is equal to the sum of the equity and debt funds, is not changed when the ratio between its parts is changed. An important role in justification of Modigliani–Miller statements an existence of an arbitral awards opportunities for the committed markets plays. Two identical companies, differing only by the leverage level, must have the same value. If this is not the case, the arbitration aligns business cost: investors of less cost company can invest capital in a company of more value. Selling of shares of the first company and buying of stock of the second company will continue until the values of both companies are not equalized.

Most of Modigliani and Miller assumptions (Modigliani and Miller 1958), of course, are unrealistic. Some assumptions can be removed without changing the conclusions of the model. However, assuming no costs of bankruptcy and the absence of taxes (or the presence of corporate taxes only) are crucial–the change of these assumptions alters conclusions. The last two assumptions rule out the possibility of signaling theory and agency costs theory and, thus, also constitute a critical prerequisite (Fig. 3.4).

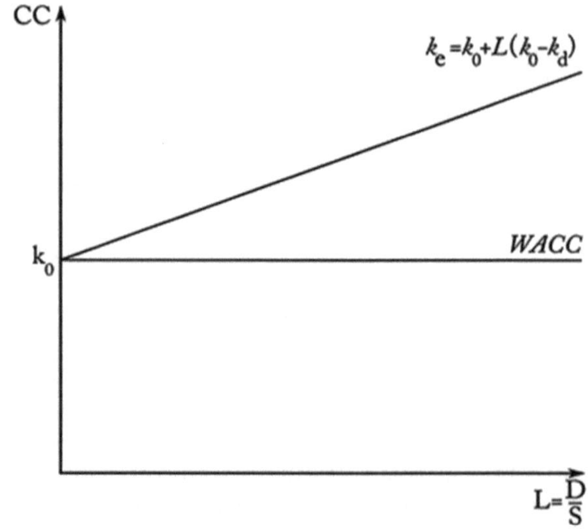

Fig. 3.4 Dependence of equity cost k_e and WACC on leverage level L within Modigliani–Miller theory without taxes

3.3.2 *Modigliani–Miller Theory with Taxes*

In the real situation, taxes on profit of companies always exist. Since the interest paid on debt are excluded from the tax base—it leads to the so—called effect of "tax shield": value of the company that used the borrowed capital (leverage company) is higher than the value of the company that financed entirely by the equity (non-leverage company). The value of the "tax shield" for 1 year is equal to $k_d\, D\, T$, where D—the value of debt, T–the income tax rate, and k_d—the interest on the debt (or debt capital cost) (Modigliani and Miller 1963). The value of the "tax shield" for perpetuity company for all time of its existence is equal to (we used the formula for the sum of terms of an infinitely decreasing geometric progression).

$$(\mathrm{PV})_{\mathrm{TS}} = k_d DT \sum_{t=1}^{\infty} (1 + k_d)^{-t} = DT \tag{3.5}$$

and the cost of leverage company is equal to

$$V = V_0 + DT, \tag{3.6}$$

where V_0 is the value of financially independent company.

Thus, we obtain the following result obtained by Modigliani and Miller (1963):

The value of financially dependent company is equal to the value of the company of the same risk group used no leverage, increased by the value of tax shield arising from financial leverage, and equal to the product of rate of corporate income tax T and the value of debt D.

Let us now get the expression for the equity capital cost of the company under the existence of corporate taxes.

Accounting that $V_0 = \mathrm{CF}/k_0$ and that the ratio of debt capital $w_\mathrm{d} = D/V$, one gets

$$V = \mathrm{CF}/k_0 + w_\mathrm{d} VT. \tag{3.7}$$

Because the value of leverage company is $V = \mathrm{CF}/\mathrm{WACC}$, for weighted average cost of capital, WACC, we get

$$\mathrm{WACC} = k_0(1 - w_\mathrm{d} T). \tag{3.8}$$

From here the dependence of WACC on leverage $L = D/S$ becomes the following:

$$\mathrm{WACC} = k_0(1 - LT/(1 + L)). \tag{3.9}$$

On the other hand, on definition of the weighted average cost of capital with "tax shield" accounting, we have

$$\mathrm{WACC} = k_0 w_\mathrm{e} + k_\mathrm{d} w_\mathrm{d}(1 - T). \tag{3.10}$$

Equating Eqs. (3.9) and (3.11), one gets

$$k_0(1 - w_\mathrm{d} T) = k_0 w_\mathrm{e} + k_\mathrm{d} w_\mathrm{d}(1 - T) \tag{3.11}$$

and from here, for equity cost, we get the following expression:

$$\begin{aligned} k_\mathrm{e} &= k_0 \frac{(1 - w_\mathrm{d} T)}{w_\mathrm{e}} - k_\mathrm{d} \frac{w_\mathrm{d}}{w_\mathrm{e}}(1 - T) = k_0 \frac{1}{w_\mathrm{e}} - k_0 \frac{w_\mathrm{d}}{w_\mathrm{e}} T - k_\mathrm{d} \frac{D}{S}(1 - T) \\ &= k_0 \frac{D + S}{S} - k_0 \frac{D}{S} T - k_\mathrm{d} \frac{D}{S}(1 - T) = k_0 + L(1 - T)(k_0 - k_\mathrm{d}). \end{aligned} \tag{3.12}$$

So, we get the following statement obtained by Modigliani and Miller (1963):

Equity cost of leverage company k_e paying tax on profit could be found as equity cost of financially independent company k_0 of the same group of risk, plus premium for risk, the value which is equal to production of difference $(k_0 - k_\mathrm{d})$ on leverage level *L*and on tax shield (*1 – T*).

It should be noted that the formula (Eq. 3.12) is different from the formula (Eq. 3.4) without tax only by the multiplier $(1 - T)$ in term, indicating a premium for risk. As the multiplier is less than unit, the corporate tax on profits leads to the fact that capital is growing with the increasing of financial leverage, slower than it would have been without them.

Analysis of formulas (Eqs. 3.4, 3.9, and 3.12) leads to following conclusions. When leverage grows:

1. Value of company increases.

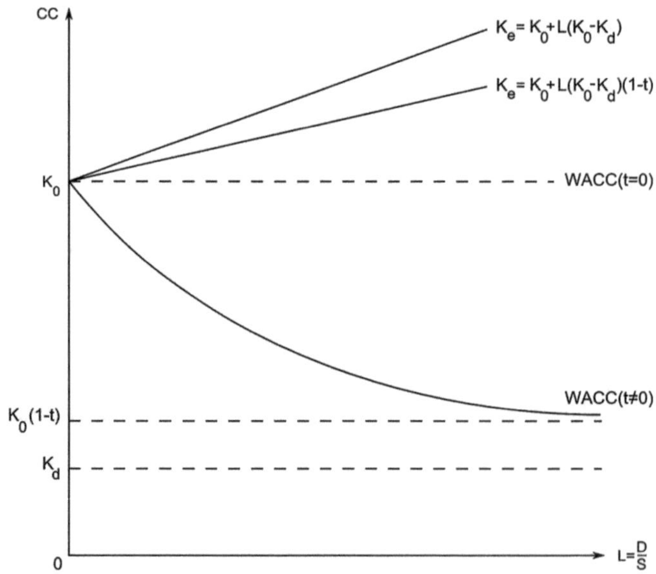

Fig. 3.5 Dependence of equity capital cost, debt cost, and WACC on leverage in Modigliani–Miller theory without taxes ($t = 0$) and with taxes ($t \neq 0$)

2. Weighted average cost of capital WACC decreases from k_0 (at $L = 0$) up to $k_0(1 - T)$ (at $L = \infty$) (when the company is funded solely by borrowed funds).
3. Equity cost increases linearly from k_0 (at $L = 0$) up to ∞ (at $L = \infty$).

Within their theory, Modigliani and Miller (1963) had come to the following conclusions. With the growth of financial leverage (Fig. 3.5):

1. The company value increases.
2. The weighted average cost of capital decreases from k_0 (for $L = 0$) up to $k_0(1 - T)$ (for $L = \infty$,, when the company is financed entirely with borrowed funds).
3. The cost of equity capital increases linearly from k_0 (for $L = 0$) up to ∞ (for $L = \infty$).

3.3.3 Main Assumptions of Modigliani–Miller Theory

The most important assumptions of the Modigliani–Miller theory are as following:

1. Investors are behaving rationally and instantaneously, see profit opportunity, inadequate investment risk. Therefore, the possibility of a stable situation of the arbitration, i.e., obtain the risk–free profit on the difference in prices for the same asset cannot be kept any length of time–reasonable investors quickly take advantage of it for their own purposes and equalize conditions in the market.

This means that in a developed financial market capital, the same risk should be rewarded by the same rate of return.

2. Investment and financial market opportunities should be equally accessible to all categories of investors–whether institutional or individual investors, large or small, rapidly growing or stable, or experienced or relatively inexperienced.
3. Transaction costs associated with funding are very small. In practice, the magnitude of transaction costs is inversely proportional to the amount of finance involved, so this assumption is more consistent with reality than the large sums involved: i.e., in attracting small amounts, the transaction costs can be high, while, as in attracting large loans, as well as during placement of shares at a significant amount, the transaction costs can be ignored.
4. Investors get money and provide funds to borrowers at risk–free rate. In all probability, this assumption is due to the fact that the lender seeks to protect himself by using one or other guarantees, pledge of assets, the right to pay claims on third parties, and the treaty provisions restricting the freedom of the borrower to act to the detriment of the creditor. Lender's risk is really small, but its position can be considered risk free with respect to the position of the borrower and, accordingly, should be rewarded by a risk–free rate of return.
5. Companies have only two types of assets: risk–free debt capital and risky equity capital.
6. There is no possibility of bankruptcy, i.e., irrespective of what the level of financial leverage of the company–borrowers are reached–bankruptcy is not threatening them. Thus, bankruptcy costs are absent.
7. There are no corporate taxes and taxes on personal income of investors. If the personal income tax can indeed be neglected, because the assets of the company separated from the assets of shareholders, the corporate income taxes should be considered in the development of more realistic theories (which was done by Modigliani and Miller in their second paper devoted to the capital structure (Modigliani et al., 1963).
8. Companies are in the same class of risky companies.
9. All financial flows are perpetuity.
10. Companies have the same information.
11. Management of the company maximizes the capitalization of the company.

3.3.4 Modifications of Modigliani–Miller Theory

Taking into Account Market Risk: Hamada Model

Robert Hamada (1969) unites Capital Asset Pricing Model (CAPM) with Modigliani–Miller model taxation. As a result, he derived the following formula for calculation of the equity cost of financially dependent company, including both financial and business risk of company:

$$k_e = k_F + (k_M - k_F)b_U + (k_M - k_F)b_U\frac{D}{S}(1 - T), \tag{3.13}$$

where b_U is the β-coefficient of the company of the same group of business risk, that the company under consideration, but with zero financial leverage. The formula (Eq. 3.13) represents the desired profitability of equity capital k_e as a sum of three components: risk-free profitability k_F, compensating to shareholders a temporary value of their money, premium for business risk $(k_M - k_F)b_U$, and premium for financial risk $(k_M - k_F)b_U\frac{D}{S}(1 - T)$.

If the company does not have borrowing ($D = 0$), the financial risk factor will be equal to zero (the third term is drawn to zero), and its owners will only receive the premium for business risk.

To apply the Hamada equation, specialists in practice, in most cases, use book value of equity capital as its approach of market value. Nevertheless, the Hamada formula implies the use of market value of the assets.

It should be noted also that the formula (Eq. 3.13) can be used to derive other equation, using which you can analyze the impact of financial leverage on β–factor of company shares.

Equating CAPM formula to equity cost, we get:

$$k_F + (k_M - k_F)b_U = k_F + (k_M - k_F)b_U + (k_M - k_F)b_U\frac{D}{S}(1 - T) \tag{3.14}$$

or

$$b = b_U\left(1 + \frac{D}{S}(1 - T)\right). \tag{3.15}$$

In this way, the assumptions on which Modigliani–Miller theory and CAPM are based, β-factor of equity capital of financially dependent company is equal to β-factor of financially independent company, corrected on tax on profit rate and applied leverage level. Consequently, market risk of the company, measured by a factor b, depends on both the business risk of the company, a measure of which is b_U,, and on the financial risk b, which is calculated by the formula (Eq. 3.15).

Note, that Hamada's empirical result regarding the inclusion of financial risk alongside business risk, as described by the classical CAPM model, was shown by Brusov et al. (2024) to be inaccurate. Brusov et al. created an innovative model, CAPM 2.0, which correctly describes financial risk alongside business risk (Brusov et al. 2024). It was shown that along with the renormalization of the beta coefficient to the level of leverage described by the Hamada model, an additional term appears in the model, that depends on leverage level, L, debt cost, k_d, risk free profitability, k_F, and tax corrector, (1-T). This term is absent in Hamada's model and can be noticeable at high leverage levels L and large differences between debt cost, k_d and risk free profitability, k_F.

In conclusion, here are the formulas for calculating the capital costs within the CAPM model [in parenthesis, there are formulas within the Modigliani–Miller theory (Modigliani and Miller 1958, 1963, 1966)].

The equity cost for company without debt capital:

$$k_e = k_F + \left(\bar{k}_M - k_F\right)\beta_U, \ (k_e = k_0). \tag{3.16}$$

The equity cost for company with debt capital:

$$k_e = k_F + \left(\bar{k}_M - k_F\right)\beta_e, \ (k_e = k_0 + (1 - T)(k_0 - k_d)L). \tag{3.17}$$

The debt cost:

$$k_d = k_F + \left(\bar{k}_M - k_F\right)\beta_d, (k_d = k_F; \beta_d = 0). \tag{3.18}$$

The weighted average cost of capital WACC

$$\text{WACC} = k_e w_e + k_d w_d (1 - T), \quad (\text{WACC} = k_0(1 - Tw_d)). \tag{3.19}$$

The Cost of Capital Under Risky Debt Another hypothesis of Modigliani and Miller was the suggestion about free of risk debt (in their theory, there are two types of assets: risky equity and free of risk debt). However, if we assume the risk of bankruptcy of company (and, accordingly, the ability to nonpayment of loans), the situation may change. Stiglitz (1969) and Rubinstein (1973) have shown that the conclusions concerning the total value of company do not change as compared to the findings derived by Modigliani and Miller under assumptions about free of risk debt (Modigliani and Miller 1958, 1963, 1966). However, the debt cost is changed. If previously, under assumption about the free of risk debt, it (debt cost) was regarded as a constant $k_d = k_F$, now it is not a constant. This claim is based on the work by Hsia (1981), where based on the models of pricing options, Modigliani–Miller and CAPM, it was shown that if one uses the formula for the net discount income, a term, reflecting tax protection on debt, should be discounted at the rate

$$k_d' = k_F + (k_0 - k_F)N(-d_1)\frac{1}{w_d}, \tag{3.20}$$

where

$$d_1 = \frac{-\ln w_d + k_F t}{\sigma\sqrt{t}} k_F + \frac{1}{2}\sigma\sqrt{t}, \tag{3.21}$$

here t—a moment of payment a credit, $N(-d_1)$—cumulative normal distribution of probability of random value d_1.

The Account of Corporate and Individual Taxes (Miller Model)

In the second article, Modigliani and Miller (1963) considered taxation of corporate profits, but did not take into account the presence in the economy of individual taxes of investors.

Merton Miller (1997) has introduced the model, demonstrating impact of leverage on the company value with account of the corporate and individual taxes (Miller 1976).

To describe his model, we will enter the following legends: T_C—tax on corporate profits rate, T_S—the tax rate on income of an individual investor from his ownership by stock of corporation, T_D—tax rate on interest income from the provision of investor—individuals of credits to other investors and companies. Income from shares partly comes in the form of a dividend and, in part, as capital profits, so that T_S is a weighted average value of effective rates of tax on dividends and capital profits on shares, while the income from the provision of loans usually comes in the form of the interests. The last are usually taxed at a higher rate. In the light of the individual taxes, and with the same assumptions that have been made for Modigliani–Miller models previously, the financially independent company value can be determined as follows:

$$V_U = \frac{\text{EBIT}(1 - T_C)(1 - T_S)}{k_0}. \tag{3.22}$$

A term $(1 - T_S)$ allows to take into account the individual taxes in the formula. In this way, numerator indicates which part of the operating company's profit remains in the possession of the investors, after the company will pay taxes on their profits, and its shareholders then will pay individual taxes on income from stock ownership. Since individual taxes reduce profits, remaining in the disposal of investors, the last, at other things being equal circumstances, also reduce and an overall assessment of the financially independent company value.

We will assess the financially dependent company under condition of a double taxation of income investors. To start, let us divide the annual cash flows of financially dependent company CF_L into flows sent to its shareholders CF_e and the flows belonging to debt owners CF_d, with account of both corporation tax on profits and on the income of individuals:

$$\text{CF}_L = \text{CF}_e + \text{CF}_d = (\text{EBIT} - I)(1 - T_C)(1 - T_S) + I(1 - T_D), \tag{3.23}$$

where I is the annual interest payments on debt.

The formula (Eq. 3.23) can also be rewritten as follows:

$$\begin{aligned} \text{CF}_L &= \text{CF}_e + \text{CF}_d \\ &= \text{EBIT}(1 - T_C)(1 - T_S) - I(1 - T_C)(1 - T_S) + I(1 - T_D). \end{aligned} \tag{3.24}$$

The first term of the equation (Eq. 3.24) corresponds to cash flow after taxes for financially independent company, shown in equation (Eq. 3.22), which shows its present value. The second and the third terms of the equation, reflecting the financial dependence, corresponds to cash flows related to the debt financing, which, as previously, is considered as free of risk. Their present values are obtained by discounting by risk-free nominal rate on debt k_d.

By combining the present values of all three terms, we get the company value under using the debt financing and in the presence of all types of taxation:

$$V_U = \frac{\text{EBIT}(1 - T_C)(1 - T_S)}{k_0} - \frac{I(1 - T_C)(1 - T_S)}{k_d} + \frac{I(1 - T_d)}{k_d}. \tag{3.25}$$

First term in (Eq. 3.25) is identical to V_U in formula (Eq. 3.22). Accounting this and combining two last terms, we get the following formula:

$$V_L = V_U + \frac{I(1 - T_d)}{k_d}\left[1 - \frac{(1 - T_C)(1 - T_S)}{(1 - T_d)}\right]. \tag{3.26}$$

The amount of paid interests with taking into account the taxation, divided by the desired profitability of debt capital,

$$\frac{I(1 - T_d)}{k_d} \tag{3.27}$$

is equal to market value of the debt D. Substituting D in the previous formula, we get the final expression, which is known as a formula of a Miller model:

$$V_L = V_U + \left[1 - \frac{(1 - T_C)(1 - T_S)}{(1 - T_d)}\right]D. \tag{3.28}$$

The Miller model allows you to obtain an estimate of the value of financially dependent company, taking into account the corporate tax, as well as tax on individuals. The Miller formula (Eq. 3.28) has several important consequences:

1. Second term of sum,

$$\left[1 - \frac{(1 - T_C)(1 - T_S)}{(1 - T_d)}\right]D, \tag{3.29}$$

represents the gains from use of debt capital. This term replaces the tax on profit of corporation rate in the Modigliani–Miller model with corporate taxes:

$$V_L = V_U + TD. \tag{3.30}$$

2. If we ignore taxes, a term (Eq. 3.29) will be equal to zero. Thus, in this case, the formula (Eq. 3.28) is transformed into the original version of the Modigliani–Miller model without taxes.
3. If we neglect taxes on individuals, the considering term becomes $1-(1-T_C)=T_C$, so, in this case, (Eq. 3.28) becomes a Modigliani–Miller Model with corporate taxes (Eq. 3.30).
4. If the shareholder receives profit only in the form of dividend, and if effective tax rates on income from shares and bonds are equal ($T_S = T_D$), the terms $1-T_S$ and $1-T_D$ are shrinking, and the factor for D in (Eq. 3.29) again is equal to T_C.
5. If the shareholder receives dividends, and income from capital, the situation is changed.

   In this case, effective tax rates on income from shares and bonds are not equal. Let's take a look at common case, when individual taxes on income for the company shares are less than individual taxes of creditors. This encourages investors to purchase the shares of the company compared to purchasing the bonds of the company. In this case, $T_S < T_D$. Then factor in D in (Eq. 3.28) β has a look

$$\beta = 1 - \frac{(1-T_C)(1-T_S)}{(1-T_d)} = 1-(1-T_C)\alpha$$
$$= 1-(1-T_C)(1+\gamma) = T_C + \gamma(T_C - 1) < T_C. \quad (3.31)$$

   It is less than T_C, because $\gamma > 0,\ T_C < 1$, therefore, in this case, the effect of using of debt financing, although there is, but it is less, than in the absence of individual taxes. In other words, the effect of tax shields for the company in this case decreases, and it becomes less than the above individual taxes of creditors (individual taxes for the obligations of the company) in comparison with the individual income tax on shares.
6. Let's take a look at case $T_S > T_D$, when individual income taxes on shares are bigger than individual taxes creditors. the factor B takes view

$$\beta = 1 - \frac{(1-T_C)(1-T_S)}{(1-T_d)} = 1-(1-T_C)\alpha$$
$$= 1-(1-T_C)(1-\gamma) = T_C + \gamma(1-T_C) > T_C. \quad (3.32)$$

   It is bigger than T_C, because $\gamma > 0, T_C < 1$; therefore, in this case, the effect of use of debt financing is increased compared with the case of the absence of individual taxes.
7. If $(1-T_C)(1-T_S) = 1-T_D$, then this term is zero, and the effect of using debt financing will also be zero. This means that the benefits of the use of tax shields as a result of the application of debt financing will be fully offset by additional losses of investors, associated with a higher tax rate on interest on income of individuals. In this case, the capital structure will not affect the company value

and its capital cost—in other words, you can apply Modigliani–Miller theory without tax (Modigliani and Miller 1958).

In his paper, Miller (1976) claimed that companies on average will use issuance of shares and debt securities in such a way as to result in taxation of investors' income to be optimal. In such an equilibrium state will occur equality

$$(1 - T_{\mathrm{C}})(1 - T_{\mathrm{S}}) = 1 - T_{\mathrm{D}}, \tag{3.33}$$

and thus, as we have pointed out above, capital structure will not affect the market company value and its capital cost. Thus, by Miller, the conclusions on the irrelevance of the capital structure, made on the base of the original Modigliani–Miller model with zero taxes, remain in force.

Subsequently, researchers adapted and checked the Miller results. Their works, as a rule, have been devoted to the Miller's conclusion concerning the absence of the gains from the use of the debt capital by the company. In the United States, an effective tax rate on the income of shareholders is lower than the one on the income of creditors, but, nevertheless, the product $(1 - T_{\mathrm{C}})(1 - T_{\mathrm{S}})$ is less than $1 - T_{\mathrm{D}}$. Consequently, the companies may receive the benefit from use of debt financing. However, in the Miller's work, in fact, has been shown that the distinction of rates of individual taxes on income of shareholders and creditors to some extent compensates the advantages of use of debt financing, and, in this way, the tax benefits of debt are less than anticipated at a more earlier Modigliani–Miller model, where only corporate taxes have been taken into account.

The General WACC Formula

A more general formula for WACC, than in the famous Modigliani–Miller theory (MM) has been derived and discussed by a few authors in 2006–2007 (Farber et al. 2006; Fernandez 2006; Berk and De Marzo 2007; Harris and Pringle 1985). It takes the following form (Eqs. [2.18] in Farber et al. [2006]).

$$WACC = k_0(1 - w_d t) - k_d t w_d + k_{TS} t w_d \tag{3.34}$$

where k_O is the required return on unleveraged company, k_d is the required return on its debt, k_{TS} is the expected return on the tax shield and t is the corporate taxes rate.

This formula is derived from the definition of the weighted average cost of capital and the balance sheet identity (for a similar presentation, see Berk and De Marzo (2007). At any point in time, it should therefore be verified, regardless of whether returns are annually or continuously compounded.

Practical applicability of Eq. (3.34) (while it is fairly general) requires additional conditions. Indeed, when the WACC is constant over time, the value of a leveraged company can be computed by discounting with the WACC of the unlevered free cash-flows. Therefore, it is interesting to consider the special cases when WACC is constant. The resulting formulas can also be found in textbooks (Brealey et al. 2005; Ross et al. 2005).

It was assumed by Modigliani and Miller in 1963, that the debt value D is constant. As the expected after-tax cash-flow of the unleveraged company is fixed, V_0 is also constant. By this assumption, $k_{TS} = k_D$ and the value of the tax shield is TS = tD. Therefore, the capitalization of the leveraged company V is a constant and the general WACC Formula (3.34) simplifies to a constant WACC:

$$WACC = k_0(1 - w_d T) \tag{3.35}$$

However, our opinion is that "classical" Modigliani–Miller (MM) theory, which suggests that the expected returns on the debt k_d and the tax shield k_{TS} are equals (because both of them have debt nature), is much more reasonable and in our paper we modify the "classical" Modigliani–Miller (MM) theory, which is still widely used in practice.

Trade–Off Theory

The world-famous **trade-off theory** has been considered the cornerstone in the solution of the problem of optimal capital structure for a company for many decades and is still used today for decision analysis on capital structure. Below we give two examples.

Frank, M., and Goyal, V., in 2009, "examines the relative importance of many factors in the capital structure decisions of publicly traded American firms from 1950 to 2003. The most reliable factors for explaining market leverage are: median industry leverage (+ effect on leverage), market-to-book assets ratio (−), tangibility (+), profits (−), log of assets (+), and expected inflation (+)". In addition, the authors have found that "dividend-paying firms tend to have lower leverage. When considering book leverage, somewhat similar effects are found. However, for book leverage, the impact of firm size, the market-to-book ratio, and the effect of inflation are not reliable". The empirical evidence seems to be reasonably consistent with some versions of the trade-off theory of capital structure.

Serrasqueiro, Z., & Caetano, A., in 2015, analyzed "to what extent decisions on the capital structure of small and medium-sized enterprises (SMEs) are closer to the assumptions of trade-off theory or to the assumptions of hierarchy theory. They used a sample of small and medium-sized enterprises located in the Portuguese hinterland, using dynamic LSDVC as the valuation method, and the empirical evidence suggests that the most profitable and oldest SMEs are less leveraged, confirming Pecking Order Theory's forecasts. Larger SMEs are leveraging more borrowing, confirming the predictions of trade-off theory and hierarchy theory. In addition, SMEs are significantly adjusting their current debt levels towards the optimal debt ratio, which is consistent with the predictions of the compromise theory. It was concluded that theories of compromise and hierarchy are not mutually exclusive in explaining capital structure decisions of small and medium–sized enterprises".

However, the bankruptcy of trade-off theory has been proven by Brusov et al. in 2013. They have shown that risky debt financing (and growing credit rate near the bankruptcy) in contrast to waiting results does not lead to growing of weighted average cost of capital, WACC, which still decreases with leverage. This means the absence of minimum in the dependence of WACC on leverage level as well as the absence of maximum in the dependence of company capitalization on leverage. Thus, the well-known trade-off theory lacks an optimal capital structure. The explanation for this fact was made by Brusov et al. in 2013 by analyzing the dependence of the cost of equity capital on the leverage level on the assumption that debt capital is risky.

Modigliani–Miller have considered tax shields from the interest on debt can increase the value of companies. In 1980, De Angelo and Masulis moved further in the theoretical examination of tax shields. They have noted that there are tax deductibles for companies other than debt to reduce their corporate tax burden and debt and non-debt tax shields should be accounted for. Depreciation, investment tax credits, or net-loss carry forwards could represents examples of such kind of non-debt tax shields. The first to test for these tax effects (suggested by DeAngelo and Masulis in 1980) has been carried out by Bradley, Jarrell and Kim in 1983. In contrast to the prediction in De Angelo and Masulis, 1980, by regressing company-specific debt-to-value ratios on non-debt tax shields, they have shown that debt is positively related to non-debt tax shields as measured by depreciation and investment tax credits. Titman and Wessels in 1988 found that "their results do not provide support for an effect on debt ratios arising from non-debt tax shields…". It was pointed out in 2003 by Graham, if a company invests heavily and uses debt financing to invest, a positive relation between such proxies for non-debt tax shield and debt may result. A mechanical positive relation of this type overwhelms and renders any substitution effects between debt and non-debt tax shields.

The original theory by Nobel Prize Winners Modigliani and Miller (1958, 1963, 1966) has been modified by many authors and above we shortly discussed some of them. In next paragraph we will generalize for the first time the Modigliani–Miller theory for the case of variable profit.

In conclusion, we present in Table 3.1 classification and summary of main theories of capital structures of company.

Table 3.1 Classification and summary of main theories of capital structures of company

Theory		Main thesis
Traditional theory		Empirical theory, existing before appearance of the first quantitative theory of capital structures (Modigliani–Miller theory) in 1958 (Modigliani and Miller 1958, 1963, 1966). Weighted average cost of capital depends on capital structures of company. There is an optimal dependence on capital structures of company
Modigliani–Miller theory (MM)	Without taxes	Capital cost and capitalization of the company are irrelevant on the capital structures of company
	With taxes	Weighted average cost of capital is decreased with leverage level, equity cost is increased linearly with leverage level, and capitalization of the company is increased with leverage level continuously
Brusov–Filatova–Orekhova theory (BFO-1)	For arbitrary age Without inflation	BFO theory (Brusov and Filatova 2011; Brusov et al. 2011a, b, c, 2012a, b, 2013a, b, 2014a, b; Filatova et al. 2008; Brusova 2011) has replaced the famous theory of capital cost and capital structure by Nobel laureates, Modigliani and Miller (1958, 1963, 1966) . The authors have moved from the assumption of Modigliani–Miller concerning the perpetuity (infinite time of life) of companies and further elaborated quantitative theory of valuation of core parameters of financial activities of companies with arbitrary age. Results of modern BFO theory turn out to be quite different from that of Modigliani–Miller theory. It shows that later, via its perpetuity, underestimates the assessment of weighted average cost of capital and the equity cost of the company and substantially overestimates the assessment of the capitalization of the company. Such an incorrect assessment of key performance indicators of financial activities of companies has led to an underestimation of risks involved, and impossibility, or serious difficulties in adequate managerial decision-making, which was one of the implicit reasons of global financial crisis of 2008 year. In the BFO theory, in investments at certain values of return-on-investment, there is an optimum investment structure. As well authors have developed a new mechanism of formation of the company optimal capital structure, different from suggested by trade-off theory
	For arbitrary age With inflation	Inflation not only increases the equity cost and the weighted average cost of capital, but as well it changes their dependence on leverage. In particular, it increases growing rate of equity cost with leverage. Capitalization of the company is decreased under accounting of inflation

(continued)

Table 3.1 (continued)

Theory		Main thesis
	For arbitrary age With increased financial distress costs and risk of bankruptcy	In BFO theory, with increased financial distress costs and risk of bankruptcy, the optimal capital structure is absent, which means that trade-off theory does NOT work
Brusov–Filatova–Orekhova theory (BFO-2)	For arbitrary lifetime	In perpetuity limit (Modigliani–Miller theory) time of life of company and company age turns out to be the same: both of them are infinite. When we move from the assumption of Modigliani–Miller concerning the perpetuity of companies these concepts (time of life of company and company age) become different and one should distinct them under generalization of Modigliani–Miller theory with respect to finite *n* Thus we have developed two kinds of finite *n*—theories: BFO-1 and BFO-3. BFO-1 theory is related to companies with arbitrary age and BFO-2 theory is related to companies with arbitrary life-time companies. By other words, BFO-1 is applicable for most interesting case of companies that reached the age of *n*-years and continue to exist on the market, and allows to analyze the financial condition of the operating companies. BFO-2 theory allows examine the financial status of the companies which ceased to exist, i.e., of those for which *n* means not age, but a life-time, i.e., the time of existence. A lot of schemes of termination of activities of the company can exist: bankruptcy, merger, acquisition, etc. One of those schemes, when the value of the debt capital *D* becomes zero at the time of termination of activity of company *n*, is considered in Chapter 3 and comparision of results of BFO-1 and BFO-2 has been done

(continued)

Table 3.1 (continued)

Theory		Main thesis
Brusov–Filatova–Orekhova theory (BFO-3)	For rating needs	A new approach to rating methodology has been developed in Chapters 21–23. Chapters 21 and 22 are devoted to rating of non-financial issuers, while Chapter 23 is devoted to long-term project rating. The key factors of a new approach are: (1) The adequate use of discounting of financial flows virtually not used in existing rating methodologies, (2) The incorporation of rating parameters (financial "ratios") into the modern theory of capital structure (Brusov–Filatova–Orekhova (BFO-3 theory) (in Chapters 21 into its perpetuity limit). This on the one hand allows use the powerful tools of this theory in the rating, and on the other hand it ensures the correct discount rates when discounting of financial flows. The interplay between rating ratios and leverage level which can be quite important in rating is discussed as well. All these create a new base for rating methodologies. New approach to ratings and rating methodologies allows to issue more correct ratings of issuers, makes the rating methodologies more understandable and transperant
Trade-off theory	Static	The static trade-off theory is developed with accounting of tax on profit and bankruptcy cost. It attempts to explain the optimal capital structure in terms of the balancing act between the benefits of debt (tax shield from interest deduction) and the disadvantage of debt (from the increased financial distress and expected bankruptcy costs). The tax shield benefit is the corporate income tax rate multiplied by the market value of debt and the expected bankruptcy costs are the probability of bankruptcy multiplied by the estimated bankruptcy costs
		Does not take into account the costs of the adaptation of financial capital structure to the optimal one, economic behavior of managers, owners, and other participants of economical process, as well as a number of other factors

(continued)

Table 3.1 (continued)

Theory		Main thesis
		As it has been shown in BFO theory, the optimal capital structure is absent in trade-off theory
	Dynamic	The dynamic trade-off models assume that costs of constant capital adjustment are high and thus firms will change capital structure only if benefits exceed costs. Therefore, there is an optimal range, outside of each leverage changes but remains unchanged inside. Companies try to adjust their leverage when it reaches the boundary of the optimal range. Subject to types of adjustment costs firms reach target ratio faster or slower. Proportional changes imply slight correction, whereas fixed changes imply considerable costs. In the dynamic model, correct decision on financial structure capital of the company in this period depends on the profit, which the company hopes to receive in the next period
		In BFO theory, with increased financial distress costs and risk of bankruptcy, the optimal capital structure is absent, which means that trade-off theory does NOT work: in static version as well as in dynamic one
Accounting of transaction cost		Accounting of the recapitalization transaction costs for the company, in which these costs are high, leads to the conclusion that a more cost-effective is not to modify financial capital structure, even if it is not optimal, during a certain period of time. The actual and target capital structure may vary because of the tool costs
Accounting of asymmetry of information		At the real financial markets, information is asymmetric (managers of the companies have owned more reliable information than investors and creditors), and rationality of economic subjects is limited
Signaling theory		Information asymmetry may be reduced on the basis of certain signals for creditors and investors, related to the behavior of managers on the capital market. It should take into account the previous development of the company and the current and projected cost-effectiveness of activities

(continued)

Table 3.1 (continued)

Theory		Main thesis
Pecking order theory		The pecking order theory is the preferred, and empirically observed, sequence of financing type to raise capital. That is, firms first tap retained earnings (internal equity) finance, second source is debt, and the last source is issuing new common stock shares (external equity). The empirical evidence of nonfinancial firm debt ratios coupled with the decision-making process of top management and the board of directors point to greater adherence to the pecking order theory
Theories of conflict of interests	Theory of agency costs	Management of the company may take decisions that are contrary to the interests of the shareholders or creditors, respectively; the costs are necessary to monitor its actions. An effective tool for resolving agent problem is the correct selection of compensation package (the share of participation of agent in property, bonus, stock options), allowing to link revenue of managers with the dynamics of equity capital and to provide motivation for managers to its (equity capital) conservation and growt
	Theory of corporate control and costs monitoring	If asymmetries of information exist, creditors, providing the capital, are interested in the possibility of the implementation of the self-monitoring of the effectiveness of its use and return. Costs for monitoring, as a rule, put on the company owners by their inclusion into credit rate. The level of monitoring costs depends on the scale of the business; therefore, with the increase of the business scale, the weighted average cost of capital of the company grows and company market value is reduced
	Theory of stakeholders	Stakeholder theory is a theory that identifies and models the groups that are stakeholders of a corporation or project. The diversity and the intersection of stakeholders' interests and different assessment by them of acceptable risk generate conditions for conflict of their interest, that is, making some corrections into the process of optimizing financial capital structure

(continued)

Table 3.1 (continued)

Theory		Main thesis
Behavioral theories	Manager investment autonomy	Managers implement those decisions, which, from their point of view, will be positively perceived by investors and, respectively, positively affect the market value of companies: when the market value of shares of a company and the degree of consensus of expectations of managers and investors are high, the company has an additional issue of shares, and in the opposite situation, it uses debt instruments. In this way, the financial capital structure is more influenced by investors, the expectations of which are taken into account by managers
	The equity market timing theory	Leverage level is determined by market dynamics. Equity market timing theory means that company should issue shares at high price and repurchase them at low price. The idea is to exploit temporary fluctuations in the equity cost relative to the cost of other forms of capital
	Information cascades	In order to save costs and to avoid errors, financial capital structure can be formed not on the basis of the calculations of optimal capital structure or depending on available in different periods of company life funding sources, but borrow from other companies that have successful, reputable managers (companies' leaders), as well as using (in the wake of the majority) the most popular methods of management of capital structure

References

Berk J, DeMarzo P (2007) Corporate finance. Pearson-Addison Wesley, Boston
Bradley M, Jarrell GA, Kim EH (1984) On the existence of an optimal capital structure: theory and evidence. J Financ 39:857–878
Brealey R, Myers S, Allen F (2005) Principle of corporate finance, 7th edn. McGraw Hill, USA, New York
Brusov P, Filatova P, Orekhova N (2013a) Absence of an optimal capital structure in the famous tradeoff theory! J Rev Glob Econ 2:94–116
Brusov P, Filatova P, Orekhova N (2014a) Mechanism of formation of the company optimal capital structure, different from suggested by trade off theory. Cogent Econ Financ 2:1–13. https://doi.org/10.1080/23322039.2013.946150
Brusov P, Filatova T, Eskindarov M, Orehova N (2012a) Influence of debt financing on the effectiveness of the finite duration investment project. Appl Financ Econ 22(13):1043–1052
Brusov P, Filatova T, Eskindarov M, Orehova N (2012b) Hidden global causes of the global financial crisis. J Rev Glob Econ 1:106–111
Brusov P, Filatova T, Orehova N (2013b) A qualitatively new effect in corporative finance: abnormal dependence of cost of equity of company on leverage. J Rev Glob Econ 2:183–193
Brusov P, Filatova T, Orehova N (2014b) Inflation in Brusov–Filatova–Orekhova theory and in its perpetuity limit-Modigliani–Miller theory. J Rev Glob Econ 3:175–185
Brusov P, Filatova T, Orehova N, Eskindarov M (2015) Modern corporate finance, investment and taxation, 1st ed. Springer International Publishing, pp 1–368
Brusov P, Filatova T, Orehova N et al (2011a) Influence of debt financing on the effectiveness of the investment project within the Modigliani–Miller theory. Res J Econ Bus ICT (UK) 2:11–15
Brusov P, Filatova T, Orehova N, Brusov PP, Brusova N (2011b) From Modigliani–Miller to general theory of capital cost and capital structure of the company. Res J Econ Bus ICT 2:16–21
Brusov P, Filatova T, Orehova N, Brusova A (2011c) Weighted average cost of capital in the theory of Modigliani–Miller, modified for a finite life-time company. Appl Financ Econ 21(11):815–824
Brusov P, Filatova T, Orehova N, Kulk V (2018a) A "golden age" of the companies: conditions of its existence. J Rev Glob Econ 7:88–103
Brusov P, Filatova T, Orehova N, Kulk V (2018b) Rating methodology: new look and New Horizons. J Rev Glob Econ 7:63–87
Brusov P, Filatova T, Orehova N, Kulk V (2018c) Rating: new approach. J Rev Glob Econ 7:37–62
Brusov P, Filatova T, Orehova N, Kulk WI (2018d) New meaningful effects in modern capital structure theory. J Rev Glob Econ 7:104–122
Brusov PN, Filatova TV, Kulik VL (2024) Capital Asset Pricing Model (CAPM) 2.0: account of business and financial risk. finance: theory and practice 28(2):128–142. https://doi.org/10.26794/2587-5671-2024-28-2-128-142
Brusov PN, Filatova TV, Orekhova NP (2021) Ratings: critical analysis and new approaches of quantitative and qualitative methodology 1–369
Brusov PN, Filatova TV, Orekhova NP (2022) Generalized Modigliani–Miller Theory: applications in corporate finance, investments, taxation and ratings 1–362
Brusov PN, Filatova TV, Orekhova NP (2023) The Brusov–Filatova–Orekhova Theory of Capital Structure: Applications in Corporate Finance. Taxation and Ratings Investments 1–769
Brusov PN, Filatova TV (2011) From Modigliani–Miller to general theory of capital cost and capital structure of the company. Financ Credit 435:2–8
Brusov PN, Filatova TV (2025a) Business valuation and company value: new qualitative approaches considering business and financial risks 1–654
Brusov PN, Filatova TV (2025b) Efficiency of investment projects: modern investment models and their applications 1–843
Brusova A (2011) A comparison of the three methods of estimation of weighted average cost of capital and equity cost of company. Financ Anal Prob Sol 34(76):36–42
Farber A, Gillet R, Szafarz A (2006) A general formula for the WACC. Int J Bus 11(2):211–218

Fernandez P (2006) A general formula for the WACC: a comment. Int J Bus 2006(11/2):219
Filatova T, Orehova N, Brusova A (2008) Weighted average cost of capital in the theory of Modigliani–Miller, modified for a finite life-time company. Bull FU 48:68–77
Frank M, Goyal V (2009) Capital structure decisions: which factors are reliably important? Financ Manag 38(1):1–37. https://doi.org/10.1111/j.1755-053X.2009.01026.x
Sheridan T, Wessels R (1988) The determinants of capital structure choice. J Financ 43:1–19
Graham JR (2003) Taxes and corporate finance: a review. Rev Financ Stud 16:1075–1129
Hamada R (1969) Portfolio analysis, market equilibrium, and corporate finance. J Financ 24(1):13–31
Harris R, Pringle J (1985) Risk-adjusted discount rates—Extension form the average-risk case. J Financ Res 8(3):237–243
Harry DA, Masulis RW (1980) Optimal capital structure under corporate and personal taxation. J Financ Econ 8:3–29
Hsia C (1981) Coherence of the modern theories of finance. Financ Rev 16(1):27–42
Miller M (1976) Debt and Taxes. J Financ 32(2):261–275
Miller M (1997) Merton Miller on derivatives. Wiley, New York, NY
Modigliani F, Miller M (1958) The cost of capital, corporate finance, and the theory of investment. Am Econ Rev 48:261–297
Modigliani F, Miller M (1963) Corporate income taxes and the cost of capital: a correction. Am Econ Rev 53:147–175
Modigliani F, Miller M (1966) Some estimates of the cost of capital to the electric utility industry 1954–1957. Am Econ Rev 56:333–391
Myers S (2001) Capital structure. J Econ Perspect 15(2):81–102
Ross S, Westerfiel R, Jaffee D (2005) Corporate finance, 7th edn. McGraw Hill, USA, New York
Rubinstein M (1973) A mean–variance synthesis of corporate financial theory. J Financ 28:167–181
Stiglitz J (1969) A re–examination of the Modigliani–Miller theorem. Am Econ Rev 59(5):784–793

Chapter 4
Modern Theory of Capital Cost and Capital Structure: Brusov–Filatova–Orekhova Theory (BFO Theory)

As we discussed in Chapter 3, one of the serious limitations of the Modigliani–Miller theory is the suggestion about perpetuity of the companies. In 2008, Brusov–Filatova–Orekhova (Filatova et al. 2008) have lifted up this limitation and have shown that the accounting of the finite life–time (or finite age) of the company leads to significant changes of all Modigliani–Miller results (Modigliani and Miller 1958, 1963, 1966): capitalization of the company is changed, as well as the equity cost, k_e, and the weighted average cost of capital, WACC, in the presence of corporative taxes. Besides, a number of qualitatively new effects in corporate finance, obtained in Brusov–Filatova–Orekhova theory (See recently published monographs by the authors at Springer Nature Publishing (Brusov et al. 2021, 2022, 2023; Brusov and Filatova 2025a, b), are absent in Modigliani–Miller theory.

Only in the absence of corporate taxes, we give a rigorous proof of the Brusov–Filatova–Orekhova theorem that equity cost, k_e, as well as its weighted average cost, WACC, does not depend on the life-time (or age) of the company, so the Modigliani–Miller theory could be generalized for arbitrary life-time (arbitrary age) companies.

Until recently (before 2008, when the first paper by Brusov–Filatova–Orekhova (Filatova et al. 2008 has appeared), the basic theory (and the first quantitative one) of the cost of capital and capital structure of companies was the theory by Nobel Prize winners Modigliani and Miller (Modigliani and Miller 1958, 1963, 1966). One of the serious limitations of the Modigliani–Miller theory is the suggestion about perpetuity of the companies. We lift up this limitation and show that the accounting of the finite life-time (finite age) of the company leads to change of the equity cost, k_e, as well as of the weighted average cost of capital, WACC, in the presence of corporate taxes. The effect of leverage on the cost of equity capital of the company, k_e, with an arbitrary life-time, and its weighted average cost of WACC is investigated. We give a rigorous proof of the Brusov–Filatova–Orekhova theorem that in the absence of corporate taxes, cost of company equity, k_e, as well as its weighted average cost, WACC, does not depend on the age (life-time) of the company.

P. Brusov and T. Filatova, *Taxes and Taxation*, Contributions to Finance and Accounting, https://doi.org/10.1007/978-3-032-11077-0_4

4.1 Companies of Arbitrary Age and Companies with Arbitrary Life-time: Brusov–Filatova–Orekhova Equation

Let us consider companies of arbitrary age and companies with arbitrary life-time.

In perpetuity limit (Modigliani–Miller theory) ***time of life of company*** and ***company age*** turn out to be the same: both of them are infinite. When we move from the assumption of Modigliani–Miller concerning the perpetuity of companies these concepts (time of life of company and company age) become different and one should distinct them under generalization of Modigliani–Miller theory with respect to finite n.

Thus we have developed two kinds of finite n—theories: BFO-1 and BFO-2. BFO-1 theory is related to companies with arbitrary age and BFO-2 theory is related to companies with arbitrary life-time companies (Brusov (2018a, b), Brusov et al. (2015, 2018a, 2018c, 2018d, 2018e, 2018f, 2018g, 2019, 2020, 2024; Filatova et al. (2018)) (See also recently published monographs by the authors at Springer Nature Publishing (Brusov et al. 2021, 2022, 2023; Brusov and Filatova 2025a, b). By other words, BFO-1 is applicable for the most interesting case of companies that reached the age of n-years and continue to exist on the market, and allows to analyze the financial state of the operating companies. BFO-2 theory allows examine the financial status of the companies which ceased to exist, i.e., of those companies for which n means not age, but a life-time, i.e., the time of existence. A lot of schemes of termination of activities of the company can exist: bankruptcy, merger, acquisition, etc. One of those schemes, when the value of the debt capital D becomes zero at the time of termination of activity of company n, is considered in this Chapter below (paragraph 4.5) and comparision of results of BFO-1 and BFO-2 has been done as well.

To start with the case of finite n let us first of all, find the value of tax shield, TS, of the company for n years

$$\mathrm{TS} = k_{\mathrm{d}}DT\sum_{t=1}^{n}(1+k_{\mathrm{d}})^{-t} = DT\big[1-(1+k_{\mathrm{d}})^{-n}\big]. \tag{4.1}$$

(We used the formula for the sum of n terms of a geometric progression).

Here, D is the value of debt capital; k_{d} the cost of debt capital; and T the tax on profit rate.

Next, we use the Modigliani–Miller theorem (Modigliani and Miller 1958, 1963, 1966):

The value of financially dependent company is equal to the value of the company of the same risk group used no leverage, increased by the value of tax shield arising from financial leverage, and equal to the product of rate of corporate income tax T and the value of debt D.

$$V = V_0 + DT\ . \tag{4.2}$$

This theorem was formulated by Modigliani and Miller for perpetuity companies, but we modify it for a company of arbitrary age.

$$\begin{aligned} V &= V_0 + \mathrm{TS} = V_0 + k_{\mathrm{d}}DT \sum_{t=1}^{\infty}(1+k_{\mathrm{d}})^{-t} \\ &= V_0 + w_{\mathrm{d}}VT\left[1-(1+k_{\mathrm{d}})^{-n}\right], \end{aligned} \tag{4.3}$$

$$V\left(1 - w_{\mathrm{d}}VT\left[1-(1+k_{\mathrm{d}})^{-n}\right]\right) = V_0. \tag{4.4}$$

There is a common use of the following two formulas for the cost of the financially independent and financially dependent companies (Modigliani and Miller 1958, 1963, 1966):

$$V_0 = \mathrm{CF}/k_0 \text{ and } \quad V = \mathrm{CF}/\mathrm{WACC}. \tag{4.5}$$

However, these almost always used formulas were derived for perpetuity company, and in case of a company of finite age (or with a finite life-time), they must be modified in the same manner as the value of tax shields (Brusov and Filatova 2011; Brusov et al. 2011a, b, c, 2012a, b, 2013a, b, 2014a, b; Filatova et al. 2008):

$$\begin{aligned} V_0 &= \mathrm{CF}\left[1-(1+k_0)^{-n}\right]/k_0; \\ V &= \mathrm{CF}\left[1-(1+\mathrm{WACC})^{-n}\right]/\mathrm{WACC}. \end{aligned} \tag{4.6}$$

From formula (Eq. 4.4), we get Brusov–Filatova–Orekhova equation for WACC (Filatova et al. 2008):

$$\frac{1-(1+\mathrm{WACC})^{-n}}{\mathrm{WACC}} = \frac{1-(1+k_0)^{-n}}{k_0\left[1-\omega_{\mathrm{d}}T\left(1-(1+k_{\mathrm{d}})^{-n}\right)\right]}. \tag{4.7}$$

Here, S—the value of equity capital of the company, $w_{\mathrm{d}} = \frac{D}{D+S}$—the share of debt capital, $k_{\mathrm{e}}, w_{\mathrm{e}} = \frac{S}{D+S}$—the cost and the share of the equity capital of the company, and $L = D/S$—financial leverage.

At $n = 1$, we get Myers (Myers 2001) formula for 1-year company

$$\mathrm{WACC} = k_0 - \frac{(1+k_0)k_{\mathrm{d}}}{1+k_{\mathrm{d}}} w_{\mathrm{d}}T \tag{4.8}$$

For $n = 2$, one has

$$\frac{1-(1+\mathrm{WACC})^{-2}}{\mathrm{WACC}} = \frac{1-(1+k_0)^{-2}}{k_0\left[1-\omega_{\mathrm{d}}T\left(1-(1+k_{\mathrm{d}})^{-2}\right)\right]}. \tag{4.9}$$

This equation can be solved for WACC analytically:

$$\mathrm{WACC} = \frac{1 - 2\alpha \pm \sqrt{4\alpha + 1}}{2\alpha}, \tag{4.10}$$

where

$$\alpha = \frac{2 + k_0}{(1 + k_0)^2 \left[1 - \omega_d T \frac{2k_d + k_d^2}{(1+k_d)^2}\right]}. \tag{4.11}$$

For $n = 3$ and $n = 4$, equation for the WACC becomes more complicated, but it still can be solved analytically, while for $n > 4$, it can be solved only numerically.

We would like to make **an important methodological notice**: taking into account the finite life-time of the company, all formulas, without exception, should be received with use formulas (Eq. 4.6) instead of their perpetuity limits (Eq. 4.5).

Below, we will describe the algorithm for the numerical solution of the equation (Eq. 4.7).

Algorithm for Finding WACC in Case of Companies of Arbitrary Age

Let us return back to n-year project (n-year company). We have the following equation for WACC in n-year case:

$$\frac{1 - (1 + \mathrm{WACC})^{-n}}{\mathrm{WACC}} - A(n) = 0, \tag{4.12}$$

where,

$$A(n) = \frac{1 - (1 + k_0)^{-n}}{k_0\left[1 - \omega_d T\left(1 - (1 + k_d)^{-n}\right)\right]}. \tag{4.13}$$

The algorithm of the solving of the Eq. (4.12) should be as follows:

1. Putting the values of parameters k_0, ω_d, T and given n, we calculate $A(n)$;
2. We determine two WACC values, for which the left part of the Eq. (4.12) has opposite signs. It is obvious that as these two values we can use WACC_1 and WACC_∞, because $\mathrm{WACC}_1 > \mathrm{WACC}_n > \mathrm{WACC}_\infty$ for finite $n \geq 2$.
3. Using, for example, the bisection method, we can solve the Eq. (4.12) numerically.

In MS Excel, it is possible to solve the Eq. (4.7) much easily by using the option "matching of parameter": we will use it through the monograph.

4.2 Comparison of Modigliani–Miller Results (Perpetuity Company) with Myers Results (1-Year Company) and Brusov–Filatova–Orekhova Ones (Company of Arbitrary Age)

Myers (2001) has compared his result for 1-year company (project) (Eq. 4.8) with Modigliani and Miller's result for perpetuity limits (Eq. 4.8). He has used the following values of parameters:

$$k_0 = 8\ \% \div 24\ \%;\ k_d = 7\ \%; T = 50\ \%;\ w_d = 0\ \% \div 60\ \%$$

and estimated the difference in the WACC values following from the formulas (Eq. 4.8). We did make the similar calculations for 2-, 3-,5-, and 10-year project for the same set of parameters, and we have gotten the following results, shown in Tables [Table 4.1 (second line (bulk)), Table 4.2 (second line (bulk)), and Table 4.4)] and corresponding figures (Figs. 4.1, 4.2, and 4.3).

For a graphic illustration of the results, we use data for $n = 1, 2, \infty$, which adequately reflect the results we have obtained.

Discussion of Results

1. From Table 4.1 and Fig. 4.1, it is obvious that WACC is maximum for 1-year company (project) and decreases with the life-time (age) of the company (project) and reaches the minimum in the Modigliani–Miller perpetuity case. Dependence of all WACC values on debt share w_d turns out to be linear at any equity cost k_0 for all considered durations of the project (life-time values of the companies). It is natural for 1-year project because it is described by Myers linear formula (4.8) as well as, in the Modigliani–Miller perpetuity case, described by the formula (3.8) (from Chapter 3), which is linear too, but it is surprise for 2-year project, where formula for WACC (4.7) is obviously nonlinear.

   The negative slope in WACC increases with the equity cost k_0.
2. As it follows from the Table 4.2 and Fig. 4.3, the dependence of the average ratios $\overline{r} = \langle \Delta_1/\Delta_2 \rangle$ on debt share w_d is quite weak and can be considered as almost constant. The value of this constant increases practically linear with the equity cost k_0 from 1.22 at $k_0 = 10\,\%$ up to 9.69 at $k_0 = 24\,\%$ (see Fig. 4.4).
3. The relative difference between 1-year and 2-year projects increases when the equity cost k_0 decreases. At the same time, the relative difference between 2-year project and perpetuity MM project increases with the equity cost k_0.

   We can also show below at Table 4.3 and Fig. 4.5 the dependence of the WACC on leverage level L for$n = 1$, $n = 3$, and $n = \infty$.

   From Table 4.3 and Fig. 4.5 it is obviously that WACC has a maximum for one year company and decreases with the age (life-time) of the company, reaching the minimum in the Modigliani–Miller perpetuity case (Note, however, that this

Table 4.1 WACC dependence on debt share w_d for different values of equity cost k_0 for companies with different life-time n

k_0	n	$w_d = 10\%$	20%	30%	40%	50%	60%
$k_0 = 8\,\%$	$n = 1$	7.6%	7.3	6.9	6.6	6.2	5.9
	$n = 2$	**7.52**	**7.08**	**6.6**	**6.17**	**5.67**	**5.21**
	$n = \infty$	7.6	7.2	6.8	6.4	6.0	5.6
$k_0 = 10\,\%$	$n = 1$	9.7	9.3	8.9	8.6	8.2	7.8
	$n = 2$	**9.51**	**9.05**	**8.59**	**8.13**	**7.64**	**7.16**
	$n = \infty$	9.5	9.0	8.5	8.0	7.5	7.0
$k_0 = 12\,\%$	$n = 1$	11.6	11.3	10.9	10.5	10.2	9.8
	$n = 2$	**11.51**	**11.02**	**10.54**	**10.07**	**9.6**	**9.09**
	$n = 3$	**11.46**	**10.93**	**10.39**	**9.85**	**9.31**	**8.77**
	$n = 5$	**11.42**	**10.83**	**10.25**	**9.66**	**9.06**	**8.46**
	$n = 10$	**11.396**	**10.786**	**10.1695**	**9.5455**	**8.914**	**8.2745**
	$n = \infty$	11.4	10.8	10.2	9.6	9.0	8.4
$k_0 = 16\,\%$	$n = 1$	15.62	15.2	14.9	14.5	14.1	13.7
	$n = 2$	**15.52**	**14.99**	**14.5**	**13.98**	**13.47**	**12.96**
	$n = 3$	**15.44**	**14.88**	**14.31**	**13.75**	**13.18**	**12.61**
	$n = 5$	**15.38**	**14.76**	**14.14**	**13.51**	**12.88**	**12.24**
	$n = 10$	**15.34**	**14.67**	**13.99**	**13.31**	**12.62**	**11.92**
	$n = \infty$	15.2	14.4	13.6	12.8	12.0	11.2
$k_0 = 20\,\%$	$n = 1$	19.6	19.2	18.8	18.4	18.1	17.7
	$n = 2$	**19.45**	**18.97**	**18.45**	**17.93**	**17.37**	**16.86**
	$n = 3$	**19.41**	**18.82**	**18.23**	**17.64**	**17.05**	**16.45**
	$n = 5$	**19.35**	**18.69**	**18.03**	**17.36**	**16.70**	**16.03**
	$n = 10$	**19.27**	**18.54**	**17.80**	**17.05**	**16.30**	**15.54**
	$n = \infty$	19.0	18.0	17.0	16.0	15.0	14.0
$k_0 = 24\,\%$	$n = 1$	23.6	23.2	22.8	22.4	22.0	21.6
	$n = 2$	**23.46**	**22.94**	**22.37**	**21.80**	**21.30**	**20.75**
	$n = 3$	**23.39**	**22.77**	**22.15**	**21.54**	**20.91**	**20.29**
	$n = 5$	**23.31**	**22.61**	**21.91**	**21.21**	**20.51**	**19.80**
	$n = 10$	**23.21**	**22.40**	**21.60**	**20.78**	**19.96**	**19.13**
	$n = \infty$	22.8	21.6	20.4	19.2	18.0	16.8

not always be so via the effect of "golden age" of the company [Brusov et al. 2018c]).

Table 4.2 Dependence of the differences $\Delta_1 = \text{WACC}_1 - \text{WACC}_\infty$ (first line), $\Delta_2 = \text{WACC}_1 - \text{WACC}_2$ [second line (bulk)], and their ratio $r = \Delta_1/\Delta_2$ (third line) on debt share w_d for different values of equity cost k_0

	$w_d = 10\,\%$	20%	30%	40%	50%	60%
$k_0 = 10\,\%$	0.20	0.30	0.4	0.60	0.7	0.8
	0.19	**0.25**	**0.31**	**0.47**	**0.56**	**0.64**
	1.05	1.2	1.29	1.28	1.25	1.25
$k_0 = 12\,\%$	0.2	0.5	0.7	0.9	1.2	1.4
	0.09	**0.28**	**0.36**	**0.43**	**0.6**	**0.71**
	2.22	1.76	1.94	2.09	2	1.97
$k_0 = 16\,\%$	0.4	0.8	1.3	1.7	2.1	2.5
	0.08	**0.21**	**0.4**	**0.52**	**0.63**	**0.74**
	5.0	3.81	3.25	3.27	3.33	3.38
$k_0 = 20\,\%$	0.6	1.2	1.8	2.4	3.1	3.7
	0.15	**0.23**	**0.35**	**0.47**	**0.73**	**0.84**
	4.0	5.22	5.14	5.11	4.25	4.4
$k_0 = 24\,\%$	0.8	1.6	2.4	3.2	4.0	4.8
	0.14	**0.26**	**0.43**	**0.6**	**0.7**	**0.85**
	5.7	6.15	5.58	5.33	5.71	5.65

Note that data for equity cost $k_0 = 8\,\%$ turn out to be a little bit uncertain: this could be related to the fact that this value of equity cost is quite close to value of interest rate of the debt $k_d = 7\,\%$. For all other values of equity cost, the results are reproducible and very informative and are discussed below

4.3 Brusov–Filatova–Orekhova Theorem

Case of Absence of Corporate Taxes

Modigliani–Miller theory in case of absence of corporate taxes gives the following results for dependence of WACC and equity cost k_e on leverage:

1. $V_0 = V_L;\quad \text{CF}/k_0 = \text{CF}/\text{WACC},\quad \text{and thus WACC} = k_0.$ (4.14)

2. $\text{WACC} = w_e \cdot k_e + w_d \cdot k_d$; and thus

$$k_e = \frac{\text{WACC} - w_d \cdot k_d}{w_e} = \frac{k_0 - \frac{L}{1+L}k_d}{\frac{1}{1+L}} = k_0 + L(k_0 - k_d). \tag{4.15}$$

For the finite life-time (finite age) companies, Modigliani–Miller theorem about equality of value of financially independent and financially dependent companies ($V_0 = V_L$) has the following view:

$$V_0 = V_L;$$

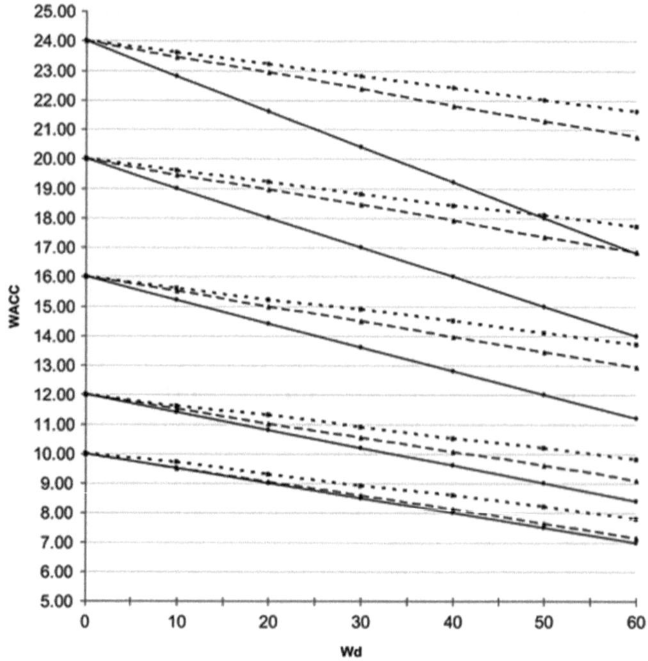

Fig. 4.1 The dependence of the WACC on debt share w_d for companies with different life-time n for different cost of equity, k_0 (from Table 4.1)

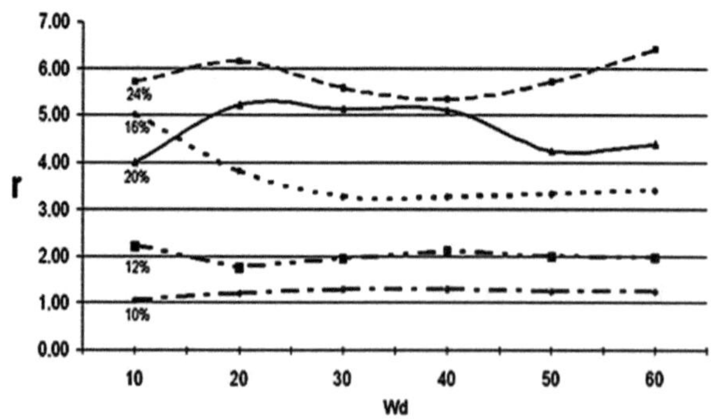

Fig. 4.2 Dependence of the ratio $r = \Delta_1/\Delta_2$ of differences $\Delta_1 = \text{WACC}_1 - \text{WACC}_\infty$ and $\Delta_2 = \text{WACC}_1 - \text{WACC}_2$ on debt share w_d for different values of equity cost k_0 (from Table 4.2)

$$\text{CF} \cdot \frac{\left[1 - (1 + k_0)^{-n}\right]}{k_0} = \text{CF} \cdot \frac{\left[1 - (1 + \text{WACC})^{-n}\right]}{\text{WACC}}. \tag{4.16}$$

Using this relation, we prove an important Brusov–Filatova–Orekhova theorem:

Under the absence of corporate taxes, the equity cost of the company, k_e, as well as its weighted average cost of capital, WACC, does not depend on the life-time (age) of the company and is equal, respectively, to

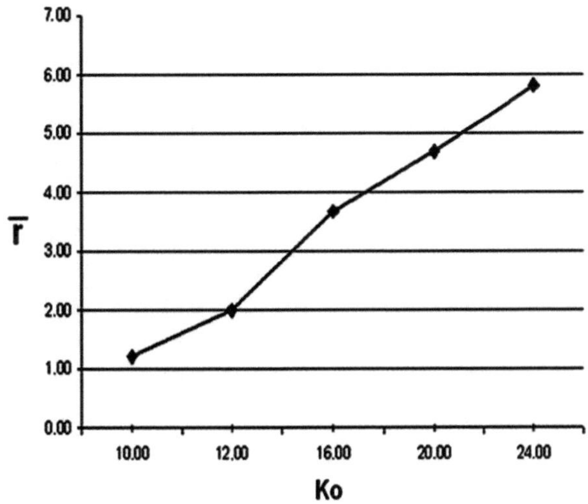

Fig. 4.3 Dependence of the average values of ratio $\overline{r} = \langle \Delta_1/\Delta_2 \rangle$ on the equity cost, k_0

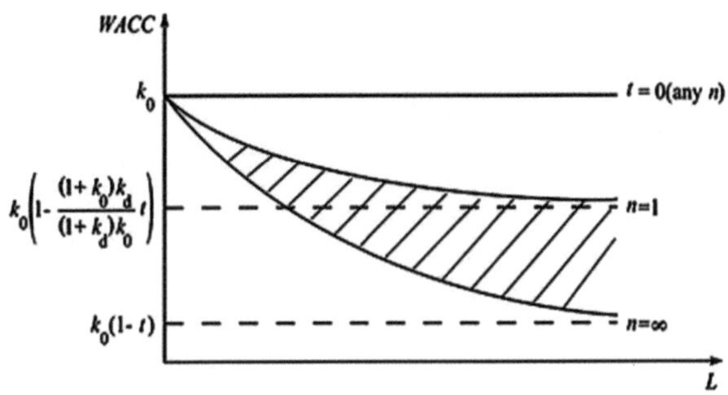

Fig. 4.4 The dependence of the WACC on leverage in the absence of corporate taxes [the horizontal line ($t = 0$)], as well as in the presence of corporate taxes [for 1-year ($n = 1$) and perpetuity companies ($n = \infty$)]. Curves for the WACC of companies with an intermediate life-time (age) ($1 < n < \infty$) lie within the shaded region

$$k_e = k_0 + L(k_0 - k_d); \quad \text{WACC} = k_0. \tag{4.17}$$

Let us consider first the one- and two-year companies

a. For 1-year company, one has from (4.15)

$$\frac{1-(1+k_0)^{-1}}{k_0} = \frac{1-(1+\text{WACC})^{-1}}{\text{WACC}}, \tag{4.18}$$

and thus

$$\frac{1}{1+k_0} = \frac{1}{1+\text{WACC}}. \tag{4.19}$$

Table 4.3 The dependence of the WACC on leverage level L for $n = 1$, $n = 3$, and $n = \infty$

L	K_0	K_d	t	W_d	WACC n = 1	WACC n = 3	WACC (MM)
0	0.2	0.1	0.2	0.00	20.00%	20.00%	20.00%
1	0.2	0.1	0.2	0.50	18.91%	18.41%	18.00%
2	0.2	0.1	0.2	0.67	18.55%	17.87%	17.33%
3	0.2	0.1	0.2	0.75	18.36%	17.61%	17.00%
4	0.2	0.1	0.2	0.80	18.25%	17.44%	16.80%
5	0.2	0.1	0.2	0.83	18.18%	17.34%	16.67%
6	0.2	0.1	0.2	0.86	18.13%	17.26%	16.57%
7	0.2	0.1	0.2	0.88	18.09%	17.20%	16.50%
8	0.2	0.1	0.2	0.89	18.06%	17.16%	16.44%
9	0.2	0.1	0.2	0.90	18.04%	17.12%	16.40%
10	0.2	0.1	0.2	0.91	18.02%	17.09%	16.36%

Table 4.4 Average (by debt share w_d) values of ratios $\overline{r} = \langle \Delta_1/\Delta_2 \rangle$ for $k_0 = 10\%$; 12%; 16%; 20%; and 24%

k_0	10%	12%	16%	20%	24%
$\overline{r} =< \Delta_1/\Delta_2 >$	1.22	2.00	3.67	4.69	3.69

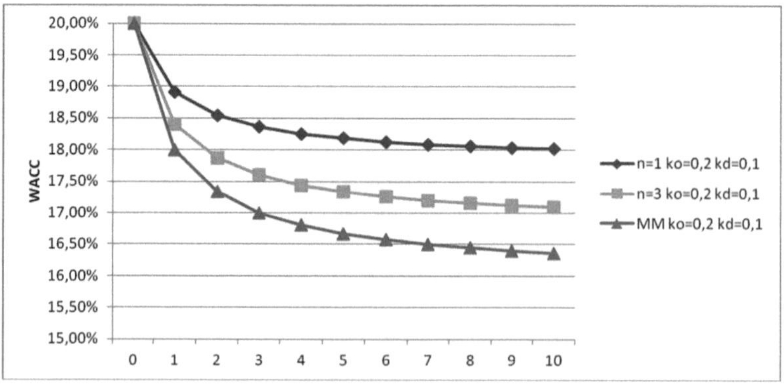

Fig. 4.5 Dependence of WACC on leverage level for $n = 1$, $n = 3$ and $n = \infty$

Hence

$$\text{WACC} = k_0. \tag{4.20}$$

Formula for equity cost $k_e = k_0 + L(k_0 - k_d)$ now obtained by substituting WACC = k_0 into (4.14).

b. For two-year company, one has from (4.15)

$$\frac{\left[1-(1+k_0)^{-2}\right]}{k_0}=\frac{\left[1-(1+\mathrm{WACC})^{-2}\right]}{\mathrm{WACC}},$$

and thus

$$\frac{2+k_0}{(1+k_0)^2}=\frac{2+\mathrm{WACC}}{(1+\mathrm{WACC})^2}. \quad (4.21)$$

Denoting $\alpha=\frac{2+k_0}{(1+k_0)^2}$, we get the following quadratic equation for WACC:

$$\alpha\cdot\mathrm{WACC}^2+(2\alpha-1)\cdot\mathrm{WACC}+(\alpha-2)=0. \quad (4.22)$$

It has two solutions

$$\mathrm{WACC}_{1,2}=\frac{1-2\alpha\pm\sqrt{4\alpha+1}}{2\alpha}. \quad (4.23)$$

Substituting $\alpha=\frac{2+k_0}{(1+k_0)^2}$, we get

$$\mathrm{WACC}_{1,2}=\frac{\left(k_0^2-3\right)\pm(k_0+3)(1+k_0)}{2(2+k_0)}. \quad (4.24)$$

$$\mathrm{WACC}_1=k_0;\quad \mathrm{WACC}_2=-\frac{2k_0+3}{k_0+2}<0. \quad (4.25)$$

The second root is negative, but the weighted average cost of capital can only be positive, so only one value remains

$$\mathrm{WACC}_1=k_0.$$

c. For company with arbitrary life–time, n, Brusov–Filatova–Orekhova formula (4.15) gives

$$\frac{1-(1+k_0)^{-n}}{k_0}=\frac{1-(1+\mathrm{WACC})^{-n}}{\mathrm{WACC}}. \quad (4.26)$$

For a fixed k_0, (Eq. 4.25) is an equation of $(n+1)$—degree relative to WACC. It has $n+1$ roots (in general complex). One of the roots, as a direct substitution shows, is always $\mathrm{WACC}=k_0$.. Investigation of the remaining roots is difficult and not a part of our problem.

Formula for equity cost $k_e=k_0+L(k_0-k_d)$ is now obtained by substituting $\mathrm{WACC}=k_0$ into (Eq. 4.14).

Thus, we have proved the Brusov–Filatova–Orekhova theorem.

Case of the Presence of Corporate Taxes

Modigliani–Miller theory in case of presence of corporate taxes gives the following results for dependence of WACC and equity cost k_e on leverage:

1. WACC

$$V_L = V_0 + Dt;\ D = w_d V_L; \tag{4.27}$$

$$\begin{aligned}\text{CF}/\text{WACC} &= \text{CF}/k_0 + Dt \\ &= \text{CF}/k_0 + w_d t \text{CF}/\text{WACC},\end{aligned} \tag{4.28}$$

$$\frac{1 - w_d t}{\text{WACC}} = \frac{1}{k_0}; \tag{4.29}$$

$$\text{WACC} = k_0(1 - w_d t) = k_0\left(1 - \frac{L}{1+L}t\right). \tag{4.30}$$

Thus, WACC decreases with leverage from k_0 [in the absence of debt financing ($L = 0$)] up to $k_0(1 - t)$ (at $L = \infty$).

2. The equity cost k_e

$$\text{WACC} = k_0(1 - w_d t) = w_e \cdot k_e + w_d \cdot k_d(1 - t);$$

and thus

$$\begin{aligned}k_e &= \frac{\text{WACC} - w_d \cdot k_d \cdot (1-t)}{w_e} = \frac{k_0(1 - w_d t) - \frac{L}{1+L}k_d(1-t)}{\frac{1}{1+L}} \\ &= k_0 + L(k_0 - k_d)(1 - t).\end{aligned} \tag{4.31}$$

4.4 From Modigliani–Miller to General Theory of Capital Cost and Capital Structure

Let us consider, how the weighted average cost of capital, WACC, and the cost of equity capital, k_e, will be changed when taking into account the finite age of the company.

a. one-year company

From (4.7), one has

$$\frac{1 - (1 + \text{WACC})^{-n}}{\text{WACC}} = \frac{1 - (1 + k_0)^{-n}}{k_0\left[1 - w_d t\left(1 - (1 + k_d)^{-n}\right)\right]}. \tag{4.32}$$

For one-year company, we get

$$\frac{1-(1+\text{WACC})^{-1}}{\text{WACC}}=\frac{1-(1+k_0)^{-1}}{k_0\left[1-w_d t\left(1-(1+k_d)^{-1}\right)\right]} \tag{4.33}$$

From (Eq. 4.33), we obtain the well-known Myers formula (Eq. 4.8), which is the particular case of Brusov–Filatova–Orekhova formula (Eq. 4.7).

$$\text{WACC}=k_0-\frac{1+k_0}{1+k_d}k_d w_d t.$$

Thus

$$\text{WACC}=k_0\left(1-\frac{(1+k_0)\cdot k_d}{(1+k_d)\cdot k_0}\cdot\frac{L}{1+L}t\right). \tag{4.34}$$

Thus, WACC decreases with leverage from k_0 [in the absence of debt financing ($L=0$)] up to $k_0\left(1-\frac{(1+k_0)\cdot k_d}{(1+k_d)\cdot k_0}t\right)$ (at $L=\infty$).

Equating the right part of Eq. (4.34) to general expression for WACC

$$WACC=w_e\cdot k_e+w_d\cdot k_d(1-t), \tag{4.35}$$

one gets

$$k_0-\frac{1+k_0}{1+k_d}k_d w_d t=w_e\cdot k_e+w_d\cdot k_d(1-t). \tag{4.36}$$

Thus

$$\begin{aligned}k_e&=\frac{1}{w_e}\left[k_0-\frac{1+k_0}{1+k_d}k_d w_d t-k_d w_d(1-t)\right]\\&=(1+L)k_0-L\frac{k_d}{1+k_d}[(1+k_0)t+(1+k_d)(1-t)]\\&=k_0+L(k_0-k_d)\left(1-\frac{k_d}{1+k_d}t\right).\end{aligned}$$

$$k_e=k_0+L(k_0-k_d)\left(1-\frac{k_d}{1+k_d}t\right). \tag{4.37}$$

So we see that in case of one-year company, the perpetuity limit.

$k_e=k_0+L(k_0-k_d)(1-t)$ is replaced by (Eq. 4.37).

Difference is due to different values of the tax shield for a one-year company and perpetuity one (Fig. 4.6).

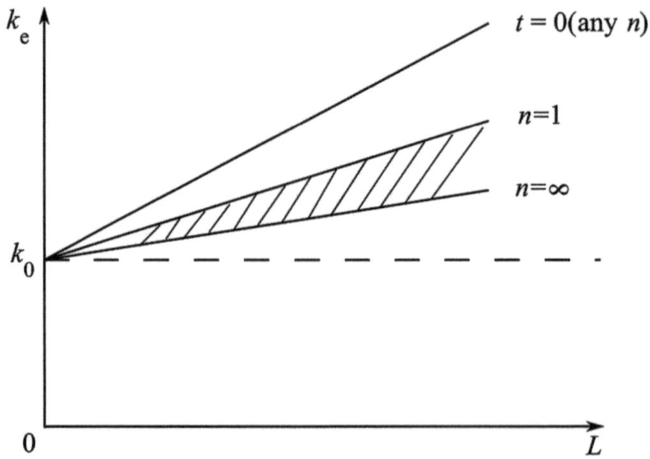

Fig. 4.6 Dependence of the equity cost, k_e, on leverage in the absence of corporate taxes [the upper line ($t = 0$)], as well as in the presence of corporate taxes [for one-year ($n = 1$) and perpetuity companies ($n = \infty$)]. Dependences of the cost of equity capital of companies, k_e, of an intermediate age ($1 < n < \infty$) lie within the shaded region

Let us investigate the question of the tax shield value for companies with different life-time (age) in more detail.

Tax Shield

General expression for the tax shield for n-year company has the form (Brusov–Filatova–Orekhova)

$$\mathrm{TS} = \sum_{i=1}^{n} \frac{k_d D t}{(1+k_d)^i} = \frac{k_d D t\left[1-(1+k_d)^{-n}\right]}{(1+k_d)\left(1-(1+k_d)^{-1}\right)} = Dt\left[1-(1+k_d)^{-n}\right]. \quad (4.38)$$

1. In perpetuity limit ($n \to \infty$), tax shield is equal to $\mathrm{TS}_\infty = Dt$, which leads to the so–called effect of the tax shield associated with the appearance of a factor (tax corrector) $(1-t)$ in the equity cost $k_e = k_0 + L(k_0 - k_d)(1-t)$.
2. For the one-year company, tax shield value is equal to

$$\mathrm{TS}_1 = Dt\left(1-(1+k_d)^{-1}\right) = Dtk_d/(1+k_d). \quad (4.39)$$

This leads to appearance of a factor $\left(1 - \frac{k_d}{1+k_d} t\right)$ in the equity cost (Eq. 4.36) $k_e = k_0 + L(k_0 - k_d)\left(1 - \frac{k_d}{1+k_d} t\right)$.

3. Tax shield for a two-year company is equal to

$$\mathrm{TS}_2 = Dt\left(1-(1+k_d)^{-2}\right) = Dtk_d(2+k_d)/(1+k_d)^2 \quad (4.40)$$

and if the analogy with one-year company will keep, then factor $(1 - t)$ in the Modigliani–Miller theory would be replaced by the factor

$$\left(1 - \frac{k_\mathrm{d}(2 + k_\mathrm{d})}{(1 + k_\mathrm{d})^2} t\right). \tag{4.41}$$

However, due to a nonlinear relation between WACC and k_0 and k_d in Brusov–Filatova–Orekhova formula (Eqs. 4.9, 4.10, and 4.11) for two-year company (and companies of bigger age), such a simple analogy is no longer observed, and the calculations become more complex.

4.5 BFO Theory in the Case, When the Company Ceased to Exist at the Time Moment N (BFO-2 Theory)

From the output of the BFO formula it follows that developed ideology is applied to companies which have reached the age of n-years and continue to exist on the market, while the theory of MM is only applicable to an infinitely old (perpetuity) companies. By other words, BFO is applicable for most interesting case of companies that reached the age of n-years and continue to exist on the market, and allows to analyze the financial condition of the operating companies.

However, the BFO theory allows also to examine the financial status of the companies which ceased to exist, i.e., of those for which n means not age, but a life-time, i.e., the time of existence. A lot of schemes of termination of activities of the company can exist: bankruptcy, merger, acquisition, etc. Below we consider one of those schemes, when the value of the debt capital D becomes zero at the time of termination of activity of company n: in this case the BFO theory requires minimal upgrades, showed below.

From the formula for the capitalization of the company (4.1), it is easy to get an estimation for the "residual capitalization" of the company, discounted to the time moment k:

$$\begin{aligned} V_k &= \sum_{t=k+1}^{n} \frac{\mathrm{CF}}{(1 + \mathrm{WACC})^t} \\ &= \frac{\mathrm{CF}}{\mathrm{WACC}}\left[1 - (1 + \mathrm{WACC})^{-(n-k)}\right]. \end{aligned} \tag{4.42}$$

Using the formula

$$V_k = w_\mathrm{d} D, \tag{4.43}$$

we obtain an expression for the tax shield for n years subject to the termination of the activities of the company at the moment n:

$$
\begin{aligned}
TS_n &= tk_\mathrm{d}w_\mathrm{d}\sum_{k=1}^{n}\frac{V_{k-1}}{(1+k_\mathrm{d})^k}\\
&= \frac{tk_\mathrm{d}w_\mathrm{d}CF}{\mathrm{WACC}}\sum_{k=1}^{n}\frac{1-(1+\mathrm{WACC})^{-(n-k+1)}}{(1+k_\mathrm{d})^k}\\
&= \frac{tk_\mathrm{d}w_\mathrm{d}}{\mathrm{WACC}}\left[\frac{1-(1+k_\mathrm{d})^{-n}}{k_\mathrm{d}}-\frac{(1+k_\mathrm{d})^{-n}-(1+\mathrm{WACC})^{-n}}{\mathrm{WACC}-k_\mathrm{d}}\right].
\end{aligned}
\tag{4.44}
$$

Substituting this expression into Eq. (4.3)

$$V_L = V_0 + (TS)_n$$

one gets the equation (let us call it BFO-2)

$$
\begin{aligned}
\frac{1-(1+\mathrm{WACC})^{-n}}{\mathrm{WACC}} = &\frac{1-(1+k_0)^{-n}}{k_0}\\
&+\frac{tk_\mathrm{d}w_\mathrm{d}}{\mathrm{WACC}}\left[\frac{1-(1+k_\mathrm{d})^{-n}}{k_\mathrm{d}}-\frac{(1+k_\mathrm{d})^{-n}-(1+\mathrm{WACC})^{-n}}{\mathrm{WACC}-k_\mathrm{d}}\right],
\end{aligned}
\tag{4.45}
$$

from which one can find the WACC for companies with arbitrary life-time n, provided that the company ceases to function at the time moment n.

Below in the monograph, we investigate the companies that have reached the age of n-years and continue to exist on the market, i.e., we will use formula BFO (9.7), but in this paragraph we present some results obtained from the formula BFO-2 (4.45).

4.5.1 Application of Formula BFO-2

Formula BFO-2 (4.45) in MS Excel takes a following form:

$$
\begin{aligned}
&\Big(\big(1-(1+C4)^{(-H4)}\big)/C4\Big)-\\
&\Big(\Big(\big(1-(1+D4)^{(-H4)}\big)/D4\Big)+\Big(\big((G4*E4*F4)/C4\big)*\Big(\big(1-(1+E4)^{(-H4)}\big)/E4\Big)-\\
&\Big(\big((1+E4)^{(-H4)}-(1+C4)^{(-H4)}\big)/(C4-E4)\Big)\Big)\Big)\Big)=0.
\end{aligned}
\tag{4.46}
$$

Using it we get the following results for dependence of WACC on leverage level L, life-time n, and on tax on profit rate t (Figs. 4.7, 4.8, and 4.9).

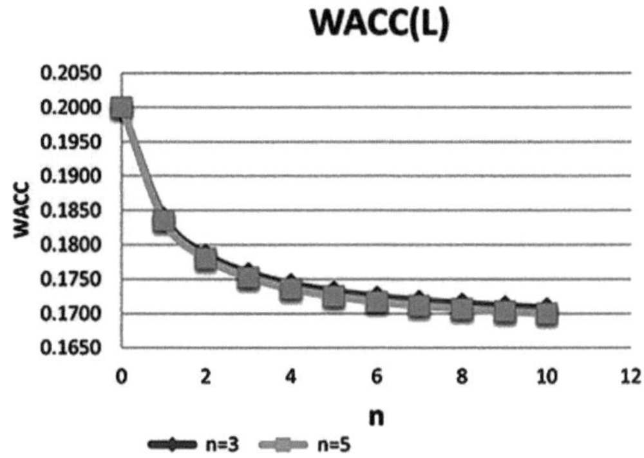

Fig. 4.7 The dependence of the WACC on leverage level L for $n = 3$ and $n = 5$; $k_0 = 0.2$; $k_d = 0.15$

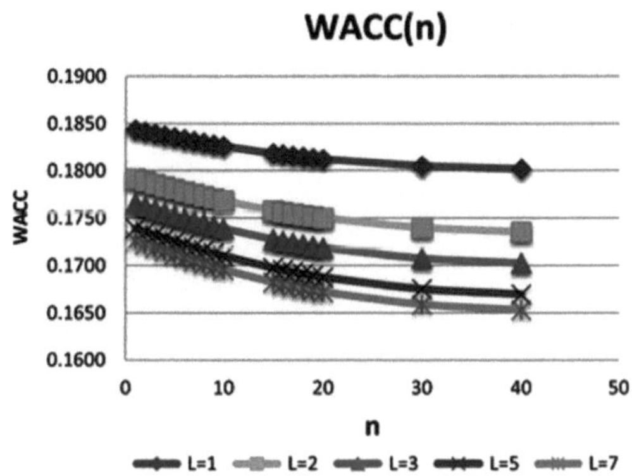

Fig. 4.8 The dependence of the WACC on life-time n at different leverage level L

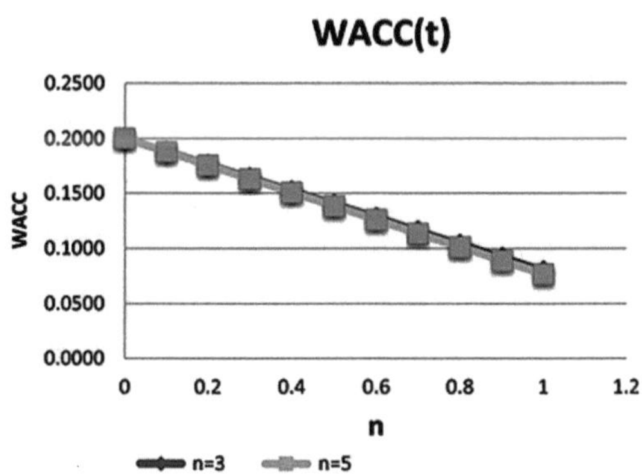

Fig. 4.9 The dependence of the WACC on tax on profit rate t for $n = 3$ and $n = 5$; $k_0 = 0.2$; $k_d = 0.15$

4.5.2 Comparison of Results Obtained from Formulas BFO and BFO-2

Let us compare results obtained from formulas BFO and BFO-2 (Figs. 4.10, 4.11, 4.12, and 4.13).

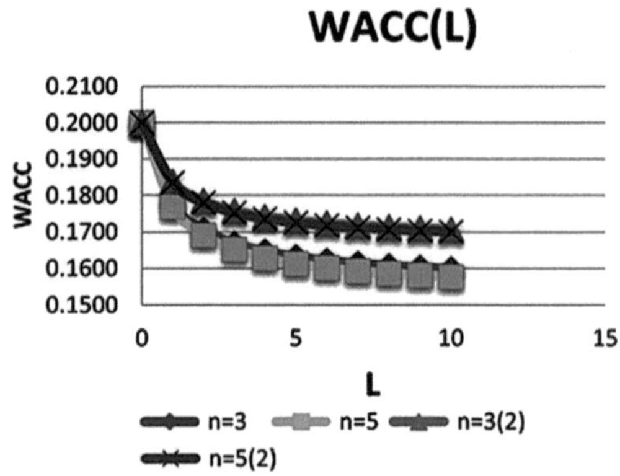

Fig. 4.10 Comparison of the dependence of the WACC on leverage level L for $n = 3$ and $n = 5$ from formulas BFO and BFO-2

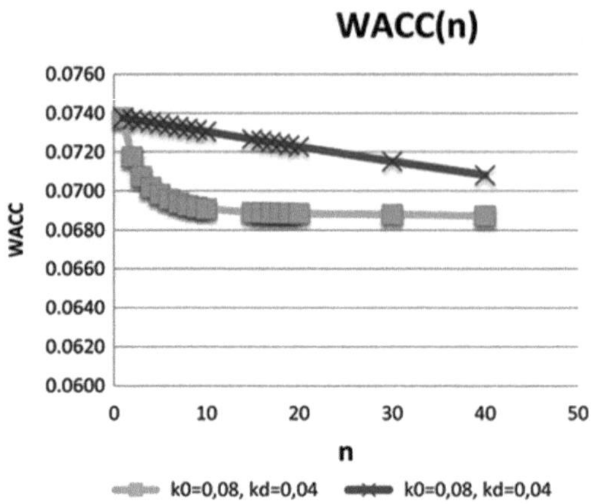

Fig. 4.11 Comparison of the dependence of the WACC on life–time n from formulas BFO (*lower curve*) and BFO-2 (*upper curve*); $k_0 = 0.08;\ k_d = 0.04$

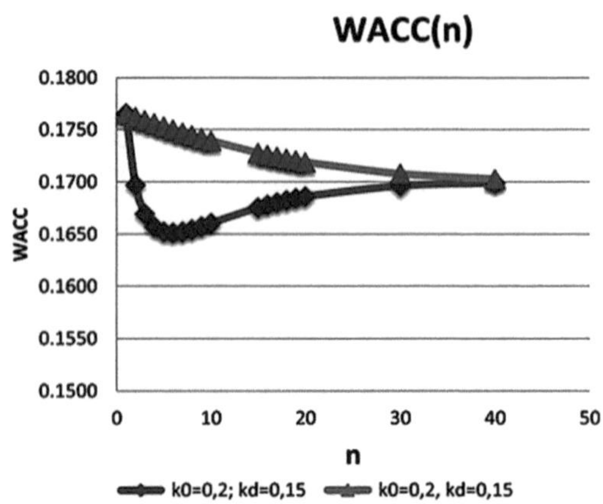

Fig. 4.12 Comparison of the dependence of the WACC on life-time n from formulas BFO (*lower curve*) and BFO-2 (*upper curve*); $k_0 = 0.2;\ k_d = 0.15; L = 3$

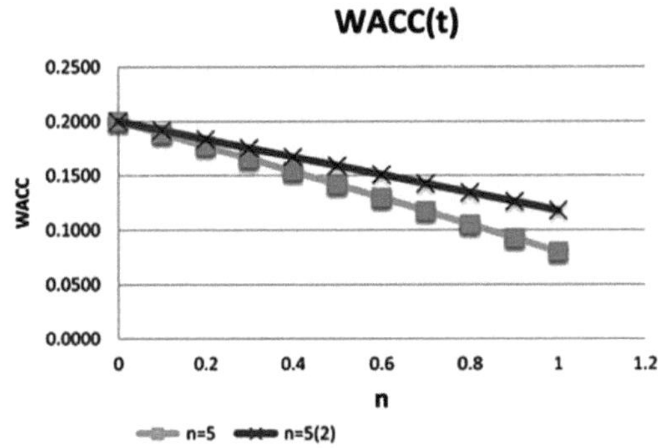

Fig. 4.13 Comparison of the dependence of the WACC on tax on profit rate t from formulas BFO (*lower curve*) and BFO-2 (*upper curve*); $k_0 = 0.2$; $k_d = 0.15$; $n = 5$

Comparison of results obtained from formulas BFO and BFO-2 shows that WACC values (at the same values of other parameters) turn out to be higher for the companies which ceased to exist at the time moment n, than for companies which have reached the age of n-years and continue to exist on the market. By other words, the companies which ceased to exist at the time moment n can attract a capital at higher rate, than for companies which have reached the age of n-years and continue to exist on the market.

We will develop the detailed investigation of the companies which ceased to exist at the time moment n (described by formula BFO-2) somewhere also and in this monograph we will limit ourselves by consideration of the companies which have reached the age of n-years and continue to exist on the market (described by formula BFO).

4.6 Conclusions

In this Chapter, an important step towards a general theory of capital cost and capital structure of the company has been done. For this, perpetuity theory of Nobel Prize winners Modigliani and Miller, which was until recently (until 2008) the main and the basic theory of capital cost and capital structure of companies, has been extended to the case of companies of arbitrary age and of companies with an arbitrary age (life-time), as well as for projects of arbitrary duration.

We show that taking into account the finite age of the company or the finite life-time of the company in the presence of corporate taxes leads to a change in the equity cost of the company, k_e, as well as in its weighted average cost, WACC, and company capitalization, V.

Thus, we have removed one of the most serious limitations of the theory of Modigliani–Miller, connected with the assumption of perpetuity of the companies. The effect of leverage on the cost of equity capital, k_e, of the company of an arbitrary age or with arbitrary life-time and its weighted average cost, WACC, is investigated. We give a rigorous proof of an important Brusov–Filatova–Orekhova theorem that

Table 4.5 Comparison of results, obtained within Modigliani–Miller theory and within general Brusov–Filatova–Orekhova theory

Financial parameter	Modigliani–Miller (MM) results	Brusov–Filatova–Orekhova (BFO) results
Capitalization of financially independent company	$V_0 = \text{CF}/k_0$	$V_0 = \frac{\text{CF}}{k_0}\left[1-(1+k_0)^{-n}\right]$
Capitalization of leverage (financially dependent) company	$V = \text{CF}/\text{WACC}$	$V = \frac{\text{CF}}{\text{WACC}}\left[1-(1+\text{WACC})^{-n}\right]$
Tax shield	$(TS)_\infty = DT$	BFO-1:$TS_n = DT\left[1-(1+k_d)^{-n}\right]$
		BFO-2:$\text{TS}_n =$ $\frac{T \cdot k_d \cdot w_d}{\text{WACC}}\left[\frac{1-(1+k_d)^{-n}}{k_d} - \frac{(1+k_d)^{-n}-(1+\text{WACC})^{-n}}{\text{WACC}-k_d}\right]$
Modigliani–Miller theorem with taxes	$V = V_0 + DT$	$V = V_0 + DT\left[1-(1+k_d)^{-n}\right]$
Weighted average cost of capital, WACC	$\text{WACC} =$ $= k_0(1-w_d t)$	BFO-1: $\frac{1-(1+\text{WACC})^{-n}}{\text{WACC}} = \frac{1-(1+k_0)^{-n}}{k_0\left[1-\omega_d T(1-(1+k_d)^{-n})\right]}$
		BFO-2: $\frac{1-(1+\text{WACC})^{-n}}{\text{WACC}} = \frac{1-(1+k_0)^{-n}}{k_0} + \frac{Tk_d w_d}{\text{WACC}} \cdot \left[\frac{1-(1+k_d)^{-n}}{k_d} - \frac{(1+k_d)^{-n}-(1+\text{WACC})^{-n}}{\text{WACC}-k_d}\right]$
Equity cost, k_e	$k_e = k_0 +$ $+L(k_0 - k_d)(1-t)$	$k_e = (1+L) \cdot \text{WACC} -$ $-k_d L(1-T)$

in the absence of corporate tax, equity cost of companies, k_e, as well as its weighted average cost, WACC, does not depend on the life-time (age) of the company.

We summarize the difference in results obtained within modern Brusov–Filatova–Orekhova theory and within classical Modigliani–Miller one in Table 4.5.

The first four formulas from the right–hand column are sometimes used in practice, but there are several significant nuances. First–these formulas do not take account of the residual value of the company, and only take into account the operating flows and this must be borne in mind. Second–these formulas contain the weighted average cost of capital of the company, WACC. If it is estimated within the traditional approach or the theory of Modigliani–Miller, it gives a lower WACC value, than the real value, and, therefore, overestimates the capitalization of both financially dependent and financially independent companies. Therefore, in order to assess a company's capitalization by the first two formulas, one needs to use Brusov–Filatova–Orekhova formulas for weighted average cost of capital, WACC, and equity cost, k_e.

To calculate the equity cost in BFO approximation (last line in Table 4.5), one first needs to use Brusov–Filatova–Orekhova formula for weighted average cost of capital, WACC (Filatova et al. 2008).

References

Brusov P (2018a) Editorial. J Rev Glob Econ 7:i–v. SCOPUS

Brusov P (2018b) Editorial: Introduction on special issue on the banking system and financial markets of Russia and other countries: problems and prospects. J Rev Glob Econ 7:i–vi. SCOPUS

Brusov PN, Filatova TV, Kulik VL (2024) Capital Asset Pricing Model (CAPM) 2.0: Account of business and financial risk. Finance: Theory and practice 28(2):128–142. https://doi.org/10.26794/2587-5671-2024-28-2-128-142

Brusov PN, Filatova TV, Orekhova NP (2018a) Modern corporate finance and investments, monograph. Knorus Publishing House, Moscow, p 517

Brusov PN, Filatova TV, Orekhova NP (2021) Ratings: Critical analysis and new approaches of quantitative and qualitative methodology 1–369

Brusov PN, Filatova TV, Orekhova NP (2022) Generalized Modigliani–Miller Theory: Applications in corporate finance, investments, taxation and ratings 1–362

Brusov PN, Filatova TV, Orekhova NP (2023) The Brusov–Filatova–Orekhova Theory of capital structure: Applications in corporate finance. Taxation and Ratings Investments 1–769

Brusov PN, Filatova TV (2025a) Business valuation and company value: New qualitative approaches considering business and financial risks 1–654

Brusov PN, Filatova TV (2025b) Efficiency of investment projects: Modern investment models and their applications 1–843

Brusov P, Filatova T, Orehova N, Eskindarov M (2015) Modern corporate finance, investments and taxation. Springer International Publishing, Switzerland, 373 p. monograph, SCOPUS. https://www.springer.com/gp/book/9783319147314

Brusov P, Filatova T, Orehova N, Eskindarov M (2018b) Modern corporate finance, investments, taxation and ratings. Springer Nature Publishing, Switzerland, 571 p. monograph

Brusov PN, Filatova TV, Orekhova NP, Kulik VL (2018c) Rating: new approach. J Rev Glob Econ 7:37–62. SCOPUS. https://doi.org/10.6000/1929-7092.2018.07.05

Brusov PN, Filatova TV, Orekhova NP, Kulik VL (2018d) A "golden age" of the companies: conditions of its existence. J Rev Glob Econ 7:88–109. SCOPUS. https://doi.org/10.6000/1929-7092.2018.07.07

Brusov PN, Filatova TV, Orekhova NP, Kulik VL (2018e) Rating methodology: new look and new horizons. J Rev Glob Econ 7:63–87. SCOPUS. https://doi.org/10.6000/1929-7092.2018.07.06

Brusov PN, Filatova TV, Orekhova NP, Kulik VL, Chang S-I, Lin YCG (2020) Modification of the Modigliani–Miller theory for the case of advance payments of tax on profit. J Rev Glob Econ 9:257–268

Brusov PN, Filatova TV, Orekhova NP, Kulik VL, Weil I (2018f) New meaningful effects in modern capital structure theory. J Rev Glob Econ 7:104–122. SCOPUS. https://doi.org/10.6000/1929-7092.2018.07.08

Brusov PN, Filatova TV, Orekhova NP, Kulik VL, Weil I (2019) Ratings of the investment projects of arbitrary durations: new methodology. J Rev Glob Econ 8:437–448. SCOPUS. https://doi.org/10.6000/1929-7092.2019.08.37

Brusov P, Filatova T, Orekhova N, Kulik V, Weil I, Brailov A (2018g) The impact of the central bank key rate and commercial banks credit rates on creating and maintaining of a favorable investment climate in the country. J Rev Glob Econ 7:360–376. SCOPUS. https://doi.org/10.6000/1929-7092.2018.07.31

Filatova TV, Brusov PN, Orekhova NP, Kulik VL (2018) Ratings of the long-term projects: new approach. J Rev Glob Econ 7:645–661. SCOPUS. https://doi.org/10.6000/1929-7092.2018.07.59

Filatova T, Orehova N, Brusova A (2008) Weighted average cost of capital in the theory of Modigliani–Miller, modified for a finite life-time company. Bull FU 48:68–77

Modigliani F, Miller M (1958) The cost of capital, corporate finance, and the theory of investment. Am Econ Rev 48:261–297

Modigliani F, Miller M (1963) Corporate income taxes and the cost of capital: a correction. Am Econ Rev 53:147–175
Modigliani F, Miller M (1966) Some estimates of the cost of capital to the electric utility industry 1954–1957. Am Econ Rev 56:333–391
Myers S (2001) Capital structure. J Econ Perspect 15(2):81–102

Chapter 5
The Modigliani–Miller Theory with Arbitrary Frequency of Payment of Tax on Profit

5.1 Introduction

5.1.1 Literature Review

In their first paper Modigliani and Miller (1958) (Brusov et al. 2015, 2018a, 2020; Modigliani and Miller 1958) consider the problem of capital cost and capital structure for perpetuity companies without any taxes. In the second article, Modigliani and Miller (1963) (Brusov et al. 2015, 2018a, 2020; Modigliani and Miller 1963) considered taxation of corporate profits, but did not take into account the presence in the economy of individual taxes of investors. Merton Miller (1977) (Brusov et al. 2015, 2018a, 2020; Miller 1977) has introduced the model, demonstrating impact of leverage on the company value with account of the corporate and individual taxes. To describe his model, we will enter the following legends: T_C–tax on corporate profits rate, T_S–the tax rate on income of an individual investor from his ownership by stock of corporation, T_D–tax rate on interest income from the provision of investor–individuals of credits to other investors and companies. Income from shares partly comes in the form of a dividend and, in part, as capital profits, so that T_S is a weighted average value of effective rates of tax on dividends and capital profits on shares, while the income from the provision of loans usually comes in the form of the interests. The last are usually taxed at a higher rate. In the light of the individual taxes, and with the same assumptions that have been made for Modigliani–Miller models previously, the financially independent company value can be determined as follows:

$$V_U = \frac{\text{EBIT}(1 - T_C)(1 - T_S)}{k_0}. \tag{5.1}$$

A term $(1 - T_S)$ allows to take into account the individual taxes in the formula. In this way, numerator indicates which part of the operating company's profit remains

P. Brusov and T. Filatova, *Taxes and Taxation*, Contributions to Finance and Accounting, https://doi.org/10.1007/978-3-032-11077-0_5

in the possession of the investors, after the company will pay taxes on their profits, and its shareholders then will pay individual taxes on income from stock ownership. Since individual taxes reduce profits, remaining in the disposal of investors, the last, at other things being equal circumstances, also reduce and an overall assessment of the financially independent company value.

Robert Hamada (1969) (Brusov et al. 2015, 2018a, 2020; Hamada 1969) unites Capital Asset Pricing Model (CAPM) with Modigliani–Miller model taxation. As a result, he derived the following formula for calculation of the equity cost of financially dependent company, including both financial and business risk of company:

$$k_e = k_F + (k_M - k_F)b_U + (k_M - k_F)b_U\frac{D}{S}(1 - T), \tag{5.2}$$

where b_U is the β–coefficient of the company of the same group of business risk, that the company under consideration, but with zero financial leverage. The formula represents the desired profitability of equity capital k_e as a sum of three components: risk–free profitability k_F, compensating to shareholders a temporary value of their money, premium for business risk $(k_M - k_F)b_U$, and premium for financial risk $(k_M - k_F)b_U\frac{D}{S}(1 - T)$.

If the company does not have borrowing ($D = 0$), the financial risk factor will be equal to zero (the third term is drawn to zero), and its owners will only receive the premium for business risk.

Note, that Hamada's empirical result regarding the inclusion of financial risk along with the business risk, which is described by the classical CAPM model, was shown by Brusov et al. (2024) to be inaccurate. Brusov et al. have created an innovative model, CAPM 2.0, which correctly describes financial risk along with the business risk (Brusov et al.2024). It was shown that along with the renormalization of the beta coefficient β to the level of leverage described by the Hamada model, an additional term appears in the model, that depends on leverage level, L, debt cost, kd, risk free profitability, kF, and tax corrector,. This term is absent in Hamada's model and can be noticeable at high leverage levels and large differences between debt cost, kd and risk free profitability, kF.

More general formula for the WACC, then famous Modigliani–Miller (MM) one has been derived and discussed by a few authors (Farber et al. 2006; Fernandez 2007; Harris and Pringle 1985; Miles and Ezzel 1980; Ross et al. 2005; Taggart 1991; DeMarzo 1998). It takes the following form (Eq. [5.18] in FGS, 2006 [Farber et al. 2006])

$$WACC = k_O(1 - w_d T) - k_d t w_d + k_{TS} t w_d \tag{5.3}$$

where k_O, k_d and k_{TS} are the expected returns respectively on the unlevered firm, the debt and the tax shield, V is the value of the levered firm, VTS is the value of the tax shield, D is the value of the debt and TC is the corporate tax rate.

This formula is derived from the balance sheet identity and the definition of the weighted average cost of capital (for a similar presentation, see Berk and De Marzo

2007). It should therefore be verified at any point in time, whatever returns are annually or continuously compounded.

Although Eq. (5.3) is fully general, its practical applicability requires additional conditions. Indeed, when the WACC is constant over time, the value of a levered firm can be computed by discounting with the WACC the unlevered free cash–flows. Therefore, we pay a special attention to the special cases that make the WACC constant. The resulting particular formulas can also be found in textbooks (Ross et al. 2005).

First, Modigliani and Miller (1963) assume that the level of debt D is constant. Then, as the expected after–tax cash–flow of the unlevered firm is fixed, V_0 is also constant. By assumption, $k_{TS} = k_D$ and the value of the tax shield is TS = tD. Therefore, the value of the firm V is a constant and the general WACC formula (5.15) simplifies to a constant WACC:

$$WACC = k_0(1 - w_d T) \tag{5.4}$$

But our opinion is that "classical" Modigliani–Miller (MM) theory, which coming from the suggestion that the expected returns on the debt k_d and the tax shield k_{TS} are equals (because both of them have debt nature), is much more reasonable and in our paper we modify namely "classical" Modigliani–Miller (MM) theory, which is still widely used in practice.

One of the most serious limitations of the Modigliani–Miller theory is the suggestion about perpetuity of the companies. In 2008, Brusov–Filatova–Orekhova (Brusov 2018a, b; Brusov et al. 2015, 2018a, b, c, d, e, f, g, 2019, 2020; Filatova et al. 2008, 2018), have lifted up this limitation and have shown that the accounting of the finite life–time (or finite age) of the company leads to significant changes of all Modigliani–Miller results (Modigliani and Miller 1958, 1963, 1977): capitalization of the company is changed, as well as the equity cost, k_e, and the weighted average cost of capital, WACC, in the presence of corporative taxes. Besides, a number of qualitatively new effects in corporate finance, obtained in Brusov–Filatova–Orekhova theory (Brusov et al. 2015, 2018a, b, c, d, e, f, g, 2019, 2020; Brusov 2018a, b; Filatova et al. 2008, 2018), are absent in Modigliani–Miller theory (Modigliani and Miller 1958, 1963, 1977). (See also recently published monographs by the authors at Springer Nature Publishing (Brusov et al. 2021, 2022, 2023; Brusov and Filatova 2025a, b).

The famous Brusov–Filatova–Orekhova formula for weighted average cost of capital, WACC, has the following form

$$\frac{1-(1+WACC)^{-n}}{WACC} = \frac{1-(1+k_0)^{-n}}{k_0\left[1-\omega_d T\left(1-(1+k_d)^{-n}\right)\right]}. \tag{5.5}$$

Here, S—the value of own (equity) capital of the company, $w_d = \frac{D}{D+S}$—the share of debt capital; k_e, $w_e = \frac{S}{D+S}$—the cost and the share of the equity of the company, $L = D/S$—financial leverage.

A lot of meaningful effects has been discovered within BFO theory: these effects are absent within MM theory. BFO theory has destroyed some main existing principles of financial management: among them trade off theory, which was considered as keystone of formation of optimal capital structure of the company during many decades and **bankruptcy of which has been proven** by Brusov–Filatova–Orekhova (Brusov et al. 2015, 2018a, b, c, d, e, f, g, 2019, 2020, 2018; Brusov 2018a, b; Filatova et al. 2008; Brusov et al. 2021, 2022, 2023; Brusov and Filatova 2025a, b).

5.1.2 Focus and Objective of the Chapter

The tax shield plays a crucial role in both main capital structure theories: Brusov–Filatova–Orekhova (BFO theory) and its perpetuity limit Modigliani–Miller theory. How it is formed influences the results of both theories. Both of them describes the case of annual payments of tax of profit, but in practice these payments are made more frequent: semiannually, quarterly, monthly. While a return is not required more than once a year, businesses may be responsible for filing estimated taxes based on profits earned. This requirement is dependent on showing a profit. For example, sole proprietors must file estimated taxes on profits quarterly, on the 15th day of April, June, September and January. In Russia tax on profit payments could be made annually, quarterly, monthly. In current paper we show that the account of frequency of payment of tax on profit within the Modigliani–Miller theory turns out to be very important and leads to significant consequences.

To study this problem we modify the Modigliani–Miller theory for the case of arbitrary frequency of payment of tax on profit and show that:

- all Modigliani–Miller theorems, statements and all formulas change;
- all main financial indicators, such as the weighted average cost of capital, WACC, company value, V and equity cost, k_e depend on the frequency of tax on profit payments. This allows to company manage WACC, V, k_e etc. by choosing the number of payments of tax of profit p per year;
- increase the number of payments of tax of profit per year leads to decrease of the cost of attracting capital and increase of the company value;
- obtained results allow to company choose the number of payments of tax of profit per year, as many, as it is profitable to it (of course, within actual tax legislation);
- in case of income tax payments more than once per year (at $p \neq 1$), as it takes place in practice, the weighted average cost of capital, WACC, company value, V and equity cost, k_e start depend on k_d, while in ordinary (classical) Modigliani–Miller theory all these values DO NOT depend on k_d.
- the tilt angle of the curve of equity cost, k_e (L), decreases with the number of payments of tax of profit p, this modifies the dividend policy of the company, because the economically justified value of dividends is equal to equity cost.

5.2 Modification of the Modigliani–Miller Theory for the Case of Arbitrary Frequency of Payments of Tax on Profit

5.2.1 Tax Shield

Let us calculate first the tax shield in the Modigliani–Miller theory for the case of p payments of tax on profit per year

$$TS = \frac{k_d Dt}{p(1+k_d)^{1/p}} + \frac{k_d Dt}{p(1+k_d)^{2/p}} + \frac{k_d Dt}{p(1+k_d)^{3/p}} + \ldots \tag{5.6}$$

TS represents a geometric progression with denominator $q = \frac{1}{(1+k_d)^{1/p}}$.

Summing the progression, one gets

$$TS = \frac{k_d Dt}{p(1+k_d)^{1/p}\left(1-(1+k_d)^{-1/p}\right)} = \frac{k_d Dt}{p\left((1+k_d)^{1/p}-1\right)}. \tag{5.7}$$

Note, that in case of classical Modigliani–Miller theory

$$TS = Dt. \tag{5.8}$$

It is easy to get this result from (5.7), putting the frequency of payments of tax on profit p=1.

5.2.2 The Weighted Average Cost of Capital, WACC

Let us now calculate the weighted average cost of capital, WACC, in the Modigliani–Miller theory for the case of p payments of tax on profit per year.

From the Modigliani–Miller theorem we have for the company value V

$$V = V_0 + TS. \tag{5.9}$$

Putting expression (5.7) for TS, we get

$$V = V_0 + \frac{k_d Dt}{p\left((1+k_d)^{1/p}-1\right)}. \tag{5.10}$$

Substituting $D = w_d V$, one gets

$$V\left(1-\frac{k_d w_d t}{p\left((1+k_d)^{1/p}-1\right)}\right)=V_0. \tag{5.11}$$

Accounting, that

$$V=\frac{CF}{WACC};\ V_0=\frac{CF}{k_0}, \tag{5.12}$$

we have

$$\frac{CF}{WACC}\cdot\left(1-\frac{k_d w_d t}{p\left((1+k_d)^{1/p}-1\right)}\right)=\frac{CF}{k_0}. \tag{5.13}$$

From here we arrive to the expression for the weighted average cost of capital, WACC, for the case of p payments of tax on profit per year.

$$WACC=k_0\cdot\left(1-\frac{k_d w_d t}{p\left((1+k_d)^{1/p}-1\right)}\right). \tag{5.14}$$

Note, that in case of classical Modigliani–Miller theory

$$WACC=k_0\cdot(1-w_d t). \tag{5.15}$$

It is easy to get this result from (5.14), putting the frequency of payments of tax on profit per year $p=1$.

5.2.3 Company Value, V

Let us now calculate the company value, V, in the Modigliani–Miller theory for the case of p payments of tax on profit per year.

Putting WACC value into first formula of (5.12) one gets for company value, V

$$V=\frac{CF}{WACC}=\frac{CF}{k_0\cdot\left(1-\frac{k_d w_d t}{p\left((1+k_d)^{1/p}-1\right)}\right)}. \tag{5.16}$$

In case of "classical" Modigliani–Miller theory one has

$$V = \frac{CF}{WACC} = \frac{CF}{k_0 \cdot (1 - w_d t)}. \tag{5.17}$$

It is easy to get this result from (5.16), putting the frequency of payments of tax on profit per year $p = 1$.

5.2.4 Equity Cost, k_e

Let us now calculate the equity cost, k_e, in the Modigliani–Miller theory for the case of p payments of tax on profit per year.

General expression for the weighted average cost of capital, WACC, upon definition has the following form

$$WACC = k_e w_e + k_d w_d (1 - t). \tag{5.18}$$

We get from (5.18) the following formula for the equity cost, k_e,

$$k_e = \frac{WACC}{w_e} - \frac{k_d w_d (1 - t)}{w_e}. \tag{5.19}$$

Accounting from (5.14) the expression for the weighted average cost of capital, WACC,

$$WACC = k_0 \cdot \left(1 - \frac{k_d w_d t}{p\left((1 + k_d)^{1/p} - 1\right)}\right), \tag{5.20}$$

one gets

$$\begin{aligned} k_e &= \frac{k_0}{w_e} \cdot \left(1 - \frac{k_d w_d t}{p\left((1 + k_d)^{1/p} - 1\right)}\right) - \frac{k_d w_d (1 - t)}{w_e} \\ &= k_0 \cdot \left(1 + L - \frac{k_d L t}{p\left((1 + k_d)^{1/p} - 1\right)}\right) - k_d L (1 - t) \\ &= k_0 + L\left(k_0 - k_d (1 - t) - \frac{k_0 k_d t}{p\left((1 + k_d)^{1/p} - 1\right)}\right). \end{aligned} \tag{5.21}$$

Thus, we have the following formula for the equity cost, k_e, in case of arbitrary frequency of payment of tax on profit

$$k_e = k_0 + L\left(k_0 - k_d(1-t) - \frac{k_0 k_d t}{p\left((1+k_d)^{1/p} - 1\right)}\right) \tag{5.22}$$

From this formula it is easy to get "classical" Modigliani–Miller expression for the equity cost, k_e, in case of annual payment of tax on profit, putting $p = 1$

$$k_e = k_0 + L(k_0 - k_d)(1-t) \tag{5.23}$$

Thus, from Sects. 5.2.1, 5.2.2, 5.2.3, and 5.2.4 we come to conclusion, that in case of income tax payments more than once per year (at $p \neq 1$), as it takes place in practice, the weighted average cost of capital, WACC, company value, V and equity cost, k_e start depend on k_d, while in ordinary (classical) Modigliani–Miller theory all these values DO NOT depend on k_d.

In subsequent paragraphs (Sects. 5.3, 5.4, and 5.5) we will study numerically with use of Microsoft Excel the dependence of the main financial indicators of the company (the weighted average cost of capital, WACC, the company value, V, the cost of equity, k_d, on leverage level L for cases of practical interest with respect to equity and debt costs and frequency of payment of tax on profit *p*.

5.3 Dependence of the Weighted Average Cost of Capital, WACC, on Leverage Level L

5.3.1 Dependence of the Weighted Average Cost of Capital, WACC, on Leverage Level L at Different p *and Fixed* K_d

Let us start from the study numerically with use of Microsoft Excel of the dependence of the weighted average cost of capital, WACC, on leverage level L at different *p* and fixed k_d, using obtained by us formula (5.14)

$$WACC = k_0 \cdot \left(1 - \frac{k_d w_d t}{p\left((1+k_d)^{1/p} - 1\right)}\right).$$

From Tables 5.1, 5.2, 5.3, 5.4, and 5.5 and Figs. 5.1, 5.2, and 5.3 it is seen, that the weighted average cost of capital, WACC, decreses with leverage level L at all values of frequency of payments of tax on profit *p*. With increase of *p* WACC decreases. As we'll see below, this will lead to increase of company value, V, with *p*.

To demonstrate, that above conclusion takes place for all values of equity cost (at zero leverage level L) k_0, we consider one more example: $k_0 = 0.22$ and different *p* = 2; 4; 12.

Table 5.1 Dependence of WACC on leverage level L at $k_0 = 0.2$, $k_d = 0.16$ and $p = 1$

L	T	K_0	K_d	*P*	WACC
0	0.2	0.2	0.16	1	0.200000
1	0.2	0.2	0.16	1	0.180000
2	0.2	0.2	0.16	1	0.173333
3	0.2	0.2	0.16	1	0.170000
4	0.2	0.2	0.16	1	0.168000
5	0.2	0.2	0.16	1	0.166667
6	0.2	0.2	0.16	1	0.165714
7	0.2	0.2	0.16	1	0.165000
8	0.2	0.2	0.16	1	0.164444
9	0.2	0.2	0.16	1	0.164000
10	0.2	0.2	0.16	1	0.163636

Table 5.2 Dependence of WACC on leverage level L at $k_0 = 0.2$, $k_d = 0.16$ and $p = 2$

L	T	K_0	K_d	*p*	WACC
0	0.2	0.2	0.16	2	0.200000
1	0.2	0.2	0.16	2	0.179230
2	0.2	0.2	0.16	2	0.172306
3	0.2	0.2	0.16	2	0.168845
4	0.2	0.2	0.16	2	0.166767
5	0.2	0.2	0.16	2	0.165383
6	0.2	0.2	0.16	2	0.164394
7	0.2	0.2	0.16	2	0.163652
8	0.2	0.2	0.16	2	0.163075
9	0.2	0.2	0.16	2	0.162613
10	0.2	0.2	0.16	2	0.162236

5.3.2 Dependence of the Weighted Average Cost of Capital, WACC, on Leverage Level L at Different K_d and Fixed p

In this paragraph we investigate the dependence of the weighted average cost of capital, WACC, on leverage level L at different values of debt cost k_d and fixed *p*.

From Tables 5.6, 5.7, 5.8, 5.9, 5.10, 5.11, 5.12, and 5.13 and Figs. 5.3, 5.4, 5.5, 5.6 and 5.7 it is seen, that in case of income tax payments more than once per year (at $p \neq 1$), as it takes place in practice, the weighted average cost of capital, WACC, (and as we'll see below, company value, V and equity cost, k_e start depend on debt cost, k_d, while in ordinary (classical) Modigliani–Miller theory all these values DO NOT depend on k_d). The weighted average cost of capital, WACC, decreses with

Table 5.3 Dependence of WACC on leverage level L at $k_0 = 0.2$, $k_d = 0.16$ and $p = 4$

L	T	K_0	K_d	p	WACC
0	0.2	0.2	0.16	4	0.200000
1	0.2	0.2	0.16	4	0.178837
2	0.2	0.2	0.16	4	0.171783
3	0.2	0.2	0.16	4	0.168256
4	0.2	0.2	0.16	4	0.166139
5	0.2	0.2	0.16	4	0.164728
6	0.2	0.2	0.16	4	0.163721
7	0.2	0.2	0.16	4	0.162965
8	0.2	0.2	0.16	4	0.162377
9	0.2	0.2	0.16	4	0.161907
10	0.2	0.2	0.16	4	0.161522

Table 5.4 Dependence of WACC on leverage level L at $k_0 = 0.2$, $k_d = 0.16$ and $p = 12$

L	T	K_0	K_d	p	WACC
0	0.2	0.2	0.16	12	0.200000
1	0.2	0.2	0.16	12	0.178573
2	0.2	0.2	0.16	12	0.171430
3	0.2	0.2	0.16	12	0.167859
4	0.2	0.2	0.16	12	0.165716
5	0.2	0.2	0.16	12	0.164288
6	0.2	0.2	0.16	12	0.163267
7	0.2	0.2	0.16	12	0.162502
8	0.2	0.2	0.16	12	0.161907
9	0.2	0.2	0.16	12	0.161431
10	0.2	0.2	0.16	12	0.161041

leverage level L at all values of debt cost k_d and fixed frequency of payments of tax on profit p. With increase of k_d WACC decreases. This is connected to the fact that the increase of k_d increases the value of tax shield in case of income tax payments more than once per year (at $p \neq 1$). Note, that in "classical" Modigliani–Miller theory with one income tax payment per year all financial indicators don't depend on debt cost, k_d.

Table 5.5 Dependence of WACC on leverage level L at $k_0 = 0.22$ and different $p = 2; 4; 12$

L	WACC		
	$p = 2$	$p = 4$	$p = 12$
0	0.2200	0.2200	0.2200
1	0.1970	0.1964	0.1960
2	0.1893	0.1886	0.1881
3	0.1854	0.1846	0.1841
4	0.1831	0.1823	0.1817
5	0.1816	0.1807	0.1801
6	0.1805	0.1796	0.1789
7	0.1797	0.1787	0.1781
8	0.1790	0.1781	0.1774
9	0.1785	0.1775	0.1769
10	0.1781	0.1771	0.1765

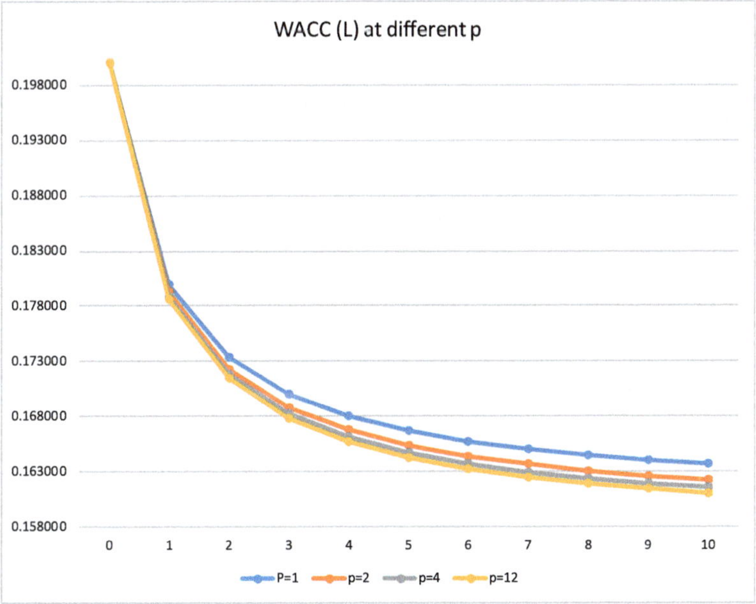

Fig. 5.1 Dependence of the weighted average cost of capital, WACC, on leverage level L at different p and fixed $k_d = 0.16$

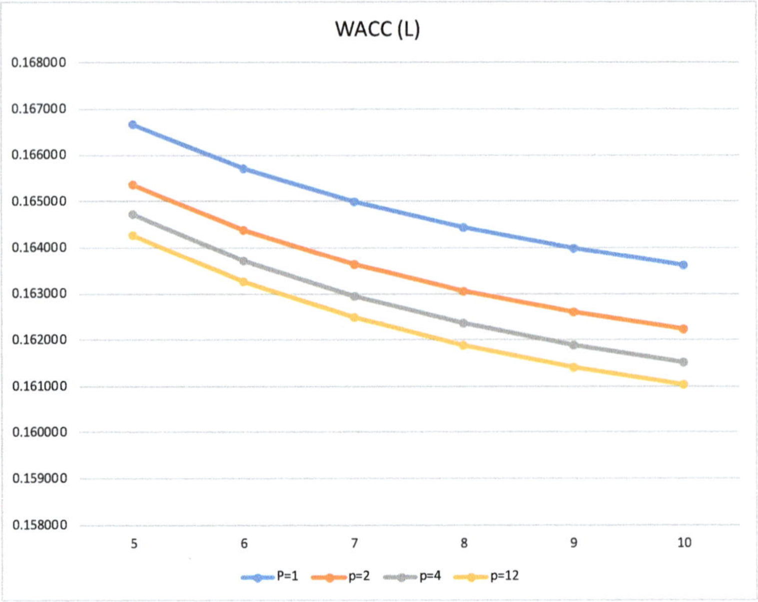

Fig. 5.2 Dependence of the weighted average cost of capital, WACC, on leverage level L at different p and fixed $k_d = 0.16$ (larger scale)

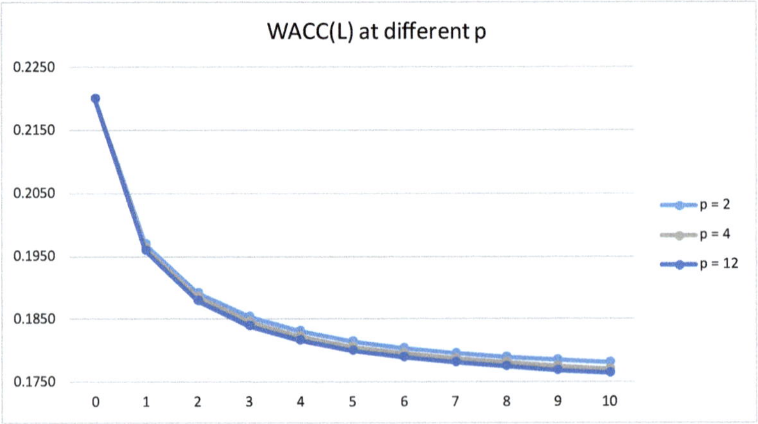

Fig. 5.3 Dependence of the weighted average cost of capital, WACC, on leverage level L at different p and fixed $k_0 = 0.22$

Table 5.6 Dependence of WACC on leverage level L at $k_0 = 0.2$, $k_d = 0.18$ and $p = 1$

L	T	K_0	K_d	p	WACC
0	0.2	0.2	0.18	12	0.20000
1	0.2	0.2	0.18	12	0.17840
2	0.2	0.2	0.18	12	0.17120
3	0.2	0.2	0.18	12	0.16760
4	0.2	0.2	0.18	12	0.16544
5	0.2	0.2	0.18	12	0.16400
6	0.2	0.2	0.18	12	0.16297
7	0.2	0.2	0.18	12	0.16220
8	0.2	0.2	0.18	12	0.16160
9	0.2	0.2	0.18	12	0.16112
10	0.2	0.2	0.18	12	0.16073

Table 5.7 Dependence of WACC on leverage level L at $k_0 = 0.2$, $k_d = 0.16$ and $p = 12$

L	T	K_0	K_d	p	WACC
0	0.2	0.2	0.16	12	0.20000
1	0.2	0.2	0.16	12	0.17857
2	0.2	0.2	0.16	12	0.17143
3	0.2	0.2	0.16	12	0.16786
4	0.2	0.2	0.16	12	0.16572
5	0.2	0.2	0.16	12	0.16429
6	0.2	0.2	0.16	12	0.16327
7	0.2	0.2	0.16	12	0.16250
8	0.2	0.2	0.16	12	0.16191
9	0.2	0.2	0.16	12	0.16143
10	0.2	0.2	0.16	12	0.16104

5.4 Dependence of the Company Capitalization, V, on Leverage Level L

In this section we study the dependence of the company capitalization, V, on leverage level L for the following situations: (1) at different $p = 1; 2; 4; 12$ and fixed $k_d = 0.16$; (2) for fixed p and at different values of debt cost $k_d = 0.18; 0.16; 0.14; 012$.

Table 5.8 Dependence of WACC on leverage level L at $k_0 = 0.2$, $k_d = 0.14$ and $p = 12$

L	T	K_0	K_d	p	WACC
0	0.2	0.2	0.14	12	0.20000
1	0.2	0.2	0.14	12	0.17875
2	0.2	0.2	0.14	12	0.17166
3	0.2	0.2	0.14	12	0.16812
4	0.2	0.2	0.14	12	0.16600
5	0.2	0.2	0.14	12	0.16458
6	0.2	0.2	0.14	12	0.16357
7	0.2	0.2	0.14	12	0.16281
8	0.2	0.2	0.14	12	0.16222
9	0.2	0.2	0.14	12	0.16174
10	0.2	0.2	0.14	12	0.16136

Table 5.9 Dependence of WACC on leverage level L at $k_0 = 0.2$, $k_d = 0.12$ and $p = 12$

L	T	K_0	K_d	p	WACC
0	0.2	0.2	0.12	12	0.20000
1	0.2	0.2	0.12	12	0.17892
2	0.2	0.2	0.12	12	0.17190
3	0.2	0.2	0.12	12	0.16838
4	0.2	0.2	0.12	12	0.16628
5	0.2	0.2	0.12	12	0.16487
6	0.2	0.2	0.12	12	0.16387
7	0.2	0.2	0.12	12	0.16311
8	0.2	0.2	0.12	12	0.16253
9	0.2	0.2	0.12	12	0.16206
10	0.2	0.2	0.12	12	0.16168

5.4.1 *Dependence of the Company Capitalization, V, on Leverage Level L at Different* p *and Fixed* K_d

Obtained results on the dependence of the company capitalization, V, on leverage level L at different $p = 1; 2; 4; 12$ and fixed $k_d = 0.16$ (Tables 5.14, 5.15, 5.16, and 5.17 and Figs. 5.8 and 5.9) show that the company capitalization, V, increases with p and reach maximum at $p = 12$. This means, that for company is more profitable to pay tax on profit as much more frequently as tax legislation allows.

Table 5.10 Dependence of WACC on leverage level L at $k_0 = 0.2$, $k_d = 0.18$ and $p = 4$

L	T	K_0	K_d	p	WACC
0	0.2	0.2	0.18	4	0.20000
1	0.2	0.2	0.18	4	0.17870
2	0.2	0.2	0.18	4	0.17160
3	0.2	0.2	0.18	4	0.16804
4	0.2	0.2	0.18	4	0.16591
5	0.2	0.2	0.18	4	0.16449
6	0.2	0.2	0.18	4	0.16348
7	0.2	0.2	0.18	4	0.16272
8	0.2	0.2	0.18	4	0.16213
9	0.2	0.2	0.18	4	0.16165
10	0.2	0.2	0.18	4	0.16127

Table 5.11 Dependence of WACC on leverage level L at $k_0 = 0.2$, $k_d = 0.16$ and $p = 4$

L	T	K_0	K_d	p	WACC
0	0.2	0.2	0.16	4	0.20000
1	0.2	0.2	0.16	4	0.17884
2	0.2	0.2	0.16	4	0.17178
3	0.2	0.2	0.16	4	0.16826
4	0.2	0.2	0.16	4	0.16614
5	0.2	0.2	0.16	4	0.16473
6	0.2	0.2	0.16	4	0.16372
7	0.2	0.2	0.16	4	0.16296
8	0.2	0.2	0.16	4	0.16238
9	0.2	0.2	0.16	4	0.16191
10	0.2	0.2	0.16	4	0.16152

5.4.2 Dependence of the Company Capitalization, V, on Leverage Level L at Different K_d and Fixed p

Let us now study the dependence of the company capitalization, V, on leverage level L for fixed p and at different values of debt cost $k_d = 0.18; 0.16; 0.14; 012$.

Obtained results on the dependence of the company capitalization, V, on leverage level L at fixed p (but for $p = 1; 2; 4; 12$) and different $k_d = 12\%; 14\%; 16\%; 18\%$ (Tables 5.18, 5.19, 5.20, 5.21, 5.22, 5.23, 5.24, 5.25, 5.26, 5.27, 5.28, and 5.29 and Figs. 5.10, 5.11, 5.12, 5.13, 5.14, and 5.15) show that the company capitalization, V, increases with k_d at each value of fixed p and reach maximum at $k_d = 18\%$. This corresponds to decrease of the weighted average cost of capital, WACC, with k_d at

Table 5.12 Dependence of WACC on leverage level L at $k_0 = 0.2$, $k_d = 0.14$ and $p = 4$

L	T	K_0	K_d	p	WACC
0	0.2	0.2	0.14	4	0.20000
1	0.2	0.2	0.14	4	0.17898
2	0.2	0.2	0.14	4	0.17197
3	0.2	0.2	0.14	4	0.16847
4	0.2	0.2	0.14	4	0.16637
5	0.2	0.2	0.14	4	0.16496
6	0.2	0.2	0.14	4	0.16396
7	0.2	0.2	0.14	4	0.16321
8	0.2	0.2	0.14	4	0.16263
9	0.2	0.2	0.14	4	0.16216
10	0.2	0.2	0.14	4	0.16178

Table 5.13 Dependence of WACC on leverage level L at $k_0 = 0.2$, $k_d = 0.12$ and $p = 4$

L	T	K_0	K_d	p	WACC
0	0.2	0.2	0.12	4	0.20000
1	0.2	0.2	0.12	4	0.17912
2	0.2	0.2	0.12	4	0.17216
3	0.2	0.2	0.12	4	0.16868
4	0.2	0.2	0.12	4	0.16659
5	0.2	0.2	0.12	4	0.16520
6	0.2	0.2	0.12	4	0.16421
7	0.2	0.2	0.12	4	0.16346
8	0.2	0.2	0.12	4	0.16288
9	0.2	0.2	0.12	4	0.16242
10	0.2	0.2	0.12	4	0.16204

fixed p, obtained by us in Sect. 5.3. This is connected to the fact that the increase of k_d increases the value of tax shield in case of income tax payments more than once per year (at $p \neq 1$). Note, that in "classical" Modigliani–Miller theory with one income tax payment per year all financial indicators, including company capitalization, V, don't depend on debt cost, k_d.

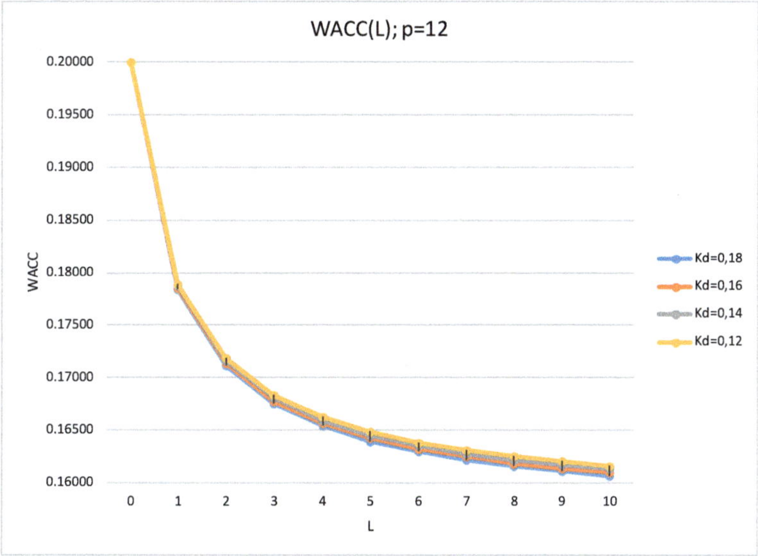

Fig. 5.4 Dependence of the weighted average cost of capital, WACC, on leverage level L at different k_d (12%; 14%; 16%; 18%) and fixed $p = 12$

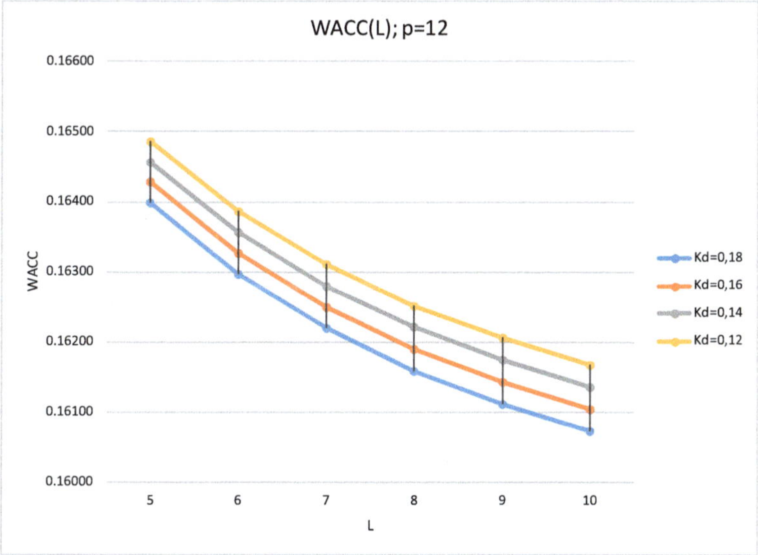

Fig. 5.5 Dependence of the weighted average cost of capital, WACC, on leverage level L at different k_d (12%; 14%; 16%; 18%) and fixed $p = 12$ (larger scale)

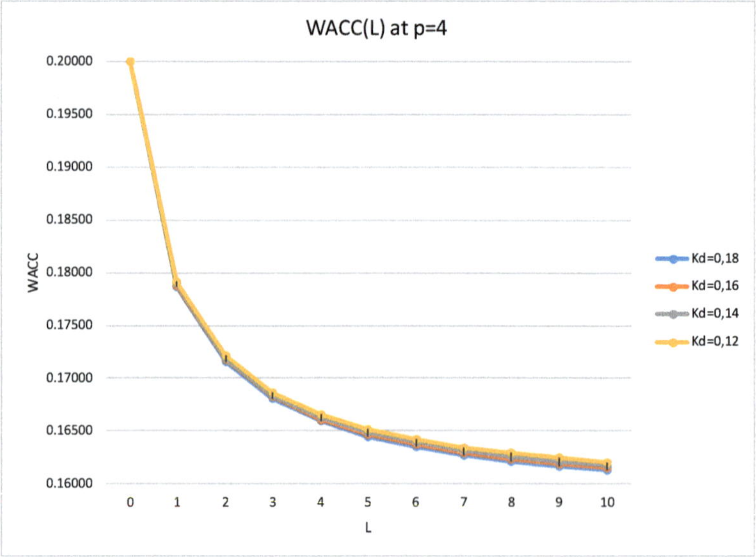

Fig. 5.6 Dependence of the weighted average cost of capital, WACC, on leverage level L at different k_d (12%; 14%; 16%; 18%) and fixed $p = 4$

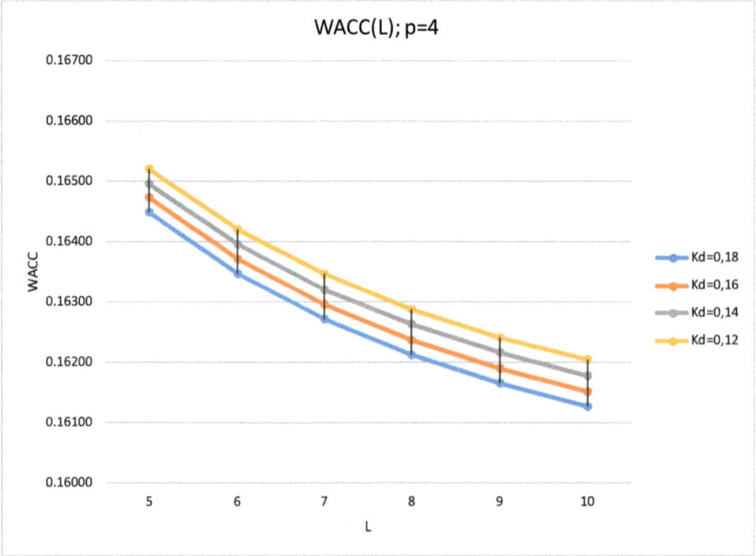

Fig. 5.7 Dependence of the weighted average cost of capital, WACC, on leverage level L at different k_d (12%; 14%; 16%; 18%) and fixed $p = 4$ (larger scale)

Table 5.14 Dependence of the company capitalization, V, on leverage level L at $p = 1$, $k_d = 0.16$

L	T	K_0	K_d	CF	p	V
0	0.2	0.2	0.16	1000	1	5000.00
1	0.2	0.2	0.16	1000	1	5555.56
2	0.2	0.2	0.16	1000	1	5769.23
3	0.2	0.2	0.16	1000	1	5882.35
4	0.2	0.2	0.16	1000	1	5952.38
5	0.2	0.2	0.16	1000	1	6000.00
6	0.2	0.2	0.16	1000	1	6034.48
7	0.2	0.2	0.16	1000	1	6060.61
8	0.2	0.2	0.16	1000	1	6081.08
9	0.2	0.2	0.16	1000	1	6097.56
10	0.2	0.2	0.16	1000	1	6111.11

Table 5.15 Dependence of the company capitalization, V, on leverage level L at $p = 2$, $k_d = 0.16$

L	T	K_0	K_d	CF	p	V
0	0.2	0.2	0.16	1000	2	5000.00
1	0.2	0.2	0.16	1000	2	5579.43
2	0.2	0.2	0.16	1000	2	5803.62
3	0.2	0.2	0.16	1000	2	5922.61
4	0.2	0.2	0.16	1000	2	5996.37
5	0.2	0.2	0.16	1000	2	6046.58
6	0.2	0.2	0.16	1000	2	6082.96
7	0.2	0.2	0.16	1000	2	6110.53
8	0.2	0.2	0.16	1000	2	6132.15
9	0.2	0.2	0.16	1000	2	6149.55
10	0.2	0.2	0.16	1000	2	6163.87

5.5 Dependence of the Equity Cost, k_e, on Leverage Level L

In this section we study the dependence of the equity cost, k_e, on leverage level L for the following situations: (1) at different $p = 1; 2; 4; 12$ and fixed $k_d = 0.16$; (2) for fixed p and at different values of debt cost $k_d = 0.18; 0.16; 0.14; 012$.

Table 5.16 Dependence of the company capitalization, V, on leverage level L at $p = 4$, $k_d = 0.16$

L	T	K_0	K_d	CF	p	V
0	0.2	0.2	0.16	1000	4	5000.00
1	0.2	0.2	0.16	1000	4	5591.68
2	0.2	0.2	0.16	1000	4	5821.31
3	0.2	0.2	0.16	1000	4	5943.34
4	0.2	0.2	0.16	1000	4	6019.04
5	0.2	0.2	0.16	1000	4	6070.60
6	0.2	0.2	0.16	1000	4	6107.96
7	0.2	0.2	0.16	1000	4	6136.29
8	0.2	0.2	0.16	1000	4	6158.51
9	0.2	0.2	0.16	1000	4	6176.39
10	0.2	0.2	0.16	1000	4	6191.11

Table 5.17 Dependence of the company capitalization, V, on leverage level L at $p = 12$, $k_d = 0.16$

L	T	K_0	K_d	CF	p	V
0	0.2	0.2	0.16	1000	12	5000.00
1	0.2	0.2	0.16	1000	12	5599.96
2	0.2	0.2	0.16	1000	12	5833.28
3	0.2	0.2	0.16	1000	12	5957.38
4	0.2	0.2	0.16	1000	12	6034.41
5	0.2	0.2	0.16	1000	12	6086.88
6	0.2	0.2	0.16	1000	12	6124.92
7	0.2	0.2	0.16	1000	12	6153.77
8	0.2	0.2	0.16	1000	12	6176.39
9	0.2	0.2	0.16	1000	12	6194.61
10	0.2	0.2	0.16	1000	12	6209.59

5.5.1 Dependence of the Equity Cost, k_e, on Leverage Level L at Different p and Fixed $k_d = 0.16$

Let us start from the study of the dependence of the equity cost, k_e, on leverage level L at different p and fixed $k_d = 0.16$.

Obtained results on the dependence of the equity cost, k_e, on leverage level L at fixed $k_d = 16\%$ and different $p = 1; 2; 4; 12$ (Tables 5.30, 5.31, 5.32, and 5.33 and Figs. 5.16 and 5.17) show that the tilt angle of the curve of equity cost, k_e (L), decreases with the number of payments of tax of profit p, this modifies the dividend policy of the company, because the economically justified value of dividends is equal to equity cost. Note, that in "classical" Modigliani–Miller theory with one income tax

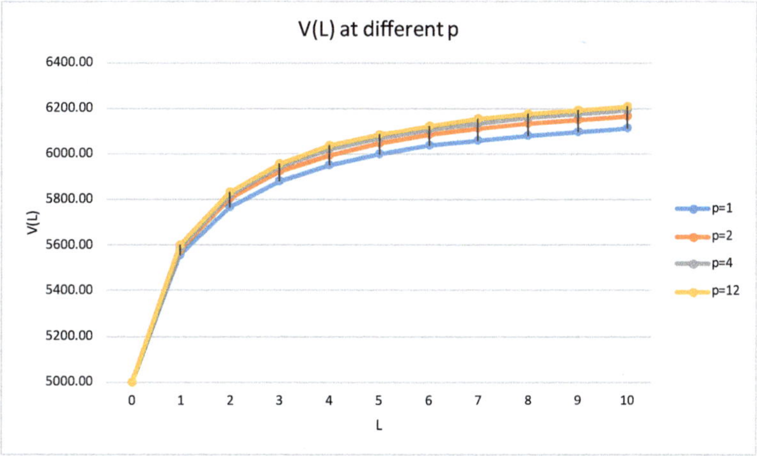

Fig. 5.8 Dependence of the company capitalization, V, on leverage level L at difference *p* (1; 2; 4; 12) and fixed $k_d = 0.16$

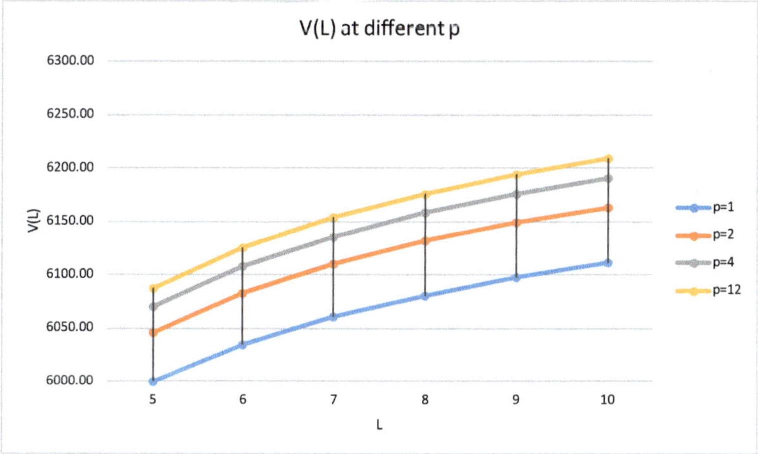

Fig. 5.9 Dependence of the company capitalization, V, on leverage level L at difference *p* (1; 2; 4; 12) and fixed $k_d = 0.16$ (larger scale)

payment per year all financial indicators, including the equity cost, k_e, don't depend on debt cost, k_d.

Table 5.18 Dependence of the company capitalization, V, on leverage level L at $p = 2$ and $k_d = 0.18$

L	T	K_0	K_d	CF	p	V
0	0.2	0.2	0.18	1000	2	5000.00
1	0.2	0.2	0.18	1000	2	5582.31
2	0.2	0.2	0.18	1000	2	5807.78
3	0.2	0.2	0.18	1000	2	5927.48
4	0.2	0.2	0.18	1000	2	6001.70
5	0.2	0.2	0.18	1000	2	6052.22
6	0.2	0.2	0.18	1000	2	6088.83
7	0.2	0.2	0.18	1000	2	6116.58
8	0.2	0.2	0.18	1000	2	6138.34
9	0.2	0.2	0.18	1000	2	6155.85
10	0.2	0.2	0.18	1000	2	6170.26

Table 5.19 Dependence of the company capitalization, V, on leverage level L at $p = 2$ and $k_d = 0.16$

L	T	K_0	K_d	CF	p	V
0	0.2	0.2	0.16	1000	2	5000.00
1	0.2	0.2	0.16	1000	2	5579.43
2	0.2	0.2	0.16	1000	2	5803.62
3	0.2	0.2	0.16	1000	2	5922.61
4	0.2	0.2	0.16	1000	2	5996.37
5	0.2	0.2	0.16	1000	2	6046.58
6	0.2	0.2	0.16	1000	2	6082.96
7	0.2	0.2	0.16	1000	2	6110.53
8	0.2	0.2	0.16	1000	2	6132.15
9	0.2	0.2	0.16	1000	2	6149.55
10	0.2	0.2	0.16	1000	2	6163.87

5.5.2 Dependence of the Equity Cost, k_e, on Leverage Level L at Different K_d and Fixed $p = 2$

In this section we study the dependence of the equity cost, k_e, on leverage level L at different $k_d = 18\%; 16\%; 14\%; 12\%$ and fixed number of income tax payments per year $p = 2$.

Conclusions. Obtained results on the dependence of the equity cost, k_e, on leverage level L at fixed but different $p = 1; 2; 4; 12$ and different values of debt cost k_d (Tables 5.34, 5.35, 5.36, 5.37, 5.38, 5.39, 5.40, 5.41, 5.42, 5.43, 5.44, and 5.45 and Figs. 5.18, 5.19, and 5.20) show that the tilt angle of the curve of equity cost,

Table 5.20 Dependence of the company capitalization, V, on leverage level L at $p = 2$ and $k_d = 0.14$

L	T	K_0	K_d	CF	p	V
0	0.2	0.2	0.14	1000	2	5000.00
1	0.2	0.2	0.14	1000	2	5576.53
2	0.2	0.2	0.14	1000	2	5799.44
3	0.2	0.2	0.14	1000	2	5917.71
4	0.2	0.2	0.14	1000	2	5991.01
5	0.2	0.2	0.14	1000	2	6040.90
6	0.2	0.2	0.14	1000	2	6077.05
7	0.2	0.2	0.14	1000	2	6104.44
8	0.2	0.2	0.14	1000	2	6125.92
9	0.2	0.2	0.14	1000	2	6143.21
10	0.2	0.2	0.14	1000	2	6157.43

Table 5.21 Dependence of the company capitalization, V, on leverage level L at $p = 2$ and $k_d = 0.12$

L	T	K_0	K_d	CF	p	V
0	0.2	0.2	0.12	1000	2	5000.00
1	0.2	0.2	0.12	1000	2	5573.61
2	0.2	0.2	0.12	1000	2	5795.22
3	0.2	0.2	0.12	1000	2	5912.77
4	0.2	0.2	0.12	1000	2	5985.62
5	0.2	0.2	0.12	1000	2	6035.19
6	0.2	0.2	0.12	1000	2	6071.10
7	0.2	0.2	0.12	1000	2	6098.31
8	0.2	0.2	0.12	1000	2	6119.65
9	0.2	0.2	0.12	1000	2	6136.83
10	0.2	0.2	0.12	1000	2	6150.96

k_e (L), decreases with the increase of values of debt cost k_d: this modifies the dividend policy of the company, because the economically justified value of dividends is equal to equity cost. Note, that in "classical" Modigliani–Miller theory with one income tax payment per year all financial indicators, including the equity cost, k_e, don't depend on debt cost, k_d.

Table 5.22 Dependence of the company capitalization, V, on leverage level L at $k_d = 0.18$ and fixed $p = 4$

L	T	K_0	K_d	CF	p	V
0	0.2	0.2	0.18	1000	4	5000.00
1	0.2	0.2	0.18	1000	4	5596.08
2	0.2	0.2	0.18	1000	4	5827.66
3	0.2	0.2	0.18	1000	4	5950.79
4	0.2	0.2	0.18	1000	4	6027.20
5	0.2	0.2	0.18	1000	4	6079.24
6	0.2	0.2	0.18	1000	4	6116.97
7	0.2	0.2	0.18	1000	4	6145.57
8	0.2	0.2	0.18	1000	4	6168.00
9	0.2	0.2	0.18	1000	4	6186.06
10	0.2	0.2	0.18	1000	4	6200.92

Table 5.23 Dependence of the company capitalization, V, on leverage level L at $k_d = 0.16$ and fixed $p = 4$

L	T	K_0	K_d	CF	p	V
0	0.2	0.2	0.16	1000	4	5000.00
1	0.2	0.2	0.16	1000	4	5591.68
2	0.2	0.2	0.16	1000	4	5821.31
3	0.2	0.2	0.16	1000	4	5943.34
4	0.2	0.2	0.16	1000	4	6019.04
5	0.2	0.2	0.16	1000	4	6070.60
6	0.2	0.2	0.16	1000	4	6107.96
7	0.2	0.2	0.16	1000	4	6136.29
8	0.2	0.2	0.16	1000	4	6158.51
9	0.2	0.2	0.16	1000	4	6176.39
10	0.2	0.2	0.16	1000	4	6191.11

5.6 Conclusions

The tax shield plays a crucial role in both main capital structure theories: Brusov–Filatova–Orekhova (BFO theory) and its perpetuity limit Modigliani–Miller theory. The way it is formed affects the results of the theories. Both of them describes the case of annual payments of tax of profit, but in practice these payments are made more frequent: semiannually, quarterly, monthly. While a return is not required more than once a year, businesses may be responsible for filing estimated taxes based on profits earned. This requirement is dependent on showing a profit. For example, sole proprietors must file estimated taxes on profits quarterly, on the 15th day of

Table 5.24 Dependence of the company capitalization, V, on leverage level L at $k_d = 0.14$ and fixed $p = 4$

L	T	K_0	K_d	CF	p	V
0	0.2	0.2	0.14	1000	4	5000.00
1	0.2	0.2	0.14	1000	4	5587.26
2	0.2	0.2	0.14	1000	4	5814.92
3	0.2	0.2	0.14	1000	4	5935.85
4	0.2	0.2	0.14	1000	4	6010.85
5	0.2	0.2	0.14	1000	4	6061.91
6	0.2	0.2	0.14	1000	4	6098.92
7	0.2	0.2	0.14	1000	4	6126.98
8	0.2	0.2	0.14	1000	4	6148.98
9	0.2	0.2	0.14	1000	4	6166.69
10	0.2	0.2	0.14	1000	4	6181.26

Table 5.25 Dependence of the company capitalization, V, on leverage level L at different k_d – 0.12 and fixed $p = 4$

L	T	K_0	K_d	CF	p	V
0	0.2	0.2	0.12	1000	4	5000.00
1	0.2	0.2	0.12	1000	4	5582.81
2	0.2	0.2	0.12	1000	4	5808.49
3	0.2	0.2	0.12	1000	4	5928.32
4	0.2	0.2	0.12	1000	4	6002.62
5	0.2	0.2	0.12	1000	4	6053.19
6	0.2	0.2	0.12	1000	4	6089.84
7	0.2	0.2	0.12	1000	4	6117.62
8	0.2	0.2	0.12	1000	4	6139.41
9	0.2	0.2	0.12	1000	4	6156.94
10	0.2	0.2	0.12	1000	4	6171.37

April, June, September and January. In Russia tax on profit payments could be made annually, quarterly, monthly. We show in current paper that the account of frequency of payment of tax on profit turns out to be very important and leads to significant consequences.

To study this problem we modify the Modigliani–Miller theory for the case of arbitrary frequency of payment of tax on profit and show that:

- all Modigliani–Miller statements and all formulas change,
- in case of income tax payments more than once per year (at $p \neq 1$), as it takes place in practice, the weighted average cost of capital, WACC, company value, V and

Table 5.26 Dependence of the company capitalization, V, on leverage level L at $k_d = 0.18$ and fixed $p = 12$

L	T	K_0	K_d	CF	p	V
0	0.2	0.2	0.18	1000	12	5000.00
1	0.2	0.2	0.18	1000	12	5605.40
2	0.2	0.2	0.18	1000	12	5841.15
3	0.2	0.2	0.18	1000	12	5966.63
4	0.2	0.2	0.18	1000	12	6044.53
5	0.2	0.2	0.18	1000	12	6097.61
6	0.2	0.2	0.18	1000	12	6136.09
7	0.2	0.2	0.18	1000	12	6165.28
8	0.2	0.2	0.18	1000	12	6188.17
9	0.2	0.2	0.18	1000	12	6206.60
10	0.2	0.2	0.18	1000	12	6221.77

Table 5.27 Dependence of the company capitalization, V, on leverage level L at $k_d = 0.16$ and fixed $p = 12$

L	T	K_0	K_d	CF	p	V
0	0.2	0.2	0.16	1000	12	5000.00
1	0.2	0.2	0.16	1000	12	5599.96
2	0.2	0.2	0.16	1000	12	5833.28
3	0.2	0.2	0.16	1000	12	5957.38
4	0.2	0.2	0.16	1000	12	6034.41
5	0.2	0.2	0.16	1000	12	6086.88
6	0.2	0.2	0.16	1000	12	6124.92
7	0.2	0.2	0.16	1000	12	6153.77
8	0.2	0.2	0.16	1000	12	6176.39
9	0.2	0.2	0.16	1000	12	6194.61
10	0.2	0.2	0.16	1000	12	6209.59

equity cost, k_e start depend on k_d, while in ordinary (classical) Modigliani–Miller theory all these values DO NOT depend on k_d.

- obtained results allow to company choose the number of payments of tax of profit per year, as many, as it is profitable to it (of course, within actual tax legislation);
- the tilt angle of the curve of equity cost, $k_e(L)$, decreases with p, this modifies the dividend policy of the company, because the economically justified value of dividends is equal to equity cost.
- one more influence of taxes within Modigliani–Miller theory is found: under accounting the number of payments of the tax of profit influent on all main indicators of the company: the weighted average cost of capital, WACC, company

Table 5.28 Dependence of the company capitalization, V, on leverage level L at $k_d = 0.14$ and fixed $p = 12$

L	T	K_0	K_d	CF	p	V
0	0.2	0.2	0.14	1000	12	5000.00
1	0.2	0.2	0.14	1000	12	5594.50
2	0.2	0.2	0.14	1000	12	5825.38
3	0.2	0.2	0.14	1000	12	5948.11
4	0.2	0.2	0.14	1000	12	6024.27
5	0.2	0.2	0.14	1000	12	6076.13
6	0.2	0.2	0.14	1000	12	6113.73
7	0.2	0.2	0.14	1000	12	6142.23
8	0.2	0.2	0.14	1000	12	6164.58
9	0.2	0.2	0.14	1000	12	6182.59
10	0.2	0.2	0.14	1000	12	6197.39

Table 5.29 Dependence of the company capitalization, V, on leverage level L at $k_d = 0.12$ and fixed $p = 12$

L	T	K_0	K_d	CF	p	V
0	0.2	0.2	0.12	1000	12	5000.00
1	0.2	0.2	0.12	1000	12	5589.01
2	0.2	0.2	0.12	1000	12	5817.45
3	0.2	0.2	0.12	1000	12	5938.82
4	0.2	0.2	0.12	1000	12	6014.10
5	0.2	0.2	0.12	1000	12	6065.35
6	0.2	0.2	0.12	1000	12	6102.50
7	0.2	0.2	0.12	1000	12	6130.67
8	0.2	0.2	0.12	1000	12	6152.75
9	0.2	0.2	0.12	1000	12	6170.53
10	0.2	0.2	0.12	1000	12	6185.16

value, V, equity cost, k_e etc. This allows to company manage WACC, V, k_e etc. by choosing the number of payments of tax of profit p.

It turns out that increase the number of payments of tax of profit per year leads to decrease of the cost of attracting capital and increase of the company value. More frequent payments of income tax are beneficial for both parties: for the company and for the tax regulator: for the company, this leads to an increase in the value of the company, and for the tax regulator, earlier payments are beneficial due to the time value of money.

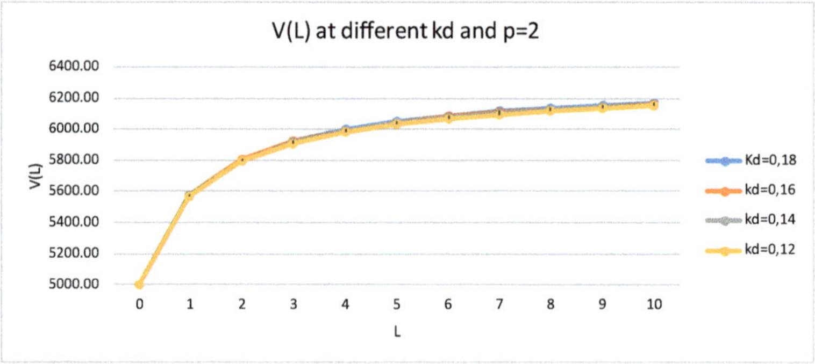

Fig. 5.10 Dependence of the company capitalization, V, on leverage level L at different k_d (12%; 14%; 16%; 18%) and fixed $p = 2$

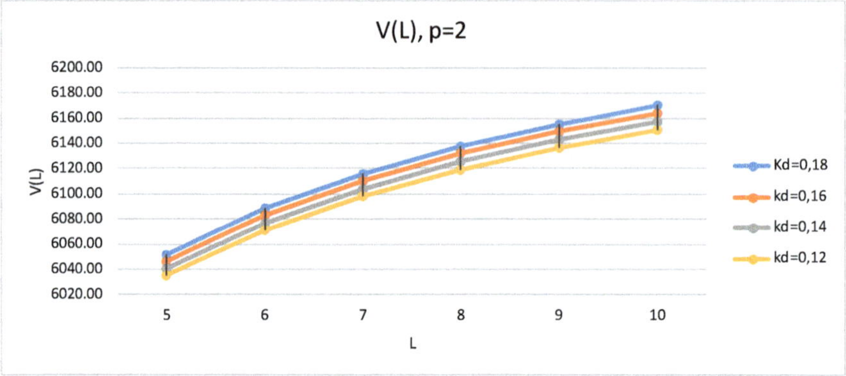

Fig. 5.11 Dependence of the company capitalization, V, on leverage level L at different k_d (12%; 14%; 16%; 18%) and fixed $p = 2$ (larger scale)

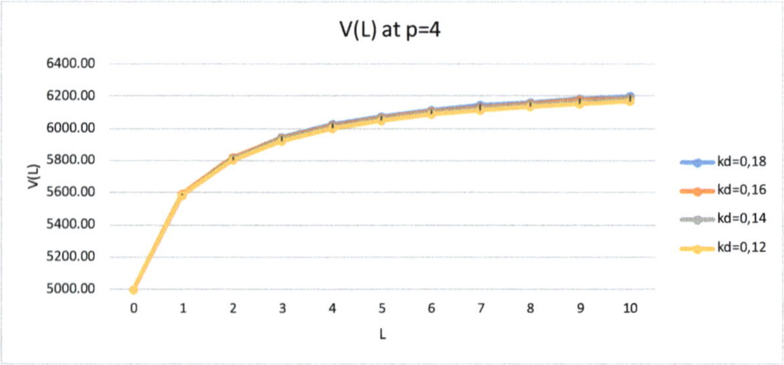

Fig. 5.12 Dependence of the company capitalization, V, on leverage level L at different k_d (12%; 14%; 16%; 18%) and fixed $p = 4$

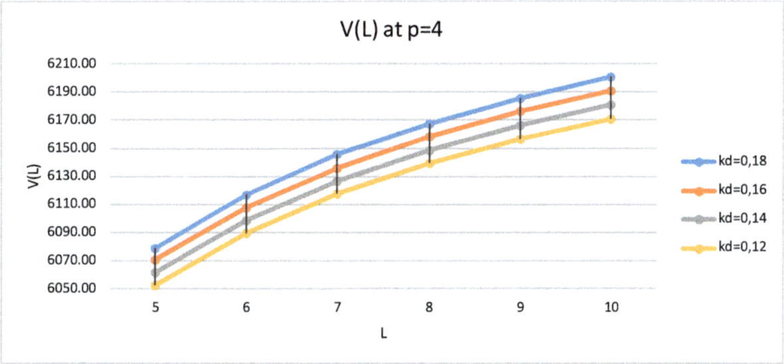

Fig. 5.13 Dependence of the company capitalization, V, on leverage level L at different k_d (12%; 14%; 16%; 18%) and fixed $p = 4$ (larger scale)

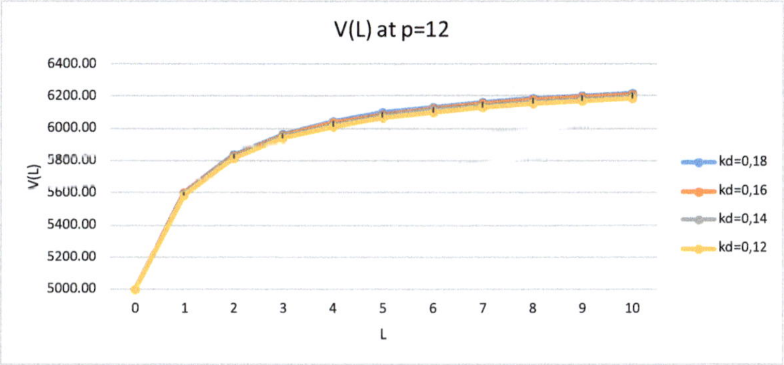

Fig. 5.14 Dependence of the company capitalization, V, on leverage level L at different k_d (12%; 14%; 16%; 18%) and fixed $p = 12$

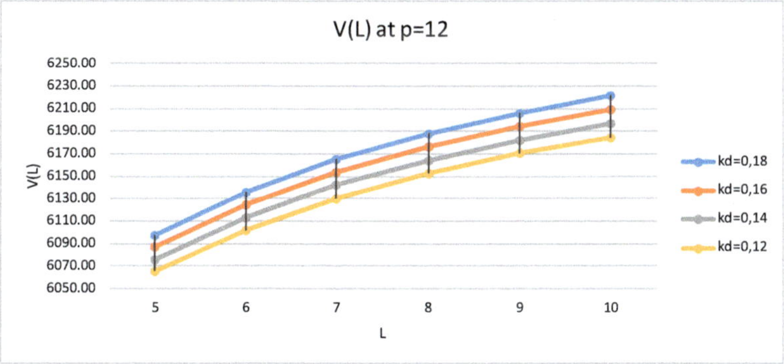

Fig. 5.15 Dependence of the company capitalization, V, on leverage level L at different k_d (12%; 14%; 16%; 18%) and fixed $p = 12$ (larger scale)

Table 5.30 Dependence of the equity cost, k_e, on leverage level L at $p = 1$ and fixed $k_d = 0.16$

L	T	K_0	K_d	p	K_e
0	0.2	0.2	0.16	1	0.2000
1	0.2	0.2	0.16	1	0.2320
2	0.2	0.2	0.16	1	0.2640
3	0.2	0.2	0.16	1	0.2960
4	0.2	0.2	0.16	1	0.3280
5	0.2	0.2	0.16	1	0.3600
6	0.2	0.2	0.16	1	0.3920
7	0.2	0.2	0.16	1	0.4240
8	0.2	0.2	0.16	1	0.4560
9	0.2	0.2	0.16	1	0.4880
10	0.2	0.2	0.16	1	0.5200

Table 5.31 Dependence of the equity cost, k_e, on leverage level L at $p = 2$ and fixed $k_d = 0.16$

L	T	K_0	K_d	p	K_e
0	0.2	0.2	0.16	2	0.2000
1	0.2	0.2	0.16	2	0.2305
2	0.2	0.2	0.16	2	0.2609
3	0.2	0.2	0.16	2	0.2914
4	0.2	0.2	0.16	2	0.3218
5	0.2	0.2	0.16	2	0.3523
6	0.2	0.2	0.16	2	0.3828
7	0.2	0.2	0.16	2	0.4132
8	0.2	0.2	0.16	2	0.4437
9	0.2	0.2	0.16	2	0.4741
10	0.2	0.2	0.16	2	0.5046

Table 5.32 Dependence of the equity cost, k_e, on leverage level L at $p = 4$ and fixed $k_d = 0.16$

L	T	K_0	K_d	p	K_e
0	0.2	0.2	0.16	4	0.2000
1	0.2	0.2	0.16	4	0.2297
2	0.2	0.2	0.16	4	0.2593
3	0.2	0.2	0.16	4	0.2890
4	0.2	0.2	0.16	4	0.3187
5	0.2	0.2	0.16	4	0.3484
6	0.2	0.2	0.16	4	0.3780
7	0.2	0.2	0.16	4	0.4077
8	0.2	0.2	0.16	4	0.4374
9	0.2	0.2	0.16	4	0.4671
10	0.2	0.2	0.16	4	0.4967

Table 5.33 Dependence of the equity cost, k_e, on leverage level L at $p = 12$ and fixed $k_d = 0.16$

L	T	K_0	K_d	P	K_e
0	0.2	0.2	0.16	12	0.2000
1	0.2	0.2	0.16	12	0.2291
2	0.2	0.2	0.16	12	0.2583
3	0.2	0.2	0.16	12	0.2874
4	0.2	0.2	0.16	12	0.3166
5	0.2	0.2	0.16	12	0.3457
6	0.2	0.2	0.16	12	0.3749
7	0.2	0.2	0.16	12	0.4040
8	0.2	0.2	0.16	12	0.4332
9	0.2	0.2	0.16	12	0.4623
10	0.2	0.2	0.16	12	0.4915

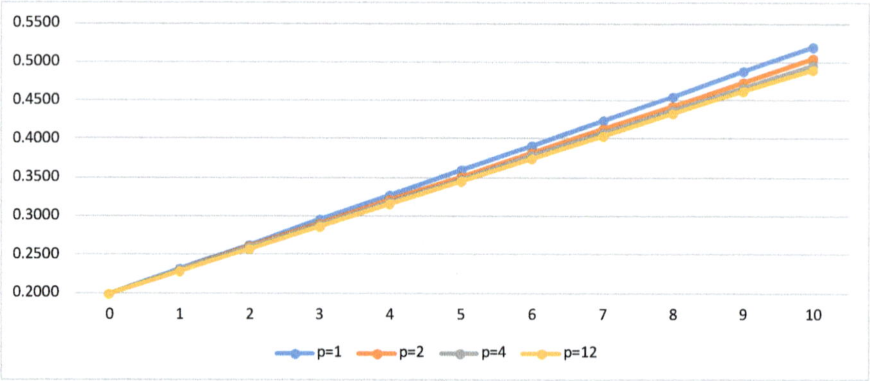

Fig. 5.16 Dependence of the equity cost, k_e, on leverage level L at different *p* (1; 2; 4; 12) and fixed $k_d = 0.16$

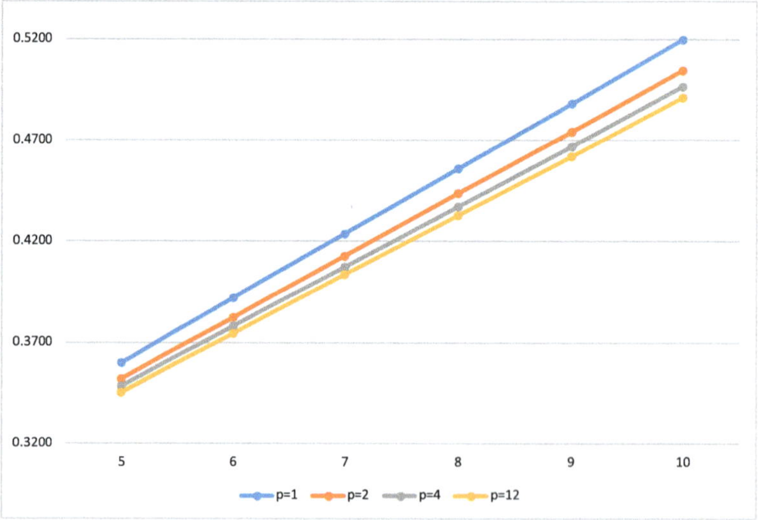

Fig. 5.17 Dependence of the equity cost, k_e, on leverage level L at different *p* (1; 2; 4; 12) and fixed $k_d = 0.16$ (lager scale)

Table 5.34 Dependence of the equity cost, k_e, on leverage level L at $p = 2$ and fixed $k_d = 0.18$

L	T	K_0	K_d	p	K_e
0	0.2	0.2	0.18	2	0.2000
1	0.2	0.2	0.18	2	0.2143
2	0.2	0.2	0.18	2	0.2285
3	0.2	0.2	0.18	2	0.2428
4	0.2	0.2	0.18	2	0.2571
5	0.2	0.2	0.18	2	0.2714
6	0.2	0.2	0.18	2	0.2856
7	0.2	0.2	0.18	2	0.2999
8	0.2	0.2	0.18	2	0.3142
9	0.2	0.2	0.18	2	0.3285
10	0.2	0.2	0.18	2	0.3427

Table 5.35 Dependence of the equity cost, k_e, on leverage level L at $p = 2$ and fixed $k_d = 0.16$

L	T	K_0	K_d	p	K_e
0	0.2	0.2	0.16	2	0.2000
1	0.2	0.2	0.16	2	0.2305
2	0.2	0.2	0.16	2	0.2609
3	0.2	0.2	0.16	2	0.2914
4	0.2	0.2	0.16	2	0.3218
5	0.2	0.2	0.16	2	0.3523
6	0.2	0.2	0.16	2	0.3828
7	0.2	0.2	0.16	2	0.4132
8	0.2	0.2	0.16	2	0.4437
9	0.2	0.2	0.16	2	0.4741
10	0.2	0.2	0.16	2	0.5046

Table 5.36 Dependence of the equity cost, k_e, on leverage level L at $p = 2$ and fixed $k_d = 0.14$

L	T	K_0	K_d	P	K_e
0	0.2	0.2	0.14	2	0.2000
1	0.2	0.2	0.14	2	0.2466
2	0.2	0.2	0.14	2	0.2933
3	0.2	0.2	0.14	2	0.3399
4	0.2	0.2	0.14	2	0.3866
5	0.2	0.2	0.14	2	0.4332
6	0.2	0.2	0.14	2	0.4799
7	0.2	0.2	0.14	2	0.5265
8	0.2	0.2	0.14	2	0.5732
9	0.2	0.2	0.14	2	0.6198
10	0.2	0.2	0.14	2	0.6665

Table 5.37 Dependence of the equity cost, k_e, on leverage level L at $p = 2$ and fixed $k_d = 0.12$

L	T	K_0	K_d	p	K_e
0	0.2	0.2	0.12	2	0.2000
1	0.2	0.2	0.12	2	0.2628
2	0.2	0.2	0.12	2	0.3257
3	0.2	0.2	0.12	2	0.3885
4	0.2	0.2	0.12	2	0.4513
5	0.2	0.2	0.12	2	0.5142
6	0.2	0.2	0.12	2	0.5770
7	0.2	0.2	0.12	2	0.6398
8	0.2	0.2	0.12	2	0.7027
9	0.2	0.2	0.12	2	0.7655
10	0.2	0.2	0.12	2	0.8283

Table 5.38 Dependence of the equity cost, k_e, on leverage level L at $k_d = 0.18$ and fixed $p = 4$

L	T	K_0	K_d	P	K_e
0	0.2	0.2	0.18	4	0.2000
1	0.2	0.2	0.18	4	0.2134
2	0.2	0.2	0.18	4	0.2268
3	0.2	0.2	0.18	4	0.2402
4	0.2	0.2	0.18	4	0.2536
5	0.2	0.2	0.18	4	0.2670
6	0.2	0.2	0.18	4	0.2804
7	0.2	0.2	0.18	4	0.2938
8	0.2	0.2	0.18	4	0.3071
9	0.2	0.2	0.18	4	0.3205
10	0.2	0.2	0.18	4	0.3339

Table 5.39 Dependence of the equity cost, k_e, on leverage level L at $k_d = 0.16$ and fixed $p = 4$

L	T	K_0	K_d	p	K_e
0	0.2	0.2	0.16	4	0.2000
1	0.2	0.2	0.16	4	0.2297
2	0.2	0.2	0.16	4	0.2593
3	0.2	0.2	0.16	4	0.2890
4	0.2	0.2	0.16	4	0.3187
5	0.2	0.2	0.16	4	0.3484
6	0.2	0.2	0.16	4	0.3780
7	0.2	0.2	0.16	4	0.4077
8	0.2	0.2	0.16	4	0.4374
9	0.2	0.2	0.16	4	0.4671
10	0.2	0.2	0.16	4	0.4967

Table 5.40 Dependence of the equity cost, k_e, on leverage level L at $k_d = 0.14$ and fixed $p = 4$

L	T	K_0	K_d	p	K_e
0	0.2	0.2	0.14	4	0.2000
1	0.2	0.2	0.14	4	0.2460
2	0.2	0.2	0.14	4	0.2919
3	0.2	0.2	0.14	4	0.3379
4	0.2	0.2	0.14	4	0.3838
5	0.2	0.2	0.14	4	0.4298
6	0.2	0.2	0.14	4	0.4757
7	0.2	0.2	0.14	4	0.5217
8	0.2	0.2	0.14	4	0.5677
9	0.2	0.2	0.14	4	0.6136
10	0.2	0.2	0.14	4	0.6596

Table 5.41 Dependence of the equity cost, k_e, on leverage level L at $k_d = 0.12$ and fixed $p = 4$

L	T	K_0	K_d	P	K_e
0	0.2	0.2	0.12	4	0.2000
1	0.2	0.2	0.12	4	0.2622
2	0.2	0.2	0.12	4	0.3245
3	0.2	0.2	0.12	4	0.3867
4	0.2	0.2	0.12	4	0.4490
5	0.2	0.2	0.12	4	0.5112
6	0.2	0.2	0.12	4	0.5735
7	0.2	0.2	0.12	4	0.6357
8	0.2	0.2	0.12	4	0.6979
9	0.2	0.2	0.12	4	0.7602
10	0.2	0.2	0.12	4	0.8224

Table 5.42 Dependence of the equity cost, k_e, on leverage level L at $k_d = 0.18$ and fixed $p = 12$

L	T	K_0	K_d	p	K_e
0	0.2	0.2	0.18	12	0.2000
1	0.2	0.2	0.18	12	0.2128
2	0.2	0.2	0.18	12	0.2256
3	0.2	0.2	0.18	12	0.2384
4	0.2	0.2	0.18	12	0.2512
5	0.2	0.2	0.18	12	0.2640
6	0.2	0.2	0.18	12	0.2768
7	0.2	0.2	0.18	12	0.2896
8	0.2	0.2	0.18	12	0.3024
9	0.2	0.2	0.18	12	0.3152
10	0.2	0.2	0.18	12	0.3280

Table 5.43 Dependence of the equity cost, k_e, on leverage level L at $k_d = 0.16$ and fixed $p = 12$

L	T	K_0	K_d	p	K_e
0	0.2	0.2	0.16	12	0.2000
1	0.2	0.2	0.16	12	0.2291
2	0.2	0.2	0.16	12	0.2583
3	0.2	0.2	0.16	12	0.2874
4	0.2	0.2	0.16	12	0.3166
5	0.2	0.2	0.16	12	0.3457
6	0.2	0.2	0.16	12	0.3749
7	0.2	0.2	0.16	12	0.4040
8	0.2	0.2	0.16	12	0.4332
9	0.2	0.2	0.16	12	0.4623
10	0.2	0.2	0.16	12	0.4915

Table 5.44 Dependence of the equity cost, k_e, on leverage level L at $k_d = 0.14$ and fixed $p = 12$

L	T	K_0	K_d	p	K_e
0	0.2	0.2	0.14	12	0.2000
1	0.2	0.2	0.14	12	0.2455
2	0.2	0.2	0.14	12	0.2910
3	0.2	0.2	0.14	12	0.3365
4	0.2	0.2	0.14	12	0.3820
5	0.2	0.2	0.14	12	0.4275
6	0.2	0.2	0.14	12	0.4730
7	0.2	0.2	0.14	12	0.5185
8	0.2	0.2	0.14	12	0.5640
9	0.2	0.2	0.14	12	0.6094
10	0.2	0.2	0.14	12	0.6549

Table 5.45 Dependence of the equity cost, k_e, on leverage level L at $k_d = 0.12$ and fixed $p = 12$

L	T	K_0	K_d	p	K_e
0	0.2	0.2	0.12	12	0.2000
1	0.2	0.2	0.12	12	0.2618
2	0.2	0.2	0.12	12	0.3237
3	0.2	0.2	0.12	12	0.3855
4	0.2	0.2	0.12	12	0.4474
5	0.2	0.2	0.12	12	0.5092
6	0.2	0.2	0.12	12	0.5711
7	0.2	0.2	0.12	12	0.6329
8	0.2	0.2	0.12	12	0.6948
9	0.2	0.2	0.12	12	0.7566
10	0.2	0.2	0.12	12	0.8185

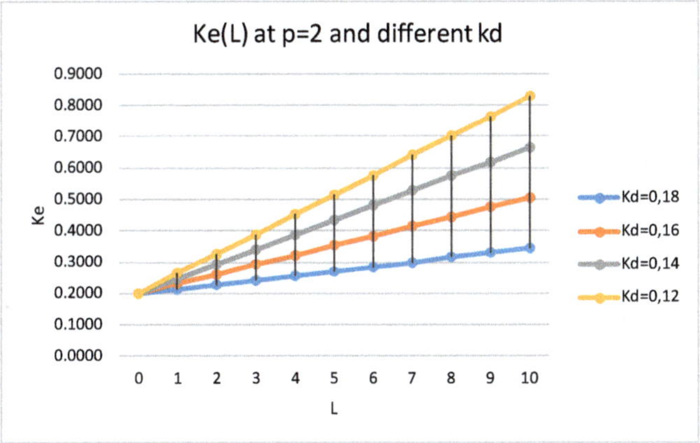

Fig. 5.18 Dependence of the equity cost, k_e, on leverage level L at different k_d (12%; 14%; 16%; 18%) and fixed $p = 2$

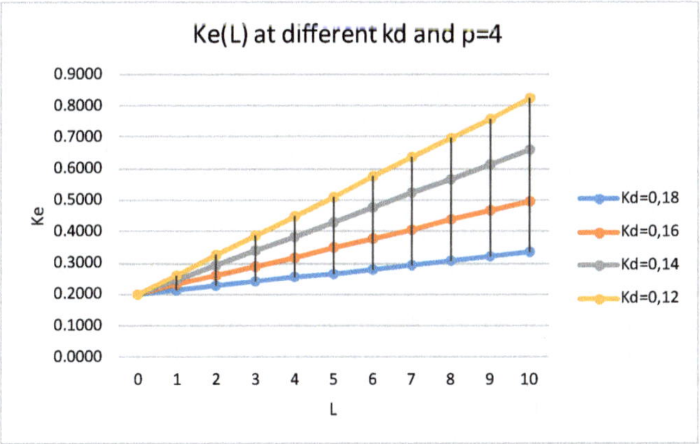

Fig. 5.19 Dependence of the equity cost, k_e, on leverage level L at different k_d (12%; 14%; 16%; 18%) and fixed $p = 4$

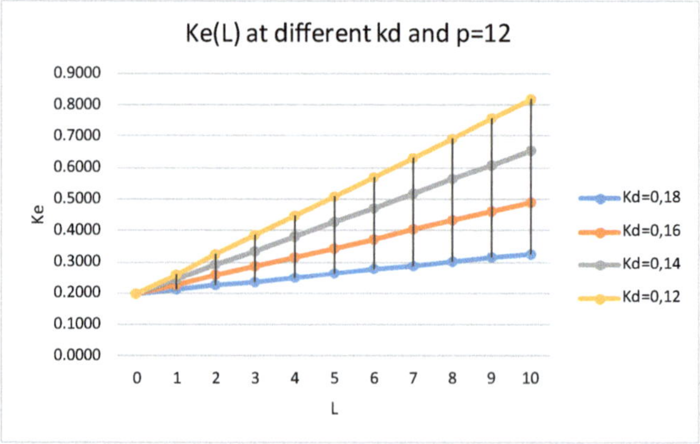

Fig. 5.20 Dependence of the equity cost, k_e, on leverage level L at different k_d (12%; 14%; 16%; 18%) and fixed $p = 12$

References

Berk J, DeMarzo P (2007) Corporate finance. Pearson-Addison Wesley, Boston

Brusov P (2018a) Editorial: introduction on special issue on the banking system and financial markets of Russia and other countries: problems and prospects. J Rev Glob Econ 7:i–vi

Brusov P (2018b) Editorial. J Rev Glob Econ 7:i–v, SCOPUS

Brusov PN, Filatova TV (2025a) Business valuation and company value: New qualitative approaches considering business and financial risks 1–654

Brusov PN, Filatova TV (2025b) Efficiency of investment projects: Modern investment models and their applications 1–843

Brusov PN, Filatova TV, Kulik VL (2024) Capital Asset Pricing Model (CAPM) 2.0: Account of business and financial risk. Finance: Theory and practice 28(2):128–142. https://doi.org/10.26794/2587-5671-2024-28-2-128-142

Brusov PN, Filatova TV, Orekhova NP (2021) Ratings: Critical analysis and new approaches of quantitative and qualitative methodology 1–369

Brusov PN, Filatova TV, Orekhova NP (2022) Generalized Modigliani–Miller Theory: Applications in corporate finance, investments, taxation and ratings 1–362

Brusov PN, Filatova TV, Orekhova NP (2023) The Brusov–Filatova–Orekhova Theory of Capital Structure: Applications in Corporate Finance. Taxation and Ratings Investments 1–769

Brusov P, Filatova T, Orehova N, Eskindarov M (2015) Modern corporate finance, investments and taxation. Springer International Publishing, Switzerland, p 373, monograph. https://www.springer.com/gp/book/9783319147314

Brusov P, Filatova T, Orehova N, Eskindarov M (2018), Modern corporate finance, investments, taxation and ratings. Springer Nature Publishing, Switzerland, p 571, monograph

Brusov PN, Filatova TV, Orekhova NP, Kulik VL (2018) Rating: new approach. J Rev Glob Econ 7:37– 62. https://doi.org/10.6000/1929-7092.2018.07.05

Brusov PN, Filatova TV, Orekhova NP, Kulik VL (2018) A "golden age" of the companies: conditions of its existence. J Rev Glob Econ 7:88–103. https://doi.org/10.6000/1929-7092.2018.07.07

Brusov PN, Filatova TV, Orekhova NP (2018d) Kulik VL. J Rev Glob Econ 7:63–87. https://doi.org/10.6000/1929-7092.2018.07.06

Brusov PN, Filatova TV, Orekhova NP, Kulik VL (2018e) New meaningful effects in modern capital structure theory. J Rev Glob Econ 7:104–122. https://doi.org/10.6000/1929-7092.2018.07.08

Brusov P, Filatova T, Orekhova N, Kulik V, Weil I, Brailov A (2018f) The impact of the central bank key rate and commercial banks credit rates on creating and maintaining of a favorable investment climate in the country. J Rev Glob Econ 7:360–376, SCOPUS. https://doi.org/10.6000/1929-7092.2018.07.31

Brusov PN, Filatova TV, Orekhova NP (2018g) Modern corporate finance and investments, monograph. Knorus publishing house, Moscow, p 517

Brusov PN, Filatova TV, Orekhova NP, Kulik VL, Weil I (2019) Ratings of the investment projects of arbitrary durations: new methodology. J Rev Glob Econ 8:437–448. https://doi.org/10.6000/1929-7092.2019.08.37

Brusov P, Filatova T, Orehova N (2020) Ratings: Critical analysis and new approaches of quantitative and qualitative methodology. Springer Nature Publishing, Switzerland, monograph, https://www.springer.com/de/book/9783030562427

DeMarzo PM (1988) An extension of the Modigliani–Miller theorem to stochastic economies with incomplete markets and interdependent securities. J Econ Theory 45(2):353–369

Farber A, Gillet R, Szafarz A (2006) A general formula for the WACC. Int J Bus 11(2):211–218

Fernandez P (2007) "A General Formula for the WACC: a Comment". Int J Bus this issue.

Filatova T, Orehova N, Brusova A (2008) Weighted average cost of capital in the theory of Modigliani-Miller, modified for a finite life–time company. Bull FU 48:68–77

Filatova TV, Brusov PN, Orekhova NP, Kulik VL (2018) Ratings of the long–term projects: new approach. J Rev Glob Econ 7:645–661. https://doi.org/10.6000/1929-7092.2018.07.59

Hamada R (1969) Portfolio analysis, market equilibrium, and corporate finance. J Financ 13 31

Harris R, Pringle J (1985) Risk–adjusted discount rates—extension form the average-risk case. J Financ Res 8(3):237–244

Miles JA, Ezzel JR (1980) The weighted average cost of capital, perfect capital markets and project life: a clarification. J Financ Quant Anal 15(3):719–730

Miller M (1977) Debt and taxes. J Financ 32(2):261–275. https://doi.org/10.1111/j.1540-6261.1977.tb03267.x

Modigliani F, Miller M (1958) The cost of capital, corporate finance, and the theory of investment. Am Econ Rev 48:261–297

Modigliani F, Miller M (1963) Corporate income taxes and the cost of capital: a correction. Am Econ Rev 53:147–175

Modigliani F, Miller M (1966) Some estimates of the cost of capital to the electric utility industry 1954–1957. Am Econ Rev 56:333–391

Ross S, Westerfiel R, Jaffee D (2005) Corporate finance, 7th edn. McGraw Hill, New York

Taggart RA (1991) Consistent valuation and cost of capital expressions with corporate and personal taxes. Financ Manag 20:8–20

Chapter 6
Modification of the Modigliani–Miller Theory for the Case of Advance Tax on Profit Payments

6.1 Introduction

One of the most important and serious assumptions of the Modigliani–Miller theory is that all financial flows as well as all companies are perpetuity. In current Chapter we discuss one more limitation of Modigliani–Miller theory: a method of tax on profit payments. Modigliani–Miller theory accounts these payments as annuity–immediate while in practice these payments are often making in advance and thus should be accounting as annuity–due. We generalize the Modigliani–Miller theory for the case of advance tax on profit payments, which is widely used in practice, and show that this leads to some important consequences, which change seriously all the main statements by Modigliani and Miller (Brusov et al. 2020). The modified Modigliani–Miller theory (MMM theory) is the second of the three main theories which consists the base for conducting of modification of existing rating methodologies. In this Chapter we describe the main results of MMM theory.

The first serious study (and first quantitative study) of influence of capital structure of the company on its indicators of activities was the work by Nobel Prize Winners Modigliani and Miller. Their theory has a lot of limitations. One of the most important and serious assumptions of the Modigliani–Miller theory is that all financial flows as well as all companies are perpetuity. This limitation was lift out by Brusov–Filatova–Orekhova in 2008 (Filatova et al. 2008), who have created BFO theory–modern theory of capital cost and capital structure for companies of arbitrary age (Brusov et al. 2021, 2022, 2023; Brusov and Filatova 2025a, b).

Despite the fact that the Modigliani–Miller theory is currently a particular case of the general theory of capital cost and capital structure—Brusov–Filatova–Orekhova (BFO) theory—it is still widely used at the West.

In current Chapter we discuss one more limitation of Modigliani–Miller theory: a method of tax on profit payments. Modigliani–Miller theory accounts these payments as annuity–immediate while in practice these payments are making in advance and thus should be accounting as annuity–due.

P. Brusov and T. Filatova, *Taxes and Taxation*, Contributions to Finance and Accounting, https://doi.org/10.1007/978-3-032-11077-0_6

We generalize the Modigliani–Miller theory for the case of advance tax on profit payments, which is widely used in practice, and show that this leads to some important consequences, which change seriously all the main statements by Modigliani and Miller. These consequences are as following: WACC starts depend on debt cost k_d, WACC turns out to be lower than in case of classical Modigliani–Miller theory and thus company capitalization becomes higher than in ordinary Modigliani–Miller theory. We show that equity dependence on leverage level L is still linear, but the tilt angle with respect to L-axis turns out to be smaller: this could lead to modification of the dividend policy of the company.

Correct account of a method of tax on profit payments demonstrates that shortcomings of Modigliani–Miller theory are dipper, than everybody suggested: the underestimation of WACC really turns out to be bigger, as well as overestimation of the capitalization of the company. This means that systematic risks arising from the use of modified Modigliani–Miller theory (which is more correct than "classical" one) in practice is higher than it was suggested by the "classical" version of this theory.

6.2 Modified Modigliani–Miller Theory in Case of Advance Tax Payments

6.2.1 Tax Shield in Case of Advance Tax Payments

Modigliani–Miller theory accounts these payments as annuity–immediate while in practice these payments are making in advance and thus should be accounting as annuity–due.

To calculate tax shield *TS* in case of advance tax payments one should use annuity–due (Fig. 6.1).

$$\begin{aligned} TS &= k_d Dt + \frac{k_d Dt}{(1+k_d)} + \frac{k_d Dt}{(1+k_d)^2} + \cdots \\ &= \frac{k_d Dt}{\left(1-(1+k_d)^{-1}\right)} = Dt(1+k_d) \end{aligned} \tag{6.1}$$

This expression is different from the case of classical Modigliani–Miller theory (which used annuity–immediate) (Fig. 6.2).

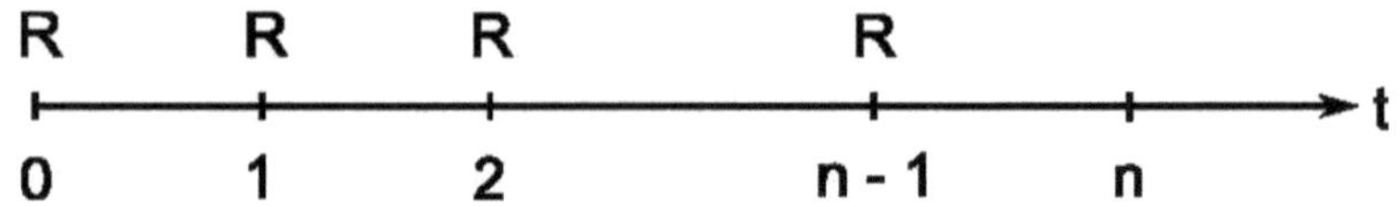

Fig. 6.1 Annuity–due

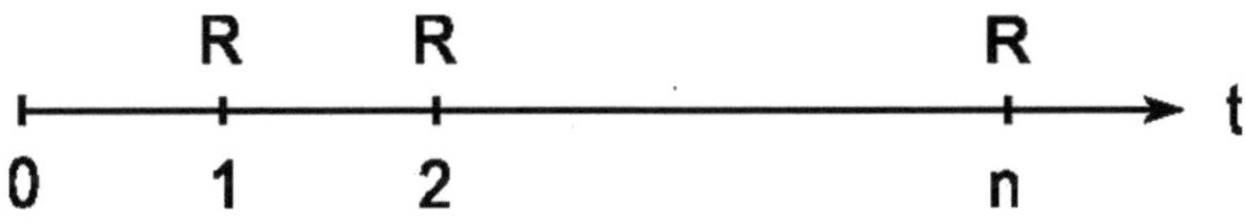

Fig. 6.2 Annuity–immediate

$$TS = \frac{k_d Dt}{(1+k_d)} + \frac{k_d Dt}{(1+k_d)^2} + \ldots = \frac{k_d Dt}{(1+k_d)\left(1-(1+k_d)^{-1}\right)} = Dt \qquad (6.2)$$

Thus in the former case tax shield *TS* is bigger by multiplyer (1 + k_d). This is connected with the time value of money: money today is more expensive than money tomorrow due to the possibility of their alternative investment.

6.2.2 Capitalization of the Company

Modigliani–Miller theorem for capitalization of the company

$$V = V_0 + TS \qquad (6.3)$$

takes the following form

$$V = V_0 + Dt(1 + k_d). \qquad (6.4)$$

Thus, we arrive to the following statement, which modifies the original Modigliani and Miller.

The value of financially dependent company making tax on profit payments in advance is equal to the value of the company of the same risk group used no leverage, increased by the value of tax shield arising from financial leverage, and equal to the product of rate of corporate income tax t, the value of debt D and multiplyer (1 + k_d***).***

Substituting $D = w_d \cdot V$.

one has

$$V(1 - w_d t(1 + k_d)) = V_0$$

$$\frac{CF}{WACC} \cdot (1 - w_d t(1 + k_d)) = \frac{CF}{k_0}$$

And for WACC we have the following formula:

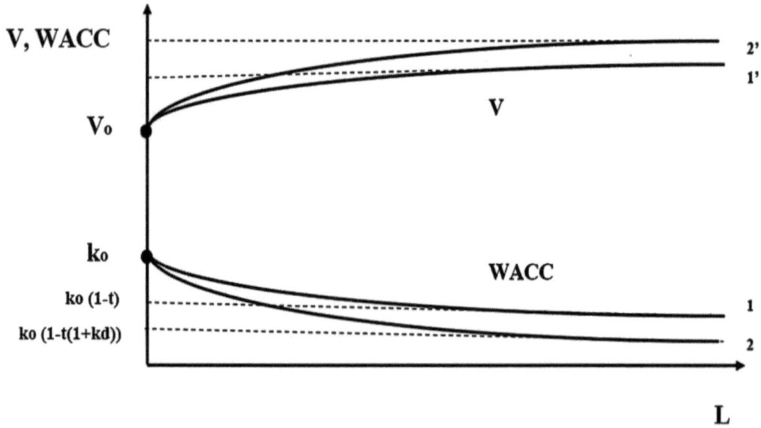

Fig. 6.3 Dependence of company capitalization, V and WACC on leverage level in "classical". Modigliani–Miller theory (curve 1′ and curve 1) and in "modified" Modigliani–Miller theory (curve 2′ and curve 2)

$$WACC = k_0(1 - w_d t(1 + k_d)). \tag{6.5}$$

$$\text{At } L \to \infty\ WACC = k_0(1 - t(1 + k_d)). \tag{6.6}$$

This expression is different from the similar one in classical Modigliani–Miller theory

$$WACC = k_0(1 - w_d t)$$

At $L \to \infty$ $WACC = k_0(1 - t)$.

From these expressions it is seen that WACC decreases with L, achieving lower value $WACC = k_0(1 - t(1 + k_d))$ at $L \to \infty$ in considering case comparing with the classical Modigliani–Miller theory $WACC = k_0(1 - t)$.

This means also, that company capitalization becomes higher than in ordinary Modigliani–Miller theory (Fig. 6.3).

6.2.3 Equity Cost

Let us find equity cost.

$$WACC = k_e w_e + k_d w_d (1 - t). \tag{6.7}$$

Equating (6.5) and (6.7), we obtain

$$k_0(1 - w_d t(1 + k_d)) = k_e w_e + k_d w_d (1 - t) \tag{6.8}$$

whence we get the following expression for the equity cost:

$$\begin{aligned} k_e &= k_0 \frac{(1 - w_d t(1 + k_d))}{w_e} - k_d \frac{w_d}{w_e}(1 - t) = \\ &= k_0 \frac{1}{w_e} - k_0 \frac{w_d}{w_e}(1 + k_d) \cdot t - k_d \frac{D}{S}(1 - t) = \\ &= k_0 \frac{D + S}{S} - k_0 \frac{D}{S}(1 + k_d) \cdot t - k_d \frac{D}{S}(1 - t) = \\ &= k_0 + L[(1 - t)(k_0 - k_d) - k_0 k_d t]. \end{aligned} \tag{6.9}$$

Finally, we have for the equity cost

$$k_e = k_0 + L[(1 - t)(k_0 - k_d) - k_0 k_d t]. \tag{6.10}$$

Thus, we arrive to the following statement, which modifies the original Modigliani and Millcr (Fig. 6.4).

Equity cost of leverage company $k_e$making tax on profit payments in advance could be found as equity cost of financially independent company $k_0$of the same group of risk, plus premium for risk, the value which is equal to production of leverage level Lon production of difference ($k_0 - k_d$)and tax shield ($1 - t$), decreasing by the value $k_0 k_d t$.

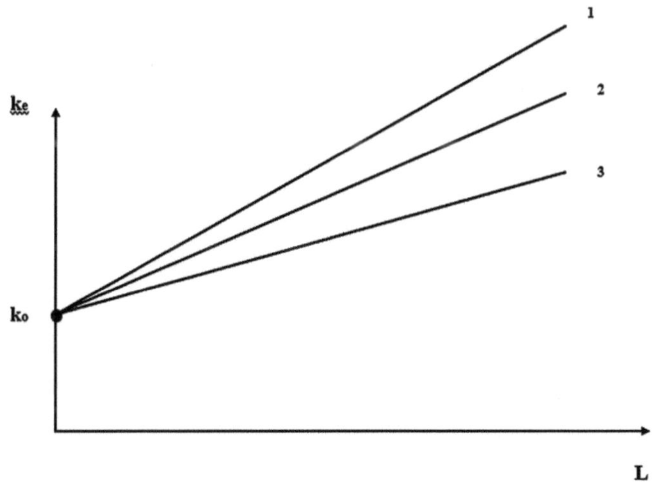

Fig. 6.4 Dependence of equity cost of the company, k_e, on leverage level in "classical". Modigliani–Miller theory (curve 2), in "modified" Modigliani–Miller theory (curve 3) and for financially independent company (t = 0) (curve 1)

This means, that equity cost dependence on leverage level L is still linear, but the tilt angle with respect to L-axis turns out to be smaller $tg\alpha = (k_0 - k_d) \cdot (1 - t) - k_0 k_d t$.

This could lead to modification of the dividend policy of the company, because the equity cost represents itself economically sound value of dividends. Thus, company could decreases the value of dividends.

6.3 The Dependence of the Weighted Average Cost of Capital, WACC, on Leverage Level in "Classical" Modigliani–Miller Theory (MM Theory) and in Modified Modigliani–Miller Theory (MMM Theory)

Let us compare the dependence of the weighted average cost of capital, WACC, on leverage level in "classical" Modigliani–Miller theory (MM theory) and in modified Modigliani–Miller theory (MMM theory). Study of such dependence is very important, because, the weighted average cost of capital, WACC, plays the role of discount rate in operating financial flows discounting as well as of financial flows in rating methodologies. WACC's value determines as well the capitalization of the company $V = CF / WACC$. We use Microsoft Excel for calculations.

From the Tables 6.1, 6.2, 6.3, 6.4 and from Fig. 6.5 it is seen that WACC in MMM theory turns out to be lower than in case of classical Modigliani–Miller theory and thus company capitalization becomes higher than in ordinary Modigliani–Miller theory. It is seen, that WACC decreases with debt cost k_d.

Table 6.1 Dependence of WACC on leverage level in "classical" Modigliani–Miller theory

K_0	L	t	WACC
0.2	0	0.2	0.2000
0.2	1	0.2	0.1800
0.2	2	0.2	0.1733
0.2	3	0.2	0.1700
0.2	4	0.2	0.1680
0.2	5	0.2	0.1667
0.2	6	0.2	0.1657
0.2	7	0.2	0.1650
0.2	8	0.2	0.1644
0.2	9	0.2	0.1640
0.2	10	0.2	0.1636

Table 6.2 Dependence of WACC on leverage level in modified Modigliani–Miller theory (MMM theory) at $k_d = 0.18$

K_0	L	t	k_d	WACC
0.2	0	0.2	0.18	0.2000
0.2	1	0.2	0.18	0.1764
0.2	2	0.2	0.18	0.1685
0.2	3	0.2	0.18	0.1646
0.2	4	0.2	0.18	0.1622
0.2	5	0.2	0.18	0.1607
0.2	6	0.2	0.18	0.1595
0.2	7	0.2	0.18	0.1587
0.2	8	0.2	0.18	0.1580
0.2	9	0.2	0.18	0.1575
0.2	10	0.2	0.18	0.1571

Table 6.3 Dependence of WACC on leverage level in modified Modigliani–Miller theory (MMM theory) at $k_d = 0.14$

K_0	L	t	k_d	WACC
0.2	0	0.2	0.14	0.2000
0.2	1	0.2	0.14	0.1772
0.2	2	0.2	0.14	0.1696
0.2	3	0.2	0.14	0.1658
0.2	4	0.2	0.14	0.1635
0.2	5	0.2	0.14	0.1620
0.2	6	0.2	0.14	0.1609
0.2	7	0.2	0.14	0.1601
0.2	8	0.2	0.14	0.1595
0.2	9	0.2	0.14	0.1590
0.2	10	0.2	0.14	0.1585

Correct account of a method of tax on profit payments demonstrates that shortcomings of Modigliani–Miller theory are dipper, than everybody suggested: the underestimation of WACC really turns out to be bigger, as well as overestimation of the capitalization of the company. This means that systematic risks arising from the use of modified Modigliani–Miller theory (MMM theory) (which is more correct than "classical" one) in practice are higher than it was suggested by the "classical" version of this theory.

Table 6.4 Dependence of WACC on leverage level in modified Modigliani–Miller theory (MMM theory) at $k_d = 0.1$

K_0	L	t	k_d	WACC
0.2	0	0.2	0.1	0.2000
0.2	1	0.2	0.1	0.1780
0.2	2	0.2	0.1	0.1707
0.2	3	0.2	0.1	0.1670
0.2	4	0.2	0.1	0.1648
0.2	5	0.2	0.1	0.1633
0.2	6	0.2	0.1	0.1623
0.2	7	0.2	0.1	0.1615
0.2	8	0.2	0.1	0.1609
0.2	9	0.2	0.1	0.1604
0.2	10	0.2	0.1	0.1600

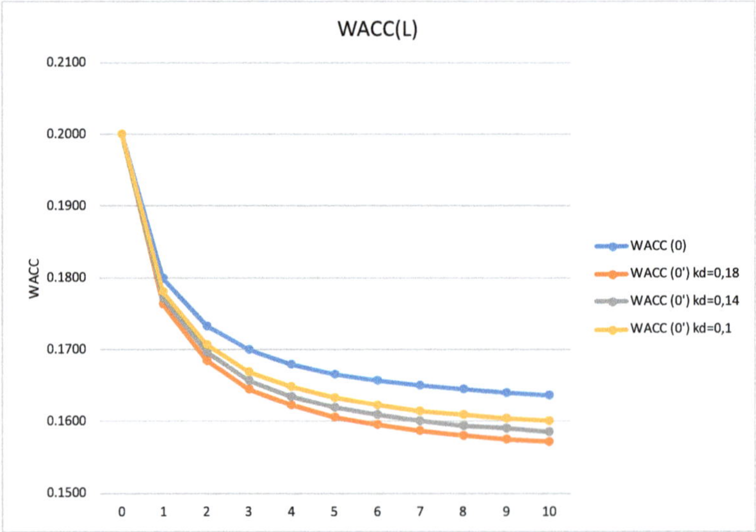

Fig. 6.5 Dependence of WACC on leverage level L: in "classical" Modigliani–Miller theory (curve WACC(0)) and in modified Modigliani–Miller theory (MMM theory) at different values of debt cost: $k_d = 0.18$; $k_d = 0.14$; $k_d = 0.1$ (curves WACC(0′))

6.4 Conclusions

Despite the fact that the Modigliani–Miller theory is currently a particular case of the general theory of capital cost and capital structure—Brusov–Filatova–Orekhova (BFO) theory—it is still widely used at the West. We generalize the Modigliani–Miller theory for the case of advance tax on profit payments, which is widely used in practice, and show that this leads to some important consequences, which change seriously all the main statements by Modigliani and Miller. These consequences are as following: WACC starts depend on debt cost k_d, WACC turns out to be lower than in case of classical Modigliani–Miller theory and thus company capitalization becomes higher than in ordinary Modigliani–Miller theory.

We study as well the equity cost dependence on leverage level L and show that it is still linear, but the tilt angle with respect to L–axis turns out to be smaller in MMM theory $tg\alpha = (k_0 - k_d) \cdot (1 - t) - k_0 k_d t$, than in classical Modigliani–Miller theory $tg\alpha = (k_0 - k_d) \cdot (1 - t)$. This could lead to modification of the dividend policy of the company, because the equity cost represents itself economically sound value of dividends. Thus, company could decreases the value of dividends, which they should pay to shareholders.

Correct account of a method of tax on profit payments demonstrates that shortcom-ings of Modigliani–Miller theory are dipper, than everybody suggested: the under-estimation of WACC really turns out to be bigger, as well as overestimation of the capitalization of the company. This means that systematic risks arising from the use of modified Modigliani–Miller theory (which is more correct than "classical" one) in practice is higher than it was suggested by the "classical" version of this theory.

References

Brusov P (2018a) Editorial: introduction on special issue on the banking system and financial markets of Russia and other countries: problems and prospects. J Rev Glob Econ 7:i–vi, SCOPUS

Brusov P (2018b) Editorial. J Rev Glob Econ 7:i–v, SCOPUS

Brusov PN, Filatova TV (2025a) Business valuation and company value: new qualitative approaches considering business and financial risks. Springer Nature Publishing, pp 1–654

Brusov PN, Filatova TV (2025b) Efficiency of investment projects: modern investment models and their applications. Springer Nature Publishing, pp.1-843

Brusov PN, Filatova TV, Orekhova NP (2018a) Modern corporate finance and investments, monograph. Knorus Publishing House, Moscow, p 517

Brusov P, Filatova T, Orekhova N, Eskindarov M (2015) Modern corporate finance, investments and taxation. Springer International Publishing, Switzerland, 373 p. monograph, SCOPUS. https://www.springer.com/gp/book/9783319147314

Brusov P, Filatova T, Orekhova N, Eskindarov M (2018b) Modern corporate finance, investments, taxation and ratings. Springer Nature Publishing, Switzerland, 571 p. monograph

Brusov PN, Filatova TV, Orekhova NP (2021) Ratings: critical analysis and new approaches of quantitative and qualitative methodology. Springer Nature Publishing, pp 1–369

Brusov PN, Filatova TV, Orekhova NP (2022) Generalized Modigliani–Miller Theory: applications in corporate finance, investments, taxation and ratings. Springer Nature Publishing, pp 1–362

Brusov PN, Filatova TV, Orekhova NP (2023) The Brusov–Filatova–Orekhova theory of capital structure: applications in corporate finance, investments, taxation and ratings. Springer Nature Publishing, pp 1–769

Brusov PN, Filatova TV, Orekhova NP, Kulik VL (2018b) Ratings of the long-term projects: new approach. J Rev Glob Econ 7:645–661, SCOPUS. https://doi.org/10.6000/1929-7092.2016.07.59

Brusov PN, Filatova TV, Orekhova NP, Kulik VL (2018c) Rating: new approach. J Rev Glob Econ 7:37–62 SCOPUS. https://doi.org/10.6000/1929-7092.2016.07.05

Brusov PN, Filatova TV, Orekhova NP, Kulik VL (2018d) A "golden age" of the companies: conditions of its existence. J Rev Glob Econ 7:88–103. SCOPUS. https://doi.org/10.6000/1929-7092.2016.07.07

Brusov PN, Filatova TV, Orekhova NP, Kulik VL (2018e) Rating methodology: new look and new horizons. J Rev Glob Econ 7:63–87. SCOPUS. https://doi.org/10.6000/1929-7092.2016.07.06

Brusov PN, Filatova TV, Orekhova NP, Kulik VL, Chang S-I, Lin YCG (2020) Modification of the Modigliani–Miller theory for the case of advance payments of tax on profit. J Rev Glob Econ 9:257–266

Brusov PN, Filatova TV, Orekhova NP, Kulik VL, Weil I (2018f) New meaningful effects in modern capital structure theory. J Rev Glob Econ 7:104–122. SCOPUS https://doi.org/10.6000/1929-7092.2016.07.08

Brusov PN, Filatova TV, Orekhova NP, Kulik VL, Weil I (2019) Ratings of the investment projects of arbitrary durations: new methodology. J Rev Glob Econ 8:437–446. SCOPUS. https://doi.org/10.6000/1929-7092.2019.06.37

Brusov P, Filatova T, Orekhova N, Kulik V, Weil I, Brailov A (2018g) The impact of the central bank key rate and commercial banks credit rates on creating and maintaining of a favorable investment climate in the country. J Rev Glob Econ 7:360–376. SCOPUS https://doi.org/10.6000/1929-7092.2016.07.31

Filatova T, Orehova N, Brusova A (2008) Weighted average cost of capital in the theory of Modigliani–Miller, modified for a finite life-time company. Bull FU 48:68–77

Modigliani F, Miller M (1958) The cost of capital, corporate finance, and the theory of investment. Am Econ Rev 48:261–297

Modigliani F, Miller M (1963) Corporate income taxes and the cost of capital: a correction. Am Econ Rev 53:147–175

Modigliani F, Miller M (1966) Some estimates of the cost of capital to the electric utility industry 1954–1957. Am Econ Rev 56:333–391

Myers S (2001) Capital structure. J Econ Perspect 15(2):81–102

Chapter 7
How Frequently Should Companies Pay Tax on Profit

7.1 Introduction

Brusov and Filatova (2021) have modified the Modigliani–Miller theory for the case of arbitrary frequency of payment of tax on profit and have shown that the account of frequency of payment of tax on profit within the Modigliani–Miller theory turns out to be very important and leads to significant consequences:

– all Modigliani–Miller theorems, statements and all formulas change;
– all main financial indicators, such as the weighted average cost of capital, WACC, company value, V and equity cost, k_e depend on the frequency of tax on profit payments. This allows to company manage WACC, V, k_e etc. by choosing the number of payments of tax of profit p per year;
– obtained results allow to company choose the number of payments of tax of profit per year, as many, as it is profitable to it (of course, within actual tax legislation);
– in case of income tax payments more than once per year(at $p \neq 1$), as it takes place in practice, the weighted average cost of capital, WACC, company value, V and equity cost, k_e start depend on k_d, while in ordinary (classical) Modigliani–Miller theory all these values **DO NOT depend on** k_d.
– the tilt angle of the curve of equity cost, k_e (L), decreases with the number of payments of tax of profit p, this modifies the dividend policy of the company, because the economically justified value of dividends is equal to equity cost.

As it was shown in that paper (Brusov and Filatova 2021), more frequent payments of income tax are beneficial for both parties: for the company and for the tax regulator: for the company, this leads to decrease of the cost of attracting capital and thus to an increase in the value of the company, and for the tax regulator, earlier payments are beneficial due to the time value of money.

But companies could pay tax of profit in advance and as we show in current paper this fact changes drastically the main conclusion: more frequent payments of income tax are **NOT** beneficial for the company: this leads to increase of the cost of attracting

P. Brusov and T. Filatova, *Taxes and Taxation*, Contributions to Finance and Accounting, https://doi.org/10.1007/978-3-032-11077-0_7

capital and thus to decrease in the value of the company, but for the tax regulator it remains beneficial: earlier payments are beneficial due to the time value of money.

The structure of the chapter is as following:

1. We give a literature review for Modigliani–Miller theory and for its modifications.
2. We modify the Modigliani–Miller theory for the case of frequent payment of tax on profit (in case of advanced payments) and get modified Modigliani–Miller theorems as well as new formulas for the weighted average cost of capital, WACC, for the equity cost, k_e, and for the capitalization of the company, V.
3. Within new Modified Modigliani–Miller theory (MMM theory) we study the dependence of the main financial indicators of the company (WACC, k_e, V) on leverage level L, on debt cost k_d and on tax on profit t at different frequency of payments of tax on profit (at the end of period and in advance).
4. Based on obtained results we come to some very important conclusions, which allow company choose the method of payments of tax of profit (at the end of period or in advance) and number of payments of tax of profit per year, as many, as it is profitable to it (of course, within actual tax legislation).

7.2 Literature Review

In their first paper Modigliani and Miller (1958) considered the problem of capital cost and capital structure for perpetuity companies without any taxes. In the second article, Modigliani and Miller (1963) considered taxation of corporate profits, but did not take into account the presence in the economy of individual taxes of investors. Merton Miller (1977) has introduced the model, demonstrating impact of leverage on the company value with account of the corporate and individual taxes. To describe his model, we will enter the following legends: T_C–tax on corporate profits rate, T_S–the tax rate on income of an individual investor from his ownership by stock of corporation, T_D–tax rate on interest income from the provision of investor–individuals of credits to other investors and companies. Income from shares partly comes in the form of a dividend and, in part, as capital profits, so that T_S is a weighted average value of effective rates of tax on dividends and capital profits on shares, while the income from the provision of loans usually comes in the form of the interests. The last are usually taxed at a higher rate. In the light of the individual taxes, and with the same assumptions that have been made for Modigliani–Miller models previously, the financially independent company value can be determined as follows:

$$V_U = \frac{\text{EBIT}(1 - T_C)(1 - T_S)}{k_0}. \tag{7.1}$$

A term $(1 - T_S)$ allows to take into account the individual taxes in the formula. In this way, numerator indicates which part of the operating company's profit remains in the possession of the investors, after the company will pay taxes on their profits, and its shareholders then will pay individual taxes on income from stock ownership.

Since individual taxes reduce profits, remaining in the disposal of investors, the last, at other things being equal circumstances, also reduce and an overall assessment of the financially independent company value.

Robert Hamada (1969) unites Capital Asset Pricing Model (CAPM) with Modigliani–Miller model taxation. As a result, he derived the following formula for calculation of the equity cost of financially dependent company, including both financial and business risk of company:

$$k_e = k_F + (k_M - k_F)b_U + (k_M - k_F)b_U\frac{D}{S}(1 - T), \tag{7.2}$$

where b_U is the β–coefficient of the company of the same group of business risk, that the company under consideration, but with zero financial leverage. The formula (7.2) represents the desired profitability of equity capital k_e as a sum of three components: risk–free profitability k_F, compensating to shareholders a temporary value of their money, premium for business risk $(k_M - k_F)b_U$, and premium for financial risk $(k_M - k_F)b_U\frac{D}{S}(1 - T)$.

If the company does not have borrowing ($D = 0$), the financial risk factor will be equal to zero (the third term is drawn to zero), and its owners will only receive the premium for business risk.

Note, that Hamada's empirical result regarding the inclusion of financial risk alongside business risk, as described by the classical CAPM model, was shown by Brusov et al. (2024) to be inaccurate. Brusov et al. created an innovative model, CAPM 2.0, which correctly describes financial risk alongside business risk (Brusov et al. 2024). It was shown that along with the renormalization of the beta coefficient to the level of leverage described by the Hamada model, an additional term appears in the model, that depends on leverage level, L, debt cost, kd, risk free profitability, kF, and tax corrector, (1-T). This term is absent in Hamada's model and can be noticeable at high leverage levels and large differences between debt cost, kd and risk free profitability, kF. More general formula for the WACC, then famous Modigliani–Miller (MM) one has been derived and discussed by a few authors (Farber et al. 2007; Fernandez 2007; Harris and Pringle 1985; Miles and Ezzel 1980; De Marzo 1988; Arzac and Glosten 2005; Brusov et al. 2015; Myers 2001; Sethi et al. 1991; Taggart 1991). It takes the following form

$$WACC = k_0(1 - w_d T) - k_d t w_d + k_{TS} t w_d \tag{7.3}$$

where k_0, k_d and k_{TS} are the expected returns respectively on the unlevered firm, the debt and the tax shield, V is the value of the levered firm, VTS is the value of the tax shield, D is the value of the debt and TC is the corporate tax rate.

This formula is derived from the balance sheet identity and the definition of the weighted average cost of capital (for a similar presentation, see Berk and De Marzo 2020). It should therefore be verified at any point in time, whatever returns are annually or continuously compounded.

Although Eq. (7.3) is fully general, its practical applicability requires additional conditions. Indeed, when the WACC is constant over time, the value of a levered firm can be computed by discounting with the WACC the unlevered free cash–flows. Therefore, we pay a special attention to the special cases that make the WACC constant. The resulting particular formulas can also be found in textbooks (Ross et al. 2005).

First, Modigliani and Miller (1963) assume that the level of debt D is constant. Then, as the expected after–tax cash–flow of the unlevered firm is fixed, V_0 is also constant. By assumption, $k_{TS} = k_D$ and the value of the tax shield is TS = tD. Therefore, the value of the firm V is a constant and the general WACC formula (7.3) simplifies to a constant WACC:

$$WACC = k_0(1 - w_d T) \tag{7.4}$$

But our opinion is that "classical" Modigliani–Miller (MM) theory, which coming from the suggestion that the expected returns on the debt k_d and the tax shield k_{TS} are equals (because both of them have debt nature), is much more reasonable and in our paper we modify namely "classical" Modigliani–Miller (MM) theory, which is still widely used in practice.

Recently the Modigliani–Miller theory has been modified by Brusov et al. (2019, 2021) into two ways: it was applied for rating methodologies needs and it was generalized for the case of advance payments of tax on profit, which are widely used in practice (MMM theory). As well Brusov et al. (2019, 2021, 2022, 2023) and Brusov and Filatova (2025a, b) used the Modified Modigliani–Miller theory (MMM theory) and apply it for rating methodologies needs. The financial "ratios" (main rating parameters) were introduced into MMM theory. The dependence of the weighted average cost of capital (WACC), which plays the role of discount rate in financial flows discounting in rating methodologies, on coverage and leverage ratios is analyzed. Obtained results will help improve the existing rating methodologies.

One of the most serious limitations of the Modigliani–Miller theory is the suggestion about perpetuity of the companies. In 2008, Brusov–Filatova–Orekhova (Filatova et al. 2008) have lifted up this limitation and have shown that the accounting of the finite age (or finite life–time) of the company leads to significant changes of all Modigliani–Miller results (Modigliani and Miller 1958, 1963, 1966): capitalization of the company is changed, as well as the equity cost, k_e, and the weighted average cost of capital, WACC, in the presence of corporative taxes. Besides, a number of qualitatively new effects in corporate finance, obtained within Brusov–Filatova–Orekhova theory (BFO theory) (Brusov et al. 2018a, b, c, d, e, f, g, 2019, 2020a, b, c; Filatova et al. 2018; Brusov 2018a, b), are absent in Modigliani–Miller theory (1958, 1963).

The famous Brusov–Filatova–Orekhova formula for weighted average cost of capital, WACC, has the following form

$$\frac{1-(1+WACC)^{-n}}{WACC} = \frac{1-(1+k_0)^{-n}}{k_0\left[1-\omega_d T\left(1-(1+k_d)^{-n}\right)\right]}. \tag{7.5}$$

Here, S—the value of own (equity) capital of the company, $w_d = \frac{D}{D+S}$—the share of debt capital; k_e, $w_e = \frac{S}{D+S}$—the cost and the share of the equity of the company, $L = D/S$—financial leverage.

A lot of meaningful effects has been discovered within BFO theory: these effects are absent within Modigliani–Miller theory. BFO theory has destroyed some main existing principles of financial management: among them trade off theory, which was considered as keystone of formation of optimal capital structure of the company during many decades and **bankruptcy of which has been proven** by Brusov–Filatova–Orekhova.

7.3 Focus and Objective of the Chapter

The tax shield plays a crucial role in both main capital structure theories: Brusov–Filatova–Orekhova (BFO theory) and its perpetuity limit Modigliani–Miller theory. How it is formed influences the results of both theories. Both of them describes the case of annual payments of tax of profit, but in practice these payments are made more frequent: semiannually, quarterly, monthly. While a return is not required more than once a year, businesses may be responsible for filing estimated taxes based on profits earned. This requirement is dependent on showing a profit. For example, sole proprietors must file estimated taxes on profits quarterly, on the 15th day of April, June, September and January. In Russia tax on profit payments could be made annually, quarterly, monthly. Brusov and Filatova (2021) have shown that the account of frequency of payment of tax on profit within the Modigliani–Miller theory turns out to be very important and leads to significant consequences.

To study this problem they have modified the Modigliani–Miller theory for the case of arbitrary frequency of payment of tax on profit and show that:

- all Modigliani–Miller theorems, statements and all formulas change;
- all main financial indicators, such as the weighted average cost of capital, WACC, company value, V and equity cost, k_e depend on the frequency of tax on profit payments. This allows to company manage WACC, V, k_e etc. by choosing the number of payments of tax of profit p per year;
- increase the number of payments of tax of profit per year leads to decrease of the cost of attracting capital and increase of the company value;
- obtained results allow to company choose the number of payments of tax of profit per year, as many, as it is profitable to it (of course, within actual tax legislation);
- in case of income tax payments more than once per year (at $p \neq 1$), as it takes place in practice, the weighted average cost of capital, WACC, company value, V and equity cost, k_e start depend on k_d, while in ordinary (classical) Modigliani–Miller theory all these values DO NOT depend on k_d.

– the tilt angle of the curve of equity cost, k_e (L), decreases with the number of payments of tax of profit p, this modifies the dividend policy of the company, because the economically justified value of dividends is equal to equity cost.

As it was shown in that paper (Brusov and Filatova 2021), more frequent payments of income tax are beneficial for both parties: for the company and for the tax regulator: for the company, this leads to decrease of the cost of attracting capital and thus to an increase in the value of the company, and for the tax regulator, earlier payments are beneficial due to the time value of money.

But companies could pay tax of profit in advance and as we show in current paper this fact changes drastically the main conclusion: more frequent payments of income tax are **NOT** beneficial for the company: this leads to increase of the cost of attracting capital and thus to decrease in the value of the company, but for the tax regulator it remains beneficial: earlier payments are beneficial due to the time value of money.

7.4 Modification of the Modigliani–Miller Theory for the Case of Arbitrary Frequency of Advanced Payments of Tax on Profit

7.4.1 Tax Shield

Let us calculate first the tax shield *TS* in the Modigliani–Miller theory in the case of arbitrary frequency (p per year) of advanced payments of tax on profit

$$TS = \frac{k_d Dt}{p} + \frac{k_d Dt}{p(1+k_d)^{1/p}} + \frac{k_d Dt}{p(1+k_d)^{2/p}} + \ldots \tag{7.6}$$

(*TS*) represents a geometric progression with denominator $q = \frac{1}{(1+k_d)^{1/p}}$.

Here D is debt value, k_d is debt cost,t is tax on profit rate, p is the frequency of payments of tax on profit.

Summing the progression, one gets

$$TS = \frac{k_d Dt}{p\left(1-(1+k_d)^{-1/p}\right)} = \frac{k_d Dt \cdot (1+k_d)^{1/p}}{p\left((1+k_d)^{1/p}-1\right)}. \tag{7.7}$$

Note, that in case of classical Modigliani–Miller theory, modified by us for the case of one advanced payment of tax on profit per year

$$TS = Dt(1 + k_d). \tag{7.8}$$

It is easy to get this result from (7.7), putting p = 1.

7.4.2 The Weighted Average Cost of Capital, WACC

Let us calculate now the weighted average cost of capital, WACC in the Modigliani–Miller theory in the case of arbitrary frequency (*p* per year) of advanced payments of tax on profit.

From the Modigliani–Miller theorem we have for the company value V

$$V = V_0 + TS. \tag{7.9}$$

Here V_0 is the financially independent company value.

Putting expression for tax shield TS, we get

$$V = V_0 + \frac{k_d Dt \cdot (1 + k_d)^{1/p}}{p\left((1 + k_d)^{1/p} - 1\right)}. \tag{7.10}$$

Substituting $D = w_d V$, one gets

$$V\left(1 - \frac{k_d w_d t \cdot (1 + k_d)^{1/p}}{p\left((1 + k_d)^{1/p} - 1\right)}\right) = V_0. \tag{7.11}$$

Accounting, that

$$V = \frac{CF}{WACC};\ V_0 = \frac{CF}{k_0}, \tag{7.12}$$

we have

$$\frac{CF}{WACC} \cdot \left(1 - \frac{k_d w_d t \cdot (1 + k_d)^{1/p}}{p\left((1 + k_d)^{1/p} - 1\right)}\right) = \frac{CF}{k_0}. \tag{7.13}$$

From here we arrive to the expression for the weighted average cost of capital, WACC,

$$WACC = k_0 \cdot \left(1 - \frac{k_d w_d t \cdot (1+k_d)^{1/p}}{p\left((1+k_d)^{1/p} - 1\right)} \right). \tag{7.14}$$

Note, that in case of classical Modigliani–Miller theory, modified by us for the case of one advanced payment of tax on profit per year

$$WACC = k_0 \cdot (1 - w_d t \cdot (1+k_d)). \tag{7.15}$$

It is easy to get this result from (7.14), putting p = 1.

7.4.3 Company Value, V

Let us calculate now the company value, V, in the Modigliani–Miller theory in the case of arbitrary frequency (p per year) of advanced payments of tax on profit.

Putting WACC value into first formula of (7.12) one gets for company value, V

$$V = \frac{CF}{WACC} = \frac{CF}{k_0 \cdot \left(1 - \frac{k_d w_d t \cdot (1+k_d)^{1/p}}{p\left((1+k_d)^{1/p} - 1\right)} \right)}. \tag{7.16}$$

Here *CF* is the profit of the company per year, w_d is the debt share.

In case of classical Modigliani–Miller theory, modified by us for the case of one advanced payment of tax on profit per year (Brusov et al. 2020a, b, c), one has

$$V = \frac{CF}{WACC} = \frac{CF}{k_0 \cdot (1 - w_d t(1+k_d))}. \tag{7.17}$$

It is easy to get this result from (7.16), putting p = 1.

7.4.4 Equity Cost

Let us calculate now the equity cost, k_d, in the Modigliani–Miller theory in the case of arbitrary frequency (p per year) of advanced payments of tax on profit.

For the weighted average cost of capital, WACC, we have from formula (7.14).

$$WACC = k_0 \cdot \left(1 - \frac{k_d w_d t \cdot (1+k_d)^{1/p}}{p\left((1+k_d)^{1/p} - 1\right)}\right). \tag{7.18}$$

From other side, upon definition one has

$$WACC = k_e w_e + k_d w_d (1-t). \tag{7.19}$$

From (7.19) we get

$$k_e = \frac{WACC}{w_e} - \frac{k_d w_d (1-t)}{w_e} \tag{7.20}$$

Putting (7.18) into (7.20), we arrive to expression for equity cost k_e

$$\begin{aligned} k_e &= \frac{k_0}{w_e} \cdot \left(1 - \frac{k_d w_d t \cdot (1+k_d)^{1/p}}{p\left((1+k_d)^{1/p} - 1\right)}\right) - \frac{k_d w_d (1-t)}{w_e} = \\ &= k_0 \cdot \left(1 + L - \frac{k_d L t \cdot (1+k_d)^{1/p}}{p\left((1+k_d)^{1/p} - 1\right)}\right) - k_d L (1-t) = \\ &= k_0 + L\left(k_0 - k_d(1-t) - \frac{k_0 k_d t \cdot (1+k_d)^{1/p}}{p\left((1+k_d)^{1/p} - 1\right)}\right) \end{aligned} \tag{7.21}$$

Finally, one has

$$k_e = k_0 + L\left(k_0 - k_d(1-t) - \frac{k_0 k_d t \cdot (1+k_d)^{1/p}}{p\left((1+k_d)^{1/p} - 1\right)}\right) \tag{7.22}$$

In case of classical Modigliani–Miller theory, modified by us for the case of one advanced payment of tax on profit per year (Brusov et al. 2020a, b, c), one has.

$$k_e = k_0 + L(k_0 - k_d \cdot (1-t) - k_0 t(1+k_d)). \tag{7.23}$$

Putting in formula (7.22) p = 1, it is easy to get formula (7.23).

7.5 Dependence of the Weighted Average Cost of Capital, WACC, on Leverage Level L

7.5.1 Dependence of the Weighted Average Cost of Capital, WACC, on Leverage Level L at Different P and Fixed k_d

Let us start from the study numerically with use of Microsoft Excel of the dependence of the weighted average cost of capital, WACC, on leverage level L at different frequency of payments p and fixed debt cost k_d, using obtained by us formulas

$$WACC = k_0 \cdot \left(1 - \frac{k_d w_d t}{p\left((1+k_d)^{1/p} - 1\right)}\right) \text{ and}$$

$$WACC = k_0 \cdot \left(1 - \frac{k_d w_d t \cdot (1+k_d)^{1/p}}{p\left((1+k_d)^{1/p} - 1\right)}\right).$$

From Tables 7.1, 7.2, 7.3, 7.4 and Figs. 7.1, 7.2 it is seen, that the weighted average cost of capital, WACC, decreases with leverage level L at all values of frequency of payments of tax on profit p. With increase of the frequency of payments of tax on profit per year p WACC (1) decreases in the case of payments at the ends of the periods and WACC (2) increases in the case of advanced payments of tax on profit. As we'll see below, this will lead to increase of company value, V, with increase of p in the case (1) and to decrease of company value, V, with increase of p in the case (2).

Note, that the weighted average cost of capital, WACC, in the case of advanced payments of tax on profit for all values of frequency of payments turns out to be low than for any values of frequency of payments in the case of payments at the ends of the periods.

Table 7.1 Dependence of WACC on leverage level L at $k_0 = 0.2$, $k_d = 0.16$ and $p = 1$

k_0	k_d	w_d	L	t	p	i	WACC
0.2	0.16	0	0	0.2	1	1.16	0.2
0.2	0.16	0.5	1	0.2	1	1.16	0.18
0.2	0.16	0.666667	2	0.2	1	1.16	0.173333
0.2	0.16	0.75	3	0.2	1	1.16	0.17
0.2	0.16	0.8	4	0.2	1	1.16	0.168
0.2	0.16	0.833333	5	0.2	1	1.16	0.166667
0.2	0.16	0.857143	6	0.2	1	1.16	0.165714
0.2	0.16	0.875	7	0.2	1	1.16	0.165
0.2	0.16	0.888889	8	0.2	1	1.16	0.164444
0.2	0.16	0.9	9	0.2	1	1.16	0.164
0.2	0.16	0.909091	10	0.2	1	1.16	0.163636

Table 7.2 Dependence of WACC on leverage level L at $k_0 = 0.2$, $k_d = 0.16$ and $p = 12$

k_0	k_d	w_d	L	t	p	i	WACC
0.2	0.16	0	0	0.2	12	1.012445	0.2
0.2	0.16	0.5	1	0.2	12	1.012445	0.178573
0.2	0.16	0.666667	2	0.2	12	1.012445	0.17143
0.2	0.16	0.75	3	0.2	12	1.012445	0.167859
0.2	0.16	0.8	4	0.2	12	1.012445	0.165716
0.2	0.16	0.833333	5	0.2	12	1.012445	0.164288
0.2	0.16	0.857143	6	0.2	12	1.012445	0.163267
0.2	0.16	0.875	7	0.2	12	1.012445	0.162502
0.2	0.16	0.888889	8	0.2	12	1.012445	0.161907
0.2	0.16	0.9	9	0.2	12	1.012445	0.161431
0.2	0.16	0.909091	10	0.2	12	1.012445	0.161041

Table 7.3 Dependence of WACC on leverage level L at $k_0 = 0.2$, $k_d = 0.16$ and $p = 1$ (advanced payment of tax of profit)

k_0	k_d	w_d	L	t	p	i	WACC
0.2	0.16	0	0	0.2	1	1.16	0.2
0.2	0.16	0.5	1	0.2	1	1.16	0.1768
0.2	0.16	0.666667	2	0.2	1	1.16	0.169067
0.2	0.16	0.75	3	0.2	1	1.16	0.1652
0.2	0.16	0.8	4	0.2	1	1.16	0.16288
0.2	0.16	0.833333	5	0.2	1	1.16	0.161333
0.2	0.16	0.857143	6	0.2	1	1.16	0.160229
0.2	0.16	0.875	7	0.2	1	1.16	0.1594
0.2	0.16	0.888889	8	0.2	1	1.16	0.158756
0.2	0.16	0.9	9	0.2	1	1.16	0.15824
0.2	0.16	0.909091	10	0.2	1	1.16	0.157818

Table 7.4 Dependence of WACC on leverage level L at $k_0 = 0.2$, $k_d = 0.16$ and $p = 12$ (advanced payment of tax of profit)

k_0	k_d	w_d	L	t	p	i	WACC
0.2	0.16	0	0	0.2	12	1.012445	0.2
0.2	0.16	0.5	1	0.2	12	1.012445	0.178306
0.2	0.16	0.666667	2	0.2	12	1.012445	0.171075
0.2	0.16	0.75	3	0.2	12	1.012445	0.167459
0.2	0.16	0.8	4	0.2	12	1.012445	0.16529
0.2	0.16	0.833333	5	0.2	12	1.012445	0.163843
0.2	0.16	0.857143	6	0.2	12	1.012445	0.16281
0.2	0.16	0.875	7	0.2	12	1.012445	0.162035
0.2	0.16	0.888889	8	0.2	12	1.012445	0.161433
0.2	0.16	0.9	9	0.2	12	1.012445	0.160951
0.2	0.16	0.909091	10	0.2	12	1.012445	0.160556

7.5.2 Dependence of the Weighted Average Cost of Capital, WACC, and of Company Value, V, on Debt Cost Value k_d at Fixed Value of Leverage Level L and Fixed P

In this paragraph we investigate the dependence of the weighted average cost of capital, WACC, and of company value, V on debt cost value k_d at fixed value of leverage level L and fixed p.

From Tables 7.5, 7.6, 7.7, 7.8 and Fig. 7.3 it is seen, that the weighted average cost of capital, WACC, decreases with increase of debt cost value k_d, except the

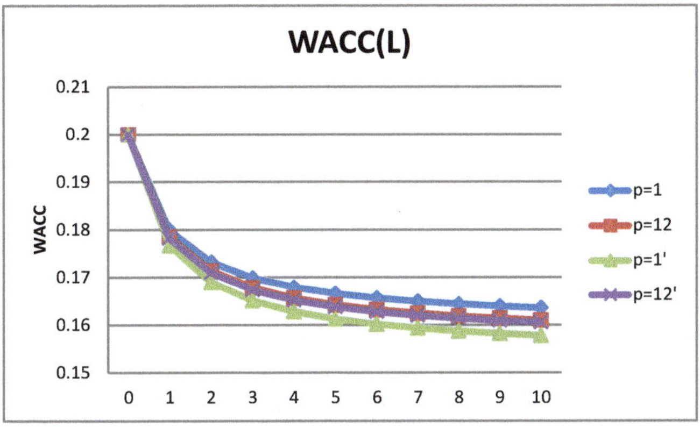

Fig. 7.1 Dependence of the weighted average cost of capital, WACC, on leverage level L at different p and fixed $k_d = 0.16$

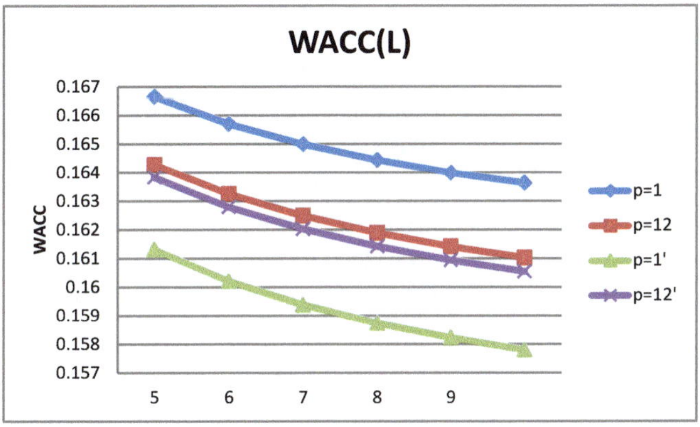

Fig. 7.2 Dependence of the weighted average cost of capital, WACC, on leverage level L at different p and fixed $k_d = 0.16$ (larger scale)

classical MM case $p = 1$ and payment at the end of the period. It supports obtained by us result that account of each of two effects (either advanced payments of tax on profit, or more frequent than once per year payments) leads to dependence of all main financial indicators, such as the weighted average cost of capital, WACC, company value, V, equity cost, k_e, etc. on debt cost value k_d, while in the classical MM case these financial indicators DO NOT depend on debt cost value k_d.

Similar to previous paragraph it is seen, that with increase of the frequency of payments of tax on profit per year p WACC (1) decreases in the case of payments at the ends of the periods and WACC (2) increases in the case of advanced payments of tax on profit. As we'll see below, this will lead to increase of company value, V, with increase of p in the case (1) and to decrease of company value, V, with increase of p in the case (2).

Table 7.5 Dependence of WACC on debt cost value k_d at $k_0 = 0.2$, AT $L = 1$ and $p = 1$

k_0	k_d	w_d	L	t	p	i	WACC	CF	V	k_e
0.2	0.08	0.5	1	0.2	1	1.08	0.18	1000	5555.556	0.296
0.2	0.09	0.5	1	0.2	1	1.09	0.18	1000	5555.556	0.288
0.2	0.1	0.5	1	0.2	1	1.1	0.18	1000	5555.556	0.28
0.2	0.11	0.5	1	0.2	1	1.11	0.18	1000	5555.556	0.272
0.2	0.12	0.5	1	0.2	1	1.12	0.18	1000	5555.556	0.264
0.2	0.13	0.5	1	0.2	1	1.13	0.18	1000	5555.556	0.256
0.2	0.14	0.5	1	0.2	1	1.14	0.18	1000	5555.556	0.248
0.2	0.15	0.5	1	0.2	1	1.15	0.18	1000	5555.556	0.24
0.2	0.16	0.5	1	0.2	1	1.16	0.18	1000	5555.556	0.232
0.2	0.17	0.5	1	0.2	1	1.17	0.18	1000	5555.556	0.224
0.2	0.18	0.5	1	0.2	1	1.18	0.18	1000	5555.556	0.216

Table 7.6 Dependence of WACC on debt cost value k_d at $k_0 = 0.2$, AT $L = 1$ and $p = 12$

k_0	k_d	w_d	L	t	p	i	WACC	CF	V	k_e
0.2	0.08	0.5	1	0.2	12	1.006434	0.179277	1000	5577.965	0.294554
0.2	0.09	0.5	1	0.2	12	1.007207	0.179188	1000	5580.736	0.286376
0.2	0.1	0.5	1	0.2	12	1.007974	0.179099	1000	5583.501	0.278198
0.2	0.11	0.5	1	0.2	12	1.008735	0.179011	1000	5586.259	0.270021
0.2	0.12	0.5	1	0.2	12	1.009489	0.178923	1000	5589.012	0.261845
0.2	0.13	0.5	1	0.2	12	1.010237	0.178835	1000	5591.758	0.253669
0.2	0.14	0.5	1	0.2	12	1.010979	0.178747	1000	5594.499	0.245494
0.2	0.15	0.5	1	0.2	12	1.011715	0.17866	1000	5597.234	0.237319
0.2	0.16	0.5	1	0.2	12	1.012445	0.178573	1000	5599.963	0.229145
0.2	0.17	0.5	1	0.2	12	1.01317	0.178486	1000	5602.686	0.220972
0.2	0.18	0.5	1	0.2	12	1.013888	0.178399	1000	5605.404	0.212799

Note, that the weighted average cost of capital, WACC, in the case of advanced payments of tax on profit for all values of frequency of payments turns out to be low than for any values of frequency of payments in the case of payments at the ends of the periods.

From Tables 7.5, 7.6, 7.7, 7.8 and Fig. 7.4 it is seen, that the company value, V, increases with increase of debt cost value k_d, except the classical Modigliani–Miller theory case $p = 1$ and payment at the end of the period, when V remains constant. It supports obtained by us result that account of each of two effects (either advanced payments of tax on profit, or more frequent than once per year) leads to dependence of all main financial indicators, such as the weighted average cost of capital, WACC, company value, V, equity cost, k_e, etc. on debt cost value k_d, while in the classical

Table 7.7 Dependence of WACC on debt cost value k_d at $k_0 = 0.2$, at $L = 1$ and $p = 1$ (for advanced payments of tax of profit)

k_0	k_d	w_d	L	t	p	i	WACC	CF	V	k_e
0.2	0.08	0.5	1	0.2	1	1.08	0.1784	1000	5605.381	0.2928
0.2	0.09	0.5	1	0.2	1	1.09	0.1782	1000	5611.672	0.2844
0.2	0.1	0.5	1	0.2	1	1.1	0.178	1000	5617.978	0.276
0.2	0.11	0.5	1	0.2	1	1.11	0.1778	1000	5624.297	0.2676
0.2	0.12	0.5	1	0.2	1	1.12	0.1776	1000	5630.631	0.2592
0.2	0.13	0.5	1	0.2	1	1.13	0.1774	1000	5636.979	0.2508
0.2	0.14	0.5	1	0.2	1	1.14	0.1772	1000	5643.341	0.2424
0.2	0.15	0.5	1	0.2	1	1.15	0.177	1000	5649.718	0.234
0.2	0.16	0.5	1	0.2	1	1.16	0.1768	1000	5656.109	0.2256
0.2	0.17	0.5	1	0.2	1	1.17	0.1766	1000	5662.514	0.2172
0.2	0.18	0.5	1	0.2	1	1.18	0.1764	1000	5668.934	0.2088

Table 7.8 Dependence of WACC on debt cost value k_d at $k_0 = 0.2$, at $L = 1$ and $p = 12$ (for advanced payments of tax of profit)

k_0	k_d	w_d	L	t	p	i	WACC	CF	V	k_e
0.2	0.08	0.5	1	0.2	12	1.006434	0.179144	1000	5582.116	0.294287
0.2	0.09	0.5	1	0.2	12	1.007207	0.179038	1000	5585.412	0.286076
0.2	0.1	0.5	1	0.2	12	1.007974	0.178932	1000	5588.702	0.277865
0.2	0.11	0.5	1	0.2	12	1.008735	0.178827	1000	5591.986	0.269655
0.2	0.12	0.5	1	0.2	12	1.009489	0.178723	1000	5595.266	0.261445
0.2	0.13	0.5	1	0.2	12	1.010237	0.178618	1000	5598.541	0.253236
0.2	0.14	0.5	1	0.2	12	1.010979	0.178514	1000	5601.811	0.245027
0.2	0.15	0.5	1	0.2	12	1.011715	0.17841	1000	5605.077	0.236819
0.2	0.16	0.5	1	0.2	12	1.012445	0.178306	1000	5608.338	0.228612
0.2	0.17	0.5	1	0.2	12	1.01317	0.178202	1000	5611.594	0.220405
0.2	0.18	0.5	1	0.2	12	1.013888	0.178099	1000	5614.846	0.212199

Modigliani–Miller theory case these financial indicators DO NOT depend on debt cost value k_d.

Similar to previous paragraph it is seen, that with increase of the frequency of payments of tax on profit per year p the company value, V, (1) increases in the case of payments at the ends of the periods and WACC (2) decreases in the case of advanced payments of tax on profit.

Note, that the company value, V, in the case of advanced payments of tax on profit for all values of frequency of payments turns out to be higher than for any values of frequency of payments in the case of payments at the ends of the periods.

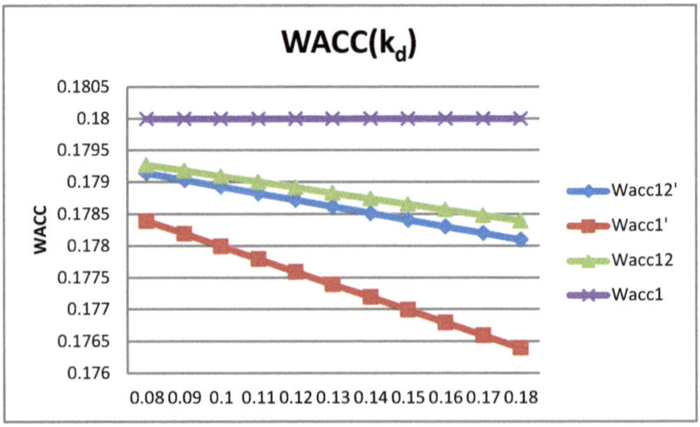

Fig. 7.3 Dependence of WACC on debt cost value k_d at $k_0 = 0.2$, at $L = 1$ and $p = 1$ and $p = 12$ ($'$ means advanced payments of tax of profit)

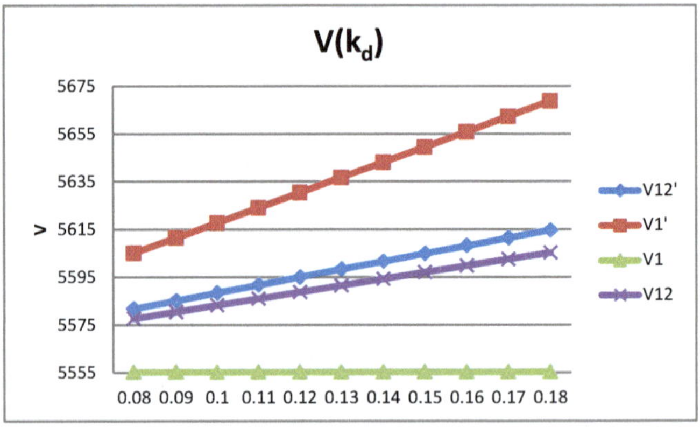

Fig. 7.4 Dependence of company value V on debt cost value k_d at $k_0 = 0.2$, at $L = 1$ and $p = 1$ and $p = 12$ ($'$ means advanced payments of tax of profit)

7.6 Dependence of the Company Capitalization, V, on Leverage Level L

7.6.1 Dependence of the Company Capitalization, Vv, on Leverage Level L at Different P and Fixed k_d

Let us now calculate the dependence of the company capitalization, V, on leverage level L at different p and fixed k_d.

From Tables 7.9, 7.10, 7.11, 7.12 and Figs. 7.5 and 7.6 it is seen, that the company value, V, increases with the increase of leverage level L for all frequencies of payment of tax on profit per year p.

Table 7.9 Dependence of the company capitalization on leverage level L at $k_d = 0.16$ and at $p = 1$

k_0	k_d	w_d	L	t	p	i	WACC	CF	V
0.2	0.16	0	0	0.2	1	1.16	0.2	1000	5000
0.2	0.16	0.5	1	0.2	1	1.16	0.18	1000	5555.556
0.2	0.16	0.666667	2	0.2	1	1.16	0.173333	1000	5769.231
0.2	0.16	0.75	3	0.2	1	1.16	0.17	1000	5882.353
0.2	0.16	0.8	4	0.2	1	1.16	0.168	1000	5952.381
0.2	0.16	0.833333	5	0.2	1	1.16	0.166667	1000	6000
0.2	0.16	0.857143	6	0.2	1	1.16	0.165714	1000	6034.483
0.2	0.16	0.875	7	0.2	1	1.16	0.165	1000	6060.606
0.2	0.16	0.888889	8	0.2	1	1.16	0.164444	1000	6081.081
0.2	0.16	0.9	9	0.2	1	1.16	0.164	1000	6097.561
0.2	0.16	0.909091	10	0.2	1	1.16	0.163636	1000	6111.111

Table 7.10 Dependence of the company capitalization on leverage level L at $k_d = 0.16$ and at $p = 12$

k_0	k_d	w_d	L	t	p	i	WACC	CF	V
0.2	0.16	0	0	0.2	12	1.012445	0.2	1000	5000
0.2	0.16	0.5	1	0.2	12	1.012445	0.178573	1000	5599.963
0.2	0.16	0.666667	2	0.2	12	1.012445	0.17143	1000	5833.279
0.2	0.16	0.75	3	0.2	12	1.012445	0.167859	1000	5957.383
0.2	0.16	0.8	4	0.2	12	1.012445	0.165716	1000	6034.413
0.2	0.16	0.833333	5	0.2	12	1.012445	0.164288	1000	6086.883
0.2	0.16	0.857143	6	0.2	12	1.012445	0.163267	1000	6124.923
0.2	0.16	0.875	7	0.2	12	1.012445	0.162502	1000	6153.767
0.2	0.16	0.888889	8	0.2	12	1.012445	0.161907	1000	6176.39
0.2	0.16	0.9	9	0.2	12	1.012445	0.161431	1000	6194.608
0.2	0.16	0.909091	10	0.2	12	1.012445	0.161041	1000	6209.594

While in case of payments at the end of the periods the company value, V, increases with the increase of the frequency of payment of tax on profit per year p, in case of advanced payments of tax on profit the company value, V, decreases with the increase of the frequency of payment of tax on profit per year p. These facts consistent with the dependence of the weighted average cost of capital, WACC, on the leverage level L.

All the company values, V, in case of advanced payments of tax on profit turns out to be bigger than in case of payments at the end of the periods. Thus if the companies tend to increase their capitalization, they should pay tax on profit (1) in advance; (2) as seldom as tax legislation allows.

Table 7.11 Dependence of the company capitalization on leverage level L at $k_d = 0.16$ and at $p = 1$ (for advanced payments of tax of profit)

k_0	k_d	w_d	L	t	p	i	WACC	CF	V
0.2	0.16	0	0	0.2	1	1.16	0.2	1000	5000
0.2	0.16	0.5	1	0.2	1	1.16	0.1768	1000	5656.109
0.2	0.16	0.666667	2	0.2	1	1.16	0.169067	1000	5914.826
0.2	0.16	0.75	3	0.2	1	1.16	0.1652	1000	6053.269
0.2	0.16	0.8	4	0.2	1	1.16	0.16288	1000	6139.489
0.2	0.16	0.833333	5	0.2	1	1.16	0.161333	1000	6198.347
0.2	0.16	0.857143	6	0.2	1	1.16	0.160229	1000	6241.084
0.2	0.16	0.875	7	0.2	1	1.16	0.1594	1000	6273.526
0.2	0.16	0.888889	8	0.2	1	1.16	0.158756	1000	6298.992
0.2	0.16	0.9	9	0.2	1	1.16	0.15824	1000	6319.515
0.2	0.16	0.909091	10	0.2	1	1.16	0.157818	1000	6336.406

Table 7.12 Dependence of the company capitalization on leverage level L at $k_d = 0.16$ and at $p = 12$ (for advanced payments of tax of profit)

k_0	k_d	w_d	L	t	p	i	WACC	CF	V
0.2	0.16	0	0	0.2	12	1.012445	0.2	1000	5000
0.2	0.16	0.5	1	0.2	12	1.012445	0.178306	1000	5608.338
0.2	0.16	0.666667	2	0.2	12	1.012445	0.171075	1000	5845.403
0.2	0.16	0.75	3	0.2	12	1.012445	0.167459	1000	5971.613
0.2	0.16	0.8	4	0.2	12	1.012445	0.16529	1000	6049.99
0.2	0.16	0.833333	5	0.2	12	1.012445	0.163843	1000	6103.394
0.2	0.16	0.857143	6	0.2	12	1.012445	0.16281	1000	6142.121
0.2	0.16	0.875	7	0.2	12	1.012445	0.162035	1000	6171.49
0.2	0.16	0.888889	8	0.2	12	1.012445	0.161433	1000	6194.528
0.2	0.16	0.9	9	0.2	12	1.012445	0.160951	1000	6213.082
0.2	0.16	0.909091	10	0.2	12	1.012445	0.160556	1000	6228.345

7.7 Dependence of the Equity Cost, k_e, on Leverage Level L

Let us now calculate the dependence of the equity cost, k_e, on leverage level L at different p and fixed k_d.

From Tables 7.13, 7.14, 7.15, 7.16 and Figs. 7.7, 7.8, 7.9 it is seen, that the equity cost, k_e, linearly increases with the increase of leverage level L for all frequencies of payment of tax on profit per year p.

While in the case of tax on profit payments at the end of the periods the tilt of the curve of the equity cost, k_e, decreases with the increase of the frequency of payment of tax on profit per year p, in case of the advanced payments of tax on

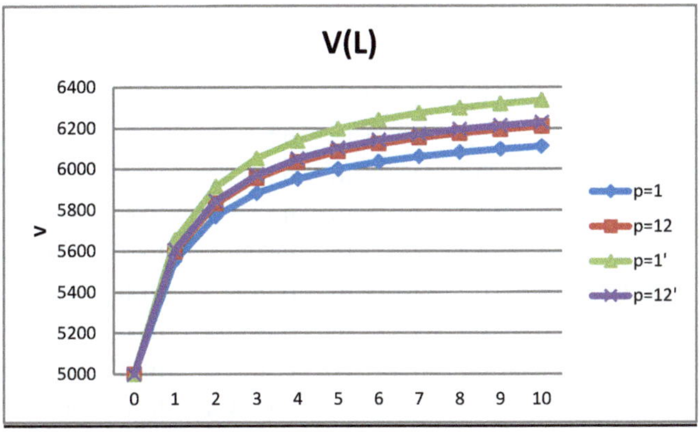

Fig. 7.5 Dependence of the company capitalization, V, on leverage level L at $k_d = 0.16$ and $p = 1$ and 12 (′ means advanced payment of tax of profit)

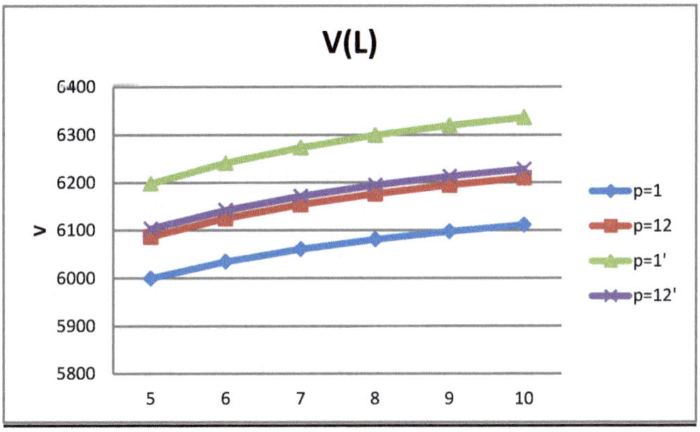

Fig. 7.6 Dependence of the company capitalization, V, on leverage level L at $k_d = 0.16$ and $p = 1$ and 12 (′ means advanced payment of tax of profit) (larger scale)

profit, the tilt of the curve of the equity cost, k_e, increases with the increase of the frequency of payment of tax on profit per year p. These facts should be accounted when developing the company's dividend policy, because the value of the equity cost, k_e, is the economically justified amount of dividends.

The company's dividend policy should be as following:

1. *If the company would like* ***to minimize the dividend payments****:*
   - in case of payments of tax on profit at the ends of periods they should be as frequently as tax legislation allows.
   - in case of advanced payments of tax on profit they should be as seldom as tax legislation allows.

Table 7.13 Dependence of the equity cost, k_e, on leverage level L at $k_d = 0.16$ and at $p = 1$

k_0	k_d	w_d	L	t	p	i	WACC	CF	V	k_e
0.2	0.16	0	0	0.2	1	1.16	0.2	1000	5000	0.2
0.2	0.16	0.5	1	0.2	1	1.16	0.18	1000	5555.556	0.232
0.2	0.16	0.666667	2	0.2	1	1.16	0.173333	1000	5769.231	0.264
0.2	0.16	0.75	3	0.2	1	1.16	0.17	1000	5882.353	0.296
0.2	0.16	0.8	4	0.2	1	1.16	0.168	1000	5952.381	0.328
0.2	0.16	0.833333	5	0.2	1	1.16	0.166667	1000	6000	0.36
0.2	0.16	0.857143	6	0.2	1	1.16	0.165714	1000	6034.483	0.392
0.2	0.16	0.875	7	0.2	1	1.16	0.165	1000	6060.606	0.424
0.2	0.16	0.888889	8	0.2	1	1.16	0.164444	1000	6081.081	0.456
0.2	0.16	0.9	9	0.2	1	1.16	0.164	1000	6097.561	0.488
0.2	0.16	0.909091	10	0.2	1	1.16	0.163636	1000	6111.111	0.52

Table 7.14 Dependence of the equity cost, k_e, on leverage level L at $k_d = 0.16$ and at $p = 12$

k_0	k_d	w_d	L	t	p	i	WACC	CF	V	k_e
0.2	0.16	0	0	0.2	12	1.012445	0.2	1000	5000	0.2
0.2	0.16	0.5	1	0.2	12	1.012445	0.178573	1000	5599.963	0.229145
0.2	0.16	0.666667	2	0.2	12	1.012445	0.17143	1000	5833.279	0.25829
0.2	0.16	0.75	3	0.2	12	1.012445	0.167859	1000	5957.383	0.287436
0.2	0.16	0.8	4	0.2	12	1.012445	0.165716	1000	6034.413	0.316581
0.2	0.16	0.833333	5	0.2	12	1.012445	0.164288	1000	6086.883	0.345726
0.2	0.16	0.857143	6	0.2	12	1.012445	0.163267	1000	6124.923	0.374871
0.2	0.16	0.875	7	0.2	12	1.012445	0.162502	1000	6153.767	0.404017
0.2	0.16	0.888889	8	0.2	12	1.012445	0.161907	1000	6176.39	0.433162
0.2	0.16	0.9	9	0.2	12	1.012445	0.161431	1000	6194.608	0.462307
0.2	0.16	0.909091	10	0.2	12	1.012445	0.161041	1000	6209.594	0.491452

2. *If the company would like* ***to maximize the dividend payments****:*
   - in case of payments of tax on profit at the ends of periods they should be as seldom as tax legislation allows.
   - in case of advanced payments of tax on profit they should be as frequently as tax legislation allows.

Table 7.15 Dependence of the equity cost, k_e, on leverage level L at $k_d = 0.16$ and at $p = 1$ (for advanced payments of tax of profit)

k_0	k_d	w_d	L	t	p	i	WACC	CF	V	k_e
0.2	0.16	0	0	0.2	1	1.16	0.2	1000	5000	0.2
0.2	0.16	0.5	1	0.2	1	1.16	0.1768	1000	5656.109	0.2256
0.2	0.16	0.666667	2	0.2	1	1.16	0.169067	1000	5914.826	0.2512
0.2	0.16	0.75	3	0.2	1	1.16	0.1652	1000	6053.269	0.2768
0.2	0.16	0.8	4	0.2	1	1.16	0.16288	1000	6139.489	0.3024
0.2	0.16	0.833333	5	0.2	1	1.16	0.161333	1000	6198.347	0.328
0.2	0.16	0.857143	6	0.2	1	1.16	0.160229	1000	6241.084	0.3536
0.2	0.16	0.875	7	0.2	1	1.16	0.1594	1000	6273.526	0.3792
0.2	0.16	0.888889	8	0.2	1	1.16	0.158756	1000	6298.992	0.4048
0.2	0.16	0.9	9	0.2	1	1.16	0.15824	1000	6319.515	0.4304
0.2	0.16	0.909091	10	0.2	1	1.16	0.157818	1000	6336.406	0.456

Table 7.16 Dependence of the equity cost, k_e, on leverage level L at $k_d = 0.16$ and at $p = 12$ (for advanced payments of tax of profit)

k_0	k_d	w_d	L	t	p	i	WACC	CF	V	k_e
0.2	0.16	0	0	0.2	12	1.012445	0.2	1000	5000	0.2
0.2	0.16	0.5	1	0.2	12	1.012445	0.178306	1000	5608.338	0.228612
0.2	0.16	0.666667	2	0.2	12	1.012445	0.171075	1000	5845.403	0.257224
0.2	0.16	0.75	3	0.2	12	1.012445	0.167459	1000	5971.613	0.285836
0.2	0.16	0.8	4	0.2	12	1.012445	0.16529	1000	6049.99	0.314448
0.2	0.16	0.833333	5	0.2	12	1.012445	0.163843	1000	6103.394	0.34306
0.2	0.16	0.857143	6	0.2	12	1.012445	0.16281	1000	6142.121	0.371671
0.2	0.16	0.875	7	0.2	12	1.012445	0.162035	1000	6171.49	0.400283
0.2	0.16	0.888889	8	0.2	12	1.012445	0.161433	1000	6194.528	0.428895
0.2	0.16	0.9	9	0.2	12	1.012445	0.160951	1000	6213.082	0.457507
0.2	0.16	0.909091	10	0.2	12	1.012445	0.160556	1000	6228.345	0.486119

7.8 Dependence of the Equity Cost, k_e, and the Weighted Average Cost of Capital, WACC, on Tax on Profit Value t

In this paragraph we study the dependence of the equity cost, k_e, and the weighted average cost of capital, WACC, on tax on profit value.

Let us first analyze the dependence of the equity cost, k_e, on tax on profit value t at different p and fixed debt cost k_d.

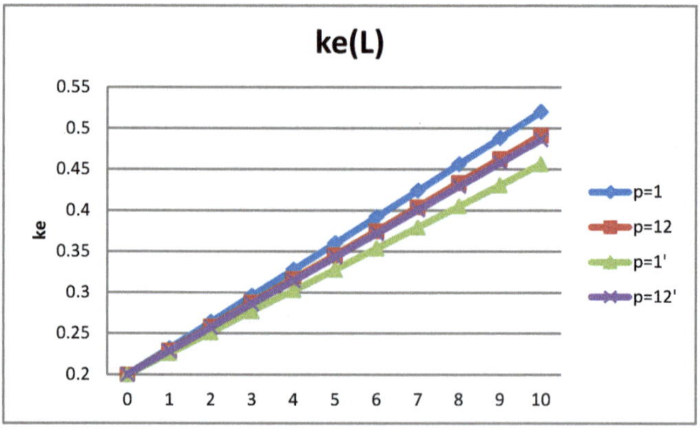

Fig. 7.7 Dependence of the dependence of the equity cost, k_e, on leverage level L at different p and fixed $k_d = 0.16$ (′ means advanced payment of tax of profit)

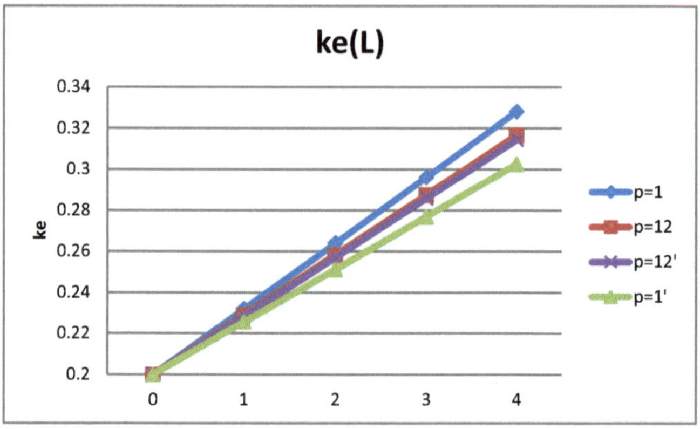

Fig. 7.8 Dependence of the dependence of the equity cost, k_e, on leverage level L at different p and fixed $k_d = 0.16$ (′ means advanced payment of tax of profit) (larger scale)

From Tables 7.17, 7.18, 7.19, 7.20 and Figs. 7.10 and 7.11 it is seen, that the equity cost, k_e, decreases with the increase of on tax on profit value t for all frequencies of payment of tax on profit per year p.

While in case of payments at the end of the periods the equity cost, k_e, decreases with the increase of the frequency of payments of tax on profit per year p (negative tilt of the curve $k_e(t)$ increases on modulus), in case of advanced payments of tax on profit t the equity cost, k_e, increases with the increase of the frequency of payment of tax on profit per year p (negative tilt of the curve $k_e(t)$ increases on modulus).

All the equity cost, k_e, values in case of advanced payments of tax on profit turns out to be lower than in case of payments at the end of the periods.

Let us now analyze the dependence of the weighted average cost of capital, WACC, on tax on profit value at different p and fixed debt cost k_d.

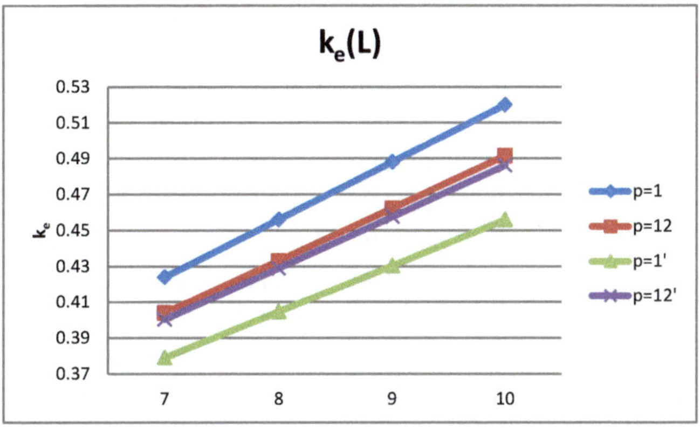

Fig. 7.9 Dependence of the dependence of the equity cost, k_e, on leverage level L at different p and fixed $k_d = 0.16$ (′ means advanced payment of tax of profit) (larger scale)

Table 7.17 Dependence of the equity cost, k_e, and the weighted average cost of capital, WACC, on tax on profit value at p = 1

k_0	k_d	w_d	L	t	p	i	WACC	CF	V	k_e
0.2	0.16	0.5	1	0	1	1.16	0.2	1000	5000	0.24
0.2	0.16	0.5	1	0.1	1	1.16	0.19	1000	5263.158	0.236
0.2	0.16	0.5	1	0.2	1	1.16	0.18	1000	5555.556	0.232
0.2	0.16	0.5	1	0.3	1	1.16	0.17	1000	5882.353	0.228
0.2	0.16	0.5	1	0.4	1	1.16	0.16	1000	6250	0.224
0.2	0.16	0.5	1	0.5	1	1.16	0.15	1000	6666.667	0.22
0.2	0.16	0.5	1	0.6	1	1.16	0.14	1000	7142.857	0.216
0.2	0.16	0.5	1	0.7	1	1.16	0.13	1000	7692.308	0.212
0.2	0.16	0.5	1	0.8	1	1.16	0.12	1000	8333.333	0.208
0.2	0.16	0.5	1	0.9	1	1.16	0.11	1000	9090.909	0.204
0.2	0.16	0.5	1	1	1	1.16	0.1	1000	10,000	0.2

From Tables 7.17, 7.18, 7.19, 7.20 and Figs. 7.10 and 7.11 it is seen, that the weighted average cost of capital, WACC, decreases with the increase of on tax on profit value t for all frequencies of payment of tax on profit per year p.

While in case of payments at the end of the periods the weighted average cost of capital, WACC, decreases with the increase of the frequency of payments of tax on profit per year p (negative tilt of the curve WACC(t) increases on modulus), in case of advanced payments of tax on profit t the weighted average cost of capital, WACC, increases with the increase of the frequency of payment of tax on profit per year p (negative tilt of the curve WACC(t) increases on modulus).

Table 7.18 Dependence of the equity cost, k_e, and the weighted average cost of capital, WACC, on tax on profit value at p = 12

k_0	k_d	w_d	L	t	p	i	WACC	CF	V	k_e
0.2	0.16	0.5	1	0	12	1.012445	0.2	1000	5000	0.24
0.2	0.16	0.5	1	0.1	12	1.012445	0.189286	1000	5283.002	0.234573
0.2	0.16	0.5	1	0.2	12	1.012445	0.178573	1000	5599.963	0.229145
0.2	0.16	0.5	1	0.3	12	1.012445	0.167859	1000	5957.383	0.223718
0.2	0.16	0.5	1	0.4	12	1.012445	0.157145	1000	6363.54	0.21829
0.2	0.16	0.5	1	0.5	12	1.012445	0.146432	1000	6829.129	0.212863
0.2	0.16	0.5	1	0.6	12	1.012445	0.135718	1000	7368.227	0.207436
0.2	0.16	0.5	1	0.7	12	1.012445	0.125004	1000	7999.733	0.202008
0.2	0.16	0.5	1	0.8	12	1.012445	0.11429	1000	8749.634	0.196581
0.2	0.16	0.5	1	0.9	12	1.012445	0.103577	1000	9654.672	0.191154
0.2	0.16	0.5	1	1	12	1.012445	0.092863	1000	10,768.54	0.185726

Table 7.19 Dependence of the equity cost, k_e, and the weighted average cost of capital, WACC, on tax on profit value at p = 1 (for advanced payments of tax of profit)

k_0	k_d	w_d	L	t	p	i	WACC	CF	V	k_e
0.2	0.16	0.5	1	0	1	1.16	0.2	1000	5000	0.24
0.2	0.16	0.5	1	0.1	1	1.16	0.1884	1000	5307.856	0.2328
0.2	0.16	0.5	1	0.2	1	1.16	0.1768	1000	5656.109	0.2256
0.2	0.16	0.5	1	0.3	1	1.16	0.1652	1000	6053.269	0.2184
0.2	0.16	0.5	1	0.4	1	1.16	0.1536	1000	657.417	0.2112
0.2	0.16	0.5	1	0.5	1	1.16	0.142	1000	7042.254	0.204
0.2	0.16	0.5	1	0.6	1	1.16	0.1304	1000	7668.712	0.1968
0.2	0.16	0.5	1	0.7	1	1.16	0.1188	1000	8417.508	0.1896
0.2	0.16	0.5	1	0.8	1	1.16	0.1072	1000	9328.358	0.1824
0.2	0.16	0.5	1	0.9	1	1.16	0.0956	1000	10,460.25	0.1752
0.2	0.16	0.5	1	1	1	1.16	0.084	1000	11,904.76	0.168

All the weighted average cost of capital, WACC, values in case of advanced payments of tax on profit turns out to be lower than in case of payments at the end of the periods.

7.9 Discussions

Let us discuss the main obtained results.

Table 7.20 Dependence of the equity cost, k_e, and the weighted average cost of capital, WACC, on tax on profit value at $p = 12$ (for advanced payments of tax of profit)

k_0	k_d	w_d	L	t	p	i	WACC	CF	V	k_e
0.2	0.16	0.5	1	0	12	1.012445	0.2	1000	5000	0.24
0.2	0.16	0.5	1	0.1	12	1.012445	0.189153	1000	5286.726	0.234306
0.2	0.16	0.5	1	0.2	12	1.012445	0.178306	1000	5608.338	0.228612
0.2	0.16	0.5	1	0.3	12	1.012445	0.167459	1000	5971.613	0.222918
0.2	0.16	0.5	1	0.4	12	1.012445	0.156612	1000	6385.21	0.217224
0.2	0.16	0.5	1	0.5	12	1.012445	0.145765	1000	6860.363	0.21153
0.2	0.16	0.5	1	0.6	12	1.012445	0.134918	1000	7411.917	0.205836
0.2	0.16	0.5	1	0.7	12	1.012445	0.124071	1000	8059.911	0.200142
0.2	0.16	0.5	1	0.8	12	1.012445	0.113224	1000	8832.063	0.194448
0.2	0.16	0.5	1	0.9	12	1.012445	0.102377	1000	9767.838	0.188754
0.2	0.16	0.5	1	1	12	1.012445	0.09153	1000	10,925.41	0.18306

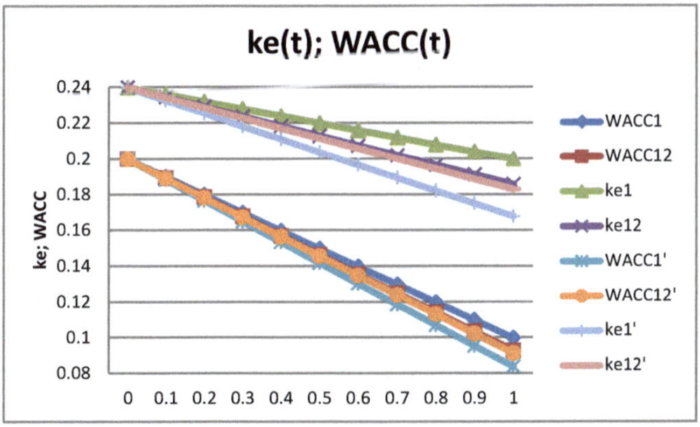

Fig. 7.10 Dependence of the equity cost, k_e, and the weighted average cost of capital, WACC, on tax on profit value at different p and fixed $k_d = 0.16$ (′ means advanced payment of tax of profit)

1. The weighted average cost of capital, WACC, decreases with leverage level L at all values of frequency of payments of tax on profit p. With increase of the frequency of payments of tax on profit per year p the weighted average cost of capital, WACC, (1) decreases in the case of payments at the ends of the periods and WACC (2) increases in the case of advanced payments of tax on profit. Note, that the weighted average cost of capital, WACC, in the case of advanced payments of tax on profit for all values of frequency of payments turns out to be low than for any values of frequency of payments in the case of payments at the ends of the periods.

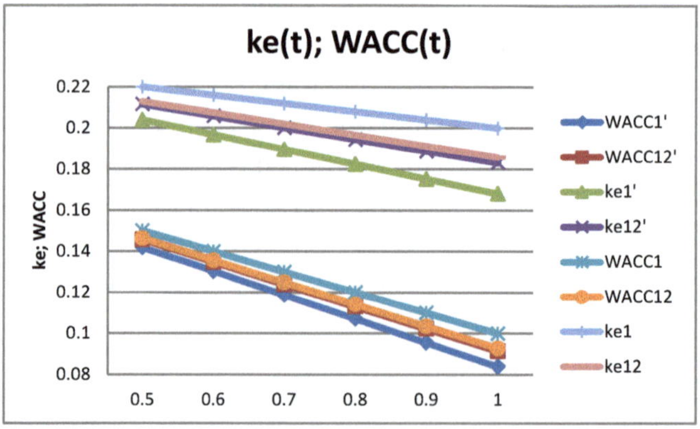

Fig. 7.11 Dependence of the dependence of the equity cost, k_e, and the weighted average cost of capital, WACC, on tax on profit value at different p and fixed $k_d = 0.16$ ($'$ means advanced payment of tax of profit) (larger scale)

2. The weighted average cost of capital, WACC, decreases with increase of debt cost value k_d, except the classical Modigliani–Miller case $p = 1$ and payment at the end of the period. It supports obtained by us result that account of each of two effects (either advanced payments of tax on profit, or more frequent than once per year) leads to dependence of all main financial indicators, such as the weighted average cost of capital, WACC, company value, V, equity cost, k_e, etc. on debt cost value k_d, while in the classical Modigliani–Miller case these financial indicators DO NOT depend on debt cost value k_d.

   Similar to previous paragraph it is seen, that with increase of the frequency of payments of tax on profit per year p WACC (1) decreases in the case of payments at the ends of the periods and WACC (2) increases in the case of advanced payments of tax on profit. As we'll see below, this will lead to increase of company value, V, with increase of p in the case (1) and to decrease of company value, V, with increase of p in the case (2).

   Note, that the weighted average cost of capital, WACC, in the case of advanced payments of tax on profit for all values of frequency of payments turns out to be low than for any values of frequency of payments in the case of payments at the ends of the periods.
3. The company value, V, increases with the increase of leverage level L for all frequencies of payment of tax on profit per year p.

   While in case of payments at the end of the periods the company value, V, increases with the increase of the frequency of payment of tax on profit per year p, in case of advanced payments of tax on profit the company value, V, decreases with the increase of the frequency of payment of tax on profit per year p. These facts consistent with the dependence of the weighted average cost of capital, WACC, on the leverage level L.

All the company values, V, in case of advanced payments of tax on profit turns out to be bigger than in case of payments at the end of the periods. Thus if the companies tend to increase their capitalization, they should pay tax on profit (1) in advance; (2) as seldom as tax legislation allows.

4. The equity cost, k_e, linearly increases with the increase of leverage level L for all frequencies of payment of tax on profit per year p.

   While in the case of tax on profit payments at the end of the periods the tilt of the curve of the equity cost, k_e, decreases with the increase of the frequency of payment of tax on profit per year p, in case of the advanced payments of tax on profit, the tilt of the curve of the equity cost, k_e, increases with the increase of the frequency of payment of tax on profit per year p. These facts should be accounted when developing the company's dividend policy, because the value of the equity cost, k_e, is the economically justified amount of dividends.

   The company's dividend policy should be as following:

   1. *If the company would like* ***to minimize the dividend payments****:*

      – in case of payments of tax on profit at the ends of periods they should be as frequently as tax legislation allows.
      – in case of advanced payments of tax on profit they should be as seldom as tax legislation allows.

   2. *If the company would like* ***to maximize the dividend payments****:*

      – in case of payments of tax on profit at the ends of periods they should be as seldom as tax legislation allows.
      – in case of advanced payments of tax on profit they should be as frequently as tax legislation allows.

5. The equity cost, k_e, decreases with the increase of on tax on profit value t for all frequencies of payment of tax on profit per year p.

   While in case of payments at the end of the periods the equity cost, k_e, decreases with the increase of the frequency of payments of tax on profit per year p (negative tilt of the curve k_e (t) increases on modulus), in case of advanced payments of tax on profit t the equity cost, k_e, increases with the increase of the frequency of payment of tax on profit per year p (negative tilt of the curve $k_e(t)$ increases on modulus).

   All the equity cost, k_e, values in case of advanced payments of tax on profit turns out to be lower than in case of payments at the end of the periods.

   The weighted average cost of capital, WACC, decreases with the increase of on tax on profit value t for all frequencies of payment of tax on profit per year p.

   While in case of payments at the end of the periods the weighted average cost of capital, WACC, decreases with the increase of the frequency of payments of tax on profit per year p (negative tilt of the curve WACC(t) increases on modulus), in case of advanced payments of tax on profit t the weighted average cost of capital, WACC, increases with the increase of the frequency of payment of tax on profit per year p (negative tilt of the curve WACC(t) increases on modulus).

All the weighted average cost of capital, WACC, values in case of advanced payments of tax on profit turns out to be lower than in case of payments at the end of the periods.

7.10 Conclusions

Brusov and Filatova (2021) have modified the Modigliani–Miller theory for the case of arbitrary frequency of payment of tax on profit t and show that the account of frequency of payment of tax on profit within the Modigliani–Miller theory turns out to be very important and leads to significant consequences: (1) all Modigliani–Miller theorems, statements and all formulas change; (2) all main financial indicators, such as the weighted average cost of capital, WACC, company value, V and equity cost, k_e depend on the frequency of tax on profit payments p; (3) this allows to company choose the number of payments of tax of profit per year, as many, as it is profitable to it (of course, within actual tax legislation).

As it was shown in that paper (Brusov and Filatova 2021), more frequent payments of income tax are beneficial for both parties: for the company and for the tax regulator: for the company, this leads to decrease of the cost of attracting capital and thus to an increase in the value of the company, and for the tax regulator, earlier payments are beneficial due to the time value of money.

But companies could (and sometimes should) pay tax of profit in advance. In current paper we use two modifications of the Modigliani–Miller theory simultaneously: (1) frequent payments of income tax; (2) advance payments of income tax and show that this fact changes drastically the main conclusions of the paper (Brusov and Filatova 2021): more frequent payments of income tax are **NOT** beneficial for the company: this leads to increase of the cost of attracting capital (the weighted average cost of capital, WACC, and the equity cost, k_e,) and thus to decrease in the value of the company, but for the tax regulator it remains beneficial: earlier payments are beneficial due to the time value of money.

Thus, the main conclusions of current Chapter are as follows:

1. for payments of tax of profit at the end of periods more frequent payments of income tax are beneficial for both parties: for the company and for the tax regulator: (1) for the company, this leads to decrease of the cost of attracting capital, WACC, and thus to an increase in the value of the company, V, and (2) for the tax regulator, more frequent payments are beneficial due to the time value of money.
2. for payments of tax of profit in advance more frequent payments of income tax are NOT beneficial for the company: this leads to increase of the cost of attracting capital, WACC, and thus to decrease in the value of the company, V, but for the tax regulator it remains beneficial: earlier payments are beneficial due to the time value of money.

References

Arzac ER, Glosten LR (2005) A reconsideration of tax shield valuation. Eur Financ Manag 11(4):453–461

Berk J, De Marzo P (2020) Corporate finance. Pearson-Addison Wesley, Boston

Brusov P (2018a) Editorial: introduction on special issue on the banking system and financial markets of Russia and other countries: problems and prospects. J Rev Glob Econ 7:i–vi

Brusov P (2018b) Editorial. J Rev Glob Econ 7:i–v

Brusov P, Filatova T (2021) The Modigliani–Miller theory with arbitrary frequency of payment of tax on profit. Mathematics 9(11):1198. https://doi.org/10.3390/math9111198

Brusov PN, Filatova TV (2025a) Business valuation and company value: new qualitative approaches considering business and financial risks. Springer Nature Publishing, pp 1–654

Brusov PN, Filatova TV (2025b) Efficiency of investment projects: modern investment models and their applications. Springer Nature Publishing, pp 1–843

Brusov PN, Filatova TV, Kulik VL (2024) Capital Asset Pricing Model (CAPM) 2.0: account of business and financial risk. Finance: Theory Prac 28(2):128–142. https://doi.org/10.26794/2587-5671-2024-28-2-128-142

Brusov PN, Filatova TV, Orekhova NP (2018a) Modern corporate finance and investments. Knorus Publishing House, Moscow, 517 p

Brusov P, Filatova T, Orekhova N (2020a) Ratings: critical analysis and new approaches of quantitative and qualitative methodology. Springer Nature Publishing, Switzerland. https://www.springer.com/de/book/9783030562427

Brusov P, Filatova T, Orekhova N, Eskindarov M (2015) Modern corporate finance, investments and taxation. Springer International Publishing, Switzerland, 373 p. https://www.springer.com/gp/book/9783319147314

Brusov P, Filatova T, Orekhova N, Eskindarov M (2018b) Modern corporate finance, investments, taxation and ratings. Springer Nature Publishing, Switzerland, 571 p

Brusov PN, Filatova TV, Orekhova NP, Kulik VL (2018c) Rating: new approach. J Rev Glob Econ 7: 37–62. https://doi.org/10.6000/1929-7092.2018.07.05

Brusov PN, Filatova TV, Orekhova NP, Kulik VL (2018d) A “golden age” of the companies: conditions of its existence. J Rev Glob Econ 7:88–103. https://doi.org/10.6000/1929-7092.2018.07.07

Brusov PN, Filatova TV, Orekhova NP, Kulik VL (2018e) Rating methodology: new look and new horizons. J Rev Glob Econ 7:63–87. https://doi.org/10.6000/1929-7092.2018.07.06

Brusov PN, Filatova TV, Orekhova NP, Kulik VL, Chang S-I, Lin YCG (2020b) Application of the Modigliani–Miller theory, modified for the case of advance payments of tax on profit, in rating methodologies. J Rev Glob Econ 9:282–292. https://doi.org/10.6000/1929-7092.2020.09.28

Brusov PN, Filatova TV, Orekhova NP, Kulik VL, Chang S-I, Lin YCG (2020c) Modification of the Modigliani–Miller theory for the case of advance payments of tax on profit. J Rev Glob Econ 9:257–267. https://doi.org/10.6000/1929-7092.2020.09.25

Brusov PN, Filatova TV, Orekhova NP, Kulik VL, Weil I (2018f) New meaningful effects in modern capital structure theory. J Rev Glob Econ 7:104–122. https://doi.org/10.6000/1929-7092.2018.07.08

Brusov PN, Filatova TV, Orekhova NP, Kulik VL, Weil I (2019) Ratings of the investment projects of arbitrary durations: new methodology. J Rev Glob Econ 8:437–448. https://doi.org/10.6000/1929-7092.2019.08.37

Brusov P, Filatova T, Orekhova N, Kulik V, Weil I, Brailov A (2018g) The impact of the central bank key rate and commercial banks credit rates on creating and maintaining of a favorable investment climate in the country. J Rev Glob Econ 7:360–376. https://doi.org/10.6000/1929-7092.2018.07.31

Brusov PN, Filatova TV, Orekhova NP (2021) Ratings: critical analysis and new approaches of quantitative and qualitative methodology. Springer Nature Publishing, pp 1–369

Brusov PN, Filatova TV, Orekhova NP (2022) Generalized Modigliani–Miller Theory: applications in corporate finance, investments, taxation and ratings. Springer Nature Publishing, pp 1–362

Brusov PN, Filatova TV, Orekhova NP (2023) The Brusov–Filatova–Orekhova theory of capital structure: applications in corporate finance, investments, taxation and ratings. Springer Nature Publishing, pp 1–769

De Marzo PM (1988) An extension of the Modigliani–Miller theorem to stochastic economies with incomplete markets and interdependent securities. J Econ Theory 45(2):353–369

Farber A, Gillet R, Szafarz A (2007) A general formula for the WACC. Int J Bus 11(2):211–218

Fernandez P (2007) A general formula for the WACC: a comment. Int J Bus, this issue

Filatova TV, Brusov PN, Orekhova NP, Kulik VL (2018a) Ratings of the long-term projects: new approach. J Rev Glob Econ 7:645–661. https://doi.org/10.6000/1929-7092.2018.07.59

Filatova T, Orekhova N, Brusova A (2008) Weighted average cost of capital in the theory of Modigliani–Miller, modified for a finite life-time company. Bull FU 48:68–77

Hamada R (1969) Portfolio analysis, market equilibrium, and corporate finance. J Financ 24(1):13–31

Harris R, Pringle J (1985) Risk-adjusted discount rates—extension form the average-risk case. J Financ Res 8(3):237–244

Miles JA, Ezzel JR (1980) The weighted average cost of capital, perfect capital markets and project life: a clarification. J Financ Quant Anal 15(3):719–730

Miller M (1977) Debt and taxes. J Financ 32(2):261–275. https://doi.org/10.1111/j.1540-6261.1977.tb03267.x

Modigliani F, Miller M (1958) The cost of capital, corporate finance, and the theory of investment. Am Econ Rev 48:261–297

Modigliani F, Miller M (1963) Corporate income taxes and the cost of capital: a correction. Am Econ Rev 53:147–175

Modigliani F, Miller M (1966) Some estimates of the cost of capital to the electric utility industry 1954–1957. Am Econ Rev 56:333–391

Myers S (2001) Capital structure. J Econ Perspect 15(2):81–102

Ross S, Westerfiel R, Jaffee D (2005) Corporate finance, 7th edn. McGraw Hill, New York

Sethi SP, Derzko NA, Lehoczky JP (1991) A stochastic extension of the Miller–Modigliani framework. Math Financ 1(4):57–76

Taggart RA (1991) Consistent valuation and cost of capital expressions with corporate and personal taxes. Financ Manag 20:8–20

Chapter 8
Generalization of the Modigliani–Miller Theory for the Case of Variable Profit

In this Chapter for the first time we have generalized the world-famous theory by Nobel Prize winners Modigliani and Miller for the case of variable profit, which significantly extends the application of the theory in practice, specifically in business valuation, ratings, corporate finance, etc. We demonstrate that all the theorems, statements and formulae of Modigliani and Miller are changed significantly. Wc combine theoretical and numerical (by MS Excel) considerations. The following results are obtained:

1. Discount rate for leverage company changes from the weighted average cost of capital, WACC, to WACC–g (where g is growing rate), for a financially independent company from k_0 to k_0–g. This means that WACC and k_0 are no longer the discount rates as it takes place in case of classical Modigliani–Miller theory with constant profit. WACC grows with g, while real discount rates WACC–g and k_0–g decrease with g. This leads to an increase of company capitalization with g.

2. The tilt angle of the equity cost $k_e(L)$ grows with g. This should change the dividend policy of the company, because the economically justified value of dividends is equal to equity cost.

3. A qualitatively new effect in corporate finance has been discovered: at rate $g < g^*$ the slope of the curve $k_e(L)$ turns out to be negative, which could significantly alter the principles of the company's dividend policy.

8.1 Introduction

The original theory by Nobel Prize Winners Modigliani and Miller (Modigliani and Miller 1958, 1963, 1966) has been modified by many authors and we shortly discuss some of these (Brusov and Filatova 2021, 2025a, b; Brusov et al. 2020c, 2021a, 2021,

P. Brusov and T. Filatova, *Taxes and Taxation*, Contributions to Finance and Accounting, https://doi.org/10.1007/978-3-032-11077-0_8

2022, 2023; Harry and Masulis 1980; Sheridan and Wessels 1988). A few important modifications have been done by the authors of this monograph (Brusov et al. 2015, 2018; Filatova et al. 2008), who created the general theory of capital cost and capital structure, the Brusov–Filatova–Orekhova (BFO) theory, which generalized the Modigliani–Miller theory for the case of companies of arbitrary age (and arbitrary lifetime), as well as for the case of advance payments of tax on profit (Brusov et al. 2020a), for rating needs (Brusov et al. 2020b), as well as for variable debt cost (Brusov et al. 2021b). Note that a stochastic extension of the Miller–Modigliani theory has been created by some authors Sethi et al. (1991), De Marzo (1988).

In the current Chapter for the first time we have generalized the world-famous theory by Nobel Prize winners Modigliani and Miller for the case of variable profit (Brusov et al. 2021b), which significantly extends the application of the theory in practice, specifically in business valuation, ratings, investments and in other areas of the economy and of finance. We consider the case of growing profit as well as decreasing profit and show that all theorems, all statements by Modigliani and Miller (and all their main formulas) are changed significantly.

Within the new Generalized Modigliani–Miller theory (GMM theory), we study the dependence of the weighted average cost of capital, WACC, the equity cost, k_e, the discount rate, *i*, and the capitalization of the company, V, on leverage level L. Some important results have been obtained, which allows for the development of a new approach to financial policy and financial strategy for the company. Some of these are as follows:

- The discount rate for a leveraged company changes from the weighted average cost of capital, WACC, to WACC–g (where g is growth rate), for an unleveraged company from k_0 to k_0–g. This means that WACC and k_0 are no longer the discount rates they are in the case of classical Modigliani–Miller theory with constant profit.
- All curves WACC(L) for different values of g start from one point, k_0. They decrease with L at $g < k_0$ and increase at $g > k_0$. It turns out that WACC grows with g, while real discount rates WACC–g and k_0–g decrease with g. This leads to an increase of company capitalization along with g: V = CF/WACC–g. Knowing the correct value of the discount rate allows for management of companies' financial flows.
- The equity cost, k_e, which grows linearly with the leverage level, increases with g: the tilt angle k_e (L) grows along with the growth rate g.

A qualitatively new effect in corporate finance has been discovered: at rate $g < g^*$ the slope of the curve k_e (L) turns out to be negative. Two these effects, which are absent in classical Modigliani–Miller theory, could significantly alter the principles behind the company's dividend policy, because the economically justified value of dividends is equal to equity cost.

The final effect is similar to the qualitatively new effect in corporate finance that was discovered by Brusov–Filatova–Orekhova within the BFO theory: the abnormal dependence of equity cost on leverage level at tax on profit rate T, which exceeds rate value T*. This discovery also significantly alters the principles behind the company's dividend policy.

The current paper, contrary to papers on (stochastically) growing cash flows, can be directly applied for calculation of all the main indicators for companies. The results obtained will have applications in corporate finance, business valuation, ratings, etc.

The structure of the Chapter is as follows:

1. We give an introduction to the traditional approach of the Modigliani–Miller theory and to its modifications.

   - We generalize the Modigliani–Miller theory to the case of variable profit and obtain generalized Modigliani–Miller theorems, as well as new formulae for the weighted average cost of capital, WACC, equity cost, k_e, discount rate, i, and capitalization of the company, V.
   - Within the new Generalized Modigliani–Miller theory (GMM theory), we numerically study (with MS Excel) the dependence of the main financial indicators of the company (WACC, k_e, i, V) on leverage level L.
   - We discuss the results obtained and based on these, we arrive at some important conclusions.

Below we discuss the problem of capital structure.

Capital structure is the relationship between the debt and the equity capital of the company. Does capital structure impact the main financial indicators of the company, such as the cost of capital, profit, value of the company, etc., and, if so, how? The choice of an optimal capital structure, i.e., a capital structure that maximizes the company's capitalization, *V*, and minimizes the weighted average cost of capital, WACC, is one of the most important problems to be solved by the financial manager and senior management of a company. The first quantitative study of the impact of company capital structure on its financial indicators was performed by Modigliani and Miller (1958). Before 1958, the traditional approach, based on empirical data analysis, was used.

8.1.1 The Traditional Approach

The traditional approach supposes that the weighted average cost of capital, WACC, and the associated company capitalization value, $V = \mathrm{CF}/\mathrm{WACC}$,, depend on the capital structure (the level of leverage (*L*)). The reason for this is that the debt cost always turns out to be lower than the equity cost because the first one has lower risk, due to the fact that, in the event of bankruptcy, creditor claims are met prior to shareholders claims.

Thus, if the firm increases the share of lower-cost debt capital in the overall capital structure, this will lead to a lower weighted average cost of capital and WACC up to the limit, which does not cause violation of financial sustainability or result in increase of bankruptcy risk.

Investor profitability is required and the cost of equity grows with the leverage level; however, its growth has not lead to compensation of benefits from the increasing use of lower-cost debt capital. Therefore, at a low leverage level WACC decreases with the increase of leverage $L = D/S$ and company capitalization increases. At a high leverage level when the risk of bankruptcy becomes higher, WACC may increase with the increase of leverage L and company capitalization decreases. Thus, the tradeoff between advantages of debt financing at a low leverage level and its shortcomings at a high leverage level forms an optimal capital structure, which maximizes the company capitalization, V, and minimizes the weighted average cost of capital, WACC.

The traditional approach has existed up to 1958, when the first quantitative theory by Modigliani and Miller has appeared (Modigliani and Miller 1958).

8.1.2 Modigliani–Miller Theory Without Taxes

In their first paper, Modigliani and Miller (MM) (1958) under a lot of assumptions (there are no taxes, no bankruptcy costs, no transaction costs, perfect financial markets exist with symmetry information, equivalence in borrowing costs for both companies and investors, etc.), came to the conclusions that choosing of the ratio between the debt and equity capital does not affect company value as well as capital costs (Fig. 8.1). These conclusions were fundamentally different from the conclusions of the traditional approach.

Modigliani and Miller, under the above assumptions, have analyzed the impact of financial leverage, assuming the absence of any taxes (on corporate profit as well as individual one). They have formulated and proven two following theorems.

Without taxes, the total cost of any company is determined by the value of its EBIT (Earnings Before Interest and Taxes), discounted with fixed rate k_0, corresponding to group of business risk of this company:

$$V = V_0 = \frac{EBIT}{k_0} \tag{8.1}$$

This leads to the following expressions for WACC:

$$WACC = k_0 \tag{8.2}$$

Note, that k_0 here and below is the weighted average cost of capital, WACC for an unleveraged company. For a leveraged company, k_0 is the equity cost (and weighted average cost of capital, WACC) at zero leverage level ($L = 0$).

From the first Modigliani–Miller theorem [1], it is easy to derive an expression for the equity capital cost:

$$\text{WACC} = k_0 = k_e w_e + k_d w_d. \tag{8.3}$$

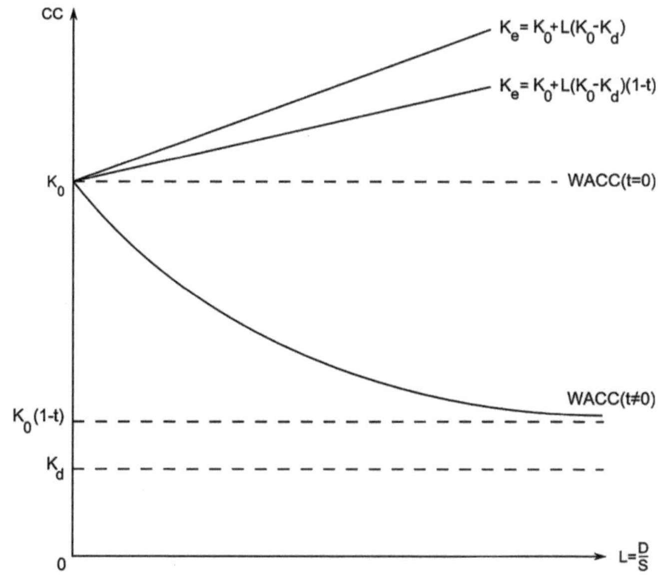

Fig. 8.1 Dependence of equity capital cost, debt cost and WACC on leverage in Modigliani–Miller theory without taxes ($t = 0$) and with taxes ($t \neq 0$)

Finding from here k_e, one gets

$$k_e = \frac{k_0}{w_e} - k_d\frac{w_d}{w_e} = \frac{k_0(S+D)}{S} - k_d\frac{D}{S}$$
$$= k_0 + (k_0 - k_d)\frac{D}{S} = k_0 + (k_0 - k_d)L \tag{8.4}$$

Here,

D	value of debt capital of the company;
S	value of equity capital of the company;
$k_d, w_d = \frac{D}{D+S}$	cost and fraction of debt capital of the company;
$k_e, w_e = \frac{S}{D+S}$	cost and fraction of equity capital of the company;
$L = D/S$	financial leverage;
WACC	weighted average cost of capital

Thus, we come to second theorem of Modigliani–Miller theory regarding the equity cost of a leveraged company (Modigliani and Miller 1958).

The equity cost of a leveraged company (k_e) could be found as k_0(the cost of equity of an unleveraged company with the same asset risk), plus premium for risk, which is equal to the product of difference $(k_0 - k_d)$and leverage level L:

$$k_e = k_0 + L(k_0 - k_d) \tag{8.5}$$

Formula (8.5) shows that equity cost of the company increases linearly with is leverage level.

8.2 Some Modifications of Modigliani–Miller Theory

8.2.1 Modigliani–Miller Theory with Taxes

In 1963 Modigliani and Miller (1963) accounted for the effect of corporate taxes and obtained the following result for the capitalization value of a leveraged company, V:

$$V = V_0 + DT, \tag{8.6}$$

where V_0 is the value of unleveraged company, D is the debt value and T is the corporate taxes on profit rate.

The value of a leveraged company is equal to the value of the unleveraged company with the same asset risk, plus the value of tax shield arising from financial leverage, which is equal to the product of corporate income tax rate (T) and the debt value (D).

The following section presents the formal derivation result for WACC and the equity capital cost (k_e) of the company with consideration of corporate taxes.

Weighted Average Cost of Capital, WACC

$$V = V_0 + DT$$

$$V(1 - w_d T) = V_0 \tag{8.7}$$

$$\frac{CF}{WACC}(1 - w_d T) = \frac{CF}{k_0} \tag{8.8}$$

$$WACC = k_0 \cdot (1 - w_d t) \tag{8.9}$$

The above is a very important formula for weighted average cost of capital (WACC) and is one of the main results of the Modigliani–Miller theory with taxes.

Equity Cost

Let us derive formula for equity cost.

On definition of the weighted average cost of capital with "tax shield", we have:

$$\text{WACC} = k_0 w_e + k_d w_d (1 - T). \tag{8.10}$$

Equating Eqs. (8.9) and (8.10), one gets:

$$k_0(1 - w_d T) = k_0 w_e + k_d w_d (1 - T) \tag{8.11}$$

and from here, for equity cost, we develop the following expression:

$$\begin{aligned} k_e &= k_0 \frac{(1 - w_d T)}{w_e} - k_d \frac{w_d}{w_e}(1 - T) = k_0 \frac{1}{w_e} - k_0 \frac{w_d}{w_e} T - k_d \frac{D}{S}(1 - T) \\ &= k_0 \frac{D + S}{S} - k_0 \frac{D}{S} T - k_d \frac{D}{S}(1 - T) = k_0 + L(1 - T)(k_0 - k_d). \end{aligned} \tag{8.12}$$

Therefore, we see the following theorem obtained by Modigliani and Miller in 1963:

Equity cost of leveraged company (k_e) could be found as equity cost of unleveraged company (k_0) with the same business risk, plus premium for risk, the value of which is equal to the triple product of difference between the cost of capital for an unleveraged firm and cost of debt $(k_0 - k_d)$, **, leverage level ($L = \frac{D}{S}$)) and tax corrector (*1 – T*).**

It should be noted that Formula (8.12) is different from Formula (8.5) without tax only by the multiplier (1 – *T*), suggesting the tax benefit of debt will lower the cost of equity as well.

Analysis of Formulas (8.5), (8.9) and (8.12) leads to the following conclusions. When leverage grows:

1. The value of company increases.
- The weighted average cost of capital WACC decreases from k_0 (at $L = 0$) up to $k_0(1 - T)$ (at $L = \infty$) (when the company is funded solely by borrowed funds).
- Equity cost increases linearly from k_0 (at $L = 0$) up to ∞ (at $L = \infty$).

Within their theory, Modigliani and Miller (1963) came to the following conclusions regarding the growth of financial leverage (Fig. 8.1).

8.2.2 *Taking into Account Market Risk: Hamada Model*

In 1969 Hamada united CAPM (Capital Asset Pricing Model) and Modigliani–Miller theory with taxes. For the equity cost of a leveraged company, the following formula has been derived, which includes financial and business risk of company:

$$k_e = k_F + (k_M - k_F)b_U + (k_M - k_F)b_U\frac{D}{S}(1 - T), \tag{8.13}$$

here b_U is the CAPM βeta of the unleveraged company with the same asset risk as the leveraged company under consideration. Formula (8.13) represents the cost of equity (k_e) for a leveraged firm as a sum of three components: risk-free rate (k_F), risk premium for business/asset risk $(k_M - k_F)b_U$ and risk premium for financial risk $(k_M - k_F)b_U\frac{D}{S}(1 - T)$.

If the company does not have borrowing ($D = 0$), the financial risk factor will be equal to zero (the third term is drawn to zero), and equity holder will only require the premium for business/asset risk.

Note, that Hamada's empirical result regarding the inclusion of financial risk alongside business risk, as described by the classical CAPM model, was shown by Brusov et al. (2024) to be inaccurate. Brusov et al. created an innovative model, CAPM 2.0, which correctly describes financial risk alongside business risk (Brusov et al. 2024). It was shown that along with the renormalization of the beta coefficient to the level of leverage described by the Hamada model, an additional term appears in the model, that depends on leverage level, L, debt cost, k_d, risk free profitability, k_F, and tax corrector, (1-T). This term is absent in Hamada's model and can be noticeable at high leverage levels and large differences between debt cost, kd and risk free profitability, k_F.

8.2.3 The Account of Corporate and Individual Taxes (Miller Model)

In their second article, Modigliani and Miller (1963) only considered corporate taxes benefit of debt but did not take into account the effect of individual investors' income taxes.

In 1977 Merton Miller (1977) have developed such a model, showing the influence of financial leverage on the capitalization of the company when the effects of both corporate and individual taxes are accounted for, i.e., there is double taxation on corporate earnings. We will use the following definitions: T_C—corporate taxes rate and T_S—a weighted average value of effective taxes rates on dividends and capital gains on shares. With the same other assumptions that have been made for Modigliani–Miller models previously, the unleveraged company value can be determined as follows:

$$V_U = \frac{\text{EBIT}(1 - T_C)(1 - T_S)}{k_0}.$$

A term $(1 - T_S)$ accounts for the individual taxes. The numerator in (1) indicates which part of the operating company's profit remains in the possession of the investors, after the company earnings are taxed twice: by corporate taxes and individual taxes. Since individual taxes reduce investors' residual income, it also reduces the overall assessment of the unleveraged company value.

8.2.4 Brusov–Filatova–Orekhova (BFO) Theory

One of the most serious limitations of the Modigliani–Miller theory is the suggestion about the perpetuity of the companies. In 2008, Brusov–Filatova–Orekhova (Filatova et al. 2008) have considered this limitation and showed that accounting for the finite lifetime length (or arbitrary age n) of the company leads to significant changes of all Modigliani–Miller results (Modigliani and Miller 1958, 1963, 1966): capitalization of the company V is changed, as well as the equity cost, k_e, and the weighted average cost of capital, WACC, in the presence of corporative taxes. Moreover, a number of new findings for corporate finance, in the Brusov–Filatova–Orekhova theory (Brusov et al. 2015, 2018; Filatova et al. 2008), are absent in Modigliani–Miller theory.

The formula for weighted average cost of capital (WACC) for the company with arbitrary age n, as derived by Brusov–Filatova–Orekhova, has the following form (Brusov et al. 2015, 2018; Filatova et al. 2008):

$$\frac{1-(1+WACC)^{-n}}{WACC}=\frac{1-(1+k_0)^{-n}}{k_0\left[1-w_d T\left(1-(1+k_d)^{-n}\right)\right]} \tag{8.14}$$

Here, $w_d(=\frac{D}{D+S})$ is the debt share; k_0 is the cost of capital for an unleveraged firm with the same asset risk; k_d the cost of debt; T denotes the corporate taxes rate; and n stands for the firm's lifetime length (age).

A perpetuity (Modigliani–Miller) limit could be easily obtained from (8.14), substituting $n \to \infty$.

A lot of meaningful effects have been discovered within the BFO theory: these effects are absent within MM theory. BFO theory has challenged some main existing principles of financial management: among them the Trade-off theory, which has been prevailing for many decades and established the foundation to claim the existence of an optimal capital structure for firms. However, BFO theory has proven the bankruptcy of Trade-off theory (Brusov et al. 2015, 2018).

8.2.5 The General WACC Formula

A more general formula for WACC, than in the famous Modigliani–Miller theory (MM) has been derived and discussed by a few authors in 2006–2007 (Farber et al. 2006; Fernandez 2006; Berk and De Marzo 2007; Harris and Pringle 1985). It takes the following form (Eq. [18] in Farber et al. [2006])

$$WACC = k_0(1 - w_d t) - k_d t w_d + k_{TS} t w_d \tag{8.15}$$

where k_0 is the required return on unleveraged company, k_d is the required return on its debt, k_{TS} is the expected return on the tax shield and t is the corporate taxes rate.

This formula is derived from the definition of the weighted average cost of capital and the balance sheet identity (for a similar presentation, see (Berk and De Marzo 2007). At any point in time, it should therefore be verified, regardless of whether returns are annually or continuously compounded.

Practical applicability of Eq. (8.15) (while it is fairly general) requires additional conditions. Indeed, when the WACC is constant over time, the value of a leveraged company can be computed by discounting with the WACC of the unlevered free cash-flows. Therefore, it is interesting to consider the special cases when WACC is constant. The resulting formulas can also be found in textbooks (Brealey et al. 2005; Ross et al. 2005).

It was assumed by Modigliani and Miller in 1963 that the debt value D is constant. As the expected after-tax cash-flow of the unleveraged company is fixed, V_0 is also constant. By this assumption, $k_{TS} = k_D$ and the value of the tax shield is $TS = tD$. Therefore, the capitalization of the leveraged company V is a constant and the general WACC Formula (8.15) simplifies to a constant WACC:

$$WACC = k_0(1 - w_d T)$$

However, our opinion is that "classical" Modigliani–Miller (MM) theory, which suggests that the expected returns on the debt k_d and the tax shield k_{TS} are equals (because both of them have debt nature), is much more reasonable and in our paper we modify the "classical" Modigliani–Miller (MM) theory, which is still widely used in practice.

8.2.6 Trade-Off Theory

The world-famous **Trade-off theory** has been considered the cornerstone in the solution of the problem of optimal capital structure for a company for many decades and is still used today for decision analysis on capital structure. Below we give two examples.

Frank and Goyal (2009) in their paper, "examines the relative importance of many factors in the capital structure decisions of publicly traded American firms from 1950 to 2003. The most reliable factors for explaining market leverage are: median industry leverage (+ effect on leverage), market-to-book assets ratio (−), tangibility (+), profits (−), log of assets (+), and expected inflation (+)". In addition, the authors have found that "dividend-paying firms tend to have lower leverage. When considering book leverage, somewhat similar effects are found. However, for book leverage, the impact of firm size, the market-to-book ratio, and the effect of inflation are not reliable". The empirical evidence seems to be reasonably consistent with some versions of the Trade-off theory of capital structure.

Serrasqueiro and Caetano (2015), analyzed "to what extent decisions on the capital structure of small and medium-sized enterprises (SMEs) are closer to the assumptions of Trade-off theory or to the assumptions of hierarchy theory. They used a sample of small and medium-sized enterprises located in the Portuguese hinterland, using dynamic LSDVC as the valuation method, and the empirical evidence suggests that the most profitable and oldest SMEs are less leveraged, confirming Pecking Order Theory 's forecasts. Larger SMEs are leveraging more borrowing, confirming the predictions of Trade-off theory and hierarchy theory. In addition, SMEs are significantly adjusting their current debt levels towards the optimal debt ratio, which is consistent with the predictions of the compromise theory. It was concluded that theories of compromise and hierarchy are not mutually exclusive in explaining capital structure decisions of small and medium-sized enterprises".

However, the bankruptcy of Trade-off theory has been proven by Brusov et al. in 2013 (Brusov et al. 2018). They have shown that risky debt financing (and growing credit rate near the bankruptcy) in contrast to waiting results does not lead to growing of weighted average cost of capital, WACC, which still decreases with leverage. This means the absence of minimum in the dependence of WACC on leverage level as well as the absence of maximum in the dependence of company capitalization on leverage. Thus, the well-known Trade-off theory lacks an optimal capital structure. The explanation for this fact was made by Brusov et al. in 2013 (Brusov et al. 2018) by analyzing the dependence of the cost of equity capital on the leverage level on the assumption that debt capital is risky.

Modigliani–Miller have considered tax shields from the interest on debt can increase the value of companies. In 1980, De Angelo and Masulis moved further in the theoretical examination of tax shields. They have noted that there are tax deductibles for companies other than debt to reduce their corporate tax burden and debt and non-debt tax shields should be accounted for. Depreciation, investment tax credits, or net-loss carry forwards could represents examples of such kind of non-debt tax shields. The first to test for these tax effects (suggested by De Angelo and Masulis in 1980) has been carried out by Bradley et al. (1984). In contrast to the prediction in De Angelo and Masulis (1980), by regressing company-specific debt-to-value ratios on non-debt tax shields, they have shown that debt is positively related to non-debt tax shields as measured by depreciation and investment tax credits. Titman and Wessels in 1988 found that "their results do not provide support for an effect on debt ratios arising from non-debt tax shields…". It was pointed out in 2003 by Graham, if a company invests heavily and uses debt financing to invest, a positive relation between such proxies for non-debt tax shield and debt may result. A mechanical positive relation of this type overwhelms and renders any substitution effects between debt and non-debt tax shields.

The original theory by Nobel Prize Winners Modigliani and Miller (Modigliani and Miller 1958, 1963, 1966) has been modified by many authors and above we shortly discussed some of them. In next paragraph we will generalize for the first time the Modigliani–Miller theory for the case of variable profit.

8.3 Generalization of the Modigliani–Miller Theory for the Case of Variable Profit

8.3.1 Modigliani–Miller Theory Without Taxes

Company Value, V

In this part we generalize for the first time the world-famous theory by Nobel Prize winners Modigliani and Miller for the case of variable profit. Let us calculate capitalization for leverage company, assuming profit per period grows with growth rate g.

$$V = \frac{CF}{1 + WACC} + \frac{CF(1+g)}{(1 + WACC)^2} + \frac{CF(1+g)^2}{(1 + WACC)^3} + \ldots + \frac{CF(1+g)^{n-1}}{(1 + WACC)^n} \tag{8.16}$$

Here, CF is the annual profit of company, $WACC$ is the weighted average cost of capital.

This is geometric progression with denominator

$$\hat{g} = \frac{1+g}{1+WACC} \tag{8.17}$$

Summing (8.16), one gets

$$V = \frac{CF}{1+WACC} \cdot \frac{1}{1 - \frac{1+g}{1+WACC}} = \frac{CF}{WACC - g} \tag{8.18}$$

Let us calculate the capitalization for a financially independent company

$$V_0 = \frac{CF}{1+k_0} + \frac{CF(1+g)}{(1+k_0)^2} + \frac{CF(1+g)^2}{(1+k_0)^3} + \ldots + \frac{CF(1+g)^{n-1}}{(1+k_0)^n} \tag{8.19}$$

This is geometric progression with denominator

$$\hat{g} = \frac{1+g}{1+k_0} \tag{8.20}$$

Summing (8.19), one gets

$$V_0 = \frac{CF}{1+k_0} \cdot \frac{1}{1 - \frac{1+g}{1+k_0}} = \frac{CF}{k_0 - g} \tag{8.21}$$

The original first theorem by Modigliani–Miller changes by the following one:

Without taxes, the total cost of any company with growing profit with rate g is determined by the value of its EBIT—Earnings Before Interest and Taxes—discounted with fixed rate $k_0 - g$, corresponding to group of business risk of this company:

$$V = V_0 = \frac{EBIT}{k_0 - g} \tag{8.22}$$

Note, that this formula for company capitalization is similar to one of the Gordon Growth Model (GGM), which assumes a company is perpetuity and pays dividends per share that increase at a constant rate. To estimate the value of a stock, the model takes the infinite series of dividends per share and discounts them back into the present using the required rate of return.

$$P = \frac{DPS_1}{k_e - g} \tag{8.23}$$

where *p*—value of stock;

DPS_1—expected Dividends one year from now (next period);

k_e—required rate of return for equity investors (equity cost);

g—growth rate in dividends forever.

Note that, despite some formal similarities, these are not the same model. In our model, CF is the company's annual income (not dividends), and we study all the financial indicators of the company (WACC, V, k_e, i, etc.), all of them (except V) are absent in Gordon's growth model.

The Weighted Average Cost of Capital, WACC

Below we calculate the WACC value.

$$V = V_0$$

$$\frac{CF}{WACC - g} = \frac{CF}{k_0 - g}$$

$$WACC = k_0 \tag{8.24}$$

It is seen, that the WACC value turns out to be the same as in case of classical Modigliani–Miller theory with constant profit.

Equity Cost, k_e

It is easy to show that the expression for equity cost turns out to be the same as in case of classical Modigliani–Miller theory with constant profit

$$k_e = k_0 + (k_0 - k_d)L. \tag{8.25}$$

Therefore, as we show in the case of the Modigliani–Miller theory without taxes accounting of variable profit changes the first of three Modigliani–Miller theorems only. As we show below, in the case of the Modigliani–Miller theory with taxes (practically interesting case) all three Modigliani–Miller theorems (concerning value of the company, V, its WACC and its equity cost, k_e) change significantly.

8.3.2 *Modigliani–Miller Theory with Taxes*

The Weighted Average Cost of Capital, WACC

The following result is obtained by Modigliani and Miller (1963):

The value of leveraged company is equal to the value of the company of the same risk group used no leverage, increased by the value of tax shield arising from financial leverage, and equal to the product of rate of corporate income tax T and the value of debt D.

$$V = V_0 + DT \tag{8.26}$$

From here it is easy to get expression for WACC (see above).

$$V(1 - w_d T) = V_0 \tag{8.27}$$

$$\frac{CF}{WACC}(1 - w_d T) = \frac{CF}{k_0} \tag{8.28}$$

$$WACC = k_0 \cdot (1 - w_d t) \tag{8.29}$$

Under variable profit, as we have seen above in the case of Modigliani–Miller theory without taxes, one has the same statement for capitalization, but discount rates are different:

$$WACC \to WACC - g$$

$$k_0 \to k_0 - g \tag{8.30}$$

$$\frac{CF}{WACC - g}(1 - w_d T) = \frac{CF}{k_0 - g} \tag{8.31}$$

$$WACC - g = (k_0 - g) \cdot (1 - w_d T) \tag{8.32}$$

$$WACC = (k_0 - g) \cdot (1 - w_d T) + g \tag{8.33}$$

This expression for WACC is different from the original result for WACC by Modigliani and Miller (8.29):

$$WACC = k_0 \cdot (1 - w_d T)$$

In order to understand the character of dependence of WACC(L) let us calculate the derivative of WACC with respect to L using Eq. (8.33):

$$WACC = (k_0 - g) \cdot (1 - w_d T) + g = k_0 - (k_0 - g) \cdot T \cdot \frac{L}{1 + L} \tag{8.34}$$

$$WACC_{L'} = -\frac{(k_0 - g) \cdot T}{(1 + L)^2} \tag{8.35}$$

At $g < k_0$ the derivative $WACC_{L'}$ is negative, thus $WACC(L)$ decreases with L, while at the $g > k_0$ derivative $WACC_{L'}$ is positive and $WACC(L)$ increases with L. We will see these effects in part 8.4 under numerical calculations.

The Company Value, V

For the company value from the Formulas (8.30) and (8.32) we get the following formula

$$V = \frac{CF}{WACC - g} = \frac{CF}{(k_0 - g) \cdot (1 - w_d t)} \tag{8.36}$$

We should note that in case of growing rate g equals to equity cost (at L = 0) k_0, the company value V becomes infinite. This is the limitation of the perpetuity Modigliani–Miller theory. As we will see in our future publications such kind of restriction is absent for companies of finite ages when we consider the generalization of BFO theory for the case of variable profit.

Equity Cost, k_e

Let us calculate the equity cost k_e. From (8.33) we have for the weighted average cost of capital, WACC,

$$WACC = (k_0 - g) \cdot (1 - w_d T) + g \tag{8.37}$$

As well according to the definition of the weighted average cost of capital, considering the "tax shield" we have

$$WACC = k_e w_e + k_d w_d (1 - T) \tag{8.38}$$

Equating (8.37) and (8.38), we obtain

$$(k_0 - g) \cdot (1 - w_d T) + g = k_e w_e + k_d w_d (1 - T) \tag{8.39}$$

whence we get the following expression for the cost of equity:

$$\begin{aligned} k_e &= WACC(1 + L) - Lk_d(1 - T) = \\ k_0 &+ L \cdot \left[(k_0 - k_d) \cdot (1 - T) + gT\right] \end{aligned} \tag{8.40}$$

This expression is different from Formula (8.12) in case of the classical Modigliani–Miller theory with tax. Thus, we have the following modified statement for equity cost within Generalized Modigliani–Miller theory.

Equity cost of leverage company $k_e$could be found as equity cost of unleveraged company $k_0$of the same group of risk, plus premium for risk, the value which is equal to production of leverage level Lon sum of production of difference $(k_0 - k_d)$on tax corrector and gT:

$$k_e = k_0 + L\left[(k_0 - k_d)(1 - T) + gT\right] \tag{8.41}$$

The Qualitatively New Effect in Corporate Finance

From the Formula (8.41) it is seen that with decrease of g tilt angle of straight $k_e(L)$ decreases and at some value of g = g*

$$k_e = k_0 \tag{8.42}$$

Let us find g* value. Equating $k_e$tok_0 in Formula (8.41), one has

$$L\left[(k_0 - k_d)(1 - T) + gT\right] = 0$$

and from here we find g*

$$g* = -\frac{(k_0 - k_d)(1 - T)}{T} \tag{8.43}$$

It is clear that at with growth rate g < g* the slope of the straight $k_e(L)$ turns out to be negative.

Thus, the qualitatively new effect in corporate finance has been discovered: at growth rate g < g* the slope of the straight $k_e(L)$ turns out to be negative. This effect, which is absent in the classical Modigliani–Miller theory, could significantly alter the principles of the company's dividend policy. Rating methodology takes into account the company's dividend policy, thus the results obtained could change the credit rating of an issuer.

We have shown in Sect. 3, that in case of the Modigliani–Miller theory with taxes, generalized for the case of variable profit all three Modigliani–Miller statements (concerning value of the company, V, the weighted average cost of capital, WACC, and its equity cost, k_e) change significantly. The consequences of such changes will be investigated numerically in next part.

8.4 Results and Discussions

In this section we study numerically (within Microsoft Excel) the dependence of the weighted average cost of capital, WACC, discount rate, i, company value, V, and equity cost, k_e, on leverage level L in the Generalized Modigliani–Miller theory (GMM theory) at two values of equity cost k_0 (0.2 and 0.3) and different values of growth rate, g. The obtained results are discussed.

8.4.1 Dependence of WACC on Leverage Level L in Generalized Modigliani–Miller Theory (GMM Theory) at $k_0 = 0.2$ and Different Values of g (0.4; 0.3; 0.2; 0.0; −0.2; −0.3; −0.4)

We study first the dependence of the weighted average cost of capital, WACC, on leverage level L in Generalized Modigliani–Miller theory (GMM theory) at $k_0 = 0.2$ and different values of g (0.4; 0.3; 0.2; 0.0; −0.2; −0.3; −0.4).

The results of Table 8.1 are shown in Fig. 8.2.

From Fig. 8.2 it is seen that all curves WACC(L) for different g start from one point k_0, in this case from point (0; 0.2). They decrease with leverage level L at g < 0.2 (at g = 0; ± 0.2; −0.3; −0.4) and increase at g > 0.2 (at g = 0.3; 0.4). The curves WACC(L) increase with growth rate, g. Note, that cut-off value of g, which separate increasing curves WACC(L) from decreasing ones is equal to $k_0 = 0.2$, and WACC is constant at g = k_0 and equal to k_0. Below we check this observation at different value of k_0 ($k_0 = 0.3$).

Table 8.1 Dependence of WACC on leverage level L in Generalized Modigliani–Miller theory (GMM theory) at $k_0 = 0.2$ and $g = 0.4; 0.3; 0.2; 0.0; -0.2; -0.3; -0.4$

L	T	k0	WACC						
			g = 0.4	g = 0.3	g = 0.2	g = 0	g = −0.2	g = −0.3	g = −0.4
0	0.2	0.2	0.20000	0.20000	0.20000	0.20000	0.20000	0.20000	0.20000
1	0.2	0.2	0.22000	0.21000	0.20000	0.18000	0.16000	0.15000	0.14000
2	0.2	0.2	0.22667	0.21333	0.20000	0.17333	0.14667	0.13333	0.12000
3	0.2	0.2	0.23000	0.21500	0.20000	0.17000	0.14000	0.12500	0.11000
4	0.2	0.2	0.23200	0.21600	0.20000	0.16800	0.13600	0.12000	0.10400
5	0.2	0.2	0.23333	0.21667	0.20000	0.16667	0.13333	0.11667	0.10000
6	0.2	0.2	0.23429	0.21714	0.20000	0.16571	0.13143	0.11429	0.09714
7	0.2	0.2	0.23500	0.21750	0.20000	0.16500	0.13000	0.11250	0.09500
8	0.2	0.2	0.23556	0.21778	0.20000	0.16444	0.12889	0.11111	0.09333
9	0.2	0.2	0.23600	0.21800	0.20000	0.16400	0.12800	0.11000	0.09200
10	0.2	0.2	0.23636	0.21818	0.20000	0.16364	0.12727	0.10909	0.09091

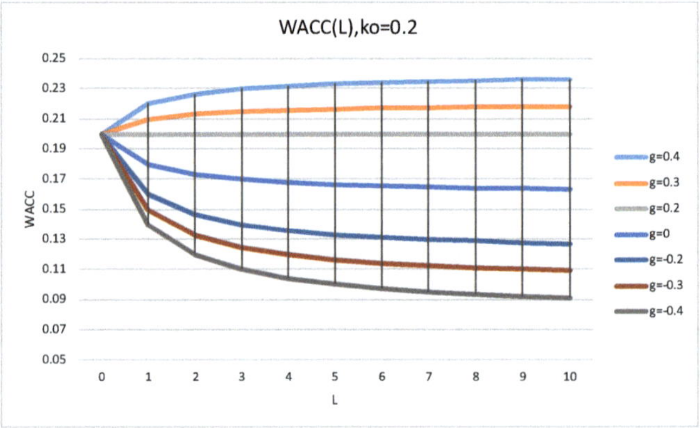

Fig. 8.2 Dependence of WACC on leverage level L in Generalized Modigliani–Miller theory (GMM theory) at $k_0 = 0.2$ and $g = 0; \pm 0.2; \pm 0.3; \pm 0.4$

8.4.2 Dependence of the Weighted Average Cost of Capital WACC on Leverage Level L in Generalized Modigliani–Miller Theory (GMM Theory) at $k_0 = 0.3$ and Different Values of g

Let us study the dependence of WACC on leverage level L in Generalized Modigliani–Miller theory (GMM theory) at $k_0 = 0.3$ and different values of g.

The results of Table 8.2 are shown in Fig. 8.3.

Table 8.2 Dependence of WACC on leverage level L in Generalized Modigliani–Miller theory (GMM theory) at $k_0 = 0.3$ and $g = 0; \pm 0.2; - 0.3; - 0.4$

L	T	k0	WACC						
			g = 0.4	**g = 0.3**	**g = 0.2**	**g = 0**	**g = − 0.2**	**g = − 0.3**	**g = − 0.4**
0	0.2	0.3	0.300	0.300	0.300	0.300	0.300	0.300	0.300
1	0.2	0.3	0.310	0.300	0.290	0.270	0.250	0.240	0.230
2	0.2	0.3	0.313	0.300	0.287	0.260	0.233	0.220	0.207
3	0.2	0.3	0.315	0.300	0.285	0.255	0.225	0.210	0.195
4	0.2	0.3	0.316	0.300	0.284	0.252	0.220	0.204	0.188
5	0.2	0.3	0.317	0.300	0.283	0.250	0.217	0.200	0.183
6	0.2	0.3	0.317	0.300	0.283	0.249	0.214	0.197	0.180
7	0.2	0.3	0.318	0.300	0.283	0.248	0.213	0.195	0.178
8	0.2	0.3	0.318	0.300	0.282	0.247	0.211	0.193	0.176
9	0.2	0.3	0.318	0.300	0.282	0.246	0.210	0.192	0.174
10	0.2	0.3	0.318	0.300	0.282	0.245	0.209	0.191	0.173

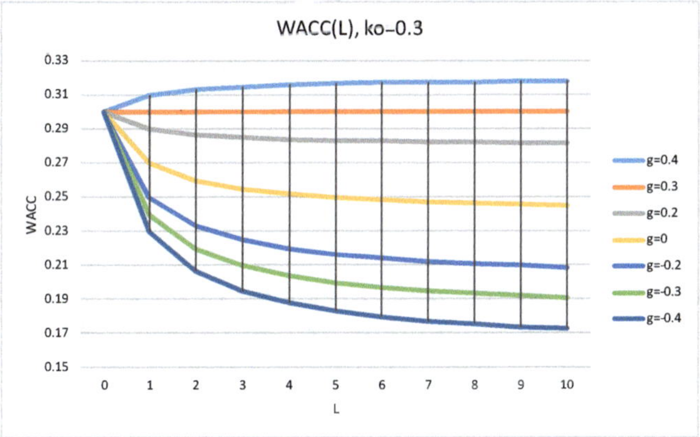

Fig. 8.3 Dependence of WACC on leverage level L in Generalized Modigliani–Miller theory (GMM theory) at $k_0 = 0.3$ and $g = 0; \pm 0.2; \pm 0.3; \pm 0.4$

From Fig. 8.3 it is seen that all curves WACC(L) for different g start from one point, k_0, in this case from (0; 0.3). They decrease with L at $g < 0.3$ (at $g = 0; \pm 0.2; \pm 0.3; - 0.4$) and increase at $g > 0.3$ (at $g = 0.4$). Note, that thr cut-off value of g, which separate increasing curves WACC(L) from decreasing ones as in above case is equal to k_0 ($k_0 = 0.3$), and WACC is constant at $g = k_0$ and equal to k_0. Therefore, our observation that this conclusion is valid at different value of k_0 is right.

From Figs. 8.2 and 8.3 it is seen that all curves WACC(L) for different g start from one point, k_0. They decrease with L at $g < k_0$ and increase at $g > k_0$. It turns out that WACC grows with g, while, as we will see below, real discount rates WACC–g and k_0–g decrease with g. This leads to increase of company capitalization with g: V = CF/WACC–g.

8.4.3 Dependence of Discount Rate I on Leverage Level L in Generalized Modigliani–Miller Theory (GMM Theory) at $k_0 = 0.2$ and Different Values of g

Discount rate for the leverage company change from the weighted average cost of capital, WACC, to WACC–g (where g is growth rate), for a financially independent company from k_0 to k_0–g. This means that WACC and k_0 are no longer the discount rates as it takes place in case of the classical Modigliani–Miller theory with constant profit. Below we study the dependence of discount rate i on leverage level L in Generalized Modigliani–Miller theory (GMM theory) at two values of k_0 (0.2; 0.3) and different values of g (−0.4; −0.3; −0.2; 0.0; 0.1; 0.15; 0.2; 0.3; 0.4). Let us start from $k_0 = 0.2$.

The results of Table 8.3 are shown in Fig. 8.4.

From Fig. 8.4 it is seen that discount rate i decreases with leverage level L at growth values $g < k_0$ (at g = 0; 0.1; 0.15; ±0.2; −0.3; −0.4). Discount rate i in contrast to WACC decreases with g: this provides the increase of company value V with g.

At $g > k_0$ discount rate i increases with L, but being negative it is not shown in Fig. 8.4.

8.4.4 Dependence of Discount Rate I on Leverage Level L in Generalized Modigliani–Miller Theory (GMM Theory) at $k_0 = 0.3$ and Different Values of g

Let us study the dependence of discount rate i on leverage level L in Generalized Modigliani–Miller theory (GMM theory) at $k_0 = 0.3$ and different values of g.

The results of Table 8.4 are shown in Fig. 8.5.

From Fig. 8.5 it is seen that discount rate i decreases with leverage level L at growth values at $g < k_0$ (at g = 0; 0.1; 0.15; ±0.2; −0.3; −0.4). Discount rate i in opposite to WACC decreases with g: this provides the increase of company value V with g.

At $g > k_0$ discount rate i increases with L, but being negative it is not shown in Fig. 8.5.

From Figs. 8.4 and 8.5 it is seen that for $k_0 = 0.2$ and 0.3 discount rate i decreases with g: this provides the increase of company value V with g. Discount rate i decreases with L at $g < k_0$ (at g = 0; 0.1; 0.15; ±0.2; −0.3; −0.4). At $g > k_0$ discount rate i increases with L, but being negative it is not shown in Figs. 8.4 and 8.5.

Table 8.3 Dependence of discount rate i on leverage level L in Generalized Modigliani–Miller theory (GMM theory) at $k_0 = 0.2$ and $g = -0.4; -0.3; -0.2; 0.0; 0.1; 0.15; 0.2; 0.3; 0.4$

L	t	k_0	i								
			g = 0.4	**g = 0.3**	**g = 0.2**	**g = 0.15**	**g = 0.1**	**g = 0**	**g = − 0.2**	**g = − 0.3**	**g = − 0.4**
0	0.2	0.2	−0.200	−0.100	0.000	0.050	0.100	0.200	0.400	0.500	0.600
1	0.2	0.2	−0.180	−0.090	0.000	0.045	0.090	0.180	0.360	0.450	0.540
2	0.2	0.2	−0.173	−0.087	0.000	0.043	0.087	0.173	0.347	0.433	0.520
3	0.2	0.2	−0.170	−0.085	0.000	0.043	0.085	0.170	0.340	0.425	0.510
4	0.2	0.2	−0.168	−0.084	0.000	0.042	0.084	0.168	0.336	0.420	0.504
5	0.2	0.2	−0.167	−0.083	0.000	0.042	0.083	0.167	0.333	0.417	0.500
6	0.2	0.2	−0.166	−0.083	0.000	0.041	0.083	0.166	0.331	0.414	0.497
7	0.2	0.2	−0.165	−0.083	0.000	0.041	0.083	0.165	0.330	0.413	0.495
8	0.2	0.2	−0.164	−0.082	0.000	0.041	0.082	0.164	0.329	0.411	0.493
9	0.2	0.2	−0.164	−0.082	0.000	0.041	0.082	0.164	0.328	0.410	0.492
10	0.2	0.2	−0.164	−0.082	0.000	0.041	0.082	0.164	0.327	0.409	0.491

8.4.5 Dependence of Company Value V on Leverage Level L in Generalized Modigliani–Miller Theory (GMM Theory) at $k_0 = 0.2$ and Different Values of g

Let us study the dependence of company value V on leverage level L in Generalized Modigliani–Miller theory (GMM theory) at $k_0 = 0.2$ and different values of g.

The results of Table 8.5 are shown in Fig. 8.6.

From Fig. 8.6 it is seen, that at $k_0 = 0.2$ and $g = 0; 0.1; 0.15; -0.2; -0.3; -0.4$ the company value V at fixed growth rate g increases with leverage level L in Generalized Modigliani–Miller theory (GMM theory). The company value V also increases with growth rate g.

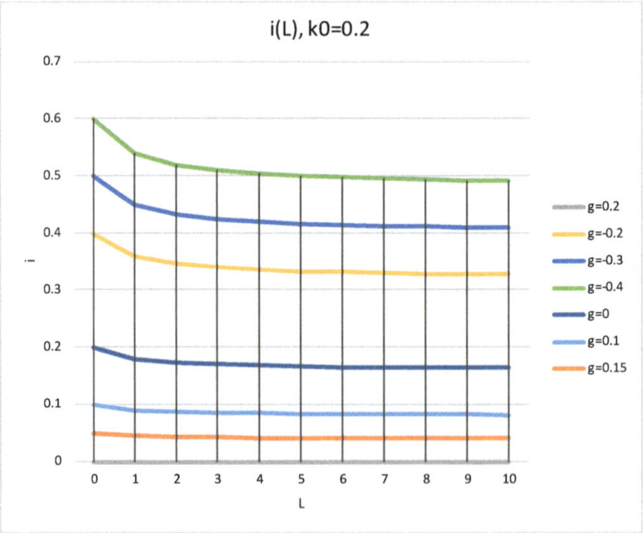

Fig. 8.4 Dependence of discount rate i on leverage level L in Generalized Modigliani–Miller theory (GMM theory) at $k_0 = 0.2$ and $g = 0; 0.1; 0.15; \pm 0.2; -0.3; -0.4$

8.4.6 Dependence of Company Value V on Leverage Level L in Generalized Modigliani–Miller Theory (GMM Theory) at $k_0 = 0.3$ and Different Values of g

Let us study the dependence of company value V on leverage level L in Generalized Modigliani–Miller theory (GMM theory) at $k_0 = 0.3$ and different values of g.

The results of Table 8.6 are shown in Fig. 8.7.

From Fig. 8.7 it is seen, that at $k_0 = 0.3$ and $g = 0; 0.1; 0.15; -0.2; -0.3; -0.4$ the company value V at fixed growth rate g increases with leverage level L in Generalized Modigliani–Miller theory (GMM theory). The company value V as well increases with growth rate g.

From Figs. 8.6 and 8.7 it is seen, that at two values of k_0 (0.2; 0.3) and $g = 0; 0.1; 0.15; -0.2; -0.3; -0.4$ the company value V at fixed growth rate g increases with leverage level L in Generalized Modigliani–Miller theory (GMM theory). The company value V as well increases with growth rate g.

We should note that in case of growing rate g equals to equity cost (at $L = 0$) k_0, the company value V becomes infinite. This is the limitation of the perpetuity Modigliani–Miller theory. As one can see in our future publications where we will consider the generalization of BFO theory for the case of variable profit such kind of restriction is absent for companies of finite ages.

Table 8.4 Dependence of discount rate i on leverage level L in Generalized Modigliani–Miller theory (GMM theory) at $k_0 = 0.3$ and $g = 0; 0.1; 0.15; \pm0.2; \pm0.3;\pm0.4$

L	T	k_0	i								
			g = 0.4	**g = 0.3**	**g = 0.2**	**g = 0.15**	**g = 0.1**	**g = 0**	**g = − 0.2**	**g = − 0.3**	**g = − 0.4**
0	0.2	0.3	− 0.100	0.000	0.100	0.150	0.200	0.300	0.500	0.600	0.700
1	0.2	0.3	− 0.090	0.000	0.090	0.135	0.180	0.270	0.450	0.540	0.630
2	0.2	0.3	− 0.087	0.000	0.087	0.130	0.173	0.260	0.433	0.520	0.607
3	0.2	0.3	− 0.085	0.000	0.085	0.128	0.170	0.255	0.425	0.510	0.595
4	0.2	0.3	− 0.084	0.000	0.084	0.126	0.168	0.252	0.420	0.504	0.588
5	0.2	0.3	− 0.083	0.000	0.083	0.125	0.167	0.250	0.417	0.500	0.583
6	0.2	0.3	− 0.083	0.000	0.083	0.124	0.166	0.249	0.414	0.497	0.580
7	0.2	0.3	− 0.083	0.000	0.083	0.124	0.165	0.248	0.413	0.495	0.578
8	0.2	0.3	− 0.082	0.000	0.082	0.123	0.164	0.247	0.411	0.493	0.576
9	0.2	0.3	− 0.082	0.000	0.082	0.123	0.164	0.246	0.410	0.492	0.574
10	0.2	0.3	− 0.082	0.000	0.082	0.123	0.164	0.245	0.409	0.491	0.573

8.4.7 *Dependence of Equity Cost k_e on Leverage Level L in Generalized Modigliani–Miller Theory (GMM Theory) at $k_0 = 0.2$ and Different Values of g (0; ±0.2;±0.3;±0.4)*

The economically justified value of dividends is equal to equity cost. Thus, knowing the dependence of equity cost of company on leverage level L, on growth rate g is very important, because it could impact the dividend policy of the company and help to company management to develop reasonable dividend policy.

Below we study the dependence of equity cost k_e on leverage level L in Generalized Modigliani–Miller theory (GMM theory) at $k_0 = 0.2$ and different values of g (0; ±0.2; ±0.3; ±0.4).

The results of Table 8.7 are shown in Fig. 8.8.

We have investigated the dependence of equity cost k_e on leverage level L in the Generalized Modigliani–Miller theory (GMM theory) at $k_0 = 0.2$ and $g = 0$;

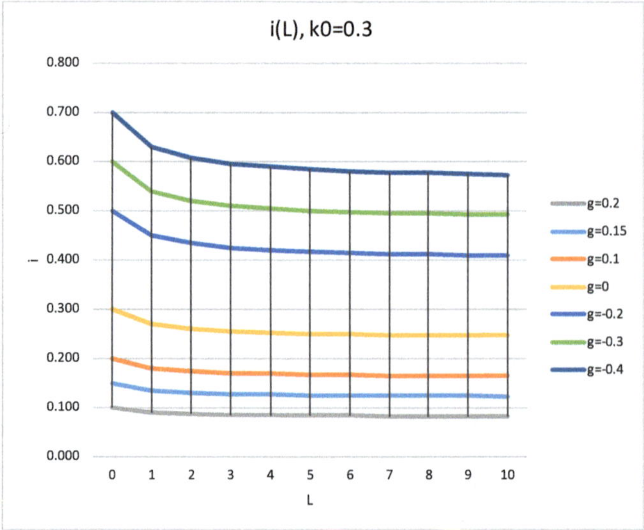

Fig. 8.5 Dependence of discount rate i on leverage level L in Generalized Modigliani–Miller theory (GMM theory) at $k_0 = 0.3$ and $g = 0; 0.1; 0.15; \pm 0.2; -0.3; -0.4$

Table 8.5 Dependence of company value V on leverage level L in Generalized Modigliani–Miller theory (GMM theory) at $k_0 = 0.2$ and different values of $g = 0.0; 0.1; 0.15; -0.2; -0.3; -0.4$

L	t	k_0	kd	CF	V					
					g = 0.1	**g = 0.15**	**g = 0**	**g = − 0.2**	**g = − 0.3**	**g = − 0.4**
0	0.2	0.2	0.16	100	1000	2000	500	250	200	166.6667
1	0.2	0.2	0.16	100	118.111	2222.222	555.5556	277.7778	222.2222	185.1852
2	0.2	0.2	0.16	100	1153.846	2307.692	576.9231	288.4615	230.7692	192.3077
3	0.2	0.2	0.16	100	1176.471	2352.941	588.2353	294.1176	235.2941	196.0784
4	0.2	0.2	0.16	100	1190.476	2380.952	595.2381	297.619	238.0952	198.4127
5	0.2	0.2	0.16	100	1200	2400	600	300	240	200
6	0.2	0.2	0.16	100	1206.897	2413.793	603.4483	301.7241	241.3793	201.1494
7	0.2	0.2	0.16	100	1212.121	2424.242	606.0606	303.0303	242.4242	202.0202
8	0.2	0.2	0.16	100	1216.216	2432.432	608.1081	304.0541	243.2432	202.7027
9	0.2	0.2	0.16	100	1219.512	2439.024	609.7561	304.878	243.9024	203.252
10	0.2	0.2	0.16	100	1222.222	2444.444	68.1111	305.5556	244.4444	203.7037

±0.2;±0.3; ±0.4. From Fig. 8.8 it is seen that the equity cost, k_e, which linearly grows with leverage level L increases with g: the tilt angle k_e (L) grows with g. It is interesting, that at $k_0 = 0.2$; $k_d = 0.16$ and at $g^* = -0.16$ in accordance with formula $g^* = -\frac{(k_0 - k_d)\cdot(1-T)}{T}$ the equity cost k_e turns out to be equal to k_0 and does not change with leverage level L.

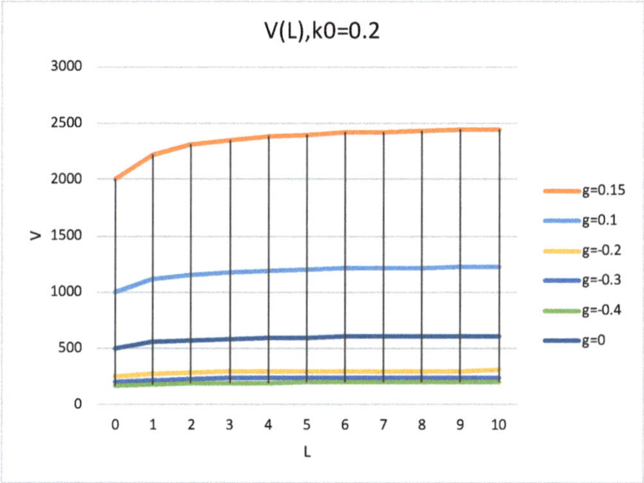

Fig. 8.6 Dependence of company value V on leverage level L in Generalized Modigliani–Miller theory (GMM theory) at $k_0 = 0.2$ and $g = 0; 0.1; 0.15; -0.2; -0.3; -0.4$

This should change the dividend policy of the company, because the economically justified value of dividends is equal to equity cost.

8.4.8 Dependence of Equity Cost k_e on Leverage Level L in Generalized Modigliani–Miller Theory (GMM Theory) at $k_0 = 0.3$ and Different Values of g

Presented below is the dependence of equity cost k_e on leverage level L in the Generalized Modigliani–Miller theory (GMM theory) at $k_0 = 0.3$ and different values of g (0; ±0.2; ±0.3;±0.4).

The results of Table 8.8 are shown in Fig. 8.9.

We have investigated the dependence of equity cost k_e on leverage level L in the Generalized Modigliani–Miller theory (GMM theory) at $k_0 = 0.3$ and $g = 0; \pm 0.2; \pm 0.3; \pm 0.4$. From Fig. 8.9 it is seen that the equity cost, k_e, which linearly grows with leverage level increases with g: the tilt angle k_e (L) grows with g. It is interesting, that at $k_0 = 0.3$; $k_d = 0.22$ and at $g^* = -0.32$ in accordance with Formula (8.43) the equity cost k_e turns out to be equal to k_0 and does not change with leverage level L.

Here, we have investigated the dependence of equity cost k_e on leverage level L in Generalized Modigliani–Miller theory (GMM theory) at two values of k_0 (0.2 and 0.3) and different values of g. The equity cost, k_e, which linearly grows with leverage level increases with g: the tilt angle k_e (L) grows with g. This should change the dividend policy of the company, because the economically justified value of dividends is equal to equity cost.

Table 8.6 Dependence of company value V on leverage level L in Generalized Modigliani–Miller theory (GMM theory) at $k_0 = 0.3$ and $g = 0.25$

L	t	k_0	kd	CF	V						
					g = 0.1	**g = 0.15**	**g = 0.25**	**g = 0**	**g = − 0.2**	**g = − 0.3**	**g = − 0.4**
0	0.2	0.3	0.16	100	500	666.6667	2000	333.3333	200	166.6667	142.8571
1	0.2	0.3	0.16	100	555.5556	740.7407	2222.222	370.3704	222.2222	185.1852	158.7302
2	0.2	0.3	0.16	100	576.9231	769.2308	2307.692	384.6154	230.7692	192.3077	164.8352
3	0.2	0.3	0.16	100	588.2353	784.3137	2352.941	392.1569	235.2941	196.0784	168.0672
4	0.2	0.3	0.16	100	595.2381	793.6508	2380.952	396.8254	238.0952	198.4127	170.068
5	0.2	0.3	0.16	100	600	800	2400	400	240	200	171.4286
6	0.2	0.3	0.16	100	603.4483	804.5977	2413.793	402.2989	241.3793	201.1494	172.4138
7	0.2	0.3	0.16	100	606.0606	808.0808	2424.242	404.0404	242.4242	202.0202	173.1602
8	0.2	0.3	0.16	100	608.1081	810.8108	2432.432	405.4054	243.2432	202.7027	173.7452
9	0.2	0.3	0.16	100	609.7561	813.0081	2439.024	406.5041	243.9024	203.252	174.216
10	0.2	0.3	0.16	100	68.1111	814.8148	2444.444	407.4074	244.4444	203.7037	174.6032

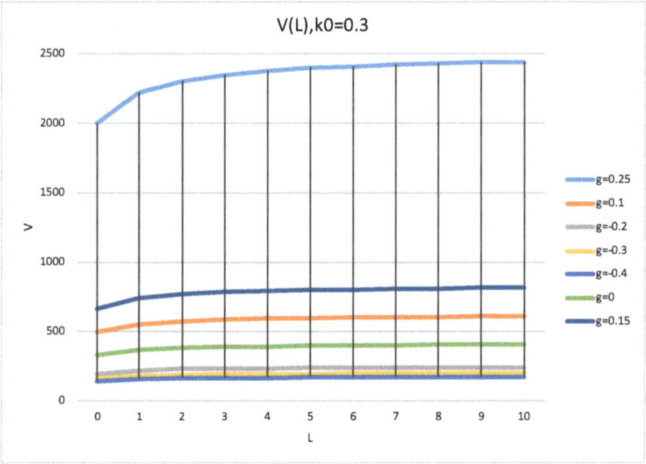

Fig. 8.7 Dependence of company value V on leverage level L in Generalized Modigliani–Miller theory (GMM theory) at $k_0 = 0.3$ and $g = 0; 0.1; 0.15; 0.25; -0.2; -0.3; -0.4$

Table 8.7 Dependence of equity cost k_e on leverage level L in Generalized Modigliani–Miller theory (GMM theory) at $k_0 = 0.2$ and different values of g (0; ±0.2; ±0.3; ±0.4)

L	T	k_0	kd	k_e						
				g = 0.4	**g = 0.3**	**g = 0.2**	**g = 0**	**g = − 0.2**	**g = − 0.3**	**g = − 0.4**
0	0.2	0.2	0.16	0.2	0.2	0.2	0.2	0.2	0.2	0.2
1	0.2	0.2	0.16	0.312	0.292	0.272	0.232	0.192	0.172	0.152
2	0.2	0.2	0.16	0.424	0.384	0.344	0.264	0.184	0.144	0.104
3	0.2	0.2	0.16	0.536	0.476	0.416	0.296	0.176	0.116	0.056
4	0.2	0.2	0.16	0.648	0.568	0.488	0.328	0.168	0.088	0.008
5	0.2	0.2	0.16	0.76	0.66	0.560	0.360	0.16	0.060	− 0.040
6	0.2	0.2	0.16	0.872	0.752	0.632	0.392	0.152	0.032	− 0.088
7	0.2	0.2	0.16	0.984	0.844	0.704	0.424	0.144	0.004	− 0.136
8	0.2	0.2	0.16	1.096	0.936	0.776	0.456	0.136	− 0.024	− 0.184
9	0.2	0.2	0.16	1.208	1.028	0.848	0.488	0.128	− 0.052	− 0.232
10	0.2	0.2	0.16	1.320	1.120	0.920	0.520	0.120	− 0.080	− 0.280

It is interesting, that at $k_0 = 0.2$; $k_d = 0.16$ and at $g^* = -0.16$ and at $k_0 = 0.3$; $k_d = 0.22$ and at $g^* = -0.32$ in accordance with Formula (43) the equity cost k_e turns out to be equal to k_0 and does not change with leverage level L.

The qualitatively new effect in corporate finance has been discovered: at rate $g < g^*$ the slope of the curve k_e (L) turns out to be negative. This effect, which is absent in classical Modigliani–Miller theory, could significantly alter the principles of the company's dividend policy.

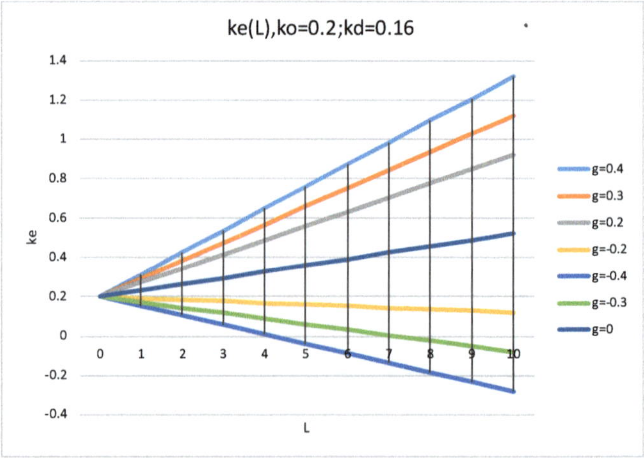

Fig. 8.8 Dependence of equity cost k_e on leverage level L in Generalized Modigliani–Miller theory (GMM theory) at $k_0 = 0.2$; $k_d = 0.16$ and $g = 0; \pm 0.2; \pm 0.3; \pm 0.4$

Table 8.8 Dependence of equity cost k_e on leverage level L in Generalized Modigliani–Miller theory (GMM theory) at $k_0 = 0.3$ and different g (0; ±0.2;±0.3; ±0.4)

L	T	k_0	kd	k_e						
				g = 0.4	g = 0.3	g = 0.2	g = 0	g = − 0.2	g = − 0.3	g = − 0.4
0	0.2	0.3	0.16	0.3	0.3	0.3	0.3	0.3	0.3	0.3
1	0.2	0.3	0.16	0.444	0.424	0.404	0.364	0.324	0.304	0.284
2	0.2	0.3	0.16	0.588	0.548	0.508	0.428	0.348	0.308	0.268
3	0.2	0.3	0.16	0.732	0.672	0.612	0.492	0.372	0.312	0.252
4	0.2	0.3	0.16	0.876	0.796	0.716	0.556	0.396	0.316	0.236
5	0.2	0.3	0.16	1.020	0.920	0.820	0.620	0.420	0.32	0.220
6	0.2	0.3	0.16	1.164	1.044	0.924	0.684	0.444	0.324	0.204
7	0.2	0.3	0.16	1.308	1.168	1.028	0.748	0.468	0.328	0.188
8	0.2	0.3	0.16	1.452	1.292	1.132	0.812	0.492	0.332	0.172
9	0.2	0.3	0.16	1.596	1.416	1.236	0.876	0.516	0.336	0.156
10	0.2	0.3	0.16	1.740	1.540	1.340	0.940	0.540	0.340	0.140

The last effect is similar to the qualitatively new effect in corporate finance, which has been discovered by Brusov–Filatova–Orekhova within the BFO theory [4]: abnormal dependence of equity cost k_e on leverage level at tax on profit rate T, which exceed some rate value T*: this discovery also significantly alters the principles of the company's dividend policy.

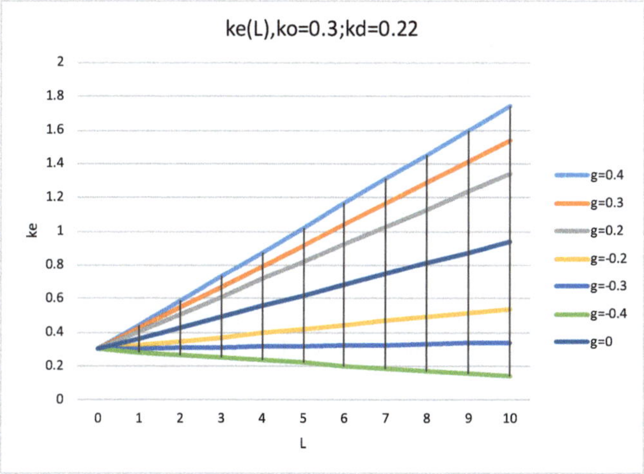

Fig. 8.9 Dependence of equity cost k_e on leverage level L in Generalized Modigliani–Miller theory (GMM theory) at $k_0 = 0.3$; $k_d = 0.22$ and $g = 0; \pm 0.2; \pm 0.3; \pm 0.4$

8.5 Conclusions

The main purpose of the current study is to generalize the Modigliani–Miller theory by taking into account one of the most important conditions of companies real functioning: variable profit. We use analytical and numerical methods: we derive all main formulas of the Generalized Modigliani–Miller theory theoretically and then use them to obtain all the main financial indicators of company and their dependences on different parameters by MS Excel. The generalized Modigliani–Miller theory significantly extends its application in practice, especially in business valuation, in ratings and in other areas of economy and finance. We consider the case of growing profit as well as decreasing of profit and show, that all the statements by Modigliani and Miller change significantly.

Within the new Generalized Modigliani–Miller theory (GMM theory), we study the dependence of the weighted average cost of capital, WACC, the cost of equity, k_e, the discount rate *i* and the capitalization of the company, V, on leverage level L at different values of growth rate g and obtained the following results:

1. Discount rate for leverage company changes from the weighted average cost of capital, WACC, to WACC–g (where g is growing rate), for a financially independent company from k_0 to k_0–g. This means that WACC and k_0 are no longer the discount rates as it takes place in case of classical Modigliani–Miller theory with constant profit.
2. All curves WACC(L) for different g start from one point, k_0. They decrease with L at $g < k_0$ and increase at $g > k_0$. It turns out that WACC grows with g, while real discount rates WACC–g and k_0–g decrease with g. This leads to increase of company capitalization with g: V = CF/WACC–g.

3. We have investigated the dependence of equity cost k_e on leverage level L in the Generalized Modigliani–Miller theory (GMM theory) at two values of k_0 (0.2 and 0.3) and different values of g. The equity cost, k_e, which linearly grows with leverage level L increases with g: the tilt angle k_e (L) grows with g. This should change the dividend policy of the company, because the economically justified value of dividends is equal to equity cost.

It is interesting, that at $k_0 = 0.2$; $k_d = 0.16$ and at $g^* = -0.16$ and at $k_0 = 0.3$; $k_d = 0.22$ and at $g^* = -0.32$ in accordance with Formula (43) the equity cost k_e turns out to be equal to k_0 and does not change with leverage level L.

A new qualitative finding related to corporate finance has been discovered in this study: at rate $g < g^*$ the slope of the curve k_e (L) turns out to be negative. This effect, which is absent in the classical Modigliani–Miller theory, could significantly alter the principles of the company's dividend policy. Rating methodology should take into account the company's dividend policy [5], thus such results obtained could change the credit rating of an issuer.

The last effect found in this study is similar to the qualitatively new effect in corporate finance, discussed above, which has been discovered by Brusov–Filatova–Orekhova within BFO theory: abnormal dependence of equity cost on leverage level when corporate taxes rate T exceeds some rate value T*; this discovery also significantly alters the principles of the company's dividend policy.

Thus, within the new Generalized Modigliani–Miller theory, a lot of significant implications are obtained, allowing us to develop new approach to financial policy and financial strategy of the company.

Note that the limitations of the Generalized Modigliani–Miller theory are similar to the limitations of the classical Modigliani–Miller theory and are connected with the numerous assumptions of classical Modigliani–Miller theory [1–3]. Therefore, the direction of future research is clear: we will consider the generalization of BFO theory, which describes the companies of arbitrary age, for the case of variable profit. The limitations of the Generalized Modigliani–Miller theory will be absent in the generalized BFO theory, which is valid for companies of an arbitrary age.

The Generalized Modigliani–Miller theory could and should be used in corporate finance and corporate management, in investments, business valuation, taxation, ratings, etc., for more correct assessments and more qualified management decisions.

Authors planning further development of the Modigliani–Miller theory should account for practical conditions of business and its application in all mentioned above areas. In particular, more frequent payments of tax of profit will be considered, combination of this case with advance payments of tax of profit, modification of BFO theory (which is valid for the companies of arbitrary ages) for the case of variable profit.

References

Berk J, De Marzo P (2007) Corporate finance. Pearson-Addison Wesley, Boston
Bradley M, Jarrell GA, Kim EH (1984) On the existence of an optimal capital structure: theory and evidence. J Financ 39:857–878
Brealey R, Myers S, Allen F (2005) Principle of corporate finance, 7th edn. McGraw Hill, New York, USA
Brusov P, Filatova T (2021) The Modigliani–Miller theory with arbitrary frequency of payment of tax on profit. Mathematics 9(11):1198 (WoS Q1)
Brusov PN, Filatova TV (2025a) Business valuation and company value: new qualitative approaches considering business and financial risks. Springer Nature Publishing, pp 1–654
Brusov PN, Filatova TV (2025b) Efficiency of investment projects: modern investment models and their applications. Springer Nature Publishing, pp 1–843
Brusov P, Filatova T, Chang S–I, Lin G (2021a) Innovative investment models with frequent payments of tax on income and of interest on debt. Mathematics 9(13):1491 (WoS Q1)
Brusov PN, Filatova TV, Kulik VL (2024) Capital Asset Pricing Model (CAPM) 2.0: account of business and financial risk. Finance: Theory Prac 28(2):128–142. https://doi.org/10.26794/2587-5671-2024-28-2-128-142
Brusov P, Filatova T, Orekhova N (2020a) Ratings: critical analysis and new approaches of quantitative and qualitative methodology. Springer Nature Publishing, Switzerland, pp 1–369. https://www.springer.com/de/book/9783030562427
Brusov P, Filatova T, Orekhova N, Eskindarov M (2018) Modern corporate finance, investments, taxation and ratings, 2nd edn. Springer Nature Publishing, Switzerland, pp 1–571
Brusov P, Filatova T, Orekhova N, Kulik V, Chang S–I, Lin G (2021b) Generalization of the Modigliani–Miller theory for the case of variable profit. Mathematics 9(11):1286 (WoS Q1)
Brusov PN, Filatova TV, Orekhova NP, Kulik VL, Chang S-I, Lin YCG (2020b) Modification of the Modigliani–Miller theory for the case of advance payments of tax on profit. J Rev Glob Econ 9:257–267
Brusov PN, Filatova TV, Orekhova NP, Kulik VL, Chang S-I, Lin YCG (2020c) Application of the Modigliani-Miller theory, modified for the case of advance payments of tax on profit, in rating methodologies. J Rev Glob Econ 9:282–292
Brusov PN, Filatova TV, Orekhova NP (2021) Ratings: critical analysis and new approaches of quantitative and qualitative methodology. Springer Nature Publishing, pp 1–369
Brusov PN, Filatova TV, Orekhova NP (2022) Generalized Modigliani–Miller Theory: applications in corporate finance, investments, taxation and ratings. Springer Nature Publishing, pp 1–362
Brusov PN, Filatova TV, Orekhova NP (2023) The Brusov–Filatova–Orekhova theory of capital structure: applications in corporate finance, investments, taxation and ratings. Springer Nature Publishing, pp 1–769
De Marzo PM (1988) An extension of the Modigliani-Miller theorem to stochastic economies with incomplete markets and interdependent securities. J Econ Theory 45(2):353–369
Farber A, Gillet R, Szafarz A (2006) A general formula for the WACC. Int J Bus 11(2):211–218
Fernandez P (2006) A general formula for the WACC: a comment. Int J Bus 11(2):219
Frank M, Goyal V (2009) Capital structure decisions: which factors are reliably important? Financ Manag 38(1):1–37. https://doi.org/10.1111/j.1755-053X.2009.01026.x
Graham JR (2003) Taxes and corporate finance: a review. Rev Financ Stud 16:1075–1129
Hamada R (1969) Portfolio analysis, market equilibrium, and corporate finance. J Financ 24(1):13–31
Harris R, Pringle J (1985) Risk-adjusted discount rates—extension form the average-risk case. J Financ Res 8(3):237–244
Harry DA, Masulis RW (1980) Optimal capital structure under corporate and personal taxation. J Financ Econ 8:3–29
Miller M (1977) Debt and taxes. J Financ 32(2):261–275. https://doi.org/10.1111/j.1540-6261.1977.tb03267.x

Modigliani F, Miller M (1958) The cost of capital, corporate finance, and the theory of investment. Am Econ Rev 48:261–297
Modigliani F, Miller M (1963) Corporate income taxes and the cost of capital: a correction. Am Econ Rev 53:147–175
Modigliani F, Miller M (1966) Some estimates of the cost of capital to the electric utility industry 1954–1957. Am Econ Rev 56:333–391
Ross S, Westerfiel R, Jaffee D (2005) Corporate finance, 7th edn. McGraw Hill, New York, USA
Sethi SP, Derzko NA, Lehoczky JP (1991) A stochastic extension of the Miller–Modigliani framework. Math Financ 1(4):57–76
Sheridan T, Wessels R (1988) The determinants of capital structure choice. J Financ 43:1–19

Chapter 9
Inflation in Brusov–Filatova–Orekhova Theory and in Its Perpetuity Limit—Modigliani–Miller Theory

9.1 Introduction

Studying the impact of inflation on taxes and the possible reverse impact of taxes on inflation is an extremely important issue due to the fact that in any country there are both taxes and inflation.

In this Chapter the influence of inflation on capital cost and capitalization of the company within modern theory of capital cost and capital structure—Brusov–Filatova–Orekhova theory (BFO theory) (Brusov et al. 2011a, b, c, d, 2012a, b, 2013a, b, 2014a, b, 2021, 2022, 2023, 2024; Filatova et al. 2008; Brusova 2011 and Brusov and Filatova 2011, 2025a, b) and within its perpetuity limit–Modigliani–Miller theory (Modigliani et al. 1958, 1963, 1966) is investigated. By direct incorporation of inflation into both theories, it is shown for the first time, that inflation not only increases the equity cost and the weighted average cost of capital, but as well it changes their dependence on leverage. In particular, it increases growing rate of equity cost with leverage. Capitalization of the company is decreased under accounting of inflation.

Created more than half a century ago by Nobel Prize winners Modigliani and Miller theory of capital cost and capital structure (Modigliani et al. 1958, 1963, 1966) did not account a lot of factors of a real economy, such as taxing, bankruptcy, unperfected capital markets, inflation and many others. But while taxing has been included into consideration by authors themselves and some other limitations have been taken off by their followers, direct incorporation of inflation to Modigliani–Miller theory is absent still now.

The influence of inflation on valuation of capital cost of company and its capitalization is investigated within Modigliani–Miller theory (MM) (Modigliani et al. 1958, 1963, 1966), which is now outdate, but still widely used at the West, as well as within modern theory of capital cost and capital structure—Brusov–Filatova–Orekhova theory (BFO theory) (Brusov et al. 2011a, b, c, d, 2012a, b, 2013a, b, 2014a, b; Filatova et al. 2008), which should replaced Modigliani–Miller theory (Modigliani et al. 1958, 1963, 1966). It is shown, that inflation not only increases

P. Brusov and T. Filatova, *Taxes and Taxation*, Contributions to Finance and Accounting, https://doi.org/10.1007/978-3-032-11077-0_9

the equity cost and the weighted average cost of capital, but as well it changes their dependence on leverage. In particular, it increases growing rate of equity cost with leverage. Capitalization of the company is decreased under accounting of inflation.

We start from the study of inflation within Modigliani–Miller theory without taxing (Modigliani et al. 1958), than with taxing (Modigliani et al. 1963) and finally within modern theory of capital cost and capital structure–Brusov–Filatova–Orekhova theory (BFO theory) (Brusov et al. 2011a, b, c, d, 2012a, b, 2013a, b, 2014a, b, Filatova et al. 2008).

9.2 Accounting of Inflation in Modigliani–Miller Theory Without Taxes

Note, that any modification of Modigliani–Miller theory, as well as of any other one, requires going behind the frame of modified theory. Thus, in current case we should go behind the frame of perpetuity of the company (remind to reader, that Modigliani–Miller theory describes only perpetuity companies–companies with infinite lifetime), come to the companies with finite lifetime, make necessary calculations and then use the perpetuity limit.

As known, in profit approach capitalization of the company is equal to discounted sum of profits of the company. Suppose that profit is constant for all periods and equal to CF, one gets for capitalization of the financially independent company V_0, existing n years at market

$$V_0 = \frac{CF}{1+k_0} + \frac{CF}{(1+k_0)^2} + \ldots + \frac{CF}{(1+k_0)^n}. \tag{9.1}$$

Here k_0 capital cost of the financially independent company.Under inflation with rate α the capitalization of the financially independent company V_0^* becomes equal to

$$V_0^* = \frac{CF}{(1+k_0)(1+\alpha)} + \frac{CF}{[(1+k_0)(1+\alpha)]^2} + \ldots + \frac{CF}{[(1+k_0)(1+\alpha)]^n}. \tag{9.2}$$

Using the formula for sum of the terms of indefinitely diminishing geometrical progression with the first term

$$a_1 = \frac{CF}{(1+k_0)(1+\alpha)} \tag{9.3}$$

and denominator

$$q = \frac{1}{(1+k_0)(1+\alpha)} \tag{9.4}$$

one gets for capitalization of the financially independent company V_0^* the following expression

$$V_0^* = \frac{a_1}{1-q} = \frac{CF}{(1+k_0)(1+\alpha)\left[1-((1+k_0)(1+\alpha))^{-1}\right]}$$
$$= \frac{CF}{(1+k_0)(1+\alpha)-1} = \frac{CF}{k_0(1+\alpha)+\alpha}.$$

$$V_0^* = \frac{CF}{k_0(1+\alpha)+\alpha}. \tag{9.5}$$

It is seen, that under accounting of inflation the capitalization of the company decreases.

At discount rate $k_0 = 10\%$ and inflation rate $\alpha = 3\%$ the decrease is equal to 5.7%, and at discount rate $k_0 = 15\%$ and inflation rate $\alpha = 7\%$ the decrease is equal to 35%. One can see that influence of inflation on the company capitalization could be significant enough and negative.

For leverage company, using debt capital one has without inflation

$$V_L = \frac{CF}{1+WACC} + \frac{CF}{(1+WACC)^2} + \ldots + \frac{CF}{(1+WACC)^n}, \tag{9.6}$$

and in perpetuity limit

$$V_L = \frac{CF}{WACC}. \tag{9.7}$$

Under accounting of inflation the capitalization of the company is equal to

$$V_L^* = \frac{CF}{(1+WACC)(1+\alpha)} + \frac{CF}{[(1+WACC)(1+\alpha)]^2}$$
$$+ \ldots + \frac{CF}{[(1+WACC)(1+\alpha)]^n}. \tag{9.8}$$

Summing the ifinite set, we get for leverage company capitalization under accounting of inflation in Modigliani–Miller limit

$$V_L^* = \frac{a_1}{1-q} = \frac{CF}{(1+WACC)(1+\alpha)\left[1-((1+WACC)(1+\alpha))^{-1}\right]}$$
$$= \frac{CF}{(1+WACC)(1+\alpha)-1} = \frac{CF}{WACC(1+\alpha)+\alpha}$$

$$V_L^* = \frac{CF}{WACC(1+\alpha)+\alpha}. \tag{9.9}$$

It is seen, that similar to the case of the financially independent company inflation decreases the company capitalization and the decrease could be significant. From the formulas (Eq. 9.7) and (Eq. 9.9) it follows that effective values of capital costs (equity and WACC) are equal to

$$k_0^* = k_0(1+\alpha)+\alpha \tag{9.10}$$

$$WACC^* = WACC \cdot (1+\alpha)+\alpha \tag{9.11}$$

Note, that both capital costs increases under inflation.

We can compare obtained results with Fisher formula for inflation.

$$i^* = \frac{i-\alpha}{1+\alpha}. \tag{9.12}$$

Solving this equation with respect to nominal rate i, one gets equation, similar (Eq. 9.10) and (Eq. 9.11)

$$i = i^* \cdot (1+\alpha)+\alpha. \tag{9.13}$$

Thus, effective capital costs in our case have meaning of nominal ones, accounting inflation.

From the Modigliani–Miller theorem, that the weighted average cost of capital WACC does not depends on leverage level (without taxing), formulating under accounting of inflation, it is easy to get expression for the equity cost:

$$WACC^* = k_0^* = k_e^* w_e + k_d^* w_d. \tag{9.14}$$

Finding from here k_e^*, one gets:

$$\begin{aligned} k_e^* &= \frac{k_0^*}{w_e} - k_d^*\frac{w_d}{w_e} = \frac{k_0^*(S+D)}{S} - k_d^*\frac{D}{S} = k_0^* + (k_0^* - k_d^*)\frac{D}{S} \\ &= k_0^* + (k_0^* - k_d^*)L \end{aligned} \tag{9.15}$$

Putting instead of k_0^*, k_d^* their expressions, one gets finally

$$\begin{aligned} k_e^* &= k_0^* + (k_0^* - k_d^*)L = k_0(1+\alpha)+\alpha \\ &\quad + L(k_0 - k_d)(1+\alpha) = (1+\alpha)[k_0 + \alpha + L(k_0 - k_d)] \end{aligned}$$

$$k_e^* = k_0(1+\alpha)+\alpha + L(k_0-k_d)(1+\alpha). \tag{9.16}$$

It is seen, that inflation not only increases the equity cost, but as well it changes its dependence on leverage. In particular, it increases growing rate of equity cost

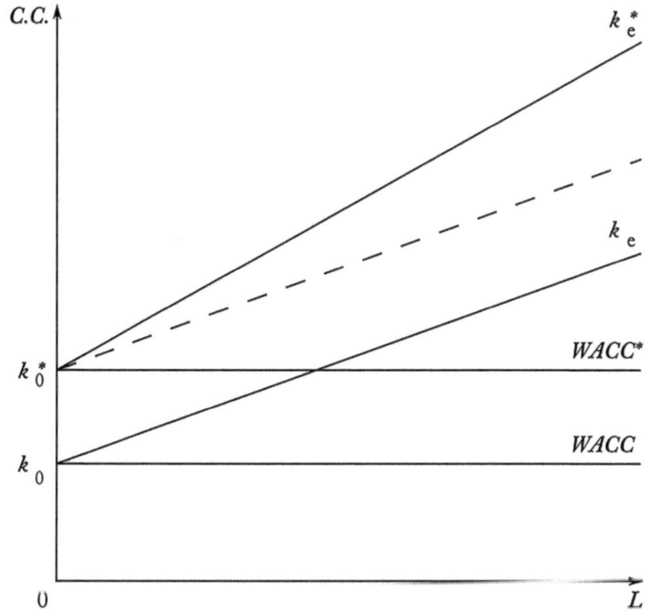

Fig. 9.1 Dependence of the equity cost and the weighted average cost of capital on leverage in the Modigliani–Miller theory without taxing under accounting of inflation. It is seen, that growing rate of equity cost increases with leverage. Axis y means capital costs—C.C

with leverage by multiplier $(1 + \alpha)$. The growing rate of equity cost with leverage, which is equal to $(k_0 - k_d)$ without inflation becomes equal to $(k_0 - k_d)(1 + \alpha)$ under accounting of inflation (Fig. 9.1).

Thus, we come to conclusion, that it is necessary to modified the second statement of the Modigliani–Miller theory (Modigliani et al. 1958) concerning the equity cost of leverage company.

2-nd Original MM Statement:

Equity cost of leverage company k_e could be found as equity cost of financially independent company k_0 of the same group of risk, plus premium for risk, which value is equal to production of difference $(k_0 - k_d)$ on leverage level *L*.

2-nd Modified MM-BFO Statement:

Under existing of inflation with rate α equity cost of leverage company k_e could be found as equity cost of financially independent company k_0 of the same group of risk, multiplied by $(1 + \alpha)$, plus inflation rate α and plus premium for risk, which value is equal to production of difference $(k_0 - k_d)$ on leverage level *L* and on multiplier $(1 + \alpha)$.

9.3 Accounting of Inflation in Modigliani–Miller Theory with Corporate Taxes

Let us calculate first the tax shield for perpetuity company under accounting of inflation

$$(PV)_{TS} = k_d^* DT \sum_{t=1}^{\infty} (1+k_d^*)^{-t} = DT \tag{9.17}$$

It is interesting to note , that inspite of dependence of each term of set on effective credit rate.

k_d^* tax shield turns out to be independent of it and equal to "inflationless" value DT and Modigliani–Miller theorem under accounting of inflation takes the form (Modigliani et al. 1963)

$$V_L^* = V_0^* + DT. \tag{9.18}$$

Substituting $D = w_d V_L^*, D = w_d V_L^*$,one gets

$$V_L^* = CF/k_0^* + w_d V_L^* T \tag{9.19}$$

or

$$V_L^*(1 - w_d T) = CF/k_0^*. \tag{9.20}$$

Because leverage company capitalization is equal to.

$V_L^* = CF/WACC^*$ for the weighted average cost of capital one has

$$WACC^* = k_0^*(1 - w_d T). \tag{9.21}$$

From (Eq. 9.21) we get the dependence of $WACC^*$ on leverage level $L = D/S$:

$$WACC^* = k_0^*(1 - LT/(1 + L)).$$

$$WACC^* = [k_0(1 + \alpha) + \alpha] \cdot (1 - w_d T) \tag{9.22}$$

On definition of the weighted average cost of capital with accounting of the tax shield one has

$$WACC^* = k_0^* w_e + k_d^* w_d (1 - T). \tag{9.23}$$

Equating right hand parts of expressions (Eq. 9.21) and (Eq. 9.23), we get

$$k_0^*(1 - w_d T) = k_0^* w_e + k_d^* w_d (1 - T), \tag{9.24}$$

from where one obtains the following expression for equity cost:

$$\begin{aligned} k_e^* &= k_0^* \frac{(1 - w_d T)}{w_e} - k_d^* \frac{w_d}{w_e}(1 - T) \\ &= k_e^* \frac{1}{w_e} - k_0^* \frac{w_d}{w_e} T - k_d^* \frac{D}{S}(1 - T) \\ &= k_0^* \frac{D + S}{S} - k_0^* \frac{D}{S} T - k_d^* \frac{D}{S}(1 - T) = k_0^* + L(1 - T)(k_0^* - k_d^*). \end{aligned}$$

$$\begin{aligned} k_e^* =& k_0^* + L(1 - T)(k_0^* - k_d^*) = [k_0(1 + \alpha) + \alpha] \\ &+ L(1 - T)(k_0 - k_d)(1 + \alpha) \end{aligned} \tag{9.25}$$

It is seen, that similar to the case without taxes inflation not only increases the equity cost, but as well it changes its dependence on leverage (Fig. 9.2). In particular, it increases growing rate of equity cost with leverage by multiplier $(1 + \alpha)$. The growing rate of equity cost with leverage, which is equal to $(k_0 - k_d)(1 - T)$ without inflation becomes equal to $(k_0 - k_d)(1 + \alpha)(1 - T)$ under accounting of inflation.

We can now reformulate the fourth statement of the Modigliani–Miller theory (Modigliani et al. 1963) concerning the equity cost of leverage company for case of accounting of inflation.

4-th Original MM Statement:

Equity cost of leverage company k_e paying tax on profit could be found as equity cost of financially independent company k_0 of the same group of risk, plus premium for risk, which value is equal to production of difference $(k_0 - k_d)$ on leverage level *L* and on tax shield (*1-T*) and on multiplier $(1 + \alpha)$.

4-th Modified MM-BFO Statement:

Equity cost of leverage company k_e paying tax on profit under existing of inflation with rate α could be found as equity cost of financially independent company k_0 of the same group of risk, multiplied by $(1 + \alpha)$, plus inflation rate α and plus premium for risk, which value is equal to production of difference $(k_0 - k_d)$ on leverage level *L*, on tax shield (*1-T*) and on multiplier $(1 + \alpha)$.

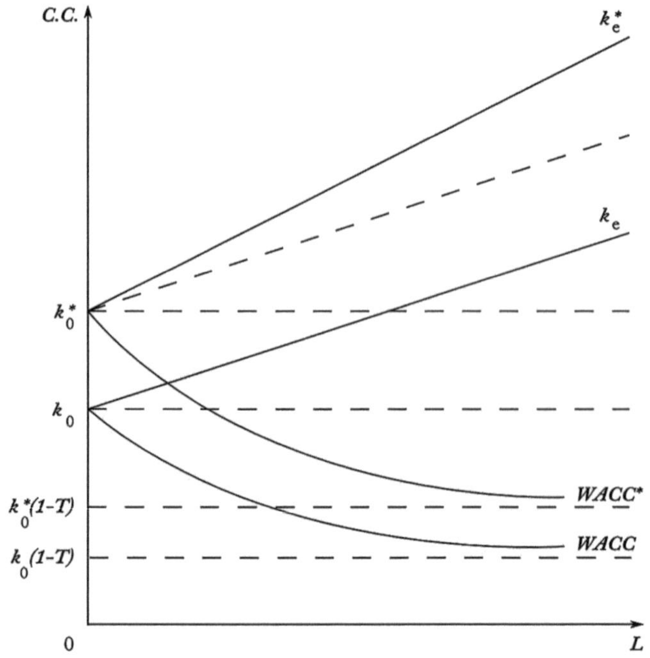

Fig. 9.2 Dependence of the equity cost and the weighted average cost of capital on leverage in the Modigliani–Miller theory with taxing under accounting of inflation. It is seen, that growing rate of equity cost increases with leverage. Axis y means capital costs—C.C

9.4 Accounting of Inflation in Brusov–Filatova–Orekhova Theory with Corporate Taxes

9.4.1 Generalized Brusov–Filatova–Orekhova Theorem

Brusov–Filatova–Orekhova, generalized the Modigliani–Miller theory for the case of the companies with arbitrary lifetime (Brusov et al. 2011a, b, c, d, 2012a, b, 2013a, b, 2014a, b; Filatova et al. 2008), have proved the following important theorem in case of absence of corporate taxing:

Without corporate taxing the equity cost k_0, as well as the weighted average cost of capital WACC do not depend on company lifetime and are equal to

$$k_e = k_0 + L(k_0 - k_d) \text{ and } WACC = k_0. \tag{9.26}$$

consequently.

Thus, the theorem has been proved, that without corporate taxes (say, in offshore zones) the Modigliani–Miller results for capital costs, in spite of the fact, that they have been obtained in perpetuity limit, remain in force for companies with arbitrary lifetime, describing by Brusov–Filatova–Orekhova theory (BFO theory). To prove this theorem Brusov, Filatova and Orekhova, of course, had to go behind Modigliani–Miller approximation.

Under accounting of inflation we can generalize this theorem (Brusov et al. 2011a, b, c, d, 2012a, b, 2013a, b, 2014a, b, Filatova et al. 2008):

9.4.2 Generalized Brusov–Filatova–Orekhova Theorem

Under accounting of inflation without corporate taxing the equity cost k_0^*, as well as the weighted average cost of capital $WACC^*$ do not depend on company lifetime and are equal to

$$k_e^* = k_0^* + L\left(k_0^* - k_d^*\right) = k_0(1+\alpha) + \alpha + L(k_0 - k_d)(1+\alpha)$$

$$\text{and} \quad WACC^* = k_0^* = k_0(1+\alpha) + \alpha \tag{9.27}$$

consequently.

Following to Brusov–Filatova–Orekhova (Brusov et al. 2011a, b, c, d, 2012a, b, 2013a, b, 2014a, b; Filatova et al. 2008), let us consider the situation for arbitrary lifetime companies with account of corporate taxing. They have derived the famous formula for weighted average cost of capital of companies with arbitrary lifetime

$$\frac{1-(1+WACC)^{-n}}{WACC} = \frac{1-(1+k_0)^{-n}}{k_0\left[1-\omega_d T\left(1-(1+k_d)^{-n}\right)\right]} \tag{9.28}$$

The application of BFO formula (9.28) is very wide: authors have applied it in corporate finance, in investments, in taxing, in business valuation, in banking and some other areas (Brusov et al. 2013b, 2011a, b***). Using this formula (9.28), one can study the dependence of the weighted average cost of capital, WACC, as well as the equity cost k_e on leverage level L, on tax on profit rate t, on lifetime of the company n and on relation between equity and debt cost. The qualitatively new effect in corporate finance has been discovered: decrease of the equity cost k_e on leverage level L, which is quite important for corporate finance in general and, in particular, for creating the adequate dividend policy.***

Below we generalize formula (9.28) under existing of inflation.

9.5 Generalized Brusov–Filatova–Orekhova Formula Under Existing of Inflation

Under existing of inflation it is necessary to replace all capital costs: the equity, the debt and the weighted average cost of capital $k_0, k_d, WACC$ by effective ones $k_0^*, k_d^*, WACC^*$, where

$$k_0^* = k_0(1+\alpha)+\alpha$$

$$k_d^* = k_d(1+\alpha)+\alpha$$

$$WACC^* = WACC \cdot (1+\alpha)+\alpha$$

Rewriting the equations for tax shield $(TS)_n$, capitalization of financially independent company V_0^* as well as for financially dependent company V_L^* for the case of existing of inflation, one gets

$$(PV)_{TS} = (TS)_n = k_d^* DT \sum_{t=1}^{n} (1+k_d^*)^{-t} = DT\left[1-\left(1+k_d^*\right)^{-n}\right] \tag{9.29}$$

$$V_0^* = CF\sum_{t=1}^{n}(1+k_0^*)^{-t} = CF\left[1-\left(1+k_0^*\right)^{-n}\right]\Big/ k_0^* \tag{9.30}$$

$$V_L^* = CF\sum_{t=1}^{n}(1+WACC^*)^{-t} = CF\left[1-\left(1+WACC^*\right)^{-n}\right]\Big/ WACC^* \tag{9.31}$$

$$V_L^* = V_0^* + (TS)_n, \tag{9.32}$$

After substitution $D = w_d V_L^*$ we have

$$V_L^* = CF/k_0^* + w_d V_L^* T \tag{9.33}$$

From here after some transformations we get generalized Brusov–Filatova–Orekhova formula under existing of inflation

$$\frac{1-(1+WACC^*)^{-n}}{WACC^*} = \frac{1-\left(1+k_0^*\right)^{-n}}{k_0^*\left[1-\omega_d T\left(1-\left(1+k_d^*\right)^{-n}\right)\right]}, \tag{9.34}$$

or after substitutions

$$k_0^* = k_0(1+\alpha)+\alpha; \qquad k_d^* = k_d(1+\alpha)+\alpha$$

one gets finally

$$\frac{1-(1+WACC^{*})^{-n}}{WACC^{*}}=\frac{1-[(1+k_0)(1+\alpha)]^{-n}}{(k_0(1+\alpha)+\alpha)\cdot\left[1-\omega_d T\left(1-((1+k_d)(1+\alpha))^{-n}\right)\right]} \tag{9.35}$$

Formula (9.35) is the generalized Brusov–Filatova–Orekhova formula under existing of inflation.

Let us show some figures, illustrating obtained results.

At Figs. 9.3 and 9.4 the dependence of the weighted average cost of capital WACC on debt ratio w_d at different inflation rate α (1 − α = 3%; 2 − α = 5%; 3 − α = 7%; 4 − α = 9%) for five—year company as well as for two–year company. It is seen that with increase of inflation rate lines, showing the dependence WACC (w_d) shift practically homogeneously to higher values.

It is seen, that difference in results for two—year company and five—year company is very small. More obviously it could be observed from below tables (Tables 9.1 and 9.2).

Below we show the dependences of the weighted average cost of capital WACC on debt ratio w_d at different tax on profit rate from $T = 10\%$ up to $T = 100\%$ at

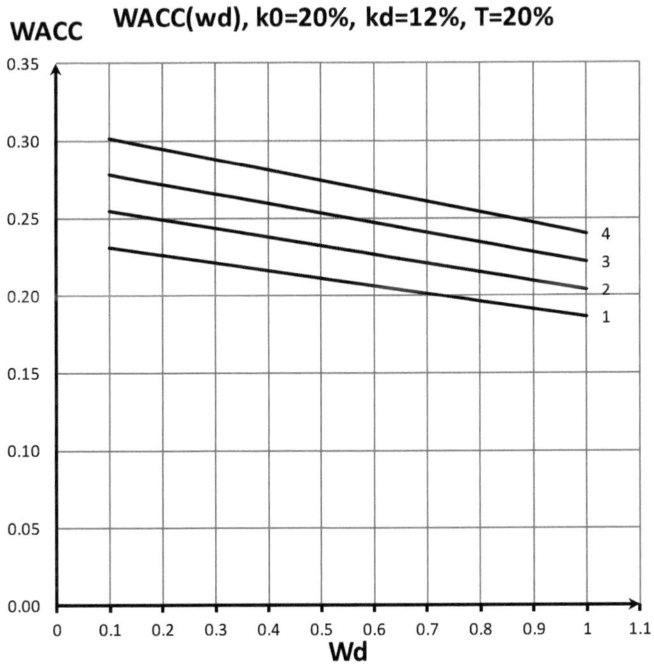

Fig. 9.3 Dependence of the weighted average cost of capital WACC on debt ratio w_d at different inflation rate α (1 − α = 3%; 2 − α = 5%; 3 − α = 7%; 4 − α = 9%) for five—year company

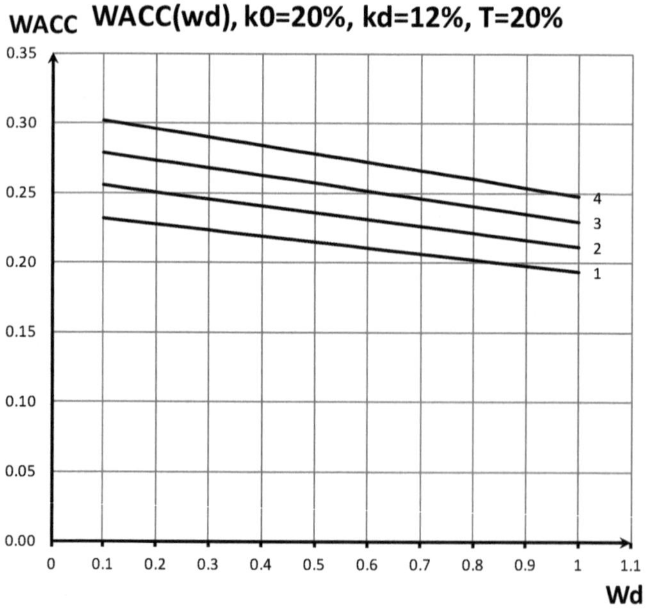

Fig. 9.4 Dependence of the weighted average cost of capital WACC on debt ratio w_d at different inflation rate α (1 – α = 3%; 2 – α = 5%; 3 – α = 7%; 4 – α = 9%) for two—year company

Table 9.1 Dependence of the weighted average cost of capital WACC on debt ratio w_d at different inflation rate α = 3%; 5%; 7%; 9% for two—year company

α \wd	0.1	0.2	0.3	0.4	0.5	0.6	0.7	0.8	0.9	1
0.03	0.2318	0.2276	0.2233	0.2191	0.2149	0.2106	0.2064	0.2021	0.1979	0.1937
0.05	0.2557	0.2503	0.2455	0.2406	0.2358	0.2309	0.2261	0.2212	0.2164	0.2115
0.07	0.2786	0.2733	0.2679	0.2626	0.2573	0.2514	0.2459	0.2404	0.2350	0.2295
0.09	0.3020	0.2960	0.2900	0.2839	0.2779	0.2720	0.2661	0.2602	0.2537	0.2476

Table 9.2 Dependence of the weighted average cost of capital WACC on debt ratio w_d at different inflation $\rho\alpha\tau\varepsilon\alpha$ = 3%; 5%; 7%; 9% for five—year company

α \wd	0.1	0.2	0.3	0.4	0.5	0.6	0.7	0.8	0.9	1
0.03	0.2311	0.2262	0.2213	0.2163	0.2113	0.2064	0.2013	0.1963	0.1912	0.1863
0.05	0.2546	0.2491	0.2434	0.2379	0.2323	0.2267	0.2210	0.2154	0.2097	0.2040
0.07	0.2781	0.2718	0.2657	0.2595	0.2534	0.2472	0.2408	0.2346	0.2283	0.2219
0.09	0.3015	0.2947	0.2879	0.2812	0.2744	0.2676	0.2608	0.2539	0.2471	0.2400

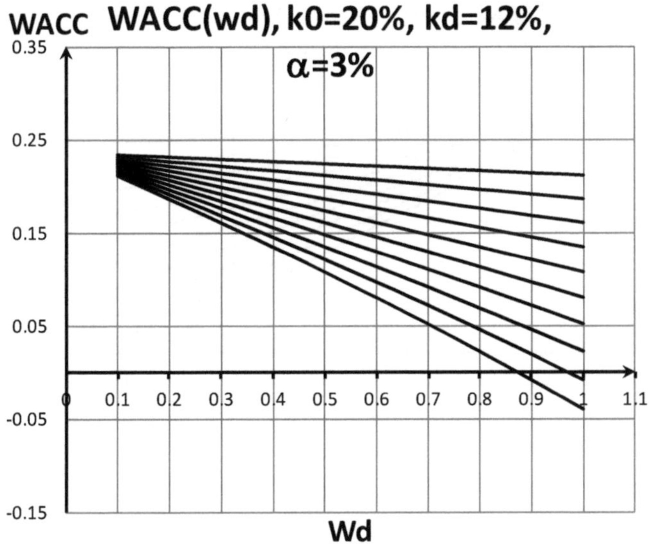

Fig. 9.5 Dependence of the weighted average cost of capital WACC on debt ratio w_d at different tax on profit rate at inflation rate α = 3% for five—year company. Tax on profit rate increases from $T = 0.1$ (upper line) up to $T = 1$ (lowest line) with step 0.1

different inflation rate α = 3%, 5%, 7%, 9% for five—year company (Figs. 9.5, 9.6, 9.7, and 9.8) as well as for two –year company (Figs. 9.9, 9.10, 9.11, and 9.12). Tax on profit rate increases from $T = 0.1$ (upper line) up to $T = 1$ (lowest line) with the step 0.1.

The analysis of Figs. 9.5, 9.6, 9.7, 9.8, 9.9, 9.10, 9.11, and 9.12 shows, that the weighted average cost of capital WACC decreases with debt ratio w_d faster with increase of tax on profit rate. The space between lines, corresponding to different tax on profit rates, increases with inflation rate. The variation range of WACC increases with inflation rate as well as with lifetime of the company.

9.6 Irregular Inflation

Above we considered inflation rate as constant. Really, as a rule, the inflation rate is a variable. It is possible to generalize all above consideration for the case of non-homogeneous inflation, introducing effective inflation for a few periods.

The effective inflation rate for a few periods $t = t_1 + t_2 + \ldots + t_n$ is equal to

$$\alpha = (1 + \alpha_1)(1 + \alpha_2) \cdot \ldots \cdot (1 + \alpha_n) - 1, \tag{9.36}$$

where $\alpha_1, \alpha_2, \ldots, \alpha_n$ are inflation rates for periods $t_1, t_2, \ldots, t_n$.

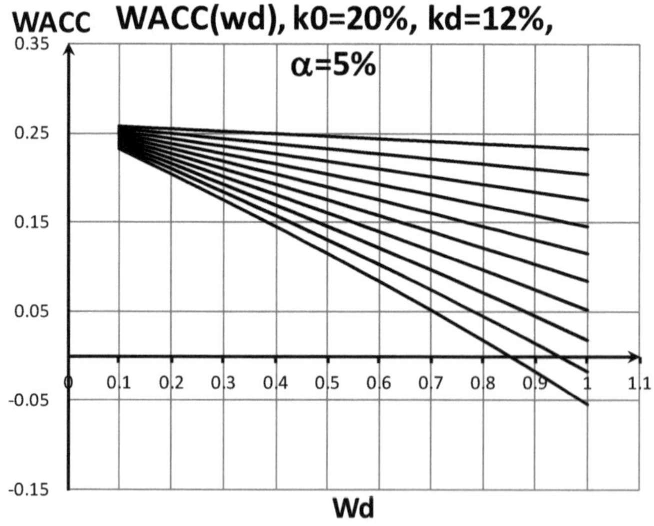

Fig. 9.6 Dependence of the weighted average cost of capital WACC on debt ratio w_d at different tax on profit rate at inflation rate $\alpha = 5\%$ for five—year company. Tax on profit rate increases from $T = 0.1$ (upper line) up to $T = 1$ (lowest line) with step 0.1

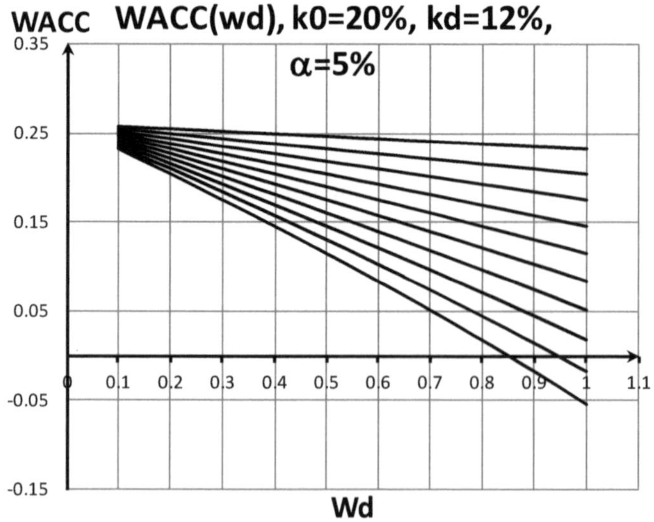

Fig. 9.7 Dependence of the weighted average cost of capital WACC on debt ratio w_d at different tax on profit rate at inflation rate $\alpha = 7\%$ for five –year company. Tax on profit rate increases from $T = 0.1$ (upper line) up to $T = 1$ (lowest line) with step 0.1

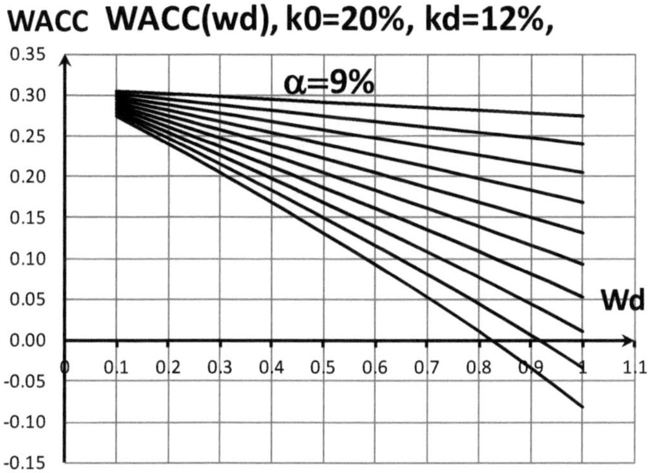

Fig. 9.8 Dependence of the weighted average cost of capital WACC on debt ratio w_d at different tax on profit rate at inflation rate $\alpha = 9\%$ for five—year company. Tax on profit rate increases from $T = 0.1$ (upper line) up to $T = 1$ (lowest line) with step 0.1

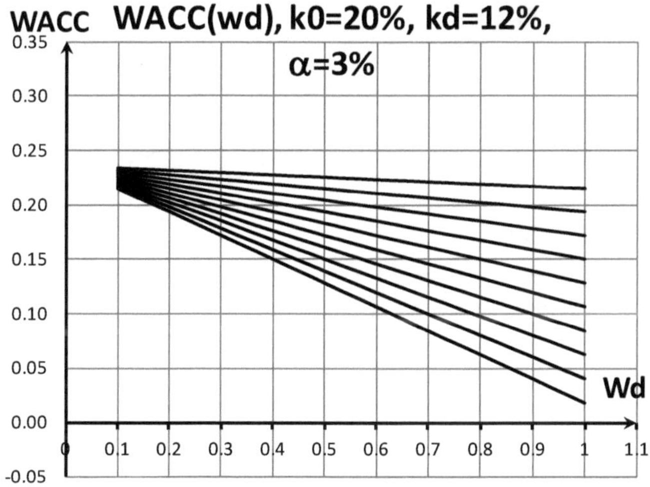

Fig. 9.9 Dependence of the weighted average cost of capital WACC on debt ratio w_d at different tax on profit rate at inflation rate $\alpha = 3\%$ for two—year company. Tax on profit rate increases from $T = 0.1$ (upper line) up to $T = 1$ (lowest line) with step 0.1

The proof of the formula (9.36) will be done below in (9.6).

In the case of non-homogeneous inflation it could be accounted in both theories: Modigliani–Miller and Brusov–Filatova–Orekhova theory (BFO theory) either through effective inflation rate, or directly upon discounting of financial flow.

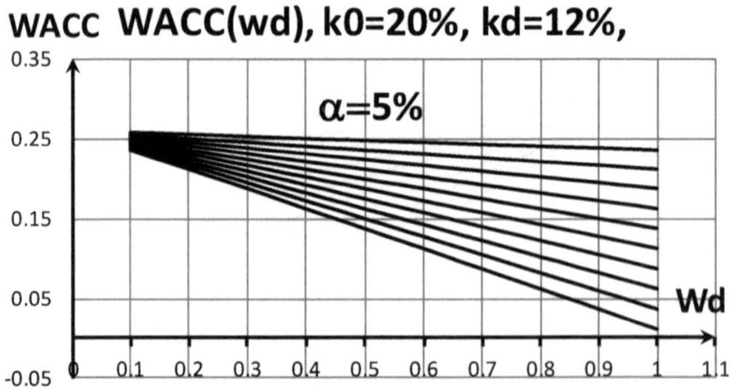

Fig. 9.10 Dependence of the weighted average cost of capital WACC on debt ratio w_d at different tax on profit rate at inflation rate $\alpha = 5\%$ for two—year company. Tax on profit rate increases from $T = 0.1$ (upper line) up to $T = 1$ (lowest line) with step 0.1

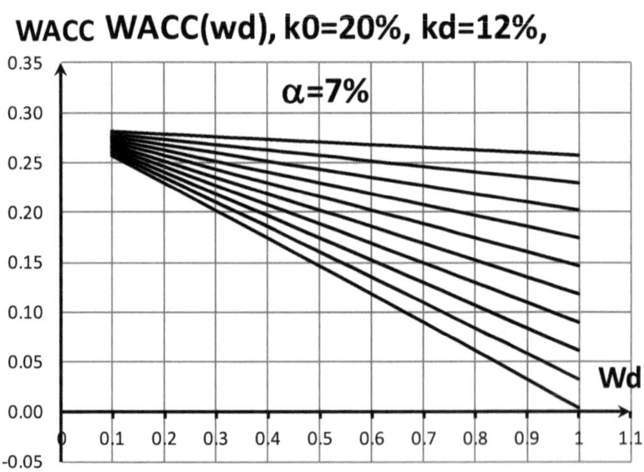

Fig. 9.11 Dependence of the weighted average cost of capital WACC on debt ratio w_d at different tax on profit rate at inflation rate $\alpha = 7\%$ for two—year company. Tax on profit rate increases from $T = 0.1$ (upper line) up to $T = 1$ (lowest line) with step 0.1

Conclusions In this Chapter the influence of inflation on capital cost and capitalization of the company within modern theory of capital cost and capital structure—Brusov–Filatova–Orekhova theory (BFO theory) (Brusov et al. 2011a, b, c, d, 2012a, b, 2013a, b, 2014a, b; Filatova et al. 2008) and in its perpetuity limit—Modigliani–Miller theory (Modigliani et al. 1958, 1963, 1966), which is now outdate, but still widely used at the West, is investigated. All basic results of Modigliani–Miller theory were modified. It is shown, that inflation not only increases the equity cost and the weighted average cost of capital, but as well it changes their dependence on leverage.

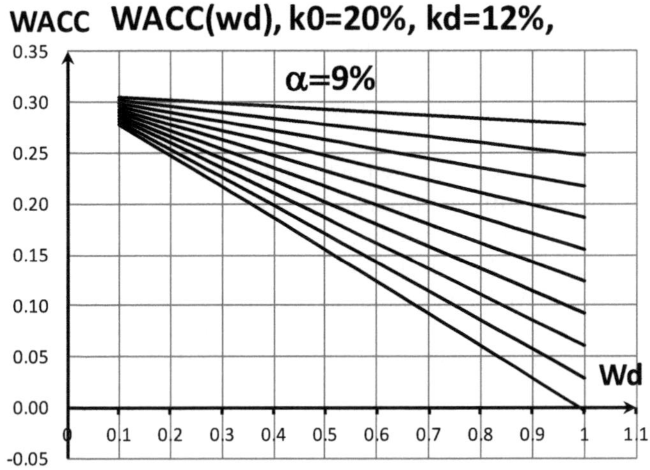

Fig. 9.12 Dependence of the weighted average cost of capital WACC on debt ratio w_d at different tax on profit rate at inflation rate $\alpha = 9\%$ for two—year company. Tax on profit rate increases from $T = 0.1$ (upper line) up to $T = 1$ (lowest line) with step 0.1

In particular, it increases growing rate of equity cost with leverage. Capitalization of the company is decreased under accounting of inflation.

Within modern theory of capital cost and capital structure—Brusov–Filatova–Orekhova theory (BFO theory) the modified equation for the weighted average cost of capital, WACC, applicable to companies with arbitrary lifetime under accounting of inflation has been derived. Modified BFO equation allow to investigate the dependence of the weighted average cost of capital, WACC, and equity cost, k_e, on leverage level L, on tax on profit rate t, on lifetime of the company n, on equity cost of financially independent company, k_0, and debt cost, k_d, as well as on inflation rate α.

Using modified BFO equation the analysis of the dependence of the weighted average cost of capital, WACC, on debt ratio, w_d, at different tax on profit rate t, as well as inflation rate α has been done.

It has been shown, that WACC decreases with debt ratio, w_d, faster at bigger tax on profit rate t. The space between lines, corresponding to different values of tax on profit rate at the same step (10%), increases with inflation rate α. The variation region (with change of tax on profit rate t) of the weighted average cost of capital, WACC, increases with inflation rate α, as well as with lifetime of the company n.

9.7 Inflation Rate for a Few Periods

Suppose that the inflation rate for the consistent time periods $t_1, t_2, \ldots, t_n$ are equal to $\alpha_1, \alpha_2, \ldots, \alpha_n$ consequently. Let us find the inflation rate α for total time period $t = t_1 + t_2 + \ldots + t_n$.

Common sense dictates that inflation rate is an additive value, so that α, at least approximately, is equal to the sum of the inflation rates $\alpha_1, \alpha_2, \ldots, \alpha_n$

$$\alpha \approx \alpha_1 + \alpha_2 + \ldots + \alpha_n. \tag{9.37}$$

Below we will get an exact expression for inflation rate for the total period of time t, and will see how it is different from an intuitive result (9.37).

At the end of the first commitment period the gained sum will be equal to the amount $S_1 = S_0(1+i)$, and with the account of inflation $S_{1\alpha} = S_0(1+i)^{t_1} / (1+\alpha_1)$. At the end of the second commitment period the gained sum will be equal to the amount $S_2 = S_0(1+i)^{t_1+t_2}$, and with the account of inflation $S_{2\alpha} = S_0(1+i)^{t_1+t_2} / (1+\alpha_1)(1+\alpha_2)$. At the end of the n–th commitment period the gained sum will be equal to the amount $S_n = S_0(1+i)^{t_1+t_2+\ldots+t_n}$, and with the account of inflation

$$S_{n\alpha} = S_0(1+i)^{t_1+t_2+\ldots+t_n} / (1+\alpha_1)(1+\alpha_2) \cdot \ldots \cdot (1+\alpha_n). \tag{9.38}$$

On the other hand, at inflation rate α for the total period at $t = t_1 + t_2 + \ldots + t_n$ at the end of this period t gained sum will be equal to

$$S_{n\alpha} = S_0(1+i)^t / (1+\alpha). \tag{9.39}$$

Equating the right-hand part of (9.38) and (9.39), we get

$$(1+\alpha_1)(1+\alpha_2) \cdot \ldots \cdot (1+\alpha_n) = 1+\alpha. \tag{9.40}$$

From where

$$\alpha = (1+\alpha_1)(1+\alpha_2) \cdot \ldots \cdot (1+\alpha_n) - 1. \tag{9.41}$$

It is easy to get a strict proof of this formula by the method of mathematical induction. Note that inflation rate for the n–periods does not depend on both of the length of constituting periods and on the period t.

For equal inflation rates $\alpha_1 = \alpha_2 = \ldots = \alpha_n$ (it is interesting to note, that herewith the time intervals $t_1, t_2, \ldots, t_n$ can be arbitrary and do not equal each other) one has

$$\alpha = (1+\alpha_1)^n - 1. \tag{9.42}$$

References

Brusova A (2011) A Comparison of the three methods of estimation of weighted average cost of capital and equity cost of company. Financ Anal: Probl Solut 34(76):36–42

Brusov PN, Filatova TV (2011) From Modigliani-Miller to general theory of capital cost and capital structure of the company. Financ Credit 435:2–8

Brusov P, Filatova T, Orehova N, Brusova A (2011a) Weighted average cost of capital in the theory of Modigliani-Miller, modified for a finite life–time company. Appl Financ Econ 21(11):815–824

Brusov P, Filatova T, Orehova N et al (2011b) From Modigliani-Miller to general theory of capital cost and capital structure of the company. Res J Econ, Bus ICT 2:16–21

Brusov P, Filatova T, Orehova N et al (2011c) Influence of debt financing on the effectiveness of the investment project within the Modigliani-Miller theory. Res J Econ Bus ICT (UK) 2:11–15

Brusov P, Filatova T, Orehova N, Brusov PP, Brusova N (2011d) From Modigliani–Miller to general theory of capital cost and capital structure of the company. Res J Econ, Bus ICT 2:16–21

Brusov P, Filatova T, Eskindarov M, Orehova N (2012a) Influence of debt financing on the effectiveness of the finite duration investment project. Appl Financ Econ 22(13):1043–1052

Brusov P, Filatova T, Eskindarov M, Orehova N (2012b) Hidden global causes of the global financial crisis. J Rev Glob Econ 1:106–111

Brusov P, Filatova P, Orekhova N (2013a) Absence of an optimal capital structure in the FA-MoUs tradeoff theory! J Rev Glob Econ 2:94–116

Brusov P, Filatova T, Orehova N (2013b) A qualitatively new effect in corporative finance: abnormal dependence of cost of equity of company on leverage. J Rev Glob Econ 2:183–193

Brusov P, Filatova P, Orekhova N (2014a) Mechanism of formation of the company optimal capital structure, different from suggested by trade off theory. Cogent Econ & Financ 2:1–13. https://doi.org/10.1080/23322039.209.946150

Brusov P, Filatova T, Orehova N (2014b) Inflation in Brusov–Filatova–Orekhova Theory and in its Perpetuity Limit–Modigliani–Miller Theory. J Rev Glob Econ 3:175–185

Brusov PN, Filatova TV, Orekhova NP (2021) Ratings: critical analysis and new approaches of quantitative and qualitative methodology. Springer Nature Publishing, pp 1–369

Brusov PN, Filatova TV, Orekhova NP (2022) Generalized Modigliani–Miller Theory: applications in corporate finance, investments, taxation and ratings. Springer Nature Publishing, pp 1–362

Brusov PN, Filatova TV, Orekhova NP (2023) The Brusov–Filatova–Orekhova theory of capital structure: applications in corporate finance, investments, taxation and ratings. Springer Nature Publishing, pp 1–769

Brusov PN, Filatova TV, Kulik VL (2024) Capital Asset Pricing Model (CAPM) 2.0: account of business and financial risk. Finance: Theory Prac 28(2):128–142. https://doi.org/10.26794/2587-5671-2024-28-2-128-142

Brusov PN, Filatova TV (2025a) Business valuation and company value: new qualitative approaches considering business and financial risks. Springer Nature Publishing, pp 1–654

Brusov PN, Filatova TV (2015b) Efficiency of investment projects: modern investment models and their applications. Springer Nature Publishing, pp.1-843

Filatova T, Orehova N, Brusova A (2008) Weighted average cost of capital in the theory of Modigliani–Miller, modified for a finite life–time company. Bull FU 48:68–77

Modigliani F, Miller M (1958) The cost of capital, corporate finance, and the theory of investment. Am Econ Rev 48:261–297

Modigliani F, Miller M (1963) Corporate income taxes and the cost of capital: a correction. Am Econ Rev 53:147–175

Modigliani F, Miller M (1966) Some estimates of the cost of capital to the electric utility industry 1954–1957. Am Econ Rev 56:333–391

Chapter 10
The Generalization of the Brusov–Filatova–Orekhova Theory for the Case of Payments of Tax on Profit with Arbitrary Frequency

10.1 Introduction

The chapter has the following structure:

In Introduction we describe some approaches to the capital structure theory: traditional approach, Modigliani–Miller theory and some of its modifications.

We generalize the Brusov–Filatova–Orekhova (BFO) theory for the case of arbitrary frequency of payments of income tax and get generalized Brusov–Filatova–Orekhova (BFO) formulas for the weighted average cost of capital, WACC, for the equity cost, ke, and for the capitalization of the company, V.

Within the generalized Brusov–Filatova–Orekhova (BFO) theory the dependence of the main financial parameters of the company (the weighted average cost of capital, WACC, equity cost, k_e, company capitalization, V) on leverage level L at different frequency of payments of income tax p is studied.

Obtained results allow come to some very important conclusions and give recommendations how frequently company should pay income tax in order to decrease the cost of attracting capital and to increase its capitalization.

10.1.1 Capital Structure of the Company

This chapter is devoted to one of the most important problem of financial management—problem of capital cost and capital structure of the company. The management by capital structure of the company (the relationship between equity and debt capital of the company) allows to company's management solve the main task—increase the company value. This relates as well with the problem of the optimal capital structure, i.e., with the capital structure, which minimizes the weighted average cost of

P. Brusov and T. Filatova, *Taxes and Taxation*, Contributions to Finance and Accounting, https://doi.org/10.1007/978-3-032-11077-0_10

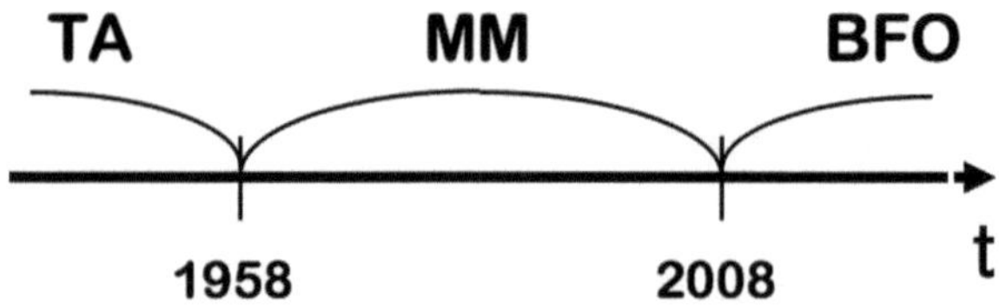

Fig. 10.1 Historical aspects of capital cost and capital structure theory: here empirical traditional approach—TA, Modigliani–Miller theory—MM, Brusov–Filatova–Orekhova theory—BFO

capital, WACC, and maximizes the value of the company, V, which is one of the most important problem in financial management. The first quantitative study of influence of capital structure of the company on its (company) financial indicators was the work by Nobel Prize winners Modigliani and Miller (1958). Before their work, the traditional approach existed, based on empirical data analysis. In 2008 the modern capital cost and capital structure theory—Brusov–Filatova–Orekhova (BFO) theory has been developed (Filatova et al. 2008; Brusov et al. 2021, 2022, 2023, 2024; Brusov and Filatova 2025a, b), which made Modigliani–Miller theory its particular case. Within BFO theory many qualitatively new effects has been discovered, which are absent within Modigliani–Miller theory. Some main existing principles of financial management have been destroyed by BFO theory, among them the world famous trade off theory (Brennan and Schwartz 1978, 1984; Leland 1994), which was considered as keystone of formation of optimal capital structure of the company during many decades. Brusov–Filatova–Orekhova have proven the bankruptcy of trade off theory and have found the cause of this (Chapter 4 in monograph [Brusov et al. 2018]). Below we briefly describe the historical development of the theory of the capital cost and the capital structure.

Figure 10.1 shows the historical development of capital cost and capital structure theory (from the empirical traditional approach, through perpetuity Modigliani–Miller theory to general capital cost and capital structure theory—Brusov–Filatova–Orekhova (BFO) theory (Brusov et al. 2018).

Myers (Myers 2001) in 2001 has considered the one–year company case and show that the weighted average cost of capital, WACC, in this case is higher than in Modigliani–Miller case, and the capitalization of the company, *V*, is less than in Modigliani–Miller case.

So, before 2008 only two results for capital structure of the company were available: Modigliani–Miller for perpetuity company (Modigliani and Miller 1958, 1963; Modigliani and Miller 1966) and Myers (Myers 2001) for one–year company (see Fig. 10.2). Wherein Brusov–Filatova–Orekhova theory has filled out whole interval between $t = 1$ and $t = \infty$. Brusov–Filatova–Orekhova theory allows calculate the company value, *V*, the weighted average cost of capital, *WACC*, the equity cost k_e and other financial parameters for arbitrary age companies and for arbitrary life–time companies. BFO theory has lead to a lot of new meaningful effects in modern capital structure theory, absent in Modigliani–Miller theory (Brusov et al. 2018).

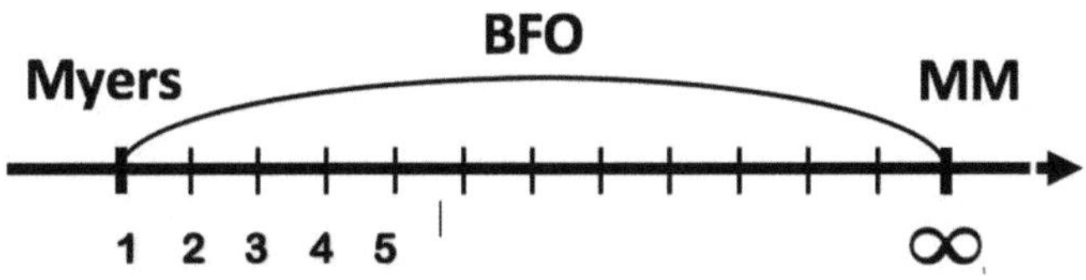

Fig. 10.2 Myers result describes one–year company, Modigliani–Miller theory (MM) corresponds to perpetuity limit, while Brusov–Filatova–Orekhova (BFO) theory fills the whole numeric axis (from n = 1 up to perpetuity limit $n = \infty$)

The main purpose of this chapter is to generalize and further develop the Brusov–Filatova–Orekhova (BFO) theory, taking into account the case of paying income tax with an arbitrary frequency (monthly, quarterly, semi–annual or annual payments), which takes place in real economic practice. Note that both major theories on the cost of capital and capital structure of the Brusov–Filatova–Orekhova (BFO) theory and its perpetuity limit, the Modigliani–Miller theory, take into account annual income tax payments. The latter was recently generalized by us to the case of an arbitrary periodicity in the payment of income tax (Filatova et al. 2022), which showed a significant change in the results of the classical Modigliani–Miller theory. Here we make this generalization for the Brusov–Filatova–Orekhova (BFO) theory.

Below we discuss the traditional approach, the Modigliani–Miller theory and its different modifications, the Brusov–Filatova–Orekhova (BFO) theory.

10.1.2 The Modigliani–Miller Theory

Before the Modigliani–Miller work, the traditional approach existed, based on empirical data analysis. In the traditional approach weighted average cost of capital, WACC, and the company value, V, depend on the capital structure, on the leverage level, L. The cost of debt is lower than cost of equity via the fact that first one has lower risk, because creditor claims are met prior to shareholders claims in the event of bankruptcy. Thus the increase of the share of lower–cost debt capital up to the values which does not cause violation of financial sustainability and growth of risk of bankruptcy leads to lower weighted average cost of capital, WACC. The required by investors profitability, which is equal to the equity cost, is growing; but its growth does not compensate the benefits from use of lower–cost debt capital. Therefore, in the traditional approach the increase of leverage level (at low leverage level) leads to decrease of WACC and to the associated increase of the value of company V. At high leverage level, financial difficulties and the risk of bankruptcy appear. The debt capital cost increases as well as the equity cost (which always increases with leverage level) and these lead to increase of WACC and decrease of company value V. Thus, competition between the advantages of debt financing at a low level of leverage and its disadvantages at a high level of leverage forms the optimal capital structure, when WACC reaches minimum and capital value V reaches maximum. This is the main point of the traditional approach and as well as trade off theory. This empirical approach has existed up to creation of the first quantitative theory by Nobel Prize Winners Modigliani and Miller (1958) (Modigliani and Miller 1958).

Modigliani and Miller (MM) in their first paper (Modigliani and Miller 1958) have come to the conclusions which were fundamentally different from the conclusions of traditional approach. Under assumptions that there are no taxes, no transaction costs, no bankruptcy costs, perfect financial markets exist with symmetry information, equivalence in borrowing costs for both companies and investors, etc., they have showed that choosing of the ratio between the debt and equity capital does not affect company value V, as well as weighted average cost of capital, WACC.

Modigliani and Miller analyzing the influence of financial leverage on V and V_0, weighted average cost of capital, WACC and k_e, get the following results: (here, EBIT–earnings before interest and taxes, k_0 is discount rate, V and V_0 are the values of levered and unlevered companies, ke is the equity cost)

$$V = V_0 = \frac{EBIT}{k_0} \tag{10.1}$$

This leads to the following expressions for weighted average cost of capital, WACC:

$$WACC = k_0. \tag{10.2}$$

Note, that k_0 here and below is the equity cost for financially independent company. For financially dependent company k_0 is the equity cost at zero leverage level (L = 0).

From (10.1), and formula for WACC definition

$$WACC = k_0 = k_e w_e + k_d w_d \tag{10.3}$$

it is easy to derive an expression for the equity capital cost.

Finding k_e, one gets

$$\begin{aligned} k_e &= \frac{k_0}{w_e} - k_d\frac{w_d}{w_e} = \frac{k_0(S+D)}{S} - k_d\frac{D}{S} \\ &= k_0 + (k_0 - k_d)\frac{D}{S} = k_0 + (k_0 - k_d)L \end{aligned} \tag{10.4}$$

Here,

D	value of debt capital of the company
S	value of equity capital of the company
$k_d, w_d = \frac{D}{D+S}$	cost and fraction of debt capital of the company.
$k_e, w_e = \frac{S}{D+S}$	cost and fraction of equity capital of the company.
$L = D/S$	financial leverage

WACC weighted average cost of capital

Thus, we have the following formula for equity cost

$$k_e = k_0 + L(k_0 - k_d) \tag{10.5}$$

Formula (10.5) shows that equity cost of the company increases linearly with leverage level.

In 1963 Modigliani and Miller (Modigliani and Miller 1963) have accounted the tax on profit and get the following formula for the cost of financially dependent company, V,

$$V = V_0 + DT, \tag{10.6}$$

where V_0 is the value of financially independent company, D is debt value and T is the tax on profit.

Below we get the expression for WACC and the equity capital cost ke of the company under the existence of corporate taxes.

Weighted Average Cost of Capital, WACC

Substituting into (10.6) $D = w_d V$, one gets

$$V(1 - w_d T) = V_0. \tag{10.7}$$

Putting $V = \frac{CF}{WACC}$; $V_0 = \frac{CF}{k_0}$ into formula (10.7), we get

$$\frac{CF}{WACC}(1 - w_d T) = \frac{CF}{k_0}. \tag{10.8}$$

Here CF is the income of the company for one period.

And from (10.8) we arrive to the expression for weighted average cost of capital, WACC

$$WACC = k_0 \cdot (1 - w_d t) \tag{10.9}$$

This formula for WACC is one of the main result of Modigliani–Miller theory with taxes.

The Equity Cost

Let us derive formula for equity cost.

On definition of the weighted average cost of capital WACC in the presence of corporate taxes, we have

$$\mathrm{WACC} = k_0 w_e + k_d w_d (1 - T). \tag{10.10}$$

Equating Eqs. (10.9) and (10.10), one gets

$$k_0(1 - w_d T) = k_0 w_e + k_d w_d (1 - T) \tag{10.11}$$

and from here, for equity cost, ke we get the following expression (Modigliani and Miller 1963):

$$\begin{aligned} k_e &= k_0 \frac{(1 - w_d T)}{w_e} - k_d \frac{w_d}{w_e}(1 - T) = k_0 \frac{1}{w_e} - k_0 \frac{w_d}{w_e} T - k_d \frac{D}{S}(1 - T) \\ &= k_0 \frac{D + S}{S} - k_0 \frac{D}{S} T - k_d \frac{D}{S}(1 - T) = k_0 + L(1 - T)(k_0 - k_d). \end{aligned} \tag{10.12}$$

The formula (10.12) is different from the formula (10.5) without tax only by the multiplier $(1 - T)$ in term, indicating a premium for risk. As the multiplier is less than unit, the corporate income tax leads to decrease of the slope of the curve $k_e(L)$ with respect to L–axis.

From formulas (10.5), (10.9) and (10.12) we get the following conclusions (see Fig. 10.3).

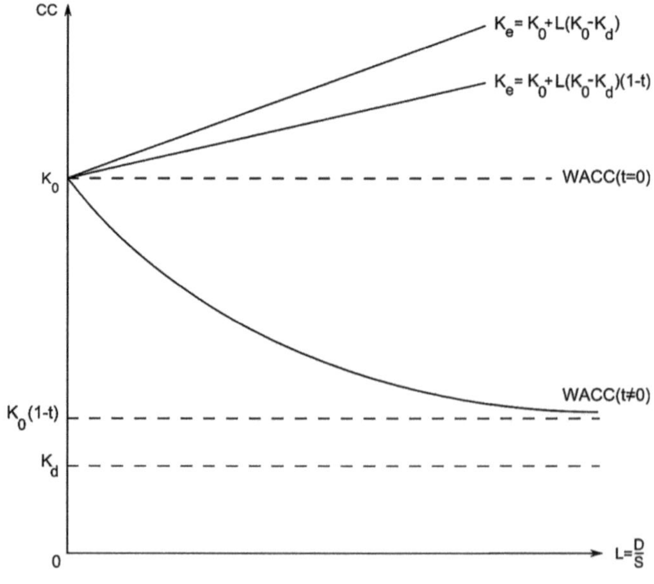

Fig. 10.3 Impact of leverage level on equity capital cost ke, and WACC within the Modigliani–Miller theory without taxes ($t = 0$) and with taxes ($t \neq 0$)

When leverage level grows:

1. Value of company, V, increases;
2. Weighted average cost of capital, WACC decreases from k_0 up to $k_0(1 - T)$ (at $L = \infty$);
3. Equity cost increases linearly from k_0 up to infinity.

10.2 Some Modifications of Modigliani–Miller Theory

10.2.1 Hamada Model: Accounting Market Risk

The Modigliani–Miller theory were united with Capital Asset Pricing Model (CAPM) in 1969 (Hamada 1969) by R. Hamada, who has derived the following formula for the leveraged company equity cost, accounting both financial and business risk of company:

$$k_e = k_F + (k_M - k_F)b_U + (k_M - k_F)b_U\frac{D}{S}(1 - T), \tag{10.13}$$

where b_U is the β–coefficient of the same group of business risk company, that the considering company, but with L = 0. The formula (10.13) represents the desired equity capital *ke* profitability as a sum of three components: risk–free profitability k_F, compensating to shareholders a temporary value of their money, premium for business risk $(k_M - k_F)b_U$, and premium for financial risk $(k_M - k_F)b_U\frac{D}{S}(1 - T)$. If the company does not have debt financing, the financial risk factor will be equal to zero (the third term is drawn to zero), and only the premium for business risk will be received by shareholders.

10.2.2 The Account of Corporate and Individual Taxes (Miller Model)

In 1963 Modigliani and Miller (Modigliani and Miller 1963) have accounted the taxation of corporate income, but the individual taxes of investors were not take into account.

The account of the corporate and individual taxes has been done by Merton Miller in 1977 (Miller 1977), who study the influence of debt financing on the company capitalization. In Miller model, the following definitions have been used: TC–the tax on corporate income rate, TS–the tax rate on income of an individual investor from his ownership by corporation stock, TD–tax rate on interest income from the provision of investor–individuals of credits to other investors and companies. Because the income from shares partly comes in the form of a dividend and, in part, as capital profits, so TS is a weighted average value of the rates of tax on capital profits on shares and on dividends, while the profit from the provision of loans usually comes in the form of the interests. The former are usually taxed at a higher rate. For the capitalization of the financially independent company one has:

$$V_{\mathrm{U}} = \frac{\mathrm{EBIT}(1 - T_{\mathrm{C}})(1 - T_{\mathrm{S}})}{k_0}. \tag{10.14}$$

A term $(1 - T_{\mathrm{S}})$ allows to take into account the individual taxes in the formula. In this way, numerator indicates which part of the operating company's profit remains in the possession of the investors, after the company will pay taxes on their profits, and its shareholders then will pay individual taxes on income from stock ownership. Since individual taxes reduce profits, remaining in the disposal of investors, the last, at other things being equal circumstances, also reduce and an overall assessment of the financially independent company value.

10.2.3 More General Case for WACC Formula

In (Farber et al. 2006; Fernandez 2006; Berk and DeMarzo 2007; Harris et al. 1985) more general than Modigliani–Miller (MM) formula for the WACC has been derived: it is described by the following formula (Farber et al. 2006)

$$WACC = k_0(1 - w_d T) - k_d t w_d + k_{TS} t w_d. \tag{10.15}$$

Here $\mathrm{k_0}$, $\mathrm{k_d}$ and $\mathrm{k_{TS}}$ are the expected returns respectively on the financially independent company, the debt and the tax shield, V is the capitalization of the financially dependent company, VTS is the tax shield value, D is the debt value and TC is the rate of corporate tax.

Formula (10.15) is derived from the WACC definition and the balance identity (see as well Berk and De Marzo 2007). Although Eq. (10.15) is general enough, some additional conditions are required its practical applicability. If the WACC is constant over time, as it stated in Farber et al. (2006) the levered company value can be found by discounting with the WACC for the unlevered free cash–flows. The resulting formulas, which describe the special cases, where the WACC is constant, can be found in textbooks (Berk and DeMarzo 2007; Harris et al. 1985).

First, Modigliani and Miller in 1963 (Modigliani and Miller 1963) assume that the level of debt D is constant. Then, as the expected after–tax cash–flow of the unlevered firm is fixed, $\mathrm{V_0}$ is also constant. By assumption, $\mathrm{k_{TS}} = \mathrm{k_D}$ and the value of the tax shield is TS = tD. Therefore, the company value V is a constant and the general WACC formula (10.15) simplifies to a constant WACC:

$$WACC = k_0(1 - w_d T)$$

We think that "classical" Modigliani–Miller (MM) theory, which suggests that the expected returns on the debt k_d and the tax shield k_{TS} are equals (because both of them have debt nature), is much more reasonable and namely the "classical" Modigliani–Miller (MM) theory, which is still widely used in practice, has been modified by us in Filatova et al. (2022).

10.2.4 Fiscal Pressure, Financial Liquidity, Financial Solvency and Financial Leverage

The problem of fiscal pressure is more current than ever in most countries. The article by Batrancea (Batrancea 2021a) was the first empirical study of the impact of fiscal pressure on the financial equilibrium of energy companies listed on the New York Stock Exchange. Empirical results obtained by econometric models showed that fiscal pressure had a stronger impact on the short–term and long–term equilibrium of electricity and oil companies than on the equilibrium of gas companies. The research could be useful for the managers of energy companies interested in estimating the evolution of company equilibrium state when considering different possible financial crises.

How financial liquidity and financial solvency influenced the performance of healthcare companies that are publicly traded on the New York Stock Exchange has been studied by Batrancea (Batrancea 2021b), who used econometric models with two–stage least squares (2SLS) panel and panel generalized method of moments (GMM). Empirical evidence showed that the financial indicators current liquidity ratio, quick liquidity ratio, and financial leverage significantly influenced company performance measured by return on assets, gross margin ratio, operating margin ratio, earnings before interest, tax, depreciation, and amortization. Strategies intended to improve business performance based on liquidity and solvency insights were also addressed.

10.2.5 Brusov–Filatova–Orekhova (BFO) Theory

The suggestion about perpetuity of the companies and of all financial flows is the most serious limitations of the Modigliani–Miller theory. This limitation have been lifted up in 2008 by Brusov, Filatova and Orekhova (Brennan and Schwartz 1984), who have created the modern theory of capital cost and capital structure, generalizing the Modigliani–Miller theory for the companies of arbitrary age (arbitrary life–time). They have shown that in this case all Modigliani–Miller results (Modigliani and Miller 1958; Filatova et al. 2008; Brennan and Schwartz 1978) significant changes: in the presence of corporative taxes capitalization of the company V is changed, as well as the equity cost, ke, and the weighted average cost of capital, WACC.

A number of qualitatively new effects in corporate finance, obtained in Brusov–Filatova–Orekhova theory (Brennan and Schwartz 1984), are absent in Modigliani–Miller theory (Modigliani and Miller 1958, 1963, 1966).

The Brusov–Filatova–Orekhova formula for weighted average cost of capital, WACC for the company of arbitrary age n, takes the following form (Brennan and Schwartz 1984)

$$\frac{1-(1+WACC)^{-n}}{WACC}=\frac{1-(1+k_0)^{-n}}{k_0\left[1-w_dT\left(1-(1+k_d)^{-n}\right)\right]}. \tag{10.16}$$

Here, S—the equity capital of the company value, $w_d = \frac{D}{D+S}$—the share of debt capital; $k_e, w_e = \frac{S}{D+S}$—the cost and the share of the equity capital of the company, $L = D/S$—leverage level.

Substituting in (10.14) $n \to \infty$, we easy arrive to the perpetuity (Modigliani–Miller) limit formula for weighted average cost of capital, WACC.

$$WACC = k_0(1 - w_dT). \tag{10.17}$$

Results of BFO theory are well known in the world literature (for example, see references [Dimitropoulos 2014; Kennedy et al. 2015; Barbi 2011; Pavel 2018; Franc-Dąbrowska et al. 2021; Angotti et al. 2018; Vergara–Novoa et al. 2018]). Some chapters (Vergara–Novoa et al. 2018) use the BFO theory in practical calculations.

The similarities and differences between BFO and MM results are shown in Table 10.1.

10.2.6 Trade–off Theory

As we mentioned above, the main theory of optimal capital structure of the company during many decades was the world famous trade–off theory (Brennan and Schwartz 1978, 1984; Leland 1994), which is still used now for decision on capital structure making. But, in 2013 Brusov et al. (Brusov et al. 2018) have proven the trade–off theory's bankruptcy. In opposite to waiting result, it was shown that suggestion of risky debt financing which causes the growing of the credit rate near the bankruptcy, does not lead to the growing of weighted average cost of capital, WACC, which still decreases with leverage level. Thus, the the minimum in the dependence of WACC on leverage level is absent as well. This means, that the world famous trade–off theory lacks an optimal capital structure. Brusov et al. in 2013 (Brusov et al. 2018) have given the explanation of this fact by analyzing the equity capital cost dependence on the leverage level on the risky debt capital assumption.

Table 10.1 The similarities and differences between BFO and MM results

	BFO	MM
Time parameter, n	Arbitrary age of companies, arbitrary life–time of companies	Perpetuity companies, perpetuity financial flows; $n = \infty$
Company age and life–time	Are different	Are the same and equal infinity
Dependence of all main financial indicators: WACC, V, ke on time parameter, n	Allow study this dependences	Time parameter, n is absent
All main financial indicators: WACC, V, ke depend on debt cost kd	Yes	None
WACC	Correct estimation; decreases with leverage level L	Underestimation; decreases with leverage level L
V	Correct estimation; increases with leverage level L	Overestimation; increases with leverage level L
Equity cost ke	Increases linearly with leverage level L	Increases linearly with leverage level L
Equity cost ke: the slope of the curve ke(L)	Less than in MM theory	Bigger than in BFO theory
ke: the slope of the curve ke (L)	**Could be negative at T > T* (qualitatively new effect)**	Always is positive **new effect is absent**
Golden and silver age effects (Brusov et al. 2018)	Exist	Absent

10.3 Modification of the Brusov–Filatova–Orekhova (BFO) Theory for Companies with Frequent Payments of Tax on Income

Below we use the following definitions:

D	value of debt capital of the company
S	value of equity capital of the company
$k_d, w_d = \frac{D}{D+S}$	cost and fraction of debt capital of the company
$k_e, w_e = \frac{S}{D+S}$	cost and fraction of equity capital of the company
$L = D/S$	financial leverage
WACC	weighted average cost of capital

k_0 is the equity cost for financially independent company;
p is the number of payments of tax on profit per year;
T is tax on profit.

10.3.1 Calculation of the Tax Shield

We start from the calculation of the tax shield within Brusov–Filatova–Orekhova theory for the case of p payments of tax on profit per year (payments are made at the end of periods). The tax shield, *TS*, for period of n–years is equal to sum of discounted values of benefits from the use of tax incentives

$$(TS)_n = \frac{k_d Dt}{p(1+k_d)^{1/p}} + \frac{k_d Dt}{p(1+k_d)^{2/p}} + \ldots. + \frac{k_d Dt}{p(1+k_d)^{np/p}} \tag{10.18}$$

We have a geometric progression with denominator $q = \frac{1}{(1+k_d)^{1/p}}$.

After summing the progression, one obtains:

$$(TS)_n = \frac{k_d Dt\left(1-(1+k_d)^{-n}\right)}{p(1+k_d)^{1/p}\left(1-(1+k_d)^{-1/p}\right)} = \frac{k_d Dt\left(1-(1+k_d)^{-n}\right)}{p\left((1+k_d)^{1/p}-1\right)} \tag{10.19}$$

In classical Brusov–Filatova–Orekhova theory (at $p = 1$):

$$(TS)_n = Dt\left(1-(1+k_d)^{-n}\right) \tag{10.20}$$

It is easy to obtain this result from (10.19), putting the frequency of payments of tax on profit $p = 1$.

10.3.2 Derivation of the Modified BFO Formula for Weighted Average Cost of Capital (WACC)

We derive now the modified formula BFO for weighted average cost of capital (WACC) for the case of p payments of tax on profit per year (payments at the end of periods).

One has for the financially dependent company value V:

$$V = V_0 + (TS)_n \tag{10.21}$$

Here V_0 is the value of a financially independent company. Putting expression (10.19) for TS, one has:

$$V = V_0 + \frac{k_d Dt\left(1-(1+k_d)^{-n}\right)}{p\left((1+k_d)^{1/p}-1\right)} \tag{10.22}$$

After substituting $D = w_d V$, we get:

$$V\left(1-\frac{k_d w_d t\left(1-(1+k_d)^{-n}\right)}{p\left((1+k_d)^{1/p}-1\right)}\right)=V_0 \tag{10.23}$$

Accounting, that the values of financially dependent company, V, and financially independent company, V_0, are respectively equal to

$$V=\frac{CF\left(1-(1+WACC)^{-n}\right)}{WACC};\ V_0=\frac{CF\left(1-(1+k_0)^{-n}\right)}{k_0} \tag{10.24}$$

one gets:

$$\frac{CF\left(1-(1+WACC)^{-n}\right)}{WACC}\cdot\left(1-\frac{k_d w_d t\left(1-(1+k_d)^{-n}\right)}{p\left((1+k_d)^{1/p}-1\right)}\right) \tag{10.25}$$

From here we derive now the modified formula BFO for weighted average cost of capital (WACC) for company of age n years for the case of p payments of tax on profit per year (payments at the end of periods)

$$\frac{1-(1+WACC)^{-n}}{WACC}=\frac{CF\left(1-(1+k_0)^{-n}\right)}{k_0\left(1-\frac{k_d w_d t\left(1-(1+k_d)^{-n}\right)}{p\left((1+k_d)^{1/p}-1\right)}\right)} \tag{10.26}$$

At $p=1$ we get **classical** BFO formula

$$\frac{1-(1+WACC)^{-n}}{WACC}=\frac{1-(1+k_0)^{-n}}{k_0\cdot\left(1-w_d t\left[1-(1+k_d)^{-n}\right]\right)} \tag{10.27}$$

10.3.3 Formulas for Capital Value, V, and Equity Cost, Ke

Below in Sect. 10.3 we will investigate the dependence of the weighted average cost of capital, WACC, capital value, V, equity cost, ke, on leverage level L at different frequency of payment of tax on profit p for three–year and six–year companies, using Microsoft Excel. For WACC we will use formula (10.10) and for capital value, V, and equity cost, ke, we will use formulas (10.28) and (10.29) respectively (see below).

Company of age n capitalization could be calculated by the following formula

$$V=\frac{CF\cdot\left(1-(1+WACC)^{-n}\right)}{WACC}. \tag{10.28}$$

k_e should be found from the equation

$$WACC = k_e w_e + k_d w_d (1 - t)$$

$$k_e = \frac{WACC}{w_e} - \frac{k_d (1 - t) w_d}{w_e} = WACC(1 + L) - L k_d (1 - t) \qquad (10.29)$$

where one should substitute WACC from the formula (10.26).

10.4 Results

In this section we study the dependence of the weighted average cost of capital, WACC, capital value, V, equity cost, ke, on leverage level L at different frequency of payment of tax on profit p for three–year and six–year companies, using Microsoft Excel. As we mentioned above, for WACC we use formula (10.10) and for capital value, V, and equity cost, ke, we use formulas (10.11) and (10.13) respectively.

We use the following parameters: $k_0 = 0.2$; $k_d = 0.18$; $t = 0.2$; $n = 3; 6$; $CF = 100$.

10.4.1 Dependence of the Weighted Average Cost of Capital, WACC, Capital Value, V, Equity Cost, Ke, on Leverage Level L at Different Frequency of Payment of Tax on Profit P *for Three–year Company*

Dependence of the Weighted Average Cost of Capital, WACC, on Leverage Level L at Different Frequency of Payment of Tax on Profit P for Three–Year Company

Dependence of the weighted average cost of capital, WACC, on leverage level L at different frequency of payments of tax on profit p **for three–year company** is shown in Table 10.2 and at Fig. 10.4.

The weighted average cost of capital, WACC, decreases with leverage level L at any frequency of payments of tax on profit p. The difference between the WACC(L) curves is maximum when moving from annual ($p = 1$) to semi–annual ($p = 2$) income tax payments and decreases when moving from semi–annual ($p = 2$) to quarterly ($p = 4$) payments and from quarterly ($p = 4$) to monthly ($p = 12$) payments.

Table 10.2 Dependence of the weighted average cost of capital, WACC, on leverage level L at different frequency of payments of tax on profit p for three–year company

L	Wd	WACC				
		$p = 1$	$p = 2$	$p = 4$	$p = 6$	$p = 12$
1	0.5	0.1749	0.1738	0.1732	0.1730	0.1728
2	0.666667	0.1664	0.1650	0.1642	0.1640	0.1637
3	0.75	0.1622	0.1605	0.1597	0.1594	0.1591
4	0.8	0.1596	0.1579	0.1570	0.1567	0.1564
5	0.833333	0.1579	0.1561	0.1552	0.1549	0.1545
6	0.857143	0.1567	0.1548	0.1539	0.1536	0.1532
7	0.875	0.1558	0.1539	0.1529	0.1526	0.1522
8	0.888889	0.1551	0.1532	0.1522	0.1518	0.1515
9	0.9	0.1545	0.1526	0.1515	0.1512	0.1509
10	0.909091	0.1541	0.1521	0.1511	0.1507	0.1504

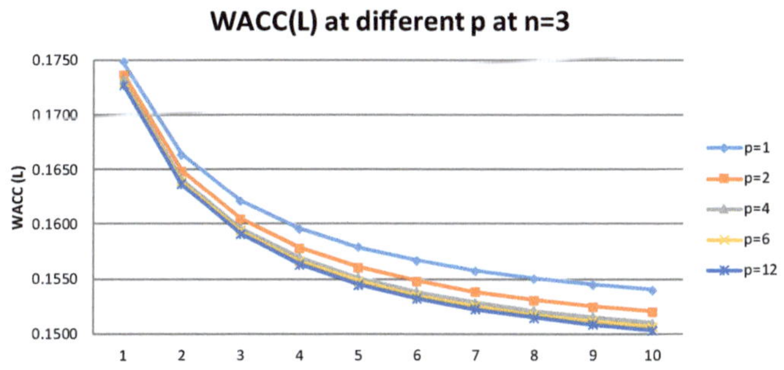

Fig. 10.4 Dependence of the weighted average cost of capital, WACC, on leverage level L at different frequency of payments of tax on profit p for three–year company

Dependence of the Company Value, on Leverage Level L at Different Frequency of Payment of Tax on Profit P for Three–Year Company

Dependence of the company value, V, on leverage level L at different frequency of payments of tax on profit p for three–year company is shown in Table 10.3 and at Fig. 10.5.

The value of company V increases with the frequency p. The largest increase occurs when moving from annual ($p = 1$) to semi–annual ($p = 2$) income tax payments and decreases when moving from semi–annual ($p = 2$) to quarterly ($p = 4$) payments and from quarterly ($p = 4$) to monthly ($p = 12$) payments.

Table 10.3 Dependence of the company value, V, on leverage level L at different frequency of payments of tax on profit p for three–year company

L	w_d	V				
		$p = 1$	$p = 2$	$p = 4$	$p = 6$	$p = 12$
1	0.5	219.2281	219.6139	219.8116	219.8781	219.9451
2	0.666667	222.2455	222.7746	223.0459	223.1373	223.2292
3	0.75	223.7856	224.3893	224.6989	224.8033	224.9082
4	0.8	224.7199	225.3694	225.7025	225.8149	225.9278
5	0.833333	225.3471	226.0275	226.3766	226.4944	226.6127
6	0.857143	225.7973	226.5000	226.8606	226.9822	227.1045
7	0.875	226.1361	226.8557	227.2250	227.3495	227.4747
8	0.888889	226.4003	227.1331	227.5091	227.6360	227.7635
9	0.9	226.6122	227.3555	227.7370	227.8657	227.9951
10	0.909091	226.7858	227.5378	227.9238	228.0540	228.1849

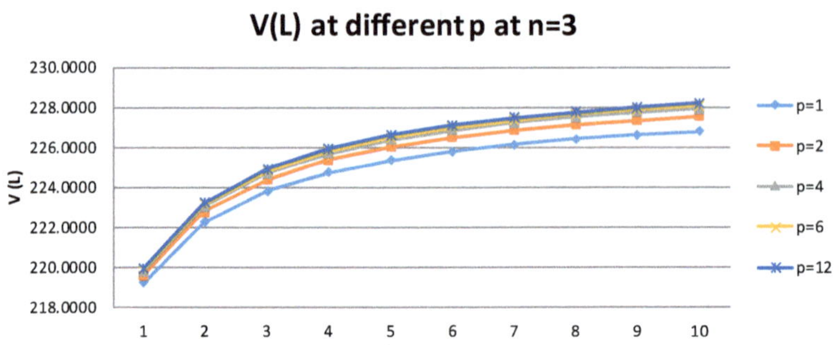

Fig. 10.5 Dependence of the company value, V, on leverage level L at different frequency of payments of tax on profit p for three–year company

Dependence of the Equity Cost, Ke, on Leverage Level L at Different Frequency of Payment of Tax on Profit P for Three–Year Company

Dependence of the equity cost, ke, on leverage level L at different frequency of payments of tax on profit p for three–year company is shown in Table 10.4 and at Fig. 10.6.

The cost of equity ke increases linearly with the level of leverage L. The slope of the curve ke(L) depends on the frequency of paying income tax: it decreases with increasing p, most rapidly when moving from annual ($p = 1$) to semi–annual ($p = 2$) payments of income tax and slower in the transition from semi–annual ($p = 2$) to quarterly ($p = 4$) payments and from quarterly ($p = 4$) to monthly ($p = 12$) payments.

Table 10.4 Dependence of the equity cost, ke, on leverage level L at different frequency of payments of tax on profit *p* for three–year company

L	w_d	ke				
		$p=1$	$p=2$	$p=4$	$p=6$	$p=12$
1	0.5	0.2057	0.2036	0.2024	0.2021	0.2017
2	0.666667	0.2113	0.2069	0.2046	0.2039	0.2031
3	0.75	0.2168	0.2102	0.2068	0.2057	0.2045
4	0.8	0.2222	0.2134	0.2089	0.2074	0.2059
5	0.833333	0.2277	0.2167	0.2111	0.2092	0.2073
6	0.857143	0.2331	0.2199	0.2132	0.2109	0.2086
7	0.875	0.2386	0.2232	0.2153	0.2126	0.2100
8	0.888889	0.2440	0.2264	0.2174	0.2144	0.2113
9	0.9	0.2495	0.2296	0.2195	0.2161	0.2127
10	0.909091	0.2549	0.2329	0.2216	0.2178	0.2140

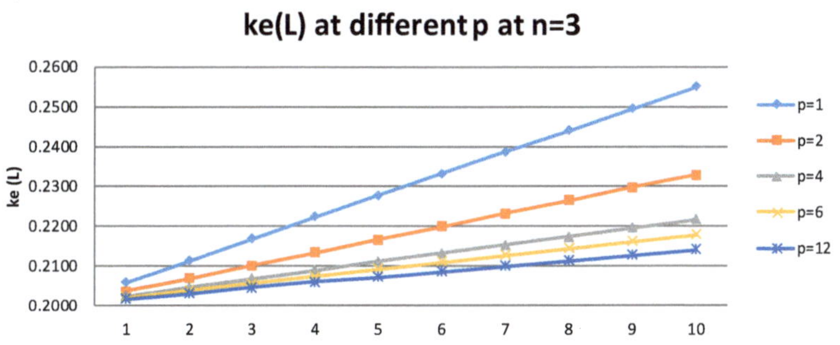

Fig. 10.6 Dependence of the equity cost, ke, on leverage level L at different frequency of payments of tax on profit *p* for three–year company

10.4.2 Dependence of the Weighted Average Cost of Capital, WACC, Capital Value, V, Equity Cost, Ke, on Leverage Level L at Different Frequency of Payment of Tax on Profit P *for Six–year Company*

Dependence of the Weighted Average Cost of Capital, WACC, on Leverage Level L at Different Frequency of Payment of Tax on Profit P for Six–Year Company

Dependence of the weighted average cost of capital, WACC, on leverage level L at different frequency of payments of tax on profit *p* for six–year company is shown in Table 10.5 and at Fig. 10.7.

We use the following parameters: $k_0 = 0.2$; $k_d = 0.18$; $t = 0.2$; $n = 6$;

Table 10.5 Dependence of the weighted average cost of capital, WACC, on leverage level L at different frequency of payments of tax on profit p for six–year company

L	w_d	WACC				
		$p = 1$	$p = 2$	$p = 4$	$p = 6$	$p = 12$
1	0.5	0.1743	0.1732	0.1726	0.1725	0.1723
2	0.666667	0.1657	0.1641	0.1634	0.1631	0.1629
3	0.75	0.1613	0.1596	0.1587	0.1584	0.1581
4	0.8	0.1586	0.1568	0.1559	0.1556	0.1553
5	0.833333	0.1569	0.1550	0.1540	0.1537	0.1534
6	0.857143	0.1556	0.1537	0.1527	0.1523	0.1520
7	0.875	0.1547	0.1527	0.1517	0.1513	0.1510
8	0.888889	0.1539	0.1519	0.1509	0.1505	0.1502
9	0.9	0.1534	0.1513	0.1502	0.1499	0.1495
10	0.909091	0.1529	0.1508	0.1497	0.1494	0.1490

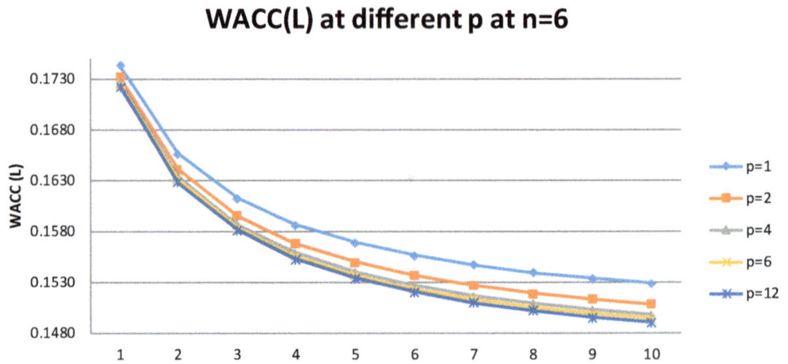

Fig. 10.7 Dependence of the weighted average cost of capital, WACC, on leverage level L at different frequency of payments of tax on profit p for six–year company

The weighted average cost of capital, WACC, decreases with leverage level L at any frequency of payments of tax on profit p. The difference between the WACC(L) curves is maximum when moving from annual ($p = 1$) to semi–annual ($p = 2$) income tax payments and decreases when moving from semi–annual ($p = 2$) to quarterly ($p = 4$) payments and from quarterly ($p = 4$) to monthly ($p = 12$) payments.

Dependence of the Company Value, V, on Leverage Level L at Different Frequency of Payment of Tax on Profit P for Six–year Company

Dependence of the company value, V, on leverage level L at different frequency of payments of tax on profit *p* for six–year company is shown in Table 10.6 and at Fig. 10.8.

The value of company V increases with the frequency *p*. The largest increase occurs when moving from annual ($p = 1$) to semi–annual ($p = 2$) income tax payments and decreases when moving from semi–annual ($p = 2$) to quarterly ($p = 4$) payments and from quarterly ($p = 4$) to monthly ($p = 12$) payments.

Table 10.6 Dependence of the company value, V, on leverage level L at different frequency of payments of tax on profit *p* for six–year company

L	w_d	V				
		$p = 1$	$p = 2$	$p = 4$	$p = 6$	$p = 12$
1	0.5	354.8940	355.9256	356.4549	356.6333	356.8127
2	0.666667	363.0242	364.4649	365.2052	365.4550	365.7063
3	0.75	367.2305	368.8900	369.7435	370.0315	370.3214
4	0.8	369.8015	371.5971	372.5210	372.8329	373.1468
5	0.833333	371.5355	373.4240	374.3960	374.7242	375.0545
6	0.857143	372.7841	374.7399	375.7468	376.0869	376.4291
7	0.875	373.7261	375.7330	376.7664	377.1154	377.4667
8	0.888889	374.4620	376.5090	377.5632	377.9193	378.2776
9	0.9	375.0529	377.1322	378.2031	378.5648	378.9289
10	0.909091	375.5377	377.6435	378.7283	379.0947	379.4635

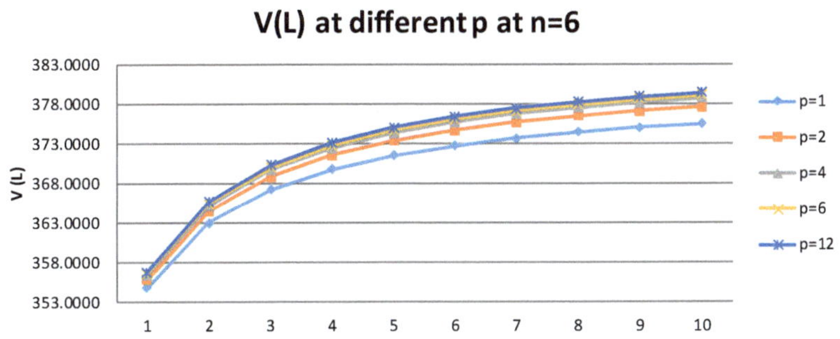

Fig. 10.8 Dependence of the company value, V, on leverage level L at different frequency of payments of tax on profit *p* for six–year company

Dependence of the Equity Cost, Ke, on Leverage Level L at Different Frequency of Payment of Tax on Profit P for Six-Year Company

Dependence of the equity cost, ke, on leverage level L at different frequency of payments of tax on profit *p* for six–year company is shown in Table 10.7 and at Fig. 10.9.

The cost of equity ke increases linearly with the level of leverage L. The slope of the curve ke(L) depends on the frequency of paying income tax: it decreases with increasing *p*, most rapidly when moving from annual ($p = 1$) to semi–annual ($p = 2$) payments of income tax and slower in the transition from semi–annual ($p = 2$) to quarterly ($p = 4$) payments and from quarterly ($p = 4$) to monthly ($p = 12$) payments.

One can see, that for a six–year–old company with monthly income tax payments **a qualitatively new anomalous effect takes place**: ke(L) decreases with an increase

Table 10.7 Dependence of the equity cost, ke, on leverage level L at different frequency of payments of tax on profit *p* for six–year company

L	w_d	ke				
		$p = 1$	$p = 2$	$p = 4$	$p = 6$	$p = 12$
1	0.5	0.2047	0.2024	0.2013	0.2009	0.2005
2	0.666667	0.2090	0.2044	0.2021	0.2013	0.2006
3	0.75	0.2131	0.2063	0.2028	0.2016	0.2005
4	0.8	0.2172	0.2081	0.2035	0.2019	0.2003
5	0.833333	0.2213	0.2099	0.2041	0.2021	0.2001
6	0.857143	0.2254	0.2117	0.2047	0.2023	0.1999
7	0.875	0.2294	0.2134	0.2052	0.2025	0.1997
8	0.888889	0.2335	0.2152	0.2058	0.2027	0.1995
9	0.9	0.2376	0.2169	0.2064	0.2029	0.1993
10	0.909091	0.2416	0.2187	0.2070	0.2030	0.1991

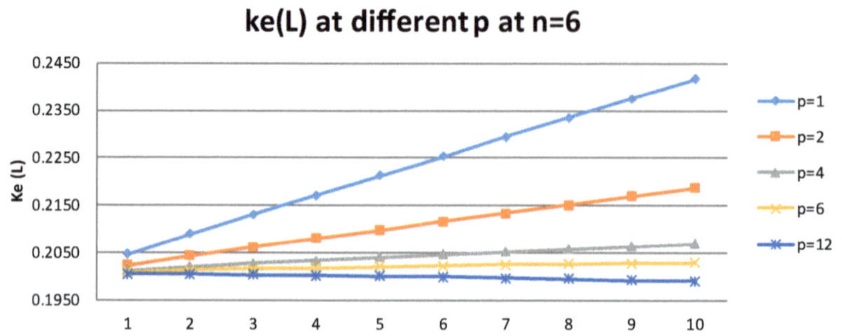

Fig. 10.9 Dependence of the equity cost, ke, on leverage level L at different frequency of payments of tax on profit *p* for six–year company

in the level of leverage L. This radically changes the company's dividend policy, since the economically justified amount of the dividends is equal to the cost of equity.

10.5 The Discussion and Conclusions

The main purpose of the chapter is bring the Brusov–Filatova–Orekhova (BFO) theory closer to economic practice, taking into account one of the features of the real functioning of companies—the frequent payments of tax on profit. We generalize for the first time the Brusov–Filatova–Orekhova (BFO) theory for the case of tax on profit payments with an arbitrary frequency. We derive modified BFO formulas and show that: (1) all BFO formulas change; (2) all main financial parameters of the company, such as company value, V, the weighted average cost of capital, WACC, and equity cost, ke, depend on the frequency of tax on profit payments. It turns out that the increase of the number of payments of tax of profit per year leads to decrease of the cost of attracting capital and increase of the company value. More frequent payments of income tax are beneficial for both parties—for the company and for the tax regulator: for the company, this leads to an increase in the value of the company, and for the tax regulator, earlier payments are beneficial due to the time value of money.

We numerically studied the dependence of the weighted average cost of capital WACC, value of company, V, cost of equity k_e on the level of leverage L at different frequency of income tax payments p for three– and six–year companies and obtained the following results. The calculation of financial indicators are made for some typical parameters of enterprises (equity and debt costs etc.).

The weighted average cost of capital, WACC, decreases with leverage level L at any frequency of payments of tax on profit p. The difference between the WACC(L) curves is maximum when moving from annual ($p = 1$) to semi–annual ($p = 2$) income tax payments and decreases when moving from semi–annual ($p = 2$) to quarterly ($p = 4$) payments and from quarterly ($p = 4$) to monthly ($p = 12$) payments.

The value of company V increases with the frequency p. The largest increase occurs when moving from annual ($p = 1$) to semi–annual ($p = 2$) income tax payments and decreases when moving from semi–annual ($p = 2$) to quarterly ($p = 4$) payments and from quarterly ($p = 4$) to monthly ($p = 12$) payments.

The cost of equity ke increases linearly with the level of leverage L. The slope of the curve ke(L) depends on the frequency of paying income tax: it decreases with increasing p, most rapidly when moving from annual ($p = 1$) to semi–annual ($p = 2$) payments of income tax and slower in the transition from semi–annual ($p = 2$) to quarterly ($p = 4$) payments and from quarterly ($p = 4$) to monthly ($p = 12$) payments.

At a certain age of the company, **a qualitatively new anomalous effect** takes place: ke(L) decreases with an increase in the level of leverage L. We obtain this result for a six–year–old company with monthly income tax payments, but it is clear that this effect should take place for the companies of different age and at different frequency of income tax payment. This radically changes the company's dividend

Table 10.8 Comparison of the impact of the frequency of income tax payments in BFO theory and in MM theory

	BFO	MM
Theorems, statements and formulas	Change	Change
All main financial indicators: WACC, V, ke	Depend on the frequency of tax on profit payments *p*	Depend on the frequency of tax on profit payments *p*
All main financial indicators: WACC, V, ke	Value of the effect of p on all indicators is higher, than in MM	Value of the effect of *p* on all indicators is smaller, than in BFO
All main financial indicators: WACC, V, ke depend on debt cost kd	At all *p*	At $p \neq 1$ only
WACC	Decreases with *p*	Decreases with *p*
V	Increases with *p*	Increases with *p*
ke: the slope of the curve ke(L)	Decreases with increasing *p*	Decreases with increasing *p*
ke: the slope of the curve ke(L)	**Could be negative (qualitatively new effect)**	Always is positive

policy, since the economically justified amount of the dividends is equal to the cost of equity.

Note, that this result remind discovery, made by us earlier (Chapter 8 in monograph [Brusov et al. 2018]): the abnormal dependence of equity cost, k_e, on leverage level L: above some value of tax on income, T^*, equity cost ke decreases with the leverage level L.

Thus, it is interesting to note, that **increase of frequency of income tax payments** ***p*** **and increase of tax on profit** ***T*** **lead to the similar abnormal effect: decrease of equity cost** $\mathbf{k_e}$ **with leverage level L.** If in the first case there are threshold values for the frequency of paying income tax, p^*, and the age of the company, n*, then in the second case there is a threshold value for income tax T^*.

In Table 10.8 we compare the impact of the frequency of income tax payments in BFO theory and in MM theory.

Recommendations

From the analysis of the results of current chapter the following recommendations could be done:

For company: company should pay tax on profit as frequently as it is possible, because in this case company value increases.

For regulator: should encourage more frequent payments of tax on profit, because earlier payments are beneficial for budget due to the time value of money.

References

Angotti M, de Lacerda Moreira R, Hipólito Bernardes do Nascimento J, Neto de Almeida Bispo O (2018) Analysis of an equity investment strategy based on accounting and financial reports in Latin American markets. Reficont 5(2):22–40

Barbi M (2011) On the risk–neutral value of debt tax shields. Appl Financ Econ 22(3):251–258. https://doi.org/10.1080/09603107.2010.613754

Batrancea L (2021a) An econometric approach regarding the impact of fiscal pressure on equilibrium: evidence from electricity gas and oil companies listed on the New York Stock Exchange. Math 9(6):630. https://doi.org/10.3390/math906063

Batrancea L (2021b) The influence of liquidity and solvency on performance within the healthcare industry: evidence from publicly listed companies. Math 9:2231. https://doi.org/10.3390/math9182231

Berk J, DeMarzo P (2007) Corporate Finance. Pearson-Addison Wesley, Boston

Brennan M, Schwartz E (1978) Corporate income taxes, valuation, and the problem of optimal capital structure. J Bus 51:103–114

Brennan M, Schwartz E (1984) Optimal financial policy and firm valuation. J Financ 39:593–607

Brusov P, Filatova T, Orehova N, Eskindarov M (2018) Modern corporate finance, investments, taxation and ratings. Springer Nature Publishing, Switzerland

Brusov PN, Filatova TV, Orekhova NP (2021) Ratings: critical analysis and new approaches of quantitative and qualitative methodology. Springer Nature Publishing, pp 1–369

Brusov PN, Filatova TV, Orekhova NP (2022) Generalized Modigliani–Miller Theory: applications in corporate finance, investments, taxation and ratings. Springer Nature Publishing, pp 1–362

Brusov PN, Filatova TV, Orekhova NP (2023) The Brusov–Filatova–Orekhova theory of capital structure: applications in corporate finance, investments, taxation and ratings. Springer Nature Publishing, pp 1–769

Brusov PN, Filatova TV, Kulik VL (2024) Capital Asset Pricing Model (CAPM) 2.0: account of business and financial risk. Finance: Theory Prac 28(2):128–142. https://doi.org/10.26794/2587-5671-2024-28-2-128-142

Brusov PN, Filatova TV (2025a) Business valuation and company value: new qualitative approaches considering business and financial risks. Springer Nature Publishing, pp 1–654

Brusov PN, Filatova TV (2015b) Efficiency of investment projects: modern investment models and their applications. Springer Nature Publishing, pp.1-843

Dimitropoulos P (2014) Capital structure and corporate governance of soccer clubs: European evidence. Manag Res Rev 37(7):658–678. https://doi.org/10.1108/MRR-09-2012-0207

Farber A, Gillet R, Szafarz A (2006) A General Formula for the WACC. Int J Bus 11(2):211–218

Fernandez P (2006) A general formula for the WACC: a comment. Int J Bus 11(2):219

Filatova T, Orehova N, Brusova A (2008) Weighted average cost of capital in the theory of Modigliani-Miller, modified for a finite life–time company. Bull FU 48:68–77

Filatova T, Brusov P, Orekhova N (2022) Impact of advance payments of tax on profit on effectiveness of investments. Math 10(4):666. https://doi.org/10.3390/math10040666

Franc-Dąbrowska J et al (2021) Energy sector risk and cost of capital assessment—companies and investors perspective. Energies 14(6):1613. https://doi.org/10.3390/en14061613

Hamada R (1969) Portfolio analysis, market equilibrium, and corporate finance. J Financ 24(1):13–31

Harris R, Pringle J (1985) Risk–adjusted discount rates—extension form the average–risk case. J Financ Res 8(3):237–244

Kennedy L, Machado C et al (2015) The relevance of capital structure on firm performance: a multivariate analysis of publicly traded Brazilian companies REPeC, Brasília 9(4):384–401. https://doi.org/10.17524/repec.v9i4.1313

Leland H (1994) Corporate debt value, bond covenants, and optimal capital structure. J Financ 49(4):1213–1252

Miller M (1977) Debt and taxes. J Financ 32(2):261–275. https://doi.org/10.1111/j.1540-6261.1977.tb03267.x

Modigliani F, Miller M (1958) The cost of capital, corporate finance, and the theory of investment. American Economic Review 48:261–297

Modigliani F, Miller M (1963) Corporate income taxes and the cost of capital: a correction. Am Econ Rev 53:147–175

Modigliani F, Miller M (1966) Some estimates of the cost of capital to the electric utility industry 1954–1957. Am Econ Rev 56:333–391

Myers S (2001) Capital structure. J Econ Perspect 15(2):81–102

Pavel Z (2018) The impact of cash flows and weighted average cost of capital to enterprise value in the oil and gas sector. J Rev Glob Econ 7:138–145

Vergara–Novoa C, Pedro Sepúlveda–Rojas J, Alfaro MD, Riveros N (2018) Cost of capital estimation for highway concessionaires in Chile. J Adv Transp. https://doi.org/10.1155/2018/2153536

Chapter 11
Benefits of Advance Payments of Tax on Profit: Consideration Within Brusov–Filatova–Orekhova (BFO) Theory

11.1 Introduction

The importance of accounting for upfront payments rests on two points: (1) companies can pay tax payments upfront with subsequent adjustments if they earn a stable and predictable income; (2) the development of a methodology for advance payments allows the regulator to expand this practice, which ensures an increase in the stability of budget revenues. As results of this chapter show the advance payments of tax on income are quite important for both parties: for companies and for regulator.

We give below the short review of evolution of the theory of capital cost and capital structure.

1. The Modigliani–Miller (MM) theory, created by Nobel Prize winners in 1958 (Modigliani and Miller 1958), was the first quantitative theory of capital structure. It was based on many restrictions, the main of which were the absence of taxes and the perpetual nature of all financial flows and companies. The first limitation was removed by the MMs themselves (Modigliani and Miller 1963, 1966) and the following formulas were obtained:

   For tax shield, TS:

$$\mathrm{TS} = \mathrm{DT}; \tag{11.1}$$

   For company value, V (financially independent company) V_0, leverage company, V:

$$V_0 = \mathrm{CF}/k_0 \quad \text{and} \quad V = \mathrm{CF}/\mathrm{WACC}. \tag{11.2}$$

   For weighted average cost of capital, WACC:

$$WACC = k_0 \cdot (1 - w_d t); \tag{11.3}$$

P. Brusov and T. Filatova, *Taxes and Taxation*, Contributions to Finance and Accounting, https://doi.org/10.1007/978-3-032-11077-0_11

For equity cost, k_e:

$$k_e = k_0 + L(k_e - k_d) \cdot (1 - t). \tag{11.4}$$

2. Hamada in 1969 (Hamada 1969) has derived the following formula for the leveraged company equity cost, accounting both financial and business risk of company, united the Modigliani–Miller theory with Capital Asset Pricing Model (CAPM):

$$k_\mathrm{e} = k_\mathrm{F} + (k_\mathrm{M} - k_\mathrm{F})b_\mathrm{U} + (k_\mathrm{M} - k_\mathrm{F})b_\mathrm{U}\frac{D}{S}(1 - T), \tag{11.5}$$

where b_U is the β–coefficient of the company of the same group of business risk, that the considering company, but with $\mathrm{L} = 0$.

3. Merton Miller in 1977 (Miller 1977) took into account the corporate and individual taxes He got for the capitalization of the financially independent company the following formula:

$$V = V_0 + \left[1 - \frac{(1 - T_C)(1 - T_S)}{(1 - T_D)}\right] \cdot D \tag{11.6}$$

Here $\mathrm{T_C}$—the tax on corporate income rate, $\mathrm{T_S}$—the tax rate on income of an individual investor from his ownership by corporation stock, $\mathrm{T_D}$—tax rate on interest income from the provision of investor–individuals of credits to other investors and companies.

4. In 2008, Brusov–Filatova–Orekhova (Brusov et al. 2018, 2021, 2022, 2023, 2024, ; Brusov and Filatova 2025a, b) have lifted up the limitation concerning the perpetuity of flows and companies and created the modern theory of capital cost and capital structure—BFO theory—which describes the companies of arbitrary age (and arbitrary life–time). The generalization of MM theory for the companies of arbitrary age (and arbitrary life–time) required the modification of the valuation of the tax shield TS, as well as of the valuation of the company capitalization: financially independent, $\mathrm{V_0}$ as well as financially dependent, V.

   The following formulas were obtained: for the tax shield, TS, company value, V, and for weighted average cost of capital WACC:

$$\mathrm{TS} = k_\mathrm{d}DT\sum_{t=1}^{n}(1 + k_\mathrm{d})^{-t} = DT\left[1 - (1 + k_\mathrm{d})^{-n}\right]. \tag{11.7}$$

$$\begin{aligned} V_0 &= \mathrm{CF}\left[1 - (1 + k_0)^{-n}\right]/k_0; \\ V &= \mathrm{CF}\left[1 - (1 + \mathrm{WACC})^{-n}\right]/\mathrm{WACC}. \end{aligned} \tag{11.8}$$

$$\frac{(1 + \mathrm{WACC})^{-n}}{\mathrm{WACC}} = \frac{1 - (1 + k_0)^{-n}}{k_0\left[1 - \omega_d T\left(1 - (1 + k_\mathrm{d})^{-n}\right)\right]}. \tag{11.9}$$

Here, S—the value of equity capital of the company, $w_{\rm d} = \frac{D}{D+S}$—the share of debt capital, $k_{\rm e}$, $w_{\rm e} = \frac{S}{D+S}$—the cost and the share of the equity capital of the company, and $L = D/S$—financial leverage, D—the value of debt capital.

At $n = 1$, from BFO formula for WACC we get Myers (Myers 2001) formula for 1–year company

$$\mathrm{WACC} = k_0 - \frac{(1 + k_0)k_{\rm d}}{1 + k_{\rm d}} w_{\rm d} T; \tag{11.10}$$

and at $n = \infty$ we get Modigliani–Miller formula for WACC (Modigliani and Miller 1963):

$$WACC = k_0 \cdot (1 - w_d t) \tag{11.11}$$

Note, that before BFO discovery in 2008 there were two results only: Modigliani–Miller for perpetuity companies (Modigliani and Miller 1958, 1963, 1966) and Myers one for a year companies (Myers 2001). The accounting of the company's finite age, as it was shown by BFO authors leads to significant changes of all Modigliani–Miller results (Modigliani and Miller 1958, 1963, 1966). Besides, a number of qualitatively new effects in corporate finance, obtained in Brusov–Filatova–Orekhova theory (Brusov et al. 2018, 2022) are absent in Modigliani–Miller theory.

5. Recently we have modified the Modigliani–Miller theory for the case of advanced payments of income tax (Brusov et al. 2022, 2020) and have shown that obtained results are quite different from ones in "classical" Modigliani–Miller theory.

11.2 Modification of the Brusov–Filatova–Orekhova (BFO) Theory for Companies with Frequent Payments of Tax on Income

11.2.1 Calculation of the Tax Shield

Let us calculate the tax shield within Brusov–Filatova–Orekhova theory for the case of advance payments of tax on profit. The tax shield, *TS*, for period of n–years is equal to sum of discounted values of benefits from the use of tax incentives

$$(TS)_n = k_d Dt + \frac{k_d Dt}{(1 + k_d)} + \frac{k_d Dt}{(1 + k_d)^2} + \ldots + \frac{k_d Dt}{(1 + k_d)^{n-1}} \tag{11.12}$$

This expression represents a geometric progression with denominator

$$q = \frac{1}{(1 + k_d)} \tag{11.13}$$

After summing the progression, one obtains:

$$(TS)_n = \frac{k_d Dt\left(1-(1+k_d)^{-n}\right)}{\left(1-(1+k_d)^{-1}\right)} = Dt\left(1-(1+k_d)^{-n}\right)(1+k_d) \tag{11.14}$$

In classical Brusov–Filatova–Orekhova theory under payments at the end of periods one has

$$(TS)_n = Dt\left(1-(1+k_d)^{-n}\right) \tag{11.15}$$

11.2.2 Company Value

For the financially dependent company value V we have:

$$V = V_0 + (TS)_n \tag{11.16}$$

$$V = V_0 + Dt\left(1-(1+k_d)^{-n}\right)\cdot(1+k_d). \tag{11.17}$$

This formula differs from the equation for company value V in case of payments of income tax at the end of the year

$$V = V_0 + Dt\left(1-(1+k_d)^{-n}\right). \tag{11.18}$$

11.2.3 The Weighted Average Cost of Capital, WACC

Substituting

$$D = w_d V \tag{11.19}$$

into (11.17), we get

$$V\left(1 - w_d t\left(1-(1+k_d)^{-n}\right)\cdot(1+k_d)\right) = V_0 \tag{11.20}$$

Using the values of financially dependent company, V, and financially independent company, V_0,

$$V = \frac{CF\left(1-(1+WACC)^{-n}\right)}{WACC}; \quad V_0 = \frac{CF}{k_0}\cdot\left(1-(1+k_0)^{-n}\right), \tag{11.21}$$

we come to the following intermediate equation

$$\begin{aligned}&\tfrac{CF\left(1-(1+WACC)^{-n}\right)}{WACC}\cdot\left(1-w_dt\cdot\left(1-(1+k_d)^{-n}\right)\right)\cdot(1+k_d)\\&=\tfrac{CF}{k_0}\cdot\left(1-(1+k_0)^{-n}\right)\end{aligned} \tag{11.22}$$

and then to the final Brusov–Filatova–Orekhova equation for WACC for the case of advanced payments of income tax

$$\frac{\left(1-(1+WACC)^{-n}\right)}{WACC}=\frac{\left(1-(1+k_0)^{-n}\right)}{k_0\left(1-w_dt\cdot\left(1-(1+k_d)^{-n}\right)\right)\cdot(1+k_d)}. \tag{11.23}$$

This formula differs from the classical Brusov–Filatova–Orekhova equation by the factor $(1+k_d)$ in the left denominator

$$\frac{\left(1-(1+WACC)^{-n}\right)}{WACC}=\frac{\left(1-(1+k_0)^{-n}\right)}{k_0\left(1-w_dt\cdot\left(1-(1+k_d)^{-n}\right)\right)} \tag{11.24}$$

Calculation of the Equity Cost

To calculate the equity cost ke one should use the equation of WACC definition

$$WACC=k_ew_e+k_dw_d(1-t) \tag{11.25}$$

from where one gets the expression for ke

$$k_e=\frac{WACC}{w_e}-\frac{k_d(1-t)w_d}{w_e}=WACC(1+L)-Lk_d(1-t). \tag{11.26}$$

One should substitute WACC from the formula (11.12), calculating the equity cost ke for the case of advanced payments of income tax and from the formula (11.13), calculating the equity cost ke for the case of payments of income tax at the end of the year.

11.3 Results

Here the dependence of the weighted average cost of capital, WACC, capital value, V, equity cost, ke, on leverage level L for three–year and six–year companies, using Microsoft Excel is being studied. We consider two types of payments of income tax: (1) at the end of the year and (2) in advance. As we mentioned above, for WACC we

Table 11.1 Dependence of the weighted average cost of capital, WACC, equity cost, ke and company value, V, on leverage level L in the cases of payments of tax on profit at the end of the year (1) and in the beginning of the year (2) for three–year company

n = 3	WACC		ke		V	
L	1	2	1	2	1	2
1	0.1749	0.1703	0.2057	0.1966	219.2281	220.8472
2	0.1664	0.1603	0.2113	0.1930	222.2455	224.4700
3	0.1622	0.1553	0.2168	0.1892	223.7856	226.3263
4	0.1596	0.1523	0.2222	0.1855	224.7199	227.4549
5	0.1579	0.1503	0.2277	0.1817	225.3471	228.2136
6	0.1567	0.1489	0.2331	0.1780	225.7973	228.7586
7	0.1558	0.1478	0.2386	0.1742	226.1361	229.1691
8	0.1551	0.1469	0.2440	0.1704	226.4003	229.4893
9	0.1545	0.1463	0.2495	0.1666	226.6122	229.7462
10	0.1541	0.1457	0.2549	0.1628	226.7858	229.9568

use formulas (11.12) and (11.13), for capital value, V, we use formulas (11.6) and (11.7) and for equity cost, ke, we use formula (11.15).

We use the following parameters: $k_0 = 0.2$; $k_d = 0.18$; $t = 0.2$; $n = 3; 6$; $CF = 100$.

11.3.1 Dependence of the Weighted Average Cost of Capital, WACC, Capital Value, V, Equity Cost, Ke, on Leverage Level L for Three–year Company

See Table 11.1 and Figs. 11.1, 11.2, and 11.3.

11.3.2 Dependence of the Weighted Average Cost of Capital, WACC, Capital Value, V, Equity Cost, Ke, on Leverage Level L for Six–year Company

See Table 11.2 and Figs. 11.4, 11.5, and 11.6.

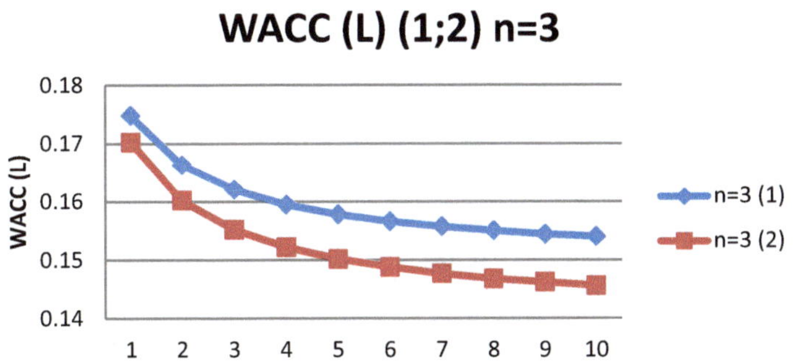

Fig. 11.1 Dependence of the weighted average cost of capital, WACC, on leverage level L in the cases of payments of tax on profit at the end of the year (1) and in the beginning of the year (2) for three–year company

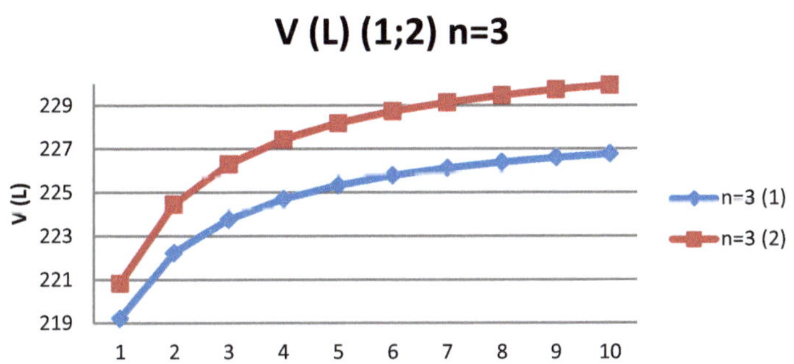

Fig. 11.2 Dependence of the company value, V, on leverage level L in the cases of payments of tax on profit at the end of the year (1) and in the beginning of the year (2) for three–year company

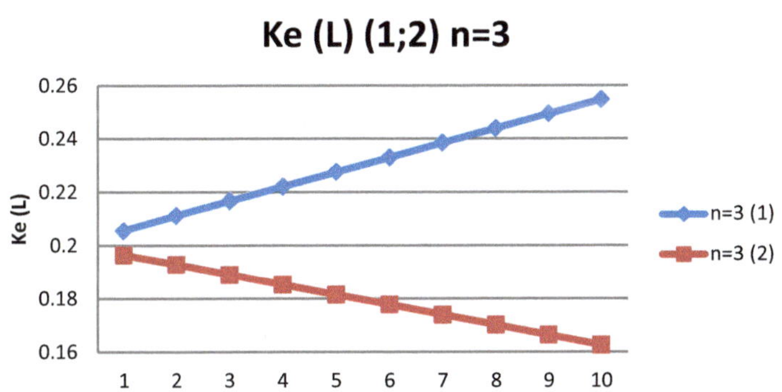

Fig. 11.3 Dependence of the equity cost, ke on leverage level L in the cases of payments of tax on profit at the end of the year (1) and in the beginning of the year (2) for three–year company

Table 11.2 Dependence of the weighted average cost of capital, WACC, equity cost, ke and company value, V, on leverage level L in the cases of payments of tax on profit at the end of the year (1) and in the beginning of the year (2) for six–year company

n = 6	WACC		ke		V	
L	1	2	1	2	1	2
1	0.1743	0.1697	0.2047	0.1953	354.8940	359.2385
2	0.1657	0.1593	0.2090	0.1900	363.0242	369.1124
3	0.1613	0.1542	0.2131	0.1846	367.2305	374.2557
4	0.1586	0.1510	0.2172	0.1791	369.8015	377.4110
5	0.1569	0.1489	0.2213	0.1736	371.5355	379.5443
6	0.1556	0.1474	0.2254	0.1680	372.7841	381.0830
7	0.1547	0.1463	0.2294	0.1624	373.7261	382.2451
8	0.1539	0.1454	0.2335	0.1569	374.4620	383.1540
9	0.1534	0.1447	0.2376	0.1513	375.0529	383.8841
10	0.1529	0.1442	0.2416	0.1457	375.5377	384.4836

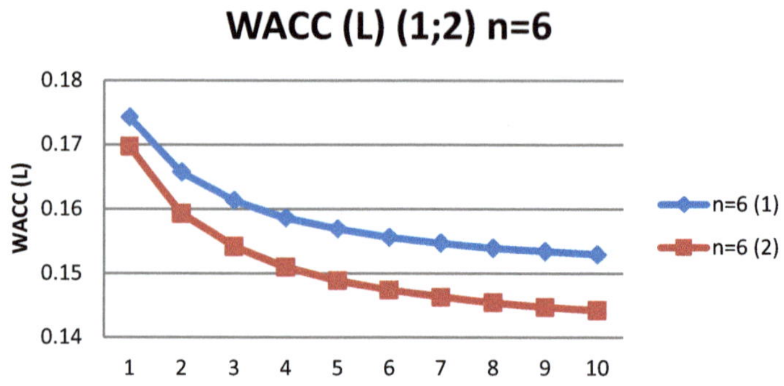

Fig. 11.4 Dependence of the weighted average cost of capital, WACC, on leverage level L in the cases of payments of tax on profit at the end of the year (1) and in the beginning of the year (2) for six–year company

11.4 Comparison of Results for three–year and Six—year Companies

See Figs. 11.7, 11.8, and 11.9.

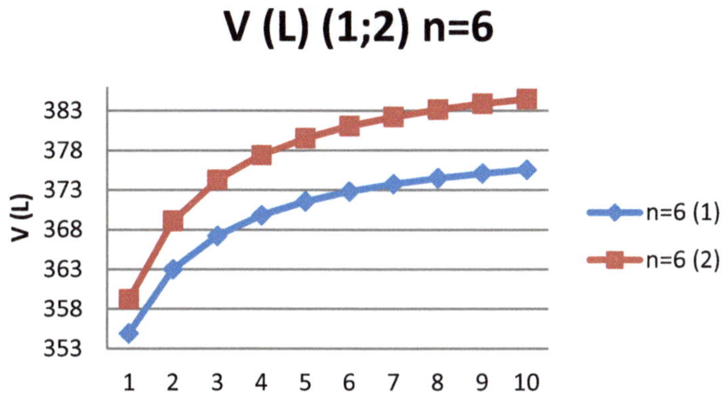

Fig. 11.5 Dependence of the company value, V, on leverage level L in the cases of payments of tax on profit at the end of the year (1) and in the beginning of the year (2) for six–year company

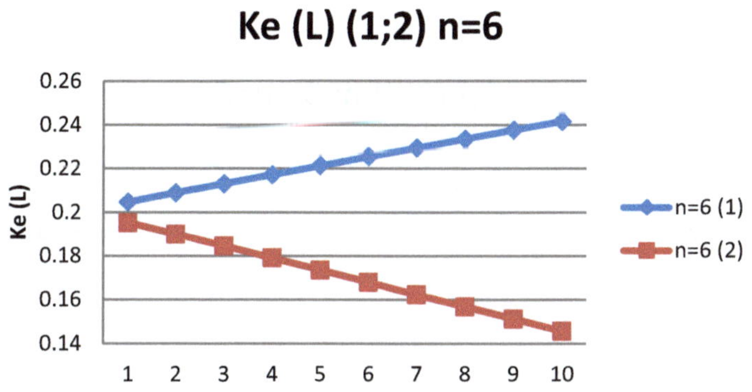

Fig. 11.6 Dependence of the equity cost, ke on leverage level L in the cases of payments of tax on profit at the end of the year (1) and in the beginning of the year (2) for six–year company

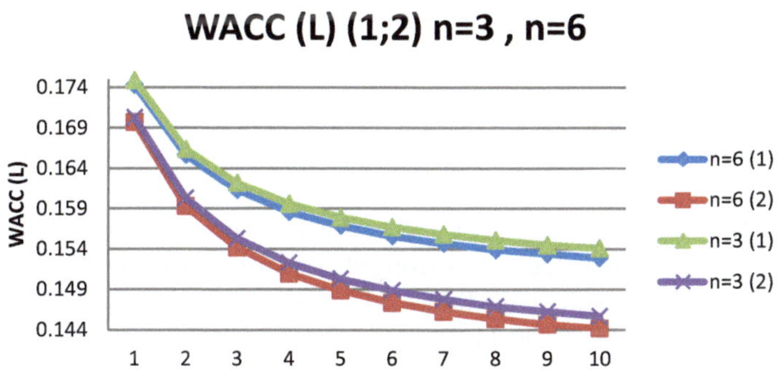

Fig. 11.7 Dependence of the weighted average cost of capital, WACC, on leverage level L in the cases of payments of tax on profit at the end of the year (1) and in the beginning of the year (2) for three–year and six—year companies

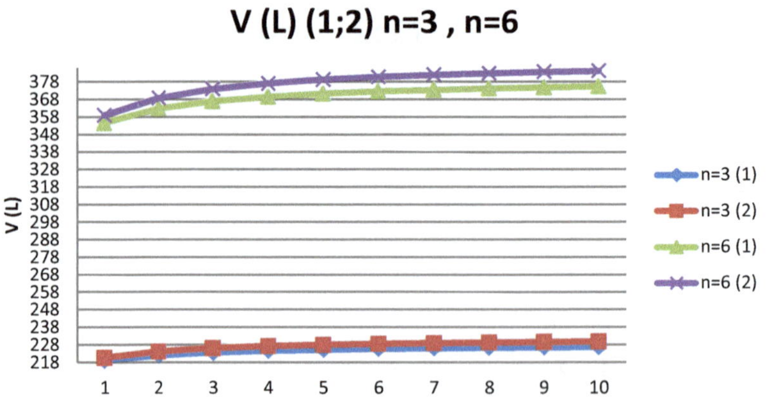

Fig. 11.8 Dependence of the company value, V, on leverage level L in the cases of payments of tax on profit at the end of the year (1) and in the beginning of the year (2) for three–year and six –year companies

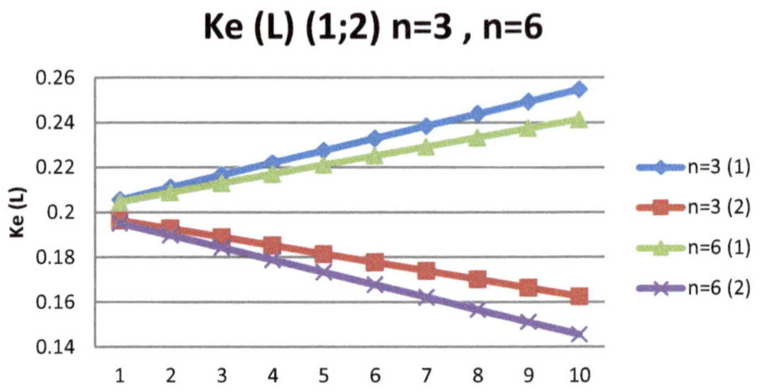

Fig. 11.9 Dependence of the equity cost, ke, on leverage level L in the cases of payments of tax on profit at the end of the year (1) and in the beginning of the year (2) for three–year and six—year companies

11.5 Discussion

We derive BFO formulas for WACC, V, ke for the case of advanced payments of income tax. Making the calculations using these formulas within Microsoft Excel we get the following results (see Tables 11.1 and 11.2 and Figs. 11.1, 11.2, 11.3, 11.4, 11.5, 11.6, 11.7, 11.8, and 11.9).

1. WACC(L) decreases with L in both cases: advanced payments of income tax and payments at the ends of years. This means that debt financing is important and should be used by company—it leads to decrease of attracting capital cost with L.

2. WACC turns out to be lower in the case of advanced payments of income tax, this tells about importance of the use of advanced payments of income tax for companies.
3. WACC decreases with company age: this is one of the important results of classical BFO theory.
4. Company value, V, increases with L in both cases, this follows from the decrease of attracting capital cost with L.
5. Company value, V, turns out to be bigger in the case of advanced payments of income tax: this tells about importance of the use of advanced payments of income tax for companies.
6. Company value, V, increases with company age.
7. Equity cost ke decreases with company age in both cases: this is one of the important results of classical BFO theory.
8. Equity cost ke increases with leverage level L in the case of payments of income tax at the end of the year.
9. Equity cost ke decreases with leverage level L in the case of advanced payments of income tax. This means the appearance of a qualitatively new effect that can greatly change the company's dividend policy, because the economically justified amount of dividends is equal to the equity cost.

11.6 Summary and conclusions

Advance income tax payments are beneficial to both parties: to companies, because they lead to decrease of cost of attracting capital and increase of company values; to regulator, because earlier replenishment of the budget ensures an increase in the stability of budget revenues. Thus the regulator should extend the practice of tax payments in advance by the companies.

An important conclusion drawn in this chapter is that the tax shield is very important and the way it is formed (payments at the end of the year or in advance) leads to very important consequences, changing all the financial indicators of the company, such as the cost of raising capital and company value and radically changing the company's dividend policy. If with payments at the end of the year, the amount of dividends should increase with the increase in the use of debt financing, with advance payments of income tax the amount of dividends should decrease with the increase in the use of debt financing: this is a pioneering result that radically changes the company's dividend policy.

References

Brusov P, Filatova T, Orehova N, Eskindarov M (2018) Modern corporate finance, investments, taxation and ratings, 2nd edn. Springer Nature Publishing, Cham, Switzerland, pp 1–571

Brusov PN, Filatova TV, Orekhova NP, Kulik VL, Chang S-I, Lin YCG (2020) Modification of the Modigliani–Miller theory for the case of advance payments of tax on profit. J Rev Glob Econ 2020(9):257–267

Brusov PN, Filatova TV, Orekhova NP (2022) Generalized Modigliani–Miller Theory: applications in corporate finance, investments, taxation and ratings. Springer Nature Publishing, pp 1–362

Brusov PN, Filatova TV, Orekhova NP (2021) Ratings: critical analysis and new approaches of quantitative and qualitative methodology. Springer Nature Publishing, pp 1–369

Brusov PN, Filatova TV, Orekhova NP (2022) Generalized Modigliani–Miller Theory: applications in corporate finance, investments, taxation and ratings. Springer Nature Publishing, pp 1–362

Brusov PN, Filatova TV, Orekhova NP (2023) The Brusov–Filatova–Orekhova theory of capital structure: applications in corporate finance, investments, taxation and ratings. Springer Nature Publishing, pp 1–769

Brusov PN, Filatova TV, Kulik VL (2024) Capital Asset Pricing Model (CAPM) 2.0: account of business and financial risk. Finance: Theory Prac 28(2):128–142. https://doi.org/10.26794/2587-5671-2024-28-2-128-142

Brusov PN, Filatova TV (2025a) Business valuation and company value: new qualitative approaches considering business and financial risks. Springer Nature Publishing, pp 1–654

Brusov PN, Filatova TV (2015b) Efficiency of investment projects: modern investment models and their applications. Springer Nature Publishing, pp.1-843

Hamada R (1969) Portfolio analysis, market equilibrium, and corporate finance. J Financ 13–31

Miller M (1977) Debt and taxes. J Financ 32(2):261–275. https://doi.org/10.1111/j.1540-6261.1977.tb03267.x

Modigliani F, Miller M (1958) The cost of capital, corporate finance, and the theory of investment. Am Econ Rev 48:261–297

Modigliani F, Miller M (1963) Corporate income taxes and the cost of capital: a correction. Am Econ Rev 53:147–175

Modigliani F, Miller M (1966) Some estimates of the cost of capital to the electric utility industry 1954–1957. Am Econ Rev 56:333–391

Myers S (2001) Capital structure. J Econ Perspect 15(2):81–102

Chapter 12
Influence of Method and Frequency of Profit Tax Payments on Company Financial Indicators

12.1 Introduction

In practice, profit tax payments are (1) made more frequently than annually and (2) can be made in advance. Recently, the Brusov–Filatova–Orekhova (BFO) theory (Brusov et al. Brusov et al. 2021, 2022, 2023, 2024; Brusov and Filatova 2025a, b) was generalized for the case of profit tax payments with an arbitrary frequency. Using modified BFO formulae, it was shown that all financial indicators of a company depend on the frequency of profit tax payments. The weighted average cost of capital (WACC) decreases with the payments and the company value increases with the payments. A new effect was thus discovered: the decrease in equity cost with an increase in the level of leverage (L). Due to the fact that the economically justified amount of dividends is equal to the equity cost, this can significantly change the dividend policy of a company.

More frequent profit tax payments are beneficial for both parties: the company and the tax regulator. For the company, this practice increases the company value and it helps the tax regulator due to the time value of money.

In current Chapter, for the first time, the Brusov–Filatova–Orekhova (BFO) theory was generalized for the case of advance profit tax payments with an arbitrary frequency. We compared the obtained results to those that we described recently for profit tax payments at the end of the financial period (Brusov et al. 2022) and found them to be totally different.

We showed that in spite the fact that the WACC decreases with the payments and the company value increases with the payments in this case (Brusov et al. 2022), the WACC values turned out to be bigger and the company value turned out to be smaller than in case of advance profit tax payments of any frequency. This underlined the importance of advance profit tax payments.

The novelty and originality of this study lie in the fact that the simultaneous influence of two effects was investigated for the first time: (1) advance profit tax payments and (2) frequent profit tax payments.

P. Brusov and T. Filatova, *Taxes and Taxation*, Contributions to Finance and Accounting, https://doi.org/10.1007/978-3-032-11077-0_12

Before this study, we generalized the Brusov–Filatova–Orekhova (BFO) theory to (1) the case of frequent profit tax payments at the end of the financial period and (2) the case of advance annual profit tax payments.

In this article, we also compared the obtained results to the results of consideration (1) and found a large difference between the results. Thus, in this chapter, an in-depth study of frequent profit tax payments was carried out for both possible cases of payments: advance and at the end of the financial period.

The robustness of the outcomes was provided by the use of the modern Brusov–Filatova–Orekhova (BFO) theory of capital cost and capital structure, which has been tested in real economic practice and its correct generalization for the case of frequent advance profit tax payments has been proven.

The structure of the chapter is as follows.

In the introduction, we present a literature review of the development of the capital structure and capital cost theory (Sect. 12.1). The Brusov–Filatova–Orekhova (BFO) theory is generalized for frequent advance profit tax payments for the first time in Sect. 12.2, The modified formulae are derived for the tax shield in Sect. 12.2.1, company value in Sect. 12.2.2 and the equity cost and WACC in Sect. 12.2.3.

In Sect. 12.3, using the generalized BFO formulae that were obtained in Sect. 12.2 and Microsoft Excel, we numerically calculate the dependence of a company's financial parameters, such as WACC, company value and equity cost, on the level of leverage for an arbitrary frequency of profit tax payment for three- and six-year-old companies (Sects. 12.3.1 and 12.3.2, respectively).

We considered frequent advance profit tax payments. In Sect. 12.3, we also compare the obtained results to those that were found previously for frequent profit tax payments tax at the end of the financial period (Brusov et al. 2022). This section also compares the results for companies of different ages (three- and six-year-old companies). In Sect. 12.4, the discussion and conclusions are presented.

12.1.1 A Literature Review on the Development of the Capital Cost and Capital Structure Theory

In this section, we present an overview of the development of the capital cost and capital structure theory. Following the traditional empirical approaches, the first quantitative theory of capital cost and capital structure was proposed the Nobel Prize winners Modigliani and Miller (the MM theory) in 1958 (Modigliani and Miller 1958). Among the many limitations of this theory, two main shortcomings can be distinguished: the non-accounting of taxes and the infinite lifetime of companies. The first constraint was removed by Modigliani and Miller themselves (Modigliani and Miller 1963, 1966), who obtained the following formulae.

The tax shield (TS) had the following form:

$$TS = DT. \tag{12.1}$$

Company value (V) and financially independent companies (V_0) were expressed as:

$$V_0 = \mathrm{CF}/k_0 \text{ and } \quad V = \mathrm{CF}/\mathrm{WACC}. \tag{12.2}$$

For *WACC*, Modigliani and Miller obtained the following formula:

$$WACC = k_0 \cdot (1 - w_d t). \tag{12.3}$$

For equity cost (k_e), they had:

$$k_e = k_0 + L(k_e - k_d) \cdot (1 - t). \tag{12.4}$$

In 1969, the capital asset pricing model (CAPM) was combined with the Modigliani–Miller theory by Hamada (Hamada 1969), which accounted for both the business and financial risk of companies and used the below formula for the equity cost (k_e) of financially dependent companies:

$$k_\mathrm{e} = k_\mathrm{F} + (k_\mathrm{M} - k_\mathrm{F})b_\mathrm{U} + (k_\mathrm{M} - k_\mathrm{F})b_\mathrm{U}\frac{D}{S}(1 - T), \tag{12.5}$$

where b_U is the β–coefficient of a company with $L = 0$.

Corporate and individual taxes were then taken into account by Miller in 1977 (Miller 1977). The following formula was obtained for unleveraged company value:

$$V = V_0 + \left[1 - \frac{(1 - T_C)(1 - T_S)}{(1 - T_D)}\right] \cdot D \tag{12.6}$$

where T_S is the profit tax rate for an individual investor for their ownership of corporation stock, T_C is the tax rate for corporate profit and T_D is the profit tax interest rate for the provision of credit to other investors or companies.

In (Farber et al. 2006; Fernandez 2006; Berk and Marzo 2007; Harris and Pringle 1985), a more general expression for *WACC* than the Modigliani–Miller (MM) version was obtained (Farber et al. 2006):

$$WACC = k_0(1 - w_d t) - k_d w_d t + k_{TS} t w_d \tag{12.7}$$

where k_0 is the equity cost of the unleveraged company, k_d is the debt cost, k_{TS} is the expected return on the tax shield, V is the leveraged company value, V_{TS} is the value of the tax shield and D is the debt value.

Derived in Berk and Marzo (2007), Formula (12.7) is more general than the Modigliani–Miller (MM) expression, so some additional conditions are necessary for its use in practice. When the WACC value is constant over time, the leveraged company value can be found by discounting the *WACC* from the unleveraged company cash flows. For this specific case, the formulae can be found in textbooks (Berk and Marzo 2007; Harris and Pringle 1985).

In 1963, Modigliani and Miller (Modigliani and Miller 1963) supposed that the level of debt was constant. The expected after-tax cash flow of a financially independent company was also fixed, thus V_0 was constant. By that assumption, $kTS = kd$ and the tax shield value was $TS = tD$. Thus, for the financially dependent company value, we used the ordinary Modigliani–Miller (MM) formula for *WACC* instead of Formula (12.7):

$$WACC = k_0(1 - w_d t) \tag{12.8}$$

From our point of view, the "classical" Modigliani–Miller (MM) theory supposed that the debt cost and expected return on the tax shield were equal (due to the fact that both of them are debt-like in nature), which is much more reasonable and so we modified the "classical" Modigliani–Miller (MM) in Brusov et al. (2020).

A study on the influence of tax pressure on the financial balance of energy companies was carried out in Batrancea 2021a. The results showed that tax pressure has a stronger influence on the financial equilibrium (both in the short term and long term) of oil and electricity companies than gas companies. These results are useful for the managers of energy companies who underestimate the evolution of the financial equilibrium of the company because they take into account various possible financial crises.

A study on the influence of financial liquidity and financial solvency on the performance of healthcare companies was conducted in Batrancea 2021b using econometric models. From the empirical evidence, it follows that certain financial parameters such as current liquidity ratio, quick liquidity ratio and financial leverage significantly influence company performance, as measured by the return on assets, gross margin ratio, operating margin ratio, taxes, earnings before interest, amortization and depreciation.

The limitation that was related to the infinite lifetime of companies was removed in 2008 by Brusov, Filatova and Orekhova (Brusov et al. 2018), who developed the modern theory of capital cost and capital structure (the BFO theory), which is applicable to companies of all ages.

Modifications to the calculations for the tax shield and company value (unleveraged, V_0; leveraged, V) were required for the generalization of the MM theory (see the formulae below):

$$\mathrm{TS} = k_d DT \sum_{t=1}^{n} (1 + k_d)^{-t} = DT\left[1 - (1 + k_d)^{-n}\right]. \tag{12.9}$$

$$V_0 = \mathrm{CF}\left[1 - (1 + k_0)^{-n}\right]/k_0; \quad V = \mathrm{CF}\left[1 - (1 + \mathrm{WACC})^{-n}\right]/\mathrm{WACC}. \tag{12.10}$$

$$\frac{1 - (1 + \mathrm{WACC})^{-n}}{\mathrm{WACC}} = \frac{1 - (1 + k_0)^{-n}}{k_0\left[1 - \omega_d T\left(1 - (1 + k_d)^{-n}\right)\right]}. \tag{12.11}$$

where S is the equity capital value, $w_{\text{d}} = \frac{D}{D+S}$ is the debt capital, k_{e}, $w_{\text{e}} = \frac{S}{D+S}$ is the equity capital, $L = D/S$ is the value of financial leverage and D is the debt value.

The Myers formula for a one-year company (Myers 2001) can be easily obtained from Formula (12.11) by substituting $n = 1$:

$$\text{WACC} = k_0 - \frac{(1+k_0)k_{\text{d}}}{1+k_{\text{d}}} w_{\text{d}} T. \tag{12.12}$$

Then, by substituting $n = \infty$, we arrive at the Modigliani–Miller formula for *WACC* (Modigliani and Miller 1958):

$$WACC = k_0 \cdot (1 - w_d t) \tag{12.13}$$

Until 2008, when the BFO theory was created, there were only two options: the Modigliani–Miller theory for perpetual companies (Modigliani and Miller 1958, 1963; Modigliani and Miller 1966) and the Myers theory for one-year companies (Myers 2001). As the authors of the BFO showed, taking the finite age of a company into account leads to significant changes in all Modigliani–Miller results (Modigliani and Miller 1958, 1963, 1966). In addition, a number of the new effects that are observed within corporate finance using the Brusov–Filatov–Orekhova theory (Brusov et al. 2018) are absent in the Modigliani–Miller theory.

In (Brusov et al. 2020), the Modigliani–Miller theory was modified for the case of advance profit tax payments and significant differences were found between the modified theory and the "classical" Modigliani–Miller theory.

In the literature, the methodology and results of the Brusov–Filatova–Orekhova (BFO) theory are well known (for example, see references [Dimitropoulos 2014; Luiz and Cruz 2015; Barbi 2011; Zhukov 2018; Franc-Dąbrowska et al. 2021; Angotti et al. 2018; Vergara-Novoa et al. 2018; Mundi et al. 2022; Sadiq et al. 2022; Becker 2022; El-Chaarani et al. 2022; Huang et al. 2020]). A number of Chapters (see, for example, [Vergara-Novoa et al. 2018; Mundi et al. 2022; Sadiq et al. 2022]) have used the BFO theory in practical calculations.

The authors of Franc-Dąbrowska et al. (2021) valuated the capital costs of energy companies by including an investor and market risk approach. The study also concerned a *WACC* intra-industry analysis the companies, which was related to the sector characteristics of revenue, total assets, company age and market capitalization.

In (Mundi et al. 2022), the influence of the overconfidence of finance managers on the capital structure decisions of family-run businesses in India was studied. It was shown that the capital structure decisions of managers could be explained by measurable managerial characteristics. In (Sadiq et al. 2022), the correlation between company risk and capital structure was explored using datasets from sugar and cement companies in Pakistan. It was shown that the role of risk assessment and capital structure is vital for the sustainable growth of companies and the increase in the wealth of shareholders.

The authors of Becker (2022) considered the adjusted present value method, the free cash flow (FCF) method, the flow-to-equity method and the relationships between these methods. The authors departed from Modigliani and Miller method and used a stationary FCF method and the Miles and Ezzell method to consider FCF as a first-order autoregressive possession. The authors derived DCF valuation formulae for annuities. The authors found (1) the correct discount rate for the tax shield when the free cash flow is a first-order autoregressive annuity and (2) the tax shield valuation of a first-order autoregressive free cash flow annuity.

The author of El-Chaarani et al. (2022) studied the impacts of internal and external corporate governance mechanisms on the financial performance of banks in the MENA region during the COVID-19 pandemic. The results showed that the corporate governance measures of the presence of independent members on the board of directors, strong legal protection, a high concentration of ownership and the lack of political pressure on board members had positive effects on the financial indicators of banks.

In (Huang et al. 2020), the influence of leverage level on the expected equity returns of listed companies was studied. The existence of an optimal capital structure to maximize the expected equity returns was discussed. The authors thought that this problem should be discussed from the perspective of maximizing shareholder wealth and not from the perspective of maximizing company value due to the existence of financial distress costs and agency costs. Using Gebhardt–Lee–Swaminathan (GLS) model to measure the implied capital costs and to measure the expected equity returns, the authors empirically found that the leverage level had a positive correlation with the equity returns of a listed company. The relationship between the leverage level and the expected equity returns appeared to an inverse "U":

- When the leverage level fell below the optimal level, increasing the leverage could increase the expected equity returns;
- When the leverage level was higher than the optimal level, deleveraging was beneficial to increase the expected equity returns.

Within a standard capital structure model, the authors of Islam and Khandaker (2015) investigated the leverage decisions of over 1500 companies that were listed in the ASX for 2000–2012 and divided the sample into mining and non-mining industries. Applying a dummy variable approach, the authors showed that there were fundamental differences between two these types of companies when making leverage decisions. It turned out that mining companies were more sensitive to profitability and asset tangibility, whereas neither profitability nor asset tangibility were significant for non-mining companies. The obtained results suggested that industry type matters for companies when making leverage decisions.

In (Barbi 2011), the authors discussed the disagreement in the financial literature about the meaning of the "value of tax shields". Although it is accepted that the tax deductibility of interest increases the value of a firm, the correct valuation of this added value is controversial. Using a risk-neutral approach, the authors derived a general formula for the valuation of tax shields, which shows that this value equals the summation of the discounted future tax savings. As soon as the authors specified a leverage level policy and cash flow dynamics, they obtained some well-known formulae for the calculation of tax shields.

12.2 The Modified Brusov–Filatova–Orekhova (BFO) Theory for the Case of Frequent Advance Profit Tax Payments

In this section, we generalize the Brusov–Filatova–Orekhova (BFO) theory for the case of frequent advance profit tax payments. The expressions for the tax shield, company value, *WACC* and equity cost are presented in Sects. 12.2.1, 12.2.2, and 12.2.3, respectively.

In this section, we use the following definitions.

D	Debt capital value
S	Equity capital value
$k_d, w_d = \frac{D}{D+S}$	Debt capital cost and share
$k_e, w_e = \frac{S}{D+S}$	Equity capital cost and share
$L = D/S$ WACC	Leverage level Weighted average cost of capital

k_0, the equity cost for a financially independent company; p, the number of payments per year; T, profit tax.

12.2.1 The Tax Shield Calculation

We started with the calculation of the tax shield for the case of frequent advance profit tax payments using the Brusov–Filatova–Orekhova theory (where p is the number of payments per year when payments are made at the beginning of the financial period). For a period of n years, the tax shield (*TS*) was equal to the sum of the discounted values of benefits from the use of tax incentives:

$$(TS)_n = \frac{k_d Dt}{p} + \frac{k_d Dt}{p(1+k_d)^{1/p}} + \frac{k_d Dt}{p(1+k_d)^{2/p}} + ... + \frac{k_d Dt}{p(1+k_d)^{np/p}} \tag{12.14}$$

We used a geometric progression with the denominator $q = \frac{1}{(1+k_d)^{1/p}}$.

After summation, we obtained:

$$(TS)_n = \frac{k_d Dt\left(1-(1+k_d)^{-n}\right)}{p\left(1-(1+k_d)^{-1/p}\right)} = \frac{k_d Dt\left(1-(1+k_d)^{-n}\right)\cdot(1+k_d)^{1/p}}{p\left((1+k_d)^{1/p}-1\right)}. \tag{12.15}$$

Using the classical Brusov–Filatova–Orekhova theory at $p = 1$, we obtained:

$$(TS)_n = Dt\left(1-(1+k_d)^{-n}\right)\cdot(1+k_d). \tag{12.16}$$

It was easy to obtain this result from Formula (12.15) by inputting the value of $p = 1$ for the number of profit tax payments.

12.2.2 Derivation of the Modified BFO Formula for the Weighted Average Cost of Capital (WACC)

We now present the modified BFO formula for the weighted average cost of capital (*WACC*) for the case of frequent advance profit tax payments (where p is the number of payments per year when the payments are made at the beginning of the financial period).

For the value of a leveraged company (V), we obtained:

$$V = V_0 + (TS)_n. \tag{12.17}$$

where V_0 is the value of an unleveraged company. By substituting Formula (12.19) for TS, we obtained:

$$V = V_0 + \frac{k_d D t\left(1 - (1 + k_d)^{-n}\right) \cdot (1 + k_d)^{1/p}}{p\left((1 + k_d)^{1/p} - 1\right)}. \tag{12.18}$$

After substituting $D = w_d V$, we obtained:

$$V\left(1 - \frac{k_d w_d t\left(1 - (1 + k_d)^{-n}\right) \cdot (1 + k_d)^{1/p}}{p\left((1 + k_d)^{1/p} - 1\right)}\right) = V_0. \tag{12.19}$$

Assuming that the values of a leveraged company (V) and an unleveraged company (V_0) were equal to:

$$V = \frac{CF\left(1 - (1 + WACC)^{-n}\right)}{WACC}; \quad V_0 = \frac{CF\left(1 - (1 + k_0)^{-n}\right)}{k_0}. \tag{12.20}$$

respectively, we obtained:

$$\frac{CF\left(1-(1+WACC)^{-n}\right)}{WACC} \cdot \left(1 - \frac{k_d w_d t\left(1-(1+k_d)^{-n}\right)\cdot(1+k_d)^{1/p}}{p\left((1+k_d)^{1/p}-1\right)}\right) = \frac{CF}{k_0} \cdot \left(1 - (1 + k_0)^{-n}\right). \tag{12.21}$$

From there, we could derive the modified BFO formula for the WACC of a company of age n years for the case of p profit tax payments per year (payments at the beginning of the financial period):

$$\frac{1-(1+WACC)^{-n}}{WACC} = \frac{CF\left(1-(1+k_0)^{-n}\right)}{k_0\left(1-\frac{k_d w_d t\left(1-(1+k_d)^{-n}\right)\cdot(1+k_d)^{1/p}}{p\left((1+k_d)^{1/p}-1\right)}\right)}. \tag{12.22}$$

For $p = 1$, we obtained the modified BFO formula for advance annual profit tax payments:

$$\frac{1-(1+WACC)^{-n}}{WACC} = \frac{1-(1+k_0)^{-n}}{k_0\cdot\left(1-w_d t\left[1-(1+k_d)^{-n}\right]\cdot(1+k_d)\right)}. \tag{12.23}$$

12.2.3 *Formulae for the Capital Value and Equity Cost*

In Sect. 12.3, we present our investigation into the impact of the frequency of profit tax payments on the dependence of the WACC, capital value and equity cost on the leverage level of companies of different ages (3 or 6 years) using Microsoft Excel. For the WACC, we used Formula (12.10) and for capital value and equity cost, we used formulae (12.24) and (12.25), respectively (see below).

The value of a company of age n could be calculated using the following formula:

$$V = \frac{CF\cdot\left(1-(1+WACC)^{-n}\right)}{WACC}. \tag{12.24}$$

Then, the equity cost could be found using the following equation:

$$WACC = k_e w_e + k_d w_d(1-t)$$

$$k_e = \frac{WACC}{w_e} - \frac{k_d(1-t)w_d}{w_e} = WACC(1+L) - Lk_d(1-t). \tag{12.25}$$

where the *WACC* value is found using Formula (12.22).

12.3 Results and Discussions

We studied the impact of the frequency of advance profit tax payments on the dependence of the WACC, capital value and equity cost on the leverage level of companies of different ages (3 or 6 years) using Microsoft Excel. We considered the advance profit tax payments using the formulae that were obtained above: Formula (12.22) was used for WACC, Formula (12.24) was used for capital value and Formula (12.25) was used for equity cost. By using the BFO theory, we could study companies of any age. Three- and six-year-old companies were considered as examples to estimate the impact of age on the financial parameters of a company. We used a large database, which can be made available to interested readers upon request. We used data that showed the influence of advance profit tax payments with an arbitrary frequency on the financial parameters of the selected companies. Then, we compared the results of the calculations of two types of profit tax payments: (1) payments at the end of the financial period (Brusov et al. 2022) and (2) at the beginning of the financial period (i.e., in advance).

The following parameters were used: $k_0 = 0.2$; $k_d = 0.18$; $t = 0.2$; $n = 3$ or 6; $CF = 100$. The chosen parameters were typical for companies and the results that were obtained using other parameters were similar and did not show any qualitative differences.

12.3.1 The Impact of the Frequency of Profit Tax Payments on the Dependence of the Weighted Average Cost of Capital, Capital Value and Equity Cost on the Leverage Level of a Three-Year-Old Company

In Tables 12.1, 12.2, and 12.3, we present the results of our study on the impact of the frequency of profit tax payments on the dependence of the *WACC*, capital value and equity cost on the leverage level of a three-year-old company with payment frequencies of $p = 1, 2, 4, 6$, and 12.

Table 12.1 The dependence of the *WACC* on the leverage level (L) of a three-year-old company for advance profit tax payments with frequencies of $p = 1, 2, 4, 6$, and 12

L	Wd	$WACC$, $n = 3$ (2)				
		$p = 1$	$p = 2$	$p = 4$	$p = 6$	$p = 12$
1	0.5	0.1703	0.1715	0.1721	0.1723	0.1725
2	0.666667	0.1603	0.1619	0.1627	0.1629	0.1632
3	0.75	0.1553	0.1571	0.1580	0.1583	0.1586
4	0.8	0.1523	0.1542	0.1552	0.1555	0.1558
5	0.833333	0.1503	0.1523	0.1533	0.1536	0.1539
6	0.857143	0.1489	0.1509	0.1519	0.1522	0.1526
7	0.875	0.1478	0.1499	0.1509	0.1512	0.1516
8	0.888889	0.1469	0.1491	0.1501	0.1505	0.1508
9	0.9	0.1463	0.1484	0.1495	0.1498	0.1502
10	0.909091	0.1457	0.1479	0.1490	0.1493	0.1497

Table 12.2 The dependence of the company value (V) on the leverage level (L) of a three-year-old company for advance profit tax payments with frequencies of $p = 1, 2, 4, 6$, and 12

L	Wd	V				
		$p = 1$	$p = 2$	$p = 4$	$p = 6$	$p = 12$
1	0.5	220.8472	220.4234	220.2163	220.1479	220.0800
2	0.666667	224.4700	223.8866	223.6018	223.5079	223.4144
3	0.75	226.3263	225.6593	225.3339	225.2266	225.1199
4	0.8	227.4549	226.7365	226.3861	226.2705	226.1557
5	0.833333	228.2136	227.4603	227.0930	226.9719	226.8515
6	0.857143	228.7586	227.9802	227.6007	227.4756	227.3512
7	0.875	229.1691	228.3717	227.9829	227.8548	227.7274
8	0.888889	229.4893	228.6771	228.2811	228.1506	228.0208
9	0.9	229.7462	228.9220	228.5202	228.3878	228.2561
10	0.909091	229.9568	229.1228	228.7162	228.5823	228.4490

Table 12.3 The dependence of the equity cost (ke) on the leverage level (L) of a three-year-old company for advance profit tax payments with frequencies of $p = 1, 2, 4, 6$, and 12

L	Wd	Ke				
		$p = 1$	$p = 2$	$p = 4$	$p = 6$	$p = 12$
1	0.5	0.1966	0.1990	0.2002	0.2005	0.2009
2	0.666667	0.1930	0.1977	0.2001	0.2008	0.2016
3	0.75	0.1892	0.1964	0.1999	0.2011	0.2022
4	0.8	0.1855	0.1951	0.1998	0.2013	0.2028
5	0.833333	0.1817	0.1937	0.1996	0.2015	0.2034
6	0.857143	0.1780	0.1923	0.1994	0.2017	0.2040
7	0.875	0.1742	0.1910	0.1992	0.2019	0.2046
8	0.888889	0.1704	0.1896	0.1990	0.2021	0.2052
9	0.9	0.1666	0.1882	0.1988	0.2023	0.2058
10	0.909091	0.1628	0.1868	0.1986	0.2025	0.2063

As can be seen from Fig. 12.1, the WACC decreased with L for all frequencies (annual, semi-annual, quarterly, monthly, etc.) of advance profit tax payments. So, the debt financing led to a decrease in the corresponding capital cost with L and thus, its use by the company was important. The *WACC* values increased with the frequency of payments, which meant that more infrequent payments were beneficial for the company. The influence of the payment frequency was stronger for annual, semi-annual and quarterly payments and decreased for monthly payments.

As can be seen from Fig. 12.2, the company value (V) increased with L for all frequencies (annual, semi-annual, quarterly, monthly, etc.) of advance profit tax payments. So, the debt financing led to an increase in the company value with L and

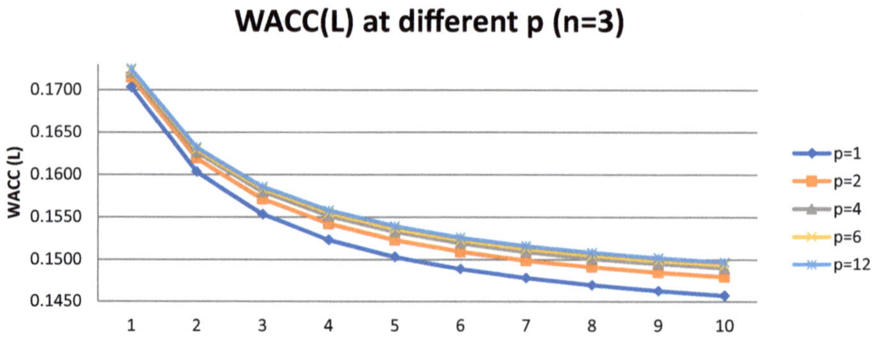

Fig. 12.1 The dependence of the WACC on the leverage level (L) of a three-year-old company for advance profit tax payments with frequencies of $p = 1, 2, 4, 6$, and 12

thus, its use by the company was important. This was consistent with the decrease in *WACC* with the leverage level, as shown in the previous section. The company value decreased with the frequency of payments, which meant that more infrequent payments were beneficial for the company. The influence of the payment frequency was stronger for annual, semi-annual and quarterly payments and decreased for monthly payments. This was consistent with the *WACC* behavior that was shown in the previous section.

As can be seen from Fig. 12.3, the equity cost (*ke*) depended on the leverage level in a linear manner. It was not expected for *ke*(L) to be linear because the BFO equation for the WACC was an $n + 1$ power equation. However, as can be seen from the figures and tables for the equity cost results, this occurred with a high accuracy. We called the relationship quasi-linear (or practically linear). Our entire extensive database showed that this was the case. The equity cost decreased for annual ($p = 1$), semi-annual ($p = 2$) and quarterly ($p = 4$) payments and increased for monthly

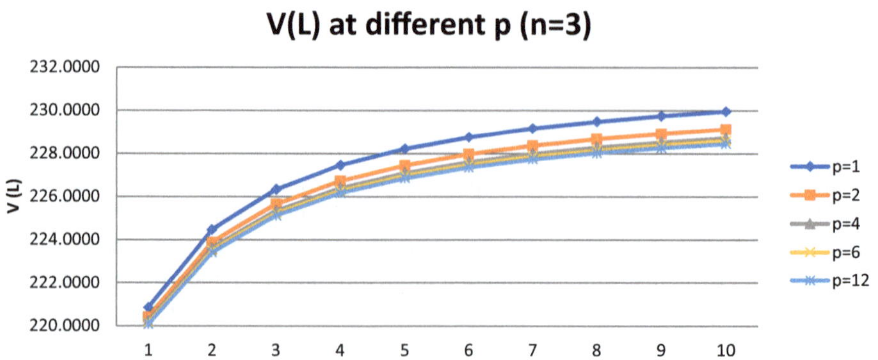

Fig. 12.2 The dependence of the company value (V) on the leverage level (L) of a three-year-old company for advance profit tax payments with frequencies of $p = 1, 2, 4, 6$, and 12

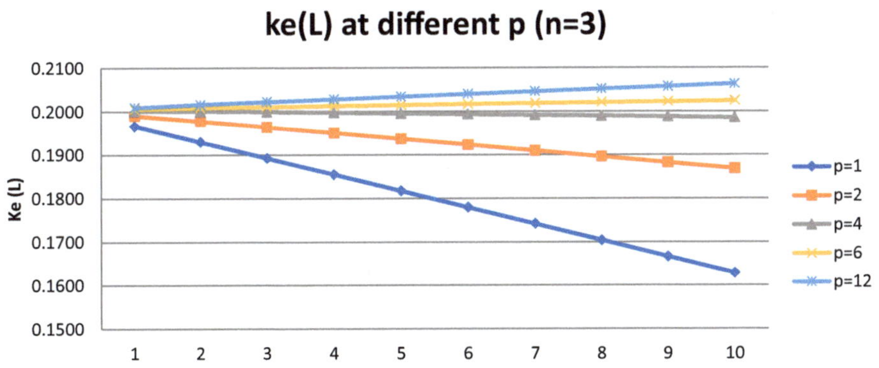

Fig. 12.3 The dependence of the equity cost (*ke*) on the leverage level (*L*) of a three-year-old company for advance profit tax payments with frequencies of $p = 1, 2, 4, 6$, and 12

($p = 12$) and bi-monthly payments ($p = 6$). The tilt angle of *ke*(L) increased with p and the transition from *ke* increasing with L to *ke* decreasing with L occurred at $p = 4$.

The economically justified amount of dividends was equal to the equity cost; therefore, the decrease in the equity cost with the leverage level signaled the discovery of a new effect that could significantly change the company's dividend policy.

Below, we compare the dependence of the WACC, company value and equity cost on the leverage level of a three-year-old company for profit tax payments that were (1) made at the end of the financial period (data from Ref. [Brusov et al. 2022]) and (2) made at the beginning of the financial period (i.e., advance payments) with frequencies of $p = 2, 4, 6$, and 12.

The comparison of the dependence of the WACC on the leverage level (L) of a three-year-old company for profit tax payments that were (1) made at the end of the financial period and (2) made at the beginning of the financial period (i.e., advance payments) with frequencies of $p = 2, 4, 6$, and 12 is shown in Fig. 12.4.

The *WACC*(L) decreased with L in both cases: advance profit tax payments and payments at the end of the financial year. This meant that debt financing was important and should be used by the company as it led to a decrease in the corresponding capital cost with L.

In the case of profit tax payments that were made at the end of the financial year, the *WACC*(L) decreased with p, while in the case of advance profit tax payments, the *WACC*(L) increased with p. However, in spite of this, the *WACC*(L) always turned out to be lower in the case of advance profit tax payments. From Fig. 12.4, it can be seen, for example, that $WACC(L = 10) = 0.1504$ at $p = 12$ for profit tax payments that were made at the end of the financial year while $WACC(L = 10) = 0.1497$ at $p = 12$ for advance profit tax payments. The *WACC*(L) curves for two these cases never crossed, i.e., the *WACC* values for advance profit tax payments always turned out to be lower than in the case of profit tax payments that were made at the end of the financial year. This demonstrated the importance of the use of advance profit tax

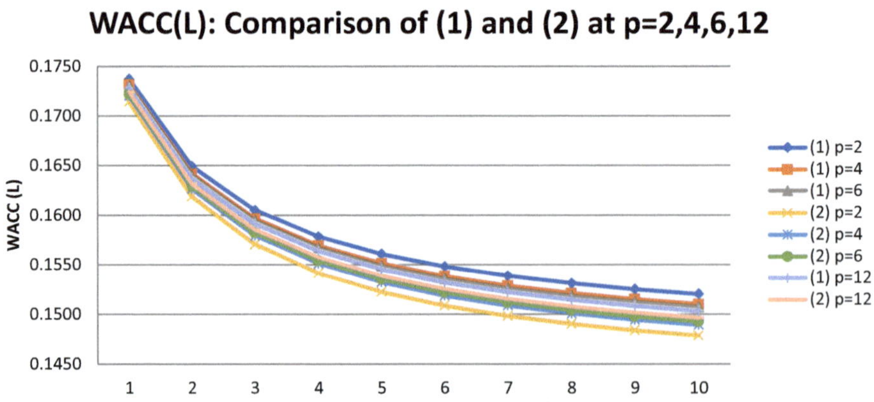

Fig. 12.4 The comparison of the dependence of the WACC on the leverage level (L) of a three-year-old company for profit tax payments that were (1) made at the end of the financial period and (2) made at the beginning of the financial period (i.e., advance payments) with frequencies of $p =$ 2, 4, 6, and 12

payments for companies because the lower values of *WACC* corresponded to higher company values.

The comparison of the dependence of the company value (V) on the leverage level (L) of a three-year-old company for profit tax payments that were (1) made at the end of the financial period and (2) made at the beginning of the financial period (i.e., advance payments) with frequencies of $p = 2$, 4, 6, and 12 is shown in Fig. 12.5.

Figure 12.5 shows that the company value increased with L for all payment frequencies (annual, semi-annual, quarterly, monthly, etc.) in both cases: advance

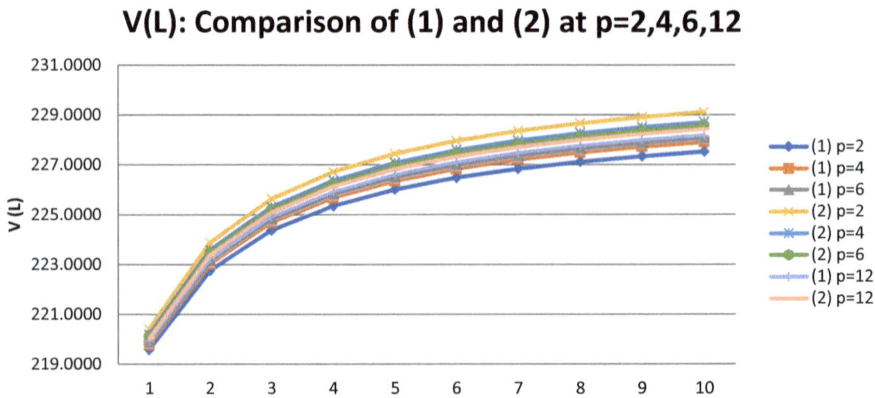

Fig. 12.5 The comparison of the dependence of the company value (V) on the leverage level (L) of a three-year-old company for profit tax payments that were (1) made at the end of the financial period and (2) made at the beginning of the financial period (i.e., advance payments) with frequencies of $p = 2$, 4, 6, and 12 is shown in Fig. 12.4

profit tax payments and payments the end of the financial period. So, the debt financing led to an increase in the company value with L and thus, it was important and should be used by the company. This was consistent with the decrease in the *WACC* with L, as shown in the previous section. The company value decreased with the frequency of payments in the case of profit tax payments being made at the beginning of the financial period (i.e., advance payments), which meant that more infrequent payments were beneficial for the company. The company value increased with the frequency of payments in the case of profit tax payments being made at the end of the financial period. However, in spite of this, $V(L)$ always turned out to be bigger in the case of advance profit tax payments. From Fig. 12.5, it can be seen, for example, that $V(L = 10) = 228.1849$ at $p = 12$ for profit tax payments that were made at the end of the financial year, while $V(L = 10) = 228.4490$ at $p = 12$ for advance profit tax payments. Note that the $V(L)$ curves that corresponded to these two cases never crossed. The influence of the payment frequency was stronger for annual, semi-annual and quarterly payments and decreased for monthly payments. This was consistent with the WACC behavior that was shown in the previous section.

The comparison of the dependence of the equity cost (*ke*) on the leverage level (L) of a three-year-old company for profit tax payments that were (1) made at the end of the financial period and (2) made at the beginning of the financial period (i.e., advance payments) with frequencies of $p = 2$, 4, 6, and 12 is shown in Fig. 12.6.

From Fig. 12.6, it can be seen that the equity cost (*ke*) depended on the leverage level (L) in a linear manner in both cases ((1) and (2)) for all values of p. In the case of profit tax payments being made at the end of the financial period, the tilt angle of $ke(L)$ decreased with p but *ke*(L) continued to increase with L for all values of p. In the case of advance profit tax payments, the tilt angle of $ke(L)$ increased with p and the transition from *ke* increasing with L to *ke* decreasing with L occurred at p

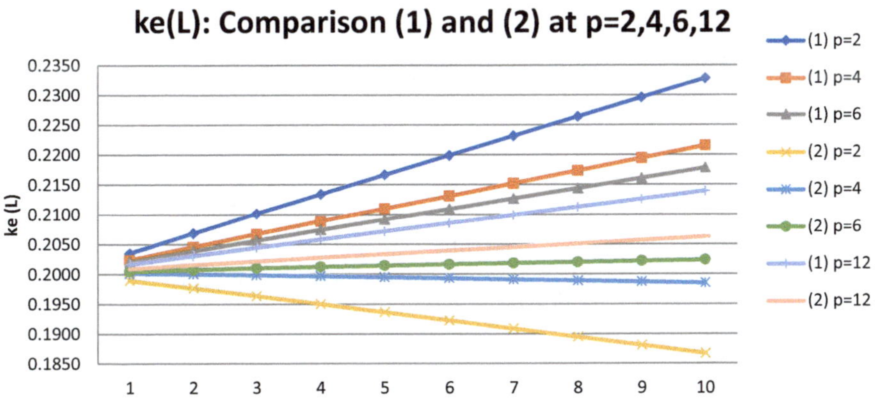

Fig. 12.6 The comparison of the dependence of the equity cost (*ke*) on the leverage level (L) of a three-year-old company for profit tax payments that were (1) made at the end of the financial period and (2) made at the beginning of the financial period (i.e., advance payments) with frequencies of $p = 2, 4, 6$, and 12

= 4. Additionally, *ke*(*L*) decreased with *L* for annual ($p = 1$), semi-annual ($p = 2$) and quarterly ($p = 4$) payments and increased for monthly ($p = 12$) and bi-monthly payments ($p = 6$). The economically justified amount of dividends was equal to the equity cost; therefore, the decrease in the equity cost with the leverage level signaled the discovery of a new effect that could significantly change the dividend policy of a company. This effect only occurred in the case of advance profit tax payments. Note that with the increase in *p*, the *ke*(*L*) curves for the two cases ((1) and (2)) approached each other but never crossed.

12.3.2 The Impact of the Frequency of Profit Tax Payments on the Dependence of the Weighted Average Cost of Capital, Capital Value and Equity Cost on the Leverage Level of a Six-Year-Old Company

In Tables 12.4, 12.5, and 12.6, we present the results of our study on the impact of the frequency of profit tax payments on the dependence of the WACC, capital value and equity cost on the leverage level of a six-year-old company with payment frequencies of $p = 1$, 2, 4, 6, and 12.

As can be seen from Fig. 12.7, the WACC decreased with *L* in the case of advance profit tax payments for all payment frequencies (annual, semi-annual, quarterly, monthly, etc.). So, debt financing led to a decrease in the corresponding capital cost with L and thus, should be used by the company. The WACC values increased with the frequency of payments, which meant that more infrequent payments were beneficial for the company. The influence of the payment frequency was stronger for annual, semi-annual and quarterly payments and decreased for monthly payments.

Table 12.4 The dependence of the WACC on the leverage level (*L*) of a six-year-old company for advance profit tax payments with frequencies of $p = 1$, 2, 4, 6, and 12

L	Wd	*WACC*, $n = 6$ (2)				
		$p = 1$	$p = 2$	$p = 4$	$p = 6$	$p = 12$
1	0.5	0.1697	0.1709	0.1715	0.1717	0.1719
2	0.666667	0.1593	0.1610	0.1618	0.1621	0.1623
3	0.75	0.1542	0.1560	0.1569	0.1572	0.1575
4	0.8	0.1510	0.1530	0.1540	0.1543	0.1546
5	0.833333	0.1489	0.1510	0.1520	0.1524	0.1527
6	0.857143	0.1474	0.1496	0.1506	0.1510	0.1513
7	0.875	0.1463	0.1485	0.1496	0.1499	0.1503
8	0.888889	0.1454	0.1477	0.1487	0.1491	0.1495
9	0.9	0.1447	0.1470	0.1481	0.1484	0.1488
10	0.909091	0.1442	0.1464	0.1475	0.1479	0.1483

Table 12.5 The dependence of the company value (V) on the leverage level (L) of a six-year-old company for advance profit tax payments with frequencies of $p = 1, 2, 4, 6$, and 12

L	Wd	V				
		$p = 1$	$p = 2$	$p = 4$	$p = 6$	$p = 12$
1	0.5	359.2385	358.0973	357.5406	357.3571	357.1746
2	0.666667	369.1124	367.5078	366.7265	366.4692	366.2133
3	0.75	374.2557	372.4010	371.4988	371.2017	370.9064
4	0.8	377.4110	375.4000	374.4222	374.1003	373.7805
5	0.833333	379.5443	377.4263	376.3969	376.0581	375.7214
6	0.857143	381.0830	378.8871	377.8201	377.4690	377.1201
7	0.875	382.2451	379.9901	378.8947	378.5342	378.1761
8	0.888889	383.1540	380.8525	379.7347	379.3669	379.0014
9	0.9	383.8841	381.5452	380.4093	380.0356	379.6643
10	0.909091	384.4836	382.1139	380.9631	380.5845	380.2084

Table 12.6 The dependence of the equity cost (ke) on the leverage level (L) of a six-year-old company for advance profit tax payments with frequencies of $p = 1, 2, 4, 6$, and 12

L	Wd	ke				
		$p = 1$	$p = 2$	$p = 4$	$p = 6$	$p = 12$
1	0.5	0.1953	0.1978	0.1990	0.1994	0.1997
2	0.666667	0.1900	0.1950	0.1974	0.1982	0.1990
3	0.75	0.1846	0.1920	0.1957	0.1969	0.1981
4	0.8	0.1791	0.1891	0.1939	0.1955	0.1971
5	0.833333	0.1736	0.1860	0.1921	0.1941	0.1961
6	0.857143	0.1680	0.1830	0.1903	0.1927	0.1951
7	0.875	0.1624	0.1799	0.1885	0.1913	0.1941
8	0.888889	0.1569	0.1769	0.1867	0.1899	0.1931
9	0.9	0.1513	0.1738	0.1848	0.1885	0.1921
10	0.909091	0.1457	0.1707	0.1830	0.1870	0.1911

As can be seen from Fig. 12.8, the company value (V) increased with L in the case of advance profit tax payments for all payment frequencies (annual, semi-annual, quarterly, monthly, etc.). This was consistent with the decrease in the WACC with the leverage level, as shown in the previous section. The company value decreased with the frequency of payments, which meant that more infrequent payments were beneficial for the company. The influence of the payment frequency was stronger for annual, semi-annual and quarterly payments and decreased for monthly payments. This was consistent with the WACC behavior that was shown in the previous section.

As can be seen from Fig. 12.9, the equity cost (ke) depended on the leverage level (L) in a linear manner. It decreased for annual ($p = 1$), semi-annual ($p = 2$)

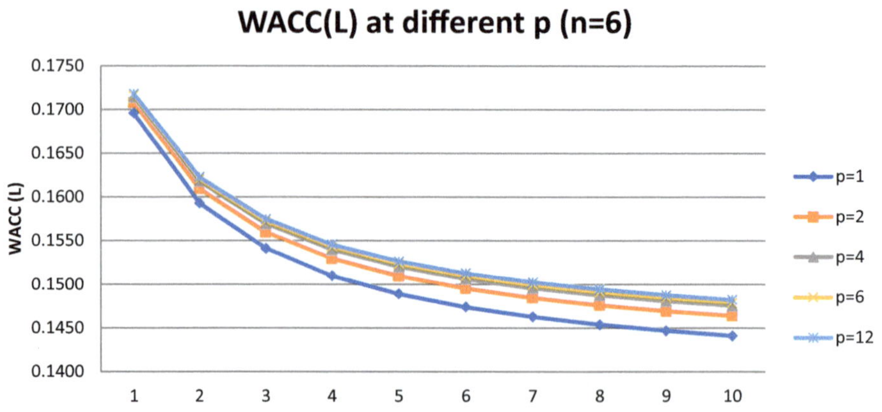

Fig. 12.7 The dependence of the *WACC* on the leverage level (L) of a six-year-old company for advance profit tax payments with frequencies of $p = 1, 2, 4, 6$, and 12

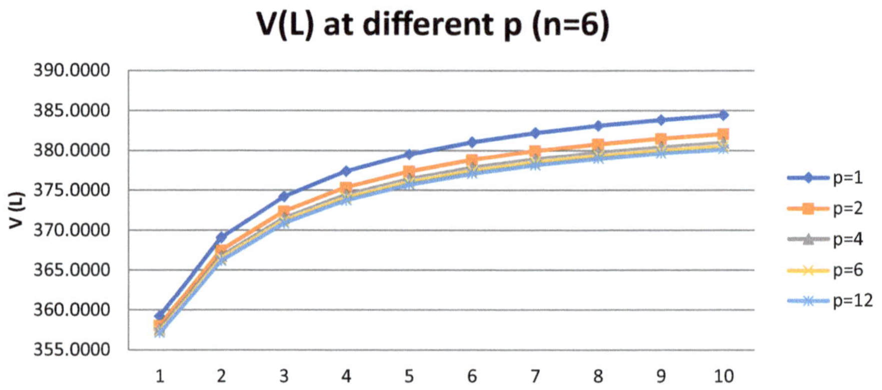

Fig. 12.8 The dependence of the company value (V) on the leverage level (L) of a six-year-old company for advance profit tax payments with frequencies of $p = 1, 2, 4, 6$, and 12

and quarterly ($p = 4$) payments and increased for monthly ($p = 12$) and bi-monthly payments ($p = 6$). The economically justified amount of dividends was equal to the equity cost; therefore, the decrease in the equity cost with the leverage level signaled the discovery of a new effect that could significantly change the dividend policy of the company. Note that for the three-year-old company, *ke* increased with L for monthly ($p = 12$) and bi-monthly payments ($p = 6$) and the transition from decreasing to increasing behavior occurred at $p = 4$.

The comparison of the dependence of the *WACC* on the leverage level (L) of a six-year-old company for profit tax payments that were (1) made at the end of the financial period and (2) made at the beginning of the financial period (i.e., advance payments) with frequencies of $p = 2, 4, 6$, and 12 is shown in Fig. 12.10.

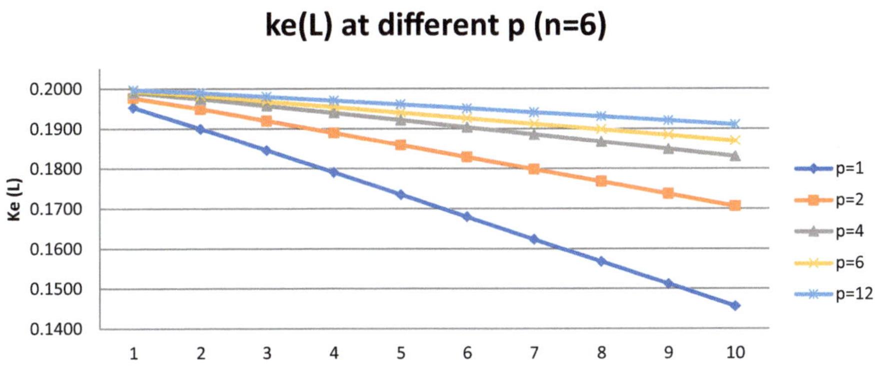

Fig. 12.9 The dependence of the equity cost (*ke*) on the leverage level (*L*) of a six-year-old company for advance profit tax payments with frequencies of $p = 1, 2, 4, 6$, and 12

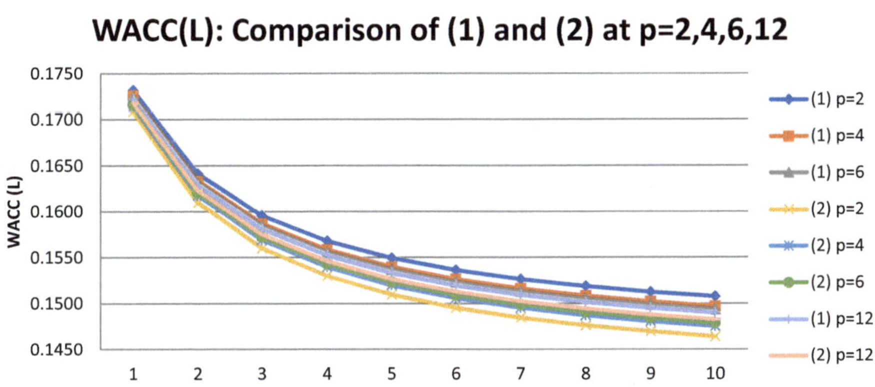

Fig. 12.10 The comparison of the dependence of the *WACC* on the leverage level (*L*) of a six-year-old company for profit tax payments that were (1) made at the end of the financial period and (2) made at the beginning of the financial period (i.e., advance payments) with frequencies of $p = 2, 4$, 6, and 12

The WACC(*L*) decreased with *L* in both cases: profit tax payments that were made at the beginning of the financial period and payments that were made at the end of the financial period. This meant that the debt financing led to a decrease in the corresponding capital cost with *L* and should be used by the company.

The *WACC*(*L*) decreased with *p* in the case of profit tax payments being made at the end of the financial period, while in the case of profit tax payments being made at the beginning of the financial period (i.e., advance payments), the *WACC*(*L*) increased with *p*. However, in spite of this, the *WACC*(*L*) always turned out to be lower in the latter case. From Fig. 12.10, it can be seen, for example, that $WACC(L = 10) = 0.1490$ at $p = 12$ for profit tax payments that were made at the end of the financial year while $WACC(L = 10) = 0.1483$ at $p = 12$ for advance profit tax payments. The *WACC*(*L*) curves for two these cases never crossed, i.e., the *WACC*

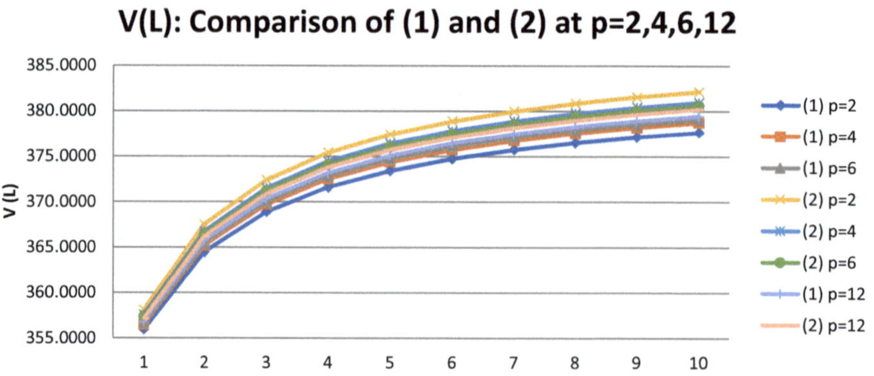

Fig. 12.11 The comparison of the dependence of the company value (V) on the leverage level (L) of a six-year-old company for profit tax payments that were (1) made at the end of the financial period and (2) made at the beginning of the financial period (i.e., advance payments) with frequencies of $p = 2, 4, 6$, and 12

values for advance profit tax payments always turned out to be lower than in the case of profit tax payments that were made at the end of the financial year. Thus, the use of advance profit tax payments was quite important for the company because the lower values of *WACC* corresponded to higher company values. This conclusion is valid for companies of any age.

The comparison of the dependence of the company cost (V) on the leverage level (L) of a six-year-old company for profit tax payments that were (1) made at the end of the financial period and (2) made at the beginning of the financial period (i.e., advance payments) with frequencies of $p = 2, 4, 6$, and 12 is shown in Fig. 12.11.

As can be seen from Fig. 12.11, the company value (V) increased with L for all payment frequencies (annual, semi-annual, quarterly, monthly, etc.) in both cases: profit tax payments that were made at the beginning of the financial period (i.e., advance payments) and profit tax payments that were made at the end of the financial period. So, the debt financing led to an increase in the company value with the leverage level and thus, should be used by the company. This was consistent with the decrease in the *WACC* with the leverage level, as shown in the previous section. The company value decreased with the frequency of payments in the case of advance profit tax payments, which meant that more infrequent payments were beneficial for the company, and increased with the frequency of payments in the case of profit tax payments that were made at the end of the financial period. However, in spite of this, the $V(L)$ always turned out to be bigger in the case of advance profit tax payments. From Fig. 12.11, it can be seen, for example, that $V(L = 10) = 379.4635$ at $p = 12$ for profit tax payments that were made at the end of the financial year while $V(L = 10) = 380.2084$ at $p = 12$ for advance profit tax payments. Note that the $V(L)$ curves that corresponded to these two cases never crossed. The influence of the payment frequency was stronger for annual, semi-annual and quarterly payments

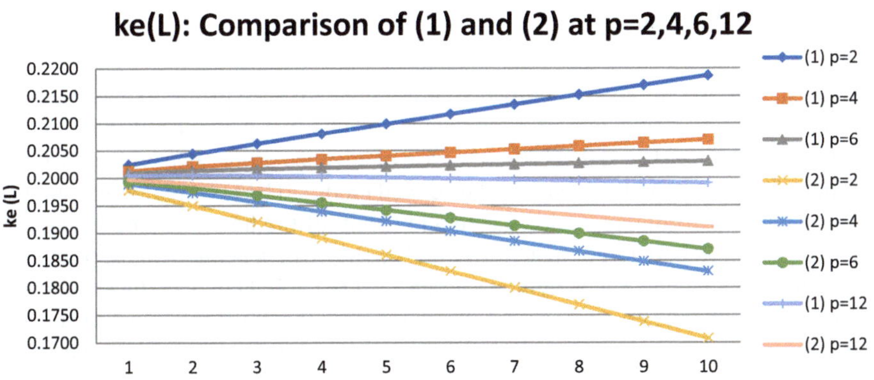

Fig. 12.12 The comparison of the dependence of the equity cost (*ke*) on the leverage level (*L*) of a six-year-old company for profit tax payments that were (1) made at the end of the financial period and (2) made at the beginning of the financial period (i.e., advance payments) with frequencies of $p = 2, 4, 6$, and 12

and decreased for monthly payments. This was consistent with the WACC behavior that was shown in the previous section.

The comparison of the dependence of the equity cost (*ke*) on the leverage level (*L*) of a six-year-old company for profit tax payments that were (1) made at the end of the financial period and (2) made at the beginning of the financial period (i.e., advance payments) with frequencies of $p = 2, 4, 6$, and 12 is shown in Fig. 12.12.

From Fig. 12.12, it can be seen that the equity cost (*ke*) depended on the leverage level (*L*) in a linear manner in both cases ((1) and (2)) for all values of *p* (similar to the case of the three-year-old company). In the case of profit tax payments that were made at the end of the financial period, the tilt angle of *ke*(*L*) decreased with *p*, but *ke*(*L*) continued to increase with L at $p = 2, 4$, and 6 and we only observed the transition to a slight decrease with leverage level at $p = 12$. Note that for the three-year-old company, this transition was absent and *ke*(*L*) increased with L for all values of *p*.

In the case of profit tax payments that were made at the beginning of the financial period (i.e., advance payments), the tilt angle of *ke*(*L*) increased with *p*, but *ke*(*L*) decreased with L for all payment frequencies. The economically justified amount of dividends was equal to the equity cost; thus, the discovery of the decrease in equity cost with the leverage level represented a new effect that could greatly change the company's dividend policy. This effect only occurred in the case of advance profit tax payments. Note that with the increase in *p*, the *ke*(*L*) curves for the two cases ((1) and (2)) approached each other but never crossed.

12.4 Conclusions

In this chapter, we studied the influence of frequent advance profit tax payments on the main financial indicators of a company. For this, we generalized the Brusov–Filatova–Orekhova (BFO) theory for the case of advance profit tax payments with an arbitrary frequency for the first time. We derived modified BFO formulae and showed that (1) all BFO formulae could change and (2) all of the financial parameters of a company, such as *WACC*, company value and equity cost, depended on the frequency of profit tax payments. The weighted average cost of capital (*WACC*) increased with the payments and the company value decreased with the payments. This meant that more infrequent payments were beneficial for the companies. The tilt angle of the equity cost (*ke*(*L*)) also increased with the payments. Depending on the company age, *ke*(*L*) either decreased with *L* for all payment frequencies or a transition from the decrease to an increase in *ke* with *L* occurred for some frequencies.

We compared the obtained results to those that we recently obtained for frequent profit tax payments that were made at the end of the financial period (Brusov et al. 2022) and found them to be totally different. We showed that in spite the fact that the *WACC* decreased with the payments and the company value increased with the payments in this case (Brusov et al. 2022), the *WACC* values turned out to be bigger and the company values turned out to be smaller than in the case of frequent advance profit tax payments for all payment frequencies. This underlined the importance of advance profit tax payments. Regulators should extend the practice of advance income tax payments to profit tax payments.

The economically justified amount of dividends was equal to the equity cost; thus, the discovered decrease in the equity cost with the leverage level represented a new effect that could greatly change a company's dividend policy. In the case of profit tax payments that were made at the end of the financial period, the tilt angle of *ke*(*L*) decreased with the payments, but *ke*(*L*) continued to increase with *L* at $p = 2$, 4, and 6 and we only observed the transition to a slight decrease with leverage level at $p = 12$. Note that for the three-year-old company, this transition was absent and *ke*(*L*) increased with *L* for all values of *p*.

In the case of advance profit tax payments, the tilt angle of *ke*(*L*) increased with the payments, but *ke*(*L*) decreased with *L* for all payment frequencies for the six-year-old company. For the three-year-old company, *ke*(*L*) decreased at $p = 1$, 2, and 4 and increased at $p = 6$ and 12. Thus, for the three-year-old company, the transition from the decreasing *ke*(*L*) behavior to the *ke*(*L*) increasing behavior occurred at $p = 6$, while for the six-year-old company, this transition was absent.

The novelty of the chapter is as follows:

1. We generalized the BFO theory for the case of advance profit tax payments with an arbitrary frequency for the first time;
2. By comparing the obtained results to those for frequent profit tax payments at the end of the financial period, we showed that in spite the fact that the WACC decreased with the payments and the company value increased with the payments, the WACC value in this case turned out to be bigger and the company value

turned out to be smaller than in case of frequent advance profit tax payments for all payment frequencies, which underlined the importance of advance profit tax payments;

3. A new effect of the dependence of equity cost on leverage level was discovered and this pioneering result could radically change the company dividend policies. In the case of advance profit tax payments, the tilt angle of *ke*(*L*) increased with the payments, but *ke*(*L*) decreased with L for all payment frequencies for the six-year-old company and at $p = 1$, 2, and 4 for the three-year-old company, although it increased at $p = 6$ and 12. Thus, for the three-year-old company, the transition from the decreasing *ke*(*L*) behavior to the increasing *ke*(*L*) behavior occurred at $p = 6$, while this transition was absent for the six-year-old company;
4. Regulator recommendations were developed to expand the practice of advance profit tax payments, which would be beneficial to both parties, the companies and the state, (1) this practice would lead to a decrease in the cost of raising capital and an increase in the company value for companies and (2) ensure an increase in the stability of budget revenues for the regulators.

There was one limitation of the current consideration: the BFO theory was used with the assumption of a constant income. We will generalize the BFO theory for the case of variable incomes in the next Chapter 13.

References

Angotti M, de Lacerda Moreira R, Hipólito Bernardes do Nascimento J, Neto de Almeida Bispo O (2018) Analysis of an equity investment strategy based on accounting and financial reports in Latin American markets. Reficont 5:22–40

Barbi M (2011) On the risk-neutral value of debt tax shields. Appl Financ Econ 22:251–258

Batrancea L (2021a) An econometric approach regarding the impact of fiscal pressure on equilibrium: evidence from electricity, gas and oil companies listed on the New York Stock Exchange. Mathematics 9:630

Batrancea L (2021b) The influence of liquidity and solvency on performance within the healthcare industry: evidence from publicly listed companies. Mathematics 9:2231

Becker DM (2022) Getting the valuation formulas right when it comes to annuities. Manag Financ 48:470

Berk J, De Marzo P (2007) *Corporate Finance*; Pearson-Addison Wesley: Boston. MA, USA

Brusov PN, Filatova TV, Kulik VL (2024) Capital asset pricing model (CAPM) 2.0: account of business and financial risk. finance: theory and practice 28(2):128–142. https://doi.org/10.26794/2587-5671-2024-28-2-128-142

Brusov P, Filatova T, Orehova N, Eskindarov M (2018) Modern corporate finance, investments, taxation and ratings, 2nd ed. Springer Nature Publishing, Cham, Switzerland pp 1–571

Brusov PN, Filatova TV, Orekhova N.P, Kulik VL, Chang SI, Lin YCG (2020) Modification of the Modigliani-Miller theory for the case of advance payments of tax on profit. J Rev Glob Econ 9:257–267

Brusov P, Filatova T, Orekhova N (2021) Ratings: critical analysis and new approaches of quantitative and qualitative methodology. Springer Nature Publishing pp.1-369

Brusov P, Filatova T, Orekhova N (2022) Generalized modigliani–miller theory: Applications in corporate finance, investments, taxation and ratings, Springer Nature Publishing pp.1-362

Brusov P, Filatova T, Orekhova N (2023) The Brusov–Filatova–Orekhova theory of capital structure: Applications in corporate finance, investments, taxation and ratings, Springer Nature Publishing pp.1-769

Brusov P, Filatova T (2025a) Business valuation and company value: New qualitative approaches considering business and financial risks, Springer Nature Publishing pp.1-654

Brusov P, Filatova T (2025b) Efficiency of investment projects: Modern investment models and their applications, Springer Nature Publishing pp.1-843

Brusov PN, Filatova TV, Orekhova NP, Kulik VL, Chang SI, Lin YCG (2022) The generalization of the Brusov–Filatova–Orekhova theory for the case of payments of tax on profit with arbitrary frequency. Mathematics 10:1343. https://doi.org/10.3390/math10081343

Dimitropoulos P (2014) Capital structure and corporate governance of soccer clubs: european evidence. Manag Res Rev 37:658–678

El-Chaarani H, Abraham R, Skaf Y (2022) The impact of corporate governance on the financial performance of the banking sector in the MENA (Middle Eastern and North African) region: an immunity test of banks for COVID-19. J Risk Financ Manag 15:82

Farber A, Gillet R, Szafarz AA (2006) General formula for the WACC. Int J Bus 11:211–218

Fernandez PA (2006) General formula for the WACC: a comment. Int J Bus 11:219

Franc-Dąbrowska J, Mądra-Sawicka M, Milewska A (2021) Energy sector risk and cost of capital assessment—companies and investors perspective. Energies 14:1613

Hamada R (1969) Portfolio analysis, market equilibrium, and corporate finance. J Financ 24:13–31

Harris R, Pringle J (1985) Risk-adjusted discount rates-extension from the average-risk case. J Financ Res 8:237–244

Huang S, Sun H, Zhao H, Zhang Y (2020) Influence of leverage on the return on equity. Syst Eng Theory Pract 40:355

Islam SZ, Khandaker S (2015) Firm leverage decisions: does industry matter? N Am J Econ Financ 31:94

Luiz K, Cruz M (2015) The relevance of capital structure on firm performance: a multivariate analysis of publicly traded Brazilian companies. REPeC Brasília 9:384–401

Miller M (1977) Debt and taxes. J Financ 32:261–275. https://doi.org/10.1111/j.1540-6261.1977.tb03267.x

Modigliani F, Miller M (1958) The cost of capital, corporate finance, and the theory of investment. Am Econ Rev 48:261–297

Modigliani F, Miller M (1963) Corporate income taxes and the cost of capital: a correction. Am Econ Rev 53:147–175

Modigliani F, Miller M (1966) Some estimates of the cost of capital to the electric utility industry 1954–1957. Am Econ Rev 56:333–391

Mundi HS, Kaur P, Murty RLN (2022) A qualitative inquiry into the capital structure decisions of overconfident finance managers of family-owned businesses in India. Qual Res Financ Mark 14:357–379

Myers S (2001) Capital structure. J Econ Perspect 15:81–102

Sadiq M, Alajlani S, Hussain MS, Bashir F, Chupradit S (2022) Impact of credit, liquidity, and systematic risk on financial structure: comparative investigation from sustainable production. Environ Sci Pollut Res Int 29:20963–20975

Vergara-Novoa C, Sepúlveda-Rojas JP, Miguel DA, Nicolás R (2018) Cost of capital estimation for highway concessionaires in Chile. J Adv Transp 2018:2153536

Zhukov P (2018) The impact of cash flows and weighted average cost of capital to enterprise value in the oil and gas sector. J Rev Glob Econ 7:138–145

Chapter 13
Generalization of the Brusov–Filatova–Orekhova Theory for the Case of Variable Income

13.1 Introduction

Among the theories of capital structure, the two main ones are the Brusov–Filatova–Orekhova (BFO) theory and the Modigliani–Miller (MM) theory, which is the eternal limit of the BFO theory. Both of them consider the case of constant income, although in practice, a company's income is, of course, variable. The generalization of these two theories of capital structure for the case of variable income is very important, since it allows them to expand their applicability in practice. Recently, we have generalized the case of variable income the Modigliani–Miller theory (Brusov et al. 2021a), and here we have generalized for the first time the case of variable income of the Brusov–Filatova–Orekhova theory. This generalization significantly expands the applicability of the modern capital structure theory, which is valid for companies of any age, and in practice, for investments, corporate finance, business valuation, banking, ratings, etc.

13.1.1 Literature Review

The Brusov–Filatova–Orekhova (BFO) theory and its perpetual limit—the theory of Nobel laureates Modigliani and Miller—study capital structure problems. Capital structure is the ratio between the company's own and borrowed capital, and asks whether capital structure affects key company metrics, such as weighted average cost of capital, WACC, cost of equity, ke, earnings, company value, and others, and if so, how? The determination of the optimal capital structure, that is, the determination of capital structure in which WACC is minimal and the company value is maximized, is one of the main problems, solved by the company's management. The Modigliani and Miller Chapter (Modigliani and Miller 1958) was the first quantitative study of

P. Brusov and T. Filatova, *Taxes and Taxation*, Contributions to Finance and Accounting, https://doi.org/10.1007/978-3-032-11077-0_13

the influence of capital structure on a company's financial parameters. Prior to this, there was a traditional approach based on empirical data analysis.

13.1.2 Before the Modigliani and Miller Work

In the traditional approach, the WACC and the value of the company, V, depend on the level of leverage, L (and, therefore, on the capital structure). Debt is always cheaper than equity, since the former has less risk, and because in the event of bankruptcy, the claims of creditors are satisfied earlier than the claims of shareholders.

Thus, an increase in the share of cheaper borrowed capital of the total capital structure to the limit that does not violate financial stability and does not increase the risk of bankruptcy leads to a decrease in the WACC and an increase in the value of the company, V.

Further increase of debt financing could lead to financial stability violation and an increase in the bankruptcy risk. WACC increases and the company value, V, decreases. The competition of advantages of debt financing and its shortcomings at low and at high leverage levels forms the optimal capital structure where WACC is minimal and the company value, V, is maximum. These traditional approach results have been used in the trade-off theory.

13.1.3 Modigliani–Miller Theory

Modigliani–Miller Theory Without Taxes

Modigliani and Miller (MM) (Modigliani and Miller 1958), under a lot of assumptions, including the absence of corporate and individual taxes, the perpetuity of all companies and all cash flows, etc., obtained results that are completely different from the results of the traditional approach: capital structure does not affect capital cost and company value.

Under the above restrictions, Modigliani and Miller have shown that without taxes, the company value, V, is equal

$$V = V_0 = \frac{EBIT}{k_0} \tag{13.1}$$

Here, EBIT is Earnings Before Interest and Taxes, k_0 is discount rate, and V_0 stands for the unlevered company value.

From (13.1) it is easy to obtain WACC:

$$WACC = k_0 \tag{13.2}$$

k_0 is the cost of equity for a company without borrowed funds, and for a company with borrowed capital, k_0 is the cost of equity with a zero level of borrowed funds ($L = 0$).

From (13.1) and the expression for WACC

$$\mathrm{WACC} = k_0 = k_e w_e + k_d w_d. \tag{13.3}$$

One can obtain the cost of equity, ke

$$\begin{aligned} k_e &= \frac{k_0}{w_e} - k_d \frac{w_d}{w_e} = \frac{k_0(S + D)}{S} - k_d \frac{D}{S} \\ &= k_0 + (k_0 - k_d)\frac{D}{S} = k_0 + (k_0 - k_d)L \end{aligned} \tag{13.4}$$

Here, WACC is weighted average cost of capital; L is leverage level; D is debt capital value; S is equity capital value; k_d and w_d are the cost and share of the company's debt capital; and k_e and w_e are the equity capital cost and share. From (13.4), it follows that the equity cost increases linearly with the leverage level.

Modigliani–Miller Theory with Taxes

Taking into account income tax, in 1963, Modigliani and Miller (Modigliani and Miller 1963; Modigliani and Miller 1966) obtained the following result for the value of the levered company, V,

$$V = V_0 + D \cdot t \tag{13.5}$$

Here, V_0 stands for the unlevered company value, t is the tax on income, and D is debt value.

From (13.5), it is easy to derive the expression for the WACC

$$WACC = k_0 \cdot (1 - w_d t) \tag{13.6}$$

From (13.6), one can obtain the formula for equity cost, ke, within the Modigliani–Miller theory with taxes

$$k_e = k_0 + L \cdot (k_0 - k_d)(1 - t) \tag{13.7}$$

Formula (13.7) differs from formula (13.4) (MM without taxes) by the factor (1 − t), which is called the tax corrector. This is less than one, so the tilt of the ke(L) curve decreases with taxes.

13.1.4 Unification of Capital Asset Pricing Model (CAPM) with Modigliani–Miller Model

Unification of Capital Asset Pricing Model (CAPM) with the Modigliani–Miller model was done in 1969 (Hamada 1969). Hamada derived the below formula for the cost of equity of a levered company, which included the financial and business risks of a company:

$$k_e = k_F + (k_M - k_F)b_U + (k_M - k_F)b_U\frac{D}{S}(1 - T), \tag{13.8}$$

where b_U is the β–coefficient of the company of the same group of business risk, that the company under consideration, but with L = 0. The formula (13.8) consists of three terms: risk-free income ability k_F, compensating shareholders a time value of their money, business risk premium $(k_M - k_F)b_U$, and financial risk premium $(k_M - k_F)b_U\frac{D}{S}(1 - T)$.

For a financially independent company, the financial risk is equal to zero (the third term disappears), and its owners will only receive the business risk premium.

Miller Model

In (Miller 1977), Miller has accounted for corporate and individual taxes to obtain the following formula for unlevered company value, V_U,

$$V_U = \frac{\text{EBIT}(1 - T_C)(1 - T_S)}{k_0}. \tag{13.9}$$

Here, T_C—tax rate on corporate income, T_S—the tax rate on incomes of an individual investor from his ownership through corporation stocks.

13.1.5 Brusov–Filatova–Orekhova (BFO) Theory

The perpetuity of all company cash flow and of a company's lifetime was one of the main restrictions of the Modigliani–Miller (MM) theory, which has been lifted up in 2008 by Brusov–Filatova–Orekhova (Brusov et al. 2018, 2021b). They generalized the MM theory for the case of the company of any age, n, and derived the following Brusov–Filatova–Orekhova formula for the WACC

$$\frac{1 - (1 + WACC)^{-n}}{WACC} = \frac{1 - (1 + k_0)^{-n}}{k_0\left[1 - w_d T\left(1 - (1 + k_d)^{-n}\right)\right]} \tag{13.10}$$

To obtain the Modigliani–Miller formula for the WACC from (13.10), one should substitute $n \to \infty$.

It was shown (Brusov et al. 2018, 2021b) that a number of innovative effects, discovered in the BFO theory, are absent in the MM theory (Modigliani and Miller 1958, 1963, 1966).

Some main existing principles of financial management spanning many decades have been destroyed by the BFO theory; among them is the keystone of optimal capital structure formation—trade-off theory, and the bankruptcy of this theory has been proven within the BFO theory (Brusov et al. 2018, 2021b).

13.1.6 Alternate WACC Formula

An alternate formula for the WACC has been suggested (Farber et al. 2006; Fernandez 2006; Berk and DeMarzo 2007; Harris and Pringle 1985). It has the form below (Eq. [13.18] in Farber et al. [2006])

$$WACC = k_0(1 - w_d t) - k_d t w_d + k_{TS} t w_d \tag{13.11}$$

Here, k_0, k_d, and k_{TS} are the returns on the financially independent company, the debt, and the tax shield, respectively, t is the corporate tax rate, and w_d is the debt share.

Although Eq. (13.11) is quite general, additional conditions are needed for practical applicability. When the WACC remains constant over time, the value of a leveraged company can be found by discounting the unleveraged free cash flows using the WACC. In this case, specific formulas can be found in textbook (Berk and DeMarzo 2007).

In the Modigliani–Miller theory (Modigliani and Miller 1963), the debt value D is constant. V_0 is also constant, as the expected after-tax cash-flow of the financially independent company is fixed. By assumption, $k_{TS} = k_d$ and the tax shield value is TS = tD. Therefore, the company value V is a constant and the alternate WACC formula (13.11) simplifies the MM formula:

$$WACC = k_0(1 - w_d t)$$

The "classical" MM theory, suggesting that the returns on the debt k_d and the tax shield k_{TS} are equals (both these values have debt nature), is much more reasonable, so this is why in Brusov et al. (2021a), we modify the "classical" MM theory, namely.

13.1.7 Trade-Off Theory

In the study of the problem of optimal capital structure of the company during many decades, the cornerstone was the world-famous trade-off theory. It is still widely used now for decisions on capital structure. In (Frank and Goyal 2009), the relative importance of different factors in capital structure decisions of publicly traded American companies has been studied. The most important factors to explain leverage level are: median industry leverage (+ effect on leverage), log of assets (+), market-to-book assets ratio (−), inflation (+), tangibility (+), and incomes (−). It was noted that companies that pay dividends tend to have lower leverage levels. The related effects have been found under considering book leverage. Authors found empirical data consistent with some trade-off theory versions.

In (Sheridan and Wessels 1988), authors compare the applicability of the trade-off theory and pecking order theory for small and medium-sized companies' decisions about capital structure. It was found that the most lucrative and oldest companies have smaller leverage levels, which confirms the forecasts of the pecking order theory. Larger companies have a higher level of leverage, which is consistent with the predictions of the trade-off theory and pecking order theory. It is concluded that the trade-off theory and pecking order theory for small and medium-sized companies are not mutually exclusive when explaining capital structure decisions.

However, in 2013, Brusov et al. (2018, 2021, 2021b, 2022, 2023, 2024) and Brusov and Filatova (2025a, b) proved the inconsistency of the trade-off theory in the framework of the BFO theory they created. It is shown that the assumption of risky debt financing does not lead to an increase in the WACC, which still decreases with increasing leverage. Thus, there is no minimum depending on the level of WACC leverage and no maximum depending on the value of the company from the level of leverage. Therefore, in the world-famous theory of trade-offs, there is no optimal capital structure. Brusov et al., in 2013 (Brusov et al. 2018, 2021b), having analyzed the equity cost dependence on the level of leverage under the assumption that debt capital is risky, gave an explanation for this fact.

The Modigliani–Miller theory proved that tax shields provided substantial gains to the company. In (Harry and Masulis 1980), the theoretical study of tax shields was continued. It was noted that companies may have tax deductibles other than debt. Such non-debt tax shields are investment tax credits, depreciation, and net-loss carry forwards. In (Bradley et al. 1984), the tax effects suggested in Harry and Masulis (1980) have been tested. In contrast to the prediction in Harry and Masulis (1980), it was shown that debt is positively related to non-debt tax shields, as measured by investment tax credits and depreciation. The results of Sheridan and Wessels (1988) do not provide support for an effect on debt ratios arising from nondebt tax shields. In (Graham 2003), it was pointed out that a positive relationship between such proxies for non-debt tax shield and debt may result if a company invests heavily and borrows to invest. Any substitution effects between debt and non-debt tax shields could be suppressed by a mechanical positive relation of this type.

The Brusov–Filatova–Orekhova (BFO) theory methodology and results are well known in the literature (for example, see references [Dimitropoulos 2014; Luiz and Cruz 2015; Barbi 2011; Franc-Dąbrowska et al. 2021; Angotti et al. 2018; Vergara–Novoa et al. 2018; Mundi et al. 2022; Becker 2022; El–Chaarani et al. 2022; Sadiq et al. 2022; Singhal et al. 2022]). Chapters (Angotti et al. 2018; Vergara–Novoa et al. 2018; Mundi et al. 2022; Singhal et al. 2022) use the BFO theory in practice. The impact on capital structure decisions of the overconfidence of finance managers of family-run businesses in India has been studied in Vergara–Novoa et al. (2018). The study concludes that manager decisions about capital structure could be explained by measurable managerial characteristics. In (Mundi et al. 2022), the correlation between capital structure and company risk was studied using datasets from Pakistani companies. It was shown that the role of capital structure and risk valuation is vital for the increase in the wealth of shareholders and the sustainable growth of companies. In (Becker 2022), the adjusted present value method, the free cash flow (FCF) method, the flow-to-equity method and the relationships between these methods have been considered. The authors used a stationary FCF method and the Miles and Ezzell method instead the Modigliani–Miller method to derive DCF valuation formulas for annuities. In (El–Chaarani et al. 2022), the influence of internal and external corporate governance mechanisms on the financial performance of banks in the MENA region is studied. It was shown that the corporate governance had positive effects on the financial indicators of banks. The energy companies capital costs by including an investor and market risk approach have been evaluated in Sadiq et al. (2022). The WACC intra-industry analysis of the companies has been done. The connection of capitalization and income ability in the BRICS banking sector has been examined in Singhal et al. (2022) under the signaling theory, the bankruptcy cost theory, the agency theory, the pecking order theory, the Modigliani and Miller theory, and the general theory of the cost of capital and capital structure—the Brusov–Filatova–Orekhova (BFO) theory. Over the past two years, the theory of capital structure has received a new impetus. A large-scale modification of both main theories of the capital structure, BFO and MM, has been carried out and continues in order to better take into account the conditions for the real functioning of companies, such as variable income, advance income tax payments, frequent income tax payments, their combinations, etc. (Brusov et al. 2021a; Brusov and Filatova 2022, 2013). A study of different aspects of emerging markets was carried out in Durana et al. (2022), Virglerova et al. (2021), Durana et al. (2021), Xu and Liu (2020), Valaskova et al. (2020, 2021a; b), and Białek-Jaworska and Klapkiv (2021). In (Xu and Liu 2020), the impact of intellectual capital on firm performance within a modified and extended VAIC model has been studied.

In the near future, the authors plan to publish a large review, which will examine in detail the problems of capital structure.

13.1.8 Materials and Methods

We combine analytical and numerical methods. First, we derive formulas for the company's leveraged value, *V*; the leverage less value of the company, V_0; the tax shield *TS*, and finally the *WACC* in the case of variable income.

Then, using Microsoft Excel, we study the dependences of the following values: weighted average cost of capital, WACC, discount rate, WACC-g, company value, V, and the cost of equity, ke, on the level of leverage, L, at different values of the growth rate, g. We have created a large database for sets of cost of equity k_0 and cost of debt kd, which is available upon request.

13.2 Modification of the BFO Theory for the Case of Companies with Variable Incomes

13.2.1 The Levered Company Value, V

Below, for the first time, we generalize the modern theory of the capital cost and capital structure—the Brusov–Filatova–Orekhova theory—to the case of variable income. We start by deriving the capitalization formula for a financially dependent company, assuming that income for the period grows with the growth rate g.

When accounting for the cost of any asset being equal to the sum of discounted values of incomes generated by this asset, one could write the capitalization for a financially dependent company's V of age, *n*, as the following expression

$$V = \frac{CF}{1+WACC} + \frac{CF(1+g)}{(1+WACC)^2} + \frac{CF(1+g)^2}{(1+WACC)^3} + \ldots + \frac{CF(1+g)^{n-1}}{(1+WACC)^n} \quad (13.12)$$

Here, *WACC* is the weighted average cost of capital, *CF* is an annual income of company, and (13.12) is geometric progression with denominator

$$g = \frac{(1+g)}{(1+WACC)} \quad (13.13)$$

Summarizing (13.12), we get the expression for the capitalization, *V*, of the levered company of age *n*

$$V = \frac{CF}{1+WACC} \cdot \frac{1-\left(\frac{1+g}{1+WACC}\right)^n}{1-\frac{1+g}{1+WACC}}$$

$$= \frac{CF}{WACC - g} \cdot \left(1 - \left(\frac{1+g}{1+WACC}\right)^n\right). \tag{13.14}$$

In the perpetuity limit ($n \to \infty$), we get the following formula for the levered company value, V,

$$V = \frac{CF}{WACC - g} \tag{13.15}$$

This formula shows that the discount rate is WACC–g, and not WACC.

13.2.2 The Unlevered Company Value, V_0

Let us now derive the capitalization formula for a financially independent company, assuming that income for the period grows with the growth rate g.

$$V_0 = \frac{CF}{1+k_0} + \frac{CF(1+g)}{(1+k_0)^2} + \frac{CF(1+g)^2}{(1+k_0)^3} + \ldots + \frac{CF(1+g)^{n-1}}{(1+k_0)^n} \tag{13.16}$$

(13.16) is geometric progression with denominator

$$g = \frac{(1+g)}{(1+k_0)} \tag{13.17}$$

Summarizing (13.16), we get the expression for the value V_0 of unlevered company of age n

$$V_0 = \frac{CF}{1+k_0} \cdot \frac{1 - \left(\frac{1+g}{1+k_0}\right)^n}{1 - \frac{1+g}{1+k_0}} = \frac{CF}{k_0 - g} \cdot \left(1 - \left(\frac{1+g}{1+k_0}\right)^n\right) \tag{13.18}$$

In the perpetuity limit ($n \to \infty$), we get the following formula for the unlevered company value, V_0,

$$V_0 = \frac{CF}{k_0 - g} \tag{13.19}$$

This formula shows that the discount rate is $k_0 - g$, and not k_0.

13.2.3 The Tax Shield Value

The tax shield for n–years is equal to

$$(TS)_n = \frac{tk_d D}{1+k_d} + \frac{tk_d D}{(1+k_d)^2} + \ldots + \frac{tk_d D}{(1+k_d)^n} \quad (13.20)$$

(13.20) is geometric progression with denominator

$$g = \frac{1}{(1+k_d)} \quad (13.21)$$

Summarizing (13.20), for the tax shield, we have

$$(TS)_n = \frac{tk_d D}{1+k_d} \cdot \frac{1-(1+k_d)^{-n}}{1-\frac{1}{1+k_d}} = Dt\big(1-(1+k_d)^{-n}\big) \quad (13.22)$$

$$(TS)_n = Dt\big(1-(1+k_d)^{-n}\big) \quad (13.23)$$

Using an analog of the first theorem by Modigliani–Miller for finite time, one gets

$$V = V_0 + (TS)_n \quad (13.24)$$

Substituting

$$D = w_d V \quad (13.25)$$

we arrive to the following expression

$$V\big(1 - w_d t\big(1-(1+k_d)^{-n}\big)\big) = V_0 \quad (13.26)$$

Substituting into this equation the values of an unlevered company, V_0 (13.18) and of levered company, V, (13.14) one gets the following expression

$$\frac{CF \cdot \left(1 - \left(\frac{1+g}{1+WACC}\right)^n\right) \cdot \left(1 - w_d t\left[1-(1+k_d)^{-n}\right]\right)}{WACC - g} = \frac{CF \cdot \left(1 - \left(\frac{1+g}{1+k_0}\right)^n\right)}{(k_0 - g)} \quad (13.27)$$

Dividing both parts by $\big(1 - w_d t\big(1-(1+k_d)^{-n}\big)\big)$, we get the BFO equation for the WACC of the company with variable income

$$\frac{1 - \left(\frac{1+g}{1+WACC}\right)^n}{WACC - g} = \frac{1 - \left(\frac{1+g}{1+k_0}\right)^n}{(k_0 - g) \cdot \left(1 - w_d t\left[1-(1+k_d)^{-n}\right]\right)} \quad (13.28)$$

This is the main theoretical result of the current chapter.

In the perpetuity limit ($n \to \infty$), we get the following equation for WACC in the case of variable income (Brusov et al. 2021a)

$$WACC - g = (k_0 - g) \cdot (1 - w_d t) \tag{13.29}$$

$$WACC = (k_0 - g) \cdot (1 - w_d t) + g \tag{13.30}$$

13.3 Results and Discussions

In order to understand the impact of a variable growth rate g on the main financial indicators of a company within the framework of the generalized theory of Brusov–Filatova–Orekhova (GBFO), we study the dependences of the following values: weighted average cost of capital, WACC, discount rate, WACC − g, company value, V, and the cost of equity, k_e, on the level of leverage L at different values of the growth rate, g. We have created a large database for sets of cost of equity k_0 and cost of debt k_d, which is available upon request. To illustrate the results obtained and the conclusions drawn below, we present below the results for the following financial parameters of the company:

$$k_0 = 0.18;\ k_d = 0.16;\ t = 0.2;\ CF = 100;\ n = 2 \text{ and}$$
$$n = 4;\ g = 0.2;\ 0.1;\ 0.0;\ -0.1;\ -0.2$$

Here, k_0 is the equity cost at zero leverage level; k_d is the debt cost; t is the tax on income; *CF* is income per period; n is the company age; L is the leverage level; and g is the growth rate.

Note that if the results for different parameters could be and are numerically different, then the qualitative effect of the variable growth rate g on the main financial indicators is similar.

13.3.1 Calculations for Two-Year Company

Calculations of Weighted Average Cost of Capital, WACC

As can be seen from Table 13.1 and Fig. 13.1, for different values of g all curves WACC(L) start from one point (0; $k_0 = 0.18$). These curves WACC(L) demonstrate the decrease of WACC with leverage level L at all g values. The curves WACC(L) increase with growth rate, g.

Table 13.1 The WACC depending on the level of leverage L at different growth rates g in Generalized Brusov–Filatova–Orekhova theory (GBFO theory) for two-year company

L	WACC, n = 2				
	g = 0.2	g = − 0.1	g = 0	g = 0.1	g = 0.2
0	0.1799864	0.1799858	0.179995	0.1799849	0.1799844
1	0.1583502	0.1583545	0.1591545	0.1594954	0.1597882
2	0.15084	0.1513935	0.1521805	0.1523026	0.1526805
3	0.1472744	0.1478992	0.148688	0.1489255	0.1493521
4	0.1451307	0.1457982	0.1465907	0.1468947	0.1473505
5	0.1436999	0.1443958	0.1451917	0.1455391	0.1460143
6	0.142677	0.1433932	0.1441921	0.1445699	0.145059
7	0.1419093	0.1426408	0.1434421	0.1438425	0.144342
8	0.141312	0.1420553	0.1428587	0.1432764	0.1437841
9	0.140834	0.1415867	0.1423919	0.1428234	0.1433376
10	0.1404427	0.1412033	0.1420099	0.1424527	0.1429721

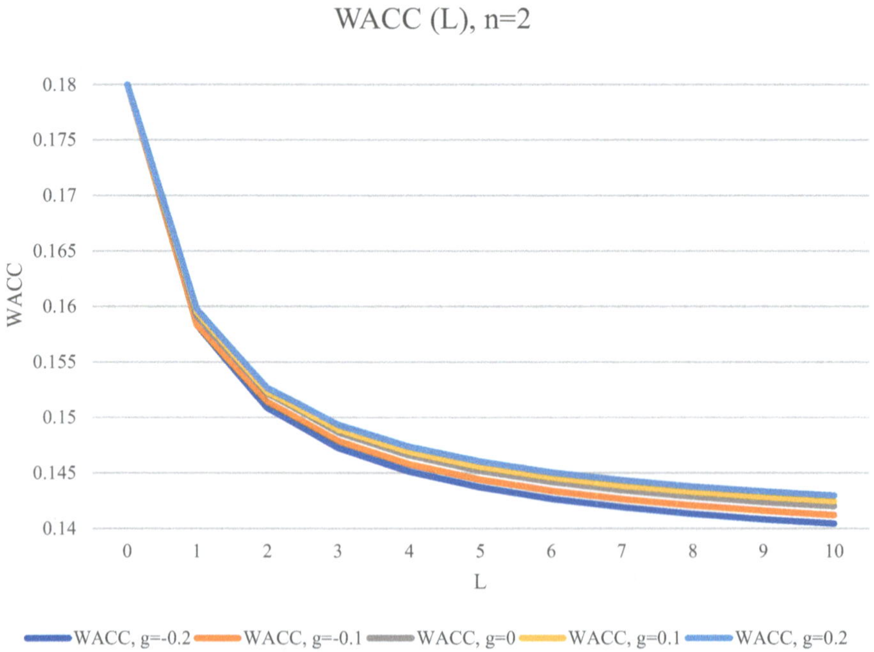

Fig. 13.1 The WACC depending on the level of leverage L at different growth rates g in Generalized Brusov–Filatova–Orekhova theory (GBFO theory) for two-year company

The results for a two-year company differ from the results for a perpetual limit—the theory of Modigliani and Miller (Brusov et al. 2021a). In the latter case, the WACC(L) curves decrease with the level of leverage L at $g < k_0$ and increase at $g > k_0$. k_0 is the threshold value g separating the increasing WACC(L) curves from the decreasing ones, and for $g = k_0$ WACC = const = k_0. In the first case (BFO theory), the WACC(L) curves decrease with increasing leverage L for all values of the growth rate g. The WACC(L) curves increase with the rate g both in the Brusov–Filatova–Orekhova theory and in the Modigliani and Miller theory. This is the first indication that WACC is no longer a discount rate, since it is intuitive that the discount rate must decrease in order to increase the value of company V. As we will see below, WACC–g and WACC–k_0 play the role of the discount rate.

The discount rate moves for a financially dependent company from the weighted average cost of capital, WACC, to WACC–g (where g is the growth rate), for a financially independent company from k_0 to k_0–g. As we intuitively understood above, this means that WACC and k0 are no longer discount rates, as is the case for the classical Brusov–Filatova–Orekhova constant income theory. Below, we study the dependence of the discount rate WACC–g on the level of leverage L in the Generalized theory of Brusov–Filatova–Orekhova (the GBFO theory) at $k_0 = 0.18$ and different values of g $(-0.2; -0.1; 0.0; 0.1; 0.2)$ for a two- and four-year company.

Calculations of the Discount Rate, WACC–g

As can be seen from Table 13.2 and Fig. 13.2, the curves (WACC–g)(L) demonstrate the decrease of WACC–g with leverage level L at all g values. The curves (WACC–g)(L) decrease with growth rate, g.

Table 13.2 The discount rate WACC–g depending on the level of leverage L at different growth rates g in Generalized Brusov–Filatova–Orekhova theory (GBFO theory) for two-year company

L	(WACC– g), n = 2				
	g = – 0.2	g = – 0.1	g = 0	g = 0.1	g = 0.2
0	0.3799864	0.2799858	0.179995	0.0799849	−0.020016
1	0.3583502	0.2583545	0.1591545	0.0594954	−0.040212
2	0.35084	0.2513935	0.1521805	0.0523026	−0.047319
3	0.3472744	0.2478992	0.148688	0.0489255	−0.050648
4	0.3451307	0.2457982	0.1465907	0.0468947	−0.052649
5	0.3436999	0.2443958	0.1451917	0.0455391	−0.053986
6	0.342677	0.2433932	0.1441921	0.0445699	−0.054941
7	0.3419093	0.2426408	0.1434421	0.0438425	−0.055658
8	0.341312	0.2420553	0.1428587	0.0432764	−0.056216
9	0.340834	0.2415867	0.1423919	0.0428234	−0.056662
10	0.3404427	0.2412033	0.1420099	0.0424527	−0.057028

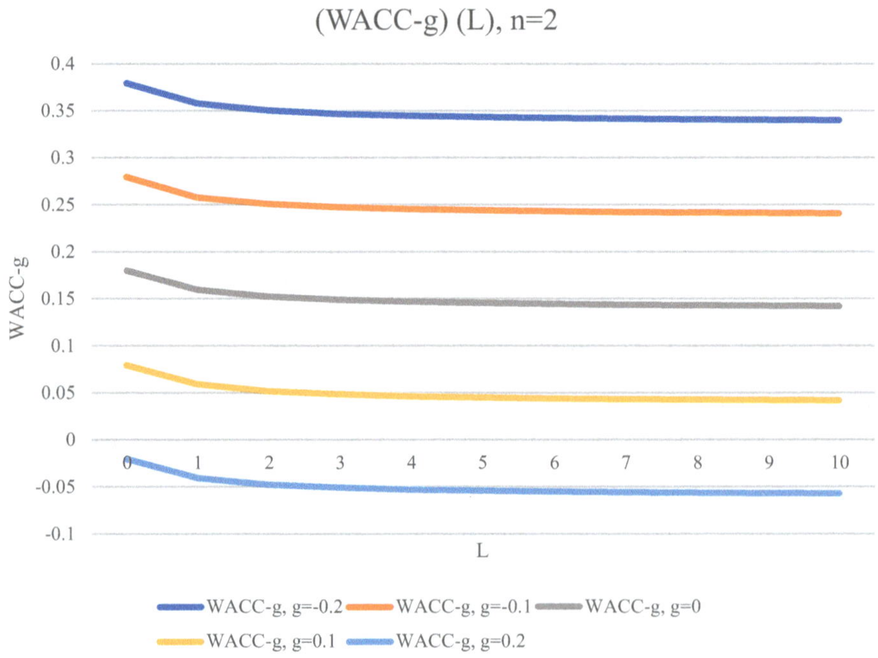

Fig. 13.2 The discount rate WACC–g depending on the level of leverage L at different growth rates g in Generalized Brusov–Filatova–Orekhova theory (GBFO theory) for two-year company

This behavior of the (WACC–g)(L) curves can be explained as follows: all WACC(L) curves originate from the same point ($L = 0$; $WACC = 0.18$). The (WACC–g)(L) curves will be ordered as follows for $L = 0$: the larger g, the lower the starting point and hence the entire graph lies, since the curves do not intersect. As we will see below, the decrease of (WACC–g)(L) with growth rate, g, will lead to an increase of the company value, V, with g.

Calculations of the Company Value, V

It is seen from Table 13.3 and Fig. 13.3 that the company value V at fixed growth rate g increases with leverage level L in the Generalized Brusov–Filatova–Orekhova theory (GBFO theory). The company value V as well increases with growth rate g. This is a consequence of a decrease in the discount rate (WACC–g)(L) with an increase in the growth rate g.

Below, we have studied the dependence of cost of equity, k_e, on leverage level L and on growth rate, g, in the Generalized Brusov–Filatova–Orekhova theory (GBFO theory) at $k_0 = 0.18$; $k_d = 0.16$; and $g = 0;\pm0.1;\pm0.2$.

Table 13.3 The company value, V, depending on the level of leverage L at different growth rates g in Generalized Brusov–Filatova–Orekhova theory (GBFO theory) for two-year company

L	V, n = 2				
	g = − 0.2	g = − 0.1	g = 0	g = 0.1	g = 0.2
0	142.20282	149.38493	156.56518	163.74916	170.93128
1	145.95218	153.40417	160.69451	168.06349	175.43476
2	147.29627	154.73958	162.12039	169.62647	177.07002
3	147.94237	155.41792	162.84303	170.36931	177.84511
4	148.3333	155.82837	163.27978	170.81878	178.31411
5	148.5953	156.10344	163.57228	171.12001	178.62842
6	148.78312	156.30063	163.78186	171.33596	178.85374
7	148.92435	156.44891	163.93941	171.49835	179.02318
8	149.03442	156.56448	164.06217	171.6249	179.15523
9	149.12261	156.65707	164.16051	171.7263	179.26104
10	149.19486	156.73293	164.24106	171.80938	179.34772

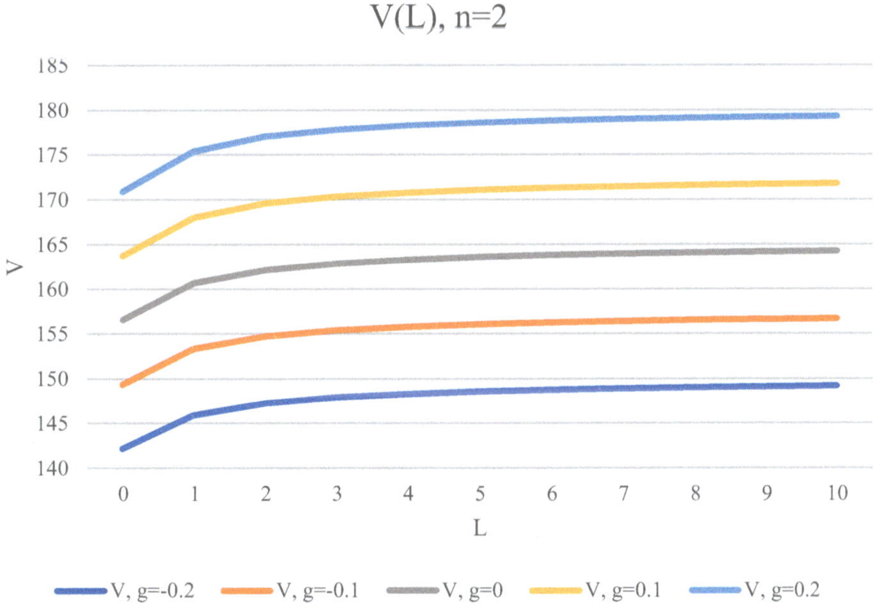

Fig. 13.3 The company value, V, depending on the level of leverage L at different growth rates g in Generalized Brusov–Filatova–Orekhova theory (GBFO theory) for two-year company

Calculations of the Equity Cost, ke

As is seen from Table 13.4 and Fig. 13.4, the equity cost, ke, practically linearly grows with leverage level L at all growth rate g values. The tilt angle ke(L) grows with g.

Table 13.4 The equity cost, ke, depending on the level of leverage L at different growth rates g in Generalized Brusov–Filatova–Orekhova theory (GBFO theory) for two-year company

L	ke, n = 2				
	g = − 0.2	g = − 0.1	g = 0	g = 0.1	g = 0.2
0	0.1799864	0.1799858	0.179995	0.1799849	0.1799844
1	0.1887005	0.1887091	0.1903091	0.1909909	0.1915764
2	0.19652	0.1981805	0.2005415	0.2009079	0.2020416
3	0.2050974	0.2075966	0.2107521	0.2117018	0.2134083
4	0.2136535	0.2169911	0.2209535	0.2224736	0.2247527
5	0.2221991	0.2263748	0.2311504	0.2332344	0.236086
6	0.2307387	0.2357525	0.2413446	0.243989	0.2474131
7	0.2392746	0.2451264	0.2515371	0.2547397	0.2587362
8	0.247808	0.2544978	0.2617285	0.2654878	0.2700568
9	0.2563397	0.2638674	0.271919	0.2762342	0.2813755
10	0.2648701	0.2732358	0.282109	0.2869792	0.292693

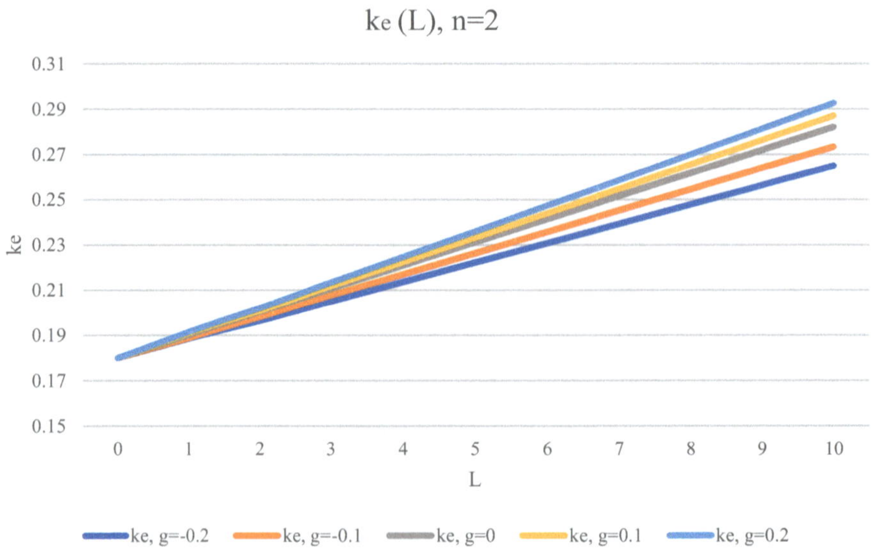

Fig. 13.4 The equity cost, ke, depending on the level of leverage L at different growth rates g in Generalized Brusov–Filatova–Orekhova theory (GBFO theory) for two-year company

13.3.2 Calculations for Four-Year Company

Below, we study the dependence of WACC, WACC–g, V, and ke on leverage level L in the Generalized Brusov–Filatova–Orekhova theory (GBFO theory) at $k_0 = 0.18$; $k_d = 0.16$; $t = 0.2$; $g = 0.2; 0.1; 0.0; -0.1; -0.2$ for a four-year company and compare obtained results with ones for a two-year company (see above).

Calculations of Weighted Average Cost of Capital, WACC

From Table 13.5 and Fig. 13.5, it follows that different values of g all curves WACC(L) start from one point (0; $k_0 = 0.18$). These curves WACC(L) demonstrate the decrease of WACC with leverage level L at all g values. The curves WACC(L) increase with growth rate, g. In this part, the results for a four-year company are similar to ones for a two-year company. There is quantitative difference between them; the splitting of the curves WACC(L) Δ for g = 0.2 and g = − 0.2 increases with g (at L = 10 Δ = 0.0018 for n = 2, while for n = 4 Δ = 0.009). In the perpetual case, ($n = \infty \Delta =$ 0.073) (Brusov et al. 2021a).

The results for a four-year company, as it was seen for a two-year company, differ from the results for the perpetual limit—the theory of Modigliani and Miller (Brusov et al. 2021a); the WACC(L) curves decrease with increasing leverage L for all values of the growth rate g. As is known from Brusov et al. (2021a), in the case of Modigliani and Miller, the WACC(L) curves decrease with the level of leverage L for $g < k_0$ and increase for $g > k_0$. Therefore, k_0 is the threshold value g separating the increasing WACC(L) curves from the decreasing ones, and for $g = k_0$ WACC = const = k_0. As we mentioned above, the increase in WACC(L) with the growth rate

Table 13.5 The WACC depending on the level of leverage L at different growth rates g in Generalized Brusov–Filatova–Orekhova theory (GBFO theory) for four-year company

L	WACC				
	g = − 0.2	g = − 0.1	g = 0	g = 0.1	g = 0.2
0	0.1799864	0.1799858	0.179995	0.1799849	0.1799844
1	0.1538597	0.1554667	0.1567983	0.1579005	0.1588493
2	0.1450677	0.1472039	0.1489781	0.1504635	0.1517081
3	0.1406528	0.1430555	0.1450509	0.1467206	0.1481196
4	0.1379983	0.1405609	0.1426891	0.1444691	0.145877
5	0.1362263	0.1388955	0.1411122	0.1429656	0.1445542
6	0.1349595	0.1377048	0.1399846	0.1418905	0.1434877
7	0.1340088	0.1368112	0.1391383	0.1410836	0.1427137
8	0.1332689	0.1361157	0.1384797	0.1404555	0.1421113
9	0.1326768	0.1355592	0.1379526	0.1399529	0.1416291
10	0.1321922	0.1351036	0.1375212	0.1395414	0.1412344

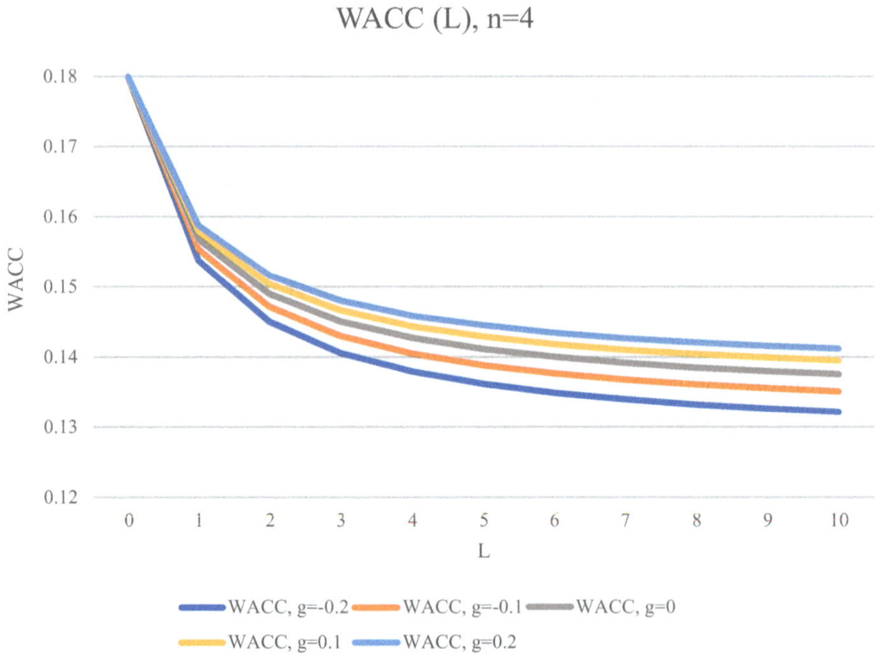

Fig. 13.5 The WACC depending on the level of leverage L at different growth rates g in Generalized Brusov–Filatova–Orekhova theory for four-year company (GBFO theory)

of g is the first indication that WACC is no longer a discount rate, since it is intuitive that the discount rate must decrease with growth rate g in order to increase the value of company V. As we will see below, WACC–g and WACC–k_0 play the role of the discount rates and satisfy the above condition.

Calculations of the Discount Rate, WACC–g

Table 13.6 and Fig. 13.6 show all the curves (WACC–g)(L) with leverage level L at all g values. The (WACC–g) values at fixed leverage level L decrease with growth rate g. This means that WACC–g is a suitable candidate for the discount rate.

As in the case of the two-year company, the behavior of (WACC–g)(L) with g growth can be explained as follows: all WACC(L) curves originate from the same point (L = 0; WACC = 0.18). The (WACC–g)(L) curves will be ordered as follows for L = 0: the larger g, the lower the starting point and hence the entire graph lies, since the curves do not intersect. As we will see below, the decrease of (WACC–g)(L) with growth rate, g, will lead to an increase of the company value, V, with g.

Table 13.6 The discount rate, WACC–g, depending on the level of leverage L at different growth rates g in Generalized Brusov–Filatova–Orekhova theory (GBFO theory) for four-year company

L	(WACC–g), n = 4				
	g = − 0.2	g = − 0.1	g = 0	g = 0.1	g = 0.2
0	0.3799864	0.2799858	0.179995	0.0799849	−0.020016
1	0.3538597	0.2554667	0.1567983	0.0579005	−0.041151
2	0.3450677	0.2472039	0.1489781	0.0504635	−0.048292
3	0.3406528	0.2430555	0.1450509	0.0467206	−0.05188
4	0.3379983	0.2405609	0.1426891	0.0444691	−0.054123
5	0.3362263	0.2388955	0.1411122	0.0429656	−0.055446
6	0.3349595	0.2377048	0.1399846	0.0418905	−0.056512
7	0.3340088	0.2368112	0.1391383	0.0410836	−0.057286
8	0.3332689	0.2361157	0.1384797	0.0404555	−0.057889
9	0.3326768	0.2355592	0.1379526	0.0399529	−0.058371
10	0.3321922	0.2351036	0.1375212	0.0395414	−0.058766

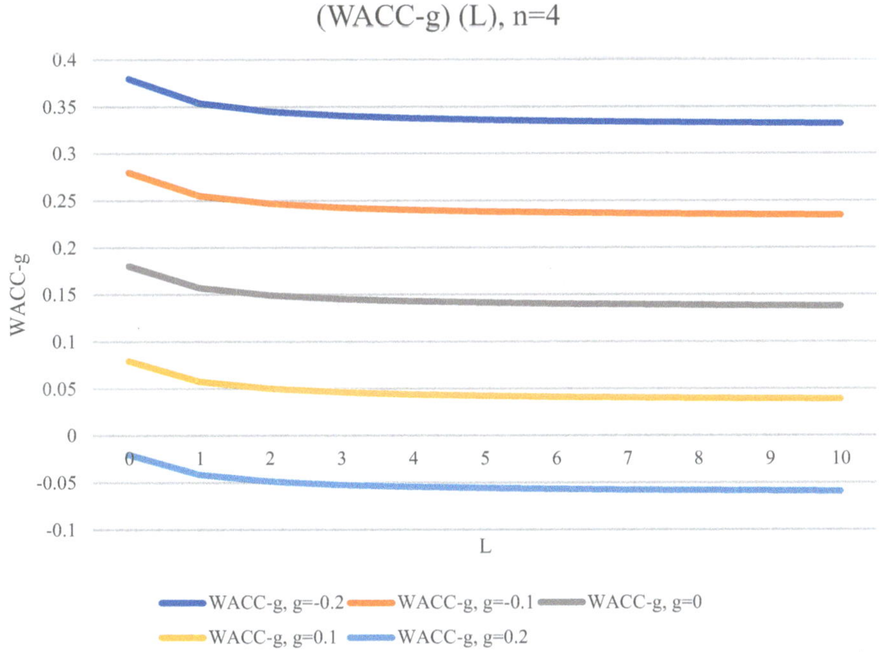

Fig. 13.6 The discount rate, WACC–g, depending on the level of leverage L at different growth rates g in Generalized Brusov–Filatova–Orekhova theory (GBFO theory) for four-year company

Table 13.7 The company value, V, depending on the level of leverage L at different growth rates g in Generalized Brusov–Filatova–Orekhova theory (GBFO theory) for four-year company

L	V, n = 4				
	g = − 0.2	g = − 0.1	g = 0	g = 0.1	g = 0.2
0	207.56615	236.28862	269.00881	306.05136	347.71061
1	217.29735	247.3597	281.61599	320.39442	363.9946
2	220.75339	251.2914	286.08901	325.47139	369.77167
3	222.5253	253.30558	288.37987	328.07604	372.72979
4	223.60263	254.53001	289.7723	329.65911	374.59742
5	224.32687	255.35305	290.70818	330.72309	375.70606
6	224.84716	255.94428	291.38042	331.48732	376.60369
7	225.23902	256.38954	291.88667	332.06283	377.25722
8	225.54478	256.73695	292.28165	332.51185	377.7671
9	225.79	257.01557	292.59842	332.87195	378.176
10	225.99105	257.244	292.85811	333.16716	378.51122

Calculations of the Company Value, V

As can be seen from Table 13.7 and Fig. 13.7, the company value V at fixed growth rate g increases with leverage level L in Generalized Brusov–Filatova–Orekhova theory (GBFO theory). The company value V increases at fixed leverage level L with growth rate g at fixed as well. This is the consequence of a decrease in the discount rate (WACC–g)(L) with an increase in the growth rate g. Comparing with the results for the two-year-old company, we see that the value of the company V increases with the age of the company: we have a range from 149 to 157 with L = 1 for g from −0.2 to 0.2 for the two- year-old company and a range from 217 to 364 with L = 1 for g from −0.2 to 0.2 for a four year old company. This is the obvious conclusion, because it is well known that the value of any asset (company, stock, bond etc.) is equal to the sum of the discounted returns generated by this asset. Since this value is proportional to the lifetime of this asset, the capitalization of the company will grow with its age.

The dependence of the cost of equity ke on the level of leverage L in the Generalized theory of Brusov–Filatova–Orekhova (GBFO theory) was studied below for a four-year company with growth rates g = 0; ±0.1; and ±0.2.

Calculations of the Cost of Equity ke

From Table 13.8 and Fig. 13.8, it can be seen that the cost of equity ke increases practically linearly with leverage level L at all growth rates g (except for g = −0.2 where we see a decrease in ke with leverage level L). The slope angle ke(L) increases

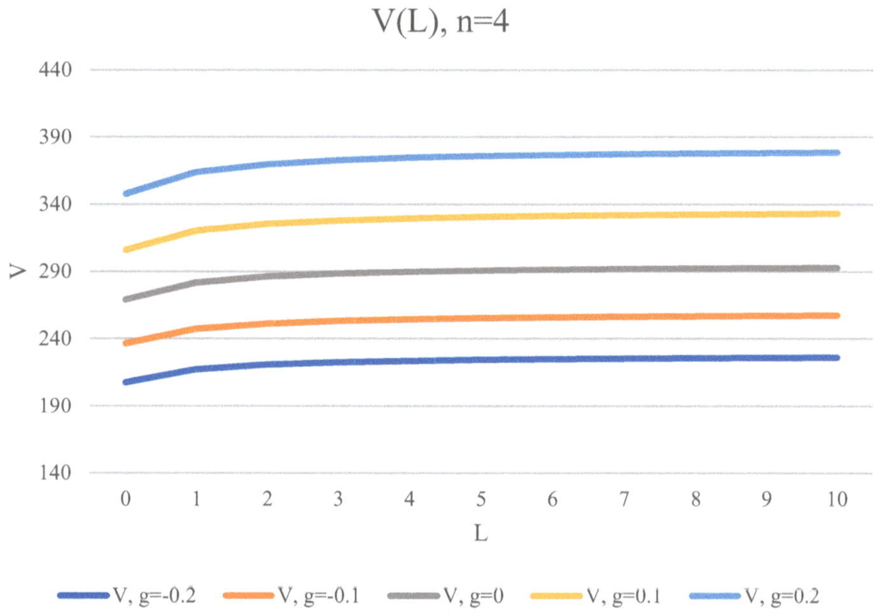

Fig. 13.7 The company value, V, depending on the level of leverage L at different growth rates g in Generalized Brusov–Filatova–Orekhova theory (GBFO theory) for four-year company

with g. This should change the dividend policy of an enterprise with variable income since, economically, the reasonable amount of dividends is equal to the cost of equity.

Table 13.8 The equity cost, ke, depending on the level of leverage L at different growth rates g in Generalized Brusov–Filatova–Orekhova theory (GBFO theory) for four-year company

L	ke, n = 4				
	$g = -0.2$	$g = -0.1$	$g = 0$	$g = 0.1$	$g = 0.2$
0	0.1799864	0.1799858	0.179995	0.1799849	0.1799844
1	0.1797193	0.1829333	0.1855967	0.187801	0.1896985
2	0.1792032	0.1856116	0.1909343	0.1953906	0.1991244
3	0.1786111	0.1882219	0.1962038	0.2028824	0.2084783
4	0.1779915	0.1908046	0.2014454	0.2103453	0.2173852
5	0.1773581	0.1933733	0.2066729	0.2177938	0.2273252
6	0.1767166	0.1959339	0.2118923	0.2252338	0.2364136
7	0.1760702	0.1984895	0.2171066	0.2326686	0.2457093
8	0.1754204	0.2010417	0.2223176	0.2400999	0.2550015
9	0.1747682	0.2035915	0.2275261	0.2475287	0.2642911
10	0.1741143	0.2061396	0.2327328	0.2549558	0.2735789

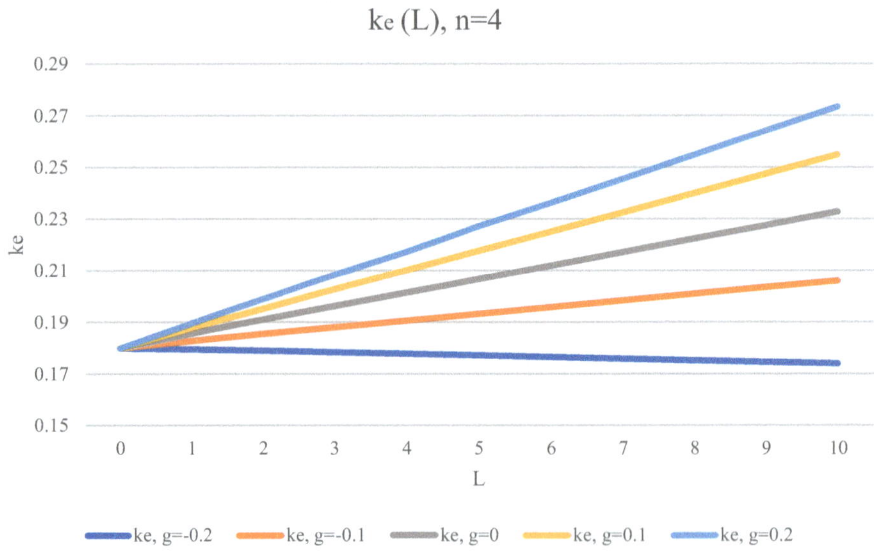

Fig. 13.8 The equity cost, ke, depending on the level of leverage L at different growth rates g in Generalized Brusov–Filatova–Orekhova theory (GBFO theory) for four-year company

However, the biggest change in the company's dividend policy is related to the discovery of a qualitatively new effect in corporate finance: at a rate $g < g^*$, the slope of the ke(L) curve turns out to be negative (one can observe this effect here for $g = -0.2$ where a decrease in ke with leverage level L takes place). This effect, which is absent in the classical Modigliani–Miller theory and the classical Brusov–Filatova–Orekhova theory with constant income, exists in the Modigliani–Miller theory with variable income and in the Brusov–Filatova–Orekhova theory with variable income at a certain age of the company, n, which exceeds some cutoff age value, n^*.

The latter effect is similar to a qualitatively new effect in corporate finance, discovered by Brusov–Filatova–Orekhova within the framework of the BFO theory (Brusov et al. 2018, 2021b): anomalous dependences of the cost of equity ke on the leverage level L when income tax T exceeds a certain value T^*. This discovery also significantly changes the principles of the company's dividend policy.

13.3.3 Comparison with the Theory of Modigliani and Miller with Variable Income

The main difference between the Modigliani–Miller (MM) theory and the Brusov–Filatova–Orekhova (BFO) theory is that the latter describes companies of an arbitrary age, whereas the former represents the eternal limit of the BFO theory and is valid only for perpetual companies (with an infinite lifetime). If there is no time factor in the MM theory, then within the framework of the modern BFO theory, it is possible to analyze the financial condition of a company of any age; in this chapter, this is done for two company ages—two and four years.

Since the MM theory is the eternal BFO limit, it is important to note that some of the results, such as the change in the discount rate from WACC to WACC–g, etc., are general, and this emphasizes the correctness of both theories and the connection between them as a connection between a general theory and its limiting case.

Along with the fundamental differences between the results of the two theories indicated above, there are also qualitative and quantitative differences. One of them is the next. The BFO results for a four-year company, as it was seen for a two-year company as well, differ from the results for the perpetual limit—the theory of Modigliani and Miller (Brusov et al. 2021a), where the WACC(L) curves decrease with increasing leverage L for all values of the growth rate g. As is known from Brusov et al. (2021a), in the case of Modigliani and Miller, the WACC(L) curves decrease with the level of leverage L for $g < k_0$ and increase for $g > k_0$.Therefore, k_0 is the threshold value g separating the increasing WACC(L) curves from the decreasing ones, and for $g = k_0$ WACC = const = k_0 (see Fig. 13.9 below).

We would like to emphasize an important observation. If in the classical versions of the Brusov–Filatova–Orekhova (BFO) theory and its perpetual limit,the theory of Nobel laureates Modigliani and Miller, where the case of constant income was considered, and where the gap between these two theories is huge (many qualitative effects that take place in the first theory, missing in the second), when taking into account the variable income, some effects of the BFO theory also take place in the Modigliani–Miller theory. This means that taking into account some effects that

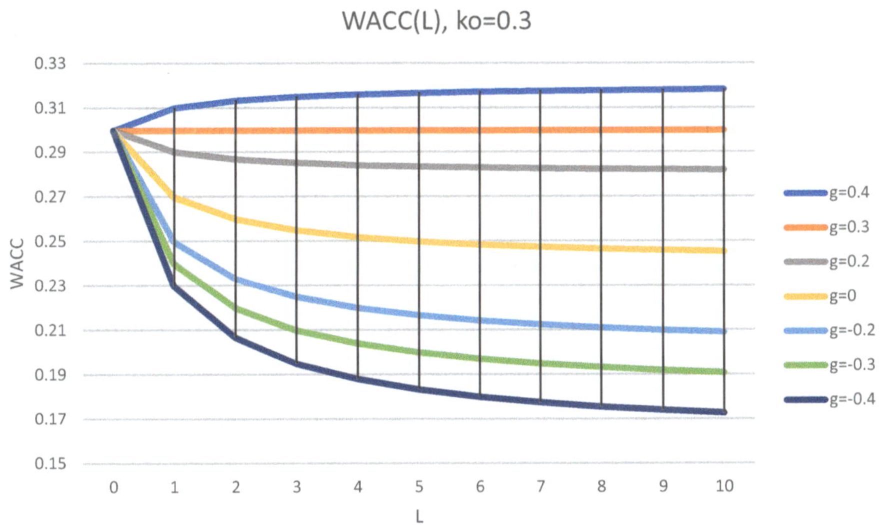

Fig. 13.9 WACC depending on leverage level L in Generalized Modigliani–Miller theory (GMM theory) at $k_0 = 0.3$ and $g = 0;\pm 0.2;\pm 0.3;\pm 0.4$ (from Brusov et al. [2021a])

are present in economic practice (for example, variable income) brings both theories closer, and even the Modigliani–Miller theory, with all its many limitations, becomes more applicable in economic practice. However, it should be remembered that the Modigliani–Miller theory is only true for perpetual companies, whereas the BFO theory is valid for companies of any age, and from this point of view, they never coincide.

13.4 Conclusions

The Brusov–Filatova–Orekhova (BFO) theory of capital cost and capital structure as well as the theory by Nobel Prize winners Modigliani and Miller (perpetuity limit of BFO theory) consider the case of constant income, whereas in practice, the income of a company is, of course, variable. Recently, we have generalized the latter for the case of variable income, and here we have generalized for the first time the Brusov–Filatova–Orekhova theory for the case of variable income.

This generalization significantly expands the applicability of this modern capital structure theory, which is valid for companies of any age, and in practice for corporate finance, business valuation, investments, banking, ratings, etc.

We have derived the generalized BFO formula for WACC and this consists of a main theoretical result of a current chapter.

From this formula and as well from using this formula in MS Excel, we show that the role of the discount rate shifts from WACC to WACC–g (where g is the growth rate) for financially dependent companies and from k_0 to k_0–g (for financially independent companies). Whereas the WACC increases with g, the actual discount rates WACC–g and k_0–g decrease with g and, accordingly, the company value, V, increases with g. For the cost of equity ke, the slope of the curve ke(L) increases with g. Since the cost of equity determines the economically justified amount of dividends, this should change the company's dividend policy. It turns out that at the rate $g < g^*$, the slope of the curve ke(L) becomes negative, which can significantly change the company's dividend policy principles. This means a qualitatively new effect on discoveries in corporate finance.

The novelty of the work is the generalization of the theory of Brusov–Filatova–Orekhova to the case of variable income, the derivation of generalized BFO formulas for the weighted average cost of capital, WACC, cost of equity, ke, company value, V, and the use of these formulas to study the influence of the growth rate g on the dependence of the main financial performance of the company on debt financing.

The importance of the current consideration is due to a couple of points:

- gives an idea of the behavior of the main financial indicators of the company with a change in the growth rate g for both cases—an increase in g and a decrease in g;

- creates a developed methodology that allows the researcher to analyze the main financial indicators of the company (capital costs, company value, etc.) for the actual conditions of the company's functioning.

Limitations of the study: a generalization of the BFO theory was carried out for the case of paying income tax at the end of reporting periods. However, in practice, these payments may also be made in advance. This determines the further direction of the study: consideration of the case of variable income when income tax is paid in advance.

References

Angotti M, de Lacerda Moreira R, Hipólito Bernardes do Nascimento J, Neto de Almeida Bispo O (2018) Analysis of an equity investment strategy based on accounting and financial reports in Latin American markets. Reficont 5:22–40

Barbi M (2011) On the risk–neutral value of debt tax shields. Appl Financ Econ 22:251–258

Becker DM (2022) Getting the valuation formulas right when it comes to annuities. Manag Financ 48:470

Berk J, DeMarzo P (2007) Corporate finance. Pearson-Addison Wesley, Boston MA USA

Białek–Jaworska A, Klapkiv L (2021) Does withholding tax on interest limit international profit–shifting by FDI? Equilib Q J Econ Econ Policy 16:11–44. https://doi.org/10.24136/eq.2021.001

Bradley M, Jarrell GA, Kim EH (1984) On the existence of an optimal capital structure: theory and evidence. J Financ 39:857–878

Brusov P, Filatova T (2013) Veniamin Kulik benefits of advance payments of tax on profit: consideration within the Brusov–Filatova–Orekhova (BFO) theory. Mathematics 2022:10. https://doi.org/10.3390/math10122013

Brusov P, Filatova T (2022) Influence of method and frequency of profit tax payments on company financial indicators. Mathematics 10:2479. https://doi.org/10.3390/math10142479

Brusov PN, Filatova TV, Kulik VL (2024) Capital Asset Pricing Model (CAPM) 2.0: Account of business and financial risk. finance: theory and practice 28(2):128-142. https://doi.org/10.26794/2587-5671-2024-28-2-128-142

Brusov P, Filatova T (2025a) Business valuation and company value: New qualitative approaches considering business and financial risks, Springer Nature Publishing pp.1–654

Brusov P, Filatova T (2025b) Efficiency of investment projects: Modern investment models and their applications, Springer Nature Publishing pp.1–843

Brusov P, Filatova T, Orehova N, Eskindarov M (2018) Modern corporate finance, investments, taxation and ratings, 2nd ed. Springer Nature Publishing, Cham, Switzerland, pp 1–571

Brusov PN, Filatova TV, Orekhova NP, Kulik VL, Chang SI, Lin YCG (2021a) Generalization of the Modigliani-Miller Theory for the Case of Variable Income. Mathematics 9:1286. https://doi.org/10.3390/math9111286

Brusov P, Filatova T, Orehova N (2021b) Ratings: Critical analysis and new approaches of quantitative and qualitative methodology. Springer Nature Publishing, Cham, Switzerland pp. 1–369. Available Online: https://www.springer.com/de/book/9783030562427

Brusov P, Filatova T, Orekhova N, (2021) Ratings: Critical analysis and new approaches of quantitative and qualitative methodology, Springer Nature Publishing pp.1–369

Brusov P, Filatova T, Orekhova N, (2022) Generalized modigliani–miller theory: Applications in corporate finance, investments, taxation and ratings, Springer Nature Publishing pp.1–362

Brusov P, Filatova T, Orekhova N, (2023) The Brusov–Filatova–Orekhova theory of capital structure: Applications in corporate finance, investments, taxation and ratings, Springer Nature Publishing pp.1–769
Dimitropoulos P (2014) Capital structure and corporate governance of soccer clubs: european evidence. Manag Res Rev 37:658–678
Durana P, Ginevicius R, Urbanski M, Podhorska I, Tumpach M (2021) Parallels and differences in earnings management of the Visegrad Four and the Baltics. J Compet 13:39–55. https://doi.org/10.7441/joc.2021.03.03
Durana P, Valaskova K, Blazek R, Palo J (2022) Metamorphoses of earnings in the transport sector of the V4 region. Mathematics 10:1204. https://doi.org/10.3390/math10081204
El–Chaarani H, Abraham R, Skaf Y (2022) The impact of corporate governance on the financial performance of the banking sector in the MENA (Middle Eastern and North African) region: an immunity test of banks for COVID–19. J Risk Financ Manag15:82
Farber A, Gillet R, Szafarz A (2006) A general formula for the WACC. Int J Bus 11:211–218
Fernandez P (2006) A general formula for the WACC: a comment. Int J Bus 11:219
Franc-Dąbrowska J, Mądra-Sawicka M, Milewska A (2021) Energy sector risk and cost of capital assessment—companies and investors perspective. Energies 14:1613
Frank M, Goyal V (2009) Capital structure decisions: which factors are reliably important? Financ Manag 38:1–37. https://doi.org/10.1111/j.1755-053X.2009.01026.x
Graham JR (2003) Taxes and corporate finance: a review. Rev Financ Stud 16:1075–1129
Hamada R (1969) Portfolio Analysis, Market Equilibrium, and Corporate Finance. J Financ 24:13–31
Harris R, Pringle J (1985) Risk-adjusted discount rates—extension form the average-risk case. J Financ Res 8:237–244
Harry DA, Masulis RW (1980) Optimal capital structure under corporate and personal taxation. J Financ Econ 8:3–29
Luiz K, Cruz M (2015) The relevance of capital structure on firm performance: a multivariate analysis of publicly traded Brazilian companies. REPeC Brasília 9:384–401
Miller M (1977) Debt and taxes. J Financ 32:261–275. https://doi.org/10.1111/j.1540-6261.1977.tb03267.x
Modigliani F, Miller M (1958) The cost of capital, corporate finance, and the theory of investment. Am Econ Rev 48:261–297
Modigliani F, Miller M (1963) Corporate income taxes and the cost of capital: A correction. Am Econ Rev 53:147–175
Modigliani F, Miller M (1966) Some estimates of the cost of capital to the electric utility industry 1954–1957. Am Econ Rev 56:333–391
Mundi HS, Kaur P, Murty RLN (2022) A qualitative inquiry into the capital structure decisions of overconfident finance managers of family–owned businesses in India. Qual Res Financ Mark 14:357–379
Sadiq M, Alajlani S, Hussain MS, Bashir F, Chupradit S (2022) Impact of credit, liquidity, and systematic risk on financial structure: comparative investigation from sustainable production. Environ Sci Pollut Res Int 29:20963–20975
Sheridan T, Wessels R (1988) The determinants of capital structure choice. J Financ 43:1–19
Singhal N, Goyal S, Sharma D, Kumari S, Nagar S (2022) Capitalization and profit ability: applicability of capital theories in BRICS banking sector. Future Bus. J. 8:30. https://doi.org/10.1186/s43093-022-00140-w
Valaskova K, Gavurova B, Durana P, Kovacova M (2020) Alter ego only four times? the case study of business profits in the Visegrad Group. EM Econ Manag 23:101–119. https://doi.org/10.15240/tul/001/2020-3-007
Valaskova K, Androniceanu A-M, Zvarikova K, Olah J (2021a) Bonds between earnings management and corporate financial stability in the context of the competitive ability of enterprises. J Compet 13:167–184. https://doi.org/10.7441/joc.2021.04.10

Valaskova K, Kliestik T, Gajdosikova D (2021b) Distinctive determinants of financial indebtedness: evidence from Slovak and Czech enterprises. Equilib Q J Econ Econ Policy 16:639–659. https://doi.org/10.24136/eq.2021.023

Vergara–Novoa C, Sepúlveda–Rojas JP, Miguel DA, Nicolás R (2018) Cost of capital estimation for highway concessionaires in Chile. J Adv Transp 2018:2153536

Virglerova Z, Ivanova E, Dvorsky J, Belas J, Krulický T (2021) Selected factors of internationalisation and their impact on the SME perception of the market risk. Oecon Copernic 12:1011–1032. https://doi.org/10.24136/oc.2021.033

Xu J, Liu F (2020) The impact of intellectual capital on firm performance: a modified and extended Vaic model. J Compet 12:161–176. https://doi.org/10.7441/joc.2010.01.10

Part III
Taxes and Investments Modern Investment Models

Chapter 14
Investment Models with Debt Repayment at the End of the Project and Their Application

14.1 Investment Models

Taxes have a significant impact on investment efficiency. In this and next chapter, we describe the modern investment models, created by the authors and well tested in the real economy. These models used by us for investigation of different problems of investments, such as influence of debt financing, leverage level, taxing, project duration, method of financing, and some other parameters on efficiency of investments and other problems. In this chapter we consider the investment models with debt repayment at the end of the project and their application while in the Chapter 15 we consider the investment models with uniform debt repayment and their application.

The effectiveness of the investment project is considered from two perspectives: the owners of equity and debt and the equity holders only. For each of these cases, NPV is calculated in two ways: with the division of credit and investment flows (and thus discounting of the payments using two different rates) and without such a division (in this case, both flows are discounted using the same rate, as which can be, obviously, chosen WACC). For each of the four situations, two cases are considered: (1) a constant value of equity S and (2) a constant value of the total invested capital $I = S + D$ (D is value of debt funds).

As it was stated above, the effectiveness of the investment project is considered from two perspectives: the owners of equity and debt and the equity holders only. In the first case, the interest and duty paid by owners of equity (negative flows) returned to the project because they are exactly equal to the flow (positive), obtained by owners of debt capital. The only effect of leverage in this case is–the effect of the tax shield, generated from the tax relief: interest on the loan is entirely included into the cost and thus reduces the tax base. After-tax flow of capital for each period in this case is equal to

$$\mathrm{NOI}(1 - t) + k_{\mathrm{d}}Dt \tag{14.1}$$

P. Brusov and T. Filatova, *Taxes and Taxation*, Contributions to Finance and Accounting, https://doi.org/10.1007/978-3-032-11077-0_14

and the value of investments at the initial time moment $T = 0$ is equal to $-I = -S - D$.

Here NOI stands for net operating income (before taxes).

In the second case, investments at the initial time moment $T = 0$ are equal to $-S$ and the flow of capital for the period (in addition to the tax shields $k_d\ Dt$ it includes a payment of interest on a loan $-k_d D$):

$$(\text{NOI} - k_d D)(1 - t). \tag{14.2}$$

Here, for simplicity, we suppose that interest on the loan will be paid in equal shares $k_d\ D$ during all periods. Note that principal repayment is made at the end of the last period.

Some variety of repayment of long-term loans will be considered below (see in this chapter).

We will consider two different ways of discounting:

1. Operating and financial flows are not separated and both are discounted, using the general rate (as which, obviously, the weighted average cost of capital (WACC) can be selected). In this case for perpetuity projects, the Modigliani–Miller formula (Modigliani and Miller 1958, 1963, 1966) for WACC will be used and for projects of finite (arbitrary) duration Brusov–Filatova–Orekhova formula Filatova et al. 2008; Brusov et al. (2015), Brusov (2018a, b), Brusov et al. (2018a, b, c, d, e, f, g, 2019, 2020), Filatova et al. (2018), and Myers (2001); Brusov et al. 2021, 2022, 2023, 2024; Brusov and Filatova 2025a, b).
2. Operating and financial flows are separated and are discounted at different rates: the operating flow at the rate which is equal to the equity cost k_e, depending on leverage, and credit flow–at the rate which is equal to the debt cost k_d, which until fairly large values of leverage remain constant and start to grow only at high values of leverage L, when there is a danger of bankruptcy.

Note that loan capital is the least risky, because interest on credit is paid after taxes in the first place. Therefore, the cost of credit will always be less than the equity cost, whether of ordinary or of preference shares $k_e > k_d$; $k_p > k_d$. Here k_e; k_p is the equity cost of ordinary or of preference shares consequently.

14.2 The Effectiveness of the Investment Project from the Perspective of the Equity Holders Only

14.2.1 With the Division of Credit and Investment Flows

Projects of Finite (Arbitrary) Duration

In this case, the expression for NPV has a view

$$\begin{aligned}\mathrm{NPV} &= -S + \sum_{i=1}^{n} \tfrac{\mathrm{NOI}(1-t)}{(1+k_e)^i} + \sum_{i=1}^{n} \tfrac{-k_d D(1-t)}{(1+k_d)^i} - \tfrac{D}{(1+k_d)^n} \\ &= -S + \frac{\mathrm{NOI}(1-t)}{k_e}\left(1 - \frac{1}{(1+k_e)^n}\right) \\ &\quad -D(1-t)\left(1 - \frac{1}{(1+k_d)^n}\right) - \frac{D}{(1+k_d)^n}.\end{aligned} \tag{14.3}$$

The last term in the first line-discounted (present) value of credit, extinguished a one-off payment at the end of the last period n.

Below we will look at two cases:

1. A constant value of the invested capital $I = S + D$ (D–debt value)
2. A constant value of equity capital S

We will start with the first case.

At a Constant Value of the Invested Capital (I = const)

In the case of a constant value of the invested capital (I = const), taking into account $D = IL/(1+L)$, $S = I/(1+L)$, one gets

$$\begin{aligned}\mathrm{NPV} = &-\tfrac{I}{1+L}\left[1 + L\left((1-t)\left(1 - \tfrac{1}{(1+k_d)^n}\right) + \tfrac{1}{(1+k_d)^n}\right)\right] \\ &+\tfrac{\mathrm{NOI}(1-t)}{k_e}\left(1 - \tfrac{1}{(1+k_e)^n}\right).\end{aligned} \tag{14.4}$$

For 1-Year Project

Putting at the Eq. (14.4) $n = 1$, one gets for NPV

$$\mathrm{NPV} = -\frac{I}{1+L}\left[1 + L\left(\frac{1 + k_d(1-t)}{(1+k_d)}\right)\right] + \frac{\mathrm{NOI}(1-t)}{1+k_e}. \tag{14.5}$$

At a Constant Value of Equity Capital (S = const)

Accounting that in the case S = const NOI is proportional to the invested capital, $\mathrm{NOI} = \beta I = \beta S(1+L)$, we get

$$\begin{aligned}\mathrm{NPV} = &-S\left[1 + L\left((1-t)\left(1 - \tfrac{1}{(1+k_d)^n}\right) + \tfrac{1}{(1+k_d)^n}\right)\right] \\ &+\tfrac{\beta S(1+L)(1-t)}{k_e}\left(1 - \tfrac{1}{(1+k_e)^n}\right).\end{aligned} \tag{14.6}$$

For 1-Year Project

Putting at the Eq. (14.6) $n = 1$, one gets for NPV

$$\mathrm{NPV} = -S\left(1 + L\left(\frac{1 + k_{\mathrm{d}}(1 - t)}{1 + k_{\mathrm{d}}}\right)\right) + \frac{\beta S(1 + L)(1 - t)}{1 + k_{\mathrm{e}}}. \tag{14.7}$$

14.2.2 *Without Flows Separation*

In this case operating and financial flows are not separated and are discounted, using the general rate (as which, obviously, WACC can be selected).

The credit reimbursable at the end of the project (at the end of the period (n)) can be discounted either at the same rate WACC or at the debt cost rate k_{d}. Now we choose a uniform rate and the first option.

$$\begin{aligned}\mathrm{NPV} &= -S + \sum_{i=1}^{n} \frac{\mathrm{NOI}(1-t) - k_{\mathrm{d}}D(1-t)}{(1+\mathrm{WACC})^i} - \frac{D}{(1+\mathrm{WACC})^n} \\ &= -S + \frac{\mathrm{NOI}(1 - t) - k_{\mathrm{d}}D(1 - t)}{\mathrm{WACC}}\left(1 - \frac{1}{(1 + \mathrm{WACC})^n}\right) \\ &\quad - \frac{D}{(1 + \mathrm{WACC})^n}.\end{aligned} \tag{14.8}$$

At a Constant Value of the Invested Capital (I = const)

In case of a constant value of the invested capital (I = const), taking into account $D = IL/(1 + L)$, $S = I/(1 + L)$, one gets

$$\begin{aligned}\mathrm{NPV} = &-\frac{I}{1+L}\left[1 + L\frac{k_{\mathrm{d}}(1-t)}{\mathrm{WACC}}\left(1 - \frac{1}{(1+\mathrm{WACC})^n}\right) + \frac{L}{(1+\mathrm{WACC})^n}\right] \\ &+ \frac{\mathrm{NOI}(1-t)}{\mathrm{WACC}}\left(1 - \frac{1}{(1+\mathrm{WACC})^n}\right).\end{aligned} \tag{14.9}$$

For 1-Year Project

Putting into Eq. (14.9) $n = 1$, one gets for NPV

$$\mathrm{NPV} = -\frac{I}{1 + L}\left[1 + L\frac{1 + k_{\mathrm{d}}(1 - t)}{1 + \mathrm{WACC}}\right] + \frac{\mathrm{NOI}(1 - t)}{1 + \mathrm{WACC}}. \tag{14.10}$$

At a Constant Value of Equity Capital (S = const)

Accounting that in the case $S = \text{const}$ NOI is proportional to the invested capital, I, $\text{NOI} = \beta I = \beta S(1 + L)$, and substituting $D = LS$, we get

$$\begin{aligned}\text{NPV} = -S + \tfrac{\text{NOI}(1-t)-k_{\text{d}}D(1-t)}{\text{WACC}}\left(1 - \tfrac{1}{(1+\text{WACC})^n}\right)\\ -\tfrac{D}{(1+\text{WACC})^n},\end{aligned} \tag{14.11}$$

$$\begin{aligned}\text{NPV} = -S\left[1 + \tfrac{Lk_{\text{d}}(1-t)}{\text{WACC}}\left(1 - \tfrac{1}{(1+\text{WACC})^n}\right) + \tfrac{L}{(1+\text{WACC})^n}\right]\\ +\tfrac{\beta S(1+L)(1-t)}{\text{WACC}}\left(1 - \tfrac{1}{(1+\text{WACC})^n}\right).\end{aligned} \tag{14.12}$$

For 1-Year Project

Putting into Eq. (14.12) $n = 1$, one gets for NPV

$$\begin{aligned}\text{NPV} = -S\left[1 + \tfrac{Lk_{\text{d}}(1-t)}{\text{WACC}}\left(1 - \tfrac{1}{(1+\text{WACC})^n}\right) + \tfrac{L}{(1+\text{WACC})^n}\right]\\ +\tfrac{\beta S(1+L)(1-t)}{\text{WACC}}\left(1 - \tfrac{1}{(1+\text{WACC})^n}\right).\end{aligned}$$

$$\text{NPV} = -S + \frac{\text{NOI}(1-t) - k_{\text{d}}D(1-t) - D}{1 + \text{WACC}}. \tag{14.13}$$

Substituting $D = LS$, $\text{NOI} = \beta I = \beta S(1 + L)$, we get

$$\text{NPV} = -S\left[1 + \frac{L(k_{\text{d}}(1-t) - 1)}{1 + \text{WACC}}\right] + \frac{\beta S(1+L)(1-t)}{1 + \text{WACC}}. \tag{14.14}$$

14.3 Modigliani–Miller Limit (Perpetuity Projects)

14.3.1 With Flows Separation

In perpetuity limit (Modigliani–Miller limit) (turning to the limit $n \to \infty$ in the relevant equations), we have

$$\text{NPV} = -S + \frac{\text{NOI}(1-t)}{k_{\text{e}}} - D(1-t). \tag{14.15}$$

At a Constant Value of the Invested Capital (I = const)

At a constant value of the invested capital ($I = \text{const}$), accounting $D = IL/(1+L)$, $S = I/(1+L)$, we get

$$\text{NPV} = -\frac{I}{1+L}(1+L(1-t)) + \frac{\text{NOI}(1-t)}{k_e}. \tag{14.16}$$

$$\text{NPV} = -\frac{I}{1+L}(1+L(1-t)) + \frac{\text{NOI}(1-t)}{k_0 + (k_0 - k_d)L(1-t)}. \tag{14.17}$$

In order to obtain Eqs. (14.17) from (14.16), we used the Modigliani–Miller formula (Modigliani and Miller 1963) for equity cost k_e for perpetuity projects:

$$k_e = k_0 + (k_0 - k_d)L(1-t). \tag{14.18}$$

At a Constant Value of Equity Capital (S = const)

Accounting $D = LS$,, we get in perpetuity limit ($n \to \infty$) (Modigliani–Miller limit)

$$\text{NPV} = -S(1+L(1-t)) + \frac{\beta S(1+L)(1-t)}{k_0 + (k_0 - k_d)Lt}. \tag{14.19}$$

14.3.2 Without Flows Separation

In perpetuity limit ($n \to \infty$) (Modigliani–Miller limit) (turning to the limit $n \to \infty$ in the relevant equations), we have

$$\text{NPV} = -S + \frac{\text{NOI}(1-t) - k_d D(1-t)}{\text{WACC}}. \tag{14.20}$$

At a Constant Value of the Invested Capital (I = const)

At a constant value of the invested capital ($I = \text{const}$), accounting $D = IL/(1+L)$, $S = I/(1+L)$, we get

$$\begin{aligned}\mathrm{NPV} &= -I\cdot\tfrac{1}{1+L}+\tfrac{\mathrm{NOI}(1-t)-I\frac{L}{1+L}k_\mathrm{d}(1-t)}{\mathrm{WACC}}\\ &= -I\cdot\frac{1}{1+L}\left[1+\frac{Lk_\mathrm{d}(1-t)}{k_0(1-Lt/(1+L))}\right]\\ &+\frac{\mathrm{NOI}(1-t)}{k_0(1-Lt/(1+L))}.\end{aligned}\tag{14.21}$$

At a Constant Value of Equity Capital (S = const)

$$\mathrm{NPV} = -S+\frac{\mathrm{NOI}(1-t)-k_\mathrm{d}D(1-t)}{\mathrm{WACC}}\tag{14.22}$$

Substituting $D = LS$, we get

$$\begin{aligned}\mathrm{NPV} &= -S\left[1+\tfrac{Lk_\mathrm{d}(1-t)}{\mathrm{WACC}}\right]+\tfrac{\mathrm{NOI}(1-t)}{\mathrm{WACC}}\\ &= -S\left[1+\tfrac{Lk_\mathrm{d}(1-t)}{k_0(1-Lt/(1+L))}\right]+\tfrac{\beta S(1+L)(1-t)}{k_0(1-Lt/(1+L))}.\end{aligned}\tag{14.23}$$

14.4 The Effectiveness of the Investment Project from the Perspective of the Owners of Equity and Debt

14.4.1 With Flows Separation

Projects of Arbitrary (Finite) Duration

In this case, operating and financial flows are separated and are discounted, using different rates: the operating flow at the rate equal to the equity cost k_e, depending on leverage, and credit flow–at the rate equal to the debt cost k_d, which until fairly large values of leverage remain constant and start to grow only at high values of leverage L, when there is a danger of bankruptcy.

$$\begin{aligned}\mathrm{NPV} &= -I+\sum_{i=1}^{n}\tfrac{\mathrm{NOI}(1-t)}{(1+k_\mathrm{e})^i}+\sum_{i=1}^{n}\tfrac{k_\mathrm{d}Dt}{(1+k_\mathrm{d})^i}\\ &= -I+\frac{\mathrm{NOI}(1-t)}{k_\mathrm{e}}\left(1-\frac{1}{(1+k_\mathrm{e})^n}\right)\\ &+Dt\left(1-\frac{1}{(1+k_\mathrm{d})^n}\right).\end{aligned}\tag{14.24}$$

Below we will consider two cases:

1. At a constant value of the invested capital ($I = S + D$ (D is the debt value)

2. At a constant value of equity capital S

We will start with the first case.

At a Constant Value of the Invested Capital (I = const)

At a constant value of the invested capital (I = const), accounting $D = IL/(1+L)$, $S = I/(1+L)$, we get

$$\begin{aligned}\mathrm{NPV} &= -I + \tfrac{\mathrm{NOI}(1-t)}{k_\mathrm{e}}\left(1 - \tfrac{1}{(1+k_\mathrm{e})^n}\right) + \tfrac{ILt}{1+L}\left(1 - \tfrac{1}{(1+k_\mathrm{d})^n}\right) \\ &= -I\left[1 - \tfrac{Lt}{1+L}\left(1 - \tfrac{1}{(1+k_\mathrm{d})^n}\right)\right] + \tfrac{\mathrm{NOI}(1-t)}{k_\mathrm{e}}\left(1 - \tfrac{1}{(1+k_\mathrm{e})^n}\right).\end{aligned} \tag{14.25}$$

At a Constant Value of Equity Capital (S = const)

Accounting $D = LS$, $I = S(1+L)$, we get

$$\begin{aligned}\mathrm{NPV} = -S - LS + \frac{\mathrm{NOI}(1-t)}{k_\mathrm{e}}\left(1 - \frac{1}{(1+k_\mathrm{e})^n}\right) \\ + Dt\left(1 - \frac{1}{(1+k_\mathrm{d})^n}\right).\end{aligned} \tag{14.26}$$

Accounting that in the case S = const NOI is not a constant, but is proportional to the invested capital, $\mathrm{NOI} = \beta I = \beta S(1+L)$, we get

$$\begin{aligned}\mathrm{NPV} = -S\left[1 + L - tL\left(1 - \tfrac{1}{(1+k_\mathrm{d})^n}\right)\right] \\ + \tfrac{\beta S(1+L)(1-t)}{k_\mathrm{e}}\left(1 - \tfrac{1}{(1+k_\mathrm{e})^n}.\right)\end{aligned} \tag{14.27}$$

For 1-Year Project

$$\mathrm{NPV} = -S\left[1 + L - tL\frac{k_\mathrm{d}}{1+k_\mathrm{d}}\right] + \frac{\beta S(1+L)(1-t)}{1+k_\mathrm{e}}. \tag{14.28}$$

14.4.2 Without Flows Separation

In this case operating and financial flows are not separated and both are discounted, using the general rate (as which, obviously, WACC can be selected):

$$\begin{aligned}\mathrm{NPV} &= -I + \sum_{i=1}^{n} \frac{\mathrm{NOI}(1-t)+k_d Dt}{(1+\mathrm{WACC})^i} \\ &= -I + \frac{\mathrm{NOI}(1-t)+k_d Dt}{\mathrm{WACC}}\left(1 - \frac{1}{(1+\mathrm{WACC})^n}\right).\end{aligned} \tag{14.29}$$

At a Constant Value of the Invested Capital (I = const)

At a constant value of the invested capital ($I = \text{const}$), we have

$$\mathrm{NPV} = -I + \frac{\mathrm{NOI}(1-t) + k_d Dt}{\mathrm{WACC}}\left(1 - \frac{1}{(1+\mathrm{WACC})^n}\right)$$

Accounting $D = IL/(1+L)$, $S = I/(1+L)$, we get

$$\begin{aligned}\mathrm{NPV} = &-I\left[1 - \frac{k_d t \frac{L}{1+L}}{k_0\left(1-\gamma \frac{L}{1+L} t\right)}\left(1 - \frac{1}{\left(1+k_0\left(1-\gamma \frac{L}{1+L} t\right)\right)^n}\right)\right] \\ &+ \frac{\mathrm{NOI}(1-t)}{k_0\left(1-\gamma \frac{L}{1+L} t\right)}\left(1 - \frac{1}{\left(1+k_0\left(1-\gamma \frac{L}{1+L} t\right)\right)^n}\right).\end{aligned} \tag{14.30}$$

For 1-Year Project

Putting at the Eq. (14.30) $n = 1$, one gets for NPV

$$\mathrm{NPV} = -I\left[1 - \frac{k_d t \frac{L}{1+L}}{1+\mathrm{WACC}}\right] + \frac{\mathrm{NOI}(1-t)}{1+\mathrm{WACC}}. \tag{14.31}$$

At a Constant Value of Equity Capital (S = const)

$$\begin{aligned}\mathrm{NPV} &= -I + \frac{\mathrm{NOI}(1-t)+k_d Dt}{\mathrm{WACC}}\left(1 - \frac{1}{(1+\mathrm{WACC})^n}\right) \\ &= -S\left[1 + L - \frac{k_d Lt}{\mathrm{WACC}}\left(1 - \frac{1}{(1+\mathrm{WACC})^n}\right)\right] \\ &\quad + \frac{\beta S(1+L)(1-t)}{\mathrm{WACC}}\left(1 - \frac{1}{(1+\mathrm{WACC})^n}\right).\end{aligned} \tag{14.32}$$

For 1-Year Project

$$\begin{aligned} \mathrm{NPV} &= -I + \tfrac{\mathrm{NOI}(1-t)+k_{\mathrm{d}}Dt}{1+\mathrm{WACC}} \\ &= -S\left[1 + L - \tfrac{k_{\mathrm{d}}Lt}{1+\mathrm{WACC}}\right] + \tfrac{\mathrm{NOI}(1-t)}{1+\mathrm{WACC}}. \end{aligned} \quad (14.33)$$

14.5 Modigliani–Miller Limit

14.5.1 With Flows Separation

In perpetuity limit ($n \to \infty$) (Modigliani–Miller limit), we have

$$\mathrm{NPV} = -I + \frac{\mathrm{NOI}(1-t)}{k_{\mathrm{e}}} + Dt. \quad (14.34)$$

At a constant value of the invested capital ($I = \mathrm{const}$), accounting $D = IL/(1+L)$, we have

$$\mathrm{NPV} = -I\left(1 - t\frac{L}{1+L}\right) + \frac{\mathrm{NOI}(1-t)}{k_{\mathrm{e}}}. \quad (14.35)$$

For equity cost k_{e} and WACC in Modigliani–Miller theory, we have consequently

$$k_{\mathrm{e}} = k_0 + (k_0 - k_{\mathrm{d}})L(1-t), \quad (14.36)$$

$$\mathrm{WACC} = k_0(1 - w_{\mathrm{d}}t) = k_0(1 - Lt/(1+L)). \quad (14.37)$$

Putting Eqs. (14.36) into (14.37), we get

$$\mathrm{NPV} = -I\left(1 - t\frac{L}{1+L}\right) + \frac{\mathrm{NOI}(1-t)}{k_0 + (k_0 - k_{\mathrm{d}})L(1-t)}. \quad (14.38)$$

At a Constant Value of Equity Capital (S = const)

Accounting $D = LS, I = S(1+L)$, in perpetuity limit ($n \to \infty$) (Modigliani–Miller limit), we have

$$\mathrm{NPV} = -S(1 + L(1-t)) + \frac{\mathrm{NOI}(1-t)}{k_0 + (k_0 - k_{\mathrm{d}})Lt}. \quad (14.39)$$

Note that in the case S = const NOI is not a constant, but is proportional to the invested capital, $\mathrm{NOI} = \beta I = \beta S(1 + L)$.

In this case, Eq. (14.38) is replaced by

$$\mathrm{NPV} = -S(1 + L(1 - t)) + \frac{\beta S(1 + L)(1 - t)}{k_0 + (k_0 - k_d)Lt}. \tag{14.40}$$

14.5.2 Without Flows Separation

In perpetuity limit ($n \to \infty$) (Modigliani–Miller limit), we have

$$\mathrm{NPV} = -I + \frac{\mathrm{NOI}(1 - t) + k_d Dt}{\mathrm{WACC}}. \tag{14.41}$$

At a constant value of the invested capital (I = const), we have

$$\begin{aligned}\mathrm{NPV} &= -I + \frac{\mathrm{NOI}(1 - t) + k_d Dt}{\mathrm{WACC}} \\ &= -I\left(1 - \frac{k_d t \frac{L}{1+L}}{k_0\left(1 - \frac{L}{1+L}t\right)}\right) + \frac{\mathrm{NOI}(1 - t)}{k_0\left(1 - \frac{L}{1+L}t\right)}.\end{aligned} \tag{14.42}$$

At a Constant Value of Equity Capital (S = const)

In perpetuity limit ($n \to \infty$) (Modigliani–Miller limit), we have

$$\mathrm{NPV} = -S\left[1 + L - \frac{k_d Lt}{\mathrm{WACC}}\right] + \frac{\mathrm{NOI}(1 - t)}{\mathrm{WACC}}. \tag{14.43}$$

$$\mathrm{NPV} = -S\left[1 + L - \frac{k_d Lt}{k_0\left(1 - \frac{L}{1+L}t\right)}\right] + \frac{\beta S(1 + L)(1 - t)}{k_0\left(1 - \frac{L}{1+L}t\right)}. \tag{14.44}$$

References

Brusov P, Filatova T, Orehova N, Eskindarov M (2015) Modern corporate finance, investments and taxation. Springer International Publishing, Switzerland, p 373. monograph, SCOPUS, https://www.springer.com/gp/book/9783319147314

Brusov P (2018a) Editorial: introduction on special issue on the Banking System and financial markets of Russia and other countries: problems and prospects. J Rev Glob Econ 7:i–vi. SCOPUS
Brusov P (2018b) Editorial. J Rev Glob Econ 7:i–v. SCOPUS
Brusov P, Filatova T (2025a) Business valuation and company value: New qualitative approaches considering business and financial risks, Springer Nature Publishing pp.1-654
Brusov P, Filatova T (2025b) Efficiency of investment projects: Modern investment models and their applications, Springer Nature Publishing pp.1-843
Brusov P, Filatova T, Kulik V (2024) Capital Asset Pricing Model (CAPM) 2.0: Account of business and financial risk. finance: theory and practice. 28(2):128-142.https://doi.org/10.26794/2587-5671-2024-28-2-128-142
Brusov P, Filatova T, Orehova N, Eskindarov M (2018a) Modern corporate finance, investments, taxation and ratings. Springer Nature Publishing, Switzerland, p 571. monograph
Brusov PN, Filatova TV, Orekhova NP, Kulik VL (2018b) Rating: new approach. J Rev Glob Econ 7:37– 62. SCOPUS, https://doi.org/10.6000/1929-7092.2018.07.05
Brusov PN, Filatova TV, Orekhova NP, Kulik VL (2018c) A "golden age" of the companies: conditions of its existence. J Rev Glob Econ 7:88–103. SCOPUS, https://doi.org/10.6000/1929-7092.2018.07.07
Brusov PN, Filatova TV, Orekhova NP, Kulik VL (2018d) Rating methodology: new look and new horizons. J Rev Glob Econ 7:63–87. SCOPUS, https://doi.org/10.6000/1929-7092.2018.07.06
Brusov PN, Filatova TV, Orekhova NP, Kulik VL, Weil I (2018e) New meaningful effects in modern capital structure theory. J Rev Glob Econ 7:104–122. SCOPUS, https://doi.org/10.6000/1929-7092.2018.07.08
Brusov P, Filatova T, Orekhova N, Kulik V, Weil I, Brailov A (2018f) The impact of the central bank key rate and commercial banks credit rates on creating and maintaining of a favorable investment climate in the country. J Rev Glob Econ 7:360–376. SCOPUS, https://doi.org/10.6000/1929-7092.2018.07.31
Brusov PN, Filatova TV, Orekhova NP (2018g) Modern corporate finance and investments, monograph. Knorus publishing house, Moscow, p 517
Brusov PN, Filatova TV, Orekhova NP, Kulik VL, Weil I (2019) Ratings of the investment projects of arbitrary durations: new methodology. J Rev Glob Econ 8:437–448. SCOPUS, https://doi.org/10.6000/1929-7092.20114.08.37
Brusov PN, Filatova TV, Orekhova NP, Kulik VL, Chang SI, Lin YCG (2020) Modification of the Modigliani–Miller theory for the case of advance payments of tax on profit. J Rev Glob Econ 9:257–268.
Brusov P, Filatova T, Orekhova N, (2021) Ratings: critical analysis and new approaches of quantitative and qualitative methodology Springer Nature Publishing pp.1-369
Brusov P, Filatova T, Orekhova N, (2022) Generalized Modigliani–Miller Theory: Applications in corporate finance, investments, taxation and ratings, Springer Nature Publishing pp.1-362
Brusov P, Filatova T, Orekhova N (2023) The Brusov–Filatova–Orekhova theory of capital structure: Applications in corporate finance, investments, taxation and ratings Springer Nature Publishing pp.1- 769
Filatova T, Orehova N, Brusova A (2008) Weighted average cost of capital in the theory of Modigliani-Miller, modified for a finite life–time company. Bull FU 48:68–77
Filatova TV, Brusov PN, Orekhova NP, Kulik VL (2018) Ratings of the long-term projects: New approach. J Rev Glob Econ 7:645–661. SCOPUS, https://doi.org/10.6000/1929-7092.2018.07.59
Modigliani F, Miller M (1958) The cost of capital, corporate finance, and the theory of investment. Am Econ Rev 48:261–297
Modigliani F, Miller M (1963) Corporate income taxes and the cost of capital: a correction. Am Econ Rev 53:147–175
Modigliani F, Miller M (1966) Some estimates of the cost of capital to the electric utility industry 1954–1957. Am Econ Rev 56:333–391
Myers S (2001) Capital structure. J Econ Perspect 15(2):81–102

Chapter 15
Investment Models with Uniform Debt Repayment and Their Application

15.1 Investment Models with Uniform Debt Repayment

In previous chapter, we have established investment models with debt repayment at the end of the project, well proven in the analysis of real investment projects. In practice, however, a scheme of uniform debt repayment during the duration of the project is more extended. In this chapter, we describe new investment models with uniform debt repayment during the duration of the investment project, quite adequately describing real investment projects. Within these models it is possible, in particular, to analyze the dependence of effectiveness of investment projects on debt financing and taxation. We will work on the modern theory of capital cost and capital structure developed by Brusov–Filatova–Orekhova (Filatova et al. 2008; Brusov (2018a, b), Brusov et al. (2015, 2018a, b, c, d, e, f, g, 2020), Filatova et al. (2018), Filatova (2018), and Myers (2001); Brusov et al. 2021, 2022, 2023, 2024; Brusov and Filatova 2025a, b) as well as on perpetuity limit (Modigliani and Miller 1958, 1963, 1966).

In this chapter we consider the application of the investment models with uniform debt repayment.

As in the case of debt repayment at the end of the project, the effectiveness of the investment project is considered from two perspectives: the owners of equity and debt and the equity holders only. In the first case, the interest and duty paid by owners of equity (negative flows) returned to the project because they are exactly equal to the flow (positive), obtained by owners of debt capital. The only effect of leverage in this case is the effect of tax shield, generated from the tax relief: interest on the loan is entirely included into the net cost and, thus, reduces the tax base. For each of these cases, NPV is calculated in two ways: with the division of credit and investment flows (and thus discounting the payments, using two different rates) and without such a division (in this case, both flows are discounted at the same rate as which, obviously, WACC can be chosen). For each of the four situations, two cases

P. Brusov and T. Filatova, *Taxes and Taxation*, Contributions to Finance and Accounting, https://doi.org/10.1007/978-3-032-11077-0_15

are considered: (1) a constant value of equity S and (2) a constant value of the total invested capital $I = S + D$ (D is value of debt funds).

The main debt repayment occurs evenly (by equal parts) at the end of each period, and the remaining debt at the end of the each period is an arithmetic progression with the difference $-D/n$

$$\left\{D, D - \frac{D}{n}, D - \frac{2D}{n}, \ldots, \frac{D}{n}\right\} = \left\{D, D\left(\frac{n-1}{n}\right), D\left(\frac{n-2}{n}\right), \ldots, \frac{D}{n}\right\} \quad (15.1)$$

Interest constitutes a sequence:

$$\left\{k_d D, k_d D\left(\frac{n-1}{n}\right), k_d D\left(\frac{n-2}{n}\right), \ldots, k_d \frac{D}{n}\right\}. \quad (15.2)$$

In the case of consideration from the point of view of equity owners and debt owners, the after-tax flow of capital for each period is equal to

$$\text{NOI}(1-t) + k_d D_i t, \quad (15.3)$$

where

$$D_i = D\frac{n-(i-1)}{n}, \quad (15.4)$$

and investments at time moment $T = 0$ are equal to $-I = -S - D$. Here NOI stands for net operating income (before tax).

In the second case (from the point of view of equity owners only), investments at the initial moment $T = 0$ are equal to $-S$, and the flow of capital for the ith period (apart from tax shields $k_d Dt$ it includes payment of interest on the loan $-k_d D_i$) is equal to

$$(\text{NOI} - k_d D_i)(1-t) - \frac{D_i}{n}. \quad (15.5)$$

We suppose that the interest on the loan and the loans itself are paid in tranches $k_d Di$ and $D \cdot \frac{n-i}{n}$ consequently during the all ith periods. We cite in Table 15.1 the sequence of debt and interest values and credit values.

As in the case of debt repayment at the end of the project, we will consider two different ways of discounting:

Table 15.1 The sequence of debt and interest values and credit values

Period number	1	2	3	...	n
Debt	D	$D \cdot \frac{n-1}{n}$	$D \cdot \frac{n-2}{n}$	...	$D \cdot \frac{1}{n}$
Interest	$k_d D$	$k_d D \cdot \frac{n-1}{n}$	$k_d D \cdot \frac{n-2}{n}$	...	$k_d D \cdot \frac{1}{n}$

1. Operating and financial flows are not separated and both are discounted, using the general rate (as which, obviously, the weighted average cost of capital (WACC) can be selected). For perpetuity projects, the Modigliani–Miller formula (Modigliani and Miller 1963) for WACC will be used and for projects of finite duration Brusov–Filatova–Orekhova formula for WACC (Filatova et al. 2008).
2. Operating and financial flows are separated and are discounted at different rates: the operating flow at the rate equal to the equity cost k_e, depending on leverage, and credit flow–at the rate equal to the debt cost k_d, which until fairly large values of leverage remain constant and start to grow only at high values of leverage L, when there is a danger of bankruptcy.

Note once again that loan capital is the least risky, because interest on credit is paid after tax in the first place. Therefore, the cost of credit will always be less than the equity cost, whether of ordinary or of preference shares $k_e > k_d; \ \ k_p > k_d$. Here $k_e; k_p$ is equity cost of ordinary or of preference shares consequently.

One can show that the present value of interest can be calculated by using the following formula, which we have been able to derive:

$$\frac{1}{a} + \frac{2}{a^2} + \frac{3}{a^3} + \cdots + \frac{n}{a^n} = \frac{a\left(1 - a^{-n}\right)}{(a-1)^2} - \frac{n}{(a-1)a^n} \tag{15.6}$$

Here $a = 1 + i$.

We will use this formula in the further calculations.

15.2 The Effectiveness of the Investment Project from the Perspective of the Equity Holders Only

15.2.1 With the Division of Credit and Investment Flows

To obtain an expression for NPV, the discounted flow values for one period, given by formulas (Eq. 15.3) and (Eq. 15.5), must be summed, using our obtained formula (Eq. 15.6), in which $a = 1 + i$, where i is the discount rate. Its accurate assessment is one of the most important advantages of BFO theory (Brusov–Filatova–Orekhova) (Filatova et al. 2008) over its perpetuity limit–Modigliani–Miller theory (Modigliani and Miller 1958, 1963, 1966).In this case, the expression for NPV has a view

$$\begin{aligned} \text{NPV} &= -S + \sum_{i=1}^{n} \frac{\text{NOI}(1-t)}{(1+k_e)^i} + \sum_{i=1}^{n} \frac{-k_d D \frac{n+1-i}{n}(1-t) - \frac{D}{n}}{(1+k_d)^i} \\ &= -S + \frac{\text{NOI}(1-t)\left(1-(1+k_e)^{-n}\right)}{k_e} \end{aligned}$$

$$-\left(\frac{D}{n}+k_{\mathrm{d}}D\frac{n+1}{n}(1-t)\right)\frac{1-(1+k_{\mathrm{d}})^{-n}}{k_{\mathrm{d}}}$$
$$+k_{\mathrm{d}}\frac{D}{n}(1-t)\left\{\frac{(1+k_{\mathrm{d}})\left[1-(1+k_{\mathrm{d}})^{-n}\right]}{k_{\mathrm{d}}^2}-\frac{n}{k_{\mathrm{d}}(1+k_{\mathrm{d}})^n}\right\} \tag{15.7}$$

In perpetuity limit (let us call it Modigliani–Miller limit), one has

$$\mathrm{NPV}=-S+\frac{\mathrm{NOI}(1-t)}{k_{\mathrm{e}}}-D(1-t) \tag{15.8}$$

15.2.2 Without Flows Separation

In this case, operating and financial flows are not separated and are discounted, using the general rate (as which, obviously, WACC can be selected).

The main debt repayment, which occurs evenly (by equal parts) at the end of each period, can be discounted either at the same rate WACC or at the debt cost rate k_{d}. Now we choose a uniform rate and the first option.

We still consider the effectiveness of the investment project from the perspective of the equity holders only.

$$NPV=-S+\sum_{i=1}^{n}\frac{NOI(1-t)-k_dD\frac{n+1-i}{n}(1-t)-\frac{D}{n}}{(1+WACC)^i}$$
$$=-S+\frac{NOI(1-t)-\frac{D}{n}-k_dD\frac{n+1}{n}(1-t)}{WACC}\cdot\left(1-\frac{1}{(1+WACC)^n}\right)$$
$$+\frac{k_dD}{n}(1-t)\left\{\frac{(1+WACC)\left[1-(1+WACC)^{-n}\right]}{WACC^2}\right.$$
$$\left.-\frac{n}{WACC(1+WACC)^n}\right\} \tag{15.9}$$

In perpetuity limit (Modigliani–Miller limit) (turning to the limit $n\to\infty$ in the relevant equations), we have

$$\mathrm{NPV}=-S+\frac{\mathrm{NOI}(1-t)-k_{\mathrm{d}}D(1-t)}{\mathrm{WACC}}. \tag{15.10}$$

Note, that formula (15.10) as well as other formulas for perpetuity limit (15.12) and (15.14) could be applied for analyze the effectiveness of the long-term investment projects.

15.3 The Effectiveness of the Investment Project from the Perspective of the Owners of Equity and Debt

15.3.1 With Flows Separation

Projects of Arbitrary (Finite) Duration

In the case of consideration from the perspective of the owners of equity and debt

$$
\begin{aligned}
\mathrm{NPV} &= -I + \sum_{i=1}^{n} \frac{\mathrm{NOI}(1-t)}{(1+k_{\mathrm{e}})^{i}} + \sum_{i=1}^{n} \frac{k_{\mathrm{d}} D \frac{n+1-i}{n} t}{(1+k_{\mathrm{d}})^{i}} \\
&= -I + \frac{\mathrm{NOI}(1-t)\left(1-(1+k_{\mathrm{e}})^{-n}\right)}{k_{\mathrm{e}}} \\
&\quad + D\frac{n+1}{n} t \cdot \left[1-(1+k_{\mathrm{d}})^{-n}\right] - k_{\mathrm{d}} \frac{D}{n} t \\
&\quad \times \left\{ \frac{(1+k_{\mathrm{d}})\left[1-(1+k_{\mathrm{d}})^{-n}\right]}{k_{\mathrm{d}}^{2}} - \frac{n}{k_{\mathrm{d}}(1+k_{\mathrm{d}})^{n}} \right\}
\end{aligned}
\tag{15.11}
$$

In perpetuity limit (Modigliani–Miller limit) (turning to the limit $n \to \infty$ in the relevant equations), we have

$$
\mathrm{NOI} = -I + \frac{\mathrm{NOI}(1-t)}{k_{\mathrm{e}}} + Dt \tag{15.12}
$$

15.3.2 Without Flows Separation

We still consider the effectiveness of the investment project from the perspective of the owners of equity and debt.

$$
\begin{aligned}
\mathrm{NPV} &= -I + \sum_{i=1}^{n} \frac{\mathrm{NOI}(1-t) + k_{\mathrm{d}} D \frac{n+1-i}{n} t}{(1+\mathrm{WACC})^{i}} \\
&= -I + \frac{\mathrm{NOI}(1-t) + k_{\mathrm{d}} D \frac{n+1}{n} t}{\mathrm{WACC}} \left(1 - \frac{1}{(1+\mathrm{WACC})^{n}}\right) \\
&\quad - \frac{k_{\mathrm{d}} D}{n} t \left\{ \frac{(1+\mathrm{WACC})\left[1-(1+\mathrm{WACC})^{-n}\right]}{\mathrm{WACC}^{2}} \right. \\
&\quad \left. - \frac{n}{\mathrm{WACC}(1+\mathrm{WACC})^{n}} \right\}
\end{aligned}
\tag{15.13}
$$

In perpetuity limit (Modigliani–Miller limit) (turning to the limit $n \to \infty$ in the relevant equations), we have

$$\text{NPV} = -I + \frac{\text{NOI}(1 - t) + k_d D t}{\text{WACC}} \tag{15.14}$$

15.4 Example of the Application of the Derived Formulas

As an example of application of the obtained formulas, let's take a look at the dependence of the NPV of project on the leverage level at three values of the tax on profit rates in the case of consideration from the perspective of the equity holders only without flows separation on operating and finance ones.

We use formula (Eq. 15.10) and the next parameters values

$$\text{NOI} = 800; \quad S = 500; \quad k_0 = 22\%; \quad k_d = 19\%; \quad T = 15\%; \quad 20\%; \quad 25\%.$$

Making the calculations in Excel, we get the data, which are shown in Fig. 15.1.

From the calculations and Fig. 15.1, one can make the following conclusions:

1. With growth of the tax on profit rate, the NPV of the project decreases and our model makes it possible to assess, for how many percent, with growth of tax on profit rate, for example, by 1%.

   It should be noted that the possibility of such evaluations is unique.

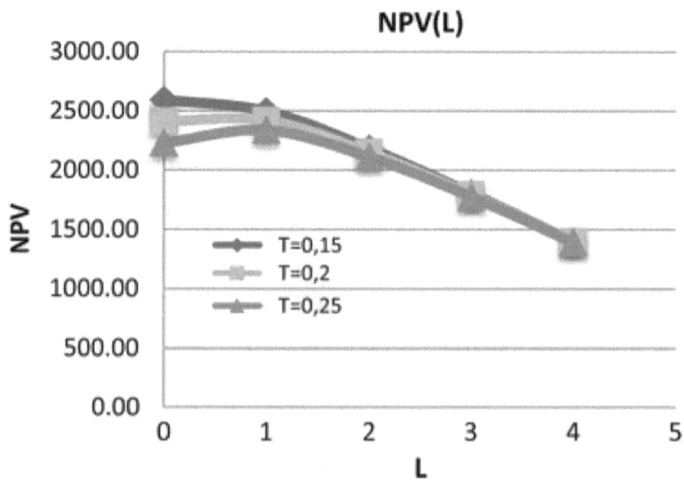

Fig. 15.1 Dependence of NPV of the project on the leverage level at three values of the tax on profit rates NOI = 800; $S = 500$; $k_0 = 22\%$; $k_d = 19\%$; $T = 15\%$; 20%; 25

2. The effect of taxation on the NPV significantly depends on the leverage level: With its increase, the impact of changing of tax on profit rate is greatly reduced. This is valid for increasing of the tax on profit rate and for its reduction.
3. At tax on profit rates 20% (as in Russia) and 25%, there is an optimum in NPV dependence on leverage. Investors should take into account the invested capital structure: in this case, they may, without special effort (only changing this structure), obtain (sometimes very substantial) gains in NPV. Note that at tax on profit rate 15%, there is no optimum in NPV dependence on leverage: NPV descends monotonically with leverage.

Conclusions New investment models with uniform debt repayment during the duration of the project, quite adequately describing real investment projects, are described. Within these models, it is possible, in particular, to analyze the dependence of effectiveness of investment projects on debt financing and taxation. We work on the modern theory of capital cost and capital structure developed by Brusov–Filatova–Orekhova as well as on perpetuity limit–MM theory.

As in the case of debt repayment at the end of the project, the effectiveness of the investment project is considered from two perspectives: the owners of equity and debt and the equity holders only. For each of these cases, NPV is calculated in two ways: with the division of credit and investment flows (and thus discounting the payments, using two different rates) and without such a division (in this case, both flows are discounted at the same rate as which, obviously, WACC can be chosen). For each of the four situations, two cases are considered: (1) a constant value of equity S and (2) a constant value of the total invested capital $I = S + D$ (D is value of debt funds).

As an example of application of the obtained formulas, the dependence of the NPV of project on the leverage level at three values of the tax on profit rate has been investigated in the case of consideration from the perspective of the equity holders only and without flows separation on operating and financial ones. It has been shown that effect of taxation on the NPV significantly depends on the leverage level: with its increase, the impact of changing of tax on profit rates is greatly reduced. This is valid for increasing of the tax on profit rate and for its reduction. The model allows investigating the dependence of effectiveness of the investment project on leverage level, on the tax on profit rate, on credit rate, on equity cost, etc.

References

Brusov P, Filatova T, Orehova N, Eskindarov M (2015) Modern corporate finance, investments and taxation. Springer International Publishing, Switzerland, p 373, monograph, SCOPUS, https://www.springer.com/gp/book/9783319147314

Brusov P (2018a) Editorial: introduction on special issue on the Banking System and financial markets of Russia and other countries: Problems and prospects. J Rev Glob Econ 7:i–vi. SCOPUS

Brusov P (2018b) Editorial. J Rev Glob Econ 7:i–v. SCOPUS

Brusov PN, Filatova TV Kulik VL (2024) Capital asset pricing model (CAPM) 2.0: Account of business and financial risk. Finance: Theory and practice. 28(2):128–142. https://doi.org/10.26794/2587-5671-2024-28-2-128-142

Brusov P, Filatova T, Orehova N, Eskindarov M (2018a) Modern corporate finance, investments, taxation and ratings. Springer Nature Publishing, Switzerland, p 571, monograph

Brusov PN, Filatova TV, Orekhova NP, Kulik VL (2018b) Rating: new approach. J Rev Glob Econ 7:37–62. SCOPUS, https://doi.org/10.6000/1929-7092.2018.07.05

Brusov PN, Filatova TV, Orekhova NP, Kulik VL (2018c) A "golden age" of the companies: conditions of its existence. J Rev Glob Econ 7:88–103. SCOPUS, https://doi.org/10.6000/1929-7092.2018.07.07

Brusov PN, Filatova TV, Orekhova NP, Kulik VL (2018d) Rating methodology: new look and new horizons. J Rev Glob Econ 7:63–87. SCOPUS, https://doi.org/10.6000/1929-7092.2018.07.06

Brusov PN, Filatova TV, Orekhova NP, Kulik VL, Weil I (2018e) New meaningful effects in modern capital structure theory. J Rev Glob Econ 7:104–122. SCOPUS, https://doi.org/10.6000/1929-7092.2018.07.08

Brusov P, Filatova T, Orekhova N, Kulik V, Weil I, Brailov A (2018f) The impact of the central bank key rate and commercial banks credit rates on creating and maintaining of a favorable investment climate in the country. J Rev Glob Econ 7:360–376. SCOPUS, https://doi.org/10.6000/1929-7092.2018.07.31

Brusov PN, Filatova TV, Orekhova NP (2018g) Modern corporate finance and investments, monograph. Knorus publishing house, Moscow, p 517

Brusov PN, Filatova TV, Orekhova NP, Kulik VL, Weil I (2019) Ratings of the investment projects of arbitrary durations: new methodology. J Rev Glob Econ 8:437–448. SCOPUS, https://doi.org/10.6000/1929-7092.2019.08.37

Brusov PN, Filatova TV, Orekhova NP, Kulik VL, Chang SI, Lin YCG (2020) Modification of the Modigliani–Miller theory for the case of advance payments of tax on profit. J Rev Glob Econ 9:257–268

Brusov PN, Filatova TV, Orekhova NP (2021) Ratings: Critical analysis and new approaches of quantitative and qualitative methodology. Springer Nature Publishing, pp.1–369

Brusov PN, Filatova TV, Orekhova NP (2022) Generalized Modigliani–Miller theory: Applications in corporate finance, investments, taxation and ratings. Springer Nature Publishing, pp.1–362

Brusov PN, Filatova TV, Orekhova NP (2023) The Brusov–Filatova–Orekhova theory of capital structure: Applications in corporate finance, investments, taxation and ratings. Springer Nature Publishing pp.1–769

Brusov PN, Filatova TV (2025a) Business valuation and company value: New qualitative approaches considering business and financial risks. Springer Nature Publishing pp.1–654

Brusov PN, Filatova TV (2025b) Efficiency of investment projects: Modern investment models and their applications. Springer Nature Publishing pp.1–843

Filatova T, Orehova N, Brusova A (2008) Weighted average cost of capital in the theory of Modigliani-Miller, modified for a finite life–time company. Bull FU 48:68–77

Filatova TV, Brusov PN, Orekhova NP, Kulik VL (2018) Ratings of the long-term projects: new approach. J Rev Glob Econ 7:645–661. SCOPUS, https://doi.org/10.6000/1929-7092.2018.07.59

Modigliani F, Miller M (1958) The cost of capital, corporate finance, and the theory of investment. Am Econ Rev 48:261–297

Modigliani F, Miller M (1963) Corporate income taxes and the cost of capital: a correction. Am Econ Rev 53:147–175

Modigliani F, Miller M (1966) Some estimates of the cost of capital to the electric utility industry 1954–1957. Am Econ Rev 56:333–391

Myers S (2001) Capital structure. J Econ Perspect 15(2):81–102

Part IV
Taxes and Investments Innovative Investment Models

Chapter 16
Innovative Investment Models with Frequent Payments of Tax on Income and of Interest on Debt

16.1 Introduction

In this chapter we continue to explore the impact of taxes on investment efficiency. Investments play a crucial role in economy and finance. Investments in tangible and intangible assets are a necessary condition for structural adjustment and economic growth. They provide the enhancement of existing basic funds and industries and the creation of new ones. The role of investment is increased many times at the current stage. In this respect, the role of the evaluation of the efficiency of investment projects, which allows for the realization of the most effective projects in the context of scarcity and limited investment resources, increases. Since virtually most investment projects use debt financing, the study of the influence of capital structure and debt financing on the efficiency of investment projects and determining the optimal capital structure is especially important at the present time. This is why in spite of the fact that a lot of different types of investment models have been developed—stochastic, dynamics (Bond and Meghir 1994), investment banking valuation models (Rosenbaum and Pearl 2013), etc.—the main problem, which has been discussed during the last few decades, is the impact of debt financing, taxation and other factors on the efficiency of investment projects and on the investment decisions of companies.

Below we review some approaches to these problems.

16.1.1 The Literature Review

Lang, L.E., Ofek, E., and Stulz, R. (Lang et al. 1996) used so–called "Tobin's q ratio" and considered companies with low Tobin's q ratios as well as high ones. Note that the q ratio, or Tobin's q ratio, equals the market value of a company divided by its assets' replacement cost. The equilibrium takes place when market value equals replacement cost. The q ratio expresses the relationship between market valuation

P. Brusov and T. Filatova, *Taxes and Taxation*, Contributions to Finance and Accounting, https://doi.org/10.1007/978-3-032-11077-0_16

and intrinsic value. It is a means of estimating the fact of whether a given business or market is undervalued or overvalued.

The authors have shown that there is a negative correlation between future growth and leverage level at the company level and, for diversified companies, at the level of business segments. This negative correlation between growth and leverage level holds for companies with low Tobin's q ratio, but not for high–q companies or companies in high–q industries. Therefore, for companies known to have good investment opportunities, leverage does not reduce growth, but it is negatively correlated to growth for companies whose growth opportunities are either not recognized by the capital markets or are not valuable enough to overcome the effects of their debt load.

Whited (Whited 1992) studied the influence of debt financing on companies' investment decisions with pharmaceutical firms in India for 11 years, from 1998 to 2009.

To study the impact of debt financing on the firms' investment decisions, Whited used pooling regression as well as random and fixed effect models. Leverage level, retained earnings, Tobin's q, sales, Return on Asset, cash flow and liquidity were considered as independent variables and investment as the dependent one. Whited considered three types of companies, depending on their size: small companies, medium companies and large companies. He showed that there is a significant positive correlation between leverage level and investment for large companies, while for medium companies a negative correlation between leverage level and investment took place.

Kang (Kang 1995) studied the connection between leverage level and investment decisions. "Interdependent tax models" were used to try to explain the specifics of company leverage levels by analyzing the interdependency between financing decisions and investment. These models account for the so–called "investment effect": the influence of investment on debt tax benefit and financial risk. One of the questions is how "investment effect" influences bond financing decisions and hence the leverage level. Different "Interdependent tax models" lead to different connections between investments and leverage levels.

Some authors mentioned a positive connection via the fact that the financial risk and hence the cost of bond financing decrease with an increase in investment at a given leverage level. A negative connection has been mentioned by DeAngelo and Masulis, 1980 (DeAngelo and Masulis 1980) and Dotan and Ravid, 1985 (Dotan and Ravid 1985). The first authors concluded this since the tax benefits of debt compete with those of capital investment. The second authors refer to the fact that financial risk and thus the cost of bond financing will increase with investment increase.

The impact of investment increase on financial risk may depend on company–specific factors, like company–specific technology (Dammon and Senbet 1988). An analysis of the impact of corporate and personal taxes on a firm's optimal investment and financing decisions under uncertainty is provided in this paper. By endogenizing firms' investment decisions, it extends the DeAngelo and Masulis capital structure model. The authors' results indicate that the existing predictions about the relationship between investment–related and debt–related tax shields must be modified in cases where investment is allowed to adjust optimally. The authors show that increases in investment–related tax shields due to changes in the corporate tax code are not necessarily associated with reductions in leverage level at the individual company level. Companies with higher investment–related tax shields (as cross–sectional analysis shows) need not have lower debt–related tax shields (normalized by expected earnings) unless all companies utilize the same production technology. Differences in production technologies across companies may thus explain why the empirical results of recent cross–sectional studies have not conformed to the predictions of DeAngelo and Masulis (DeAngelo and Masulis 1980). A model of company leverage level choice is formulated in this paper, in which corporate and differential personal taxes exist and supply–side adjustments by companies enter into the determination of equilibrium prices of debt and equity. The presence of corporate tax shield substitutes for debt such as depletion allowances, accounting depreciation and investment tax credits are shown to imply a market equilibrium in which each company has a unique interior optimum leverage level decision. The optimal leverage level model yields a number of interesting predictions regarding cross–sectional and time–series properties of firms' capital structures. Below we discuss some portfolio investment models as well as behavioral aspects of investors, which play an important role in investments.

Among those portfolio investment models is the well known Black–Litterman model, which was created by Fischer Black and Robert Litterman in 1992 (Black and Litterman 1992). They developed the model to address the problems that institutional investors have encountered the during application of modern portfolio theory in practice. Starting with an asset allocation based on the equilibrium assumption, the model then modifies that allocation by accounting the investors' opinions with respect to future asset performance.

Anthony Loviscek (Loviscek 2021) has applied the Black–Litterman model of modern portfolio theory to well–known index mutual funds–one guided by the classic 60%/40% stock/bond allocation and one based on an all–equity allocation. The period under their study is from 2000 to 2020. Although statistical evidence supports that the efficacy of a precious metal allocation is elusive, the results suggest an average allocation of about 2% for "buy–and–hold" investors who seek one. He has shown that, from 2003 to 2010 and from 2016 to 2020, the allocations were in the range of 5–10%. Other periods, however, register only a little more than 0%.

Nusret Cakici and Adam Zaremba (Cakici and Zaremba 2021), using data on 65,000 stocks from 23 countries, reconsidered the performance of the Fama–French factors in global markets. As their results showed, the value, profitability and investment factors are far less reliable than what is commonly thought. Their performance depends strongly on the geographical regions and periods examined. Moreover, most factor returns are driven by the smallest companies. Virtually no value or investment effects are present among the big companies representing most of the total market capitalization worldwide. These results cast doubt on the five–factor model's applicability in international markets, citing that the smallest companies are typically not invested in by major financial institutions.

A growing number of investors want to use firm sustainability information in their investment decision processes to avoid risk, satisfy their own asset preference, or find a new alpha–generating factor. Not too many users of environment, social and governance (ESG) data understand how ESG ratings change over time. Bahar Gidwani (Gidwani 2020) used the CSRHub data set to show that ESG ratings regress strongly toward the mean. These ratings include both data from 640 sources and from most commercial ESG ratings firms. The observed regression persists during nine years within the ratings data, for a sample set of more than 8000 firms. Newly–rated firms show even more reversion than "seasoned" firms. Firms can only rarely maintain an especially high or low ESG rating. Investors and firm managers should understand that ESG ratings are likely to change toward the mean. This however does not mean that a good firm is getting worse or a bad one is getting better.

Keith C. Brown, W. V. Harlow and Hanjiang Zhang (Brown et al. 2021) have developed statistics (holdings–based) to estimate the volatility with time of investment style characteristics of funds. They found that funds with lower levels of style volatility significantly outperform funds with higher levels of style volatility on a risk–adjusted basis. The authors have shown that style volatility has a distinct impact on fund performance in the future compared to expenses of funds or past risk–adjusted returns, with the level of indirect style volatility being the primary determinant of the overall effect. It was concluded that deciding to maintain a less volatile investment style is an important aspect of the portfolio management process.

Some behavioral aspects of investors have been considered by Marcos Escobar–Anel, Andreas Lichtenstern and Rudi Zagst (Escobar-Anel et al. 2020), who introduced a strategy generalizing the CPPI (Constant Proportion Portfolio Insurance) approach. The target of this strategy is to guarantee the investment goal or floor during participation in the performance of the assets and limiting the downside risk of the portfolio at the same time. The authors show that the strategy accounts for the following behavioral aspects of investors: a risk–averse behavior for gains, distorted probabilities recognition and a risk–seeking behavior for losses. The developed strategy turns out to be optimal within the Cumulative Prospect Theory framework by Tversky and Kahneman (Kahneman and Tversky 1996).

16.1.2 Some Problems Under the Evaluation of the Effectiveness of the Investment Projects

Some of the major problems under the evaluation of the effectiveness of investment projects are suggested as follows:

1. Which financial flows should be taken into account when calculating the parameters of efficiency of a project (NPV, IRR, etc.)?
2. How many discount rates should be used for discounting various cashflows?
3. How can these discount rates be accurately evaluated?

The first two problems are still under intensive discussion. Concerning the third issue, we need to note that, in the last decade, significant progress in the accurate determination of the cost of the equity and company weighted average cost, which just are the discount rates when evaluating the effectiveness of the project, has been achieved. The progress is mainly associated with the studies by Brusov, Filatova and Orekhova (BFO theory) (Brusov et al. 2015, 2018a; Filatova et al. 2008), in which a general theory of capital cost of the company and its capital structure was established, and the dependence of capital cost on leverage level and on the age of a company was found for the companies of arbitrary age. The main difference between their theory and Modigliani–Miller theory is that the former one removes the assumption of perpetuity for the companies under discussion, which leads to a significantly different new theory from the theory established by the Nobel laureates Modigliani and Miller (Modigliani and Miller 1958, 1963, 1966).

In modern conditions, the requirements for improving the quality of assessing the effectiveness of investments have increased. The modern investment models, which have been well–tested in real economic situations, have been developed by Brusov, Filatova and Orekhova (Brusov et al. 2021; Filatova et al. 2008). They have created long-term as well as arbitrary duration models and have considered the effectiveness of the investment project from two points of view: from the equity holders and from the owners of equity and debt. NPV in each of these cases could be calculated by two different methods: with the division of credit and investment flows and using two different discounting rates, and without such a division and using a general discounting rate (for which WACC can, obviously, be chosen).

Applying their modern investment models on the evaluation of the dependence of the effectiveness of investments on debt financing of one telecommunication company in 2010–2012 from the point of view of optimal structure of investment, the authors showed that in 2012, the company lost 675 million USD on average, because the investment structure had been far from the optimal one. The ability to calculate the correct optimal capital structure is one important feature implied by the Brusov, Filatova and Orekhova modern investment models (Brusov et al. 2015, 2018a; 2021, 2022, 2023, 2024; Brusov and Filatova 2025a, b; Filatova et al. 2008).

16.1.3 The Discount Rates

As we mentioned above, one of the most important elements of calculating the effectiveness of investment projects is the assessment of the discount rate. In the case of long-term investment models without the division of credit and investment flows, the discount rate WACC has been calculated using the Modigliani–Miller formula (Modigliani and Miller 1958, 1963, 1966)

$$WACC = k_0 \cdot (1 - w_d t) \tag{16.1}$$

while in the case of arbitrary duration models, the Brusov–Filatova–Orekhova formula for WACC (Black and Litterman 1992; Loviscek 2021; Cakici and Zaremba 2021)

$$\frac{1-(1+WACC)^{-n}}{WACC}=\frac{1-(1+k_0)^{-n}}{k_0\cdot\left(1-w_dt\left[1-(1+k_d)^{-n}\right]\right)} \tag{16.2}$$

has been used.

Here and below, WACC is the weighted average cost of capital; k_0 is the equity cost at zero leverage ($L=0$); k_d is the debt cost; w_d is the debt share; t is the tax on profit; n is the project duration; k_e is the equity cost; and L is the leverage level.

In the case of long-term investment models with the division of credit and investment flows, the discount rate for discounting the investment flows (equity cost k_e) has been calculated using the Modigliani–Miller formula (Modigliani and Miller 1958, 1963, 1966)

$$k_e=k_0+L\cdot(k_0-k_d)(1-t) \tag{16.3}$$

while in the case of arbitrary duration models, equity cost k_e has been calculated from the formula

$$WACC=k_ew_e+k_dw_d(1-t) \tag{16.4}$$

using the Brusov–Filatova–Orekhova value for WACC (Brusov et al. 2015, 2018a; Filatova et al. 2008).

The calculation methods of the discount rates (WACC, equity cost k_e) has been generalized in Brusov and Filatova (2021) for the real conditions of the implementation of investment projects: for arbitrary frequency of payment of tax on profit.

In this paper, new modern investment models, both long-term and arbitrary duration, will be created, as close as possible to real investment conditions. They will account the payments of interest on debt and of tax on income a few times per year (semi–annually, quarterly, monthly), which are applied in real economic practice. Their verification will lead to the creation of a comprehensive system of adequate and correct assessment of the effectiveness of the company's investment program and its investment strategy.

16.1.4 The Structure of the Paper

The structure of the paper is as follows:

1. In Sect. 16.1 above, we presented:
   16.1.1. The literature review.
   16.1.2. Some problems under the evaluation of the effectiveness of the investment projects.
   16.1.3. Discount rates.

2. In Sect. 16.2, we consider the effectiveness of the investment project from the perspective of the equity holders only.
   In Sect. 16.2.1, we consider a case with flow separation.
   In Sect. 16.2.2, we consider a case without flow separation.
3. In Sect. 16.3, we consider the effectiveness of the investment project from the perspective of the owners of equity and debt.
   In Sect. 16.3.1, we consider a case with flow separation.
   In Sect. 16.3.2, we consider a case without flow separation.
4. In Sect. 16.4, the problem of calculation of discount rates is discussed and expressions for their modified values are obtained.
5. In Sect. 16.5, we study numerically with the use of Microsoft Excel the effectiveness of the four models, created by us in this paper. We consider long-term projects as well as projects of arbitrary duration from two perspectives: the owners of equity and debt and the equity holders only without the division of credit and investment flows.
6. In Conclusions, we discuss obtained results and their impact on the correctness of valuation of efficiency of investment projects.

16.2 The Effectiveness of the Investment Project from the Perspective of the Equity Holders Only

We will consider the effectiveness of the investment project from two points of view: from the equity holders and from the owners of equity and debt. NPV in each of these cases could be calculated by two different methods: with the division of credit and investment flows and using two different discounting rates, and without such a division and using a general discounting rate (for which WACC can, obviously, be chosen).

The following designations are used below:

The equity value S, the investment value I, the net operating income NOI, the leverage level L, the profitability of investments β, the tax on profit t, the project duration n, the equity cost k_0, the debt cost k_d and the number of payments of interest on debt p_1 and of tax on income p_2; D is the debt value.

In the first case (from the perspective of the equity holders), at the initial moment in time, $T = 0$ investments are equal to –S and the flow of capital, CF, for the period is equal to:

$$\mathrm{CF} = (\mathrm{NOI} - k_d D)(1 - t) \tag{16.5}$$

In addition to the tax shields, $k_d Dt$ includes a payment of interest on a loan, $-k_d D$.

We suppose below that interests on the loan are paid in equal shares of $k_d D$ during all periods and principal repayment is made at the end of the project.

In the second case (from the perspective of the equity holders), the negative flows (the interest and duty paid by owners of equity) are returned to the project and they are exactly equal to the positive flows obtained by owners of debt capital. Thus, in this case the only effect of debt financing is the effect of the tax shield, generated from the tax relief: interest on the loan is entirely included in the cost and thus reduces the tax base. After–tax flow of capital, CF, for each period is equal to

$$\mathrm{CF} = \mathrm{NOI}(1 - t) + k_d Dt \tag{16.6}$$

and the value of investments at the initial moment in time $T = 0$ is equal to $-I = -S - D$.

Below two different ways of discounting will be considered:

1. If operating and financial flows are not separated, both flows are discounted by the general rate. In this case, the weighted average cost of capital (WACC) can be selected as a discounting rate. For long-term projects, we will use the Modigliani–Miller formula for WACC (Modigliani and Miller 1958, 1963, 1966), modified by us for the case of payments of interest on debt and of tax on income a few times per year (semi–annually, quarterly, monthly) and for projects of finite (arbitrary) duration we will use the Brusov–Filatova–Orekhova formula for WACC (Brusov et al. 2018a; Filatova et al. 2008), modified by us for the case of payments of interest on debt and of tax on income a few times per year (semi–annually, quarterly, monthly).
2. Operating and financial flows are separated and are discounted at different rates: the operating flow at the rate which is equal to the equity cost k_e, depending on leverage and on the number of payments of interest on debt and of tax on income, and credit flow at the rate which is equal to the debt cost k_d.

Note that loan capital is the least risky because the credit (including the interest on credit) is paid after taxes in the first place. Therefore, the cost of credit will always be less than the equity cost, whether for ordinary or for preference shares $k_e > k_d;\ k_p > k_d$. Here $k_\mathrm{e};\ k_\mathrm{p}$ is the equity cost of ordinary or of preference shares consequently.

16.2.1 *With Flow Separation*

In this case, the expression for NPV (net present value) per period has a view

$$NPV = NOI(1 - t) - k_d D(1 - t) = NOI(1 - t) + k_d Dt - k_d D \tag{16.7}$$

Here, the first term is the value of operating income from the investment project after tax deduction, the second term is the value of the tax shield, the third term is the value of interest on debt for one period.

We will need the following auxiliary formulas for summing the reduced values of financial flows (16.7) when calculating NPV:

For annual payments of interest on debt and of tax on income:

$$\sum_{i=1}^{n} \frac{1}{(1+k_d)^i} = \frac{1}{1+k_d} \cdot \frac{1-(1+k_d)^{-n}}{1-\frac{1}{1+k_d}} = \frac{1}{k_d} \cdot \left(1-(1+k_d)^{-n}\right) \tag{16.8}$$

For more frequent payments (p times per period) of interest on debt and of tax on income (semi–annually, quarterly, monthly):

$$\begin{aligned} \sum_{i=1}^{np} \frac{R}{p(1+k_d)^{i/p}} &= \frac{R}{p(1+k_d)^{1/p}} \cdot \frac{1-(1+k_d)^{-n}}{1-\frac{1}{(1+k_d)^{1/p}}} \\ &= \frac{R}{p} \cdot \frac{\left(1-(1+k_d)^{-n}\right)}{(1+k_d)^{1/p}-1} \end{aligned} \tag{16.9}$$

Similar formulas are obtained using the cost of equity k_e and WACC as the discount rates.

Summing up the given values of financial flows for each period (16.7), we obtain for NPV of n–years project in the case of separated flows:

$$\begin{aligned} NPV = &-S + \sum_{i=1}^{n} \frac{NOI(1-t)}{(1+k_e)^i} + \sum_{i=1}^{n} \frac{k_d Dt}{(1+k_d)^i} \\ &- \sum_{i=1}^{n} \frac{k_d D}{(1+k_d)^i} - \frac{D}{(1+k_d)^n} \end{aligned} \tag{16.10}$$

Here, the second term is the reduced value of operating income from the investment project, the second term is the reduced value of the tax shield, the third term is the reduced value of interest paid annually (at the end of the year), and the fourth term is the reduced value of the debt paid at the end of the project.

After summing, we have the following expression for NPV:

$$\begin{aligned} NPV = &-S + \frac{NOI(1-t)}{k_e} \cdot \left(1-\left(\frac{1}{1+k_e}\right)^n\right) + Dt\left(1-(1+k_d)^{-n}\right) \\ &-D\left(1-(1+k_d)^{-n}\right) - \frac{D}{(1+k_d)^n} \end{aligned} \tag{16.11}$$

In the case of more frequent (p–times per year) payment of income taxes (p_1) and frequent payments of interest on debt (p_2) we have:

$$\begin{aligned} NPV = &-S + \sum_{i=1}^{n} \frac{NOI(1-t)}{(1+k_e)^i} + \sum_{i=1}^{np} \frac{k_d Dt}{p_1(1+k_d)^{i/p_1}} \\ &- \sum_{i=1}^{np} \frac{k_d D}{p_2(1+k_d)^{i/p_2}} - \frac{D}{(1+k_d)^n} \end{aligned} \tag{16.12}$$

After summing, we have the following expression for NPV:

$$NPV = -S + \frac{NOI(1-t)}{k_e} \cdot \left(1 - \left(\frac{1}{1+k_e}\right)^n\right) + \frac{k_d Dt\left(1-(1+k_d)^{-n}\right)}{p_1\left((1+k_d)^{1/p_1} - 1\right)} - \frac{k_d D\left(1-(1+k_d)^{-n}\right)}{p_2\left((1+k_d)^{1/p_2} - 1\right)} - \frac{D}{(1+k_d)^n} \tag{16.13}$$

Long-Term Investment Projects

To obtain the expression for NPV of long-term investment projects, one should find the limit of (16.13) $n \to \infty$.

$$NPV = -S + \sum_{i=1}^{n} \frac{NOI(1-t)}{(1+k_e)^i} + \sum_{i=1}^{np} \frac{k_d Dt}{p_1(1+k_d)^{i/p_1}} - \sum_{i=1}^{np} \frac{k_d D}{p_2(1+k_d)^{i/p_2}} - \frac{D}{(1+k_d)^n} \tag{16.14}$$

16.2.2 Without Flow Separation

In the case of no separation between operating and financial flows, both flows are discounted by the general rate WACC. The credit reimbursable at the end of the project can be discounted either at the same rate WACC or at the debt cost rate k_d. Below, a uniform rate for WACC has been used.

Summing up the given values of financial flows for each period (16.3), we obtain for NPV of n–years project in the case without separated flows:

$$NPV = -S + \sum_{i=1}^{n} \frac{NOI(1-t)}{(1+WACC)^i} + \sum_{i=1}^{n} \frac{k_d Dt}{(1+WACC)^i} - \sum_{i=1}^{n} \frac{k_d D}{(1+WACC)^i} - \frac{D}{(1+WACC)^n} \tag{16.15}$$

After summing, we have the following expression for NPV:

$$NPV = -S + \frac{NOI(1-t)}{WACC} \cdot \left(1 - \left(\frac{1}{1+WACC}\right)^n\right) + \frac{k_d Dt\left(1-(1+WACC)^{-n}\right)}{WACC} - \frac{k_d D\left(1-(1+WACC)^{-n}\right)}{WACC} - \frac{D}{(1+WACC)^n} \tag{16.16}$$

In the case of more frequent (*p*–times per year) payment of income taxes and frequent payments of interest on the debt we have:

$$NPV = -S + \sum_{i=1}^{n} \frac{NOI(1-t)}{(1+WACC)^i} + \sum_{i=1}^{np} \frac{k_d Dt}{p_1(1+WACC)^{i/p_1}} - \sum_{i=1}^{np} \frac{k_d D}{p_2(1+WACC)^{i/p_2}} - \frac{D}{(1+WACC)^n} \quad (16.17)$$

After summing, we have the following expression for NPV:

$$NPV = -S + \frac{NOI(1-t)}{WACC} \cdot \left(1 - \left(\frac{1}{1+WACC}\right)^n\right) + \frac{k_d Dt\left(1-(1+WACC)^{-n}\right)}{p_1\left((1+WACC)^{1/p_1} - 1\right)} - \frac{k_d D\left(1-(1+WACC)^{-n}\right)}{p_2\left((1+WACC)^{1/p_2} - 1\right)} - \frac{D}{(1+WACC)^n} \quad (16.18)$$

Long-Term Investment Projects

To obtain the expression for NPV of long-term investment projects, one should find the limit of (16.18) $n \to \infty$.

$$NPV = -S + \frac{NOI(1-t)}{WACC} + \frac{k_d Dt}{p_1\left((1+WACC)^{1/p_1} - 1\right)} - \frac{k_d D}{p_2\left((1+WACC)^{1/p_2} - 1\right)} \quad (16.19)$$

16.3 The Effectiveness of the Investment Project from the Perspective of the Owners of Equity and Debt

16.3.1 With Flow Separation

In this case, operating and financial flows are separated and are discounted using different rates: the operating flow at the rate equal to the equity cost k_e, depending on leverage, and credit flow at the rate equal to the debt cost k_d, which remain constant until fairly large values of leverage and start to grow only at high values of leverage L, when there is a danger of bankruptcy.

After–tax flow of capital for each period in this case is equal to (16.6):

$$CF = NOI(1-t) + k_d Dt \tag{16.20}$$

After summing over n–periods, one gets the following expression for NPV:

$$\begin{aligned} NPV &= -I + \sum_{i=1}^{n} \frac{NOI(1-t)}{(1+k_e)^i} + \sum_{i=1}^{n} \frac{k_d Dt}{(1+k_d)^i} \\ &= -I + \frac{NOI(1-t)}{k_e}\left(1-(1+k_e)^{-n}\right) + Dt\left(1-(1+k_d)^{-n}\right) \end{aligned} \tag{16.21}$$

In the case of a few (p) payments of tax on profit per period, the expression for NPV will be modified:

$$NPV = -I + \sum_{i=1}^{n} \frac{NOI(1-t)}{(1+k_e)^i} + \sum_{i=1}^{np} \frac{k_d Dt}{p(1+k_d)^{i/p}} \tag{16.22}$$

After summing over n–periods, one gets the following modified expression for NPV:

$$NPV = -I + \frac{NOI(1-t)\left[1-(1+k_e)^{-n}\right]}{k_e} + \frac{k_d Dt\left[1-(1+k_d)^{-n}\right]}{p\left[(1+k_d)^{1/p}-1\right]} \tag{16.23}$$

To obtain the expression for NPV of long-term investment projects, one should find the limit of (16.23) $n \to \infty$.

$$NPV = -I + \frac{NOI(1-t)}{k_e} + \frac{k_d Dt}{p\left[(1+k_d)^{1/p}-1\right]} \tag{16.24}$$

16.3.2 Without Flow Separation

In the case of no separation between operating and financial flows, both flows are discounted by the general rate WACC.

After summing the expression (16.6) over n–periods, one gets the following expression for NPV:

$$NPV = -I + \sum_{i=1}^{n} \frac{NOI(1-t)}{(1+WACC)^i} + \sum_{i=1}^{n} \frac{k_d Dt}{(1+WACC)^i} \tag{16.25}$$

$$\begin{aligned} NPV = {} & -I + \tfrac{NOI(1-t)}{WACC}\left(1-(1+WACC)^{-n}\right) \\ & + \tfrac{k_d Dt}{WACC}\left(1-(1+WACC)^{-n}\right) \end{aligned} \tag{16.26}$$

In the case of a few (p) payments of tax on profit per period, the expression for NPV will be modified:

$$NPV = -I + \sum_{i=1}^{n} \frac{NOI(1-t)}{(1+WACC)^i} + \sum_{i=1}^{np} \frac{k_d Dt}{p(1+WACC)^{i/p}} \tag{16.27}$$

After summing over n–periods, one gets the following modified expression for NPV:

$$\begin{aligned} NPV = {} & -I + \tfrac{NOI(1-t)}{WACC} \cdot \left(1 - \left(\tfrac{1}{1+WACC}\right)^n\right) \\ & + \tfrac{k_d Dt\left(1-(1+WACC)^{-n}\right)}{p\left((1+WACC)^{1/p}-1\right)} \end{aligned} \tag{16.28}$$

To obtain the expression for NPV of long-term investment projects, one should find the limit of (16.28) $n \to \infty$.

$$NPV = -I + \frac{NOI(1-t)}{WACC} + \frac{k_d Dt}{p\left((1+WACC)^{1/p}-1\right)} \tag{16.29}$$

16.4 Discount Rates

In the case without the division of credit and investment flows (both flows are discounted using the same rate, for which WACC can obviously be chosen), WACC is calculated by the following formulas:

For arbitrary project duration (Kahneman and Tversky 1996):

$$\frac{1-(1+WACC)^{-n}}{WACC}=\frac{1-(1+k_0)^{-n}}{k_0\cdot\left(1-\frac{k_d w_d t}{p}\frac{\left[1-(1+k_d)^{-n}\right]}{(1+k_d)^{1/p}-1}\right)} \tag{16.30}$$

For long-term projects (Kahneman and Tversky 1996):

$$WACC=k_0\cdot\left(1-\frac{k_d w_d t}{p}\frac{1}{(1+k_d)^{1/p}-1}\right) \tag{16.31}$$

In the case of the division of credit and investment flows (and thus discounting of the payments using two different rates, equity cost k_e and debt cost k_d), k_e should be found from the equation

$$WACC=k_e w_e+k_d w_d(1-t) \tag{16.32}$$

where we substitute WACC from the formula (16.30) for a project with arbitrary duration and from the formula (16.31) for a long-term project.

Note that formulas (16.30) and (16.31) are quite different from the original formulas by Brusov–Filatova–Orekhova (Brusov et al. 2018a; Filatova et al. 2008) and Modigliani–Miller (Modigliani and Miller 1958, 1963, 1966), where payments of interest on debt and of tax on income are made once per year and are turned into them if we put $p=1$:

$$\frac{1-(1+WACC)^{-n}}{WACC}=\frac{1-(1+k_0)^{-n}}{k_0\cdot\left(1-w_d t\left[1-(1+k_d)^{-n}\right]\right)} \tag{16.33}$$

$$WACC=k_0\cdot(1-w_d t) \tag{16.34}$$

16.5 Results and Discussions

In this section, we study numerically with the use of Microsoft Excel the effectiveness of the four models created above by us. We consider long-term projects as well as projects of arbitrary duration from two perspectives: the owners of equity and debt and the equity holders only. We will study the case without flow separation. In this case, operating and financial flows are not separated and both are discounted, using the general rate, for which we select the weighted average cost of capital, WACC. Let us start from the study numerically on the dependence of the discount rates

Table 16.1 Dependence of WACC on leverage level L at $k_0 = 0.22$, $k_d = 0.14$ and different $p = 1, 6, 12$

L	WACC		
	$p = 1$	$p = 6$	$p = 12$
0	0.2200	0.2200	0.2200
1	0.1980	0.1967	0.1966
2	0.1907	0.1890	0.1888
3	0.1870	0.1851	0.1849
4	0.1848	0.1828	0.1826
5	0.1833	0.1812	0.1810
6	0.1823	0.1801	0.1799
7	0.1815	0.1793	0.1791
8	0.1809	0.1787	0.1784
9	0.1804	0.1781	0.1779
10	0.1800	0.1777	0.1775

(weighted average cost of capital, WACC) on leverage level L at different frequencies of payment of tax on profit p.

16.5.1 Numerical Calculation of the Discount Rates

The Long-Term Investment Projects

For long-term investment projects (the Modigliani–Miller limit), the discount rate (WACC) in the case of arbitrary frequency of payment of tax on profit p is described by formula (16.31) (Brusov and Filatova 2021):

$$WACC = k_0 \cdot \left(1 - \frac{k_d w_d t}{p} \frac{1}{(1+k_d)^{1/p} - 1}\right)$$

For WACC calculation, we will use the following parameters: $k_0 = 0.22$; $k_d = 0.14$; $t = 20\%$; $L = 0$; 1; 2…; 10.

Dependence of WACC on leverage level L at $k_0 = 0.22$, $k_d = 0.14$ and different $p = 1, 6, 12$ is shown in Table 16.1 and Fig. 16.1.

The Arbitrary Duration Investment Projects

For arbitrary duration investment projects, the discount rate (WACC) in the case of arbitrary frequency of payment of tax on profit p is described by formula (16.30) (modified BFO formula [Brusov and Filatova 2021]).

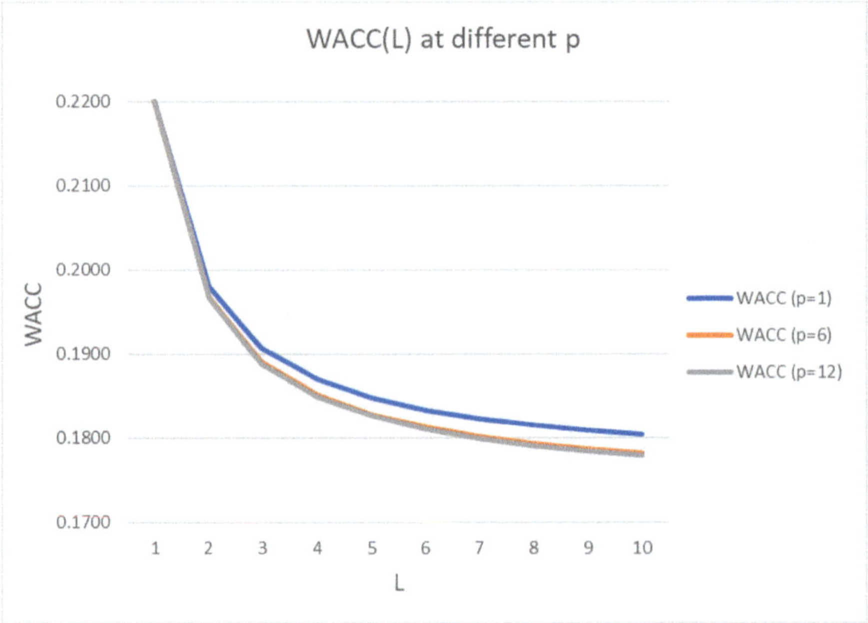

Fig. 16.1 Dependence of the weighted average cost of capital, WACC, on leverage level L at different frequencies of payments of tax on profit, $p = 1; 6; 12$

For WACC calculation, we will use the following parameters: $k_O = 0.22$; $k_d = 0.14$; $t = 20\%$; $L = 0; 1; 2\ldots; 10$; $p = 1; 6; 12$; $n = 3$

$$\frac{1-(1+WACC)^{-n}}{WACC} = \frac{1-(1+k_0)^{-n}}{k_0 \cdot \left(1 - \frac{k_d w_d t}{p} \frac{\left[1-(1+k_d)^{-n}\right]}{(1+k_d)^{1/p}-1}\right)}$$

Dependence of WACC on leverage level L at $k_O = 0.22$, $k_d = 0.14$ and different $p = 1, 6, 12$ for a three–year company is shown in Table 16.2 and Figs. 16.2 and 16.3.

Note that the dependences of WACC on leverage level L obtained above will be used below under a study of the effectiveness of long-term as well arbitrary duration investment projects, from the perspective of the owners of equity capital and of the owners of equity and debt.

Table 16.2 Dependence of WACC on leverage level L at $k_0 = 0.22$, $k_d = 0.14$ and different $p = 1, 6, 12$ for a three–year company

L	WACC		
	$p = 1$	$p = 6$	$p = 12$
0	0.2200	0.2200	0.2200
1	0.1987	0.1974	0.1973
2	0.1915	0.1899	0.1897
3	0.1879	0.1861	0.1859
4	0.1858	0.1838	0.1836
5	0.1843	0.1823	0.1821
6	0.1833	0.1812	0.1810
7	0.1825	0.1804	0.1802
8	0.1819	0.1798	0.1795
9	0.1815	0.1793	0.1790
10	0.1811	0.1788	0.1786

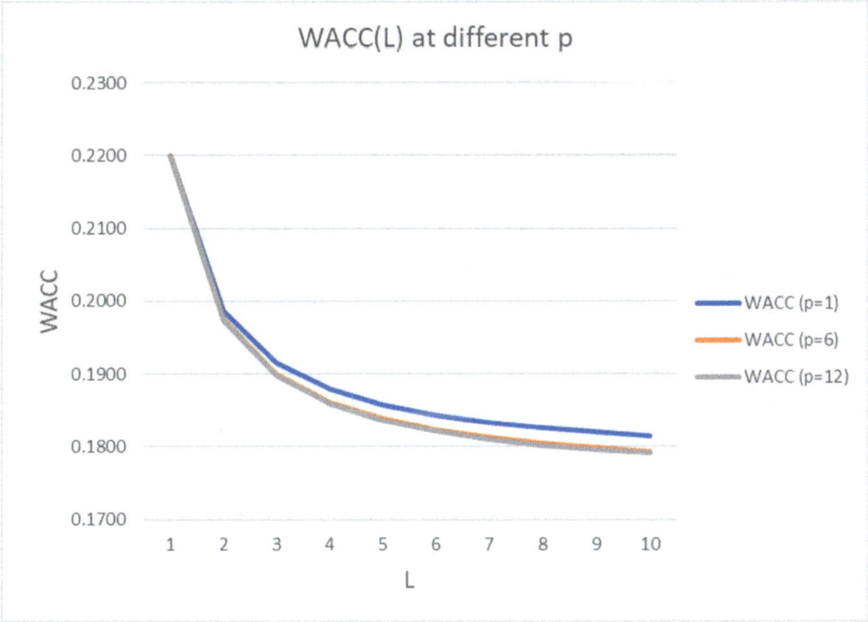

Fig. 16.2 Dependence of WACC on leverage level L at $k_0 = 0.22$, $k_d = 0.14$ and different $p = 1$, 6, 12 for a three–year project

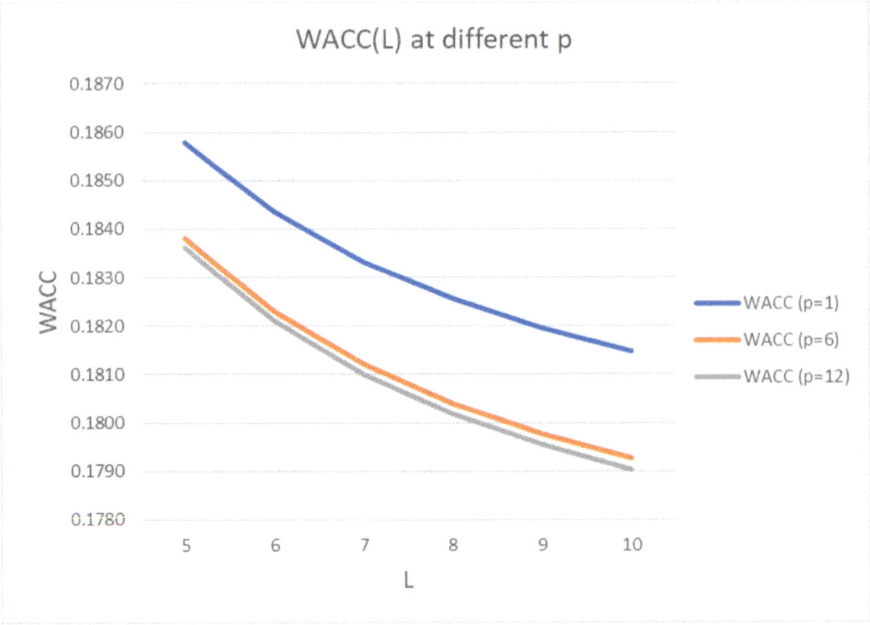

Fig. 16.3 Dependence of WACC on leverage level L at $k_0 = 0.22$, $k_d = 0.14$ and different $p = 1$, 6, 12 for a three–year project (larger scale)

16.5.2 The Effectiveness of the Long-Term Investment Project from the Perspective of the Owners of Equity Capital

For long-term investment projects, the discount rate (WACC) in the case of arbitrary frequency of payment of tax on profit p is described by formula (16.19) and for NPV one has:

$$NPV = -S + \frac{NOI(1-t)}{WACC} + \frac{k_d D t}{p_1\left((1+WACC)^{1/p_1}-1\right)} - \frac{k_d D}{p_2\left((1+WACC)^{1/p_2}-1\right)}$$

For NPV calculation, we will use the following parameters: $k_0 = 0.22$; $k_d = 0.14$; $t = 20\%$; $L = 0$; 1; 2…; 10; $p_1 = p_2 = p = 1$; 6; 12;$S = 1000$;$D = LS$; $NOI = 800$.

It is seen from Figs. 16.4 and 16.5 that in the case of considering the effectiveness of long-term investment projects for owners of equity capital, NPV will vary with the change of p, but with not much variation (it is seen from Table 16.3 and from Fig. 16.5, but not from Fig. 16.4).

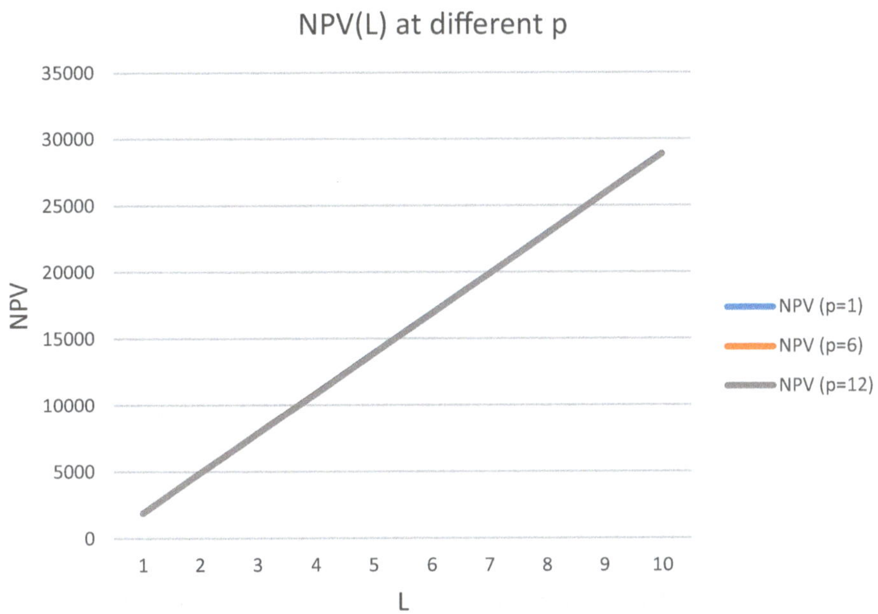

Fig. 16.4 Dependence of NPV on leverage level L at $k_0 = 0.22$, $k_d = 0.14$ and different $p = 1, 6, 12$ for a long-term project

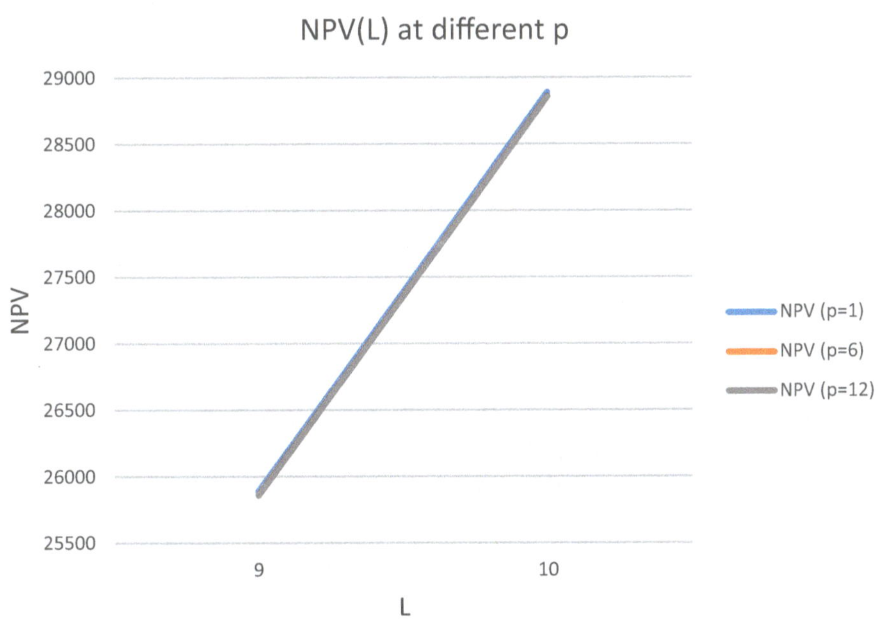

Fig. 16.5 Dependence of NPV on leverage level L at $k_0 = 0.22$, $k_d = 0.14$ and different $p = 1, 6, 12$ for a long-term project (larger scale)

Table 16.3 Dependence of WACC and NPV on leverage level L at $k_0 = 0.22$, $k_d = 0.14$ and different $p = 1, 6, 12$

L	NPV		
	$p = 1$	$p = 6$	$p = 12$
0	1909	1909	1909
1	4899	4891	4891
2	7895	7883	7882
3	10,893	10,878	10,877
4	13,892	13,874	13,873
5	16,891	16,871	16,869
6	19,890	19,868	19,866
7	22,890	22,865	22,863
8	25,889	25,863	25,860
9	28,889	28,860	28,858
10	31,889	31,858	31,855

16.5.3 The Effectiveness of the Long-Term Investment Project from the Perspective of the Owners of Equity and Debt

For long-term investment projects, NPV in the case of arbitrary frequency of payment of tax on profit p is described by formula (16.29):

$$NPV = -I + \frac{NOI(1-t)}{WACC} + \frac{k_d Dt}{p\left((1+WACC)^{1/p} - 1\right)}$$

For NPV calculation, we will use the following parameters: $k_0 = 0.22$; $k_d = 0.14$;$t = 20\%$; $L = 0;\ 1;\ 2\ldots;\ 10$; $p_1 = p_2 = p = 1;\ 6;\ 12$;$S = 1000$;$D = LS$; $NOI = 800$.

Dependence of NPV on leverage level$L$ at $k_0 = 0.22$, $k_d = 0.14$ and different $p = 1, 6, 12$ for a long-term project is shown in Table 16.4 and Figs. 16.6 and 16.7.

16.5.4 The Effectiveness of the Arbitrary Duration Investment Projects from the Perspective of the Owners of Equity Capital

For the arbitrary duration investment projects, NPV in the case of arbitrary frequency of payment of tax on profit p is described by formula (16.18):

Table 16.4 Dependence of NPV on leverage level L at $k_0 = 0.22$, $k_d = 0.14$ and different $p = 1, 6, 12$

L	NPV		
	$p = 1$	$p = 6$	$p = 12$
0	1909	1909	1909
1	4606	4659	4665
2	7364	7478	7489
3	10,139	10,316	10,334
4	12,922	13,163	13,188
5	15,709	16,015	16,047
6	18,498	18,870	18,908
7	21,289	21,726	21,771
8	24,081	24,583	24,635
9	26,874	27,441	27,500
10	29,667	30,300	30,365

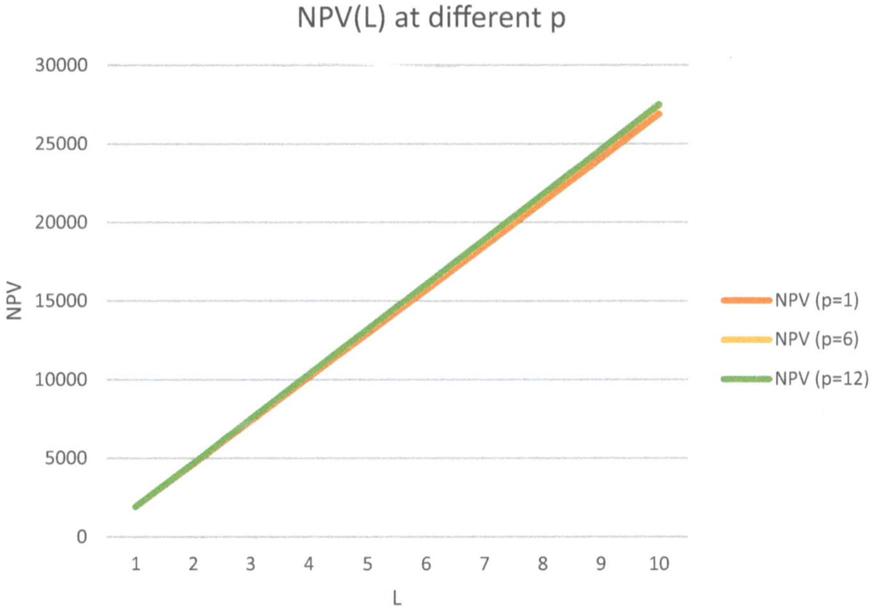

Fig. 16.6 Dependence of NPV on leverage level L at $k_0 = 0.22$, $k_d = 0.14$ and different $p = 1, 6, 12$ for a long-term project

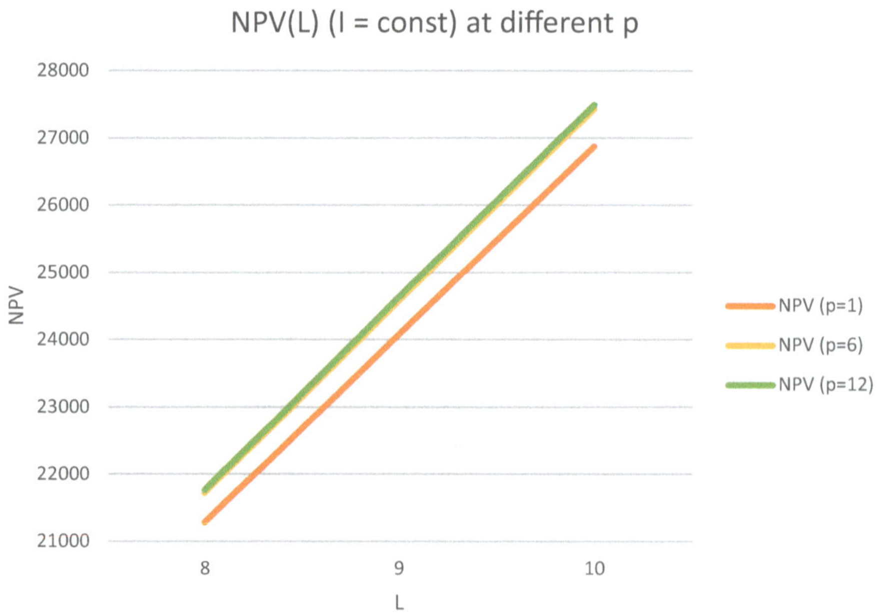

Fig. 16.7 Dependence of NPV on leverage level L at $k_0 = 0.22$, $k_d = 0.14$ and different $p = 1, 6, 12$ for a long-term project (larger scale)

$$NPV = -S + \frac{NOI(1-t)}{WACC} \cdot \left(1 - \left(\frac{1}{1+WACC}\right)^n\right) + \frac{k_d Dt\left(1-(1+WACC)^{-n}\right)}{p_1\left((1+WACC)^{1/p_1}-1\right)} - \frac{k_d D\left(1-(1+WACC)^{-n}\right)}{p_2\left((1+WACC)^{1/p_2}-1\right)} - \frac{D}{(1+WACC)^n}$$

For NPV calculation, we will use the following parameters: $k_0 = 0.22$; $k_d = 0.14$; $t = 20\%$; $L = 0; 1; 2\ldots; 10$; $p_1 = p_2 = p = 1; 6; 12$;$S = 1000$;$D = LS$; $NOI = 800$; $n = 3$.

Dependence of NPV on leverage level L at $k_0 = 0.22$, $k_d = 0.14$ and different $p = 1, 6, 12$ for a three–year project is shown in Table 16.5 and Figs. 16.8 and 16.9.

16.5.5 *The Effectiveness of the Arbitrary Duration Investment Project from the Perspective of the Owners of Equity and Debt*

For the arbitrary duration investment projects, NPV in the case of arbitrary frequency of payment of tax on profit p is described by formula (16.28):

Table 16.5 Dependence of NPV on leverage level L at $k_0 = 0.22$, $k_d = 0.14$ and different $p = 1, 6, 12$ for a three–year project

L	NPV		
	$p = 1$	$p = 6$	$p = 12$
0	307	307	307
1	885	869	867
2	1438	1406	1403
3	1985	1937	1932
4	2530	2464	2458
5	3072	2991	2983
6	3615	3516	3506
7	4156	4042	4030
8	4698	4566	4553
9	5239	5091	5076
10	5780	5615	5599

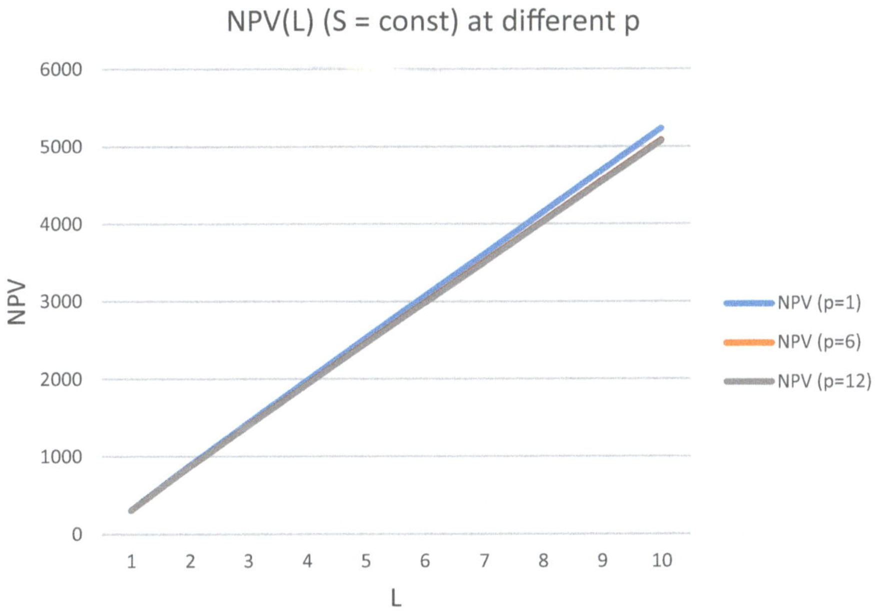

Fig. 16.8 Dependence of NPV on leverage level L at $k_0 = 0.22$, $k_d = 0.14$ and different $p = 1, 6, 12$ for a three–year project

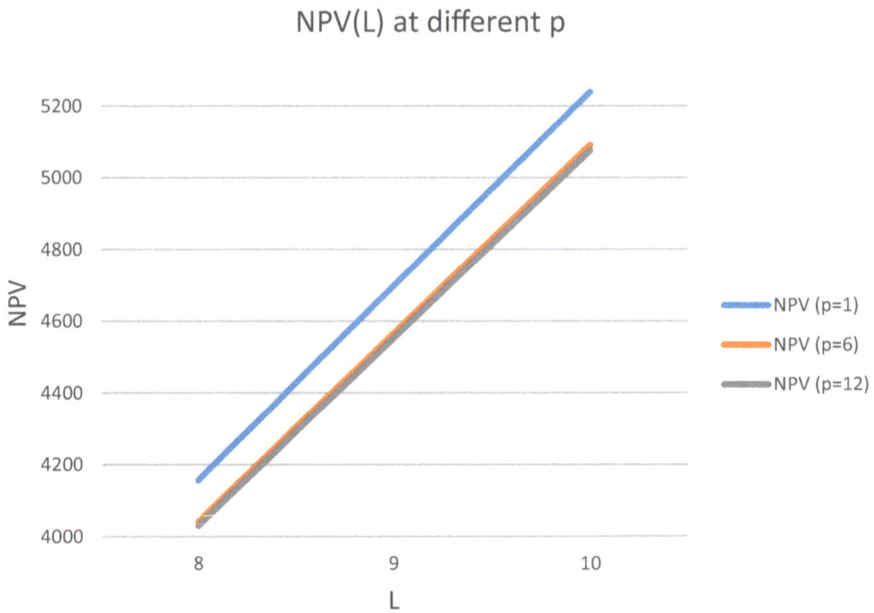

Fig. 16.9 Dependence of NPV on leverage level L at $k_0 = 0.22$, $k_d = 0.14$ and different $p = 1, 6, 12$ for a three–year project (larger scale)

$$NPV = -I + \frac{NOI(1-t)}{WACC} \cdot \left(1 - \left(\frac{1}{1 + WACC}\right)^n\right) + \frac{k_d Dt\left(1 - (1 + WACC)^{-n}\right)}{p\left((1 + WACC)^{1/p} - 1\right)}$$

For NPV calculation, we will use the following parameters: $k_0 = 0.22$; $k_d = 0.14$; $t = 20\%$; $L = 0; 1; 2\ldots; 10$; $p_1 = p_2 = p = 1; 6; 12$;$S = 1000$;$D = LS$; $NOI = 800$; $n = 3$.

Dependence of NPV on leverage level L at $k_0 = 0.22$, $k_d = 0.14$ and different $p = 1, 6, 12$ for a three–year project is shown in Table 16.6 and Figs. 16.10 and 16.11.

16.5.6 Discussions

The analysis of results from Tables 16.1, 16.2, 16.3, 16.4, 16.5, and 16.6 and Figs. 16.1, 16.2, 16.3, 16.4, 16.5, 16.6, 16.7, 16.8, 16.9, 16.10, and 16.11 shows that:

1. The weighted average cost of capital, WACC, decreases with leverage level L at all values of frequency of payments of tax on profit p (see Tables 16.1 and 16.2 and Figs. 16.1, 16.2, and 16.3);

Table 16.6 Dependence of NPV on leverage level$L$ at $k_0 = 0.22$, $k_d = 0.14$ and different $p = 1, 6, 12$ for a three–year project

L	NPV		
	$p = 1$	$p = 6$	$p = 12$
0	307	307	307
1	761	771	772
2	1218	1238	1240
3	1676	1707	1710
4	2135	2175	2179
5	2594	2644	2649
6	3053	3113	3119
7	3511	3582	3589
8	3970	4051	4059
9	4429	4520	4529
10	4888	4989	4999

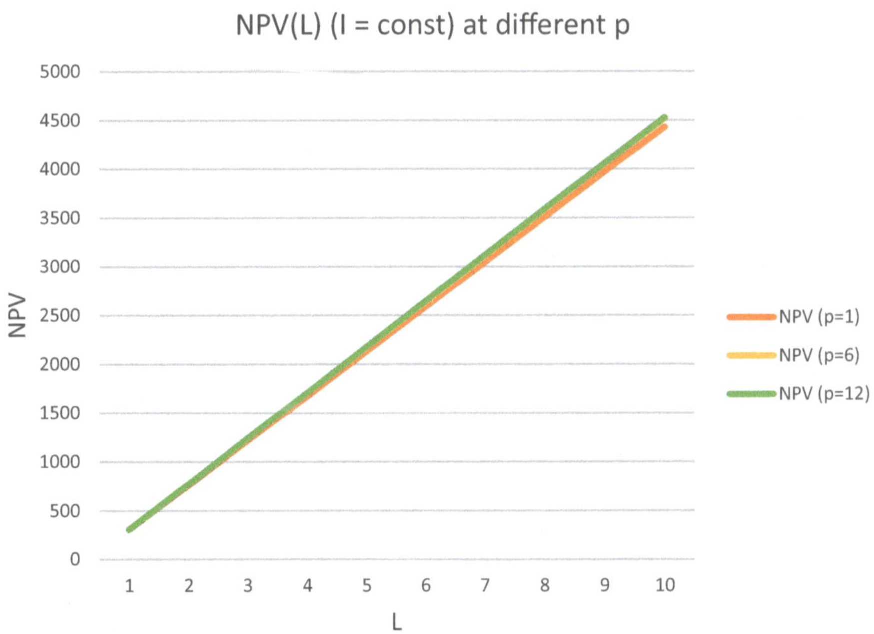

Fig. 16.10 Dependence of NPV on leverage level L at $k_0 = 0.22$, $k_d = 0.14$ and different $p = 1$, 6, 12 for a three–year project

2. With an increase in p, WACC decreases: WACC(L) curves lie lower with increase of p;
3. The difference between curves corresponding to $p = 1$ and $p = 6$ is much more than the difference between the curves corresponding to $p = 6$ and $p = 12$. This difference decreases with p. It turns out that an increase in the number of

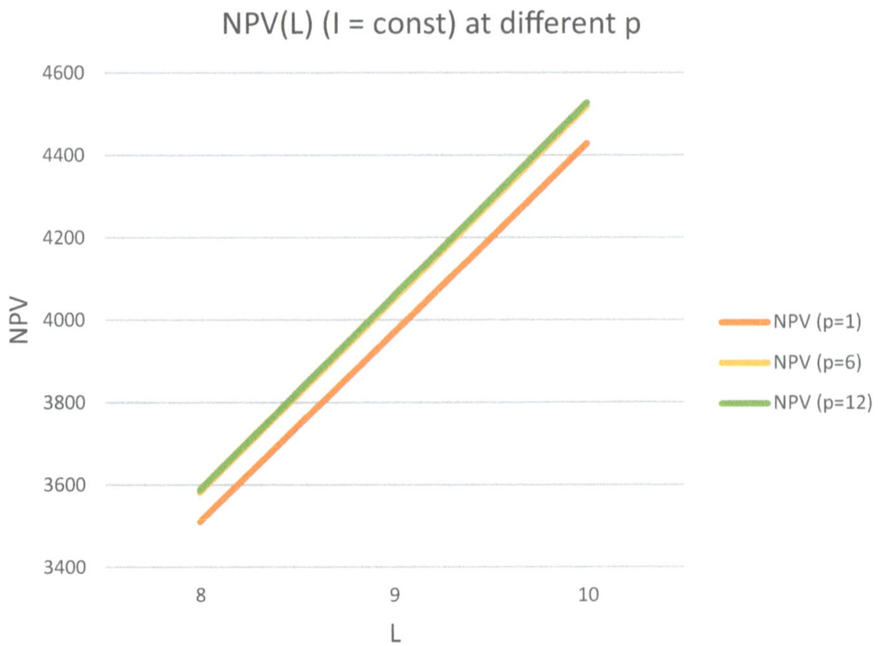

Fig. 16.11 Dependence of NPV on leverage level L at $k_0 = 0.22$, $k_d = 0.14$ and different $p = 1$, 6, 12 for a three–year project (larger scale)

payments of tax on profit per year p leads to a decrease in the cost of attracting capital (WACC). Will this decrease in the discount rate increase the effectiveness of investment projects? As we see from the Tables 16.3, 16.4, 16.5, and 16.6 and Figs. 16.4, 16.5, 16.6, 16.7, 16.8, 16.9, 16.10, and 16.11, the situation is different for owners of equity capital and for owners of equity and debt capital.

4. NPV practically linearly increases with leverage level at all values of frequency of payments of tax on profit p and all frequency of payments of interest on debt;
5. In the case of considering the effectiveness of long-term investment projects for owners of equity capital, NPV is changed with a change of p (both p_1 and p_2 are equal everywhere below) but by a very small value (it is seen in the Tables, but not in the Figures);
6. In the case of considering the effectiveness of long-term investment projects for owners of equity and debt, NPV is changed with a change of p more significantly (it is seen in the Tables and in the Figures);
7. For arbitrary duration projects, this difference in NPV with a change of p is more significant and should be accounted under valuation of the effectiveness of an investment project;
8. In the case of considering the effectiveness of an investment project for owners of equity capital, we need to note that an increase in p leads to a decrease in NPV: this means that the effectiveness of an investment project decreases with p;

9. In the case of considering the effectiveness of an investment project for owners of equity and debt capital, we need to note that the situation is opposite and an increase in p leads to increase in NPV: this means that the effectiveness of an investment project increases with p;
10. The above results show that in the former case, companies should pay tax on profit and interest on debt once per year, while in the latter case, more frequent payments are profitable for the effectiveness of an investment;
11. Thus, while for long-term projects' NPV, the impact of more frequent payments of both values p_1 and p_2 is insignificant, for arbitrary duration projects the account of the frequency of both types of payments could be important and could lead to more significant influence on the effectiveness of an investment project, decreasing it (in the former case), or increasing it (in the latter case). Note that the specific value of the effect depends on the values of the parameters in the project (k_0, k_d, n,t, S etc.).

16.6 Conclusions

There are too few investment models which can numerically valuate the effectiveness of investment projects, among them the investment models developed by the authors of this paper. Moreover, investment models are practically absent which account for the conditions of the real functioning of investment projects. This paper covers this gap in the literature and science in the field of investments and develops innovative investment models which are much closer to economic practice.

We developed here for the first time eight innovative investment models: long-term (described by Eqs. [16.14], [16.19], [16.24] and [16.29]) as well arbitrary duration (described by Eqs. [16.13], [16.18], [16.23] and [16.28]), which account payments of interest on debt and of tax on income a few times per year (semi–annually, quarterly, monthly) as it happened in practice. Note that no one before had investigated the impact of the frequency of payments of taxes and of debt interest on the effectiveness of investment projects. These investment models allow for investigation of the impact of all main parameters of investment projects (equity value S, investment value I, net operating income NOI, leverage level L, profitability of investments β, tax on profit t, project duration n, equity cost k_0, debt cost k_d and number of payments of interest on debt p_1 and of tax on income p_2) on the main indicator of effectiveness of investment projects NPV (net present value). They could be used for investigation of different problems of investments, such as the influence of debt financing, leverage level, taxing, project duration, method of financing, number of payments of interest on debt and of tax on income and some other parameters on efficiency of investments and other problems. In particular, they will improve the issue of project ratings (Brusov et al. 2018b). These new models allow for making more correct evaluations of effectiveness of investment projects long-term as well as of arbitrary duration.

Numerical calculations, conducted for four investment models (without flow separation) show that:

- In the case of considering the effectiveness of an investment project for owners of equity capital, the increase in the number of payments of tax on income and of interest on debt p leads to an decrease in NPV: this means that the effectiveness of an investment project decreases with p;
- In the case of considering the effectiveness of an investment project for owners of equity and debt capital, the increase in the number of payments of tax on income and of interest on debt p leads to an increase in NPV: this means that the effectiveness of an investment project increases with p.

In the former case, companies should pay tax on profit and interest on debt once per year, while in the latter case, more frequent payments are profitable for the effectiveness of an investment.

Thus, while for long-term projects' NPV, the impact of more frequent payments of both values p_1 and p_2 is insignificant, for arbitrary duration projects the account of the frequency of both types of payments could be important and could lead to more significant influence on the effectiveness of an investment project, decreasing it (in the former case), or increasing it (in the latter case). Note that the specific value of the effect depends on the values of the parameters in the project (k_0, k_d, n, t, S, etc.).

There are some limitations of the applicability of the proposed models:

1. For long-term projects, they are connected with the limitations of the Modigliani–Miller theory;
2. For consideration of without flow separation, they are connected with the well–known limitations of the WACC approach;
3. For arbitrary duration projects (using BFO theory), they are connected with the fact that not all the conditions of real investments are accounted yet.

The contribution of this study to finance and economics is mainly related to the goal that new modern investment models have been created to be as close as possible to real investment conditions. Our models, namely, models with payments of interest on debt and of tax on income which occur a few times per year (semi–annually, quarterly or monthly), could be more successfully applied in real economic practice.

References

Black F, Litterman R (1992) Global portfolio optimization. Financ Anal J 48:28–43

Bond S, Meghir C (1994) Dynamic investment models and the firm's financial policy. Rev Econ Study 67:197–216

Brown K, Harlow W, Zhang H (2021) Investment style volatility and mutual fund performance. J Invest Manag 19:78

Brusov P, Filatova T, Orehova N, Eskindarov M (2015) Modern corporate finance, investments and taxation. Springer International Publishing, Cham, Switzerland, pp 1–373. Available online: https://www.springer.com/gp/book/9783319147314. Accessed 29 Apr 2021

Brusov P, Filatova T, Orehova N, Eskindarov M (2018a) Modern corporate finance, investments, taxation and ratings, 2nd ed. Springer Nature Publishing, Cham, Switzerland, pp 1–571

Brusov P, Filatova T, Orehova N (2018b) Ratings: Critical analysis and new approaches of quantitative and qualitative methodology. Springer Nature Publishing, Switzerland, pp 1–379. Available online: https://www.springer.com/de/book/9783030562427. Accessed 29 Apr 2021
Brusov P, Filatova T (2021) The Modigliani-Miller theory with arbitrary frequency of payment of tax on profit. Mathematics 9:1198. https://doi.org/10.3390/math9111198
Brusov PN, Filatova TV Kulik VL (2024) Capital asset pricing model (CAPM) 2.0: Account of business and financial risk. Finance: Theory and practice. 28(2):128–142. https://doi.org/10.26794/2587-5671-2024-28-2-128-142
Brusov PN, Filatova TV, Orekhova NP (2021) Ratings: Critical analysis and new approaches of quantitative and qualitative methodology. Springer Nature Publishing, pp.1–369
Brusov PN, Filatova TV, Orekhova NP (2022) Generalized Modigliani–Miller theory: Applications in corporate finance, investments, taxation and ratings. Springer Nature Publishing, pp.1–362
Brusov PN, Filatova TV, Orekhova NP (2023) The Brusov–Filatova–Orekhova theory of capital structure: Applications in corporate finance, investments, taxation and ratings. Springer Nature Publishing, pp.1–769
Brusov PN, Filatova TV (2025a) Business valuation and company value: New qualitative approaches considering business and financial risks. Springer Nature Publishing, pp.1–654
Brusov PN, Filatova TV (2025b) Efficiency of investment projects: Modern investment models and their applications. Springer Nature Publishing, pp.1–843
Cakici N, Zaremba A (2021) Size, value, profitability, and investment effects in international stock returns: are they really there? J Invest 30:65–86. https://doi.org/10.3905/joi.2021.1.176
Dammon R, Senbet L (1988) The effect of taxes and depreciation on corporate investment and financial leverage. J Financ 43:357–373. https://doi.org/10.1111/j.1540-6261.1988.tb03944.x
DeAngelo H, Masulis R (1980) Optimal capital structure under corporate and personal taxation. J Financ Econ 8:3–29
Dotan A, Ravid S (1985) On the interaction of real and financial decisions of the firm under uncertainty. J Financ 40:501–516
Escobar-Anel M, Lichtenstern A, Zagst R (2020) Behavioral portfolio insurance strategies. Financ Mark Portf Manag 34:353–399
Filatova TV, Orekhova NP, Brusova AP (2008) Weighted average cost of capital in the theory of Modigliani-Miller, modified for a finite life–time company. Bull FU 48:68–77
Gidwani B (2020) Some issues with using ESG ratings in an investment process. J Invest 29:76–84. https://doi.org/10.3905/joi.2020.1.147
Kahneman D, Tversky A (1996) On the reality of cognitive illusions. Psychol Rev 103:582–591. https://doi.org/10.1037/0033-295X.103.3.582
Kang J (1995) The conditional relationship between financial leverage and corporate investment: Further clarification. J Bus Financ Account 22:1211–1219. https://doi.org/10.1111/j.1468-5957.1995.tb00902.x
Lang LE, Ofek E, Stulz R (1996) Leverage, investment, and firm growth. J Financ Econ 40:3–29
Loviscek A (2021) How much to invest, if any, in precious metals? A 21st–century perspective. J Invest 30:95–111. https://doi.org/10.3905/joi.2021.1.179
Modigliani F, Miller M (1958) The cost of capital, corporate finance, and the theory of investment. Am Econ Rev 48:261–297
Modigliani F, Miller M (1963) Corporate income taxes and the cost of capital: a correction. Am Econ Rev 53:147–175
Modigliani F, Miller M (1966) Some estimates of the cost of capital to the electric utility industry 1954–1957. Am Econ Rev 56:333–391
Rosenbaum J, Pearl J 2013 Investment banking valuation models. Wiley, New York, NY, USA, pp 1–342
Whited T (1992) Debt, Liquidity constraints and corporate investment: Evidence from panel data. J Financ 47:1425–1461

Chapter 17
Investment Models with Advance Frequent Payments of Tax on Profit and of Interest on Debt

17.1 Introduction

In this chapter as in previous one we continue to explore the impact of taxes on investment efficiency. Investments are quite important in economy and finance of any country. At the current stage the role of investment is increased many times as well as the role of the evaluation of the efficiency of investment projects, which allows for the realization of the most effective projects in the context of scarcity and limited investment resources, increases. Since virtually most investment projects use debt financing, the study of the influence of capital structure and debt financing on the efficiency of investment projects and determining the optimal capital structure is especially important at the present time. This is why in spite of the fact that a lot of different types of investment models have been developed—stochastic, dynamics (Bond and Meghir 1994), investment banking valuation models (Rosenbaum and Pearl 2013), etc.—the main problem, which has been discussed during the last few decades, is the impact of debt financing on the efficiency of investment projects and on the investment decisions of companies.

Recently (Brusov et al. 2021) new modern investment models have been created by us to be as close as possible to real investment conditions. We developed long-term as well as arbitrary duration models with payments of interest on debt and of tax on income a few times per year (semi-annually, quarterly and monthly), which could be applied in real economic practice. But in practice payments of tax on profit and of interest on debt could be made in advance. In current Chapter we develop the innovative investment models with frequent **advance** payments of tax on profit and of interest on debt and study the effectiveness of an investment projects within them.

We considered the effectiveness of the investment project from two points of view: the equity owners and the owners of equity and debt. NPV for each of these cases was calculated by two different methods: with the separation of credit and investment flows (and thus discounting the flows using two different rates) and without such separation (with discounting of both flows using the same rate, and the weighted

P. Brusov and T. Filatova, *Taxes and Taxation*, Contributions to Finance and Accounting, https://doi.org/10.1007/978-3-032-11077-0_17

average cost of capital, WACC, can be chosen as the rate). Numerical calculations, conducted for four investment models (without flow separation) showed that: (1) WACC decreases with p; (2) in the case of considering the effectiveness of an investment project for owners of equity capital, the increase in the number of payments of tax on income and of interest on debt p leads to a decrease in NPV: this means that the effectiveness of an investment project decreases with p; (3) in the case of considering the effectiveness of an investment project for owners of equity and debt capital, the increase in the number of payments of tax on income and of interest on debt p leads to an increase in NPV: this means that the effectiveness of an investment project increases with p. In the former case, companies should pay tax on profit and interest on debt once per year, while in the latter case, more frequent payments are profitable for the effectiveness of investment.

But in practice payments of tax on profit and of interest on debt could be made in advance. In current Chapter we develop the innovative investment models with frequent **advance** payments of tax on profit and of interest on debt and study the effectiveness of an investment projects within them.

Numerical calculations carried out for four investment models (without split flows) showed that in the case of **advance** payments of income tax and interest on debt, all the results related to the effect of the number of payments of income tax and interest on debt on the effectiveness of the investment projects are opposite to the results in the case of payments at the end of the periods obtained by us in the previous article: (1) WACC increases with p; (2) in the case of considering the effectiveness of an investment project for owners of equity capital, the increase in the number of payments of tax on income and of interest on debt p leads to a increase in NPV: this means that the effectiveness of an investment project increases with p; (3) in the case of considering the effectiveness of an investment project for owners of equity and debt capital, the increase in the number of payments of tax on income and of interest on debt p leads to the decrease in NPV: this means that the effectiveness of an investment project decreases with p. In the latter case, companies should pay tax on profit and interest on debt once per year, while in the former case, more frequent payments are profitable for the effectiveness of investment.

Thus, this means that method of payments of tax on income and of interest on debt (in advance or in the ends of periods) changes drastically the effect of the number of payments of income tax and interest on debt on the effectiveness of investments. Depending on the relationship between the investor and the lender, the investor can choose (within the framework of tax legislation):

- the frequency of payment of income tax;
- scheme for payment of income tax (in advance or at the end of periods).

The verification of developed by us the innovative investment models with frequent **advance** payments of tax on profit and of interest on debt will lead to the creation of a comprehensive system of adequate and correct assessment of the effectiveness of the company's investment program and its investment strategy for both schemes for payment of income tax (in advance or at the end of periods).

One of the most important elements of calculating the effectiveness of investment projects is the assessment of the discount rate, the calculation methods of which are generalized for the real conditions of the implementation of investment projects. Eight innovative investment models with **advance** payments of tax on profit and of interest on debt created in this paper can assist decision-makers in the optimal design, planning and control of company investments and the development of a company's investment strategy.

Obtained in current chapter and paper (Brusov et al. 2021) results help to tax regulator (Finance Ministry) understand the influence of the number of payments of tax on income and to credit regulator (Central Bank) understand the influence of the number of payments of interest on debt on the effectiveness of investment projects. These allow both regulators modify and improve tax legislation and credit policy respectively.

Comprehensive literature review of investment models has been done in Brusov et al. (2021). Below we shortly summarize it and add review of a few recent papers devoted to investigation of frequent payments of tax on income as well as advance payments of tax on income.

17.1.1 The Literature Review

Lang et al. (1992) have shown that there is a negative correlation between future growth and leverage level at the company level and, for diversified companies, at the level of business segments. This negative correlation between growth and leverage level holds for companies with low Tobin's q ratio, but not for high-q companies or companies in high-q industries (the q ratio, or Tobin's q ratio, equals the market value of a company divided by its assets' replacement cost). Therefore, for companies known to have good investment opportunities, leverage does not reduce growth, but it is negatively correlated to growth for companies whose growth opportunities are either not recognized by the capital markets or are not valuable enough to overcome the effects of their debt load.

Whited (1992) studied the influence of debt financing on companies' investment decisions and showed that there is a significant positive correlation between leverage level and investment for large companies, while for medium companies a negative correlation between leverage level and investment took place.

Kang (1995) studied the connection between leverage level and investment decisions. "Interdependent tax models" were used to try to explain the specifics of company leverage levels by analyzing the interdependency between financing decisions and investment.

Some authors mentioned a positive connection via the fact that the financial risk and hence the cost of bond financing decrease with an increase in investment at a given leverage level. A negative connection has been mentioned by DeAngelo and Masulis (1980) and Dotan and Ravid (1985). The first authors concluded this since the tax benefits of debt compete with those of capital investment. The second authors refer to the fact that financial risk and thus the cost of bond financing will increase with investment increase.

The impact of investment increase on financial risk may depend on company-specific factors, like company-specific technology (Dammon and Senbet 1988). An analysis of the impact of corporate and personal taxes on a firm's optimal investment and financing decisions under uncertainty is provided in (Dammon and Senbet 1988). By endogenizing firms' investment decisions, it extends the DeAngelo and Masulis capital structure model. The authors' results indicate that the existing predictions about the relationship between investment-related and debt-related tax shields must be modified in cases where investment is allowed to adjust optimally. Differences in production technologies across companies may thus explain why the empirical results of recent cross-sectional studies have not conformed to the predictions of DeAngelo and Masulis (1980).

Below we discuss some portfolio investment models as well as behavioral aspects of investors, which play an important role in investments.

Among those portfolio investment models is the well-known Black–Litterman model, which was created by Black and Litterman (1992). They developed the model to address the problems that institutional investors have encountered the during application of modern portfolio theory in practice. Starting with an asset allocation based on the equilibrium assumption, the model then modifies that allocation by accounting the investors' opinions with respect to future asset performance.

Anthony Loviscek (2021) has applied the Black–Litterman model of modern portfolio theory to well-known index mutual funds—one guided by the classic 60%/40% stock/bond allocation and one based on an all-equity allocation. The period under their study is from 2000 to 2020. Although statistical evidence supports that the efficacy of a precious metal allocation is elusive, the results suggest an average allocation of about 2% for "buy-and-hold" investors who seek one. He has shown that, from 2003 to 2010 and from 2016 to 2020, the allocations were in the range of 5–10%. Other periods, however, register only a little more than 0%.

Cakici and Zaremba (2021) reconsidered the performance of the Fama–French factors in global markets. As their results showed, the value, profitability and investment factors are far less reliable than what is commonly thought. Their performance depends strongly on the geographical regions and periods examined. Moreover, most factor returns are driven by the smallest companies. Virtually no value or investment effects are present among the big companies representing most of the total market capitalization worldwide. These results cast doubt on the five-factor model's applicability in international markets, citing that the smallest companies are typically not invested in by major financial institutions.

A growing number of investors want to use firm sustainability information in their investment decision processes to avoid risk, satisfy their own asset preference, or find a new alpha-generating factor. Not too many users of environment, social and governance (ESG) data understand how ESG ratings change over time. Bahar Gidwani (2020) used the CSRHub data set to show that ESG ratings regress strongly toward the mean. The observed regression persists during 9 years within the ratings data, for a sample set of more than 8000 firms. Newly-rated firms show even more reversion than "seasoned" firms. Firms can only rarely maintain an especially high or low ESG rating. Investors and firm managers should understand that ESG ratings are likely to change toward the mean. This however does not mean that a good firm is getting worse or a bad one is getting better.

Brown et al. (2021) have developed statistics (holdings-based) to estimate the volatility with time of investment style characteristics of funds. They found that funds with lower levels of style volatility significantly outperform funds with higher levels of style volatility on a risk-adjusted basis. It was concluded that deciding to maintain a less volatile investment style is an important aspect of the portfolio management process.

Some behavioral aspects of investors have been considered by Escobar-Anel et al. (2020), who introduced a strategy generalizing the CPPI (Constant Proportion Portfolio Insurance) approach. The target of this strategy is to guarantee the investment goal or floor during participation in the performance of the assets and limiting the downside risk of the portfolio at the same time. The authors show that the strategy accounts for the following behavioral aspects of investors: a risk-averse behavior for gains, distorted probabilities recognition and a risk-seeking behavior for losses. The developed strategy turns out to be optimal within the Cumulative Prospect Theory framework by Tversky and Kahneman (1996).

In current paper we study the innovative investment models with advance frequent payments of tax on income. Thus below we add review of a few recent papers devoted to investigation of frequency of payments of tax on income as well as advance payments of tax on income.

Brusov and Filatova (2021a) discuss one of the additional limitation of Modigliani–Miller theory: a method of tax on profit payments. Modigliani–Miller theory accounts these payments as annuity–immediate while in practice these payments are making in advance and thus should be accounted as annuity–due.

Brusov and Filatova (2021a) have generalized the Modigliani–Miller theory for the case of advance payments of tax on profit, which is widely used in practice, and show that this leads to some important consequences, which change seriously all the main statements by Modigliani and Miller. These consequences are as following: WACC starts to depend on debt cost k_d, WACC turns out to be lower than in case of classical Modigliani–Miller theory and thus company capitalization becomes higher than in ordinary Modigliani–Miller theory. We show that dependence of equity cost on leverage level L is still linear, but the tilt angle with respect to L–axis turns out to be smaller: this could lead to modification of the dividend policy of the company.

Correct account of a method of tax on profit payments demonstrates that shortcomings of Modigliani–Miller theory are dipper, than everybody suggested: the underestimation of WACC really turns out to be bigger, as well as overestimation of the capitalization of the company. This means that systematic risks arising from the use of modified Modigliani–Miller theory (MMM theory) (which is more correct than "classical' one) in practice are higher than it was suggested by the "classical" version of this theory.

Brusov et al. (2020b) use the modified Modigliani–Miller theory (MMM theory) and apply it for rating methodologies needs. A serious modification of MMM theory in order to use it in rating procedure has been required. The financial "ratios" were incorporated into MMM theory. The dependence of the weighted average cost of capital (WACC), which plays the role of discount rate, on coverage and leverage ratios is analyzed.

Obtained results make possible to use the power of the MMM theory in the rating and create a new base for rating methodologies.

By Brusov et al. (2021) the Modigliani–Miller theory has been generalized and developed taking into account one of the conditions of the real functioning of companies for the case of paying income tax with an arbitrary frequency (monthly, quarterly, semi-annual or annual payments). While a return is not required more than once a year, businesses may be responsible for filing estimated taxes based on profits earned. This requirement is dependent on showing a profit. For example, sole proprietors must file estimated taxes on profits quarterly, on the 15th day of April, June, September and January. In Russia, tax on profit payments could be made annually, quarterly, or monthly. Authors suppose, that more frequent payment of income tax impacts on all main financial indicators of the company and leads to some important consequences. They used analytical and numerical methods: all main formulas of the modified Modigliani–Miller theory have been derived theoretically and then used to obtain all main financial indicators of company and their dependences on different parameters by MS Excel. Authors show that: (1) all Modigliani–Miller theorems, statements and formulas change; (2) all main financial indicators, such as the weighted average cost of capital (*WACC*), company value, *V*, and equity cost, k_e, depend on the frequency of tax on profit payments; (3) in the case of income tax payments more than once per year (at $p \neq 1$), as takes place in practice, the *WACC*, company value, *V* and equity cost, and k_e start depend on debt cost, k_d, while in ordinary (classical) Modigliani–Miller theory all these values do not depend on k_d; (4) obtained results allow a company to choose the number of payments of tax on profit per year (of course, within actual tax legislation): more frequent payments of income tax are beneficial for both parties, for the company and for the tax regulator.

As we mentioned in Brusov and Filatova (2021a) some of the major problems under the evaluation of the effectiveness of investment projects are suggested as follows:

1. Which financial flows should be taken into account when calculating the parameters of efficiency of a project (NPV, IRR, etc.)?
2. How many discount rates should be used for discounting various cashflows?
3. How can these discount rates be accurately evaluated?

The first problem is still under intensive discussion. Concerning the second issue either two different discount rates could be used (equity cost, k_e and debt cost, k_d) or a general discount rate for operating and financial flows (for which WACC can, obviously, be chosen).

Concerning the third issue, we need to note that, in the last decade, significant progress in the accurate determination of the cost of the equity and company weighted average cost, which just are the discount rates when evaluating the effectiveness of the project, has been achieved. The progress is mainly associated with the studies by

Brusov, Filatova and Orekhova (BFO theory) (Brusov et al. 2015, 2018b; Filatova et al. 2008; Brusov et al. 2021, 2022, 2023, 2024; Brusov and Filatova 2025a,b), in which a general theory of capital cost of the company and its capital structure was established, and the dependence of capital cost on leverage level and on the age of a company was found for the companies of arbitrary age. The main difference between their theory and Modigliani–Miller theory is that the former one removes the assumption of perpetuity for the companies under discussion, which leads to a significantly different new theory from the theory established by the Nobel laureates Modigliani and Miller (1958, 1963, 1966).

In modern conditions, the requirements for improving the quality of assessing the effectiveness of investments have increased. The modern investment models, which have been well-tested in real economic situations, have been developed by Brusov, Filatova and Orekhova (Brusov et al. 2015, 2018b; Filatova et al. 2008). They have created long-term as well as arbitrary duration models and have considered the effectiveness of the investment project from two points of view: from the equity holders and from the owners of equity and debt. NPV in each of these cases could be calculated by two different methods: with the division of credit and investment flows and using two different discounting rates (equity cost, k_e and debt cost, k_d), and without such a division and using a general discounting rate (for which WACC can, obviously, be chosen).

17.1.2 The Discount Rates

As we mentioned above, one of the most important elements of calculating the effectiveness of investment projects is the assessment of the discount rate. In the case of long-term investment models without the division of credit and investment flows, the discount rate WACC has been calculated using the modified for advance payments Modigliani–Miller formula (Modigliani and Miller 1958, 1963, 1966)

$$WACC = k_0 \cdot (1 - w_d t \cdot (1 + k_d)) \tag{17.1}$$

while in the case of arbitrary duration models, the modified for advance payments Brusov–Filatova–Orekhova formula for WACC (Brusov et al. 2015, 2018b; Filatova et al. 2008)

$$\frac{1 - (1 + WACC)^{-n}}{WACC} = \frac{1 - (1 + k_0)^{-n}}{k_0 \cdot \left(1 - w_d t \cdot \left[1 - (1 + k_d)^{-n}\right] \cdot (1 + k_d)\right)} \tag{17.2}$$

has been used.

Note, that both formulas for the weighted average cost of capital, WACC, [Modigliani–Miller (17.1) and Brusov–Filatova–Orekhova (17.2)] in case of advance payments are different from ones in case of payments in the ends of periods

(Modigliani and Miller 1958, 1963, 1966, 2018b; Brusov et al. 2015; Filatova et al. 2008).

Here and below, WACC is the weighted average cost of capital; k_0 is the equity cost at zero leverage ($L = 0$); k_d is the debt cost; w_d is the debt share; t is the tax on profit; n is the project duration; ke is the equity cost; and L is the leverage level.

In the case of long-term investment models with the division of credit and investment flows, the discount rate for discounting the investment flows (equity cost ke) has been calculated using the Modigliani–Miller formula (Modigliani and Miller 1958, 1963, 1966)

$$k_e = k_0 + L \cdot (k_0 - k_d)(1 - t) \tag{17.3}$$

while in the case of arbitrary duration models, equity cost ke has been calculated from the formula

$$WACC = k_e w_e + k_d w_d (1 - t) \tag{17.4}$$

using the Brusov–Filatova–Orekhova value for WACC (17.2) (Brusov et al. 2015, 2018b; Filatova et al. 2008).

The calculation methods of the discount rates (WACC, equity cost k_e) has been generalized for the real conditions of the implementation of investment projects: for arbitrary frequency of payments of tax on profit (Brusov and Filatova 2021b) and for advance payments of tax on profit (Brusov et al. 2020a).

In this paper, new modern investment models, both long-term and arbitrary duration, will be created, as close as possible to real investment conditions. They will account the **advance** payments of interest on debt and of tax on income a few times per year (semi-annually, quarterly, monthly), which are applied in real economic practice. Their verification will lead to the creation of a comprehensive system of adequate and correct assessment of the effectiveness of the company's investment program and its investment strategy.

17.1.3 The Structure of the Chapter

The structure of the paper is as follows:

1. In Sect. 17.1 above, we presented:

    17.1.1. The literature review.
    17.1.2. Discount rates.

2. In Sect. 17.2, we consider the effectiveness of the investment project from the perspective of the equity holders only.

    In Sect. 17.2.1, we consider a case with flow separation.
    In Sect. 17.2.2, we consider a case without flow separation.

3. In Sect. 17.3, we consider the effectiveness of the investment project from the perspective of the owners of equity and debt.

   In Sect. 17.3.1, we consider a case with flow separation.
   In Sect. 17.3.2, we consider a case without flow separation.

4. In Sect. 17.4, the problem of calculation of discount rates is discussed and expressions for their modified values are obtained.
5. In Sect. 17.5, we study numerically with the use of Microsoft Excel the effectiveness of the four models, created by us in this paper. We consider long-term projects as well as projects of arbitrary duration from two perspectives: the owners of equity and debt and the equity holders only without the division of credit and investment flows.
6. In Conclusions, we discuss obtained results and their impact on the correctness of valuation of efficiency of investment projects. As well we compare obtained in current paper results for advance payments of tax on profit with ones, obtained by Brusov et al. (2021) for payments of tax on profit at the end of periods.

17.2 The Effectiveness of the Investment Project from the Perspective of the Equity Holders Only

We will consider the effectiveness of the investment project from two points of view: from the equity holders and from the owners of equity and debt. NPV in each of these cases could be calculated by two different methods: with the division of credit and investment flows and using two different discounting rates, and without such a division and using a general discounting rate (for which WACC can, obviously, be chosen).

The following designations are used below:

The equity value S, the investment value I, the net operating income NOI, the leverage level L, the profitability of investments β, the tax on profit t, the project duration n, the equity cost k_0, the debt cost k_d and the number of payments of interest on debt p_1 and of tax on income p_2; D is the debt value.

In the first case (from the perspective of the equity holders), at the initial moment in time, $T = 0$ investments are equal to $-S$ and the flow of capital, CF, for the period is equal to:

$$\mathrm{CF} = (\mathrm{NOI} - k_\mathrm{d}D)(1 - t). \tag{17.5}$$

In addition to the tax shields, $k_\mathrm{d}Dt$ includes a payment of interest on a loan, $-k_\mathrm{d}D$.

We suppose below that interests on the loan are paid in equal shares of $k_\mathrm{d}D$ during all periods and principal repayment is made at the end of the project.

In the second case (from the perspective of the equity and debt holders), the negative flows (the interest and duty paid by owners of equity) are returned to the project and they are exactly equal to the positive flows obtained by owners of debt capital. Thus, in this case the only effect of debt financing is the effect of the tax shield, generated from the tax relief: interest on the loan is entirely included in the cost and thus reduces the tax base. After-tax flow of capital, CF, for each period is equal to

$$\mathrm{CF} = \mathrm{NOI}(1 - t) + k_{\mathrm{d}} D t \tag{17.6}$$

and the value of investments at the initial moment in time $T = 0$ is equal to $- I = - S - D$.

Below two different ways of discounting will be considered:

(1) If operating and financial flows are not separated, both flows are discounted by the general rate. In this case, the weighted average cost of capital (WACC) can be selected as a discounting rate. For long-term projects, we will use the Modigliani–Miller formula for WACC (Modigliani and Miller 1958, 1963), modified by us for the case of payments of interest on debt and of tax on income a few times per year (semi-annually, quarterly, monthly) and for projects of finite (arbitrary) duration we will use the Brusov–Filatova–Orekhova formula for WACC (Brusov et al. 2018b; Filatova et al. 2008), modified by us for the case of payments of interest on debt and of tax on income a few times per year (semi-annually, quarterly, monthly).

(2) Operating and financial flows are separated and are discounted at different rates: the operating flow at the rate which is equal to the equity cost k_{e}, depending on leverage and on the number of payments of interest on debt and of tax on income, and credit flow at the rate which is equal to the debt cost $k_{\mathrm{d.}}$

Note that loan capital is the least risky because the credit (including the interest on credit) is paid after taxes in the first place. Therefore, the cost of credit will always be less than the equity cost, whether for ordinary or for preference shares $k_{\mathrm{e}} > k_{\mathrm{d}}$; $k_{\mathrm{p}} > k_{\mathrm{d}}$. Here k_{e}; k_{p} is the equity cost of ordinary or of preference shares consequently.

17.2.1 With Flow Separation

In this case, the expression for NPV (net present value) per period has a view

$$NPV = NOI(1 - t) - k_d D(1 - t) = NOI(1 - t) + k_d Dt - k_d D. \tag{17.7}$$

Here, the first term is the value of operating income from the investment project after tax deduction, the second term is the value of the tax shield, the third term is the value of interest on debt for one period.

We will need the following auxiliary formulas for summing the reduced values of financial flows (17.7) when calculating NPV:

For annual advance payments of interest on debt and of tax on income:

$$\sum_{i=0}^{n-1} \frac{1}{(1+k_d)^i} = \frac{1-(1+k_d)^{-n}}{1-\frac{1}{1+k_d}} = \frac{1+k_d}{k_d} \cdot \left(1-(1+k_d)^{-n}\right) \tag{17.8}$$

For more frequent advance payments [p times per period (per year)] of interest on debt and of tax on income (semi-annually, quarterly, monthly):

$$\sum_{i=0}^{np-1} \frac{R}{p(1+k_d)^{i/p}} = \frac{R}{p} \cdot \frac{1-(1+k_d)^{-n}}{1-\frac{1}{(1+k_d)^{1/p}}} = \frac{R}{p} \cdot \frac{\left(1-(1+k_d)^{-n}\right)\cdot(1+k_d)^{1/p}}{(1+k_d)^{1/p}-1} \tag{17.9}$$

Similar formulas are obtained using the cost of equity ke and WACC as the discount rates.

Summing up the given values of financial flows for each period (17.7), we obtain for NPV of n-years project in the case of separated flows:

$$NPV = -S + \sum_{i=1}^{n} \frac{NOI(1-t)}{(1+k_e)^i} + \sum_{i=0}^{n-1} \frac{k_d Dt}{(1+k_d)^i} - \sum_{i=0}^{n-1} \frac{k_d D}{(1+k_d)^i} - \frac{D}{(1+k_d)^n} \tag{17.10}$$

Here, the second term is the reduced value of operating income from the investment project, the third term is the reduced value of the tax shield, the fourth term is the reduced value of interest paid annually (at the beginning of the year), and the fifth term is the reduced value of the debt paid at the end of the project.

After summing, we have the following expression for NPV:

$$\begin{aligned} NPV = -S &+ \frac{NOI(1-t)}{k_e} \cdot \left(1-\left(\frac{1}{1+k_e}\right)^n\right) + Dt\left(1-(1+k_d)^{-n}\right)\cdot(1+k_d) \\ &- D\left(1-(1+k_d)^{-n}\right)\cdot(1+k_d) - \frac{D}{(1+k_d)^n} \end{aligned} \tag{17.11}$$

In the case of more frequent (p-times per year) advance payment of income taxes (p_1) and frequent advance payments of interest on debt (p_2) we have:

$$\begin{aligned} NPV = -S &+ \sum_{i=1}^{n} \frac{NOI(1-t)}{(1+k_e)^i} + \sum_{i=0}^{np-1} \frac{k_d Dt}{p_1(1+k_d)^{i/p_1}} \\ &- \sum_{i=01}^{np-1} \frac{k_d D}{p_2(1+k_d)^{i/p_2}} - \frac{D}{(1+k_d)^n}; \end{aligned} \tag{17.12}$$

After summing, we have the following expression for NPV:

$$NPV = -S + \frac{NOI(1-t)}{k_e} \cdot \left(1 - \left(\frac{1}{1+k_e}\right)^n\right) + \frac{k_d Dt\left(1 - (1+k_d)^{-n}\right) \cdot (1+k_d)^{1/p_1}}{p_1\left((1+k_d)^{1/p_1} - 1\right)} - \frac{k_d D\left(1 - (1+k_d)^{-n}\right) \cdot (1+k_d)^{1/p_2}}{p_2\left((1+k_d)^{1/p_2} - 1\right)} - \frac{D}{(1+k_d)^n} \quad (17.13)$$

Long-term investment projects

To obtain the expression for NPV of long-term investment projects, one should find the limit of (17.13) $n \to \infty$.

$$NPV = -S + \frac{NOI(1-t)}{k_e} + \frac{k_d Dt \cdot (1+k_d)^{1/p_1}}{p_1\left((1+k_d)^{1/p_1} - 1\right)} - \frac{k_d D \cdot (1+k_d)^{1/p_2}}{p_2\left((1+k_d)^{1/p_2} - 1\right)} \quad (17.14)$$

17.2.2 Without Flow Separation

In the case of no separation between operating and financial flows, both flows are discounted by the general rate WACC. The credit reimbursable at the end of the project can be discounted either at the same rate WACC or at the debt cost rate k_d. Below, a uniform rate for WACC has been used.

Summing up the given values of financial flows for each period (17.7), we obtain for NPV of n-years project in the case without separated flows:

$$NPV = -S + \sum_{i=1}^{n} \frac{NOI(1-t)}{(1+WACC)^i} + \sum_{i=0}^{n-1} \frac{k_d Dt}{(1+WACC)^i} - \sum_{i=0}^{n-1} \frac{k_d D}{(1+WACC)^i} - \frac{D}{(1+WACC)^n} \quad (17.15)$$

After summing, we have the following expression for NPV:

$$NPV = -S + \frac{NOI(1-t)}{WACC} \cdot \left(1 - \left(\frac{1}{1+WACC}\right)^n\right) + \frac{k_d Dt\left(1 - (1+WACC)^{-n}\right) \cdot (1+WACC)}{WACC}$$

$$-\frac{k_dD\left(1-(1+WACC)^{-n}\right)\cdot(1+WACC)}{WACC}-\frac{D}{(1+WACC)^n} \tag{17.16}$$

In the case of more frequent (p-times per year) advance payment of income taxes and frequent payments of interest on the debt we have:

$$NPV=-S+\sum_{i=1}^{n}\frac{NOI(1-t)}{(1+WACC)^i}+\sum_{i=0}^{np-1}\frac{k_dDt}{p_1(1+WACC)^{i/p_1}}$$
$$-\sum_{i=0}^{np-1}\frac{k_dD}{p_2(1+WACC)^{i/p_2}}-\frac{D}{(1+WACC)^n} \tag{17.17}$$

After summing, we have the following expression for NPV:

$$NPV=-S+\frac{NOI(1-t)}{WACC}\cdot\left(1-\left(\frac{1}{1+WACC}\right)^n\right)$$
$$+\frac{k_dDt\left(1-(1+WACC)^{-n}\right)\cdot(1+WACC)^{1/p_1}}{p_1\left((1+WACC)^{1/p_1}-1\right)}$$
$$-\frac{k_dD\left(1-(1+WACC)^{-n}\right)\cdot(1+WACC)^{1/p_2}}{p_2\left((1+WACC)^{1/p_2}-1\right)}-\frac{D}{(1+WACC)^n} \tag{17.18}$$

Long-term investment projects

To obtain the expression for NPV of long-term investment projects, one should find the limit of (17.18) $n\to\infty$.

$$NPV=-S+\frac{NOI(1-t)}{WACC}+\frac{k_dDt(1+WACC)^{1/p_1}}{p_1\left((1+WACC)^{1/p_1}-1\right)}-\frac{k_dD(1+WACC)^{1/p_2}}{p_2\left((1+WACC)^{1/p_2}-1\right)} \tag{17.19}$$

17.3 The Effectiveness of the Investment Project from the Perspective of the Owners of Equity and Debt

17.3.1 With Flow Separation

In this case, operating and financial flows are separated and are discounted using different rates: the operating flow at the rate equal to the equity cost k_e, depending on leverage, and credit flow at the rate equal to the debt cost k_d, which remain constant until fairly large values of leverage and start to grow only at high values of leverage L, when there is a danger of bankruptcy.

After-tax flow of capital for each period in this case is equal to (17.6):

$$\mathrm{CF} = NOI(1-t) + k_d Dt \tag{17.20}$$

After summing over n-periods, one gets the following expression for NPV:

$$\begin{aligned} NPV &= -I + \sum_{i=1}^{n} \frac{NOI(1-t)}{(1+k_e)^i} + \sum_{i=0}^{n-1} \frac{k_d Dt}{(1+k_d)^i} = -I \\ &+ \frac{NOI(1-t)}{k_e}\left(1-(1+k_e)^{-n}\right) + Dt\left(1-(1+k_d)^{-n}\right)\cdot(1+k_d) \end{aligned} \tag{17.21}$$

In the case of a few (p) advance payments of tax on profit per period, the expression for NPV will be modified:

$$NPV = -I + \sum_{i=1}^{n} \frac{NOI(1-t)}{(1+k_e)^i} + \sum_{i=0}^{np-1} \frac{k_d Dt}{p(1+k_d)^{i/p}} \tag{17.22}$$

After summing over n-periods, one gets the following modified expression for NPV:

$$NPV = -I + \frac{NOI(1-t)\left[1-(1+k_e)^{-n}\right]}{k_e} + \frac{k_d Dt\left[1-(1+k_d)^{-n}\right](1+k_d)^{1/p}}{p\left[(1+k_d)^{1/p}-1\right]} \tag{17.23}$$

To obtain the expression for NPV of long-term investment projects, one should find the limit of (17.23) $n \to \infty$.

$$NPV = -I + \frac{NOI(1-t)}{k_e} + \frac{k_d Dt(1+k_d)^{1/p}}{p\left[(1+k_d)^{1/p} - 1\right]} \quad (17.24)$$

17.3.2 Without Flow Separation

In the case of no separation between operating and financial flows, both flows are discounted by the general rate WACC.

After summing the expression (17.6) over n-periods, one gets the following expression for NPV:

$$NPV = -I + \sum_{i=1}^{n} \frac{NOI(1-t)}{(1+WACC)^i} + \sum_{i=0}^{n-1} \frac{k_d Dt}{(1+WACC)^i} \quad (17.25)$$

$$\begin{aligned} NPV = -I &+ \frac{NOI(1-t)}{WACC}\left(1-(1+WACC)^{-n}\right) \\ &+ \frac{k_d Dt}{WACC}\left(1-(1+WACC)^{-n}\right)(1+WACC) \end{aligned} \quad (17.26)$$

In the case of a few (p) advance payments of tax on profit per period, the expression for NPV will be modified:

$$NPV = -I + \sum_{i=1}^{n} \frac{NOI(1-t)}{(1+WACC)^i} + \sum_{i=0}^{np-1} \frac{k_d Dt}{p(1+WACC)^{i/p}} \quad (17.27)$$

After summing over n-periods, one gets the following modified expression for NPV:

$$\begin{aligned} NPV = -I &+ \frac{NOI(1-t)}{WACC} \cdot \left(1 - \left(\frac{1}{1+WACC}\right)^n\right) \\ &+ \frac{k_d Dt\left(1-(1+WACC)^{-n}\right)(1+WACC)^{1/p}}{p\left((1+WACC)^{1/p} - 1\right)} \end{aligned} \quad (17.28)$$

To obtain the expression for NPV of long-term investment projects, one should find the limit of (17.28) $n \to \infty$.

$$NPV = -I + \frac{NOI(1-t)}{WACC} \cdot + \frac{k_d Dt(1+WACC)^{1/p}}{p\left((1+WACC)^{1/p}-1\right)} \tag{17.29}$$

17.4 Discount Rates

In the case without the division of credit and investment flows (both flows are discounted using the same rate, for which WACC can obviously be chosen), WACC is calculated by the following formulas:

For arbitrary project duration (Brusov et al. 2018b):

$$\frac{1-(1+WACC)^{-n}}{WACC} = \frac{1-(1+k_0)^{-n}}{k_0 \cdot \left(1 - \frac{k_d w_d t}{p} \frac{\left[1-(1+k_d)^{-n}\right]\cdot(1+k_d)^{1/p}}{(1+k_d)^{1/p}-1}\right)} \tag{17.30}$$

For long-term projects (Modigliani and Miller 1958, 1963):

$$WACC = k_0 \cdot \left(1 - \frac{k_d w_d t}{p} \frac{(1+k_d)^{1/p}}{(1+k_d)^{1/p}-1}\right) \tag{17.31}$$

Note, that both formulas for the weighted average cost of capital, WACC [Modigliani–Miller (17.31, 17.32) and Brusov–Filatova–Orekhova (17.30)] in case of advance payments, obtained by Brusov et al. (2021) are different from ones in case of payments in the ends of periods (classical Modigliani–Miller formulas and Brusov–Filatova–Orekhova formulas).

In the case of the division of credit and investment flows (and thus discounting of the payments using two different rates, equity cost ke and debt cost kd), ke should be found from the equation

$$WACC = k_e w_e + k_d w_d (1-t) \tag{17.32}$$

where we substitute WACC from the formula (17.30) for a project with arbitrary duration and from the formula (17.31, 17.32) for a long-term project.

Note that formulas (17.30) and (17.31, 17.32) are quite different as well from the original formulas by Brusov—Filatova—Orekhova (Brusov et al. 2015, 2018b;

Filatova et al. 2008) and Modigliani–Miller (1958, 1963), where payments of interest on debt and of tax on income are made once per year at the end of the periods. They are turned into advance version of them (not original ones, which suppose the payments at the end of periods), if we put p = 1:

$$\frac{1-(1+WACC)^{-n}}{WACC}=\frac{1-(1+k_0)^{-n}}{k_0\cdot\left(1-w_dt\cdot\left[1-(1+k_d)^{-n}\right]\cdot(1+k_d)\right)} \quad (17.33)$$

$$WACC=k_0\cdot(1-w_dt\cdot(1+k_d)) \quad (17.34)$$

17.5 Results and Discussion

In this section, we study numerically with the use of Microsoft Excel the effectiveness of the four models created above by us. We consider long-term projects as well as projects of arbitrary duration from two perspectives: the owners of equity and debt and the equity holders only. We will study the case without flow separation. In this case, operating and financial flows are not separated and both are discounted, using the general rate, for which we select the weighted average cost of capital, WACC. Let us start from the study numerically on the dependence of the discount rates (weighted average cost of capital, WACC) on leverage level L at different frequencies of payment of tax on profit p.

17.5.1 Numerical Calculation of the Discount Rates

The Long-Term Investment Projects

For long-term investment projects (the Modigliani−Miller limit), the discount rate (WACC) in the case of arbitrary frequency of advance payment of tax on profit p is described by formula (17.31, 17.32) (Brusov and Filatova 2021b):

$$WACC=k_0\cdot\left(1-\frac{k_dw_dt}{p}\frac{(1+k_d)^{1/p}}{(1+k_d)^{1/p}-1}\right)$$

For WACC calculation, we will use the following parameters: $k_0 = 0.22$; $k_d = 0.14$; t = 20%; L = 0; 1; 2…; 10.

Dependence of WACC on leverage level L at k0 = 0.22, kd = 0.14 and different p = 1, 4, 12 is shown in Table 17.1 and Figs. 17.1 and 17.2.

Table 17.1 Dependence of WACC on leverage level L at $k_0 = 0.22$, $k_d = 0.14$ and different p = 1, 4, 12

L	WACC		
	p = 1	p = 4	p = 12
0	0.2200	0.2200	0.2200
1	0.1949	0.1961	0.1964
2	0.1866	0.1881	0.1885
3	0.1824	0.1842	0.1845
4	0.1799	0.1818	0.1822
5	0.1782	0.1802	0.1806
6	0.1770	0.1790	0.1795
7	0.1761	0.1782	0.1786
8	0.1754	0.1775	0.1780
9	0.1749	0.1770	0.1775
10	0.1744	0.1766	0.1770

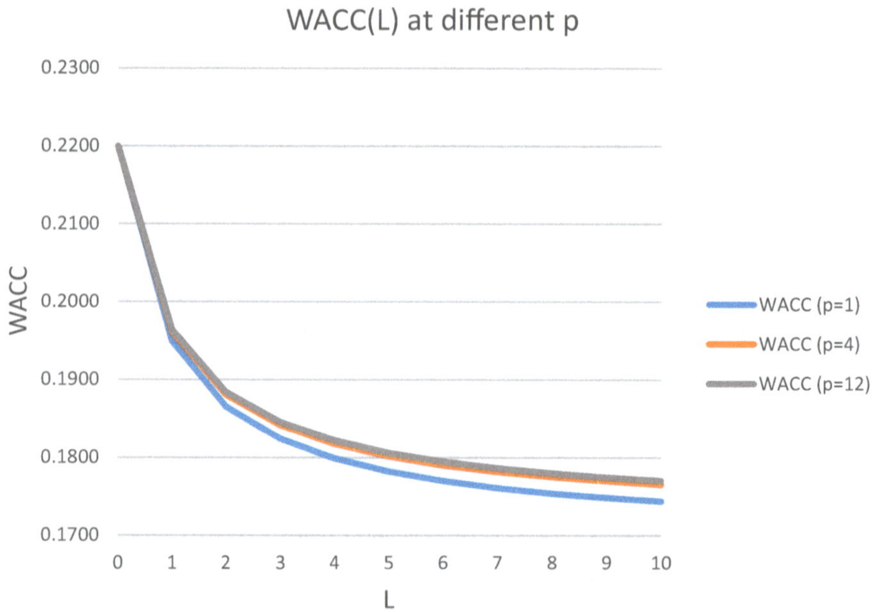

Fig. 17.1 Dependence of the weighted average cost of capital, WACC, on leverage level L at different frequencies of payments of tax on profit, p = 1; 4; 12

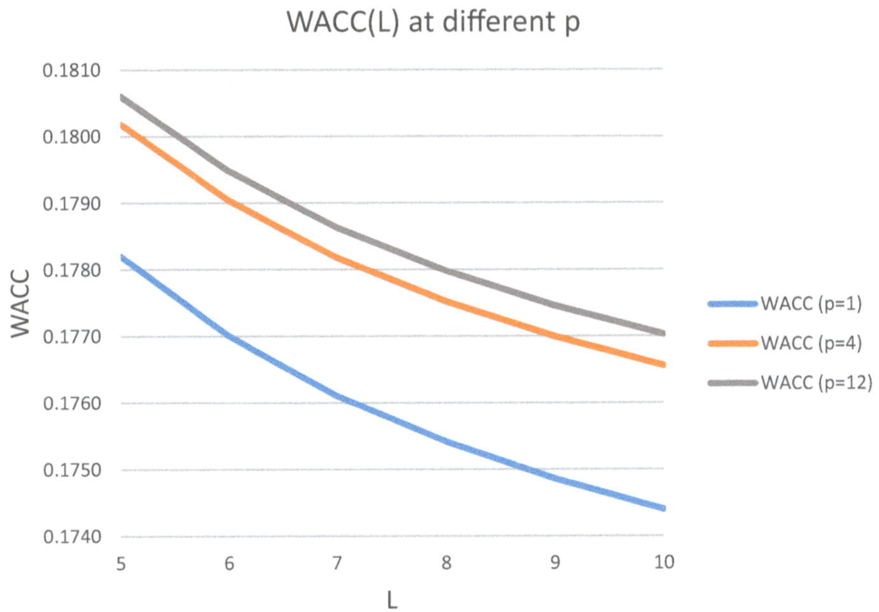

Fig. 17.2 Dependence of the weighted average cost of capital, WACC, on leverage level L at different frequencies of payments of tax on profit, p = 1; 4; 12 (larger scale)

The Arbitrary Duration Investment Projects

For arbitrary duration investment projects, the discount rate (WACC) in the case of arbitrary frequency of payment of tax on profit p is described by formula (17.30) [modified BFO formula (17.22)].

For WACC calculation, we will use the following parameters: $k_0 = 0.22$; $k_d = 0.14$; $t = 20\%$; $L = 0; 1; 2\ldots; 10$; $p = 1; 4; 12$; $n = 3$

$$\frac{1-(1+WACC)^{-n}}{WACC} = \frac{1-(1+k_0)^{-n}}{k_0 \cdot \left(1 - \frac{k_d w_d t}{p} \frac{\left[1-(1+k_d)^{-n}\right]\cdot(1+k_d)^{1/p}}{(1+k_d)^{1/p}-1}\right)}$$

Dependence of WACC on leverage level L at k0 = 0.22, kd = 0.14 and different p = 1, 6, 12 for a 3-year company is shown in Table 17.2 and Figures 17.2 and 17.3.

Note that the dependences of WACC on leverage level L obtained above will be used below under a study of the effectiveness of long-term as well arbitrary duration investment projects, from the perspective of the owners of equity capital and of the owners of equity and debt.

Table 17.2 Dependence of WACC on leverage level L at $k_0 = 0.22$, $k_d = 0.14$ and different p = 1, 4, 12 for a 3-year company

L	WACC		
	p = 1	p = 4	p = 12
0	0.2199	0.2199	0.2199
1	0.1957	0.1969	0.1971
2	0.1876	0.1892	0.1895
3	0.1836	0.1853	0.1857
4	0.1812	0.1830	0.1834
5	0.1796	0.1815	0.1819
6	0.1784	0.1804	0.1808
7	0.1775	0.1795	0.1800
8	0.1768	0.1789	0.1793
9	0.1763	0.1784	0.1788
10	0.1758	0.1780	0.1784

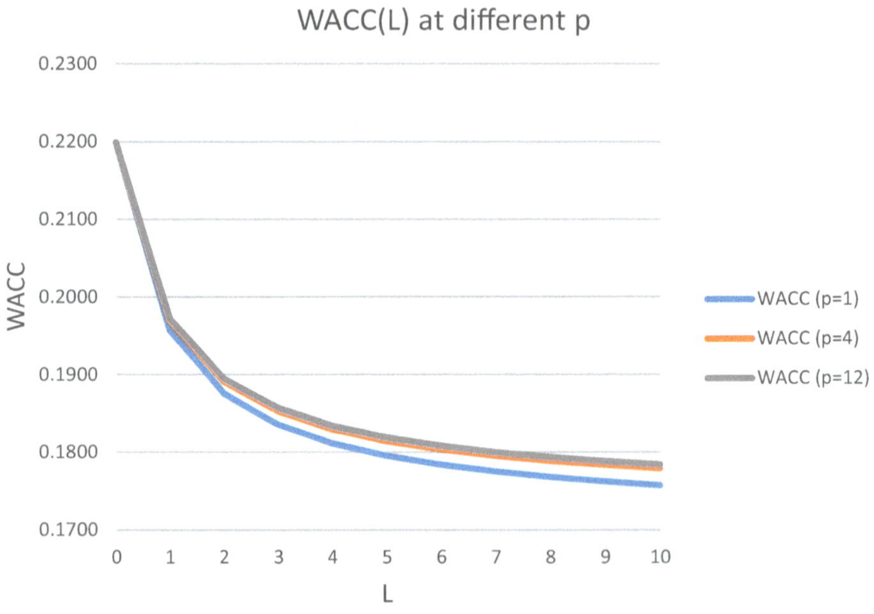

Fig. 17.3 Dependence of WACC on leverage level L at $k_0 = 0.22$, $k_d = 0.14$ and different p = 1, 4, 12 for a 3-year project

17.5.2 The Effectiveness of the Long-Term Investment Project from the Perspective of the Owners of Equity Capital

For long-term investment projects, the discount rate (WACC) in the case of arbitrary frequency of advance payment of tax on profit p is described by formula (17.19) and for NPV one has:

$$NPV = -S + \frac{NOI(1-t)}{WACC} + \frac{k_d Dt(1+WACC)^{1/p_1}}{p_1\left((1+WACC)^{1/p_1}-1\right)} - \frac{k_d D(1+WACC)^{1/p_2}}{p_2\left((1+WACC)^{1/p_2}-1\right)}$$

For NPV calculation, we will use the following parameters: $k_0 = 0.22$; $k_d = 0.14$; $t = 20\%$; L = 0; 1; 2…; 10; $p_1 = p_2 = p = 1; 4; 12$; $S = 1000$; $D = LS$; $NOI = 800$.

It is seen from Figs. 17.5 and 17.6 that in the case of considering the effectiveness of long-term investment projects for owners of equity capital, NPV will vary with the change of p, but with not much variation (it is seen from Table 17.3 and from Fig. 17.6, but not from Fig. 17.5).

Table 17.3 Dependence of WACC and NPV on leverage level L at $k_0 = 0.22$, $k_d = 0.14$ and different p = 1, 4, 12

L	NPV		
	p = 1	p = 4	p = 12
0	1909	1909	1909
1	4880	4888	4889
2	7867	7877	7880
3	10,858	10,871	10,874
4	13,852	13,866	13,869
5	16,846	16,862	16,865
6	19,841	19,858	19,862
7	22,837	22,854	22,858
8	25,833	25,851	25,855
9	28,829	28,848	28,852
10	31,825	31,844	31,850

Table 17.4 Dependence of NPV on leverage level L at $k_0 = 0.22$, $k_d = 0.14$ and different p = 1, 4, 12

L	NPV		
	p = 1	p = 4	p = 12
0	1909	1909	1909
1	4738	4687	4676
2	7648	7537	7513
3	10,581	10,408	10,371
4	13,525	13,289	13,239
5	16,474	16,175	16,111
6	19,427	19,064	18,985
7	22,382	21,954	21,862
8	25,338	24,846	24,740
9	28,295	27,738	27,618
10	31,252	30,631	30,497

17.5.3 The Effectiveness of the Long-Term Investment Project from the Perspective of the Owners of Equity and Debt

For long-term investment projects, NPV in the case of arbitrary frequency of payment of tax on profit p is described by formula (17.29):

$$NPV = -I + \frac{NOI(1-t)}{WACC} + \frac{k_d Dt(1+WACC)^{1/p}}{p\left((1+WACC)^{1/p} - 1\right)}$$

For NPV calculation, we will use the following parameters: $k_0 = 0.22$; $k_d = 0.14$; t = 20%; L = 0; 1; 2…; 10; $p_1 = p_2 = p = 1; 6; 12$; $S = 1000$; $D = LS$; $NOI = 800$.

Dependence of NPV on leverage level L at k0 = 0.22, kd = 0.14 and different p = 1, 4, 12 for a long-term project is shown in Table 17.4 and Figs. 17.7 and 17.8.

17.5.4 The Effectiveness of the Arbitrary Duration Investment Projects from the Perspective of the Owners of Equity Capital

For the arbitrary duration investment projects, NPV in the case of arbitrary frequency of payment of tax on profit p is described by formula (17.18):

Table 17.5 Dependence of NPV on leverage level L at $k_0 = 0.22$, $k_d = 0.14$ and different p = 1, 4, 12 for a 3-year project

L	NPV		
	p = 1	p = 4	p = 12
0	307	307	307
1	845	861	864
2	1359	1389	1396
3	1865	1911	1921
4	2369	2430	2444
5	2871	2948	2965
6	3373	3465	3485
7	3874	3982	4005
8	4375	4498	4525
9	4876	5014	5044
10	5376	5530	5563

$$NPV = -S + \frac{NOI(1-t)}{WACC} \cdot \left(1 - \left(\frac{1}{1+WACC}\right)^n\right) + \frac{k_d Dt\left(1-(1+WACC)^{-n}\right) \cdot (1+WACC)^{1/p_1}}{p_1\left((1+WACC)^{1/p_1} - 1\right)} - \frac{k_d D\left(1-(1+WACC)^{-n}\right) \cdot (1+WACC)^{1/p_2}}{p_2\left((1+WACC)^{1/p_2} - 1\right)} - \frac{D}{(1+WACC)^n}$$

For NPV calculation, we will use the following parameters: $k_0 = 0.22$; $k_d = 0.14$; t = 20%; L = 0; 1; 2…; 10; $p_1 = p_2 = p = 1; 6; 12$; $S = 1000$; $D = LS$; $NOI = 800$; n = 3.

Dependence of NPV on leverage level L at k0 = 0.22, kd = 0.14 and different p = 1, 4, 12 for a 3-year project is shown in Table 17.5 and Figs. 17.8 and 17.9.

17.5.5 The Effectiveness of the Arbitrary Duration Investment Project from the Perspective of the Owners of Equity and Debt

For the arbitrary duration investment projects, NPV in the case of arbitrary frequency of payment of tax on profit p is described by formula (17.28):

Table 17.6 Dependence of NPV on leverage level L at $k_0 = 0.22$, $k_d = 0.14$ and different p = 1, 4, 12 for a 3-year project

L	NPV		
	p = 1	p = 4	p = 12
0	307	307	307
1	785	776	774
2	1267	1248	1244
3	1749	1721	1714
4	2232	2194	2185
5	2714	2667	2657
6	3197	3140	3128
7	3680	3614	3599
8	4164	4087	4071
9	4648	4561	4542
10	5132	5034	5013

$$NPV = -I + \frac{NOI(1-t)}{WACC} \cdot \left(1 - \left(\frac{1}{1+WACC}\right)^n\right) + \frac{k_d Dt\left(1 - (1+WACC)^{-n}\right) \cdot (1+WACC)^{1/p}}{p\left((1+WACC)^{1/p} - 1\right)}$$

For NPV calculation, we will use the following parameters: $k_0 = 0.22$; $k_d = 0.14$; t = 20%; L = 0; 1; 2…; 10; $p_1 = p_2 = p = 1; 6; 12$; $S = 1000$; $D = LS$; $NOI = 800$; n = 3.

Dependence of NPV on leverage level L at k0 = 0.22, kd = 0.14 and different p = 1, 4, 12 for a 3-year project is shown in Table 17.6 and Figs. 17.10 and 17.11.

17.5.6 Discussion

The analysis of results from Tables 17.1, 17.2, 17.3, 17.4, 17.5 and 17.6 and Figs. 17.1 and 17.12 shows that:

(1) The weighted average cost of capital, WACC, decreases with leverage level L at all values of frequency of payments of tax on profit p (see Tables 17.1 and 17.2 and Figs. 17.1, 17.2, 17.3 and 17.4);
(2) With an increase in p, WACC increases: WACC(L) curves lie higher with increase of p;
(3) The difference between curves corresponding to p = 1 and p = 4 is much more than the difference between the curves corresponding to p = 4 and p = 12. This difference decreases with p. It turns out that an increase in the

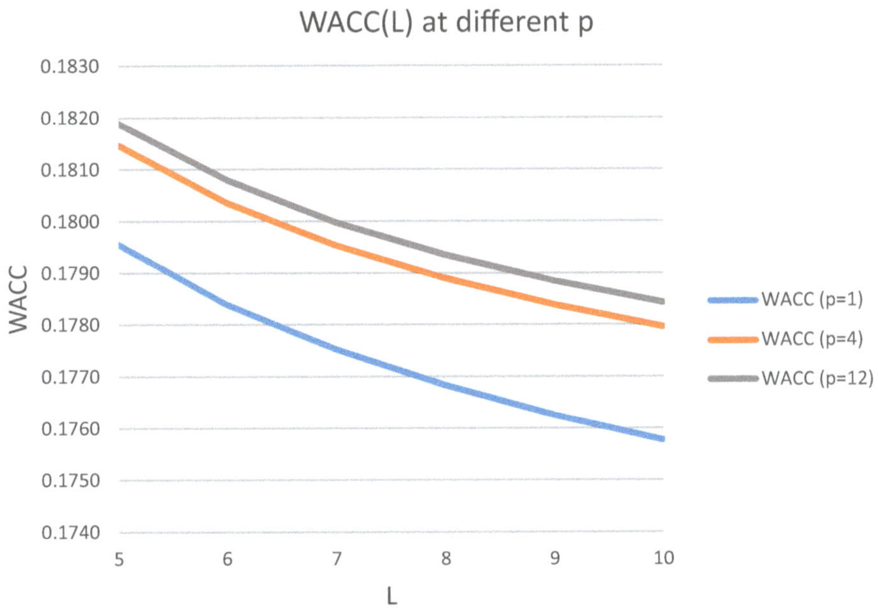

Fig. 17.4 Dependence of WACC on leverage level L at $k_0 = 0.22$, $k_d = 0.14$ and different p = 1, 4, 12 for a 3-year project (larger scale)

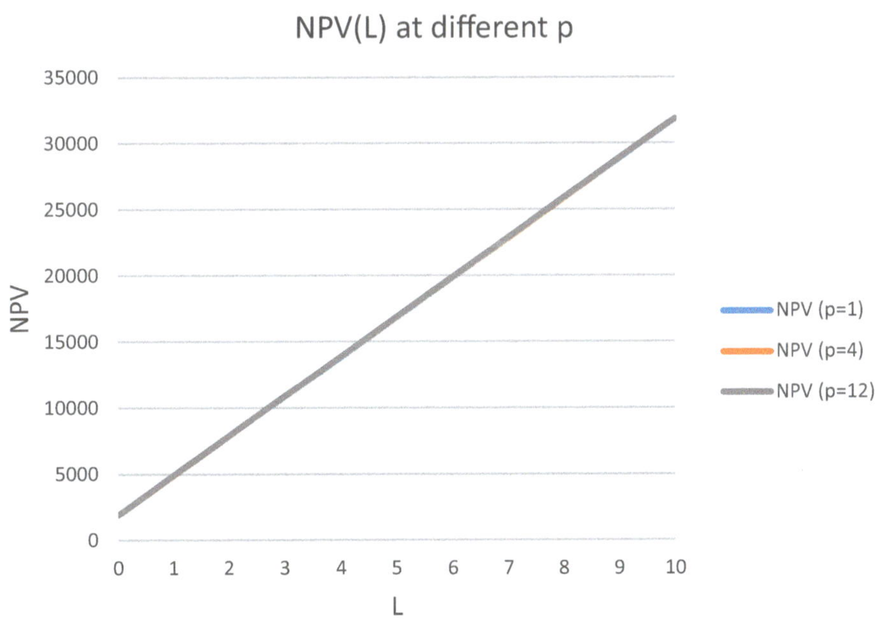

Fig. 17.5 Dependence of NPV on leverage level L at $k_0 = 0.22$, $k_d = 0.14$ and different p = 1, 4, 12 for a long-term project

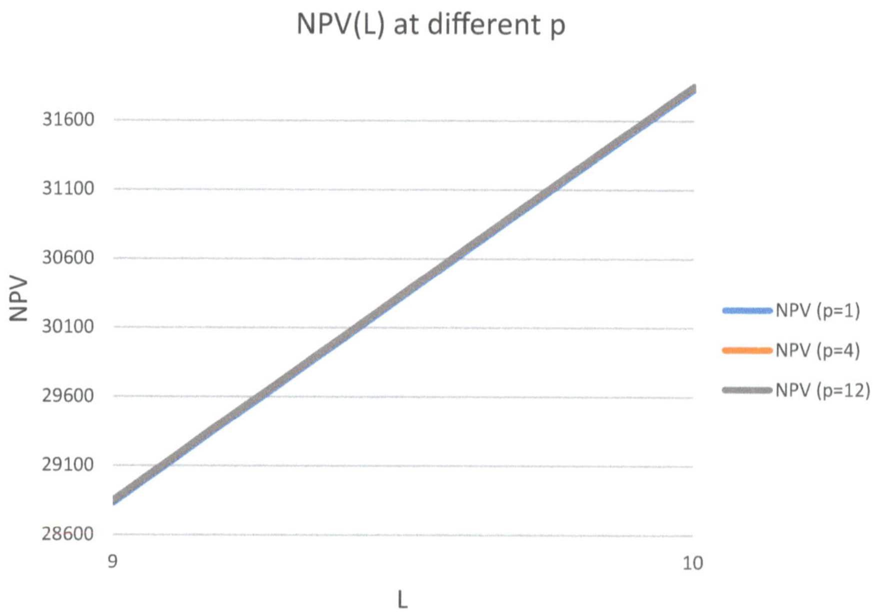

Fig. 17.6 Dependence of NPV on leverage level L at $k_0 = 0.22$, $k_d = 0.14$ and different p = 1, 4, 12 for a long-term project (larger scale)

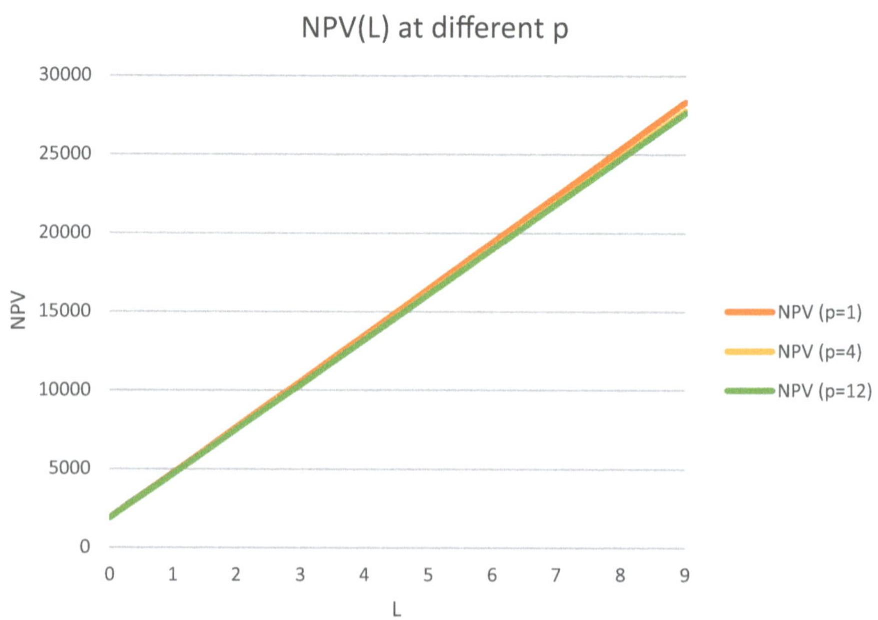

Fig. 17.7 Dependence of NPV on leverage level L at $k_0 = 0.22$, $k_d = 0.14$ and different p = 1, 4, 12 for a long-term project

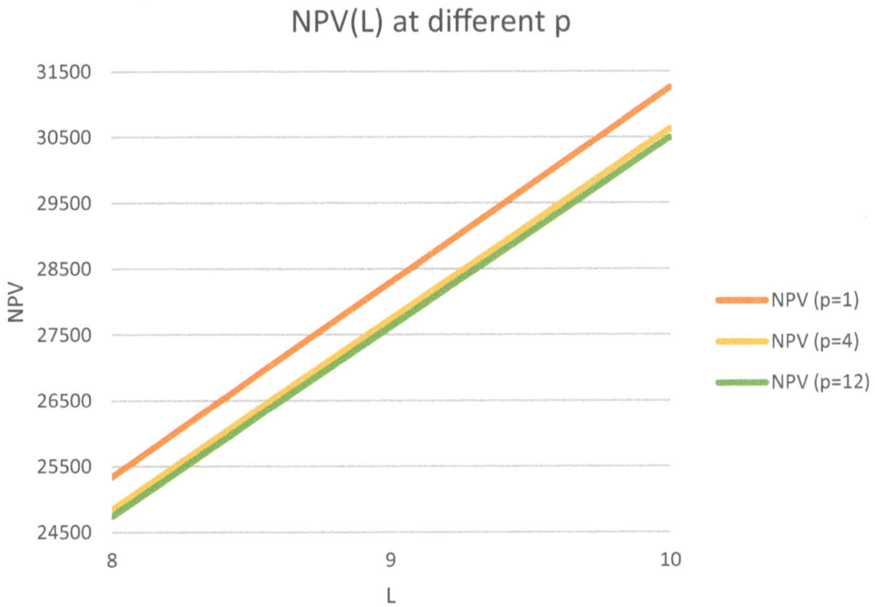

Fig. 17.8 Dependence of NPV on leverage level L at $k_0 = 0.22$, $k_d = 0.14$ and different p = 1, 4, 12 for a long-term project (larger scale)

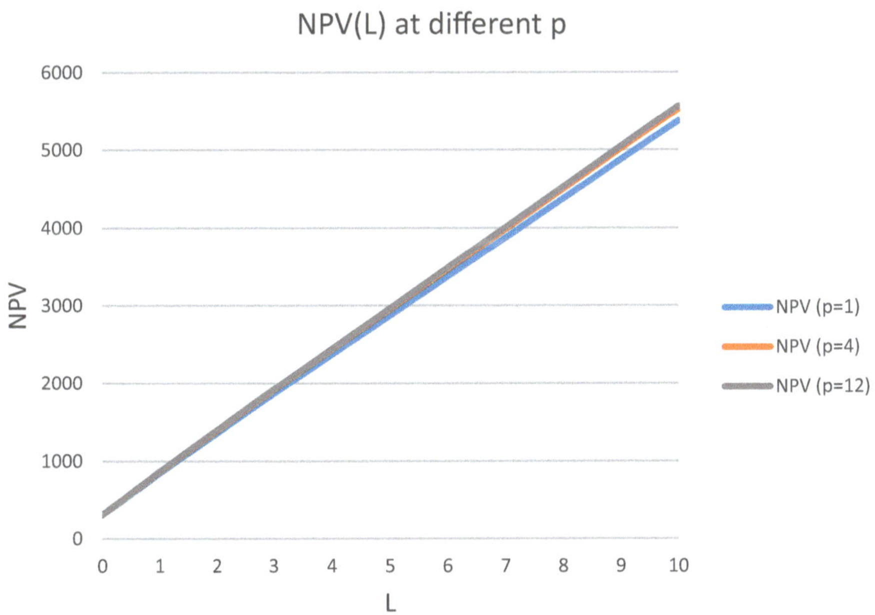

Fig. 17.9 Dependence of NPV on leverage level L at $k_0 = 0.22$, $k_d = 0.14$ and different p = 1, 6, 12 for a 3-year project

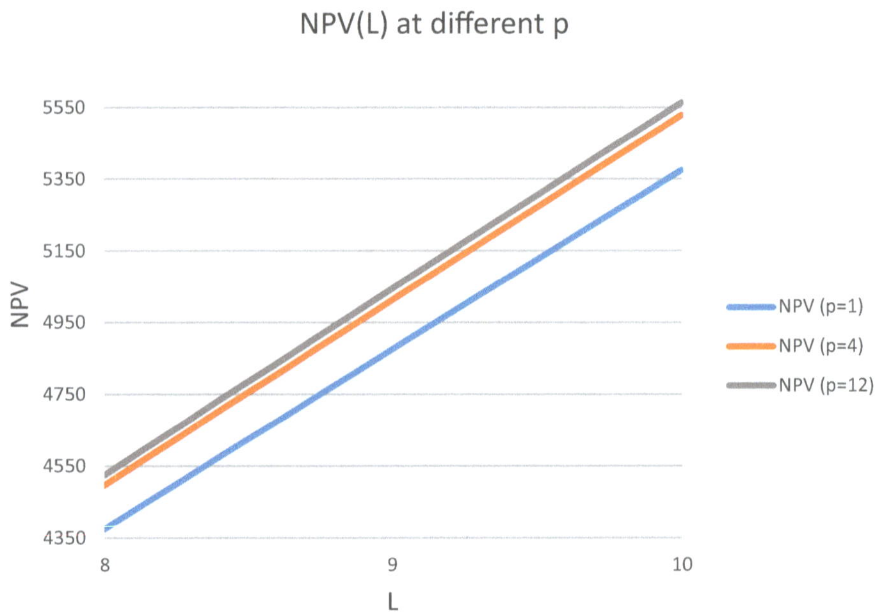

Fig. 17.10 Dependence of NPV on leverage level L at $k_0 = 0.22$, $k_d = 0.14$ and different p = 1, 4, 12 for a 3-year project (larger scale)

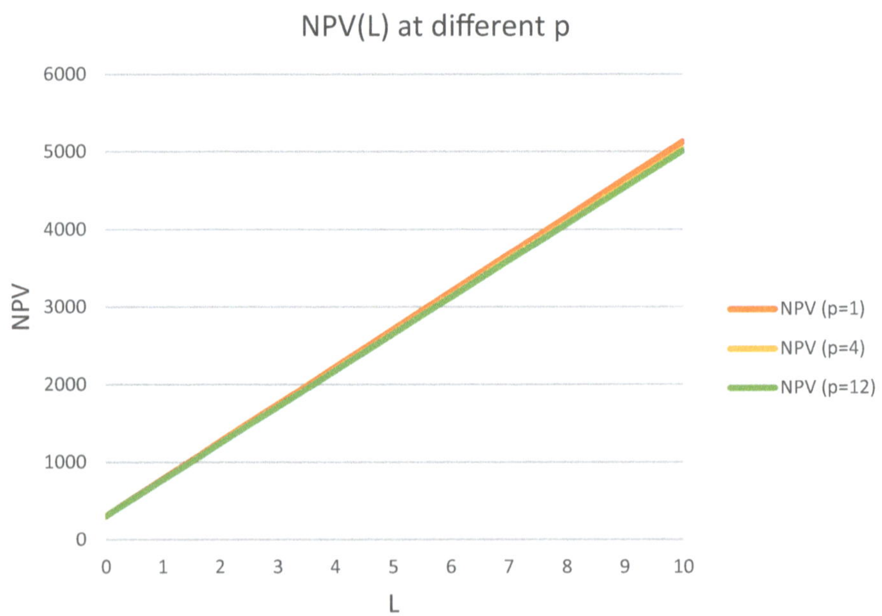

Fig. 17.11 Dependence of NPV on leverage level L at $k_0 = 0.22$, $k_d = 0.14$ and different p = 1, 4, 12 for a 3-year project

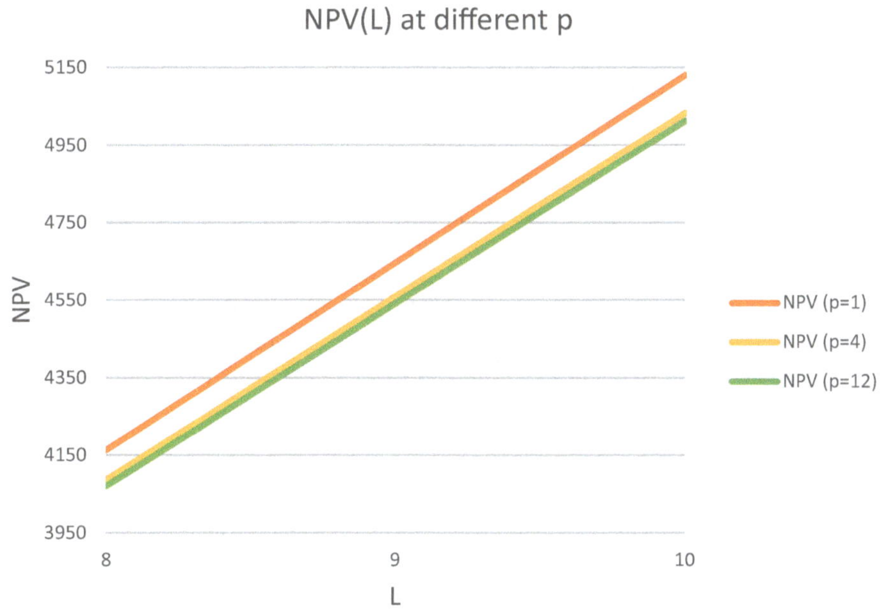

Fig. 17.12 Dependence of NPV on leverage level L at $k_0 = 0.22$, $k_d = 0.14$ and different $p = 1, 6, 12$ for a 3-year project (larger scale)

number of payments of tax on profit per year p leads to an increase in the cost of attracting capital (WACC). Will this increase in the discount rate decrease the effectiveness of investment projects? As we see from the Tables 17.3, 17.4, 17.5 and 17.6 and Figs. 17.5, 17.6, 17.7, 17.8, 17.9, 17.10, 17.11 and 17.12, the situation is different for owners of equity capital and for owners of equity and debt capital.

(4) NPV practically linearly increases with leverage level at all values of frequency of payments of tax on profit p and all frequency of payments of interest on debt;
(5) In the case of considering the effectiveness of long-term investment projects for owners of equity capital, NPV is changed with a change of p (both p_1 and p_2 are equal everywhere below) but by a very small value (it is seen in the tables, but not in the figures); NPV is growing with p.
(6) In the case of considering the effectiveness of long-term investment projects for owners of equity and debt, NPV is changed with a change of p more significantly (it is seen in the tables and in the figures); NPV decreases with p.
(7) For arbitrary duration projects, this difference in NPV with a change of p is more significant and should be accounted under valuation of the effectiveness of an investment project;
(8) In the case of considering the effectiveness of an investment project for owners of equity capital, we need to note that an increase in p leads to an increase in

NPV: this means that the effectiveness of an investment project increases with p;

(9) In the case of considering the effectiveness of an investment project for owners of equity and debt capital, we need to note that the situation is opposite and an increase in p leads to decrease in NPV: this means that the effectiveness of an investment project decreases with p;

(10) The above results show that in the latter case, companies should pay tax on profit and interest on debt once per year, while in the former case, more frequent payments are profitable for the effectiveness of an investment;

(11) Thus, while for long-term projects' NPV, the impact of more frequent payments of both values p_1 and p_2 is insignificant, for arbitrary duration projects the account of the frequency of both types of payments could be important and could lead to more significant influence on the effectiveness of an investment project, increasing it (in the former case), or decreasing it (in the latter case). Note that the specific value of the effect depends on the values of the parameters in the project (k_0, k_d, n, t, S etc.).

17.6 Conclusions

There are too few investment models which can numerically valuate the effectiveness of investment projects, among them the investment models developed by the authors of this paper. Moreover, investment models are practically absent which account for the conditions of the real functioning of investment projects. This paper covers this gap in the literature and science in the field of investments and develops innovative investment models which are much closer to economic practice.

We developed here for the first time eight innovative investment models: long-term [described by Eqs. (17.14), (17.19), (17.24) and (17.29)] as well arbitrary duration [described by Eqs. (17.13), (17.18), (17.23) and (17.28)], which account two effects: (1) payments of interest on debt and of tax on income a few times per year (semi-annually, quarterly, monthly); (2) advance payments of taxes and of debt interest, as it happened in practice. Note that no one before had investigated the impact of the frequency of payments of taxes and of debt interest and payments of taxes and of debt interest on the effectiveness of investment projects. These investment models allow for investigation of the impact of all main parameters of investment projects (equity value S, investment value I, net operating income NOI, leverage level L, profitability of investments β, tax on profit t, project duration n, equity cost k_0, debt cost k_d and number of payments of interest on debt p_1 and of tax on income p_2) on the main indicator of effectiveness of investment projects NPV (net present value). They could be used for investigation of different problems of investments, such as the influence of debt financing, leverage level, taxing, project duration, method of financing, number of payments of interest on debt and of tax on income and some other parameters on efficiency of investments and other problems. In particular, they will improve the issue of project ratings (Brusov et al. 2018a). These new models allow for making more correct evaluations of effectiveness of investment projects long-term as well as of arbitrary duration.

Numerical calculations, conducted for four investment models (without flow separation) show that:

- In the case of considering the effectiveness of an investment project for owners of equity capital, the increase in the number of payments of tax on income and of interest on debt p leads to an increase in NPV: this means that the effectiveness of an investment project increases with p;
- In the case of considering the effectiveness of an investment project for owners of equity and debt capital, the increase in the number of payments of tax on income and of interest on debt p leads to decrease in NPV: this means that the effectiveness of an investment project decreases with p.

In the latter case, companies should pay tax on profit and interest on debt once per year, while in the former case, more frequent payments are profitable for the effectiveness of an investment.

Thus, while for long-term projects' NPV, the impact of more frequent payments of both values p_1 and p_2 is insignificant, for arbitrary duration projects the account of the frequency of both types of payments could be important and could lead to more significant influence on the effectiveness of an investment project, decreasing it (in the latter case), or increasing it (in the former case). Note that the specific value of the effect depends on the values of the parameters in the project (k_0, k_d, n, t, S, etc.).

There are some limitations of the applicability of the proposed models:

(1) For long-term projects, they are connected with the limitations of the Modigliani–Miller theory;
(2) For consideration of without flow separation, they are connected with the well-known limitations of the WACC approach;
(3) For arbitrary duration projects (using BFO theory), they are connected with the fact that not all the conditions of real investments are accounted yet.

We could compare obtained by us results with ones of our paper [1], where we have frequent payments of tax on income and of interest on debt p at the end of periods. The results turn out to be opposite. In [1] we have:

(1) WACC decreases with p; (2) in the case of considering the effectiveness of an investment project for owners of equity capital, the increase in the number of payments of tax on income and of interest on debt p leads to a decrease in NPV: this means that the effectiveness of an investment project decreases with p; (3) in the case of considering the effectiveness of an investment project for owners of equity and debt capital, the increase in the number of payments of tax on income and of interest on debt p leads to an increase in NPV: this means that the effectiveness of an investment project increases with p. In the former case, companies should pay tax on profit and interest on debt once per year, while in the latter case, more frequent payments are profitable for the effectiveness of investment.

In current Chapter, where payments of income tax and interest on debt are made in advance, we have:

(1) WACC increases with p;
(2) in the case of considering the effectiveness of an investment project for owners of equity capital, the increase in the number of payments of tax on income and of interest on debt p leads to a increase in NPV: this means that the effectiveness of an investment project increases with p;
(3) in the case of considering the effectiveness of an investment project for owners of equity and debt capital, the increase in the number of payments of tax on income and of interest on debt p leads to the decrease in NPV: this means that the effectiveness of an investment project decreases with p. In the latter case, companies should pay tax on profit and interest on debt once per year, while in the former case, more frequent payments are profitable for the effectiveness of investment.

So, we have created and fully investigated eight innovative investment models with frequent payments of income tax and interest on debt in advance (current paper) and at the end of periods (Brusov et al. 2021). We have shown, that method of payments of tax on income and of interest on debt (in advance or in the ends of periods) changes drastically the effect of the number of payments of income tax and interest on debt on the effectiveness of investments. Depending on the relationship between the investor and the lender, the investor can choose (within the framework of tax legislation):

- the frequency of payment of income tax;
- scheme for payment of income tax (in advance or at the end of periods).

Obtained results help to tax regulator (Finance Ministry) understand the influence of the number of payments of tax on income and to credit regulator (Central Bank) the influence of the number of payments of interest on debt on the effectiveness of investment projects. This allow them modify and improve tax legislation and credit policy respectively.

The contribution of this study to finance and economics is mainly related to the goal that new modern investment models have been created to be as close as possible to real investment conditions. Our models, namely, models with advance payments of interest on debt and of tax on income which occur a few times per year (semi-annually, quarterly or monthly), could be more successfully applied in real economic practice.

References

Black F, Litterman R (1992) Global portfolio optimization. Financ Anal J 48:28–43

Bond S, Meghir C (1994) Dynamic investment models and the firm's financial policy. Rev Econ Study 67:197–222

Brown K, Harlow W, Zhang H (2021) Investment style volatility and mutual fund performance. J Invest Manag 19:78

Brusov P, Filatova T (2021a) The Modigliani–Miller theory with arbitrary frequency of payment of tax on profit. Mathematics 9(11):1198. https://doi.org/10.3390/math9111198

Brusov P, Filatova T (2021b) The Modigliani–Miller theory with arbitrary frequency of payment of tax on profit. Mathematics 9:1198. https://doi.org/10.3390/math9111198

Brusov PN, Filatova TV Kulik VL (2024) Capital asset pricing model (CAPM) 2.0: Account of business and financial risk. Finance: Theory and practice. 28(2):128–142. https://doi.org/10.26794/2587-5671-2024-28-2-128-142

Brusov P, Filatova T, Orehova N, Eskindarov M (2015) Modern corporate finance, investments and taxation. Springer, Cham, pp 1–373. https://www.springer.com/gp/book/9783319147314

Brusov P, Filatova T, Orehova N (2018a) Ratings: critical analysis and new approaches of quantitative and qualitative methodology. Springer, Cham, pp 1–379. Available online: https://www.springer.com/de/book/9783030562427

Brusov P, Filatova T, Orehova N, Eskindarov M (2018b) Modern corporate finance, investments, taxation and ratings, 2nd edn. Springer, Cham, pp 1–571

Brusov PN, Filatova TV, Orekhova NP, Kulik VL, Chang S-I, Lin YCG (2020a) Modification of the Modigliani–Miller theory for the case of advance payments of tax on profit. J Rev Glob Econ 9:257–267

Brusov PN, Filatova TV, Orekhova NP, Kulik VL, Chang S-I, Lin YCG (2020b) Application of the Modigliani–Miller theory, modified for the case of advance payments of tax on profit, in rating methodologies. J Rev Glob Econ 9:282–292

Brusov PN, Filatova TV, Chang S-I, Lin YCG (2021) Innovative investment models with frequent payments of tax on income and of interest on debt. Mathematics 9(13):1491. https://doi.org/10.3390/math9131491

Brusov PN, Filatova TV, Orekhova NP (2021) Ratings: Critical analysis and new approaches of quantitative and qualitative methodology. Springer Nature Publishing, pp.1–369

Brusov PN, Filatova TV, Orekhova NP (2022) Generalized Modigliani–Miller theory: Applications in corporate finance, investments, taxation and ratings. Springer Nature Publishing, pp.1–362

Brusov PN, Filatova TV, Orekhova NP (2023) The Brusov–Filatova–Orekhova theory of capital structure: Applications in corporate finance, investments, taxation and ratings. Springer Nature Publishing, pp.1–769

Brusov PN, Filatova TV (2025a) Business valuation and company value: New qualitative approaches considering business and financial risks. Springer Nature Publishing, pp.1–654

Brusov PN, Filatova TV (2025b) Efficiency of investment projects: Modern investment models and their applications. Springer Nature Publishing, pp.1–843

Business and Financial Risk. Finance: Theory and Practice. (2024) 28(2):128–142. https://doi.org/10.26794/2587-5671-2024-28-2-128-142

Cakici N, Zaremba A (2021) Size, value, profitability, and investment effects in international stock returns: Are they really there? J Invest 30:65–86. https://doi.org/10.3905/joi.2021.1.176

Dammon R, Senbet L (1988) The effect of taxes and depreciation on corporate investment and financial leverage. J Financ 43:357–373. https://doi.org/10.1111/j.1540-6261.1988.tb03944.x

DeAngelo H, Masulis R (1980) Optimal capital structure under corporate and personal taxation. J Financ Econ 8:3–29

Dotan A, Ravid S (1985) On the interaction of real and financial decisions of the firm under uncertainty. J Financ 40:501–517

Escobar-Anel M, Lichtenstern A, Zagst R (2020) Behavioral portfolio insurance strategies. Financ Mark Portf Manag 34:353–399

Filatova TV, Orekhova NP, Brusova AP (2008) Weighted average cost of capital in the theory of Modigliani–Miller, modified for a finite life-time company. Bull FU 48:68–77

Gidwani B (2020) Some issues with using ESG ratings in an investment process. J Invest 29:76–84. https://doi.org/10.3905/joi.2020.1.147

Kahneman D, Tversky A (1996) On the reality of cognitive illusions. Psychol Rev 103:582–591. https://doi.org/10.1037/0033-295X.103.3.582

Kang J (1995) The conditional relationship between financial leverage and corporate investment: further clarification. J Bus Financ Account 22:1211–1219. https://doi.org/10.1111/j.1468-5957.1995.tb00902.x

Lang LE, Ofek E, Stulz R (1992) Leverage, investment, and firm growth. J Financ Econ 40:3–29
Loviscek A (2021) How much to invest, if any, in precious metals? A 21st-century perspective. J Invest 30:95–111. https://doi.org/10.3905/joi.2021.1.179
Modigliani F, Miller M (1958) The cost of capital, corporate finance, and the theory of investment. Am Econ Rev 48:261–297
Modigliani F, Miller M (1963) Corporate income taxes and the cost of capital: a correction. Am Econ Rev 53:147–175
Modigliani F, Miller M (1966) Some estimates of the cost of capital to the electric utility industry 1954–1957. Am Econ Rev 56:333–391
Rosenbaum J, Pearl J (2013) Investment banking valuation models. Wiley, New York, pp 1–342
Whited T (1992) Debt, liquidity constraints and corporate investment: evidence from panel data. J Financ 47:1425–1461

Part V
Qualitatively New Effects in the Influence of Taxes on Investments

Chapter 18
Whether It is Possible to Increase Taxing and Conserve a Good Investment Climate in the Country?

Within investment models, developed by Brusov, Filatova, Orekhova earlier (Brusov et al. 2011a, b, c, d, 2012a, b, 2013a, b, 2014a, b; Filatova et al. 2008; Brusov and Filatova (2011); Brusova (2011); Brusov et al. 2021, 2022, 2023, 2024; Brusov and Filatova 2025a,b) the influence of tax on profit rate on effectiveness of long-term investment projects at different debt levels is investigated. It is shown, that increase of tax on profit rate from one side leads to decrease of project NPV, but from other side it leads to decrease of sensitivity of NPV with respect to leverage level. At high leverage level L the influence of tax on profit rate increase on effectiveness of investment projects becomes significantly less. We come to conclusion, that taxing could be differentiated depending on debt level of investment projects of the company: for projects with high debt level L it is possible to apply a higher tax on profit rate.

18.1 Influence of Tax on Profit Rates on the Efficiency of the Investment Projects

Basis of the modern tax systems are the following taxes: tax on profit of organizations, income tax (tax on the income of individuals), social tax (contributions into state extra budgetary funds), the sales tax (the value-added tax), tax on property of the organization. In this Chapter we investigate the influence of tax on profit rates on the efficiency of the investment projects.

The problems that we are currently investigating now, those questions which we can analyze now in all of their complexity and diversity and to which we give answers, not be tractable by analysis and assessment previously, for them one was not able to give an answer, they even not been raised in such a setting. What should be the taxes scale: flat, progressive or otherwise, differentiated, as well as tax rate has an impact on the cost of attract of company capital, its capitalization. What is cumulative effect of increase of taxes: whether the system "state-employer" will win, or will lose

P. Brusov and T. Filatova, *Taxes and Taxation*, Contributions to Finance and Accounting, https://doi.org/10.1007/978-3-032-11077-0_18

as a whole from the tax growth, and if it will lose, then how much. Whether the redistribution of income in favor of the state does not destroy the spirit of enterprise, its driving force. If tax on profit rate will increase by 1%, for how much does the cost of attractive capital of company will increase, for how much its capitalization will decrease. If by 3–6%, it should be serious reasons for such increase, but if by 0.5–1.5%, it is possible to discuss such increase.

How taxation affects the efficiency of investment? How much does the NPV of investment project will decrease, if tax on profit rate will increase by 1%? If on 5–10%, it has a strong negative impact on investment, if on the 1%, or 0.5%, or 0.25%, Regulator can accept this: this will help to the state and do not exert much to investment programs of companies.

One of the main reasons for which it has become possible to carry out such studies, has been a progress in corporate finance, has been made in recent years. It relates primarily to the establishment of a modern theory of capital cost and capital structure by Brusov, Filatova, Orekhova (BFO theory) (Brusov et al. 2011a, b, c, d, 2012a, b, 2013a, b, 2014a, b; Filatova et al. 2008) and to the creation by them in the framework of this theory of modern investment models. The BFO theory allows to make correct assessment of the financial performance of companies with arbitrary life time and of efficiency of investment projects of arbitrary duration. This distinguishes BFO theory from Modigliani–Miller theory (Modigliani et al. 1958, 1963, 1966), which is a perpetuity limit of BFO theory. Archived after the appearance of BFO theory the Modigliani–Miller theory, still heavily used in the West, despite of its obvious limitations, may, mutatis mutandis, be applied to long living stable companies and long-term investment projects. In its framework in this Chapter effects of taxation on the effectiveness of long-term investment will be investigated.

So, at present, there are two main theories, that allow to explore the effects of taxation on the efficiency of investments: perpetuity Modigliani–Miller theory (Modigliani et al. 1958, 1963, 1966) and the modern theory of capital cost and capital structure developed by Brusov, Filatova, Orekhova (Brusov et al. 2011a, b, c, d, 2012a, b, 2013a, b, 2014a, b; Filatova et al. 2008). In this Chapter we describe the first real results obtained by us within created by us investment projects in perpetuity limit, which can be applied to long-term projects.

The effectiveness of the investment project is considered from the perspectives of the equity holders. For this case, NPV is calculated in two ways: with the division of credit and investment flows (and thus discounting the payments at two different rates) and without such a division (in this case, both flows are discounted at the same rate as which, obviously, can be chosen WACC). For each of the four situations two cases are considered: 1) a constant value of equity S; 2) a constant value of the total invested capital I = S + D (D is value of debt funds).

We start first from the case with the division of credit and investment flows and then consider the case without the division of flows.

18.2 Investment Models

Let us remind shortly the main points of the investment models with debt repayment at the end of the project, well-proven in the analysis of real investment projects.

Investments at the initial time moment $T = 0$, are equal to $-S$, and the flow of capital for the period (in addition to the tax shields $k_d Dt$ it includes a payment of interest on a loan $-k_d D$)

$$(NOI - k_d D)(1 - t). \tag{18.1}$$

Here, for simplicity, we suppose that interest on the loan will be paid in equal shares $k_d D$ during all periods. Note, that principal repayment is made at the end of last period.

Here NOI—Net Operating Income (before taxes), k_d—debt cost, t—tax on profit rate.

Let us first consider the case with the division of credit and investment flows. In this case in perpetuity limit (Modigliani–Miller approximation) expression for NPV takes a following form (Brusov et al. 2011a, b, c, d, 2012a, b, 2013a, b, 2014a, b; Filatova et al. 2008)

$$NPV = -S + \frac{NOI(1 - t)}{k_e} - D(1 - t). \tag{18.2}$$

We will consider two cases: (1) a constant value of the total invested capital I = S + D (D is value of debt funds); (2) a constant value of equity S.

At a constant value of the total invested capital (I = const), accounting $D = IL/(1 + L)$, $S = I/(1 + L)$, one gets

$$NPV = -\frac{I}{1 + L}(1 + L(1 - t)) + \frac{NOI(1 - t)}{k_e}. \tag{18.3}$$

$$NPV = -\frac{I}{1 + L}(1 + L(1 - t)) + \frac{NOI(1 - t)}{k_0 + (k_0 - k_d)L(1 - t)}, \tag{18.4}$$

where $L = D/S$—leverage level; k_e—equity cost of leverage company (which uses the debt financing); k_0—equity cost of non-leverage company (which does not use the debt financing).

Under the transition from the equation (Eqs. 18.3)–(18.4) we have used the dependence of equity capital on leverage, received by Modigliani and Miller (Modigliani et al. 1958, 1963, 1966):

$$k_e = k_0 + (k_0 - k_d)L(1 - t). \tag{18.5}$$

So, we explore the equation (Eq. 18.4). A number of conclusions can be drawn from the study of dependence of NPV of the project on leverage level at different

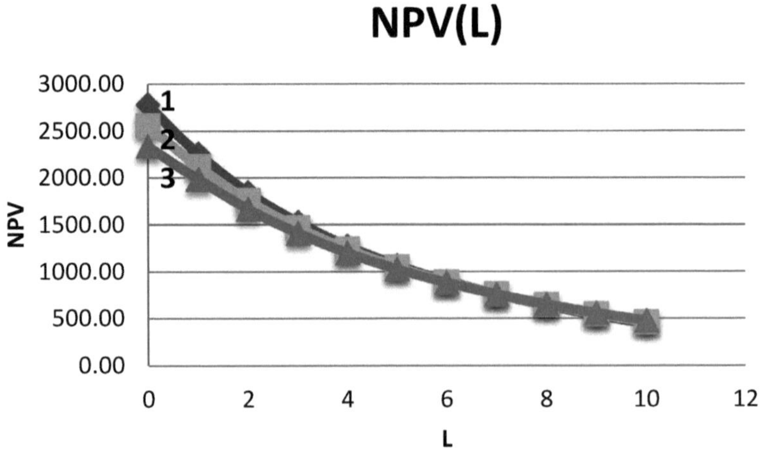

Fig. 18.1 Dependence of NPV on leverage level L at three values of tax on profit rate (1—t = 0.15; 2—t = 0.20; 3—t = 0.25), NOI = 800

values of tax on profit rates t (Fig. 18.1). It is clear that the increase of tax on profit rates leads not only to reduce of NPV of the project, but as well to decrease of the sensitivity of effectiveness of investment projects NPV to the leverage level L. At high leverage levels the influence of growth of tax on profit rates on the effectiveness of investment projects is significantly reduced.

Hence, in particular, it should be noted, that taxation can be differentiated depending on the debt financing level in the company investment projects: for projects with a high leverage level L the higher tax on profit rates t can be used. The foregoing is illustrated also at Fig. 18.2, where it is clear that the change of NPV (ΔNPV) with leverage level decreases when the tax on profit rate t grows, and as well when leverage level increases.

Let us increase our return on investment in 1.5 times (NOI = 1200 instead of 800) (Fig. 18.3). Still, the impact of the tax on profit rate on the NPV value significantly depends on the level of debt financing. So the increase in tax on profit rate by 1% from the existing (in Russia) (20%) leads to a reduction in the NPV by 44.5 units at L = 0, by 18.7 units at L = 1, by 12.2 units at L = 3, by 5 units at L = 5.

I.e. for companies with a high level of the debt financing (for example, companies in the telecommunication sector and other) an increase in tax on profit rate will have less impact on the effectiveness of their investment projects and will be less painful, than for companies with low leverage level in investment. It should be noted that the increase of NOI in 1.5 times increases NPV in 1.7 times (from 2555 up to 4333), and increases ΔNPV(L) in 1.62 at L = 0, and in 1.5 times when L = 9 (Fig. 18.4).

It is clear also that, with the increase of the leverage level L curves, describing the dependence ΔNPV(L), virtually converge, which demonstrates once again the reduction of impact of the change of the tax on profit rate t on the efficiency of investment projects with the increase of the leverage level L.

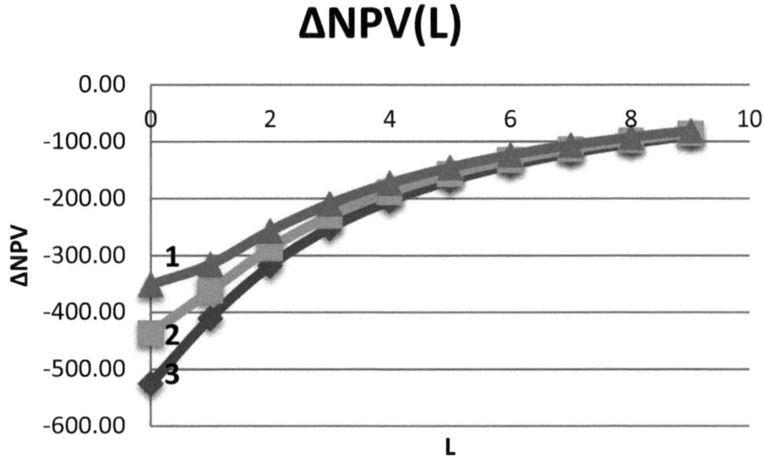

Fig. 18.2 Dependence of ΔNPV on leverage level L at three values of tax on profit rate (1—t = 0.25; 2—t = 0.20; 3—t = 0.15). NOI = 800, I = 1000

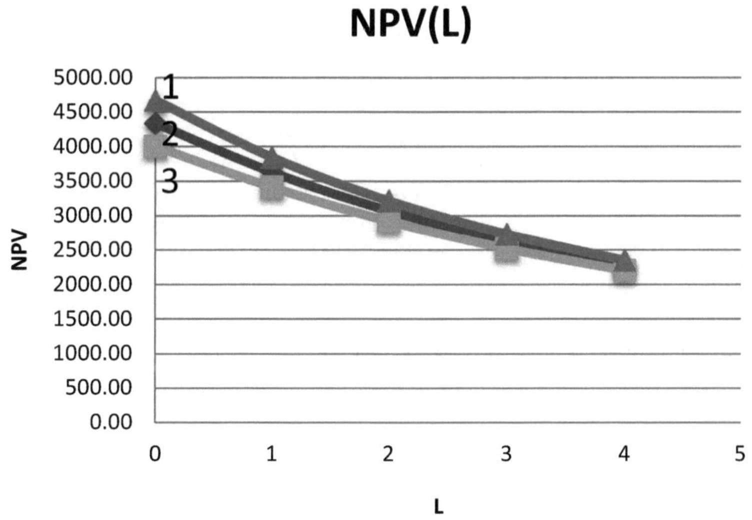

Fig. 18.3 Dependence of NPV on leverage level L at three values of tax on profit rate (1—t = 0.15; 2—t = 0.20; 3—t = 0.25), NOI = 1200, I = 1000

18.3 Borrowings Abroad

Until recently, Russian companies have preferred to borrow abroad, because overseas credits are much cheaper than domestic ones. Although relevance of studies using such loans now is not so high in connection with the West sanctions, all same,

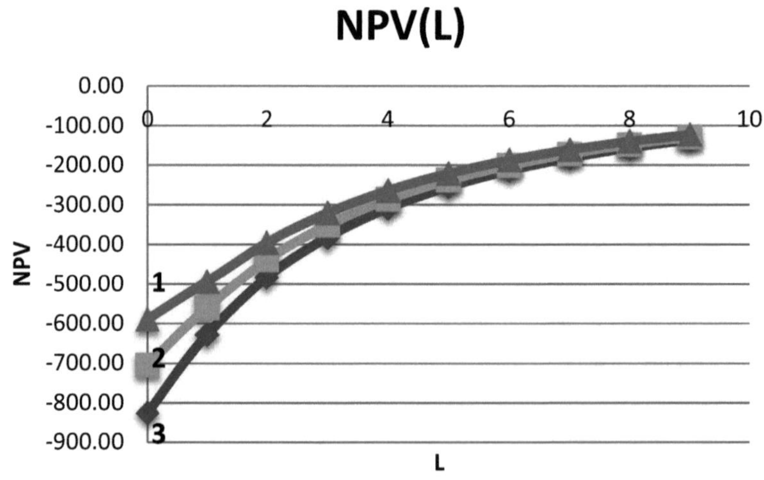

Fig. 18.4 Dependence of ΔNPV on leverage level L at three values of tax on profit rate (1—t = 0.25; 2—t = 0.20; 3—t = 0.15), NOI = 1200, I = 1000

realizing that, in the not-too-distant future, all will return to the its circles, here's a comparison of NPV dependencies on leverage at typical values of rates on credit, with borrowings abroad (k_0 = 0.1; k_d = 0.07) and with borrowings at domestic (Russian) credit market (k_0 = 0.18; k_d = 0.14). (Here k_0—equity cost of financially independent company (Fig. 18.5). ***The growing of effectiveness of investment when using cheaper foreign credit is obvious.*** The stabilization of the situation on the external credit market a detailed analysis of this case, as well as of the case of use of domestic and overseas credits can be done.

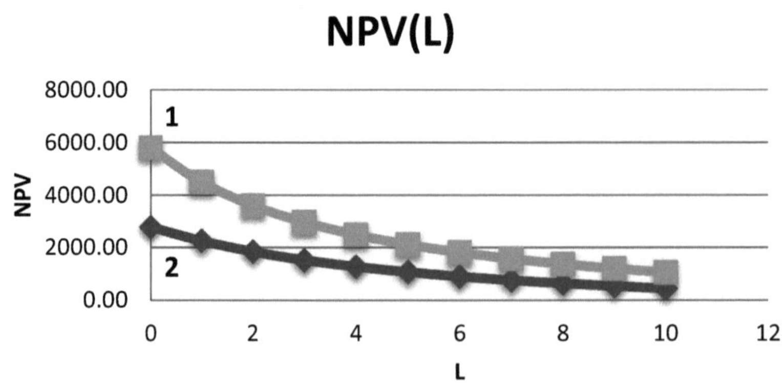

Fig. 18.5 Comparison of dependences of NPV on leverage level L at typical values of credit rates with borrowings abroad (1—k_0 = 0.1; k_d = 0.07) and with borrowings at domestic (Russian) credit market (2—k_0 = 0.18; k_d = 0.14), NOI = 800, I = 1000, t = 15%

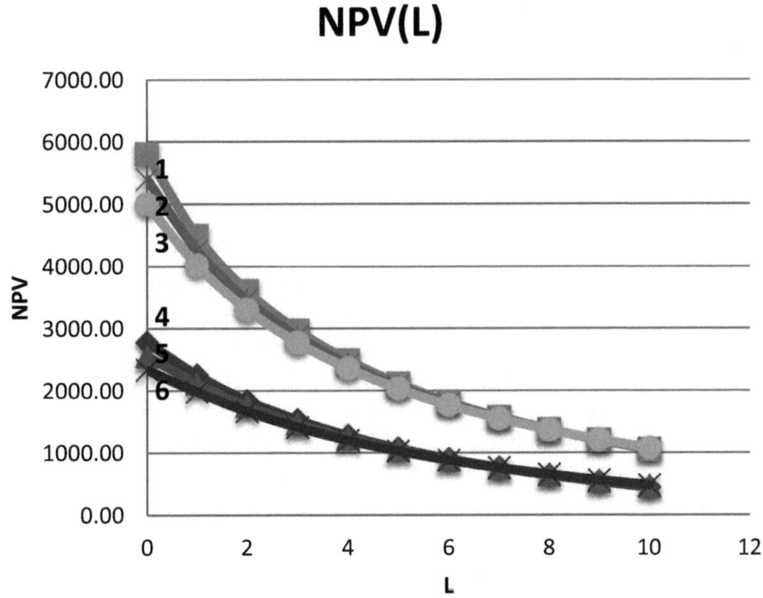

Fig. 18.6 Influence of tax on profit rates on dependence of NPV on leverage level at typical values of credit rates with borrowings abroad (lines 1–2–3) and with borrowings at domestic (Russian) credit market (lines 4–5–6)

We analyze now the impact of the tax on profit rates on dependence of NPV on leverage level at typical values of credit rates with borrowings abroad and with borrowings at domestic (Russian) credit market (Fig. 18.6).

1. $k_0 = 0.1$; $k_d = 0.07$; $T = 0.15$
2. $k_0 = 0.1$; $k_d = 0.07$; $T = 0.2$
3. $k_0 = 0.1$; $k_d = 0.07$; $T = 0.25$
4. $k_0 = 0.18$; $k_d = 0.14$; $T = 0.15$
5. $k_0 = 0.18$; $k_d = 0.14$; $T = 0.2$
6. $k_0 = 0.18$; $k_d = 0.14$; $T = 0.25$

It is clear that, at low leverage levels influence of tax on profit rates is very significant: at zero leverage the NPV drops by 80 units at increase of tax on profit rates on 1% when one borrows abroad and on 44 units when one borrows at domestic (Russian) credit market. It would seem that this could be one of the signals for borrowing within the country, however, taking into account the different values of NPV at two considering cases (ratio is 2.1), we come to the conclusion that the impact of tax on profit rates is in close proportions (ratio is 80/44 = 1.8). So it seems that after the West sanctions will be over, to borrow at the West will be more advantageous for a long time.

18.4 Dependence of NPV on Tax on Profit Rates at Different Leverage Levels

From Fig. 18.7 it is seen that dependence of NPV on tax on profit rates significantly depends on the leverage level L.

When there is no borrowing NPV linearly decreases with t with a factor—43.44 units at 1%. When L = 1 this factor (at t = 20%) is equal to—18.7 units at 1%, when L = 3 this factor (when t = 20%) is equal to—12.3 units at 1%, and when L = 5 this factor (at t = 20%) is equal to—5.8 units. at 1%. It can be seen that the influence of tax on profit rate on efficiency of investment projects drops significantly with increase of the leverage level L used in investments.

This is particularly seen at Fig. 18.8 in the dependence of ΔNPV on tax on profit rate at different leverage levels L (here ΔNPV—increment of NPV under change of t for 10%). When there is no borrowing ΔNPV = −450 and does not depend on tax on profit rate. At t = 20%: at L = 1 ΔNPV = −276.6; at L = 3 ΔNPV = −122.6; at L = 5 ΔNPV = −49. It is clear that the change of tax on profit rate affect mostly the effectiveness of the projects, funded by equity capital only, and if you use debt financing to finance the projects impact of the change of tax on profit rate drops very substantially (up to ten times).

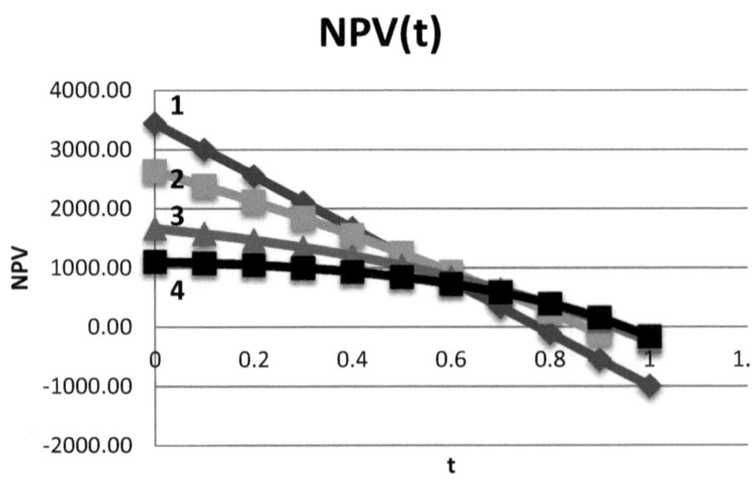

Fig. 18.7 Dependence of NPV on tax on profit rate at different leverage levels L (1—L = 0; 2—L = 1; 3—L = 3; 4—L = 5), NOI = 800, I = 1000

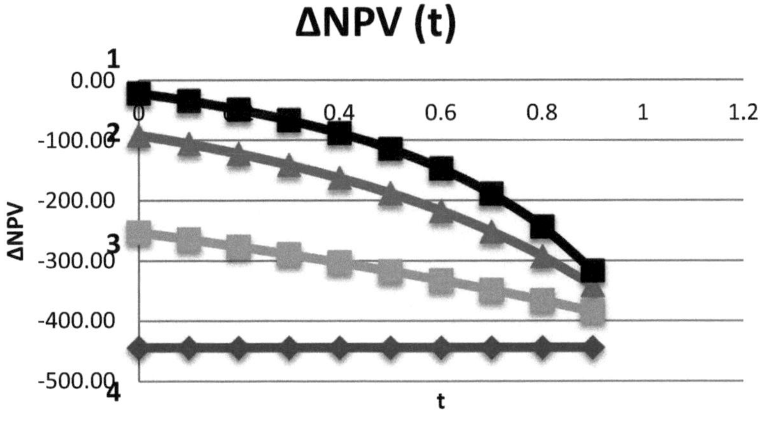

Fig. 18.8 Dependence of ΔNPV on tax on profit rate at different leverage levels L (1—L = 5; 2—L = 3; 3—L = 1; 4—L = 0), NOI = 800, I = 1000

18.5 At a Constant Value of Equity Capital (S = const)

At a constant value of equity capital (S = const), when investment growth is associated with the increased borrowing only, the dependence of NPV on leverage level is qualitatively different in nature, rather than in the case of a constant value of invested capital. Now, depending on the values of the coefficient $\beta = NOI/I$ NPV can grow with leverage level. It should be noted that, in this case (at large values of the coefficient β) the optimal structure of invested capital, in which NPV is maximized could take place. NPV in this case is described by the following expression

$$NPV = -S(1 + L(1 - t)) + \frac{\beta S(1 + L)(1 - t)}{k_0 + (k_0 - k_d)L(t - 1)}. \tag{18.6}$$

It is seen from the Fig. 18.9 that with the increase of the coefficients β value NPV and its optimal (maximum) values grow.

It follows from Fig. 18.10, that with the increase of the leverage level ΔNPV drops and either goes to the saturation (ΔNPV = 0), or becomes negative (ΔNPV < 0), and that means that there is an optimum (after ΔNPV > 0 at small leverage level L).

Below at Figs. 18.11 and 18.12 the dependencies of ΔNPV and NPV on tax on profit rate at different leverage levels and at S = 500, β = 0.8 are shown.

From Fig. 18.11 as well as from Fig. 18.9, it is seen, that at fixed tax on profit rate NPV grows with leverage level. With the increasing of tax on profit rate NPV drops, and curves, corresponding to the different leverage level converge in one point at t = 100% and NPV = −S in accordance to equation (Eq. 18.6). Change of ΔNPV with increasing of t also depends on the leverage level: with the growth of the leverage level it changes from constant (at L = 0) up to the increasingly growing at t > 30–40% at L = 1;3;5.

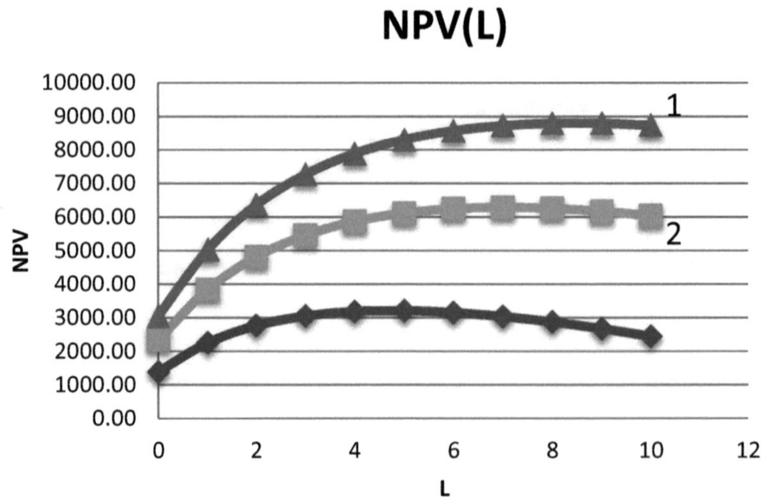

Fig. 18.9 Dependence of NPV on leverage level L at three values of β-coefficient (1—β = 1.5; 2—β = 1.2; 3—β = 0.8), S = 500

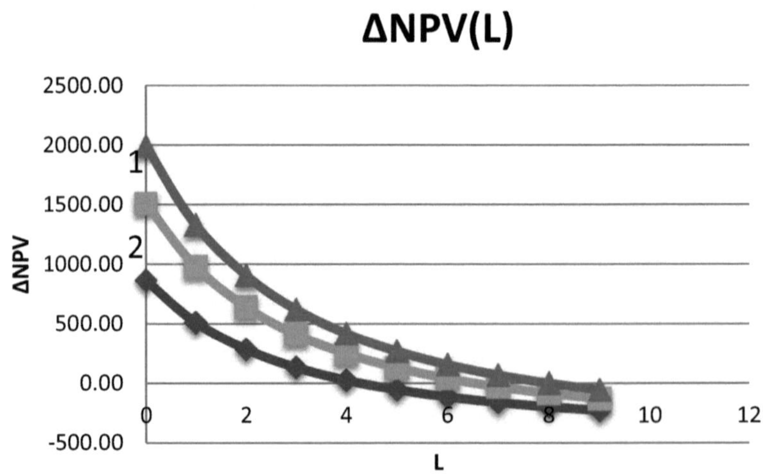

Fig. 18.10 Dependence of ΔNPV on leverage level L at three values of β—coefficient (1—β = 1.5; 2—β = 1.2; 3—β = 0.8), S = 500

18.6 Without Flows Separation

Let us consider the case without the division of credit and investment flows. In this case, both flows are discounted at the same rate as which, obviously, can be chosen WACC). In perpetuity limit ($n \to \infty$) one has

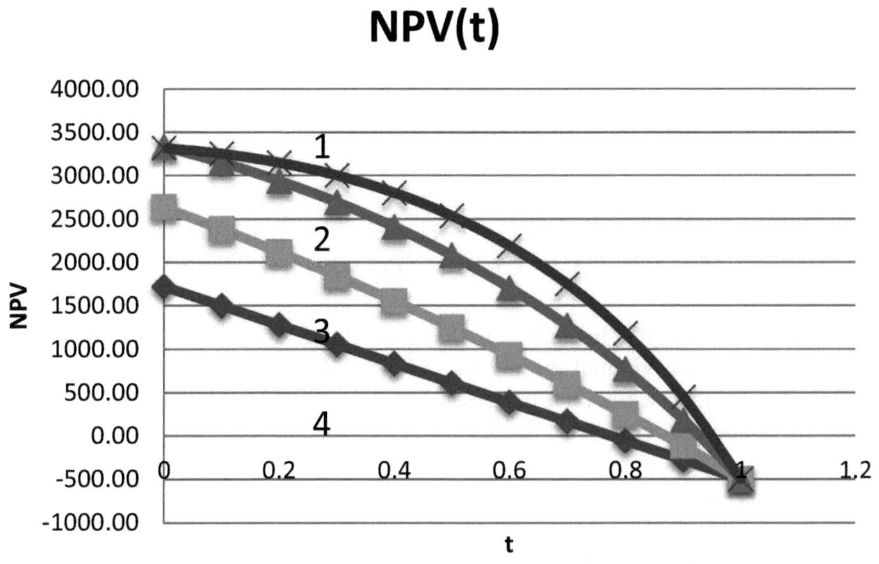

Fig. 18.11 Dependence of NPV on tax on profit rate at different leverage levels L (1—L = 5; 2—L = 3; 3—L = 1; 4—L = 0), S = 500, β = 0.8

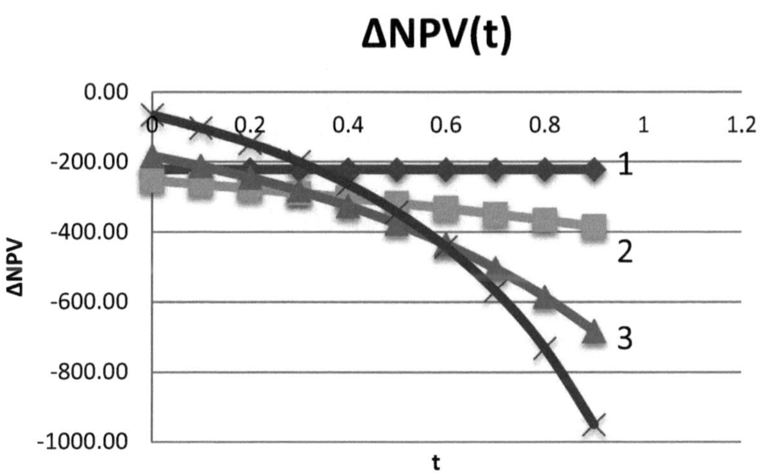

Fig. 18.12 Dependence of ΔNPV on tax on profit rate at different leverage levels L (1—L = 0; 2—L = 1; 3—L = 3; 4—L = 5), S = 500, β = 0.8

$$NPV = -S + \frac{NOI(1-t) - k_d D(1-t)}{WACC}. \tag{18.7}$$

18.6.1 At a Constant Value of the Total Invested Capital (I = const)

In case of a constant value of the total invested capital (I = const), accounting $D = IL/(1+L)$, $S = I/(1+L)$, we get

$$NPV = -I \cdot \frac{1}{1+L}\left[1 + \frac{Lk_d(1-t)}{k_0\left(1 - Lt/(1+L)\right)}\right] + \frac{NOI(1-t)}{k_0\left(1 - Lt/(1+L)\right)}. \quad (18.8)$$

It should be noted that, in contrast to the case with the division of flows, described above, in a situation without the division of flows NPV is growing with leverage level. It is seen, that, while NOI increases in 1.5 times NPV increases in 1.68 times (Figs. 18.13 and 18.14).

NPV rather quickly goes to the saturation, at L > 4 it varies weakly, and the leverage level, at which the saturation of NPV(L) takes place, practically does not depend on NOI (Fig. 18.15).

NPV falls down with growth of tax on profits rate at different leverage levels:

at L = 0 at change of tax on profits rate on 1%, NPV falls down on 1.74%;
at L = 1 at change of tax on profits rate on 1%, NPV falls down on 0.85%;
at L = 3 at change of tax on profits rate on 1%, NPV falls down on 0.43%;
at L = 5 at change of tax on profits rate on 1%, NPV falls down on 0.29%;

It is seen that, with the rising of the tax on profit rate by 1%, NPV drops the less at the higher leverage level. This confirms the conclusion, made in the previous section, that with the increase of the leverage level a negative impact of the growth of the

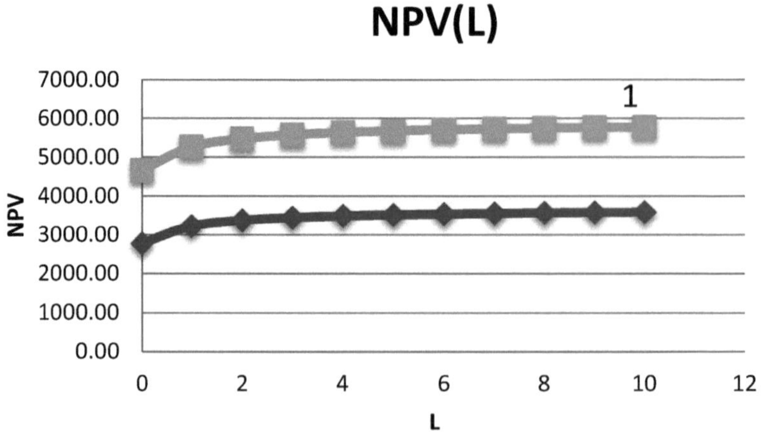

Fig. 18.13 Dependence of NPV on leverage level L at two values of NOI (1—NOI = 1200; 2—NOI = 800), I = 1000

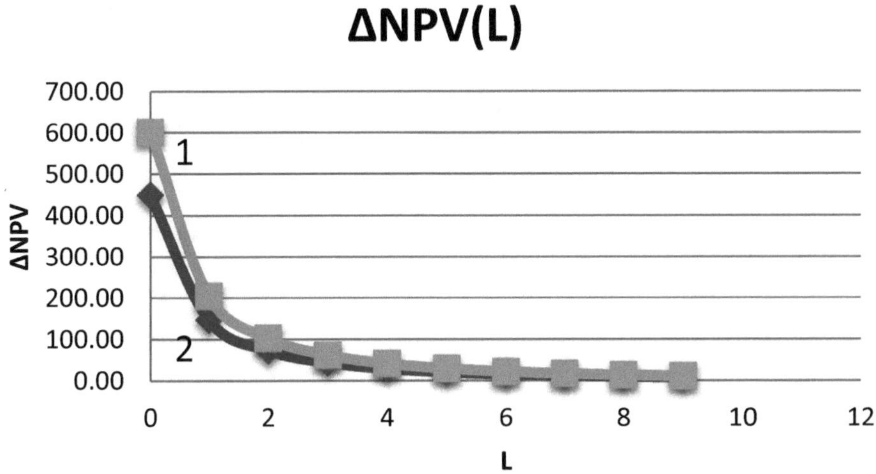

Fig. 18.14 Dependence of ΔNPV on leverage level L at two values of NOI (1—NOI = 1200; 2—NOI = 800), I = 1000

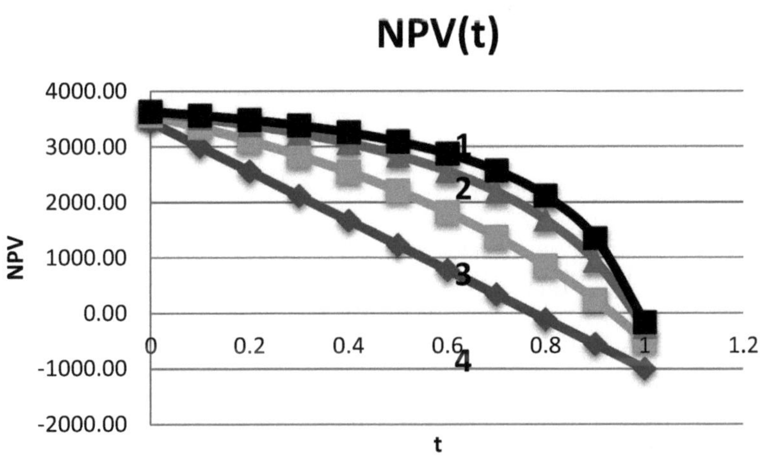

Fig. 18.15 Dependence of ΔNPV on tax on profit rate at different leverage levels L (1—L = 5; 2—L = 3; 3—L = 1; 4—L = 0), NOI = 800, I = 1000

tax on profit rate declines in a few times, allowing to the Regulator to establish the differentiated tax on profit rates (as can be seen from Fig. 18.16, the founded conclusions are true up to tax on profit rate values of 70% to 80%).

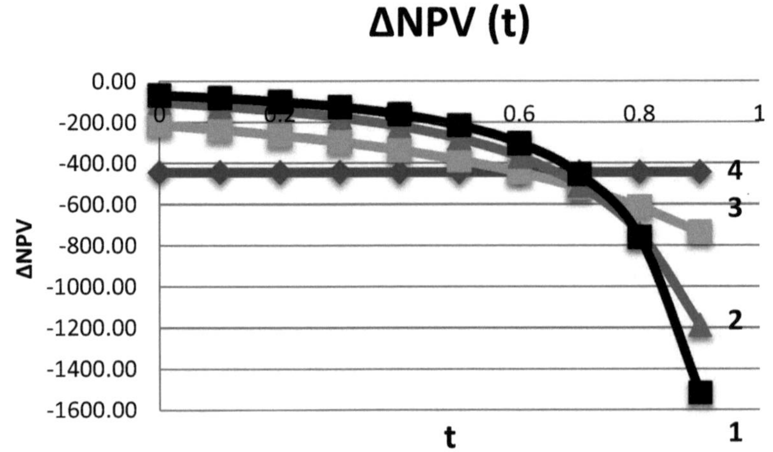

Fig. 18.16 Dependence of ΔNPV on tax on profit rate at different leverage levels L (1—L = 5; 2—L = 3; 3—L = 1; 4—L = 0), NOI = 800, I = 1000

18.6.2 At a Constant Value of Equity Capital (S = const)

$$NPV = -S + \frac{NOI(1-t) - k_d D(1-t)}{WACC}. \quad (18.9)$$

Substituting $D = LS$, one gets

$$NPV = -S\left[1 + \frac{Lk_d(1-t)}{k_0\left(1 - Lt/(1+L)\right)}\right] + \frac{\beta S(1+L)(1-t)}{k_0\left(1 - Lt/(1+L)\right)}. \quad (18.10)$$

From Fig. 18.17 it follows, that NPV grows linearly with leverage level and speed of its growth increases with grows of coefficient β.

From Fig. 18.18 it follows, that ΔNPV practically does not depend on leverage level L and at decrease of β—coefficient in 1.25 times (the transition from line 1 to line 2) ΔNPV is decreased in 1.28 times (practically so), and at decrease of β—coefficient in 1.5 times (the transition from line 2 to line 3) ΔNPV is decreased in 1.59 times (practically so).

As in case of constant value of investments (I = const), at constant equity capital value (S = const) NPV falls down with growth of tax on profit rate t at different leverage levels L.

Let's take a look at the region of changes of tax on profits rates from 0% up to 60%. In this region:

at L = 0 at change of tax on profits rate on 1%, NPV falls down on 3.6%;
at L = 1 at change of tax on profits rate on 1%, NPV falls down on 1.23%;
at L = 3 at change of tax on profits rate on 1%, NPV falls down on 0.46%;

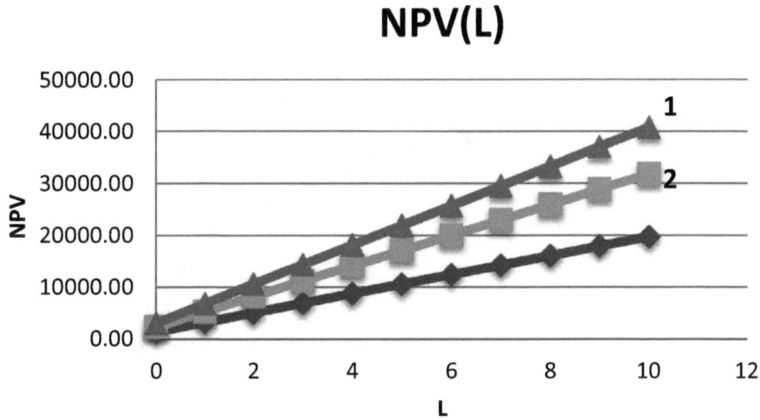

Fig. 18.17 Dependence of NPV on leverage level L at three values of β—coefficient (1—β = 1.5; 2—β = 1.2; 3—β = 0.8), S = 500

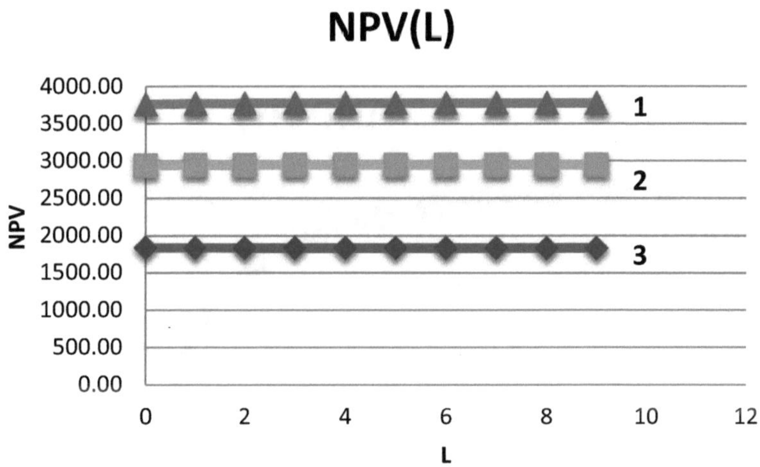

Fig. 18.18 Dependence of ΔNPV on leverage level L at three values of β—coefficient (1—β = 1.5; 2—β = 1.2; 3—β = 0.8), S = 500

at L = 5 at change of tax on profits rate on 1%, NPV falls down on 0.22%;

And so, with the increasing of the tax on profits rates at the 1%, NPV drops the less for the higher leverage level. This correlates with the conclusion made above and in the previous section, that with the increase of the leverage level a negative impact of the growth of the tax on profit rates declines in a few times, allowing the regulator to introduce differentiated tax on profits rate (as it can be seen from Figs. 18.19 and 18.20, the findings are true up to values of tax on profits rates 60%). At higher rates (that, however, is a purely theoretical interest) the situation will be different.

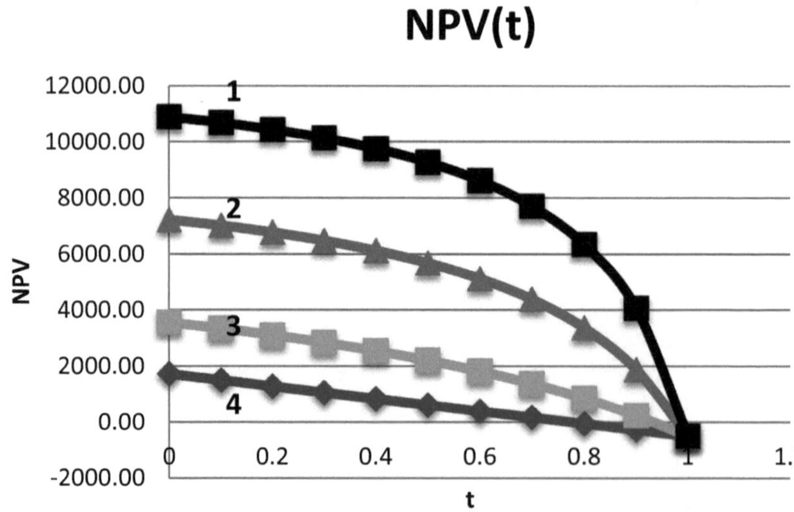

Fig. 18.19 Dependence of NPV on tax on profit rate t at different leverage levels L (1—L = 5; 2—L = 3; 3—L = 1; 4—L = 0), S = 500

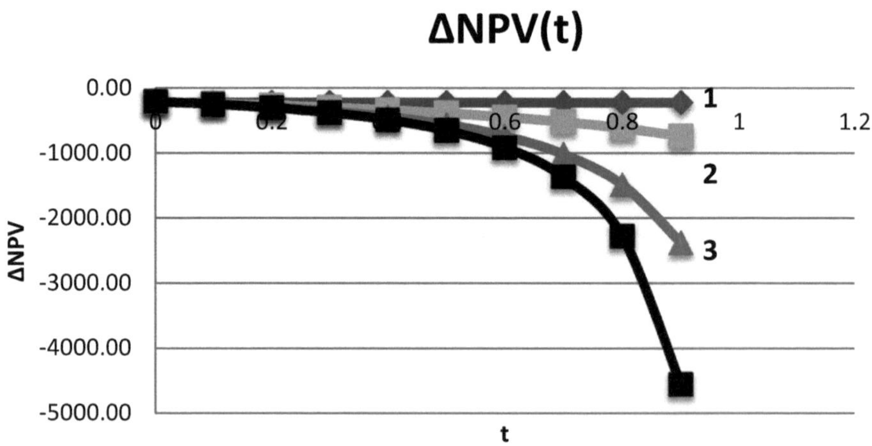

Fig. 18.20 Dependence of NPV on tax on profit rate t at different leverage levels L (1—L = 0; 2—L = 1; 3—L = 3; 4—L = 5), S = 500

18.7 Conclusions

Within investment models, developed by Brusov, Filatova, Orekhova earlier (Brusov et al. 2011a, b, c, d, 2012a, b, 2013a, b, 2014a, b; Filatova et al. 2008) the influence of tax on profit rate on effectiveness of long-term investment projects at different debt levels is investigated. The ability to obtain of quantitative estimates of such impact on the projects with various costs of equity and debt capital, at an arbitrary structure of invested capital has been demonstrated. It is shown, that increase of tax on profit rate from one side leads to decrease of project NPV, but from other side it leads to decrease of sensitivity of NPV with respect to leverage level. At high leverage level L the influence of tax on profit rate increase on effectiveness of investment projects becomes significantly less. We come to conclusion, that taxing could be differentiated depending on debt level of investment projects of the company: for projects with high debt level L it is possible to apply a higher tax on profit rate.

These recommendations, in particular, may be addressed to the Regulator. Effects of taxation on the effectiveness of investment projects depends on the level of leverage, of the project duration, of the equity cost, as well as of the level of returns on investment (NOI) and of methods of forming of invested capital. Study of all these problems, as the results of this Chapter show, may be successfully carried out within developed by Brusov, Filatova, Orekhova investment models, using discount rates, derived from the Brusov–Filatova–Orekhova (BFO) theory.

References

Brusov PN, Filatova TV (2011) From Modigliani–Miller to general theory of capital cost and capital structure of the company. Financ Credit 435:2–8

Brusov P, Filatova T, Kulik V (2024) Capital asset pricing model (CAPM) 2.0: Account of business and financial risk. Financ. theory pract. 28(2):128–142. https://doi.org/10.26794/2587-5671-2024-28-2-128-142

Brusov P, Filatova T, Orehova N, Brusova A (2011a) Weighted average cost of capital in the theory of Modigliani–Miller, modified for a finite life-time company. Appl Financ Econ 21(11):815–824

Brusov P, Filatova T, Orehova N et al (2011b) From Modigliani–Miller to general theory of capital cost and capital structure of the company. Res J Econ Bus ICT 2:16–21

Brusov P, Filatova T, Orehova N et al (2011c) Influence of debt financing on the effectiveness of the investment project within the Modigliani–Miller theory. Res J Econ Bus ICT (UK) 2:11–15

Brusov P, Filatova T, Orehova N, Brusov PP, Brusova N (2011d) From Modigliani–Miller to general theory of capital cost and capital structure of the company. Res J Econ Bus ICT 2:16–21

Brusov P, Filatova T, Eskindarov M, Orehova N (2012a) Influence of debt financing on the effectiveness of the finite duration investment project. Appl Financ Econ 22(13):1043–1052

Brusov P, Filatova T, Eskindarov M, Orehova N (2012b) Hidden global causes of the global financial crisis. J Rev Glob Econ 1:106–111

Brusov P, Filatova P, Orekhova N (2013a) Absence of an optimal capital structure in the famous tradeoff theory! J Rev Glob Econ 2:94–116

Brusov P, Filatova T, Orehova N (2013b) A qualitatively new effect in corporative finance: abnormal dependence of cost of equity of company on leverage. J Rev Glob Econ 2:183–193

Brusov P, Filatova P, Orekhova N (2014a) Mechanism of formation of the company optimal capital structure, different from suggested by trade off theory. Cogent Econ Financ 2:1–13. https://doi.org/10.1080/23322039.2014.946150

Brusov P, Filatova T, Orehova N (2014b) Inflation in Brusov–Filatova–Orekhova theory and in its perpetuity limit—Modigliani–Miller theory. J Rev Glob Econ 3:175–185

Brusova A (2011) A comparison of the three methods of estimation of weighted average cost of capital and equity cost of company. Financ Anal Problems Solut 34(76):36–42

Brusov P, Filatova T, Orehova N (2021) Ratings: Critical analysis and new approaches of quantitative and qualitative methodology. Springer Nature Publishing, pp.1–369

Brusov P, Filatova T, Orehova N (2022) Generalized Modigliani–Miller theory: Applications in corporate finance, investments, taxation and ratings. Springer Nature Publishing, pp.1–362

Brusov P, Filatova T, Orehova N (2023) The Brusov–Filatova–Orekhova theory of capital structure: Applications in corporate finance, investments, taxation and ratings. Springer Nature Publishing pp.1–769

Brusov P, Filatova T (2025a) Business valuation and company value: New qualitative approaches considering business and financial risks. Springer Nature Publishing pp.1–654

Brusov P, Filatova T (2025b) Efficiency of investment projects: Modern investment models and their applications. Springer Nature Publishing pp.1–843

Filatova T, Orehova N, Brusova A (2008) Weighted average cost of capital in the theory of Modigliani–Miller, modified for a finite life-time company. Bull FU 48:68–77

Modigliani F, Miller M (1958) The cost of capital, corporate finance, and the theory of investment. Am Econ Rev 48:261–297

Modigliani F, Miller M (1963) Corporate income taxes and the cost of capital: a correction. Am Econ Rev 53:147–175

Modigliani F, Miller M (1966) Some estimates of the cost of capital to the electric utility industry 1954–1957. Am Econ Rev 56:333–391

Chapter 19
Whether It is Possible to Increase of the Investment Efficiency, Increasing Tax on Profit Rate? An Sabnormal Influence of Growth of Tax on Profit Rate on the Efficiency of the Investment

19.1 Dependence of NPV on Leverage Level L at Fixed Levels of Tax on Profit Rates t

19.1.1 The Effectiveness of the Investment Project from the Perspective of the Equity Holders Only

In this Chapter an abnormal influence of growth of tax on profit rate on the efficiency of the investment has been discovered and the answer on the question "Whether it is possible to increase of the investment efficiency, increasing tax on profit rate?" has been done.

Investigations will be done with the division of credit and investment flows: operating and finance flows are divided and discounted using different rates: operating flows—by the rate equal to equity cost k_e, depending on leverage, and credit ones—by the rate equal to debt cost k_d, which, until a sufficiently large values of leverage levels, remains constant and starts to grow only at sufficiently high leverage values L, when a risk of bankruptcy will appear. The consideration has been done upon constant value of investment capital I.

In this case NPV is described by the following formula (Brusov et al. 2011a, b, c, d; 2012a, b; 2013a, b; 2014a, b; Filatova et al. 2008; Brusov and Filatova (2011); Brusova (2011); Brusov et al. 2021, 2022, 2023, 2024; Brusov and Filatova 2025a,b)

$$NPV = -\frac{I}{1+L}\left[1 + L\left((1-t)\left(1 - \frac{1}{(1+k_d)^n}\right) + \frac{1}{(1+k_d)^n}\right)\right] + \frac{NOI(1-t)}{k_e}\left(1 - \frac{1}{(1+k_e)^n}\right). \tag{19.1}$$

Using it we calculate NPV and ΔNPV at fixed levels of tax on profit rates t.

P. Brusov and T. Filatova, *Taxes and Taxation*, Contributions to Finance and Accounting, https://doi.org/10.1007/978-3-032-11077-0_19

5-year project

For 5-year projects we get the following results (Tables 19.1, 19.2, 19.3, 19.4, 19.5, 19.6, 19.7, 19.8, 19.9, Figs. 19.1 and 19.2).

One can see from the Fig. 19.1, that the nature of the NPV dependence on leverage at t* = 0.5: there is a transition from diminishing function NPV(L) when t < t* to growing function NPV(L) at t > t*.

Table 19.1 Dependence of NPV and ΔNPV on leverage level *L* at fixed levels of tax on profit rates t for 5-year project at t = 0.3

L	Ko	Kd	Wd	t	n	NOI	Ke	NPV	ΔNPV
0	0.18	0.14	0	0.3	5	800	0.18	751.22	4.922709
1	0.18	0.14	0.5	0.3	5	800	0.197488	756.14	−36.8599
2	0.18	0.14	0.66667	0.3	5	800	0.214367	719.28	−44.7663
3	0.18	0.14	0.75	0.3	5	800	0.231082	674.51	−46.126
4	0.18	0.14	0.8	0.3	5	800	0.24773	628.39	−45.4549
5	0.18	0.14	0.83333	0.3	5	800	0.264343	582.93	−44.027
6	0.18	0.14	0.85714	0.3	5	800	0.280937	538.90	−42.3084
7	0.18	0.14	0.875	0.3	5	800	0.297518	496.60	−40.4978
8	0.18	0.14	0.88889	0.3	5	800	0.314091	456.10	−38.6879
9	0.18	0.14	0.9	0.3	5	800	0.330658	417.41	−36.9239
10	0.18	0.14	0.90909	0.3	5	800	0.34722	380.49	

Table 19.2 Dependence of NPV and ΔNPV on leverage level *L* at fixed levels of tax on profit rates t for 5-year project at t = 0.4

L	Ko	Kd	Wd	t	n	NOI	Ke	NPV	ΔNPV
0	0.18	0.14	0	0.4	5	800	0.18	501.04	64.13345
1	0.18	0.14	0.5	0.4	5	800	0.189578	565.18	4.73089
2	0.18	0.14	0.66667	0.4	5	800	0.19803	569.91	−9.5017
3	0.18	0.14	0.75	0.4	5	800	0.206172	560.40	−14.7815
4	0.18	0.14	0.8	0.4	5	800	0.214184	545.62	−17.1025
5	0.18	0.14	0.83333	0.4	5	800	0.22213	528.52	−18.1709
6	0.18	0.14	0.85714	0.4	5	800	0.230037	510.35	−18.6246
7	0.18	0.14	0.875	0.4	5	800	0.23792	491.73	−18.7461
8	0.18	0.14	0.88889	0.4	5	800	0.245786	472.98	−18.6762
9	0.18	0.14	0.9	0.4	5	800	0.253642	454.30	−18.4911
10	0.18	0.14	0.90909	0.4	5	800	0.261488	435.81	

Table 19.3 Dependence of NPV and ΔNPV on leverage level *L* at fixed levels of tax on profit rates t for 5-year project at t = 0.5

L	Ko	Kd	Wd	t	n	NOI	Ke	NPV	ΔNPV
0	0.18	0.14	0	0.5	5	800	0.18	250.87	128.0669
1	0.18	0.14	0.5	0.5	5	800	0.181448	366.94	41.1323
2	0.18	0.14	0.66667	0.5	5	800	0.181065	408.07	22.57738
3	0.18	0.14	0.75	0.5	5	800	0.180162	430.65	15.19888
4	0.18	0.14	0.8	0.5	5	800	0.179041	445.84	11.52994
5	0.18	0.14	0.83333	0.5	5	800	0.177806	457.37	9.446706
6	0.18	0.14	0.85714	0.5	5	800	0.176505	466.82	8.154973
7	0.18	0.14	0.875	0.5	5	800	0.175162	474.98	7.302458
8	0.18	0.14	0.88889	0.5	5	800	0.173792	482.28	6.713275
9	0.18	0.14	0.9	0.5	5	800	0.172401	488.99	6.291579
10	0.18	0.14	0.90909	0.5	5	800	0.170996	495.28	

Table 19.4 Dependence of NPV and ΔNPV on leverage level *L* at fixed levels of tax on profit rates t for 5-year project at t = 0.6

L	Ko	Kd	Wd	t	n	NOI	Ke	NPV	ΔNPV
0	0.18	0.14	0	0.6	5	800	0.18	0.69	160.0655
1	0.18	0.14	0.5	0.6	5	800	0.173086	160.76	70.95083
2	0.18	0.14	0.66667	0.6	5	800	0.163424	231.71	49.78654
3	0.18	0.14	0.75	0.6	5	800	0.15296	281.50	42.12961
4	0.18	0.14	0.8	0.6	5	800	0.142153	323.63	39.00243
5	0.18	0.14	0.83333	0.6	5	800	0.131168	362.63	37.85743
6	0.18	0.14	0.85714	0.6	5	800	0.120078	400.49	37.74625
7	0.18	0.14	0.875	0.6	5	800	0.108922	438.23	38.25211
8	0.18	0.14	0.88889	0.6	5	800	0.097721	476.49	39.17065
9	0.18	0.14	0.9	0.6	5	800	0.086488	515.66	40.39427
10	0.18	0.14	0.90909	0.6	5	800	0.075231	556.05	

10-year project

For 10-year projects we get the following results (Tables 19.8, 19.9, 19.10, 19.11, 19.12, 19.13, 19.14, Figs. 19.3 and 19.4).

Perpetuity limit

In perpetuity limit $n \to \infty$ [Modigliani and Miller limit (Modigliani et al. 1958, 1963, 1966)] formula for NPV is as following (Brusov et al. 2011a, b, c, d; 2012a, b; 2013a, b; 2014a, b; Filatova et al. 2008)

Table 19.5 Dependence of NPV and ΔNPV on leverage level L at fixed levels of tax on profit rates t for 5-year project at t = 0.7

L	Ko	Kd	Wd	t	n	NOI	Ke	NPV	ΔNPV
0	0.18	0.14	0	0.7	5	800	0.18	−249.48	195.3877
1	0.18	0.14	0.5	0.7	5	800	0.16448	−54.09	92.40829
2	0.18	0.14	0.66667	0.7	5	800	0.145057	38.32	69.68464
3	0.18	0.14	0.75	0.7	5	800	0.124461	108.00	63.19622
4	0.18	0.14	0.8	0.7	5	800	0.103355	171.20	62.43475
5	0.18	0.14	0.83333	0.7	5	800	0.081982	233.63	64.46977
6	0.18	0.14	0.85714	0.7	5	800	0.060453	298.10	68.26526
7	0.18	0.14	0.875	0.7	5	800	0.038822	366.37	73.42597
8	0.18	0.14	0.88889	0.7	5	800	0.017124	439.79	79.82524
9	0.18	0.14	0.9	0.7	5	800	−0.00462	519.62	87.47314
10	0.18	0.14	0.90909	0.7	5	800	−0.0264	607.09	

Table 19.6 Dependence of NPV and ΔNPV on leverage level L at fixed levels of tax on profit rates t for 5-year project at t = 0.8

L	Ko	Kd	Wd	t	n	NOI	Ke	NPV	ΔNPV
0	0.18	0.14	0	0.8	5	800	0.18	−499.65	221.1945
1	0.18	0.14	0.5	0.8	5	800	0.155616	−278.46	103.2179
2	0.18	0.14	0.66667	0.8	5	800	0.125907	−175.24	78.69376
3	0.18	0.14	0.75	0.8	5	800	0.094544	−96.55	73.65304
4	0.18	0.14	0.8	0.8	5	800	0.062454	−22.89	76.11182
5	0.18	0.14	0.83333	0.8	5	800	0.029979	53.22	82.93806
6	0.18	0.14	0.85714	0.8	5	800	−0.00272	136.16	93.28915
7	0.18	0.14	0.875	0.8	5	800	−0.03557	229.45	107.1925
8	0.18	0.14	0.88889	0.8	5	800	−0.06852	336.64	125.1636
9	0.18	0.14	0.9	0.8	5	800	−0.10154	461.80	148.1245
10	0.18	0.14	0.90909	0.8	5	800	−0.13462	609.93	

$$NPV = -S + \frac{NOI(1-t)}{k_e} - D(1-t). \tag{19.2}$$

At constant value of investment capital ($I = \text{const}$), accounting $D = IL/(1+L)$, $S = I/(1+L)$, one gets

$$NPV = -\frac{I}{1+L}(1 + L(1-t)) + \frac{NOI(1-t)}{k_e}. \tag{19.3}$$

$$NPV = -\frac{I}{1+L}(1 + L(1-t)) + \frac{NOI(1-t)}{k_0 + (k_0 - k_d)L(1-t)}, \tag{19.4}$$

Table 19.7 Dependence of NPV and ΔNPV on leverage level *L* at fixed levels of tax on profit rates t for 5-year project at t = 0.9

L	Ko	Kd	Wd	t	n	NOI	Ke	NPV	ΔNPV
0	0.18	0.14	0	0.9	5	800	0.18	−749.83	236.5329
1	0.18	0.14	0.5	0.9	5	800	0.14648	−513.29	100.4127
2	0.18	0.14	0.66667	0.9	5	800	0.105908	−412.88	71.49601
3	0.18	0.14	0.75	0.9	5	800	0.063074	−341.38	65.36206
4	0.18	0.14	0.8	0.9	5	800	0.019228	−276.02	68.55205
5	0.18	0.14	0.83333	0.9	5	800	−0.02516	−207.47	77.93497
6	0.18	0.14	0.85714	0.9	5	800	−0.06987	−129.54	93.29474
7	0.18	0.14	0.875	0.9	5	800	−0.11479	−36.24	115.8841
8	0.18	0.14	0.88889	0.9	5	800	−0.15985	79.64	148.3017
9	0.18	0.14	0.9	0.9	5	800	−0.20501	227.94	194.9563
10	0.18	0.14	0.90909	0.9	5	800	−0.25024	422.90	

Table 19.8 Dependence of NPV and ΔNPV on leverage level *L* at fixed levels of tax on profit rates t for 10-year project at t = 0.3

L	Ko	Kd	Wd	t	n	NOI	Ke	NPV	ΔNPV
0	0.18	0.14	0	0.3	10	800	0.18	1528.69	−51.935
1	0.18	0.14	0.5	0.3	10	800	0.19907	1464.75	−101.47
2	0.18	0.14	0.66667	0.3	10	800	0.217182	1363.28	−104.843
3	0.18	0.14	0.75	0.3	10	800	0.235022	1258.44	−100.263
4	0.18	0.14	0.8	0.3	10	800	0.252747	1158.18	−93.8156
5	0.18	0.14	0.83333	0.3	10	800	0.270413	1064.36	−87.1129
6	0.18	0.14	0.85714	0.3	10	800	0.288045	977.25	−80.6768
7	0.18	0.14	0.875	0.3	10	800	0.305654	896.57	−74.6812
8	0.18	0.14	0.88889	0.3	10	800	0.323249	821.89	−69.1705
9	0.18	0.14	0.9	0.3	10	800	0.340834	752.72	−64.1369
10	0.18	0.14	0.90909	0.3	10	800	0.358411	688.58	

here $L = D/S$—leverage level; k_e—equity cost of leverage company (use the debt capital); k_0—equity cost of financially independent company.

In the transition from the equation (Eqs. 19.3)–(19.4) we have used the formula for equity capital cost, received by Modigliani and Miller [Modigliani and Miller (1958, 1963, 1966)]

$$k_e = k_0 + (k_0 - k_d)L(1 - t). \tag{19.5}$$

For perpetuity projects we get the following results (Tables 19.15, 19.16, 19.17, 19.18, 19.19, 19.20, 19.21, Figs. 19.5 and 19.6).

Table 19.9 Dependence of NPV and ΔNPV on leverage level *L* at fixed levels of tax on profit rates t for 10-year project at t = 0.4

L	Ko	Kd	Wd	t	n	NOI	Ke	NPV	ΔNPV
0	0.18	0.14	0	0.4	10	800	0.18	1157.16	61.10029
1	0.18	0.14	0.5	0.4	10	800	0.191455	1218.26	−18.517
2	0.18	0.14	0.66667	0.4	10	800	0.201083	1199.74	−35.7995
3	0.18	0.14	0.75	0.4	10	800	0.210169	1163.95	−41.1321
4	0.18	0.14	0.8	0.4	10	800	0.21902	1122.81	−42.6427
5	0.18	0.14	0.83333	0.4	10	800	0.22775	1080.17	−42.6081
6	0.18	0.14	0.85714	0.4	10	800	0.236408	1037.56	−41.8669
7	0.18	0.14	0.875	0.4	10	800	0.24502	995.70	−40.7844
8	0.18	0.14	0.88889	0.4	10	800	0.253602	954.91	−39.5386
9	0.18	0.14	0.9	0.4	10	800	0.262161	915.37	−38.2228
10	0.18	0.14	0.90909	0.4	10	800	0.270705	877.15	

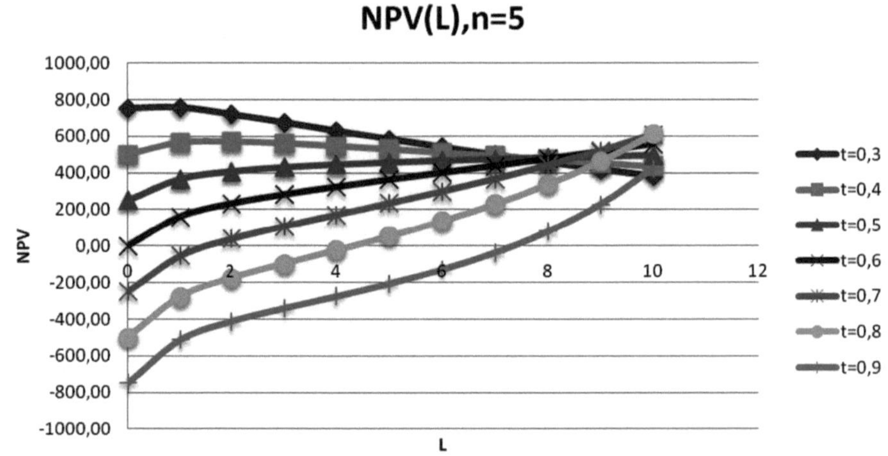

Fig. 19.1 Dependence of NPV on leverage level *L* at fixed levels of tax on profit rates t for 5-year project

19.1.2 The Effectiveness of the Investment Project from the Perspective of the Equity and Debt Holders

In this case we use the following expression for NPV (Brusov et al. 2011a, b, c, d; 2012a, b; 2013a, b; 2014a, b; Filatova et al. 2008)

$$NPV = -I\left[1 - \frac{Lt}{1+L}\left(1 - \frac{1}{(1+k_d)^n}\right)\right] + \frac{NOI(1-t)}{k_e}\left(1 - \frac{1}{(1+k_e)^n}\right) \tag{19.6}$$

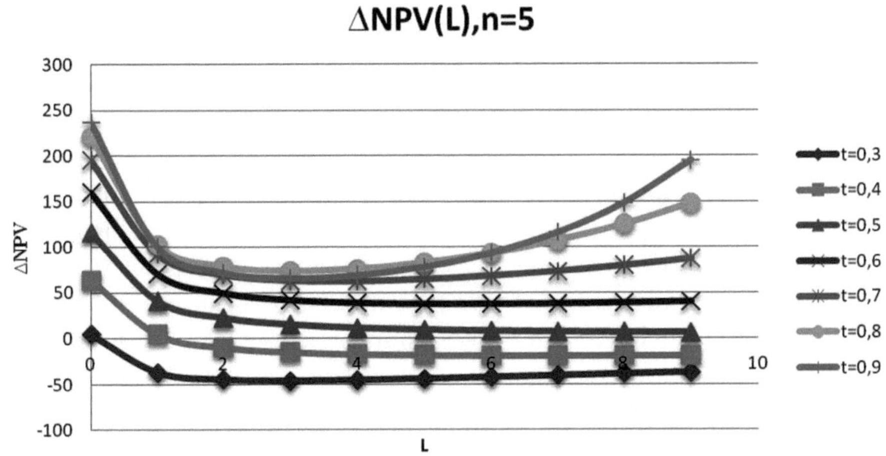

Fig. 19.2 Dependence of ΔNPV on leverage level *L* at fixed levels of tax on profit rates t for 5-year project

Table 19.10 Dependence of NPV and ΔNPV on leverage level *L* at fixed levels of tax on profit rates t for 10-year project at t = 0.5

L	Ko	Kd	Wd	t	n	NOI	Ke	NPV	ΔNPV
0	0.18	0.14	0	0.5	10	800	0.18	797.63	−44.2013
1	0.18	0.14	0.5	0.5	10	800	0.219687	753.43	−104.707
2	0.18	0.14	0.66667	0.5	10	800	0.255351	648.73	−103.671
3	0.18	0.14	0.75	0.5	10	800	0.290005	545.06	−93.6005
4	0.18	0.14	0.8	0.5	10	800	0.32421	451.45	−82.6797
5	0.18	0.14	0.83333	0.5	10	800	0.358168	368.78	−72.7174
6	0.18	0.14	0.85714	0.5	10	800	0.391982	296.06	−64.0269
7	0.18	0.14	0.875	0.5	10	800	0.425702	232.03	−56.5734
8	0.18	0.14	0.88889	0.5	10	800	0.459362	175.46	−50.1953
9	0.18	0.14	0.9	0.5	10	800	0.492979	125.26	−44.7383
10	0.18	0.14	0.90909	0.5	10	800	0.526564	80.52	

Using it we calculate the dependence of NPV and ΔNPV on leverage level *L* at fixed levels of tax on profit rates t.

5-year project

For 5-year projects we get the following results (Tables 19.22, 19.23, 19.24, 19.25, 19.26, 19.27, 19.28, Figs. 19.7 and 19.8).

Table 19.11 Dependence of NPV and ΔNPV on leverage level *L* at fixed levels of tax on profit rates t for 10-year project at t = 0.6

L	Ko	Kd	Wd	t	n	NOI	Ke	NPV	ΔNPV
0	0.18	0.14	0	0.6	10	800	0.18	438.11	244.5668
1	0.18	0.14	0.5	0.6	10	800	0.175084	682.67	125.4304
2	0.18	0.14	0.66667	0.6	10	800	0.165407	808.10	101.3662
3	0.18	0.14	0.75	0.6	10	800	0.154162	909.47	95.93652
4	0.18	0.14	0.8	0.6	10	800	0.142206	1005.41	97.02629
5	0.18	0.14	0.83333	0.6	10	800	0.129869	1102.43	101.3309
6	0.18	0.14	0.85714	0.6	10	800	0.117304	1203.76	107.7015
7	0.18	0.14	0.875	0.6	10	800	0.10459	1311.47	115.7055
8	0.18	0.14	0.88889	0.6	10	800	0.091775	1427.17	125.2046
9	0.18	0.14	0.9	0.6	10	800	0.078888	1552.38	136.2059
10	0.18	0.14	0.90909	0.6	10	800	0.065947	1688.58	

Table 19.12 Dependence of NPV and ΔNPV on leverage level *L* at fixed levels of tax on profit rates t for 10-year project at t = 0.7

L	Ko	Kd	Wd	t	n	NOI	Ke	NPV	ΔNPV
0	0.18	0.14	0	0.7	10	800	0.18	78.58	310.4744
1	0.18	0.14	0.5	0.7	10	800	0.166255	389.06	177.1979
2	0.18	0.14	0.66667	0.7	10	800	0.145497	566.25	160.5402
3	0.18	0.14	0.75	0.7	10	800	0.122295	726.79	169.9063
4	0.18	0.14	0.8	0.7	10	800	0.097953	896.70	191.9196
5	0.18	0.14	0.83333	0.7	10	800	0.072986	1088.62	224.1724
6	0.18	0.14	0.85714	0.7	10	800	0.04764	1312.79	267.4019
7	0.18	0.14	0.875	0.7	10	800	0.022047	1580.19	323.9861
8	0.18	0.14	0.88889	0.7	10	800	−0.00372	1904.18	397.7601
9	0.18	0.14	0.9	0.7	10	800	−0.0296	2301.94	494.3094
10	0.18	0.14	0.90909	0.7	10	800	−0.05558	2796.25	

10-year project

For 10-year projects we get the following results (Tables 19.29, 19.30, 19.31, 19.32, 19.33, 19.34, 19.35, Figs. 19.9 and 19.10).

Table 19.13 Dependence of NPV and ΔNPV on leverage level L at fixed levels of tax on profit rates t for 10-year project at t = 0.8

L	Ko	Kd	Wd	t	n	NOI	Ke	NPV	ΔNPV
0	0.18	0.14	0	0.8	10	800	0.18	−280.95	355.2633
1	0.18	0.14	0.5	0.8	10	800	0.156938	74.32	204.8466
2	0.18	0.14	0.66667	0.8	10	800	0.123925	279.16	198.4863
3	0.18	0.14	0.75	0.8	10	800	0.087223	477.65	232.7806
4	0.18	0.14	0.8	0.8	10	800	0.048741	710.43	297.8303
5	0.18	0.14	0.83333	0.8	10	800	0.009262	1008.26	400.9259
6	0.18	0.14	0.85714	0.8	10	800	−0.03083	1409.19	560.3743
7	0.18	0.14	0.875	0.8	10	800	−0.07133	1969.56	809.4944
8	0.18	0.14	0.88889	0.8	10	800	−0.11211	2779.06	1207.425
9	0.18	0.14	0.9	0.8	10	800	−0.1531	3986.48	1861.112
10	0.18	0.14	0.90909	0.8	10	800	−0.19424	5847.59	

Table 19.14 Dependence of NPV and ΔNPV on leverage level L at fixed levels of tax on profit rates t for 10-year project at t = 0.9

L	Ko	Kd	Wd	t	n	NOI	Ke	NPV	ΔNPV
0	0.18	0.14	0	0.9	10	800	0.18	−640.47	375.0978
1	0.18	0.14	0.5	0.9	10	800	0.147081	−265.38	194.2145
2	0.18	0.14	0.66667	0.9	10	800	0.100417	−71.16	186.9461
3	0.18	0.14	0.75	0.9	10	800	0.048303	115.79	239.586
4	0.18	0.14	0.8	0.9	10	800	−0.00655	355.37	356.4744
5	0.18	0.14	0.83333	0.9	10	800	−0.06297	711.85	583.6021
6	0.18	0.14	0.85714	0.9	10	800	−0.12039	1295.45	1032.383
7	0.18	0.14	0.875	0.9	10	800	−0.17847	2327.83	1967.211
8	0.18	0.14	0.88889	0.9	10	800	−0.23701	4295.04	4054.338
9	0.18	0.14	0.9	0.9	10	800	−0.2959	8349.38	9115.336
10	0.18	0.14	0.90909	0.9	10	800	−0.35504	17,464.72	

19.2 Dependence of NPV on Tax on Profit Rates at Fixed Leverage Levels *L*

Below we study the dependence of NPV on tax on profit rates at fixed leverage levels L.

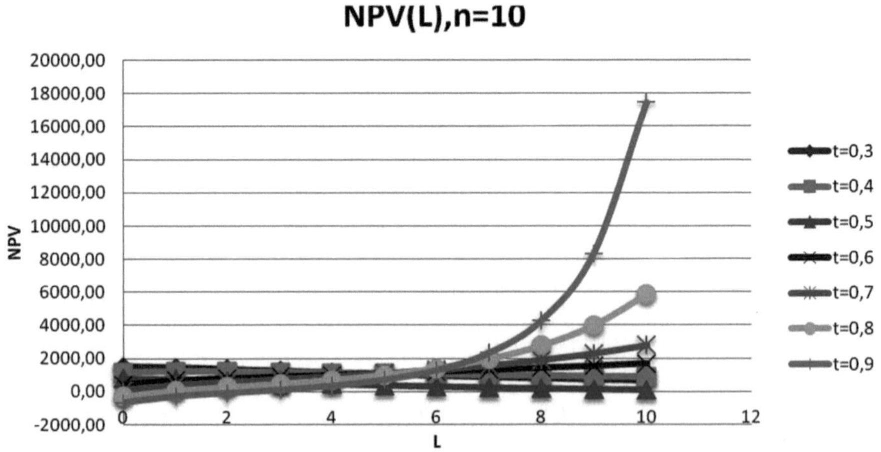

Fig. 19.3 Dependence of NPV on leverage level *L* at fixed levels of tax on profit rates t for 10-year project

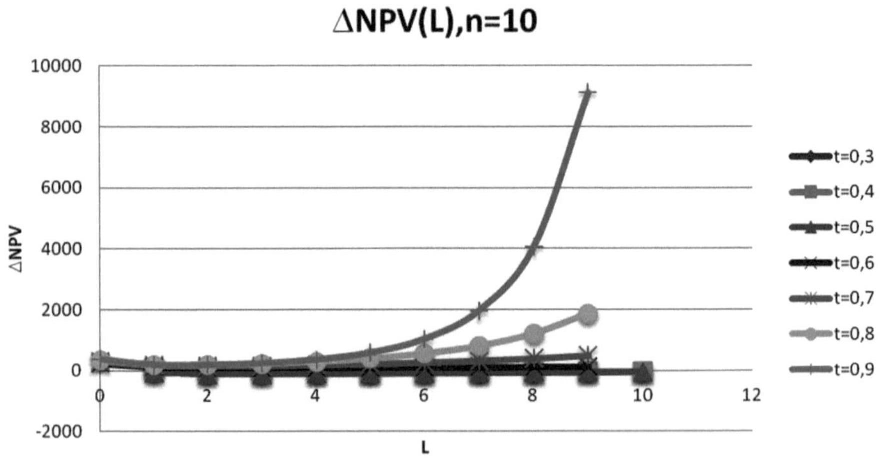

Fig. 19.4 Dependence of NPV on leverage level *L* at fixed levels of tax on profit rates t for 10-year project

19.2.1 The Effectiveness of the Investment Project from the Perspective of the Equity Holders Only

5-year project

For 5-year projects we get the following results (Tables 19.36, 19.37, 19.38, 19.39, 19.40, 19.41, Figs. 19.11 and 19.12).

Table 19.15 Dependence of NPV and ΔNPV on leverage level *L* at fixed levels of tax on profit rates t for perpetuity project at t = 0.3

L	t	k0	kd	I	NOI	NPV	ΔNPV
0	0.3	0.18	0.14	1000	800	2111.111	−268.803
1	0.3	0.18	0.14	1000	800	1842.308	−269.426
2	0.3	0.18	0.14	1000	800	1572.881	−226.669
3	0.3	0.18	0.14	1000	800	1346.212	−188.404
4	0.3	0.18	0.14	1000	800	1157.808	−157.808
5	0.3	0.18	0.14	1000	800	1000	−133.662
6	0.3	0.18	0.14	1000	800	866.3383	−114.477
7	0.3	0.18	0.14	1000	800	751.8617	−99.0564
8	0.3	0.18	0.14	1000	800	652.8053	−86.509
9	0.3	0.18	0.14	1000	800	566.2963	−76.1777
10	0.3	0.18	0.14	1000	800	490.1186	

Table 19.16 Dependence of NPV and ΔNPV on leverage level *L* at fixed levels of tax on profit rates t for perpetuity project at t = 0.4

L	t	k0	kd	I	NOI	NPV	ΔNPV
0	0.4	0.18	0.14	1000	800	1666.667	−113.725
1	0.4	0.18	0.14	1000	800	1552.941	−181.011
2	0.4	0.18	0.14	1000	800	1371.93	−167.168
3	0.4	0.18	0.14	1000	800	1204.762	−145.631
4	0.4	0.18	0.14	1000	800	1059.13	−125.797
5	0.4	0.18	0.14	1000	800	933.3333	−108.995
6	0.4	0.18	0.14	1000	800	824.3386	−95.0283
7	0.4	0.18	0.14	1000	800	729.3103	−83.4322
8	0.4	0.18	0.14	1000	800	645.8781	−73.7569
9	0.4	0.18	0.14	1000	800	572.1212	−65.6277
10	0.4	0.18	0.14	1000	800	506.4935	

10-year project

For 10-year projects we get the following results (Tables 19.42, 19.43, 19.44, 19.45, 19.46, 19.47, Figs. 19.13 and 19.14).

Perpetuity limit

For perpetuity projects we get the following results (Tables 19.48, 19.49, Fig. 19.15).

Table 19.17 Dependence of NPV and ΔNPV on leverage level *L* at fixed levels of tax on profit rates t for perpetuity project at t = 0.5

L	t	k0	kd	I	NOI	NPV	ΔNPV
0	0.5	0.18	0.14	1000	800	1222.222	27.77778
1	0.5	0.18	0.14	1000	800	1250	−98.4848
2	0.5	0.18	0.14	1000	800	1151.515	−109.848
3	0.5	0.18	0.14	1000	800	1041.667	−103.205
4	0.5	0.18	0.14	1000	800	938.4615	−93.2234
5	0.5	0.18	0.14	1000	800	845.2381	−83.3333
6	0.5	0.18	0.14	1000	800	761.9048	−74.4048
7	0.5	0.18	0.14	1000	800	687.5	−66.585
8	0.5	0.18	0.14	1000	800	620.915	−59.8039
9	0.5	0.18	0.14	1000	800	561.1111	−53.9341
10	0.5	0.18	0.14	1000	800	507.177	

Table 19.18 Dependence of NPV and ΔNPV on leverage level *L* at fixed levels of tax on profit rates t for perpetuity project at t = 0.6

L	t	k0	kd	I	NOI	NPV	ΔNPV
0	0.6	0.18	0.14	1000	800	777.7778	154.8753
1	0.6	0.18	0.14	1000	800	932.6531	−23.2191
2	0.6	0.18	0.14	1000	800	909.434	−55.9252
3	0.6	0.18	0.14	1000	800	853.5088	−62.0334
4	0.6	0.18	0.14	1000	800	791.4754	−60.7062
5	0.6	0.18	0.14	1000	800	730.7692	−57.0632
6	0.6	0.18	0.14	1000	800	673.706	−52.8156
7	0.6	0.18	0.14	1000	800	620.8904	−48.596
8	0.6	0.18	0.14	1000	800	572.2944	−44.6401
9	0.6	0.18	0.14	1000	800	527.6543	−41.0233
10	0.6	0.18	0.14	1000	800	486.631	

19.2.2 The Effectiveness of the Investment Project from the Perspective of the Equity and Debt Holders

5-year project

For 5-year projects we get the following results (Tables 19.50, 19.51, 19.52, 19.53, 19.54, 19.55, Figs. 19.16 and 19.17).

Table 19.19 Dependence of NPV and ΔNPV on leverage level *L* at fixed levels of tax on profit rates t for perpetuity project at t = 0.7

L	t	k0	kd	I	NOI	NPV	ΔNPV
0	0.7	0.18	0.14	1000	800	333.3333	266.6667
1	0.7	0.18	0.14	1000	800	600	43.13725
2	0.7	0.18	0.14	1000	800	643.1373	−7.02614
3	0.7	0.18	0.14	1000	800	636.1111	−23.4795
4	0.7	0.18	0.14	1000	800	612.6316	−29.2982
5	0.7	0.18	0.14	1000	800	583.3333	−30.9524
6	0.7	0.18	0.14	1000	800	552.381	−30.79
7	0.7	0.18	0.14	1000	800	521.5909	−29.8035
8	0.7	0.18	0.14	1000	800	491.7874	−28.4541
9	0.7	0.18	0.14	1000	800	463.3333	−26.9697
10	0.7	0.18	0.14	1000	800	436.3636	

Table 19.20 Dependence of NPV and ΔNPV on leverage level *L* at fixed levels of tax on profit rates t for perpetuity project at t = 0.8

L	t	k0	kd	I	NOI	NPV	ΔNPV
0	0.8	0.18	0.14	1000	800	−111.111	362.1749
1	0.8	0.18	0.14	1000	800	251.0638	98.59603
2	0.8	0.18	0.14	1000	800	349.6599	34.65386
3	0.8	0.18	0.14	1000	800	384.3137	10.40326
4	0.8	0.18	0.14	1000	800	394.717	−0.77759
5	0.8	0.18	0.14	1000	800	393.9394	−6.47072
6	0.8	0.18	0.14	1000	800	387.4687	−9.50257
7	0.8	0.18	0.14	1000	800	377.9661	−11.1173
8	0.8	0.18	0.14	1000	800	366.8488	−11.9282
9	0.8	0.18	0.14	1000	800	354.9206	−12.2633
10	0.8	0.18	0.14	1000	800	342.6573	

10-year projects

For 10-year projects we get the following results (Tables 19.56, 19.57, 19.58, 19.59, 19.60, 19.61, Figs. 19.18, 19.19, 19.20, 19.21).

Or more detailed

It is seen from Fig. 19.19, that falling trend at L = 0, 2, and 4 alternates by growing trend at higher leverage levels L = 6, 8, and 10.

The observed at high leverage levels (starting from L = 6) increase of NPV with growth of the tax on profit rate t takes place at all values of t, that means that this is an entirely new effect in investments which can be applied in a real economic practice for optimizing of the management of investments.

Table 19.21 Dependence of NPV and ΔNPV on leverage level *L* at fixed levels of tax on profit rates t for perpetuity project at t = 0.9

L	t	k0	kd	I	NOI	NPV	ΔNPV
0	0.9	0.18	0.14	1000	800	−555.556	440.3382
1	0.9	0.18	0.14	1000	800	−115.217	140.7493
2	0.9	0.18	0.14	1000	800	25.53191	66.13475
3	0.9	0.18	0.14	1000	800	91.66667	36.4966
4	0.9	0.18	0.14	1000	800	119.1633	21.83673
5	0.9	0.18	0.14	1000	800	150	13.58543
6	0.9	0.18	0.14	1000	800	163.5854	8.52995
7	0.9	0.18	0.14	1000	800	172.1154	5.243106
8	0.9	0.18	0.14	1000	800	177.3585	3.01188
9	0.9	0.18	0.14	1000	800	180.3704	1.447811
10	0.9	0.18	0.14	1000	800	181.8182	

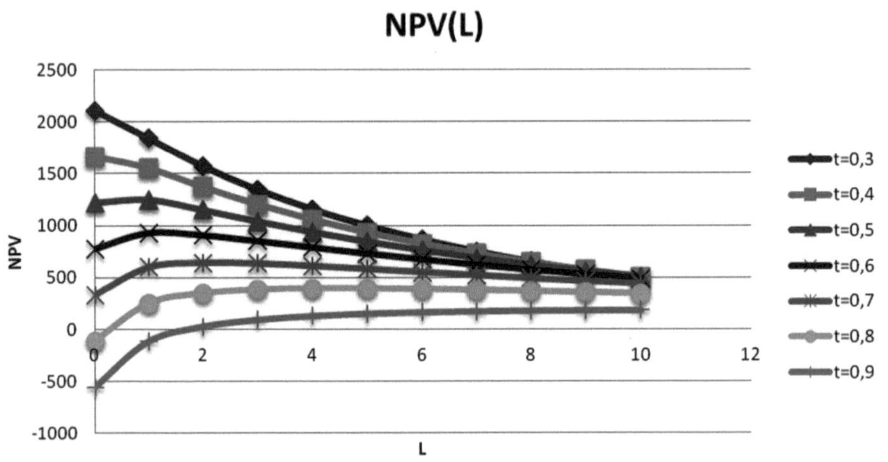

Fig. 19.5 Dependence of NPV on leverage level *L* at fixed levels of tax on profit rates t for perpetuity project

Or more detailed

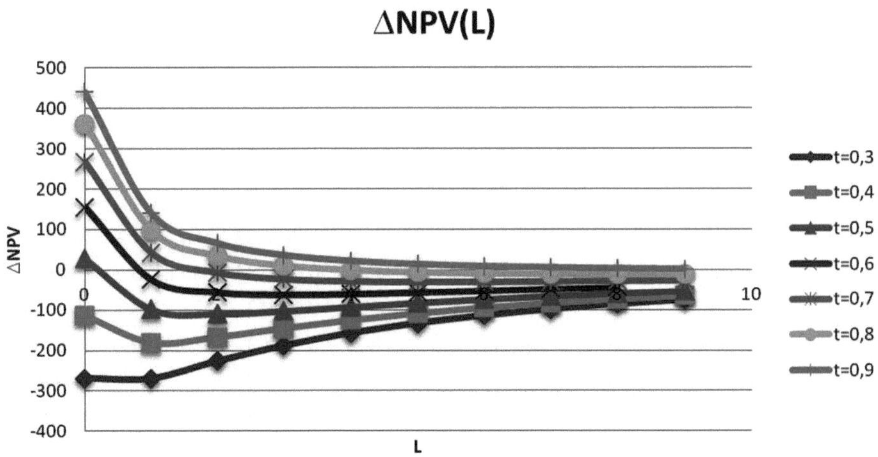

Fig. 19.6 Dependence of ΔNPV on leverage level *L* at fixed levels of tax on profit rates t for perpetuity project

Table 19.22 Dependence of NPV and ΔNPV on leverage level *L* at fixed levels of tax on profit rates t for 5-year project at t = 0.3

I	L	WACC	Ko	Kd	Wd	t	n	NOI	Ke	NPV	ΔNPV
1000	0	0.18	0.18	0.14	0	0.3	5	800	0.18	751.2158	4.922709
1000	1	0.14774	0.18	0.14	0.5	0.3	5	800	0.197488	756.1385	−36.8599
1000	2	0.13679	0.18	0.14	0.66667	0.3	5	800	0.214367	719.2786	−44.7663
1000	3	0.13127	0.18	0.14	0.75	0.3	5	800	0.231082	674.5122	−46.126
1000	4	0.12795	0.18	0.14	0.8	0.3	5	800	0.24773	619.3863	−45.4549
1000	5	0.12572	0.18	0.14	0.83333	0.3	5	800	0.264343	582.9313	−44.027
1000	6	0.12413	0.18	0.14	0.85714	0.3	5	800	0.280937	538.9044	−42.3084
1000	7	0.12294	0.18	0.14	0.875	0.3	5	800	0.297518	496.596	−40.4978
1000	8	0.12201	0.18	0.14	0.88889	0.3	5	800	0.314091	456.0982	−38.6879
1000	9	0.12127	0.18	0.14	0.9	0.3	5	800	0.330658	417.4103	−36.9239
1000	10	0.12066	0.18	0.14	0.90909	0.3	5	800	0.34722	380.4865	

19.3 Conclusions

Within modern theory of capital cost and capital structure by Brusov-Filatova-Orekhova (BFO theory) and created within this theory modern investment models influence of growth of tax on profit rate on the efficiency of the investment is investigated. It has been shown that for arbitrary duration projects as well as for perpetuity projects the growth of tax on profit rate change the nature of the NPV dependence on leverage at some value t*: there is a transition from diminishing function NPV(L)

Table 19.23 Dependence of NPV and ΔNPV on leverage level *L* at fixed levels of tax on profit rates t for 5-year project at t = 0.4

I	L	WACC	Ko	Kd	Wd	t	n	NOI	Ke	NPV	ΔNPV
1000	0	0.18	0.18	0.14	0	0.4	5	800	0.18	501.0421	64.13345
1000	1	0.13679	0.18	0.14	0.5	0.4	5	800	0.189578	565.1755	4.73089
1000	2	0.12201	0.18	0.14	0.66667	0.4	5	800	0.19803	569.9064	−9.5017
1000	3	0.11454	0.18	0.14	0.75	0.4	5	800	0.206172	560.4047	−14.7815
1000	4	0.11004	0.18	0.14	0.8	0.4	5	800	0.214184	545.6233	−17.1025
1000	5	0.10702	0.18	0.14	0.83333	0.4	5	800	0.22213	528.5208	−18.1709
1000	6	0.10486	0.18	0.14	0.85714	0.4	5	800	0.230037	510.3499	−18.6246
1000	7	0.10324	0.18	0.14	0.875	0.4	5	800	0.23792	491.7254	−18.7461
1000	8	0.10198	0.18	0.14	0.88889	0.4	5	800	0.245786	472.9793	−18.6762
1000	9	0.10096	0.18	0.14	0.9	0.4	5	800	0.253642	454.3031	−18.4911
1000	10	0.10014	0.18	0.14	0.90909	0.4	5	800	0.261488	435.812	

Table 19.24 Dependence of NPV and ΔNPV on leverage level *L* at fixed levels of tax on profit rates t for 5-year project at t = 0.5

I	L	WACC	Ko	Kd	Wd	t	n	NOI	Ke	NPV	ΔNPV
1000	0	0.18	0.18	0.14	0	0.5	5	800	0.18	250.8684	119.0669
1000	1	0.12572	0.18	0.14	0.5	0.5	5	800	0.181448	366.9353	41.1323
1000	2	0.10702	0.18	0.14	0.66667	0.5	5	800	0.181065	408.0676	22.57738
1000	3	0.09754	0.18	0.14	0.75	0.5	5	800	0.180162	430.645	15.19888
1000	4	0.09181	0.18	0.14	0.8	0.5	5	800	0.179041	445.8439	11.52994
1000	5	0.08797	0.18	0.14	0.83333	0.5	5	800	0.177806	457.3738	9.446706
1000	6	0.08522	0.18	0.14	0.85714	0.5	5	800	0.176505	466.8205	8.154973
1000	7	0.08315	0.18	0.14	0.875	0.5	5	800	0.175162	474.9755	7.302458
1000	8	0.08153	0.18	0.14	0.88889	0.5	5	800	0.173792	482.278	6.713275
1000	9	0.08024	0.18	0.14	0.9	0.5	5	800	0.172401	488.9912	6.291579
1000	10	0.07918	0.18	0.14	0.90909	0.5	5	800	0.170996	495.2828	

when t < t* to growing function NPV(L). The t* value depends on the duration of the project, cost of capital (equity and debt) values and other parameters of the project.

At high leverage levels this leads to qualitatively new effect in investments: growth of the efficiency of the investments with growth of tax on profit rate**.** Discovered effects take place under consideration from the point of view of owners of equity capital as well as from the point of view of owners of equity and debt capital.

The observed at high leverage levels (starting from L = 6) increase of NPV with growth of the tax on profit rate t takes place at all values of t, that means that this is an entirely new effect in investments which can be applied in a real economic practice for optimizing of the management of investments.

Table 19.25 Dependence of NPV and ΔNPV on leverage level L at fixed levels of tax on profit rates t for 5-year project at t = 0.6

I	L	WACC	Ko	Kd	Wd	t	n	NOI	Ke	NPV	ΔNPV
1000	0	0.18	0.18	0.14	0	0.6	5	800	0.18	0.694727	160.0655
1000	1	0.11454	0.18	0.14	0.5	0.6	5	800	0.173086	160.7602	70.95083
1000	2	0.09181	0.18	0.14	0.66667	0.6	5	800	0.163424	231.711	49.78654
1000	3	0.08024	0.18	0.14	0.75	0.6	5	800	0.15296	281.4976	42.12961
1000	4	0.07323	0.18	0.14	0.8	0.6	5	800	0.142153	323.6272	39.00243
1000	5	0.06853	0.18	0.14	0.83333	0.6	5	800	0.131168	362.6296	37.85743
1000	6	0.06515	0.18	0.14	0.85714	0.6	5	800	0.120078	400.487	37.74625
1000	7	0.06262	0.18	0.14	0.875	0.6	5	800	0.108922	438.2333	38.25211
1000	8	0.06064	0.18	0.14	0.88889	0.6	5	800	0.097721	476.4854	39.17065
1000	9	0.05905	0.18	0.14	0.9	0.6	5	800	0.086488	515.656	40.39427
1000	10	0.05775	0.18	0.14	0.90909	0.6	5	800	0.075231	556.0503	

Table 19.26 Dependence of NPV and ΔNPV on leverage level L at fixed levels of tax on profit rates t for 5-year project at t = 0.7

I	L	WACC	Ko	Kd	Wd	t	n	NOI	Ke	NPV	ΔNPV
1000	0	0.18	0.18	0.14	0	0.7	5	800	0.18	−249.479	195.3877
1000	1	0.10324	0.18	0.14	0.5	0.7	5	800	0.16448	−54.0913	92.40829
1000	2	0.07635	0.18	0.14	0.66667	0.7	5	800	0.145057	38.31702	69.68464
1000	3	0.06262	0.18	0.14	0.75	0.7	5	800	0.124461	108.0017	63.19622
1000	4	0.05427	0.18	0.14	0.8	0.7	5	800	0.103355	171.1979	62.43475
1000	5	0.04866	0.18	0.14	0.83333	0.7	5	800	0.081982	233.6326	64.46977
1000	6	0.04464	0.18	0.14	0.85714	0.7	5	800	0.060453	298.1024	68.26526
1000	7	0.0416	0.18	0.14	0.875	0.7	5	800	0.038822	366.3677	73.42597
1000	8	0.03924	0.18	0.14	0.88889	0.7	5	800	0.017124	439.7936	79.82524
1000	9	0.03734	0.18	0.14	0.9	0.7	5	800	−0.00462	519.6189	87.47314
1000	10	0.03578	0.18	0.14	0.90909	0.7	5	800	−0.0264	607.092	

So, *two very important qualitatively new effects in investments has been discovered:*

1. change the character of NPV dependence on leverage;
2. growth of the efficiency of the investments with growth of tax on profit rate.

Both effects could be used in practice to optimize the investments.

Table 19.27 Dependence of NPV and ΔNPV on leverage level *L* at fixed levels of tax on profit rates t for 5-year project at t = 0.8

I	L	WACC	Ko	Kd	Wd	t	n	NOI	Ke	NPV	ΔNPV
1000	0	0.18	0.18	0.14	0	0.8	5	800	0.18	−499.653	221.1945
1000	1	0.09181	0.18	0.14	0.5	0.8	5	800	0.155616	−278.458	103.2179
1000	2	0.06064	0.18	0.14	0.66667	0.8	5	800	0.125907	−175.24	78.69376
1000	3	0.04464	0.18	0.14	0.75	0.8	5	800	0.094544	−96.5465	73.65304
1000	4	0.03489	0.18	0.14	0.8	0.8	5	800	0.062454	−22.8934	76.11182
1000	5	0.02833	0.18	0.14	0.83333	0.8	5	800	0.029979	53.21839	82.93806
1000	6	0.02361	0.18	0.14	0.85714	0.8	5	800	−0.00272	136.1565	93.28915
1000	7	0.02005	0.18	0.14	0.875	0.8	5	800	−0.03557	229.4456	107.1925
1000	8	0.01728	0.18	0.14	0.88889	0.8	5	800	−0.06852	336.6381	125.1636
1000	9	0.01505	0.18	0.14	0.9	0.8	5	800	−0.10154	461.8017	148.1245
1000	10	0.01322	0.18	0.14	0.90909	0.8	5	800	−0.13462	609.9262	

Table 19.28 Dependence of NPV and ΔNPV on leverage level *L* at fixed levels of tax on profit rates t for 5-year project at t = 0.9

I	L	WACC	Ko	Kd	Wd	t	n	NOI	Ke	NPV	ΔNPV
1000	0	0.18	0.18	0.14	0	0.9	5	800	0.18	−749.826	236.5329
1000	1	0.08024	0.18	0.14	0.5	0.9	5	800	0.14648	−513.293	100.4127
1000	2	0.04464	0.18	0.14	0.66667	0.9	5	800	0.105908	−412.881	71.49601
1000	3	0.02627	0.18	0.14	0.75	0.9	5	800	0.063074	−341.385	65.36206
1000	4	0.01505	0.18	0.14	0.8	0.9	5	800	0.019228	−276.023	68.55205
1000	5	0.00747	0.18	0.14	0.83333	0.9	5	800	−0.02516	−207.471	77.93497
1000	6	0.00202	0.18	0.14	0.85714	0.9	5	800	−0.06987	−129.536	93.29474
1000	7	−0.0021	0.18	0.14	0.875	0.9	5	800	−0.11479	−36.2409	115.8841
1000	8	−0.0053	0.18	0.14	0.88889	0.9	5	800	−0.15985	79.64322	148.3017
1000	9	−0.0079	0.18	0.14	0.9	0.9	5	800	−0.20501	227.945	194.9563
1000	10	−0.01	0.18	0.14	0.90909	0.9	5	800	−0.25024	422.9012	

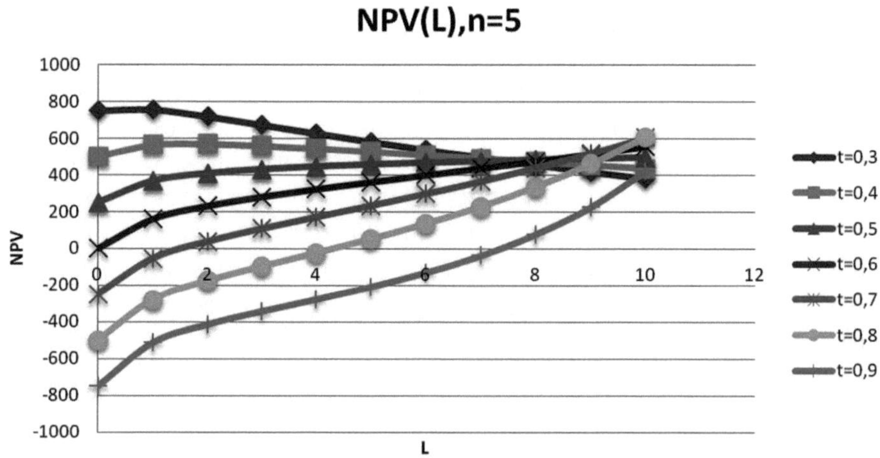

Fig. 19.7 Dependence of NPV on leverage level *L* at fixed levels of tax on profit rates t for 5-year project

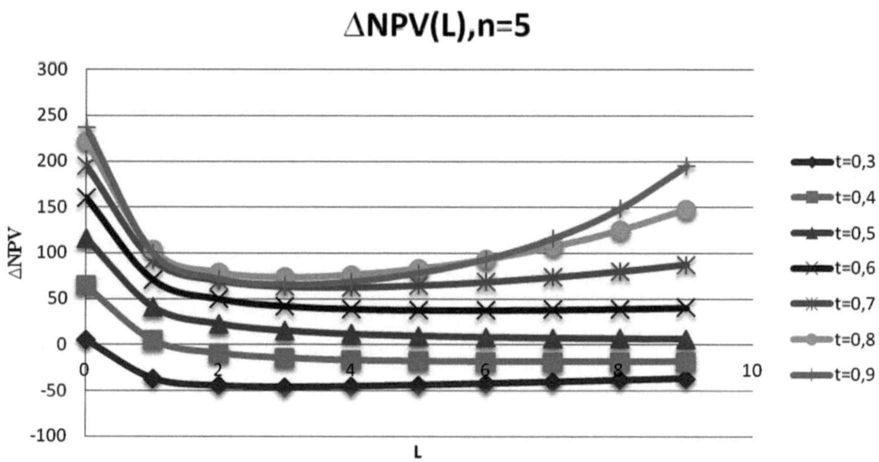

Fig. 19.8 Dependence of ΔNPV on leverage level *L* at fixed levels of tax on profit rates t for 5-year project

Table 19.29 Dependence of NPV and ΔNPV on leverage level L at fixed levels of tax on profit rates t for 10-year project at t = 0.3

I	L	WACC	Ko	Kd	Wd	t	n	NOI	Ke	NPV	ΔNPV
1000	0	0.18	0.18	0.14	0	0.3	10	800	0.18	1520.688	−51.935
1000	1	0.14854	0.18	0.14	0.5	0.3	10	800	0.19907	1464.753	−101.47
1000	2	0.13773	0.18	0.14	0.66667	0.3	10	800	0.217182	1363.283	−104.843
1000	3	0.13226	0.18	0.14	0.75	0.3	10	800	0.235022	1258.441	−100.263
1000	4	0.12895	0.18	0.14	0.8	0.3	10	800	0.252747	1158.178	−93.8156
1000	5	0.12674	0.18	0.14	0.83333	0.3	10	800	0.270413	1064.362	−87.1129
1000	6	0.12515	0.18	0.14	0.85714	0.3	10	800	0.288045	977.2493	−80.6768
1000	7	0.12396	0.18	0.14	0.875	0.3	10	800	0.305654	896.5725	−74.6812
1000	8	0.12303	0.18	0.14	0.88889	0.3	10	800	0.323249	821.8913	−69.1705
1000	9	0.12228	0.18	0.14	0.9	0.3	10	800	0.340834	752.7207	−64.1369
1000	10	0.12167	0.18	0.14	0.90909	0.3	10	800	0.358411	688.5839	

Table 19.30 Dependence of NPV and ΔNPV on leverage level L at fixed levels of tax on profit rates t for 10-year project at t = 0.4

I	L	WACC	Ko	Kd	Wd	t	n	NOI	Ke	NPV	ΔNPV
1000	0	0.18	0.18	0.14	0	0.4	10	800	0.18	1157.161	61.10029
1000	1	0.13773	0.18	0.14	0.5	0.4	10	800	0.191455	1218.262	−18.517
1000	2	0.12303	0.18	0.14	0.66667	0.4	10	800	0.201083	1199.745	−35.7995
1000	3	0.11554	0.18	0.14	0.75	0.4	10	800	0.210169	1163.945	−41.1321
1000	4	0.111	0.18	0.14	0.8	0.4	10	800	0.21902	1122.813	−42.6427
1000	5	0.10796	0.18	0.14	0.83333	0.4	10	800	0.22775	1080.17	−42.6081
1000	6	0.10577	0.18	0.14	0.85714	0.4	10	800	0.236408	1037.562	−41.8669
1000	7	0.10413	0.18	0.14	0.875	0.4	10	800	0.24502	995.6955	−40.7844
1000	8	0.10284	0.18	0.14	0.88889	0.4	10	800	0.253602	954.9111	−39.5386
1000	9	0.10182	0.18	0.14	0.9	0.4	10	800	0.262161	915.3725	−38.2228
1000	10	0.10097	0.18	0.14	0.90909	0.4	10	800	0.270705	877.1497	

Table 19.31 Dependence of NPV and ΔNPV on leverage level *L* at fixed levels of tax on profit rates t for 10-year project at t = 0.5

I	L	WACC	Ko	Kd	Wd	t	n	NOI	Ke	NPV	ΔNPV
1000	0	0.18	0.18	0.14	0	0.5	10	800	0.18	797.6345	−44.2013
1000	1	0.14484	0.20056	0.14	0.5	0.5	10	800	0.219687	753.4333	−104.707
1000	2	0.13178	0.20836	0.14	0.66667	0.5	10	800	0.255351	648.7259	−103.671
1000	3	0.125	0.21253	0.14	0.75	0.5	10	800	0.290005	545.0552	−93.6005
1000	4	0.12084	0.21513	0.14	0.8	0.5	10	800	0.32421	451.4547	−82.6797
1000	5	0.11803	0.2169	0.14	0.83333	0.5	10	800	0.358168	368.775	−72.7174
1000	6	0.116	0.21819	0.14	0.85714	0.5	10	800	0.391982	296.0576	−64.0269
1000	7	0.11446	0.21917	0.14	0.875	0.5	10	800	0.425702	232.0307	−56.5734
1000	8	0.11326	0.21994	0.14	0.88889	0.5	10	800	0.459362	175.4573	−50.1953
1000	9	0.1123	0.22055	0.14	0.9	0.5	10	800	0.492979	125.262	−44.7383
1000	10	0.11151	0.22106	0.14	0.90909	0.5	10	800	0.526564	80.52365	

Table 19.32 Dependence of NPV and ΔNPV on leverage level *L* at fixed levels of tax on profit rates t for 10-year project at t = 0.6

I	L	WACC	Ko	Kd	Wd	t	n	NOI	Kc	NPV	ΔNPV
1000	0	0.18	0.18	0.14	0	0.6	10	800	0.18	438.1076	244.5668
1000	1	0.11554	0.18	0.14	0.5	0.6	10	800	0.175084	682.6744	125.4304
1000	2	0.09247	0.18	0.14	0.66667	0.6	10	800	0.165407	808.1048	101.3662
1000	3	0.08054	0.18	0.14	0.75	0.6	10	800	0.154162	909.471	95.93652
1000	4	0.07324	0.18	0.14	0.8	0.6	10	800	0.142206	1005.408	97.02629
1000	5	0.06831	0.18	0.14	0.83333	0.6	10	800	0.129869	1102.434	101.3309
1000	6	0.06476	0.18	0.14	0.85714	0.6	10	800	0.117304	1203.765	107.7015
1000	7	0.06207	0.18	0.14	0.875	0.6	10	800	0.10459	1311.466	115.7055
1000	8	0.05998	0.18	0.14	0.88889	0.6	10	800	0.091775	1427.172	125.2046
1000	9	0.05829	0.18	0.14	0.9	0.6	10	800	0.078888	1552.376	136.2059
1000	10	0.0569	0.18	0.14	0.90909	0.6	10	800	0.065947	1688.582	

Table 19.33 Dependence of NPV and ΔNPV on leverage level *L* at fixed levels of tax on profit rates t for 10-year project at t = 0.7

I	L	WACC	Ko	Kd	Wd	t	n	NOI	Ke	NPV	ΔNPV
1000	0	0.18	0.18	0.14	0	0.7	10	800	0.18	78.58071	310.4744
1000	1	0.10413	0.18	0.14	0.5	0.7	10	800	0.166255	389.0551	177.1979
1000	2	0.0765	0.18	0.14	0.66667	0.7	10	800	0.145497	566.253	160.5402
1000	3	0.06207	0.18	0.14	0.75	0.7	10	800	0.122295	726.7932	169.9063
1000	4	0.05319	0.18	0.14	0.8	0.7	10	800	0.097953	896.6995	191.9196
1000	5	0.04716	0.18	0.14	0.83333	0.7	10	800	0.072986	1088.619	224.1724
1000	6	0.04281	0.18	0.14	0.85714	0.7	10	800	0.04764	1312.791	267.4019
1000	7	0.03951	0.18	0.14	0.875	0.7	10	800	0.022047	1580.193	323.9861
1000	8	0.03692	0.18	0.14	0.88889	0.7	10	800	−0.00372	1904.18	397.7601
1000	9	0.03484	0.18	0.14	0.9	0.7	10	800	−0.0296	2301.94	494.3094
1000	10	0.03313	0.18	0.14	0.90909	0.7	10	800	−0.05558	2796.249	

Table 19.34 Dependence of NPV and ΔNPV on leverage level *L* at fixed levels of tax on profit rates t for 10-year project at t = 0.8

I	L	WACC	Ko	Kd	Wd	t	n	NOI	Ke	NPV	ΔNPV
1000	0	0.18	0.18	0.14	0	0.8	10	800	0.18	−280.946	355.2633
1000	1	0.09247	0.18	0.14	0.5	0.8	10	800	0.156938	74.31716	204.8466
1000	2	0.05998	0.18	0.14	0.66667	0.8	10	800	0.123925	279.1638	198.4863
1000	3	0.04281	0.18	0.14	0.75	0.8	10	800	0.087223	477.6501	232.7806
1000	4	0.03215	0.18	0.14	0.8	0.8	10	800	0.048741	710.4306	297.8303
1000	5	0.02488	0.18	0.14	0.83333	0.8	10	800	0.009262	1008.261	400.9259
1000	6	0.0196	0.18	0.14	0.85714	0.8	10	800	−0.03083	1409.187	560.3743
1000	7	0.01558	0.18	0.14	0.875	0.8	10	800	−0.07133	1969.561	809.4944
1000	8	0.01243	0.18	0.14	0.88889	0.8	10	800	−0.11211	2779.056	1207.425
1000	9	0.00989	0.18	0.14	0.9	0.8	10	800	−0.1531	3986.481	1861.112
1000	10	0.0078	0.18	0.14	0.90909	0.8	10	800	−0.19424	5847.593	

Table 19.35 Dependence of NPV and ΔNPV on leverage level L at fixed levels of tax on profit rates t for 10-year project at t = 0.9

I	L	WACC	Ko	Kd	Wd	t	n	NOI	Ke	NPV	ΔNPV
1000	0	0.18	0.18	0.14	0	0.9	10	800	0.18	−640.473	375.0978
1000	1	0.08054	0.18	0.14	0.5	0.9	10	800	0.147081	−265.375	194.2145
1000	2	0.04281	0.18	0.14	0.66667	0.9	10	800	0.100417	−71.1609	186.9461
1000	3	0.02258	0.18	0.14	0.75	0.9	10	800	0.048303	115.7852	239.586
1000	4	0.00989	0.18	0.14	0.8	0.9	10	800	−0.00655	355.3712	356.4744
1000	5	0.00117	0.18	0.14	0.83333	0.9	10	800	−0.06297	711.8456	583.6021
1000	6	−0.0052	0.18	0.14	0.85714	0.9	10	800	−0.12039	1295.448	1032.383
1000	7	−0.0101	0.18	0.14	0.875	0.9	10	800	−0.17847	2327.831	1967.211
1000	8	−0.0139	0.18	0.14	0.88889	0.9	10	800	−0.23701	4295.041	4054.338
1000	9	−0.017	0.18	0.14	0.9	0.9	10	800	−0.2959	8349.379	9115.336
1000	10	−0.0195	0.18	0.14	0.90909	0.9	10	800	−0.35504	17,464.72	

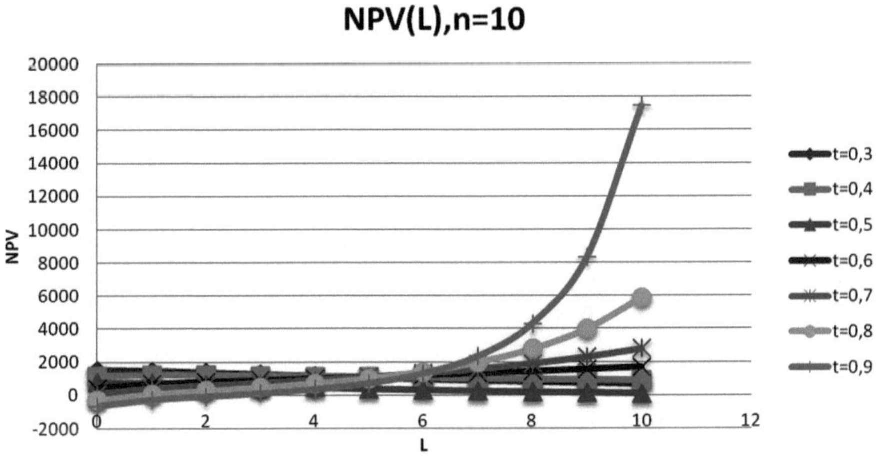

Fig. 19.9 Dependence of NPV on leverage level L at fixed levels of tax on profit rates t for 5-year project

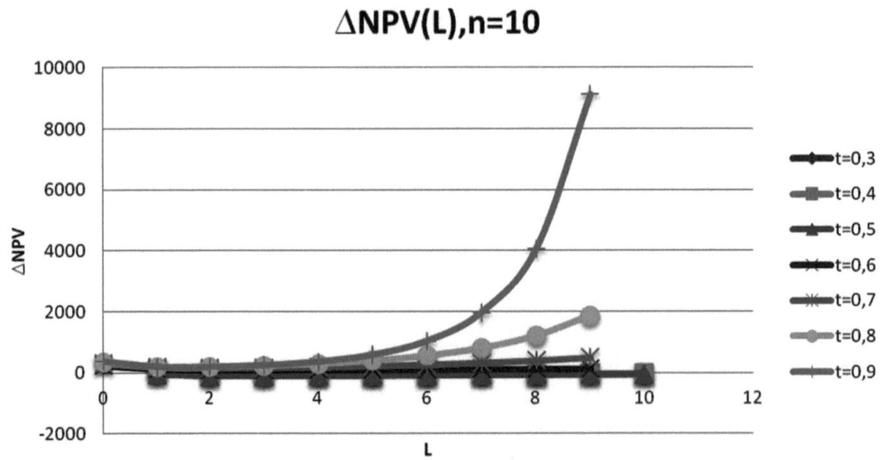

Fig. 19.10 Dependence of ΔNPV on leverage level *L* at fixed levels of tax on profit rates t for 5-year project

Table 19.36 Dependence of NPV and ΔNPV on tax on profit rate t at fixed leverage level *L* for 5-year project at L = 0

I	L	WACC	Ko	Kd	Wd	t	n	NOI	Ke	NPV	ΔNPV
1000	0	0.18	0.18	0.14	0	0	5	800	0.18	1501.74	−250.174
1000	0	0.18	0.18	0.14	0	0.1	5	800	0.18	1251.56	−250.174
1000	0	0.18	0.18	0.14	0	0.2	5	800	0.18	1001.39	−250.174
1000	0	0.18	0.18	0.14	0	0.3	5	800	0.18	751.22	−250.174
1000	0	0.18	0.18	0.14	0	0.4	5	800	0.18	501.04	−250.174
1000	0	0.18	0.18	0.14	0	0.5	5	800	0.18	250.87	−250.174
1000	0	0.18	0.18	0.14	0	0.6	5	800	0.18	0.69	−250.174
1000	0	0.18	0.18	0.14	0	0.7	5	800	0.18	−249.48	−250.174
1000	0	0.18	0.18	0.14	0	0.8	5	800	0.18	−499.65	−250.174
1000	0	0.18	0.18	0.14	0	0.9	5	800	0.18	−749.83	−250.174
1000	0	0.18	0.18	0.14	0	1	5	800	0.18	−1000.00	

Table 19.37 Dependence of NPV and ΔNPV on tax on profit rate t at fixed leverage level *L* for 5-year project at L = 2

I	L	WACC	Ko	Kd	Wd	t	n	NOI	Ke	NPV	ΔNPV
1000	2	0.18	0.18	0.14	0.66667	0	5	800	0.26	1108.06	−128.983
1000	2	0.16577	0.18	0.14	0.66667	0.1	5	800	0.245315	987.07	−129.204
1000	2	0.15137	0.18	0.14	0.66667	0.2	5	800	0.230116	857.87	−138.59
1000	2	0.13679	0.18	0.14	0.66667	0.3	5	800	0.214367	719.28	−149.372
1000	2	0.12201	0.18	0.14	0.66667	0.4	5	800	0.19803	569.91	−161.839
1000	2	0.10702	0.18	0.14	0.66667	0.5	5	800	0.181065	408.07	−176.357
1000	2	0.09181	0.18	0.14	0.66667	0.6	5	800	0.163424	231.71	−193.394
1000	2	0.07635	0.18	0.14	0.66667	0.7	5	800	0.145057	38.32	−213.557
1000	2	0.06064	0.18	0.14	0.66667	0.8	5	800	0.125907	−175.24	−237.64
1000	2	0.04464	0.18	0.14	0.66667	0.9	5	800	0.105908	−412.88	−266.698
1000	2	0.02833	0.18	0.14	0.66667	1	5	800	0.084989	−679.58	

Table 19.38 Dependence of NPV and ΔNPV on tax on profit rate t at fixed leverage level *L* for 5-year project at L = 4

I	L	WACC	Ko	Kd	Wd	t	n	NOI	Ke	NPV	ΔNPV
1000	4	0.18	0.18	0.14	0.8	0	5	800	0.34	808.33	−51.044
1000	4	0.16291	0.18	0.14	0.8	0.1	5	800	0.31053	757.29	−59.2842
1000	4	0.14556	0.18	0.14	0.8	0.2	5	800	0.279807	698.00	−69.6148
1000	4	0.12795	0.18	0.14	0.8	0.3	5	800	0.24773	628.39	−82.763
1000	4	0.11004	0.18	0.14	0.8	0.4	5	800	0.214184	545.62	−99.7794
1000	4	0.09181	0.18	0.14	0.8	0.5	5	800	0.179041	445.84	−122.217
1000	4	0.07323	0.18	0.14	0.8	0.6	5	800	0.142153	323.63	−152.429
1000	4	0.05427	0.18	0.14	0.8	0.7	5	800	0.103355	171.20	−194.091
1000	4	0.03489	0.18	0.14	0.8	0.8	5	800	0.062454	−22.89	−253.129
1000	4	0.01505	0.18	0.14	0.8	0.9	5	800	0.019228	−276.02	−339.472
1000	4	−0.0053	0.18	0.14	0.8	1	5	800	−0.02658	−615.49	

Table 19.39 Dependence of NPV and ΔNPV on tax on profit rate t at fixed leverage level L for 5-year project at L = 6

I	L	WACC	Ko	Kd	Wd	t	n	NOI	Ke	NPV	ΔNPV
1000	6	0.18	0.18	0.14	0.85714	0	5	800	0.42	574.85	−6.23744
1000	6	0.16168	0.18	0.14	0.85714	0.1	5	800	0.375729	568.61	−11.31
1000	6	0.14306	0.18	0.14	0.85714	0.2	5	800	0.329434	557.30	−18.3975
1000	6	0.12413	0.18	0.14	0.85714	0.3	5	800	0.280937	538.90	−28.5544
1000	6	0.10486	0.18	0.14	0.85714	0.4	5	800	0.230037	510.35	−43.5294
1000	6	0.08522	0.18	0.14	0.85714	0.5	5	800	0.176505	466.82	−66.3335
1000	6	0.06515	0.18	0.14	0.85714	0.6	5	800	0.120078	400.49	−102.385
1000	6	0.04464	0.18	0.14	0.85714	0.7	5	800	0.060453	298.10	−161.946
1000	6	0.02361	0.18	0.14	0.85714	0.8	5	800	−0.00272	136.16	−265.692
1000	6	0.00202	0.18	0.14	0.85714	0.9	5	800	−0.06987	−129.54	−458.495
1000	6	−0.0202	0.18	0.14	0.85714	1	5	800	−0.14147	−588.03	

Table 19.40 Dependence of NPV and ΔNPV on tax on profit rate t at fixed leverage level L for 5-year project at L = 8

I	L	WACC	Ko	Kd	Wd	t	n	NOI	Ke	NPV	ΔNPV
1000	8	0.18	0.18	0.14	0.88889	0	5	800	0.5	389.30	23.47489
1000	8	0.16099	0.18	0.14	0.88889	0.1	5	800	0.440923	412.78	22.6083
1000	8	0.14167	0.18	0.14	0.88889	0.2	5	800	0.379039	435.38	28.71462
1000	8	0.12201	0.18	0.14	0.88889	0.3	5	800	0.314091	456.10	28.88106
1000	8	0.10198	0.18	0.14	0.88889	0.4	5	800	0.245786	472.98	9.298693
1000	8	0.08153	0.18	0.14	0.88889	0.5	5	800	0.173792	482.28	−5.79258
1000	8	0.06064	0.18	0.14	0.88889	0.6	5	800	0.097721	476.49	−36.6918
1000	8	0.03924	0.18	0.14	0.88889	0.7	5	800	0.017124	439.79	−103.156
1000	8	0.01728	0.18	0.14	0.88889	0.8	5	800	−0.06852	336.64	−256.995
1000	8	−0.0053	0.18	0.14	0.88889	0.9	5	800	−0.15985	79.64	−652.415
1000	8	−0.0286	0.18	0.14	0.88889	1	5	800	−0.25759	−572.77	

Table 19.41 Dependence of NPV and ΔNPV on tax on profit rate t at fixed leverage level *L* for 5-year project at L = 10

I	L	WACC	Ko	Kd	Wd	t	n	NOI	Ke	NPV	ΔNPV
1000	10	0.18	0.18	0.14	0.90909	0	5	800	0.58	239.23	43.49836
1000	10	0.16056	0.18	0.14	0.90909	0.1	5	800	0.506115	282.73	46.87962
1000	10	0.14078	0.18	0.14	0.90909	0.2	5	800	0.428635	329.61	50.87829
1000	10	0.12066	0.18	0.14	0.90909	0.3	5	800	0.34722	380.49	55.32552
1000	10	0.10014	0.18	0.14	0.90909	0.4	5	800	0.261488	435.81	59.47085
1000	10	0.07918	0.18	0.14	0.90909	0.5	5	800	0.170996	495.28	60.76747
1000	10	0.05775	0.18	0.14	0.90909	0.6	5	800	0.075231	556.05	51.04171
1000	10	0.03578	0.18	0.14	0.90909	0.7	5	800	−0.0264	607.09	2.834166
1000	10	0.01322	0.18	0.14	0.90909	0.8	5	800	−0.13462	609.93	−187.024
1000	10	−0.01	0.18	0.14	0.90909	0.9	5	800	−0.25024	422.90	−985.964
1000	10	−0.034	0.18	0.14	0.90909	1	5	800	−0.37429	−563.06	

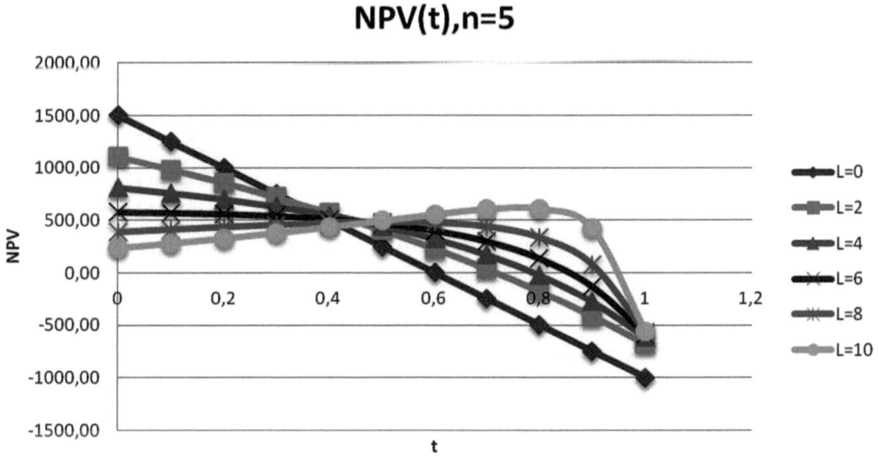

Fig. 19.11 Dependence of NPV on tax on profit rate t at fixed leverage level *L* for 5-year project

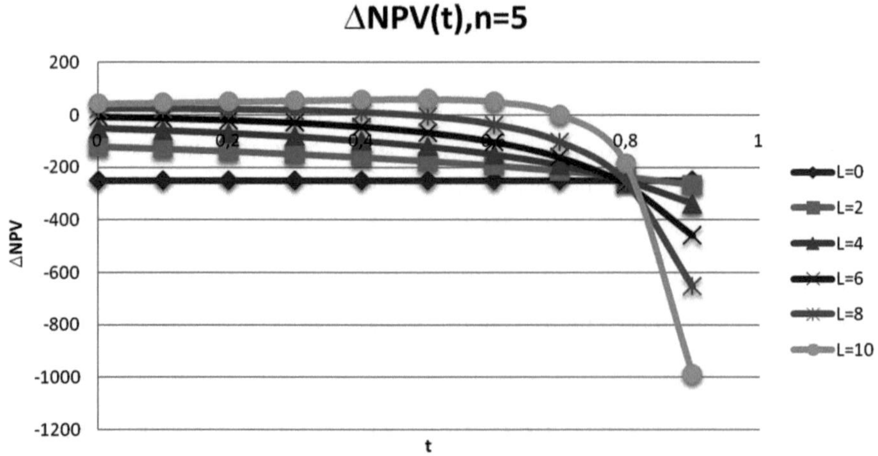

Fig. 19.12 Dependence of ΔNPV on tax on profit rate t at fixed leverage level *L* for 5-year project

Table 19.42 Dependence of NPV and ΔNPV on tax on profit rate t at fixed leverage level *L* for 10-year project at L = 0

I	L	WACC	Ko	Kd	Wd	t	n	NOI	Ke	NPV	ΔNPV
1000	0	0.18	0.18	0.14	0	0	10	800	0.18	2595.27	−359.527
1000	0	0.18	0.18	0.14	0	0.1	10	800	0.18	2235.74	−359.527
1000	0	0.18	0.18	0.14	0	0.2	10	800	0.18	1876.22	−359.527
1000	0	0.18	0.18	0.14	0	0.3	10	800	0.18	1520.69	−359.527
1000	0	0.18	0.18	0.14	0	0.4	10	800	0.18	1157.16	−359.527
1000	0	0.18	0.18	0.14	0	0.5	10	800	0.18	797.63	−359.527
1000	0	0.18	0.18	0.14	0	0.6	10	800	0.18	438.11	−359.527
1000	0	0.18	0.18	0.14	0	0.7	10	800	0.18	78.58	−359.527
1000	0	0.18	0.18	0.14	0	0.8	10	800	0.18	−280.95	−359.527
1000	0	0.18	0.18	0.14	0	0.9	10	800	0.18	−640.47	−359.527
1000	0	0.18	0.18	0.14	0	1	10	800	0.18	−1000.00	

Table 19.43 Dependence of NPV and ΔNPV on tax on profit rate t at fixed leverage level *L* for 10-year project at L = 2

I	L	WACC	Ko	Kd	Wd	t	n	NOI	Ke	NPV	ΔNPV
1000	2	0.18	0.18	0.14	0.66667	0	10	800	0.26	1771.84	−125.137
1000	2	0.16618	0.18	0.14	0.66667	0.1	10	800	0.24654	1646.71	−135.437
1000	2	0.1521	0.18	0.14	0.66667	0.2	10	800	0.232299	1511.27	−147.987
1000	2	0.13773	0.18	0.14	0.66667	0.3	10	800	0.217182	1363.28	−163.538
1000	2	0.12303	0.18	0.14	0.66667	0.4	10	800	0.201083	1199.74	−183.17
1000	2	0.10796	0.18	0.14	0.66667	0.5	10	800	0.183875	1019.58	−208.47
1000	2	0.09247	0.18	0.14	0.66667	0.6	10	800	0.165407	808.10	−241.852
1000	2	0.0765	0.18	0.14	0.66667	0.7	10	800	0.145497	566.25	−287.089
1000	2	0.05998	0.18	0.14	0.66667	0.8	10	800	0.123925	279.16	−350.325
1000	2	0.04281	0.18	0.14	0.66667	0.9	10	800	0.100417	−71.16	−442.002
1000	2	0.02488	0.18	0.14	0.66667	1	10	800	0.074631	−513.16	

Table 19.44 Dependence of NPV and ΔNPV on tax on profit rate t at fixed leverage level *L* for 10 year project at L = 4

I	L	WACC	Ko	Kd	Wd	t	n	NOI	Ke	NPV	ΔNPV
1000	4	0.18	0.18	0.14	0.8	0	10	800	0.34	1226.89	−475.625
1000	4	0.18316	0.20056	0.14	0.8	0.1	10	800	0.411801	751.26	−139.495
1000	4	0.17256	0.20836	0.14	0.8	0.2	10	800	0.414791	611.77	−74.4553
1000	4	0.15772	0.21253	0.14	0.8	0.3	10	800	0.396579	537.31	−54.8815
1000	4	0.14072	0.21513	0.14	0.8	0.4	10	800	0.367589	482.43	−52.0879
1000	4	0.12227	0.2169	0.14	0.8	0.5	10	800	0.331331	430.34	−60.1971
1000	4	0.10261	0.21819	0.14	0.8	0.6	10	800	0.289071	370.14	−80.4792
1000	4	0.08181	0.21917	0.14	0.8	0.7	10	800	0.241069	289.66	−128.753
1000	4	0.0598	0.21994	0.14	0.8	0.8	10	800	0.186991	168.91	−202.021
1000	4	0.0364	0.22055	0.14	0.8	0.9	10	800	0.126013	−33.11	−382.685
1000	4	0.01135	0.22106	0.14	0.8	1	10	800	0.056769	−415.80	

Table 19.45 Dependence of NPV and ΔNPV on tax on profit rate t at fixed leverage level *L* for 10-year project at L = 6

I	L	WACC	Ko	Kd	Wd	t	n	NOI	Ke	NPV	ΔNPV
1000	6	0.18	0.18	0.14	0.85714	0	10	800	0.42	847.62	37.06285
1000	6	0.16218	0.18	0.14	0.85714	0.1	10	800	0.379295	884.68	42.53552
1000	6	0.14392	0.18	0.14	0.85714	0.2	10	800	0.335473	927.22	50.03126
1000	6	0.12515	0.18	0.14	0.85714	0.3	10	800	0.288045	977.25	60.31305
1000	6	0.10577	0.18	0.14	0.85714	0.4	10	800	0.236408	1037.56	74.23617
1000	6	0.08569	0.18	0.14	0.85714	0.5	10	800	0.179813	1111.80	91.96624
1000	6	0.06476	0.18	0.14	0.85714	0.6	10	800	0.117304	1203.76	109.0267
1000	6	0.04281	0.18	0.14	0.85714	0.7	10	800	0.04764	1312.79	96.39537
1000	6	0.0196	0.18	0.14	0.85714	0.8	10	800	−0.03083	1409.19	−113.739
1000	6	−0.0052	0.18	0.14	0.85714	0.9	10	800	−0.12039	1295.45	−1669.51
1000	6	−0.032	0.18	0.14	0.85714	1	10	800	−0.22431	−374.07	

Table 19.46 Dependence of NPV and ΔNPV on tax on profit rate t at fixed leverage level *L* for 10-year project at L = 8

I	L	WACC	Ko	Kd	Wd	t	n	NOI	Ke	NPV	ΔNPV
1000	8	0.18	0.18	0.14	0.88889	0	10	800	0.5	572.25	67.74227
1000	8	0.16152	0.18	0.14	0.88889	0.1	10	800	0.445653	640.00	80.91054
1000	8	0.14255	0.18	0.14	0.88889	0.2	10	800	0.386973	728.91	100.9849
1000	8	0.12303	0.18	0.14	0.88889	0.3	10	800	0.323249	821.89	133.0198
1000	8	0.10284	0.18	0.14	0.88889	0.4	10	800	0.253602	954.91	187.1372
1000	8	0.08188	0.18	0.14	0.88889	0.5	10	800	0.17692	1142.05	285.1235
1000	8	0.05998	0.18	0.14	0.88889	0.6	10	800	0.091775	1427.17	477.0078
1000	8	0.03692	0.18	0.14	0.88889	0.7	10	800	−0.00372	1904.18	874.876
1000	8	0.01243	0.18	0.14	0.88889	0.8	10	800	−0.11211	2779.06	1515.986
1000	8	−0.0139	0.18	0.14	0.88889	0.9	10	800	−0.23701	4295.04	−4645.92
1000	8	−0.0426	0.18	0.14	0.88889	1	10	800	−0.38375	−350.88	

Table 19.47 Dependence of NPV and ΔNPV on tax on profit rate t at fixed leverage level L for 10-year project at L = 10

I	L	WACC	Ko	Kd	Wd	t	n	NOI	Ke	NPV	ΔNPV
1000	10	0.18	0.18	0.14	0.90909	0	10	800	0.58	365.08	85.01433
1000	10	0.16109	0.18	0.14	0.90909	0.1	10	800	0.512008	450.10	103.8568
1000	10	0.14168	0.18	0.14	0.90909	0.2	10	800	0.438456	553.96	134.6286
1000	10	0.12167	0.18	0.14	0.90909	0.3	10	800	0.358411	688.58	188.5659
1000	10	0.10097	0.18	0.14	0.90909	0.4	10	800	0.270705	877.15	292.3814
1000	10	0.07944	0.18	0.14	0.90909	0.5	10	800	0.173857	1169.53	519.0512
1000	10	0.0569	0.18	0.14	0.90909	0.6	10	800	0.065947	1688.58	1107.667
1000	10	0.03313	0.18	0.14	0.90909	0.7	10	800	−0.05558	2796.25	3051.344
1000	10	0.0078	0.18	0.14	0.90909	0.8	10	800	−0.19424	5847.59	11,617.12
1000	10	−0.0195	0.18	0.14	0.90909	0.9	10	800	−0.35504	17,464.71	−17,800.8
1000	10	−0.0496	0.18	0.14	0.90909	1	10	800	−0.54557	−336.13	

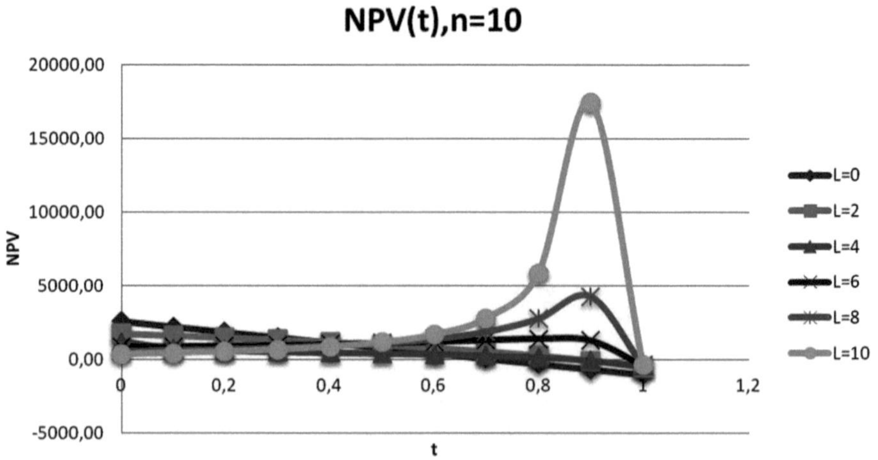

Fig. 19.13 Dependence of NPV on tax on profit rate t at fixed leverage level *L* for 10-year project

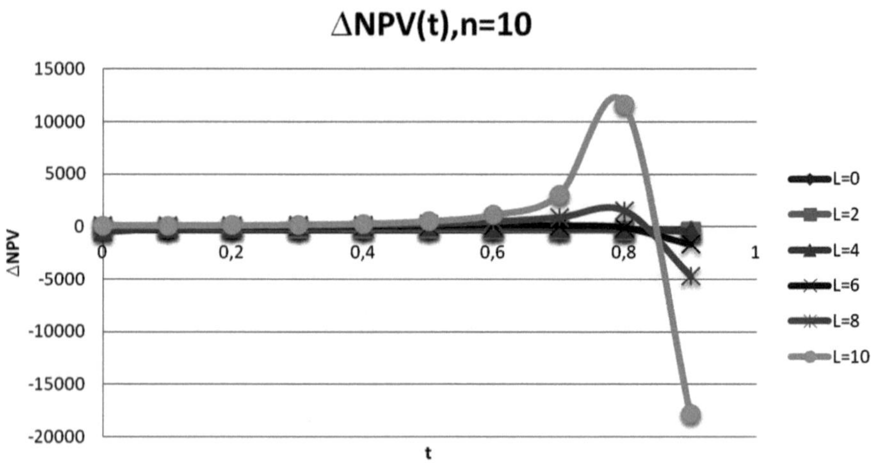

Fig. 19.14 Dependence of ΔNPV on tax on profit rate t at fixed leverage level *L* for 10-year project

Table 19.48 Dependence of NPV and ΔNPV on tax on profit rate t at fixed leverage level *L* for perpetuity project at L = 8

t	L	k0	kd	I	NOI	NPV	ΔNPV
0	8	0.18	0.14	1000	800	−32,111.1	−5003.72
0.1	8	0.18	0.14	1000	800	−37,114.8	−7713.12
0.2	8	0.18	0.14	1000	800	−44,828	−12,659.2
0.3	8	0.18	0.14	1000	800	−57,487.2	−23,580
0.4	8	0.18	0.14	1000	800	−81,067.2	−57,266.1
0.5	8	0.18	0.14	1000	800	−138,333	−326,333
0.6	8	0.18	0.14	1000	800	−464,667	816,960.8
0.7	8	0.18	0.14	1000	800	352,294.1	−222,466
0.8	8	0.18	0.14	1000	800	129,819.3	−49,261
0.9	8	0.18	0.14	1000	800	80,567.25	−21,567.3
1	8	0.18	0.14	1000	800	59,000	

Table 19.49 Dependence of NPV and ΔNPV on tax on profit rate t at fixed leverage level *L* for perpetuity project at L = 10

t	L	k0	kd	I	NOI	NPV	ΔNPV
0	10	0.18	0.14	1000	800	−41,000	−9090.91
0.1	10	0.18	0.14	1000	800	−50,090.9	−15,909.1
0.2	10	0.18	0.14	1000	800	−66,000	−32,692.3
0.3	10	0.18	0.14	1000	800	−98,692.3	−99,450.5
0.4	10	0.18	0.14	1000	800	−198,143	−8.6E + 19
0.5	10	0.18	0.14	1000	800	−8.6E + 19	8.65E + 19
0.6	10	0.18	0.14	1000	800	202,750	−99,632.4
0.7	10	0.18	0.14	1000	800	103,117.6	−33,006.5
0.8	10	0.18	0.14	1000	800	70,111.11	−16,374.3
0.9	10	0.18	0.14	1000	800	53,736.84	−9736.84
1	10	0.18	0.14	1000	800	44,000	

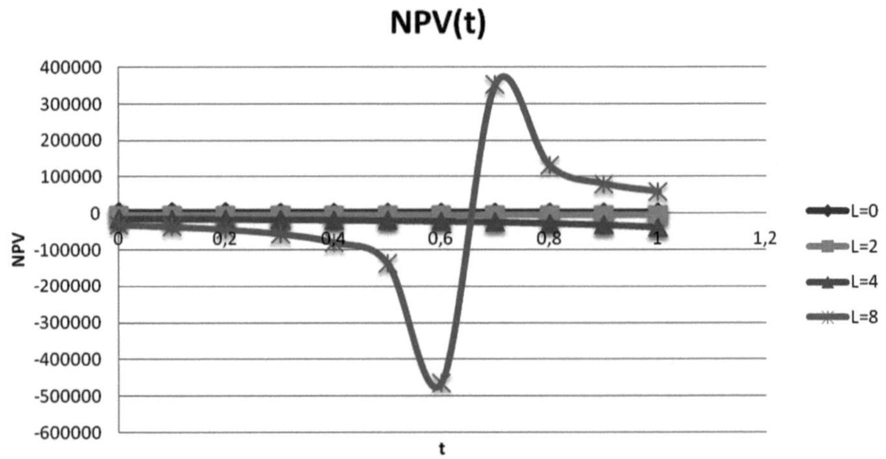

Fig. 19.15 Dependence of ΔNPV on tax on profit rate t at fixed leverage level *L* for perpetuity project

Table 19.50 Dependence of NPV and ΔNPV on tax on profit rate t at fixed leverage level *L* for 5-year project at L = 0

I	L	WACC	Ko	Kd	Wd	t	n	NOI	Ke	NPV	ΔNPV
1000	0	0.18	0.18	0.14	0	0	5	800	0.18	1501.737	−250.174
1000	0	0.18	0.18	0.14	0	0.1	5	800	0.18	1251.563	−250.174
1000	0	0.18	0.18	0.14	0	0.2	5	800	0.18	1001.389	−250.174
1000	0	0.18	0.18	0.14	0	0.3	5	800	0.18	751.2158	−250.174
1000	0	0.18	0.18	0.14	0	0.4	5	800	0.18	501.0421	−250.174
1000	0	0.18	0.18	0.14	0	0.5	5	800	0.18	250.8684	−250.174
1000	0	0.18	0.18	0.14	0	0.6	5	800	0.18	0.694727	−250.174
1000	0	0.18	0.18	0.14	0	0.7	5	800	0.18	−249.479	−250.174
1000	0	0.18	0.18	0.14	0	0.8	5	800	0.18	−499.653	−250.174
1000	0	0.18	0.18	0.14	0	0.9	5	800	0.18	−749.826	−250.174
1000	0	0.18	0.18	0.14	0	1	5	800	0.18	−1000	

Table 19.51 Dependence of NPV and ΔNPV on tax on profit rate t at fixed leverage level *L* for 5-year project at L = 2

I	L	WACC	Ko	Kd	Wd	t	n	NOI	Ke	NPV	ΔNPV
1000	2	0.18	0.18	0.14	0.66667	0	5	800	0.26	1108.057	−128.983
1000	2	0.16577	0.18	0.14	0.66667	0.1	5	800	0.245315	987.0733	−129.204
1000	2	0.15137	0.18	0.14	0.66667	0.2	5	800	0.230116	857.869	−138.59
1000	2	0.13679	0.18	0.14	0.66667	0.3	5	800	0.214367	719.2786	−149.372
1000	2	0.12201	0.18	0.14	0.66667	0.4	5	800	0.19803	569.9064	−161.839
1000	2	0.10702	0.18	0.14	0.66667	0.5	5	800	0.181065	408.0676	−176.357
1000	2	0.09181	0.18	0.14	0.66667	0.6	5	800	0.163424	231.711	−193.394
1000	2	0.07635	0.18	0.14	0.66667	0.7	5	800	0.145057	38.31702	−213.557
1000	2	0.06064	0.18	0.14	0.66667	0.8	5	800	0.125907	−175.24	−237.64
1000	2	0.04464	0.18	0.14	0.66667	0.9	5	800	0.105908	−412.881	−266.698
1000	2	0.02833	0.18	0.14	0.66667	1	5	800	0.084989	−679.579	

Table 19.52 Dependence of NPV and ΔNPV on tax on profit rate t at fixed leverage level *L* for 5-year project at L = 4

I	L	WACC	Ko	Kd	Wd	t	n	NOI	Ke	NPV	ΔNPV
1000	4	0.18	0.18	0.14	0.8	0	5	800	0.34	808.3293	−51.044
1000	4	0.16291	0.18	0.14	0.8	0.1	5	800	0.31053	757.2853	−59.2842
1000	4	0.14556	0.18	0.14	0.8	0.2	5	800	0.279807	698.0011	−69.6148
1000	4	0.12795	0.18	0.14	0.8	0.3	5	800	0.24773	628.3863	−82.763
1000	4	0.11004	0.18	0.14	0.8	0.4	5	800	0.214184	545.6233	−99.7794
1000	4	0.09181	0.18	0.14	0.8	0.5	5	800	0.179041	445.8439	−122.217
1000	4	0.07323	0.18	0.14	0.8	0.6	5	800	0.142153	323.6272	−152.429
1000	4	0.05427	0.18	0.14	0.8	0.7	5	800	0.103355	171.1979	−194.091
1000	4	0.03489	0.18	0.14	0.8	0.8	5	800	0.062454	−22.8934	−253.129
1000	4	0.01505	0.18	0.14	0.8	0.9	5	800	0.019228	−276.023	−339.472
1000	4	−0.0053	0.18	0.14	0.8	1	5	800	−0.02658	−615.495	

Table 19.53 Dependence of NPV and ΔNPV on tax on profit rate t at fixed leverage level *L* for 5-year project at L = 6

I	L	WACC	Ko	Kd	Wd	t	n	NOI	Ke	NPV	ΔNPV
1000	6	0.18	0.18	0.14	0.85714	0	5	800	0.42	574.8492	−6.23744
1000	6	0.16168	0.18	0.14	0.85714	0.1	5	800	0.375729	568.6118	−11.31
1000	6	0.14306	0.18	0.14	0.85714	0.2	5	800	0.329434	557.3019	−18.3975
1000	6	0.12413	0.18	0.14	0.85714	0.3	5	800	0.280937	538.9044	−28.5544
1000	6	0.10486	0.18	0.14	0.85714	0.4	5	800	0.230037	510.3499	−43.5294
1000	6	0.08522	0.18	0.14	0.85714	0.5	5	800	0.176505	466.8205	−66.3335
1000	6	0.06515	0.18	0.14	0.85714	0.6	5	800	0.120078	400.487	−102.385
1000	6	0.04464	0.18	0.14	0.85714	0.7	5	800	0.060453	298.1024	−161.946
1000	6	0.02361	0.18	0.14	0.85714	0.8	5	800	−0.00272	136.1565	−265.692
1000	6	0.00202	0.18	0.14	0.85714	0.9	5	800	−0.06987	−129.536	−458.495
1000	6	−0.0202	0.18	0.14	0.85714	1	5	800	−0.14147	−588.03	

Table 19.54 Dependence of NPV and ΔNPV on tax on profit rate t at fixed leverage level *L* for 5-year project at L = 8

I	L	WACC	Ko	Kd	Wd	t	n	NOI	Ke	NPV	ΔNPV
1000	8	0.18	0.18	0.14	0.88889	0	5	800	0.5	389.3004	23.47489
1000	8	0.16099	0.18	0.14	0.88889	0.1	5	800	0.440923	412.7753	22.6083
1000	8	0.14167	0.18	0.14	0.88889	0.2	5	800	0.379039	435.3836	20.71462
1000	8	0.12201	0.18	0.14	0.88889	0.3	5	800	0.314091	456.0982	20.88106
1000	8	0.10198	0.18	0.14	0.88889	0.4	5	800	0.245786	472.9793	9.298693
1000	8	0.08153	0.18	0.14	0.88889	0.5	5	800	0.173792	482.278	−5.79258
1000	8	0.06064	0.18	0.14	0.88889	0.6	5	800	0.097721	476.4854	−36.6918
1000	8	0.03924	0.18	0.14	0.88889	0.7	5	800	0.017124	439.7936	−103.156
1000	8	0.01728	0.18	0.14	0.88889	0.8	5	800	−0.06852	336.6381	−256.995
1000	8	−0.0053	0.18	0.14	0.88889	0.9	5	800	−0.15985	79.64322	−652.415
1000	8	−0.0286	0.18	0.14	0.88889	1	5	800	−0.25759	−572.772	

Table 19.55 Dependence of NPV and ΔNPV on tax on profit rate t at fixed leverage level L for 5-year project at L = 10

I	L	WACC	Ko	Kd	Wd	t	n	NOI	Ke	NPV	ΔNPV
1000	10	0.18	0.18	0.14	0.90909	0	5	800	0.58	239.2302	43.49836
1000	10	0.16056	0.18	0.14	0.90909	0.1	5	800	0.506115	282.7286	46.87962
1000	10	0.14078	0.18	0.14	0.90909	0.2	5	800	0.428635	329.6082	50.87829
1000	10	0.12066	0.18	0.14	0.90909	0.3	5	800	0.34722	380.4865	55.32552
1000	10	0.10014	0.18	0.14	0.90909	0.4	5	800	0.261488	435.812	59.47085
1000	10	0.07918	0.18	0.14	0.90909	0.5	5	800	0.170996	495.2828	60.76747
1000	10	0.05775	0.18	0.14	0.90909	0.6	5	800	0.075231	556.0503	51.04171
1000	10	0.03578	0.18	0.14	0.90909	0.7	5	800	−0.0264	607.092	2.834166
1000	10	0.01322	0.18	0.14	0.90909	0.8	5	800	−0.13462	609.9262	−187.024
1000	10	−0.01	0.18	0.14	0.90909	0.9	5	800	−0.25024	422.9017	−985.964
1000	10	−0.034	0.18	0.14	0.90909	1	5	800	−0.37429	−563.062	

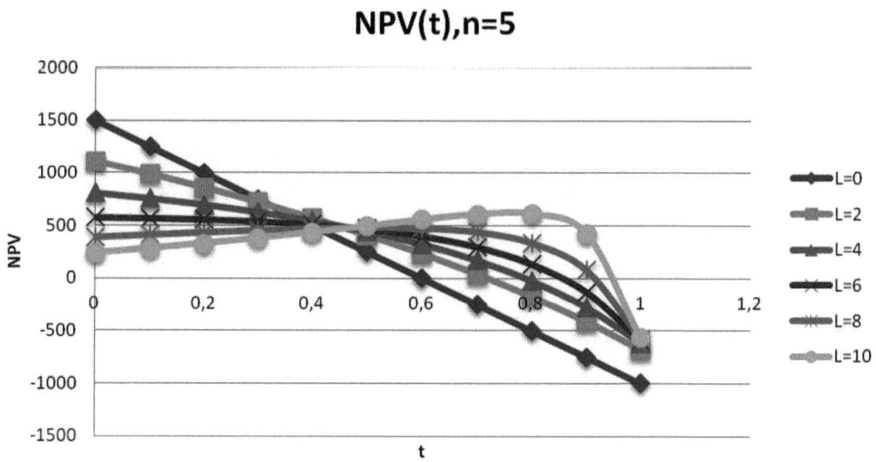

Fig. 19.16 Dependence of NPV on tax on profit rate t at fixed leverage level L for 5-year project

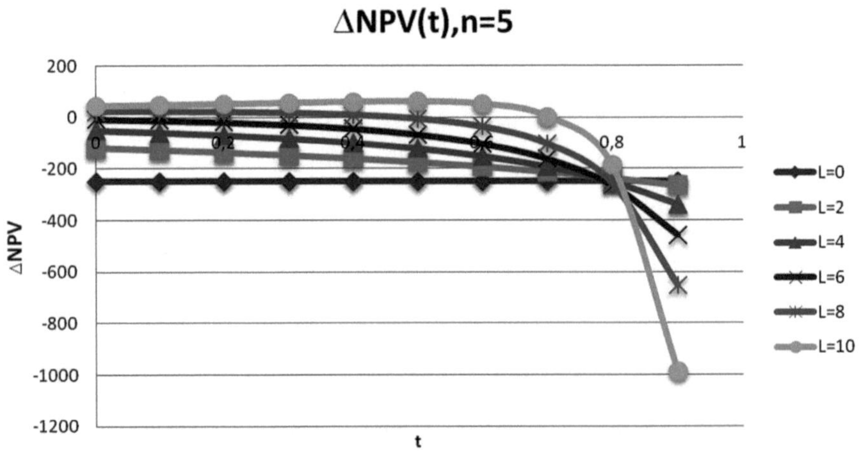

Fig. 19.17 Dependence of ΔNPV on tax on profit rate t at fixed leverage level *L* for 5-year project

Table 19.56 Dependence of NPV and ΔNPV on tax on profit rate t at fixed leverage level *L* for 10-year project at L = 0

I	L	WACC	Ko	Kd	Wd	t	n	NOI	Ke	NPV	ΔNPV
1000	0	0.18	0.18	0.14	0	0	10	800	0.18	2595.269	−359.527
1000	0	0.18	0.18	0.14	0	0.1	10	800	0.18	2235.742	−359.527
1000	0	0.18	0.18	0.14	0	0.2	10	800	0.18	1876.215	−359.527
1000	0	0.18	0.18	0.14	0	0.3	10	800	0.18	1520.688	−359.527
1000	0	0.18	0.18	0.14	0	0.4	10	800	0.18	1157.161	−359.527
1000	0	0.18	0.18	0.14	0	0.5	10	800	0.18	797.6345	−359.527
1000	0	0.18	0.18	0.14	0	0.6	10	800	0.18	438.1076	−359.527
1000	0	0.18	0.18	0.14	0	0.7	10	800	0.18	78.58071	−359.527
1000	0	0.18	0.18	0.14	0	0.8	10	800	0.18	−280.946	−359.527
1000	0	0.18	0.18	0.14	0	0.9	10	800	0.18	−640.473	−359.527
1000	0	0.18	0.18	0.14	0	1	10	800	0.18	−1000	

Table 19.57 Dependence of NPV and ΔNPV on tax on profit rate t at fixed leverage level *L* for 10-year project at L = 2

I	L	WACC	Ko	Kd	Wd	t	n	NOI	Ke	NPV	ΔNPV
1000	2	0.18	0.18	0.14	0.66667	0	10	800	0.26	1771.845	−125.137
1000	2	0.16618	0.18	0.14	0.66667	0.1	10	800	0.24654	1646.708	−135.437
1000	2	0.1521	0.18	0.14	0.66667	0.2	10	800	0.232299	1511.27	−147.987
1000	2	0.13773	0.18	0.14	0.66667	0.3	10	800	0.217182	1363.283	−163.538
1000	2	0.12303	0.18	0.14	0.66667	0.4	10	800	0.201083	1199.745	−183.17
1000	2	0.10796	0.18	0.14	0.66667	0.5	10	800	0.183875	1020.575	−208.47
1000	2	0.09247	0.18	0.14	0.66667	0.6	10	800	0.165407	808.1048	−241.852
1000	2	0.0765	0.18	0.14	0.66667	0.7	10	800	0.145497	566.253	−287.089
1000	2	0.05998	0.18	0.14	0.66667	0.8	10	800	0.123925	279.1638	−350.325
1000	2	0.04281	0.18	0.14	0.66667	0.9	10	800	0.100417	−71.1609	−442.002
1000	2	0.02488	0.18	0.14	0.66667	1	10	800	0.074631	−513.163	

Table 19.58 Dependence of NPV and ΔNPV on tax on profit rate t at fixed leverage level *L* for 10-year project at L = 4

I	L	WACC	Ko	Kd	Wd	t	n	NOI	Ke	NPV	ΔNPV
1000	4	0.18	0.18	0.14	0.8	0	10	800	0.34	1226.885	−475.625
1000	4	0.18316	0.20056	0.14	0.8	0.1	10	800	0.411801	751.2601	−139.495
1000	4	0.17256	0.20836	0.14	0.8	0.2	10	800	0.414791	611.7654	−74.4553
1000	4	0.15772	0.21253	0.14	0.8	0.3	10	800	0.396579	537.3101	−54.8815
1000	4	0.14072	0.21513	0.14	0.8	0.4	10	800	0.367589	482.4286	−52.0879
1000	4	0.12227	0.2169	0.14	0.8	0.5	10	800	0.331331	430.3407	−60.1971
1000	4	0.10261	0.21819	0.14	0.8	0.6	10	800	0.289071	370.1436	−80.4792
1000	4	0.08181	0.21917	0.14	0.8	0.7	10	800	0.241069	289.6644	−120.753
1000	4	0.0598	0.21994	0.14	0.8	0.8	10	800	0.186991	168.9112	−202.021
1000	4	0.0364	0.22055	0.14	0.8	0.9	10	800	0.126013	−33.1095	−382.685
1000	4	0.01135	0.22106	0.14	0.8	1	10	800	0.056769	−415.795	

Table 19.59 Dependence of NPV and ΔNPV on tax on profit rate t at fixed leverage level *L* for 10-year project at L = 6

I	L	WACC	Ko	Kd	Wd	t	n	NOI	Ke	NPV	ΔNPV
1000	6	0.18	0.18	0.14	0.85714	0	10	800	0.42	847.6197	37.06285
1000	6	0.16218	0.18	0.14	0.85714	0.1	10	800	0.379295	884.6825	42.53552
1000	6	0.14392	0.18	0.14	0.85714	0.2	10	800	0.335473	927.218	50.03126
1000	6	0.12515	0.18	0.14	0.85714	0.3	10	800	0.288045	977.2493	60.31305
1000	6	0.10577	0.18	0.14	0.85714	0.4	10	800	0.236408	1037.562	74.23617
1000	6	0.08569	0.18	0.14	0.85714	0.5	10	800	0.179813	1111.799	91.96624
1000	6	0.06476	0.18	0.14	0.85714	0.6	10	800	0.117304	1203.765	109.0267
1000	6	0.04281	0.18	0.14	0.85714	0.7	10	800	0.04764	1312.791	96.39537
1000	6	0.0196	0.18	0.14	0.85714	0.8	10	800	−0.03083	1409.187	−113.739
1000	6	−0.0052	0.18	0.14	0.85714	0.9	10	800	−0.12039	1295.448	−1669.51
1000	6	−0.032	0.18	0.14	0.85714	1	10	800	−0.22431	−374.066	

Table 19.60 Dependence of NPV and ΔNPV on tax on profit rate t at fixed leverage level *L* for 10-year project at L = 8

I	L	WACC	Ko	Kd	Wd	t	n	NOI	Ke	NPV	ΔNPV
1000	8	0.18	0.18	0.14	0.88889	0	10	800	0.5	572.2536	67.74227
1000	8	0.16152	0.18	0.14	0.88889	0.1	10	800	0.445653	639.9958	80.91054
1000	8	0.14255	0.18	0.14	0.88889	0.2	10	800	0.386973	720.9064	100.9849
1000	8	0.12303	0.18	0.14	0.88889	0.3	10	800	0.323249	821.8913	133.0198
1000	8	0.10284	0.18	0.14	0.88889	0.4	10	800	0.253602	954.9111	187.1372
1000	8	0.08188	0.18	0.14	0.88889	0.5	10	800	0.17692	1142.048	285.1235
1000	8	0.05998	0.18	0.14	0.88889	0.6	10	800	0.091775	1427.172	477.0078
1000	8	0.03692	0.18	0.14	0.88889	0.7	10	800	−0.00372	1904.18	874.876
1000	8	0.01243	0.18	0.14	0.88889	0.8	10	800	−0.11211	2779.056	1515.986
1000	8	−0.0139	0.18	0.14	0.88889	0.9	10	800	−0.23701	4295.041	−4645.92
1000	8	−0.0426	0.18	0.14	0.88889	1	10	800	−0.38375	−350.883	

Table 19.61 Dependence of NPV and ΔNPV on tax on profit rate t at fixed leverage level L for 10-year project at L = 10

I	L	WACC	Ko	Kd	Wd	t	n	NOI	Ke	NPV	ΔNPV
1000	10	0.18	0.18	0.14	0.90909	0	10	800	0.58	365.0841	85.01433
1000	10	0.16109	0.18	0.14	0.90909	0.1	10	800	0.512008	450.0984	103.8568
1000	10	0.14168	0.18	0.14	0.90909	0.2	10	800	0.438456	553.9552	134.6286
1000	10	0.12167	0.18	0.14	0.90909	0.3	10	800	0.358411	688.5839	188.5659
1000	10	0.10097	0.18	0.14	0.90909	0.4	10	800	0.270705	877.1497	292.3814
1000	10	0.07944	0.18	0.14	0.90909	0.5	10	800	0.173857	1169.531	519.0512
1000	10	0.0569	0.18	0.14	0.90909	0.6	10	800	0.065947	1688.582	1107.667
1000	10	0.03313	0.18	0.14	0.90909	0.7	10	800	−0.05558	2796.249	3051.344
1000	10	0.0078	0.18	0.14	0.90909	0.8	10	800	−0.19424	5847.593	11,617.12
1000	10	−0.0195	0.18	0.14	0.90909	0.9	10	800	−0.35504	17,464.71	−17,800.8
1000	10	−0.0496	0.18	0.14	0.90909	1	10	800	−0.54557	−336.131	

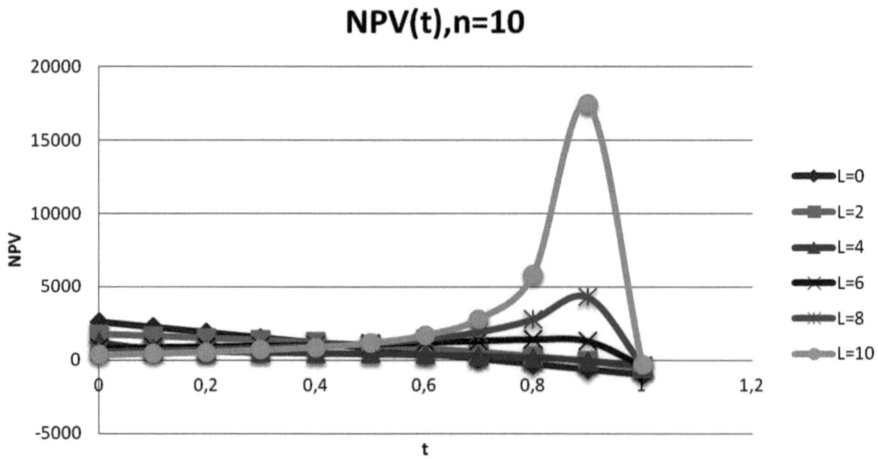

Fig. 19.18 Dependence of NPV on tax on profit rate t at fixed leverage level *L* for 10-year project

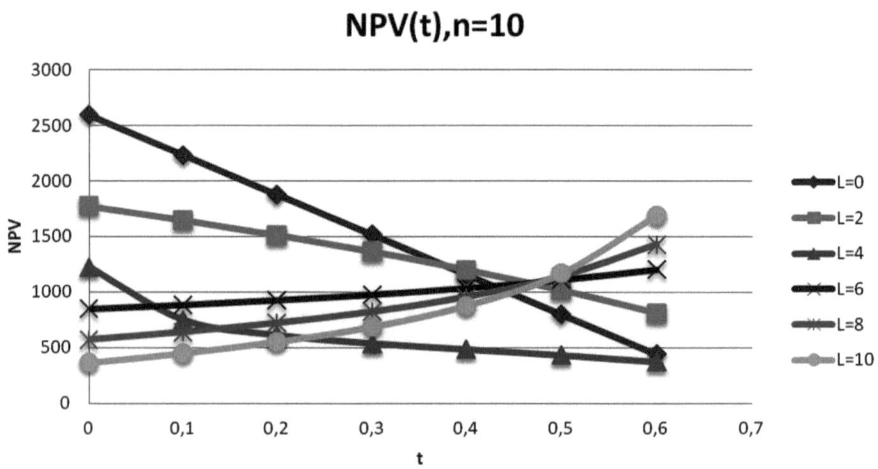

Fig. 19.19 Dependence of NPV on tax on profit rate t at fixed leverage level *L* for 10-year project (more detailed)

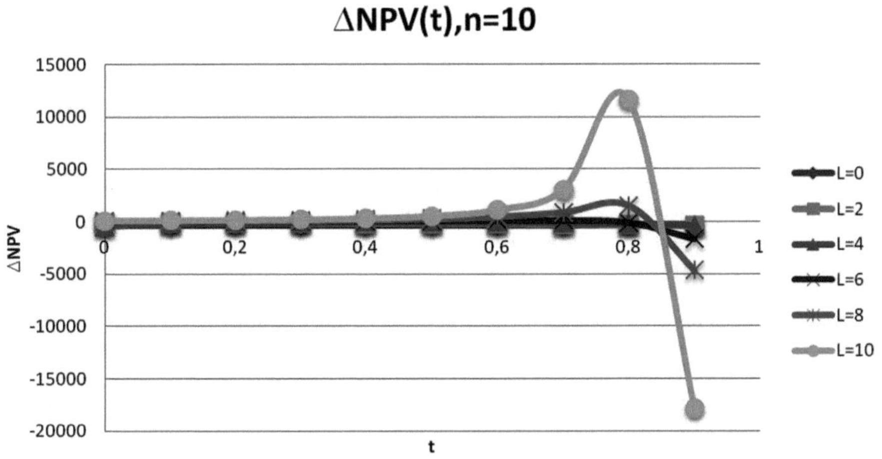

Fig. 19.20 Dependence of ΔNPV on tax on profit rate t at fixed leverage level L for 10-year project

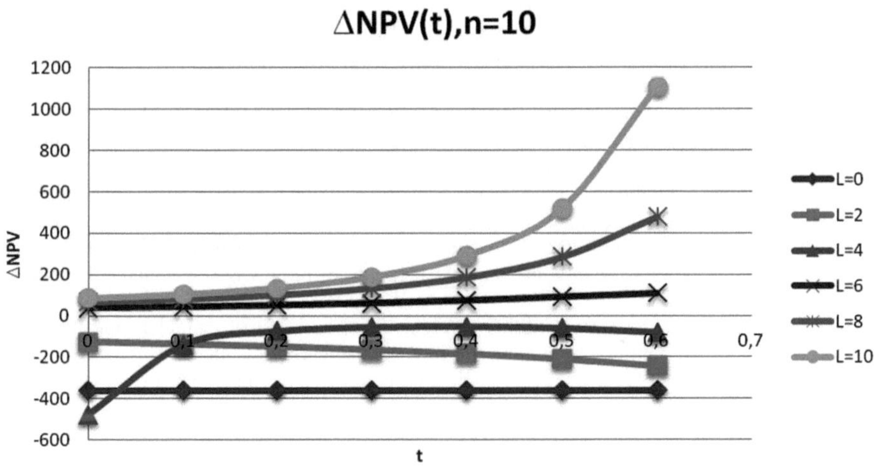

Fig. 19.21 Dependence of ΔNPV on tax on profit rate t at fixed leverage level L for 10-year project (more detailed)

References

Brusov PN, Filatova TV (2011) From Modigliani–Miller to general theory of capital cost and capital structure of the company. Financ Credit 435:2–8

Brusov P, Filatova T, Kulik V (2024) Capital Asset Pricing Model (CAPM) 2.0: Account of business and financial risk. Financ. theory pract. 28(2):128–142. https://doi.org/10.26794/2587-5671-2024-28-2-128-142

Brusov P, Filatova T (2025a) Business valuation and company value: New qualitative approaches considering business and financial risks, Springer Nature Publishing pp.1–654

Brusov P, Filatova T (2025b) Efficiency of investment projects: Modern investment models and their applications, Springer Nature Publishing pp.1–843
Brusov P, Filatova T, Orehova N, Brusova A (2011a) Weighted average cost of capital in the theory of Modigliani–Miller, modified for a finite life-time company. Appl Financ Econ 21(11):815–824
Brusov P, Filatova T, Orehova N et al (2011b) From Modigliani–Miller to general theory of capital cost and capital structure of the company. Res J Econ Bus ICT 2:16–21
Brusov P, Filatova T, Orehova N et al (2011c) Influence of debt financing on the effectiveness of the investment project within the Modigliani–Miller theory. Res J Econ Bus ICT (UK) 2:11–15
Brusov P, Filatova T, Orehova N, Brusov PP, Brusova N (2011d) From Modigliani–Miller to general theory of capital cost and capital structure of the company. Res J Econ Bus ICT 2:16–21
Brusov P, Filatova T, Eskindarov M, Orehova N (2012a) Influence of debt financing on the effectiveness of the finite duration investment project. Appl Financ Econ 22(13):1043–1052
Brusov P, Filatova T, Eskindarov M, Orehova N (2012b) Hidden global causes of the global financial crisis. J Rev Glob Econ 1:106–111
Brusov P, Filatova P, Orekhova N (2013a) Absence of an optimal capital structure in the famous tradeoff theory! J Rev Glob Econ 2:94–116
Brusov P, Filatova T, Orehova N (2013b) A qualitatively new effect in corporative finance: abnormal dependence of cost of equity of company on leverage. J Rev Glob Econ 2:183–193
Brusov P, Filatova P, Orekhova N (2014a) Mechanism of formation of the company optimal capital structure, different from suggested by trade off theory. Cogent Econ Financ 2:1–13. https://doi.org/10.1080/23322039.2014.946150
Brusov P, Filatova T, Orehova N (2014b) Inflation in Brusov–Filatova–Orekhova theory and in its perpetuity limit—Modigliani–Miller theory. J Rev Glob Econ 3:175–185
Brusova A (2011) A comparison of the three methods of estimation of weighted average cost of capital and equity cost of company. Financ Anal Problems Solut 34(76):36–42
Brusov P, Filatova T, Orehova N (2021) Ratings: Critical analysis and new approaches of quantitative and qualitative methodology, Springer Nature Publishing, pp.1–369
Brusov P, Filatova T, Orehova N (2022) Generalized modigliani–miller theory: applications in corporate finance, investments, taxation and ratings, Springer Nature Publishing, pp.1–362
Brusov P, Filatova T, Orehova N (2023) The Brusov–Filatova–Orekhova theory of capital structure: Applications in corporate finance, investments, taxation and ratings, Springer Nature Publishing pp.1–769
Filatova T, Orehova N, Brusova A (2008) Weighted average cost of capital in the theory of Modigliani–Miller, modified for a finite life-time company. Bull FU 48:68–77
Modigliani F, Miller M (1958) The cost of capital, corporate finance, and the theory of investment. Am Econ Rev 48:261–297
Modigliani F, Miller M (1963) Corporate income taxes and the cost of capital: a correction. Am Econ Rev 53:147–175
Modigliani F, Miller M (1966) Some estimates of the cost of capital to the electric utility industry 1954–1957. Am Econ Rev 56:333–391

Chapter 20
Optimizing the Investment Structure of the Telecommunication Sector Company

20.1 Introduction

Investments in tangible and intangible assets play an important role in the activities of any company. They are a necessary condition for structural adjustment and economic growth and provide the creation of new and enhancement of existing basic funds and industries. The role of investment, which is always the one of the most important, is increased many times at the current stage.

For example, in Russia a priority of budget will be the reduced of dependence of the price of oil and gas. The main issue that helps at least to start the movement on this way is, of course, investments. In this way, the role of investment at the present stage is indeed increasing dramatically. In this regard, the role of the evaluation of the efficiency of investment projects, which in the context of scarcity and limited investment resources allows the realization of the most effective projects, increases. Since virtually all investment projects use debt financing, the purpose of the study of the impact of debt financing and capital structure on the efficiency of investment projects, determining the optimal level leverage, is especially actual at the present time.

The hope to determine the optimal capital structure, in which one or more parameters of the efficiency of the project (NPV, IRR, etc.) are maximum, more than half a century has encouraged researchers to deal with the issue. Some of the major problems in the assessment of the effectiveness of the projects are the following:

- What are financial flows and why are they necessary to take into account when calculating parameters of efficiency of the project (NPV, IRR, etc.)?
- How many discount rate should be used for financial flows associated with investments?
- How can these discount rates be accurately determined?

Discussion concerning the first two problems is ongoing. On the third issue, one needs to note that, in recent years, there has been a significant progress in the accurate

P. Brusov and T. Filatova, *Taxes and Taxation*, Contributions to Finance and Accounting, https://doi.org/10.1007/978-3-032-11077-0_20

determination of the cost of the equity capital of the company and its weighted average cost, which as time and are the discount rate when evaluating the NPV of the project. The progress is associated with work performed by Brusov, Filatova, and Orekhova (Brusov and Filatova 2011; Brusov et al. 2011a, b, c, 2012a, b, 2013a, b, 2014a, b; Filatova et al. 2008; Brusova 2011; Brusov et al. (2015), Brusov et al. (2018a, b, c, d); Brusov et al. 2021, 2022, 2023, 2024; Brusov and Filatova 2025a, b), in which the general theory of capital cost of the company (equity cost as well as weighted average cost) was established and its dependence on leverage and on lifetime (age) of company was found for the companies with arbitrary lifetime (age). The main difference between their theory and theory by Modigliani and Miller is that the former one waives from the perpetuity of the companies, which leads to significant differences of a new theory from theory of Nobel laureates Modigliani and Miller (1958, 1963, 1966).

The lack of modern methods of evaluation of effectiveness of investment projects with account of the debt financing, with the correct assessment of discount rate, used in investment models, has identified the need for research. The establishment of such modern models, considering problem from the point of view of equity capital owners as well as from the point of view of equity and debt capital owners, with the use of modern theory by Brusov, Filatova, and Orekhova that assesses the equity capital cost and weighted average cost of capital of the company (Modigliani and Miller 1958, 1963, 1966), which play the role of discount rate in the investment models, can significantly contribute to the problem of the assessment of investment projects' effectiveness.

20.2 Investment Analysis and Recommendations for Telecommunication Company "Nastcom Plus"

Based on the method, developed by the authors (Brusov and Filatova 2011; Brusov et al. 2011a, b, c, 2012a, b, 2013a, b, 2014a, b; Filatova et al. 2008), let us analyze the efficiency of investments of one of the leading companies in the telecommunication sector "Nastcom Plus" for 2010–2012 from the point of view of optimal structure of investment. The source data for the analysis are presented in Table 20.1.

Quantity k_0 is the equity cost of financially independent company (or equity cost at zero leverage) and for "Nastcom Plus" is equal to 23.67% (Brusova 2011). Here are also calculated dependence of weighted average cost of capital WACC and the equity cost k_e on leverage (Fig. 20.1).

Table 20.1 Data of "Nastcom Plus" for 2010–2012

Indicator	2010	2011	2012
Investment I, million dollars	1.124	2.05	2.763
Revenue, million dollars	7204.335	8232.172	9418.773
Net operating income for the year before taxing, NOI, million dollars	2161.3	2469.174	2826
Equity cost at zero leverage, k_0, %	23.67	23.67	23.67
Debt cost $\overline{k}_d$, %	8.26	7.4	6.69
Return on investment for 1 year, $\beta = I/\mathrm{NOI}$	1.92	1.204	1.02
Amount of debt financing, %	35	50	50
Amount of equity, %	65	50	50
Leverage level, L	0.54	1	1
Amount of equity capital S, million dollars	730.6	1025	1381.5

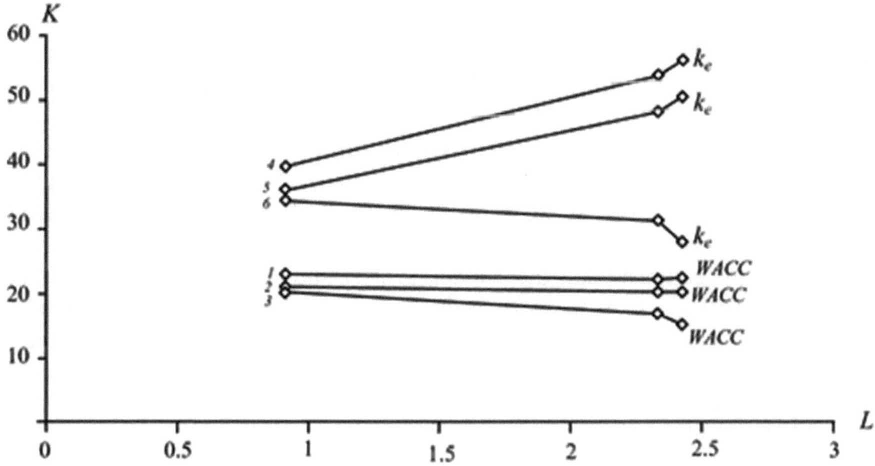

Fig. 20.1 Dependence of weighted average cost of capital WACC and the equity cost k_e on leverage: *1*, *4* within Brusov–Filatova–Orekhova theory; *2*, *5* within Modigliani–Miller theory; *3*, *6* within traditional approach

20.2.1 The Dependence of NPV on Investment Capital Structure

Analysis of investment will be continued with use of the formula provided in the works (Brusov and Filatova 2011; Brusov et al. 2011a, b, c, 2012a, b, 2013a, b, 2014a, b; Filatova et al. 2008):

$$\mathrm{NPV} = -S\left\{1 + L\left[(1-t)\left(1 - \frac{1}{(1+k_\mathrm{d})^n}\right) + \frac{1}{(1+k_\mathrm{d})^n}\right]\right\} + \frac{\beta S(1+L)(1-t)}{k_\mathrm{e}}\left[1 - \frac{1}{(1+k_\mathrm{e})^n}\right], \tag{20.1}$$

where NPV—net present value, S—equity capital amount, L—leverage level, t—tax on profit rate, k_d—debt cost, n—project duration, β—return on investment for 1 year, k_e—equity cost.

Analysis of Investments in 2010 Using company's data (Table 20.1), we compute the WACC, k_e, and NPV (Tables 20.2, 20.3, and 20.4; Figs. 20.1 and 20.2).

In the company's investment in 2010, equity capital accounted for 65%, and debt 35%, i.e., the leverage level was equal to $L = 0.54$. The term for hardware depreciation, into establishment of which investment was done, was 5 years. Curve 2 (Fig. 20.2) corresponds to dependence of NPV on leverage level for the 5-year project. Optimum NPV is achieved when $L = 2$. At this leverage level, NPV = 3624.5 million dollars.

The level leverage with which "Nastcom Plus" has carried out its investment projects ($L = 0.54$) was lying far from optimum and provided NPV = 2979.2 million dollars, which is approximately 645 million dollars less than the optimal value of NPV.

Since the equipment can be operated, after depreciation, one can estimate the NPV for a more long-term perspective. For example, for the 7-year project, the optimal leverage value is $L = 2.0$, when the NPV = 4157.6 million dollars, which is 562.8 million dollars more than nonoptimal values of NPV = 3594.8 million dollars, obtained by the company. For the 10-year project, the optimal leverage level is $L = 1.5$, with NPV = 4509.1 million dollars, which is 422.9 million dollars more than nonoptimal values of NPV = 4086.2 million dollars, obtained by the company (Fig. 20.2; Tables 20.2, 20.3, and 20.4).

Analysis of Investments in 2011 Using company's data, we compute the WACC, k_e, and NPV (Tables 20.5, 20.6, and 20.7; Fig. 20.3).

In the company's investment in 2011, equity capital accounted for 50%, and debt capital for 50% as well, i.e., the leverage level was equal to $L = 1$. The term for hardware depreciation, into establishment of which investment was done, was 5 years. Curve 2 (Fig. 20.3) corresponds to dependence of NPV on leverage level for the 5-year project. Optimum NPV is achieved approximately at $L = 1$. More accurate calculations show that the optimal value of NPV = 2133.7 million dollars is achieved when $L = 1.1$.

The level leverage with which "Nastcom Plus" has carried out its investment projects ($L = 0.1$) was lying in the vicinity of optimum and provided NPV = 2131.8 million dollars, which is just 2 million dollars less than the optimal value of NPV. You can take it that, in 2011, investment in "Nastcom Plus" company has been carried out with almost optimal structure.

Analysis of Investments in 2012 Using company's data, we compute the WACC, k_e, and NPV (Tables 20.8, 20.9, and 20.10; Fig. 20.4).

Table 20.2 Weighted average cost of capital, WACC, in 2010

Project duration n	Leverage level L										
	0	0.5	1	1.5	2	2.5	3	3.5	4	4.5	5
2	0.2367	0.2284	0.2242	0.2217	0.2201	0.2189	0.2180	0.2173	0.2167	0.2163	0.2159
5	0.2367	0.2262	0.2209	0.2177	0.2156	0.2141	0.2130	0.2121	0.2114	0.2108	0.2103
7	0.2367	0.2256	0.2199	0.2166	0.2143	0.2127	0.2116	0.2106	0.2099	0.2093	0.2087
10	0.2366	0.2250	0.2190	0.2155	0.2131	0.2114	0.2101	0.2091	0.2083	0.2076	0.2071

Table 20.3 Equity cost, k_e, in 2010

Project duration n	Leverage level L										
	0	0.5	1	1.5	2	2.5	3	3.5	4	4.5	5
2	0.2367	0.3096	0.3824	0.4552	0.5280	0.6008	0.6736	0.7464	0.8192	0.8920	0.9649
5	0.2367	0.3063	0.3758	0.4452	0.5147	0.5841	0.6536	0.7230	0.7925	0.8619	0.9314
7	0.2367	0.3053	0.3738	0.4423	0.5107	0.5791	0.6480	0.7165	0.7850	0.8535	0.9220
10	0.2366	0.3044	0.3720	0.4396	0.5071	0.5746	0.6422	0.7097	0.7772	0.8447	0.9122

Table 20.4 Net present value, NPV, in 2010, million dollars

Project duration *n*	Leverage level *L*										
	0	0.5	1	1.5	2	2.5	3	3.5	4	4.5	5
2	910.5	1181.8	1358.3	1458.5	1496.3	1482.8	1426.6	1334.6	1212.4	1064.5	894.5
5	2371.6	2979.2	3347.7	3547.1	3624.5	3612.4	3533.6	3404.2	3236.1	3038.0	2816.2
7	2939.0	3594.8	3955.1	4121.6	4157.6	4103.6	3981.6	3821.6	3619.9	3397.1	3155.1
10	3444.5	4086.2	4396.9	4509.1	4497.4	4405.3	4258.9	4074.9	3863.8	3632.7	3386.5

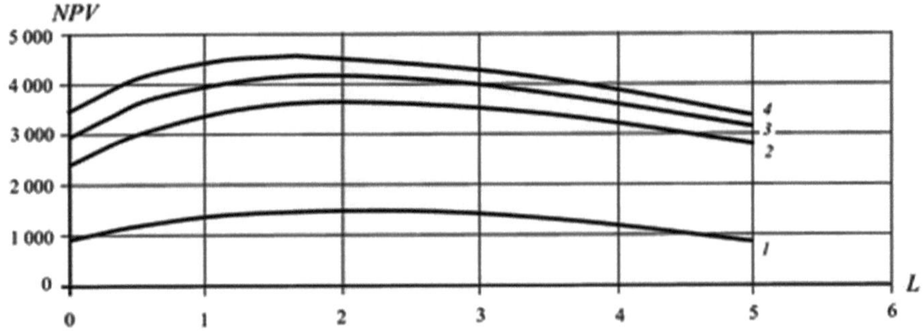

Fig. 20.2 Dependence of NPV on leverage L at $t = 20\%$ in 2010: *1* for 2-year income from investments; *2* for 5-year income from investments (the term for hardware depreciation); *3* for 7 years of investment income; *4* for 10 years of investment income

The company's investment structure in 2012 was the same as in 2011: equity capital accounted for 50%, and debt capital for 50%, i.e., the leverage level was equal to $L = 1$. The term hardware for depreciation, into establishment of which investment was done, was 5 years. Curve 2 (Fig. 20.4) corresponds to dependence of NPV on leverage level for the 5-year project. Optimum NPV is achieved when $L = 0.5$. More accurate calculations show that the optimal value of NPV = 1987.7 million dollars is achieved when $L = 0.7$ (Table 20.11, Fig. 20.5).

The level leverage, with which "Nastcom Plus" has carried out its investment projects ($L = 0.1$), did not correspond to optimum value ($L = 0.7$) and provided NPV = 1954.6 million dollars, which is 31.7 million dollars less than the optimal value of NPV (Figs. 20.4 and 20.5; Tables 20.10 and 20.11).

Since the equipment can be operated after depreciation, one can estimate the NPV for a more long-term perspective. For example, for the 7-year project, the optimal leverage value is $L = 0.65$, when the NPV = 2580.6 million dollars, which is 51.7 million dollars more than nonoptimal values of NPV = 2528.9 million dollars, obtained by the company. For the 10-year project, the optimal leverage level $L = 0.55$, with NPV = 3043.5 million dollars, which is 98 million dollars more than nonoptimal values of NPV = 2945.5 million dollars, obtained by the company.

20.2.2 The Dependence of NPV on the Equity Capital Value and Coefficient B

Let us investigate the dependence of NPV on the equity capital value and coefficient β (Tables 20.12, 20.13, 20.14, and 20.15; Figs. 20.6, 20.7, 20.8, and 20.9).

With increase of the equity value, optimum is observed for all of the values S when leverage level is approximately equal to $L = 0.7$, and the optimum value as

Table 20.5 Weighted average cost of capital, WACC, in 2011

Project duration n	Leverage level L										
	0	0.5	1	1.5	2	2.5	3	3.5	4	4.5	5
2	0.2367	0.3096	0.3824	0.4552	0.5280	0.6008	0.6736	0.7464	0.8192	0.8920	0.9649
5	0.2367	0.3063	0.3758	0.4452	0.5147	0.5841	0.6536	0.7230	0.7925	0.8619	0.9314
7	0.2367	0.3053	0.3738	0.4423	0.5107	0.5791	0.6480	0.7165	0.7850	0.8535	0.9220
10	0.2366	0.3044	0.3720	0.4396	0.5071	0.5746	0.6422	0.7097	0.7772	0.8447	0.9122

Table 20.6 Equity cost, k_e, in 2011

Project duration n	Leverage level L										
	0	0.5	1	1.5	2	2.5	3	3.5	4	4.5	5
2	0.2367	0.3142	0.3916	0.4690	0.5464	0.6239	0.7013	0.7787	0.8561	0.9335	1.0110
5	0.2367	0.3110	0.3853	0.4595	0.5338	0.6080	0.6822	0.7565	0.8307	0.9049	0.9791
7	0.2367	0.3100	0.3833	0.4565	0.5297	0.6029	0.6761	0.7493	0.8230	0.8963	0.9695
10	0.2366	0.3091	0.3813	0.4536	0.5258	0.5980	0.6702	0.7424	0.8146	0.8868	0.9589

Table 20.7 Net present value, NPV, of the company in 2011, million dollars

Project duration n	Leverage level L										
	0	0.5	1	1.5	2	2.5	3	3.5	4	4.5	5
2	418.8	460.5	415.8	302.3	133.3	−80.9	−332.5	−615.0	−923.5	−1254.0	−1603.1
5	1704.2	2025.4	2131.8	2089.9	1943.2	1721.0	1443.5	1124.7	774.8	400.9	8.5
7	2203.4	2558.0	2650.5	2576.1	2392.2	2134.4	1825.6	1480.7	1105.7	715.0	309.8
10	2648.2	2982.3	3028.1	2907.1	2685.2	2399.5	2071.6	1715.0	1338.0	946.0	542.9

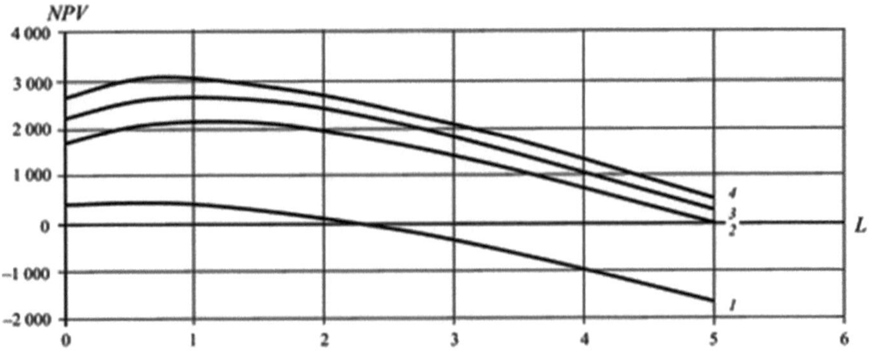

Fig. 20.3 Dependence of NPV on leverage L at t = 20% in 2011: *1* for 2-year income from investments; *2* for 5-year income from investments (the term for hardware depreciation); *3* for 7 years of investment income; *4* for 10 years of investment income

well as the NPV value is growing with increasing S, as long as the project remains effective (up to the leverage level approximately $L = 3.7$).

With the decrease of the return on investment ($\beta = 0.5$), the dependence of the NPV on leverage changes significantly: now NPV monotonically decreases with the leverage at all values of equity capital S (Fig. 20.7).

With the increase of the return on investment ($\beta = 1.5$), the NPV of the project has an optimum at all values of equity capital S at leverage level $L = 1.5$, and NPV(L) curve is going up with the increase in S until the project remains effective (up to the leverage level approximately $L = 7$). The optimum position (value L_0) almost does not depend on the equity value S ($L_0 = 1.5$). This means the possibility of a tabulation of obtained results by the known values k_0 and k_d for large values $\beta \geq 1$, when in dependence of NPV(L) there is an optimum.

With the further increase of the return on investment ($\beta = 2$), NPV of the project has an optimum for all values S at leverage level which is already approximately equal to $L = 1.8$, and the value of optimum as well as of NPV in general is growing with increasing S, until the project remains an effective (up to leverage level of order $L = 8.5$, see Fig. 20.9).

In this way, the analysis of the dependence of NPV on the equity value S and on the return on investment β allows us to conclude that in contrast to the parameters I and NOI, the change of parameters S and β, both individually and simultaneously, can significantly change the nature of the dependence of NPV on leverage level.

With the increase of return on investment (with the increased β), there is a transition from the monotonic decrease of NPV of the project with leverage (Fig. 20.7) to the existing of the optimum at all values of S (see Figs. 20.6 and 20.8). The growth of β leads to the growth of NPV as well as to the growth of the limit leverage value, up to which the project remains effective.

This means the inability of tabulation of the results, obtained in the general case of a constant value of equity capital; in this case, it is necessary to use the formulas

Table 20.8 Weighted average cost of capital, WACC, in 2012

Project duration n	Leverage level L										
	0	0.5	1	1.5	2	2.5	3	3.5	4	4.5	5
2	0.2367	0.2298	0.2264	0.2243	0.2229	0.2219	0.2212	0.2206	0.2202	0.2198	0.2195
5	0.2367	0.2278	0.2234	0.2207	0.2189	0.2176	0.2167	0.2159	0.2153	0.2148	0.2144
7	0.2367	0.2272	0.2224	0.2195	0.2176	0.2162	0.2152	0.2143	0.2137	0.2132	0.2127
10	0.2366	0.2265	0.2213	0.2183	0.2162	0.2147	0.2136	0.2127	0.2120	0.2115	0.2110

Table 20.9 Equity cost, k_e, in 2012

Project duration n	Leverage level L										
	0	0.5	1	1.5	2	2.5	3	3.5	4	4.5	5
2	0.2367	0.3180	0.3992	0.4805	0.5617	0.6430	0.7242	0.8055	0.8867	0.9680	1.0492
5	0.2367	0.3150	0.3933	0.4715	0.5497	0.6279	0.7062	0.7844	0.8626	0.9408	1.0190
7	0.2367	0.3140	0.3913	0.4685	0.5457	0.6229	0.7001	0.7772	0.8544	0.9316	1.0088
10	0.2366	0.3130	0.3892	0.4653	0.5415	0.6177	0.6938	0.7699	0.8461	0.9222	0.9983

Table 20.10 Net present value, NPV, in 2012, million dollars

Project duration n	Leverage level L										
	0	0.5	1	1.5	2	2.5	3	3.5	4	4.5	5
2	267.0	200.9	33.4	−214.0	−525.3	−888.3	−1293.4	−1733.4	−2202.4	−2695.8	−3209.9
5	1734.8	1968.9	1954.6	1771.8	1472.1	1089.6	647.1	160.6	−358.9	−903.4	−1467.2
7	2304.7	2566.9	2528.9	2304.4	1960.4	1537.2	1060.3	545.9	4.7	−556.0	−1131.2
10	2812.6	3041.6	2945.5	2667.4	2281.9	1829.9	1335.0	811.1	266.8	−292.2	−862.1

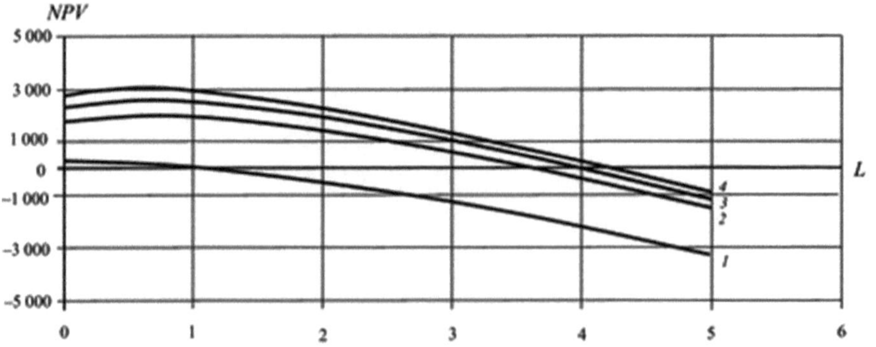

Fig. 20.4 Dependence of NPV on leverage L at $t = 20\%$ in 2012: *1* for 2-year income from investments; *2* for 5-year income from investments (the term for hardware depreciation); *3* for 7 years of investment income; *4* for 10 years of investment income

obtained by authors in their works (Brusov and Filatova 2011; Brusov et al. 2011a, b, c, 2012a, b, 2013a, b, 2014a, b; Filatova et al. 2008) to determine the NPV at the existing leverage level as well as for optimization of existing investment structure. Tabulation is possible only in the case of large β values ($\beta \geq 1$), when there is an optimum in the dependence of NPV on the leverage level.

20.3 Effects of Taxation on the Optimal Capital Structure of Companies in the Telecommunication Sector

We continue the analysis of activity of "Nastcom Plus." In this paragraph, we examine the effect of change of tax on profit rate, both in the case of its increase and decrease, on the optimal structure of investments at different project durations.

It is shown that the increase of tax on profit rate leads to the degradation (decreasing) of NPV, and the degradation is reduced with an increase of project duration. In particular, for the 5-year project (amortization period), when the tax on profit rate decreases on 1%, NPV decreases on 1.5–2.34% in different years.

The impact of change of tax on the profit rate on the optimum position while it exists (change optimum position) is changed for 2-year and 10-year projects in 2010 and for the 5-year project in the 2012 year [for 0.5–1 (in L units)]; nevertheless the optimum position turns out to be sufficiently stable (Figs. 20.10, 20.11, 20.12, 20.13, 20.14, 20.15, 20.16, 20.17, 20.18, 20.19, 20.20, and 20.21; Tables 20.16, 20.17, 20.18, 20.19, 20.20, and 20.21).

It is shown that the increase of tax on profit rate leads to the degradation (decreasing) of NPV, and the degradation is reduced with an increase of project duration. Note that for the 5-year project (amortization period), when the tax on

Table 20.11 Net present value, NPV, at leverage level from 0.5 up to 1.05 in 2012, million dollars

Project duration n	Leverage level L											
	0.5	0.55	0.6	0.65	0.7	0.75	0.8	0.85	0.9	0.95	1	1.05
2	200.9	188.3	174.8	160.2	144.8	128.4	111.1	92.9	73.9	54.1	33.4	12.0
5	1968.9	1977.0	1982.8	1986.3	1987.7	1987.0	1984.2	1979.5	1973.0	1964.6	1954.6	1942.8
7	2566.9	2574.2	2578.8	2580.6	2580.0	2576.9	2571.5	2563.9	2554.2	2542.5	2528.9	2513.5
10	3041.6	3043.5	3042.4	3038.5	3032.0	3023.1	3011.7	2998.2	2982.6	2965.0	2945.5	2924.3

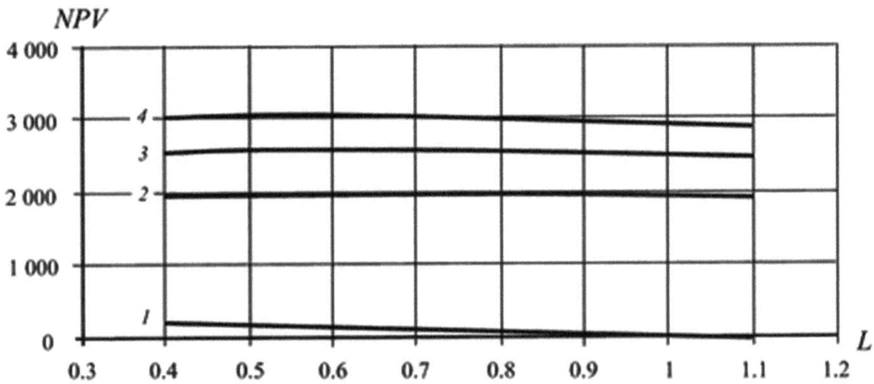

Fig. 20.5 Dependence of NPV on leverage L at $t = 20\%$ in 2012 in the vicinity of optimum: *1* for 2-year income from investments; *2* for 5-year income from investments (the term for hardware depreciation); *3* for 7 years of investment income; *4* for 10 years of investment income

profit rate decreases by 1%, NPV decreases by 2.34% in 2012, by 2.04% in 2011, and by 1.49% in 2010.

20.4 Conclusions

In 2010, the company "Nastcom Plus" worked at leverage level $L = 0.54$ instead of optimal value $L = 2.0$. The NPV loss amounted to 645 million dollars.

In 2012, the company worked at leverage level $L = 1.0$ instead of optimal value $L = 0.7$. The NPV loss amounted from 32 to 98 million dollars, depending on the term of operation of equipment.

The authors have evaluated effectiveness of investment at existing level of debt financing and have developed recommendations on the optimum level of leverage for the Russian company "Nastcom Plus" in 2010–2012.

The results indicate that if in 2011 the financial structure of the investment of "Nastcom Plus" was close to the optimal and NPV was only 2 million dollars less than the optimal value, in 2010, when the leverage level was $L = 0.54$, NPV was 645 million dollars less than optimal value (the optimal leverage level should be equal to $L = 2$).

In 2012 the leverage level, with which "Nastcom Plus" has carried out its investment projects ($L = 0.1$), did not correspond to optimum value ($L = 0.7$) and provided NPV = 1954.6 million dollars, which is 31.7 million dollars less than the optimal value of NPV (Tables 20.10 and 20.11; Figs. 20.4 and 20.5).

Since the equipment can be operated after depreciation, one can estimate the NPV for a more long-term perspective. For example, for the 7-year project, the optimal leverage value is $L = 0.65$, when the NPV = 2580.6 million dollars, which is 51.7 million dollars more than nonoptimal values of NPV = 2528.9 million dollars,

Table 20.12 Net present value, NPV, at $\beta = 1.02$, million dollars

Equity S	Leverage level L										
	0	0.5	1	1.5	2	2.5	3	3.5	4	4.5	5
1382	1734.8	1968.9	1954.6	1771.8	1472.1	1089.6	647.1	160.6	−358.9	−903.4	−1467.2
1000	1255.7	1425.2	1414.8	1282.5	1065.6	788.7	468.4	116.2	−259.8	−653.9	−1062.0
1200	1506.8	1710.2	1697.8	1539.0	1278.7	946.4	562.1	139.5	−311.8	−784.7	−1274.4
1600	2009.1	2280.3	2263.7	2052.0	1705.0	1261.9	749.5	186.0	−415.7	−1046.3	−1699.2
1800	2260.3	2565.3	2546.7	2308.5	1918.1	1419.7	843.2	209.2	−467.6	−1177.1	−1911.6

Table 20.13 Net present value, NPV, at $\beta = 0.5$, million dollars

Equity S	Leverage level L										
	0	0.5	1	1.5	2	2.5	3	3.5	4	4.5	5
1382	146.1	−71.8	−411.5	−833.8	−1313.3	−1833.5	−2383.1	−2954.2	−3541.6	−4141.1	−4750.2
1000	105.7	−52.0	−297.9	−603.5	−950.7	−1327.2	−1725.0	−2138.4	−2563.6	−2997.6	−3438.4
1200	126.9	−62.4	−357.4	−724.2	−1140.8	−1592.6	−2070.0	−2566.1	−3076.3	−3597.1	−4126.1
1600	169.2	−83.2	−476.6	−965.6	−1521.0	−2123.5	−2760.0	−3421.5	−4101.7	−4796.1	−5501.4
1800	190.3	−93.6	−536.2	−1086.3	−1711.2	−2388.9	−3105.0	−3849.2	−4614.4	−5395.6	−6189.1

Table 20.14 Net present value, NPV, at $\beta = 1.5$, million dollars

Equity S	Leverage level L										
	0	0.5	1	1.5	2	2.5	3	3.5	4	4.5	5
1382	3201.2	3852.6	4138.6	4176.9	4043.3	3787.8	3444.2	3035.8	2578.9	2085.3	1563.3
1000	2320.2	2788.7	2995.8	3023.5	2926.8	2741.8	2493.1	2197.5	1866.7	1509.4	1131.6
1200	2780.7	3346.5	3594.9	3628.2	3512.1	3290.2	2991.7	2637.0	2240.1	1811.3	1357.9
1600	3707.5	4462.0	4793.2	4837.6	4682.8	4386.9	3989.0	3515.9	2986.8	2415.1	1810.6
1800	4171.0	5019.7	5392.4	5442.3	5268.2	4935.3	4487.6	3955.4	3360.1	2716.9	2036.9

Table 20.15 Net present value, NPV, at $\beta = 2.0$, million dollars

Equity S	Leverage level L										
	0	0.5	1	1.5	2	2.5	3	3.5	4	4.5	5
1382	4728.8	5814.9	6413.7	6682.3	6721.7	6598.5	6357.9	6020.8	5639.2	5198.5	4720.0
1000	3423.0	4209.1	4642.6	4837.0	4865.5	4776.3	4602.2	4365.4	4081.9	3762.9	3416.6
1200	4107.5	5050.9	5571.1	5804.4	5838.6	5731.6	5522.6	5238.5	4898.3	4515.5	4099.9
1600	5476.7	6734.5	7428.1	7739.2	7784.8	7642.1	7363.4	6984.7	6531.1	6020.6	5466.6
1800	6161.3	7576.4	8356.6	8706.6	8757.9	8597.4	8283.9	7857.8	7347.4	6773.2	6149.9

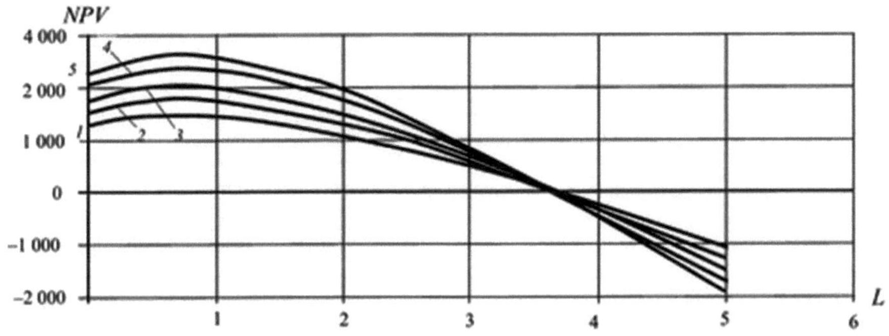

Fig. 20.6 Dependence of NPV on leverage at different values of equity cost *S* at $\beta = 1.02$, million dollars: *1 S* = 1382.2 million dollars; *2 S* = 1000 million dollars; *3 S* = 1200 million dollars; *4 S* = 1600 million dollars; *5 S* = 1800 million dollars

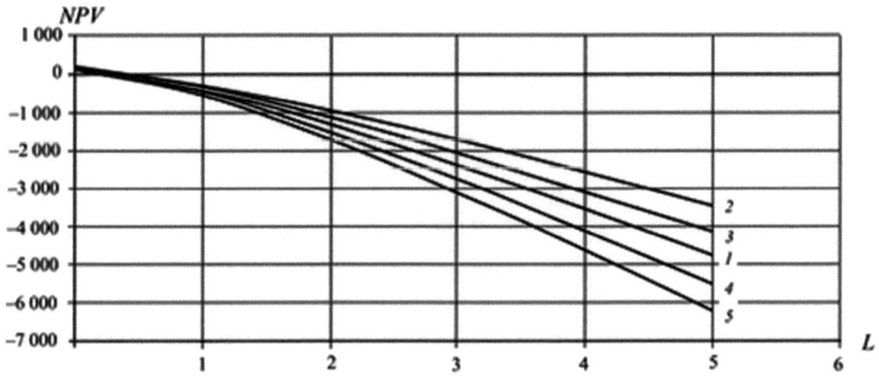

Fig. 20.7 Dependence of NPV on leverage at different values of equity cost *S* at $\beta = 0.5$, million dollars: *1 S* = 1382.2 million dollars; *2 S* = 1000 million dollars; *3 S* = 1200 million dollars; *4 S* = 1600 million dollars; *5 S* = 1800 million dollars

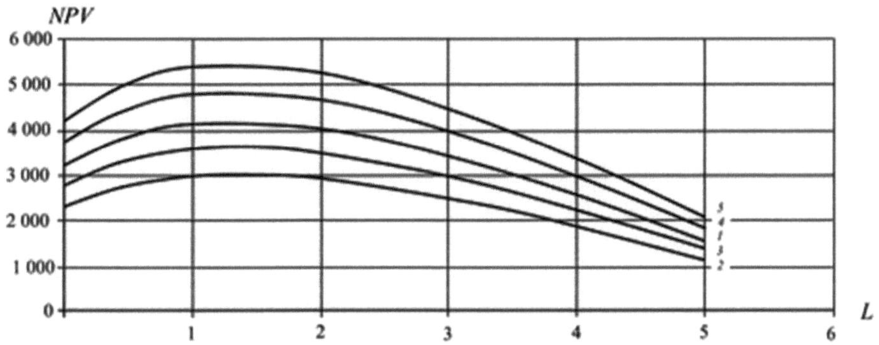

Fig. 20.8 Dependence of NPV on leverage at different values of equity cost *S* at $\beta = 1.5$, million dollars: *1 S* = 1382.2 million dollars; *2 S* = 1000 million dollars; *3 S* = 1200 million dollars; *4 S* = 1600 million dollars; *5 S* = 1800 million dollars

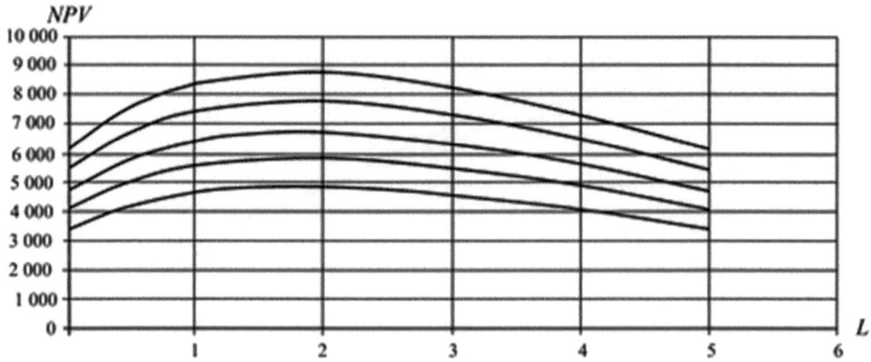

Fig. 20.9 Dependence of NPV on leverage at different values of equity cost S at $\beta = 2$, million dollars: *1* $S = 1382.2$ million dollars; *2* $S = 1000$ million dollars; *3* $S = 1200$ million dollars; *4* $S = 1600$ million dollars; *5* $S = 1800$ million dollars

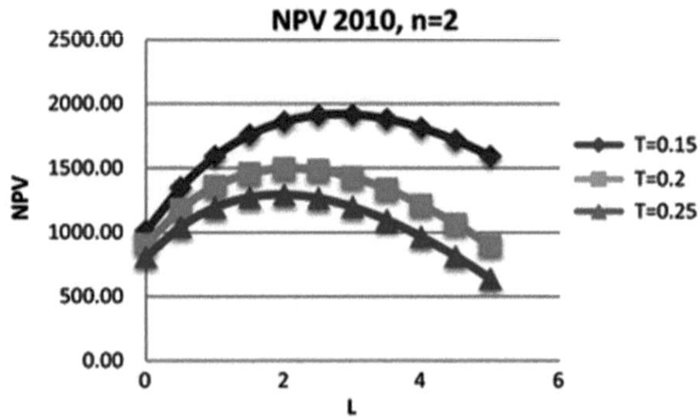

Fig. 20.10 Dependence of NPV on leverage level L for three values of tax on profit rate: $T = 15\%, 20\%, 25\%$ for the 2-year project in 2010

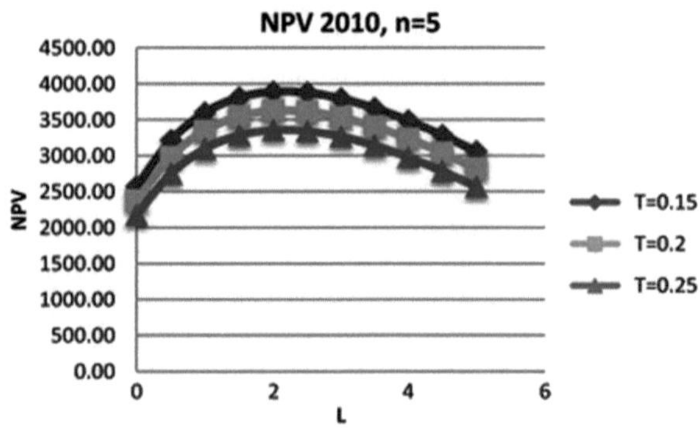

Fig. 20.11 Dependence of NPV on leverage level L for three values of tax on profit rate: $T = 15\%, 20\%, 25\%$ for the 5-year project in 2010

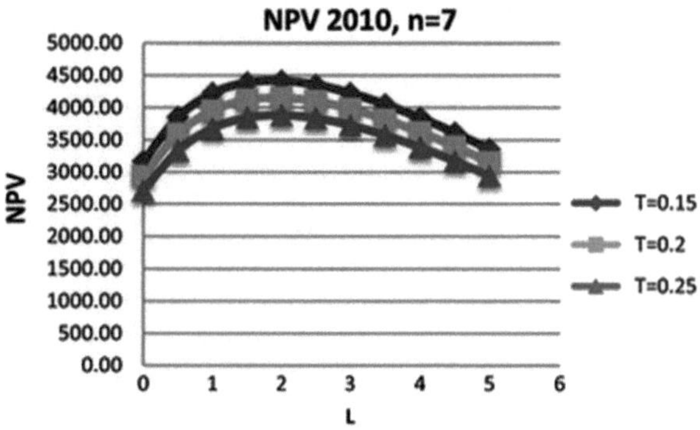

Fig. 20.12 Dependence of NPV on leverage level L for three values of tax on profit rate: $T = 15\%, 20\%, 25\%$ for the 7-year project in 2010

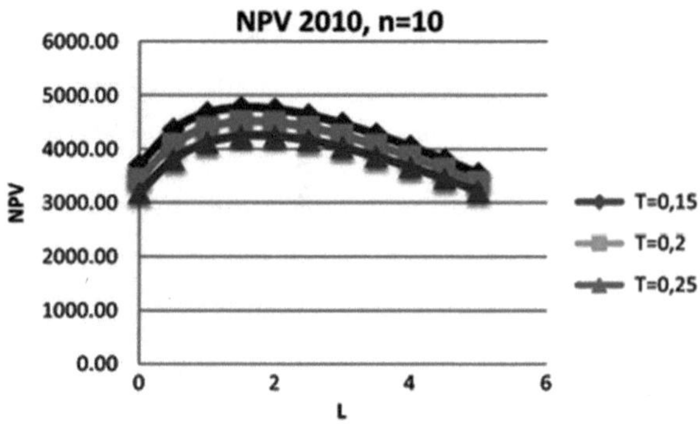

Fig. 20.13 Dependence of NPV on leverage level L for three values of tax on profit rate: $T = 15\%, 20\%, 25\%$ for the 10-year project in 2010

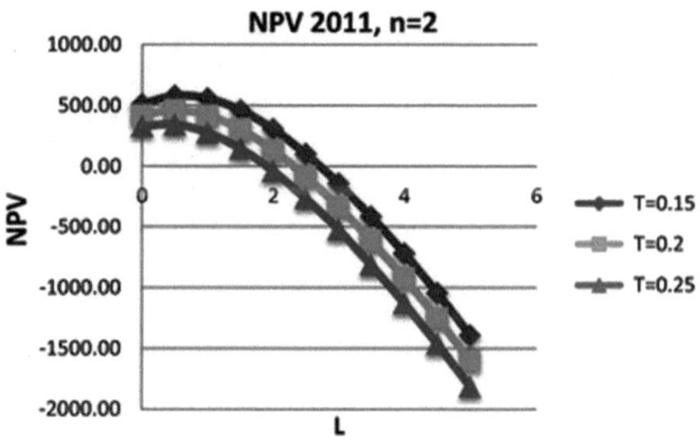

Fig. 20.14 Dependence of NPV on leverage level L for three values of tax on profit rate: $T = 15\%, 20\%, 25\%$ for the 2-year project in 2011

obtained by the company. For the 10-year project, the optimal leverage level $L = 0.55$, with NPV = 3043.5 million dollars, which is 98 million dollars more than nonoptimal values of NPV = 2945.5 million dollars, obtained by the company.

Fig. 20.15 Dependence of NPV on leverage level L for three values of tax on profit rate: $T = 15\%, 20\%, 25\%$ for the 5-year project in 2011

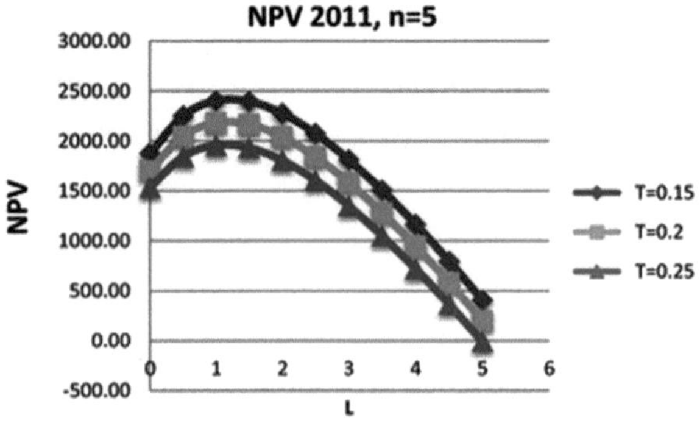

Fig. 20.16 Dependence of NPV on leverage level L for three values of tax on profit rate: $T = 15\%, 20\%, 25\%$ for the 7-year project in 2011

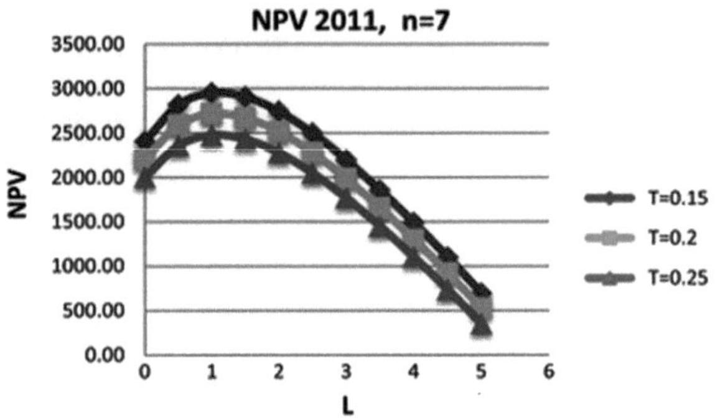

Fig. 20.17 Dependence of NPV on leverage level L for three values of tax on profit rate: $T = 15\%, 20\%, 25\%$ for the 10-year project in 2011

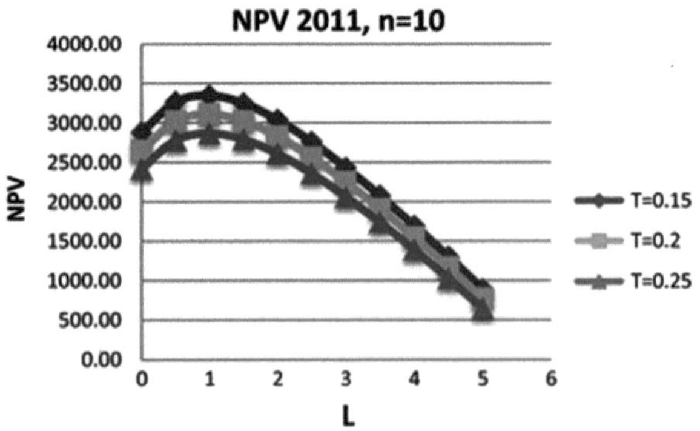

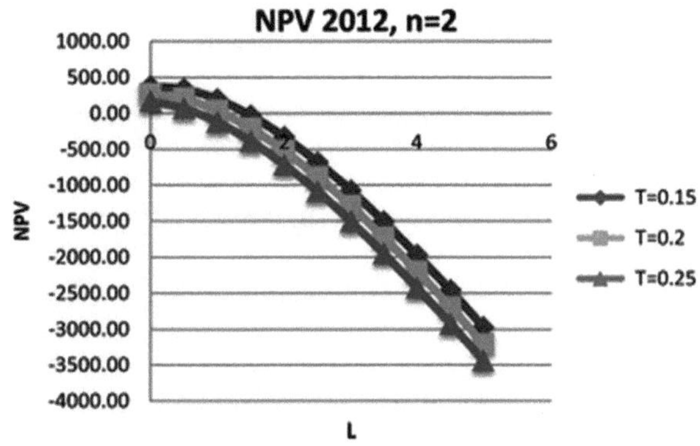

Fig. 20.18 Dependence of NPV on leverage level L for three values of tax on profit rate: $T = 15\%, 20\%, 25\%$ for the 2-year project in 2012

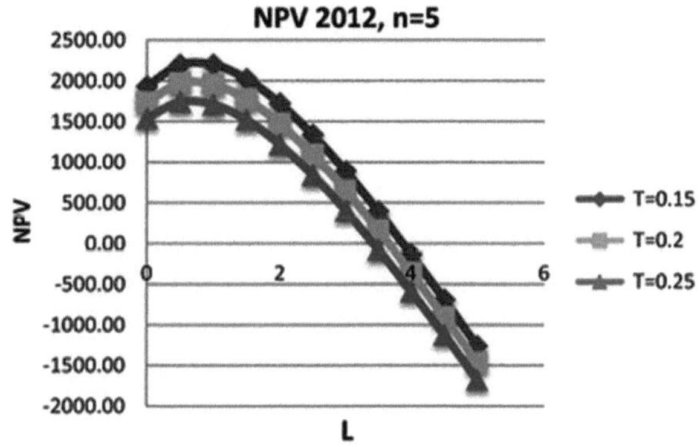

Fig. 20.19 Dependence of NPV on leverage level L for three values of tax on profit rate: $T = 15\%, 20\%, 25\%$ for the 5-year project in 2012

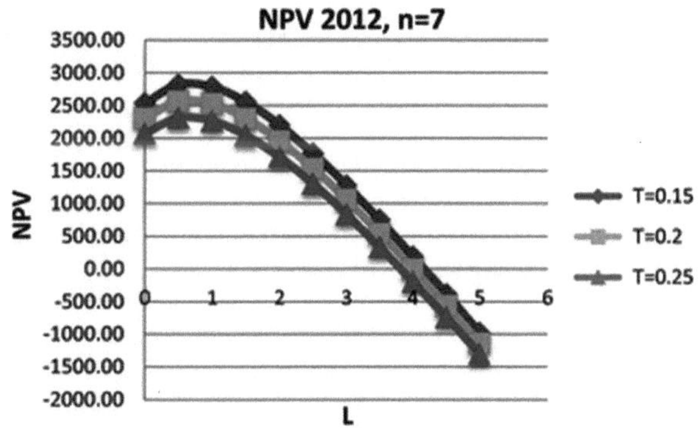

Fig. 20.20 Dependence of NPV on leverage level L for three values of tax on profit rate: $T = 15\%, 20\%, 25\%$ for the 7-year project in 2012

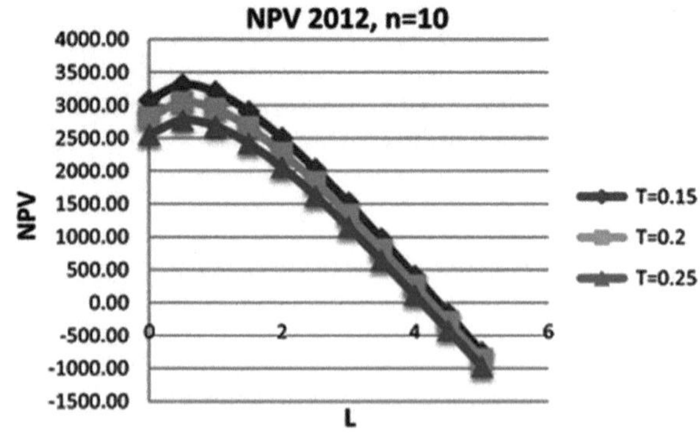

Fig. 20.21 Dependence of NPV on leverage level L for three values of tax on profit rate: $T = 15\%, 20\%, 25\%$ for the 10-year project in 2012

Table 20.16 Dependence of optimum position L_0 of investment structure in 2010 on tax on profit rate and project duration

2010, t (%)	n			
	2	5	7	10
15	3	2	2	2
20	2	2	2	1.5
25	2	2	2	2

Table 20.17 Absolute and relative change of NPV with increase/decrease of tax on profit rate on 5% (1%) in 2010

2010	$t = 20–15\%$	$t = 25–20\%$	On 5% (%)	On 1% (%)
$n = 2$	418/487	204	34	6.8
5	266	273	7.45	1.49
7	263	271	6.88	1.37
10	245	256	5.56	1.11

Table 20.18 Dependence of optimum position L_0 of investment structure in 2011 on tax on profit rate and project duration

2011, t (%)	n			
	2	5	7	10
15	0.5	1	1	1
20	0.5	1	1	1
25	0.5	1	1	1

Table 20.19 Absolute and relative change of NPV with increase/decrease of tax on profit rate on 5% (1%) in 2011

2011	$t = 20–15\%$	$t = 25–20\%$	On 5% (%)	On 1% (%)
$n = 2$	119	118	25.8	5.16
5	222	223	10.2	2.04
7	236	239	8.75	1.75
10	238	242	7.7	1.54

Table 20.20 Dependence of optimum position L_0 of investment structure in 2010 on tax on profit rate and project duration

2012, t (%)	n			
	2	5	7	10
15	0	1	0.5	0.5
20	0	0.5	0.5	0.5
25	0	0.5	0.5	0.5

Table 20.21 Absolute and relative change of NPV with increase/decrease of tax on profit rate on 5% (1%) in 2012

2012	$t = 20–15\%$	$t = 25–20\%$	On 5% (%)	On 1% (%)
$n = 2$	104	103	39	7.8
5	229	229	11.7	2.34
7	253	256	9.9	1.98
10	269	271	8.9	1.74

References

Brusov PN, Filatova TV (2011) From Modigliani–Miller to general theory of capital cost and capital structure of the company. Financ Credit 435:2–8

Brusov P, Filatova T, Orehova N, Brusova A (2011a) Weighted average cost of capital in the theory of Modigliani–Miller, modified for a finite life-time company. Appl Financ Econ 21(11):815–824

Brusov P, Filatova T, Orehova N et al (2011b) From Modigliani–Miller to general theory of capital cost and capital structure of the company. Res J Econ Bus ICT 2:16–21

Brusov P, Filatova T, Orehova N et al (2011c) Influence of debt financing on the effectiveness of the investment project within the Modigliani–Miller theory. Res J Econ Bus ICT (UK) 2:11–15

Brusov P, Filatova T, Eskindarov M, Orehova N (2012a) Influence of debt financing on the effectiveness of the finite duration investment project. Appl Financ Econ 22(13):1043–1052

Brusov P, Filatova T, Eskindarov M, Orehova N (2012b) Hidden global causes of the global financial crisis. J Rev Global Econ 1:106–111

Brusov P, Filatova T, Kulik V (2024) Capital asset pricing model (CAPM) 2.0: Account of business and financial risk. Financ. theory pract. 28(2):128–142. https://doi.org/10.26794/2587-5671-2024-28-2-128-142

Brusov P, Filatova P, Orekhova N (2013a) Absence of an optimal capital structure in the famous tradeoff theory! J Rev Global Econ 2:94–116

Brusov P, Filatova T, Orehova N (2013b) A qualitatively new effect in corporative finance: abnormal dependence of cost of equity of company on leverage. J Rev Global Econ 2:183–193
Brusov P, Filatova P, Orekhova N (2014a) Mechanism of formation of the company optimal capital structure, different from suggested by trade off theory. Cogent Econ Financ 2:1–13. https://doi.org/10.1080/23322039.2014.946150
Brusov P, Filatova T, Orehova N (2014b) Inflation in Brusov–Filatova–Orekhova theory and in its perpetuity limit—Modigliani–Miller theory. J Rev Global Econ 3:175–185
Brusov P, Filatova T, Orehova N, Eskindarov M (2015) Modern corporate finance, investment and taxation, 1st edn. Springer, London, pp 1–368
Brusov P, Filatova T, Orehova N, Kulk WI (2018a) New meaningful effects in modern capital structure theory. J Rev Global Econ 7:104–122
Brusov P, Filatova T, Orehova N, Kulk V (2018b) A "golden age" of the companies: conditions of its existence. J Rev Global Econ 7:88–103
Brusov P, Filatova T, Orehova N, Kulk V (2018c) Rating methodology: new look and new horizons. J Rev Global Econ 7:63–87
Brusov P, Filatova T, Orehova N, Kulk V (2018d) Rating: new approach. J Rev Global Econ 7:37–62
Brusova A (2011) A comparison of the three methods of estimation of weighted average cost of capital and equity cost of company. Financ Anal Prob Sol 34(76):36–42
Brusov P, Filatova T, Orehova N (2021) Ratings: Critical analysis and new approaches of quantitative and qualitative methodology, Springer Nature Publishing, pp.1–369
Brusov P, Filatova T, Orehova N (2022) Generalized Modigliani–Miller theory: Applications in corporate finance, investments, taxation and ratings, Springer Nature Publishing, pp.1–362
Brusov P, Filatova T, Orehova N (2023) The Brusov–Filatova–Orekhova theory of capital structure: Applications in corporate finance, investments, taxation and ratings Springer Nature Publishing pp.1–769
Brusov P, Filatova T (2025a) Business valuation and company calue: New qualitative approaches considering business and financial risks, Springer Nature Publishing pp.1–654
Brusov P, Filatova T (2025b) Efficiency of investment projects: Modern investment models and their applications, Springer Nature Publishing pp.1–843
Filatova T, Orehova N, Brusova A (2008) Weighted average cost of capital in the theory of Modigliani–Miller, modified for a finite life-time company. Bull FU 48:68–77
Modigliani F, Miller M (1958) The cost of capital, corporate finance, and the theory of investment. Am Econ Rev 48:261–297
Modigliani F, Miller M (1963) Corporate income taxes and the cost of capital: a correction. Am Econ Rev 53:147–175
Modigliani F, Miller M (1966) Some estimates of the cost of capital to the electric utility industry 1954–1957. Am Econ Rev 56:333–391

Chapter 21
The Role of the Central Bank and Commercial Banks in Creating and Maintaining of a Favorable Investment Climate in the Country

In this chapter we study the role of the Central Bank and commercial banks in creating and maintaining of a favorable investment climate in the country. within the framework of modern investment models created by the authors, the dependence of the efficiency of investments on the level of debt financing within a wide range of values of equity costs and debt capital costs under different project terms (long-term projects as well as projects of arbitrary duration) and different investment profitability coefficients β is investigated. the effectiveness of investments is determined by Net Present Value, NPV. the study is conducted within the framework of investment models with debt repayment at the end of the project term.

It is found that NPV depends practically linearly on leverage level L, Increasing or decreasing depending on profitability coefficient β and credit rate values k_d. the cut off credit rate values k_d*, Separating the range of increasing NPV(L) from range of decreasing NPV(L), are determined. the Central Bank should keep its key rate at the level which allow commercial banks keep their credit rates below the cut off credit rate k_d* values in order to create and maintain a favorable investment climate in the country.

21.1 Introduction

The investments play a very important role in an economy of each country. As a rule the the debt financing is always used in the investments. In current paper we determine the role of the Central Bank and commercial banks in creating and maintaining of a favorable investment climate in the country. Within the framework of modern investment models created by the authors, the dependence of the efficiency of investments on the level of debt financing within a wide range of values of equity capital costs and debt capital costs under different project terms (long-term projects as well as projects of arbitrary duration) and different investment profitability coefficients β

P. Brusov and T. Filatova, *Taxes and Taxation*, Contributions to Finance and Accounting, https://doi.org/10.1007/978-3-032-11077-0_21

is investigated. The effectiveness of investments is determined by Net Present Value, NPV. The study is conducted within the framework of investment models with debt repayment at the end of the project term.

It is found that NPV depends practically linearly on leverage level L, increasing or decreasing depending on profitability coefficient β and credit rate values k_d. The cut off credit rate values k_d*, separating the range of increasing NPV(L) from range of decreasing NPV(L) are determined. The Central Bank should keep its key rate at the level which allow to commercial banks keep their credit rates below the cut off credit rate values k_d*in order to create and maintain a favorable investment climate in the country.

21.2 Investment Models with Debt Repayment at the End of the Project

The effectiveness of the investment project could be considered from two perspectives: the owners of equity and debt and the equity holders only. For each of these cases, NPV could be calculated in two ways: with the division of credit and investment flows (and thus discounting of the payments using two different rates) and without such a division (in this case, both flows are discounted using the same rate, as which can be, obviously, chosen WACC). For each of the four situations, two cases could be considered: (1) a constant value of equity S and (2) a constant value of the total invested capital $I = S + D$ (D is value of debt funds).

As it was stated above, the effectiveness of the investment project is considered from two perspectives: the owners of equity and debt and the equity holders only. In the first case, the interest and duty paid by owners of equity (negative flows) returned to the project because they are exactly equal to the flow (positive), obtained by owners of debt capital. The only effect of leverage in this case is the effect of the tax shield, generated from the tax relief: interest on the loan is entirely included into the cost and thus reduces the tax base. After–tax flow of capital for each period in this case is equal to

$$\mathrm{NOI}(1-t)+k_{\mathrm{d}}Dt \tag{21.1}$$

and the value of investments at the initial time moment $T = 0$ is equal to $-I = -S - D$.

Here *NOI* stands for net operating income (before taxes).

In the second case, investments at the initial time moment $T = 0$ are equal to $-S$ and the flow of capital for the period (in addition to the tax shields $k_d\,Dt$ it includes a payment of interest on a loan $-k_dD$):

$$(\mathrm{NOI}-k_{\mathrm{d}}D)(1-t). \tag{21.2}$$

Here, for simplicity, we suppose that interest on the loan will be paid in equal shares $k_d\, D$ during all periods. Note that principal repayment is made at the end of the last period.

We will consider the case of discounting, when operating and financial flows are not separated and both are discounted, using the general rate (as which, obviously, the weighted average cost of capital (WACC) can be selected). In this case for long-term (perpetuity) projects, the Modigliani–Miller formula (Modigliani and Miller 1958, 1963, 1966) for WACC will be used and for projects of finite (arbitrary) duration Brusov–Filatova–Orekhova formula will be used (Brusov and Filatova 2011, 2025a, b; Brusov et al. 2011a, b, c, 2012a, b, 2013a, b, 2014a, b; 2015, 2018a, b, c, d, 2021, 2022, 2023, 2024; Filatova et al. 2008; Brusova 2011).

Note that debt capital is the least risky, because interest on credit is paid after taxes in the first place. Therefore, the cost of credit will always be less than the equity cost, whether of ordinary or of preference shares $k_e > k_d; k_p > k_d$. Here $k_e; k_p$ is the equity cost of ordinary or of preference shares consequently.

21.2.1 The Effectiveness of the Investment Project from the Perspective of the Equity Holders Only (Without Flows Separation)

In this case operating and financial flows are not separated and are discounted, using the general rate (as which, obviously, WACC can be selected).

The credit reimbursable at the end of the project [at the end of the period (n)] can be discounted either at the same rate WACC or at the debt cost rate k_d. Now we choose a uniform rate and the first option.

$$\begin{aligned}\mathrm{NPV} &= -S + \sum_{i=1}^{n} \frac{\mathrm{NOI}(1-t) - k_d D(1-t)}{(1+\mathrm{WACC})^i} - \frac{D}{(1+\mathrm{WACC})^n} \\ &= -S + \frac{\mathrm{NOI}(1-t) - k_d D(1-t)}{\mathrm{WACC}}\left(1 - \frac{1}{(1+\mathrm{WACC})^n}\right) - \frac{D}{(1+\mathrm{WACC})^n}.\end{aligned} \tag{21.3}$$

At a Constant Value of Equity Capital ($S = \mathrm{const}$)

Accounting that in the case $S = \mathrm{const}$ NOI is proportional to the invested capital, I, $\mathrm{NOI} = \beta I = \beta S(1+L)$, and substituting $D = LS$, we get

$$\mathrm{NPV} = -S + \frac{\mathrm{NOI}(1-t) - k_d D(1-t)}{\mathrm{WACC}}\left(1 - \frac{1}{(1+\mathrm{WACC})^n}\right) - \frac{D}{(1+\mathrm{WACC})^n}, \tag{21.4}$$

$$\mathrm{NPV} = -S\left[1 + \frac{Lk_{\mathrm{d}}(1-t)}{\mathrm{WACC}}\left(1 - \frac{1}{(1+\mathrm{WACC})^n}\right) + \frac{L}{(1+\mathrm{WACC})^n}\right] + \frac{\beta S(1+L)(1-t)}{\mathrm{WACC}}\left(1 - \frac{1}{(1+\mathrm{WACC})^n}\right). \tag{21.5}$$

Modigliani–Miller Limit [Long-Term (Perpetuity) Projects]

In perpetuity limit ($n \to \infty$) (Modigliani–Miller limit) (turning to the limit $n \to \infty$ in the relevant equations), we have

$$\mathrm{NPV} = -S + \frac{\mathrm{NOI}(1-t) - k_{\mathrm{d}}D(1-t)}{\mathrm{WACC}}. \tag{21.6}$$

At a Constant Value of Equity Capital (S = const)

$$\mathrm{NPV} = -S + \frac{\mathrm{NOI}(1-t) - k_{\mathrm{d}}D(1-t)}{\mathrm{WACC}} \tag{21.7}$$

Substituting $D = LS$, we get

$$\begin{aligned}\mathrm{NPV} &= -S\left[1 + \frac{Lk_{\mathrm{d}}(1-t)}{\mathrm{WACC}}\right] + \frac{\mathrm{NOI}(1-t)}{\mathrm{WACC}} \\ &= -S\left[1 + \frac{Lk_{\mathrm{d}}(1-t)}{k_0(1 - Lt/(1+L))}\right] + \frac{\beta S(1+L)(1-t)}{k_0(1 - Lt/(1+L))}.\end{aligned} \tag{21.8}$$

In last equation we substituted the perpetuity (Modigliani–Miller) formula for WACC.

$$WACC = k_0\left(1 - \frac{Lt}{1+L}\right). \tag{21.9}$$

Below we will investigate the dependence of the efficiency of investments on the level of debt financing within a wide range of values of equity costs k_0 and debt capital costs k_d under different project terms (long-term projects as well as projects of arbitrary duration) and different investment profitability coefficients β.

For long-term project calculations we use formulas (21.8) and (21.9), while for arbitrary duration project calculations we use formula (21.5) for NPV and BFO formula for WACC

$$\frac{1 - (1+\mathrm{WACC})^{-n}}{\mathrm{WACC}} = \frac{1 - (1+k_0)^{-n}}{k_0\left[1 - \omega_{\mathrm{d}}T\left(1 - (1+k_{\mathrm{d}})^{-n}\right)\right]}. \tag{21.10}$$

Here, S is the value of equity capital of the company, $w_d = \frac{D}{D+S}$—the share of debt capital, k_e, $w_e = \frac{S}{D+S}$—the cost and the share of the equity capital of the company, and $L = D/S$—financial leverage.

21.3 Modigliani–Miller Limit (Long-Term (Perpetuity) Projects)

Let us start from the long-term projects. We will study the dependence of the efficiency of investments on the level of debt financing L for the values of equity costs k_0 from 6% up to 32% and for different debt capital costs and different investment profitability coefficient β values.

21.3.1 The Dependence of the Efficiency of Investments NPV on the Level of Debt Financing L for the Values of Equity Costs $k_0 = 0.2$

Below we represent the results of calculations for equity costs $k_0 = 0.2$; debt capital costs $k_d = 0.18$; 0.16; 0.14; 0.12; 0.10; 0.08; 0.06; $S = 250$; tax on profit rate $t = 0.2$.

Results are shown in Tables 21.1, 21.2 and 21.3 and Figs. 21.1, 21.2 and 21.3.

Table 21.1 The dependence of NPV on the level of debt financing L for the values of equity costs $k_0 = 0.2$ and for different debt capital costs $k_d = 0.18$; 0.16; 0.14; 0.12; 0.10; 0.08; 0.06; S = 250; tax on profit rate t = 0.2 and investment profitability coefficient β = 0.1

L	NPV (kd = 0.18)	NPV (kd = 0.16)	NPV (kd = 0.14)	NPV (kd = 0.12)	NPV (kd = 0.1)	NPV (kd = 0.08)	NPV (kd = 0.06)
0	−150.00	−150.00	−150.00	−150.00	−150.00	−150.00	−150.00
1	−227.78	−205.56	−183.33	−161.11	−138.89	−116.67	−94.44
2	−319.23	−273.08	−226.92	−180.77	−134.62	−88.46	−42.31
3	−414.71	−344.12	−273.53	−202.94	−132.35	−61.76	8.82
4	−511.90	−416.67	−321.43	−226.19	−130.95	−35.71	59.52
5	−610.00	−490.00	−370.00	−250.00	−130.00	−10.00	110.00
6	−708.62	−563.79	−418.97	−274.14	−129.31	15.52	160.34
7	−807.58	−637.88	−468.18	−298.48	−128.79	40.91	210.61
8	−906.76	−712.16	−517.57	−322.97	−128.38	66.22	260.81
9	−1006.10	−786.59	−567.07	−347.56	−128.05	91.46	310.98
10	−1105.56	−861.11	−616.67	−372.22	−127.78	116.67	361.11

Table 21.2 The dependence of NPV on the level of debt financing L for the values of equity costs $k_0 = 0.2$ and for different debt capital costs $k_d = 0.18; 0.16; 0.14; 0.12; 0.10; 0.08; 0.06$; $S = 250$; tax on profit rate $t = 0.2$ and investment profitability coefficient $\beta = 0.12$

L	NPV (kd = 0.18)	NPV (kd = 0.16)	NPV (kd = 0.14)	NPV (kd = 0.12)	NPV (kd = 0.1)	NPV (kd = 0.08)	NPV (kd = 0.06)
0	−130.00	−130.00	−130.00	−130.00	−130.00	−130.00	−130.00
1	−183.33	−161.11	−138.89	−116.67	−94.44	−72.22	−50.00
2	−250.00	−203.85	−157.69	−111.54	−65.38	−19.23	26.92
3	−323.59	−250.00	−179.41	−108.82	−38.24	32.35	102.94
4	−392.86	−297.62	−202.38	−107.14	−11.90	83.33	178.57
5	−466.00	−346.00	−226.00	−106.00	14.00	134.00	254.00
6	−539.66	−394.83	−250.00	−105.17	39.66	184.48	329.31
7	−613.64	−443.94	−274.24	−104.55	65.15	234.85	404.55
8	−687.84	−493.24	−298.65	−104.05	90.54	285.14	479.73
9	−762.20	−542.68	−323.17	−103.66	115.85	335.37	554.88
10	−836.67	−592.22	−347.78	−103.33	141.11	385.56	630.00

Table 21.3 The dependence of NPV on the level of debt financing L for the values of equity costs $k_0 = 0.2$ and for different debt capital costs $k_d = 0.18; 0.16; 0.14; 0.12; 0.10; 0.08; 0.06$; $S = 250$; tax on profit rate $t = 0.2$ and investment profitability coefficient $\beta = 0.14$

L	NPV (kd = 0.18)	NPV (kd = 0.16)	NPV (kd = 0.14)	NPV (kd = 0.12)	NPV (kd = 0.1)	NPV (kd = 0.08)	NPV (kd = 0.06)
0	−110.00	−110.00	−110.00	−110.00	−110.00	−110.00	−110.00
1	−138.89	−116.67	−94.44	−72.22	−50.00	−27.78	−5.56
2	−180.77	−134.62	−88.46	−42.31	3.85	50.00	96.15
3	−226.47	−155.88	−85.29	−14.71	55.88	126.47	197.06
4	−273.81	−178.57	−83.33	11.90	107.14	202.38	297.62
5	−322.00	−202.00	−82.00	38.00	158.00	278.00	398.00
6	−370.69	−225.86	−81.03	63.79	208.62	353.45	498.28
7	−419.70	−250.00	−80.30	89.39	259.09	428.79	598.48
8	−468.92	−274.32	−79.73	114.86	309.46	504.05	698.65
9	−518.29	−298.78	−79.27	140.24	359.76	579.27	798.78
10	−567.78	−323.33	−78.89	165.56	410.00	654.44	898.89

1. B = 0.1

From Table 21.1 and Fig. 21.1 it is seen that NPV depends practically linearly on leverage level L, increasing or decreasing depending on credit rate value k_d. NPV(L) increases at credit rate $k_d = 0.06$ and $k_d = 0.08$. The cut off credit rate k_d* values, separating the range of increasing NPV(L) from range of decreasing NPV(L) for investment profitability coefficient $\beta = 0.1$, is equal to 0.1. At higher credit rate k_d values NPV(L) represents decreasing function.

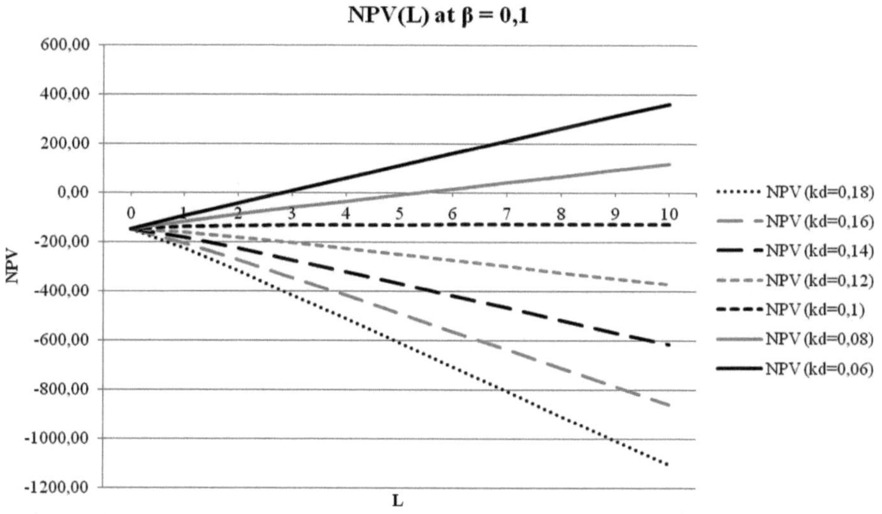

Fig. 21.1 The dependence of the Net Present Value, NPV on the leverage level L for the equity value $k_0 = 20\%$ and for different debt capital costs $k_d = 0.18; 0.16; 0.14; 0.12; 0.10; 0.08; 0.06$; $S = 250$; tax on profit rate $t = 0.2$ and investment profitability coefficient $\beta = 0.1$

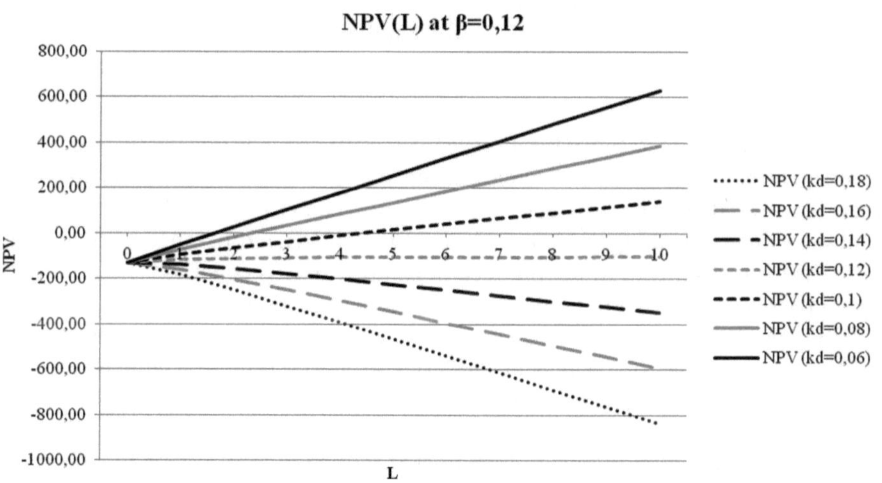

Fig. 21.2 The dependence of the Net Present Value, NPV, on the leverage level L for the equity value $k_0 = 20\%$ and for different debt capital costs $k_d = 0.18; 0.16; 0.14; 0.12; 0.10; 0.08; 0.06$; $S = 250$; tax on profit rate $t = 0.2$ and investment profitability coefficient $\beta = 0.12$

2. Β = 0.12

From Table 21.2 and Fig. 21.2 it is seen that NPV depends practically linearly on leverage level L, increasing or decreasing depending on credit rate value k_d. NPV(L) increases at credit rate $k_d = 0.06$; $k_d = 0.08$ and $k_d = 0.1$. The cut off credit rate

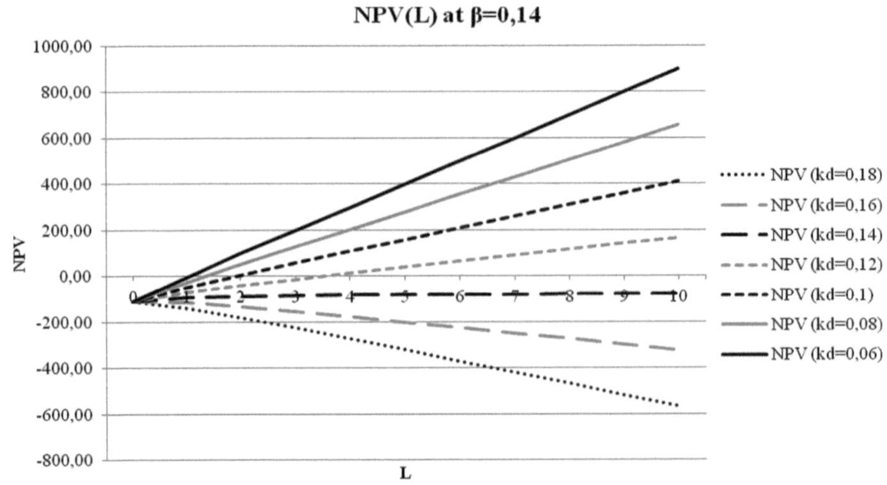

Fig. 21.3 The dependence of the Net Present Value, NPV, on the leverage level L for the equity value $k_0 = 20\%$ and for different debt capital costs $k_d = 0.18; 0.16; 0.14; 0.12; 0.10; 0.08; 0.06$; $S = 250$; tax on profit rate $t = 0.2$ and investment profitability coefficient $\beta = 0.14$

values k_d*, separating the range of increasing NPV(L) from range of decreasing NPV(L) for investment profitability coefficient $\beta = 0.12$, is equal to 0.12. At higher credit rate k_d values NPV(L) represents decreasing function.

3. B = 0.14

From Table 21.3 and Fig. 21.3 it is seen that NPV depends practically linearly on leverage level L, increasing or decreasing depending on credit rate value k_d. NPV(L) increases at credit rate $k_d = 0.06$; $k_d = 0.08$; $k_d = 0.1$ and $k_d = 0.12$. The cut off credit rate k_d* values separating the range of increasing NPV(L) from range of decreasing NPV(L) for investment profitability coefficient $\beta = 0.14$ is equal to 0.14. At higher credit rate k_d values NPV(L) represents decreasing function.

One can see that the cut off credit rate k_d* values separating the range of increasing NPV(L) from range of decreasing NPV(L) strongly correlates with investment profitability coefficient β and practically linearly depends on it.

For long-term projects (Modigliani–Miller limit) it was found that the cut off credit rate values k_d* are proportional to investment profitability coefficients β: it turns out that for equity capital cost $\mathbf{k_0 = 0.2}$ the cut off credit rate values k_d* separating the range of increasing NPV(L) from range of decreasing NPV(L) are approximately equal to investment profitability coefficient β: for investment profitability coefficient $\beta = 0.1$ k_d* is equal to 0.1; for $\beta = 0.12$ k_d* is equal to 0.12; and for investment profitability coefficient $\beta = 0.14$ k_d* is equal to 0.14. The slope of the curve NPV(L) increases with investment profitability coefficient β for the same value of credit rate k_d.

21.3.2 The Dependence of the Efficiency of Investments NPV on the Level of Debt Financing L for the Value of Equity Costs $k_0 = 0.28$

Let us consider also the case of equity capital cost $k_0 = 0.28$ and debt capital cost $k_d = 6\%;8\%;10\%;12\%;14\%;16\%;18\%;20\%;22\%;24\%$.

It is seen from Fig. 21.4 that the cut off credit rate $k_d{}^*$ value separating the range of increasing NPV(L) from range of decreasing NPV(L) is equal to 10%.

It is seen from Fig. 21.5 that the cut off credit rate value $k_d{}^*$, separating the range of increasing NPV(L) from range of decreasing NPV(L), is equal to 20%.

From Figs. 21.4 and 21.5 it follows that for $\beta = 0.1$ $k_d{}^*$ is equal to 0.1; and for investment profitability coefficient $\beta = 0.2$ $k_d{}^*$ is equal to 0.2.

We could come to conclusion that in perpetuity limit for both cases for the equity values $k_0 = 20\%$ and $k_0 = 28\%$ it turns out that the cut off credit rate $k_d{}^*$ values are equal to investment profitability coefficient β (and does not depend on the equity values k_0).

As we will see below this statement is not valid for the projects of arbitrary durations.

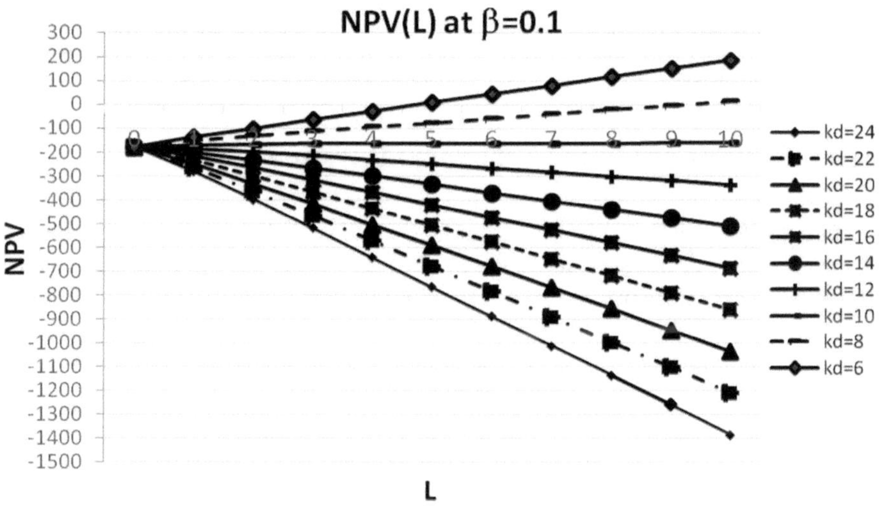

Fig. 21.4 The dependence of the Net Present Value, NPV on the leverage level L for the equity value $k_0 = 28\%$ and for different debt capital costs $k_d = 6\%;8\%;10\%;12\%;14\%;16\%;18\%;20\%;22\%;24\%$; $S = 250$; tax on profit rate $t = 0.2$ and investment profitability coefficient $\beta = 0.1$

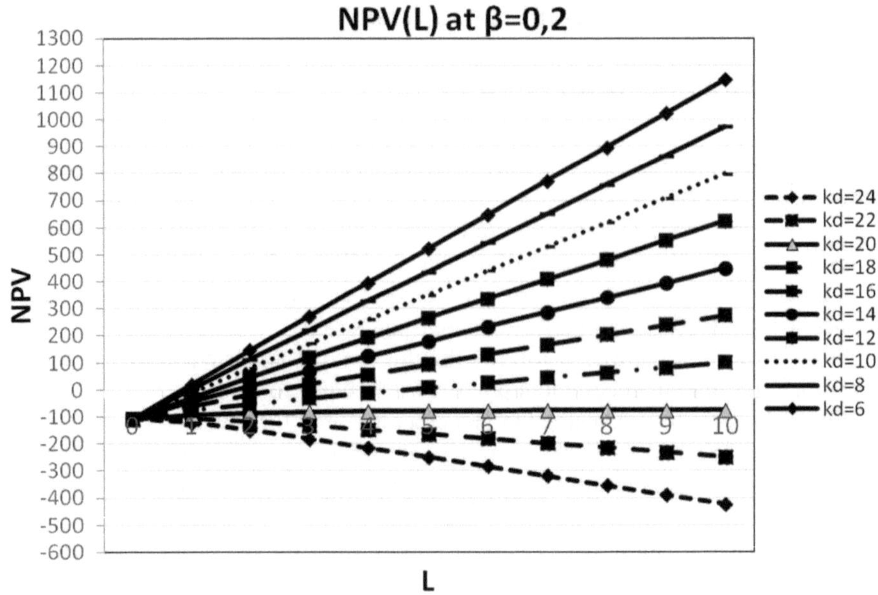

Fig. 21.5 The dependence of the Net Present Value, NPV on the leverage level L for the equity value $k_0 = 28\%$ and for different debt capital costs k_d = 6%;8%;10%;12%;14%;16%;18%;20%;22%;24%; S = 250; tax on profit rate t = 0.2 and investment profitability coefficient β = 0.2

21.4 Projects of Finite (Arbitrary) Duration

Let us consider now the projects of arbitrary durations. We will study the dependence of the efficiency of investments on the level of debt financing L for the same values of equity costs k_0 from 6% up to 32%; for different debt capital costs k_d and different investment profitability coefficient β values as well as for different project durations.

For arbitrary duration project calculations we use formula (21.5) for NPV

$$\mathrm{NPV} = -S\left[1 + \frac{Lk_d(1-t)}{\mathrm{WACC}}\left(1 - \frac{1}{(1+\mathrm{WACC})^n}\right) + \frac{L}{(1+\mathrm{WACC})^n}\right] + \frac{\beta S(1+L)(1-t)}{\mathrm{WACC}}\left(1 - \frac{1}{(1+\mathrm{WACC})^n}\right).$$

and BFO formula (21.10) for WACC

$$\frac{1-(1+\mathrm{WACC})^{-n}}{\mathrm{WACC}} = \frac{1-(1+k_0)^{-n}}{k_0\left[1-\omega_d T\left(1-(1+k_d)^{-n}\right)\right]}.$$

21.4.1 *The Dependence of the Efficiency of Investments NPV on the Level of Debt Financing L for the Values of Equity Costs $k_0 = 0.2$*

Below we represent the results of calculations for equity costs $k_0 = 0.2$; debt capital costs $k_d = 0.18; 0.16; 0.14; 0.12; 0.10; 0.08; 0.06$; $S = 250$; tax on profit rate $t = 0.2$ and project duration $n = 5$. In next part we will compare the results for project durations $n = 5$ and $n = 3$.

For arbitrary duration project calculations we use formula (21.5) for NPV and BFO formula for WACC (21.10).

Results are shown in Tables 21.4, 21.5 and 21.6 and Figs. 21.4, 21.5 and 21.6.

1. B = 0.325

From Table 21.4 and Fig. 21.6 it is seen that NPV depends practically linearly on leverage level L, increasing or decreasing depending on credit rate value k_d. NPV(L) increases at credit rate $k_d = 0.06$; $k_d = 0.08$; $k_d = 0.1$ and $k_d = 0.12$. The cut off credit rate value $k_d{}^*$, separating the range of increasing NPV(L) from range of decreasing NPV(L) for investment profitability coefficient $\beta = 0.325$, is equal to 0.14. At higher credit rates k_d values NPV(L) represents decreasing function.

2. B = 0.345

From Table 21.5 and Fig. 21.7 it is seen that NPV depends practically linearly on leverage level L, increasing or decreasing depending on credit rate value k_d. NPV(L) increases at credit rates $k_d = 0.06$; $k_d = 0.08$; $k_d = 0.1$; $k_d = 0.12$ and $k_d = 0.14$. The cut off credit rate value $k_d{}^*$, separating the range of increasing NPV(L) from range

Table 21.4 The dependence of NPV on the level of debt financing L for the values of equity costs $k_0 = 0.2$ and for different debt capital costs $k_d = 0.18; 0.16; 0.14; 0.12; 0.10; 0.08; 0.06$; $S = 250$; tax on profit rate $t = 0.2$; $\beta = 0.325$ and project duration $n = 5$

L	NPV (kd = 0.18)	NPV (kd = 0.16)	NPV (kd = 0.14)	NPV (kd = 0.12)	NPV (kd = 0.1)	NPV (kd = 0.08)	NPV (kd = 0.06)
0	−55.62	−55.62	−55.62	−55.62	−55.62	−55.62	−55.62
1	−64.27	−51.88	−39.78	−27.84	−16.10	−4.63	6.60
2	−84.87	−58.97	−33.37	−8.12	16.70	41.06	64.88
3	−109.00	−69.04	−29.55	9.40	47.74	85.35	122.14
4	−134.55	−80.39	−26.81	26.01	78.04	129.06	178.95
5	−160.82	−92.33	−24.61	42.16	107.96	172.47	235.56
6	−187.68	−104.63	−22.73	58.04	137.67	215.71	292.05
7	−214.48	−117.19	−21.05	73.87	167.24	258.85	348.47
8	−241.83	−129.90	−19.51	89.50	196.72	301.91	404.83
9	−269.07	−142.72	−18.06	105.05	226.13	344.92	461.15
10	−296.16	−155.62	−16.68	131.54	255.50	387.89	517.45

Table 21.5 The dependence of NPV on the level of debt financing L for the values of equity costs $k_0 = 0.2$ and for different debt capital costs $k_d = 0.18; 0.16; 0.14; 0.12; 0.10; 0.08; 0.06$; $S = 250$; tax on profit rate $t = 0.2$; $\beta = 0.345$ and project duration $n = 5$

L	NPV (kd = 0.18)	NPV (kd = 0.16)	NPV (kd = 0.14)	NPV (kd = 0.12)	NPV (kd = 0.1)	NPV (kd = 0.08)	NPV (kd = 0.06)
0	−43.66	−43.66	−43.66	−43.66	−43.66	−43.66	−43.66
1	−38.96	−26.63	−14.64	−2.83	8.77	23.08	31.15
2	−46.07	−23.39	4.97	29.97	54.50	78.55	102.02
3	−56.74	−17.11	22.02	60.58	98.47	135.61	171.89
4	−68.82	−15.10	37.99	90.29	141.71	192.09	241.28
5	−81.62	−13.68	53.42	119.54	184.58	248.28	310.49
6	−94.98	−12.63	68.53	148.51	227.22	304.31	379.58
7	−108.32	−11.83	83.45	177.41	269.74	360.22	448.59
8	−122.17	−11.18	98.22	206.13	312.16	416.07	517.55
9	−135.93	−10.64	112.91	234.77	354.52	471.86	586.48
10	−149.58	−10.18	127.53	263.36	396.83	527.61	655.38

Table 21.6 The dependence of NPV on the level of debt financing L for the values of equity costs $k_0 = 0.2$ and for different debt capital costs $k_d = 0.18; 0.16; 0.14; 0.12; 0.10; 0.08; 0.06$; $S = 250$; tax on profit rate $t = 0.2$; $\beta = 0.365$ and project duration $n = 5$

L	NPV (kd = 0.18)	NPV (kd = 0.16)	NPV (kd = 0.14)	NPV (kd = 0.12)	NPV (kd = 0.1)	NPV (kd = 0.08)	NPV (kd = 0.06)
0	−31.70	−31.70	−31.70	−31.70	−31.70	−31.70	−31.70
1	−13.65	−1.39	10.49	22.18	33.65	44.80	55.69
2	−7.27	18.20	43.32	68.06	92.30	116.03	139.16
3	−4.48	34.82	73.59	111.76	149.21	185.87	221.64
4	−3.08	50.20	102.79	154.56	205.39	255.13	303.62
5	−2.41	64.96	131.45	196.91	261.19	324.10	385.43
6	−2.27	79.37	159.80	238.99	316.78	392.90	467.11
7	−2.17	93.53	187.94	280.94	372.24	461.60	548.72
8	−2.50	107.54	215.96	322.76	427.60	530.22	630.28
9	−2.79	121.44	243.87	364.50	482.91	598.80	711.81
10	−3.01	135.26	271.73	406.18	538.16	667.33	793.30

of decreasing NPV(L) for investment profitability coefficient $\beta = 0.345$ is equal to 0.16. At higher credit rates k_d values NPV(L) represents decreasing function.

3. B = 0.365

From Table 21.6 and Fig. 21.8 it is seen that NPV depends practically linearly on leverage level L, increasing or decreasing depending on credit rate value k_d. NPV(L) increases at credit rate $k_d = 0.06$; $k_d = 0.08$; $k_d = 0.1$; $k_d = 0.12$; $k_d = 0.14$ and $k_d =$

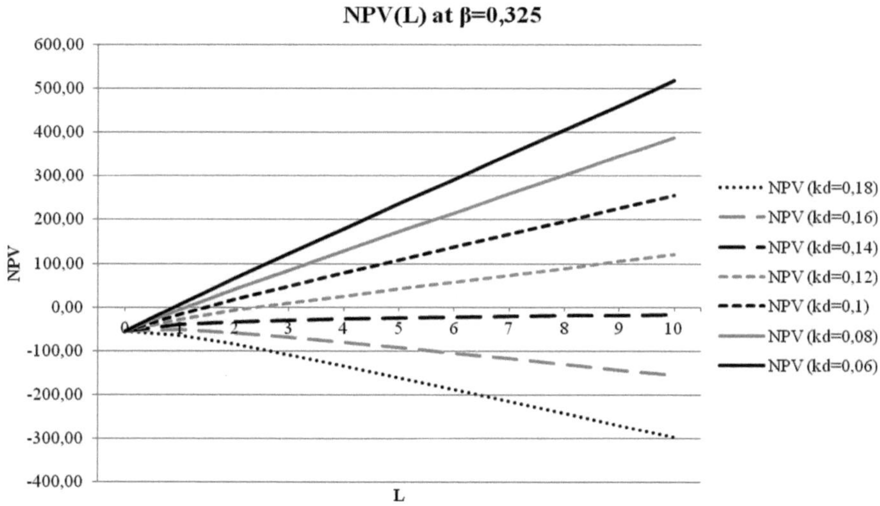

Fig. 21.6 The dependence of the Net Present Value, NPV, on the leverage level L for the equity value $k_0 = 20\%$ and for different debt capital costs $k_d = 0.18; 0.16; 0.14; 0.12; 0.10; 0.08; 0.06$; S = 250; tax on profit rate t = 0.2; investment profitability coefficient β = 0.325 and project duration n = 5

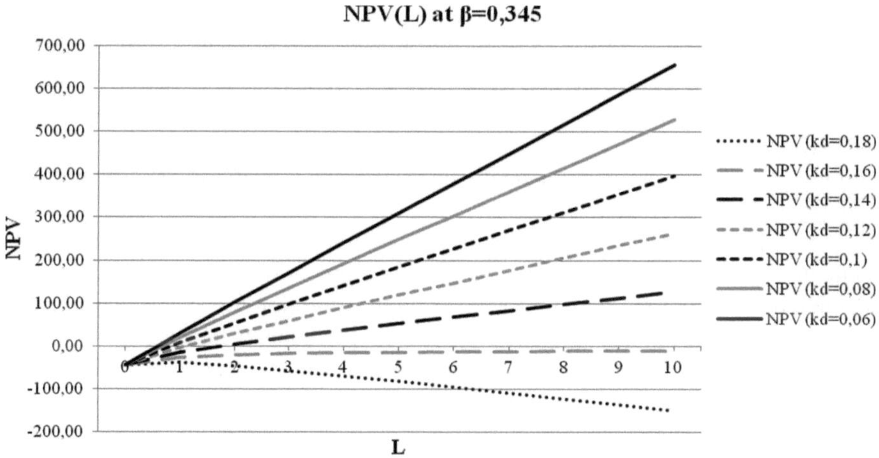

Fig. 21.7 The dependence of the Net Present Value, NPV, on the leverage level L for the equity value $k_0 = 20\%$ and for different debt capital costs $k_d = 0.18; 0.16; 0.14; 0.12; 0.10; 0.08; 0.06$; $S = 250$; tax on profit rate $t = 0.2$; investment profitability coefficient β = 0.345 and project duration n = 5

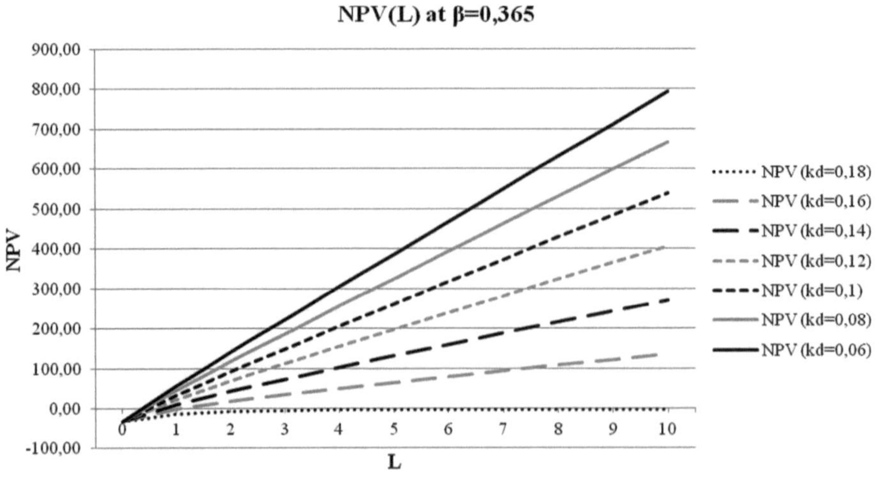

Fig. 21.8 The dependence of the Net Present Value, NPV, on the leverage level L for the equity value $k_0 = 20\%$ and for different debt capital costs $k_d = 0.18; 0.16; 0.14; 0.12; 0.10; 0.08; 0.06$; $S = 250$; tax on profit rate $t = 0.2$; investment profitability coefficient $\beta = 0.365$ and project duration $n = 5$

0.16. The cut off credit rate value k_d*, separating the range of increasing NPV(L) from the range of decreasing NPV(L) for investment profitability coefficient $\beta = 0.365$, is equal to 0.18. At higher credit rates k_d values NPV(L) represents decreasing function.

One can see that the cut off credit rate values k_d*, separating the range of increasing NPV(L) from the range of decreasing NPV(L), strongly correlate with investment profitability coefficient β and practically linearly depends on it: k_d* linearly increases with profitability coefficient β.

For arbitrary duration projects results are as folloing. The efficiency of investments strongly depends on project duration and increases with duration. One can see, that the slope of the curve NPV(L) at project duration $n = 5$ is always higher, than for project duration $n = 3$. The efficiency of investments increases with project duration and is less than for long-term (perpetuity) projects. Transition to increasing NPV(L) behavior for finite duration projects requires much higher values of investment profitability coefficient β than in case of long-term (perpetuity) projects, where k_d* is approximately equal to β: for 5-years projects the cut off credit rate values k_d* for investment profitability coefficient $\beta = 0.325$ is equal to 0.14; for investment profitability coefficient $\beta = 0.345$ is equal to 0.16; for investment profitability coefficient $\beta = 0.365$ is equal to 0.18. Thus, for finite duration projects as well as for the long-term projects cut off credit rate values k_d* turn out to be proportional to investment profitability coefficients β, but investment profitability coefficients β, is approximately twice higher than k_d*.

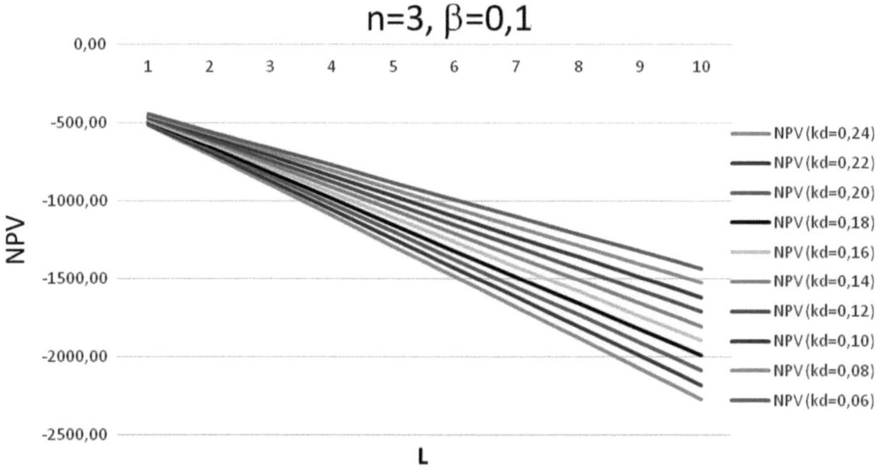

Fig. 21.9 The dependence of the Net Present Value, NPV on the leverage level L for the equity value $k_0 = 28\%$ and for different debt capital costs $k_d = 0.24;0.22;0.20;0.18; 0.16; 0.14; 0.12; 0.10; 0.08; 0.06$; $S = 250$; tax on profit rate $t = 0.2$; investment profitability coefficient $\beta = 0.1$ and project duration $n = 3$

21.4.2 The Dependence of the Efficiency of Investments NPV on the Level of Debt Financing L for the Values of Equity Costs $k_0 = 0.28$

Below at Figs. 21.9, 21.10, 21.11 and 21.12 we present the results of calculations of the dependence of the Net Present Value, NPV, on the leverage level L for the equity value $k_0 = 28\%$ and for different debt capital costs $k_d = 0.24;0.22;0.20;0.18; 0.16; 0.14; 0.12; 0.10; 0.08; 0.06$; $S = 250$; tax on profit rate $t = 0.2$; investment profitability coefficient $\beta = 0.1$ and project durations $n = 3$ and $n = 5$.

From the Figs. 21.9, 21.10, 21.11 and 21.12 one can make the following conclusions:

1. NPV decreases with debt capital cost k_d.
2. NPV increases with investment profitability coefficient β as well as with project duration.
3. The cut off value k_d* has been reached at Figs. 21.9, 21.10, 21.11 and 21.12 only at profitability coefficient $\beta = 0.2$ for 5-year project and is equal to 6%; it will increases with investment profitability coefficient β, Bigger values of β, and/or longer durations n, and/or bigger values of equity capital *S* are required in order to demonstrate the presence of a cut off value k_d* for particular project.

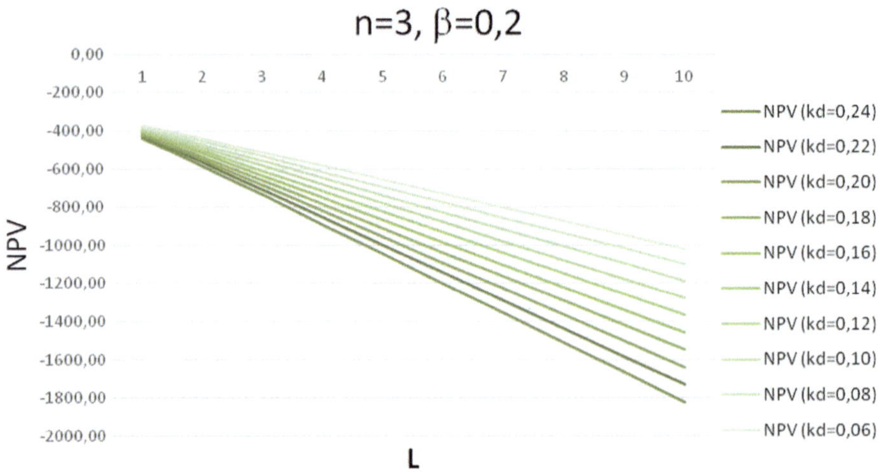

Fig. 21.10 The dependence of the Net Present Value, NPV on the leverage level L for the equity value $k_0 = 28\%$ and for different debt capital costs $k_d = 0.24;0.22;0.20;0.18;\ 0.16;\ 0.14;\ 0.12;\ 0.10;\ 0.08;\ 0.06$; S = 250; tax on profit rate t = 0.2; investment profitability coefficient β = 0.2 and project duration n = 3

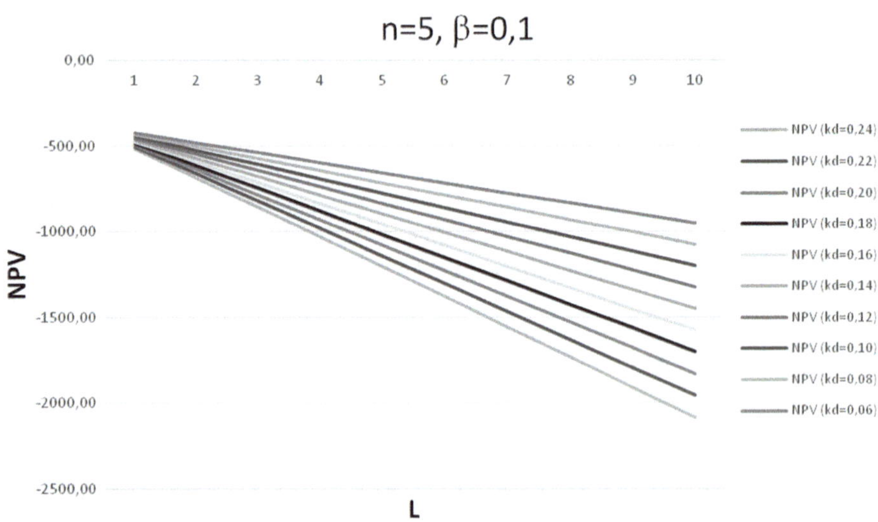

Fig. 21.11 The dependence of the Net Present Value, NPV on the leverage level L for the equity value $k_0 = 28\%$ and for different debt capital costs $k_d = 0.24;0.22;0.20;0.18;\ 0.16;\ 0.14;\ 0.12;\ 0.10;\ 0.08;\ 0.06$; S = 250; tax on profit rate t = 0.2; investment profitability coefficient β = 0.1 and project duration n = 5

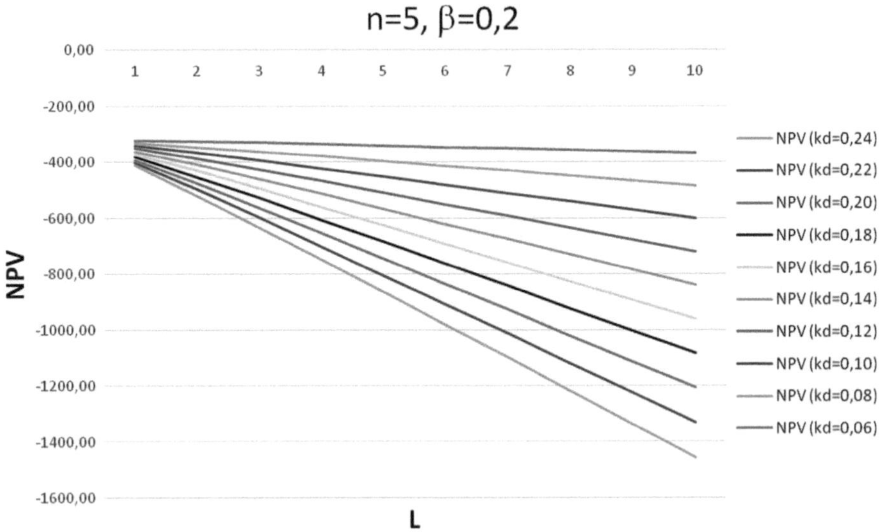

Fig. 21.12 The dependence of the Net Present Value, NPV, on the leverage level L for the equity value $k_0 = 28\%$ and for different debt capital costs $k_d = 0.24;0.22;0.20;0.18;\ 0.16;\ 0.14;\ 0.12;\ 0.10;\ 0.08;\ 0.06$; $S = 250$; tax on profit rate $t = 0.2$; investment profitability coefficient $\beta = 0.2$ and project duration $n = 5$

21.5 The Dependence of the Net Present Value, NPV, on the Leverage Level l for Projects of Different Durations

We consider the case of equity cost (at $L = 0$) $k_0 = 14\%$ and fixed value of debt cost $k_d = 0.04; 0.06; 0.08; 0.1; 0.12$ and compare the results for projects of different duration: $n = 3$ years and $n = 5$ years (Table 21.7, 21.8, 21.9, 21.10, 21.11, 21.12, 21.13, 21.14 and Figs. 21.13, 21.14, 21.15, 21.16).

Kd = 0.1

One can see, that at fixed credit rates k_0 NPV increases with project duration. The (negative) slope of NPV(L) curves decreases with project duration.

21.6 Conclusions

We study the role of the Central Bank and commercial banks in creating and maintaining of a favorable investment climate in the country. Within the framework of modern investment models created by the authors, the dependence of the efficiency of investments on the level of debt financing within a wide range of values of equity capital costs and debt capital costs under different project terms (long-term projects

Table 21.7 The dependence of the Net Present Value, NPV, on the leverage level L for the equity cost value $k_0 = 14\%$ and for debt capital costs $k_d = 0.04$; S = 250; tax on profit rate t = 0.2; investment profitability coefficient β = 0.1 and for project durations n = 3

S	L	WACC (%)	k_0	k_d	w_d	t	n	β	k_e	NPV
250	0	14.00	0.14	0.04	0.00	0.2	3	0.1	0.14	−203.57
250	1	13.34	0.14	0.04	0.50	0.2	3	0.1	0.23	−346.60
250	2	13.11	0.14	0.04	0.67	0.2	3	0.1	0.33	−491.78
250	3	13.00	0.14	0.04	0.75	0.2	3	0.1	0.42	−637.53
250	4	12.94	0.14	0.04	0.80	0.2	3	0.1	0.52	−783.49
250	5	12.89	0.14	0.04	0.83	0.2	3	0.1	0.61	−929.57
250	6	12.86	0.14	0.04	0.86	0.2	3	0.1	0.71	−1075.71
250	7	12.84	0.14	0.04	0.88	0.2	3	0.1	0.80	−1221.89
250	8	12.82	0.14	0.04	0.89	0.2	3	0.1	0.90	−1368.10
250	9	12.80	0.14	0.04	0.90	0.2	3	0.1	0.99	−1514.33
250	10	12.79	0.14	0.04	0.91	0.2	3	0.1	1.09	−1660.57

Table 21.8 The dependence of the Net Present Value, NPV, on the leverage level L for the equity cost value $k_0 = 14\%$ and for debt capital costs $k_d = 0.04$; S = 250; tax on profit rate t = 0.2; investment profitability coefficient β = 0.1 and for project durations n = 5

S	L	WACC (%)	k_0	k_d	w_d	t	n	β	k_e	NPV
250	0	14.00	0.14	0.04	0.00	0.2	5	0.1	0.14	−181.34
250	1	13.26	0.14	0.04	0.50	0.2	5	0.1	0.23	−272.31
250	2	13.01	0.14	0.04	0.67	0.2	5	0.1	0.33	−366.58
250	3	12.88	0.14	0.04	0.75	0.2	5	0.1	0.42	−461.70
250	4	12.80	0.14	0.04	0.80	0.2	5	0.1	0.51	−557.17
250	5	12.75	0.14	0.04	0.83	0.2	5	0.1	0.61	−652.81
250	6	12.72	0.14	0.04	0.86	0.2	5	0.1	0.70	−748.55
250	7	12.69	0.14	0.04	0.88	0.2	5	0.1	0.79	−844.36
250	8	12.67	0.14	0.04	0.89	0.2	5	0.1	0.88	−940.21
250	9	12.65	0.14	0.04	0.90	0.2	5	0.1	0.98	−1036.09
250	10	12.64	0.14	0.04	0.91	0.2	5	0.1	1.07	−1131.99

as well as projects of arbitrary duration) and different investment profitability coefficients β is investigated. The effectiveness of investments is determined by net present value (Net Present Value, NPV). The study is conducted within the framework of investment models with debt repayment at the end of the project term.

It is found that NPV depends practically linearly on leverage level L, increasing or decreasing depending on profitability coefficient β and credit rate value k_d. The

Table 21.9 The dependence of the Net Present Value, NPV, on the leverage level L for the equity cost value $k_0 = 14\%$ and for debt capital costs $k_d = 0.04$; S = 250; tax on profit rate t = 0.2; investment profitability coefficient $\beta = 0.2$ and for project durations n = 3

S	L	WACC (%)	k_0	k_d	w_d	t	n	β	k_e	NPV
250	0	14.00	0.14	0.04	0.00	0.2	3	0.2	0.14	−157.14
250	1	13.34	0.14	0.04	0.50	0.2	3	0.2	0.23	−252.69
250	2	13.11	0.14	0.04	0.67	0.2	3	0.2	0.33	−350.39
250	3	13.00	0.14	0.04	0.75	0.2	3	0.2	0.42	−448.64
250	4	12.94	0.14	0.04	0.80	0.2	3	0.2	0.52	−547.12
250	5	12.89	0.14	0.04	0.83	0.2	3	0.2	0.61	−645.71
250	6	12.86	0.14	0.04	0.86	0.2	3	0.2	0.71	−744.36
250	7	12.84	0.14	0.04	0.88	0.2	3	0.2	0.80	−843.05
250	8	12.82	0.14	0.04	0.89	0.2	3	0.2	0.90	−941.77
250	9	12.80	0.14	0.04	0.90	0.2	3	0.2	0.99	−1040.51
250	10	12.79	0.14	0.04	0.91	0.2	3	0.2	1.09	−1139.26

Table 21.10 The dependence of the Net Present Value, NPV, on the leverage level L for the equity cost value $k_0 = 14\%$ and for debt capital costs $k_d = 0.04$; S = 250; tax on profit rate t = 0.2; investment profitability coefficient $\beta = 0.2$ and for project durations n = 5

S	L	WACC (%)	k_0	k_d	w_d	t	n	β	k_e	NPV
250	0	14.00	0.14	0.04	0.00	0.2	5	0.2	0.14	−112.68
250	1	13.26	0.14	0.04	0.50	0.2	5	0.2	0.23	−132.50
250	2	13.01	0.14	0.04	0.67	0.2	5	0.2	0.33	−155.57
250	3	12.88	0.14	0.04	0.75	0.2	5	0.2	0.42	−179.49
250	4	12.80	0.14	0.04	0.80	0.2	5	0.2	0.51	−203.76
250	5	12.75	0.14	0.04	0.83	0.2	5	0.2	0.61	−228.20
250	6	12.72	0.14	0.04	0.86	0.2	5	0.2	0.70	−252.73
250	7	12.69	0.14	0.04	0.88	0.2	5	0.2	0.79	−277.33
250	8	12.67	0.14	0.04	0.89	0.2	5	0.2	0.88	−301.97
250	9	12.65	0.14	0.04	0.90	0.2	5	0.2	0.98	−326.65
250	10	12.64	0.14	0.04	0.91	0.2	5	0.2	1.07	−351.34

cut off credit rate values k_d* separating the range of increasing NPV(L) from range of decreasing NPV(L) are determined.

For long-term projects (Modigliani–Miller limit) it was found that the cut off credit rate values k_d* are proportional to investment profitability coefficients β: it turns out that for equity capital cost $k_0 = 0.2$ the cut off credit rate value k_d* separating the range of increasing NPV(L) from range of decreasing NPV(L) is approximately equal to investment profitability coefficient β: for investment profitability coefficient $\beta = 0.1$ k_d* is equal to 0.1; for $\beta = 0.12$ k_d* is equal to 0.12; and for investment

Table 21.11 The dependence of the Net Present Value, NPV, on the leverage level L for the equity cost value $k_0 = 14\%$ and for debt capital costs $k_d = 0.1$; S = 250; tax on profit rate t = 0.2; investment profitability coefficient $\beta = 0.2$ and for project durations n = 3

S	L	WACC (%)	k_0	k_d	w_d	t	n	β	k_e	NPV
250	0	14.00	0.14	0.10	0.00	0.2	3	0.1	0.14	−203.57
250	1	12.51	0.14	0.10	0.50	0.2	3	0.1	0.17	−377.91
250	2	12.01	0.14	0.10	0.67	0.2	3	0.1	0.20	−557.74
250	3	11.76	0.14	0.10	0.75	0.2	3	0.1	0.23	−739.00
250	4	11.61	0.14	0.10	0.80	0.2	3	0.1	0.26	−923.85
250	5	11.51	0.14	0.10	0.83	0.2	3	0.1	0.29	−1103.00
250	6	11.44	0.14	0.10	0.86	0.2	3	0.1	0.32	−1285.31
250	7	11.39	0.14	0.10	0.88	0.2	3	0.1	0.35	−1467.73
250	8	11.35	0.14	0.10	0.89	0.2	3	0.1	0.38	−1650.23
250	9	11.31	0.14	0.10	0.90	0.2	3	0.1	0.41	−1832.77
250	10	11.28	0.14	0.10	0.91	0.2	3	0.1	0.44	−2015.35

Table 21.12 The dependence of the Net Present Value, NPV, on the leverage level L for the equity cost value $k_0 = 14\%$ and for debt capital costs $k_d = 0.1$; S = 250; tax on profit rate t = 0.2; investment profitability coefficient $\beta = 0.1$ and for project durations n = 5

S	L	WACC (%)	k_0	k_d	w_d	t	n	β	k_e	NPV
250	0	14.00	0.14	0.10	0.00	0.2	5	0.1	0.14	−181.34
250	1	12.41	0.14	0.10	0.50	0.2	5	0.1	0.17	−317.91
250	2	11.88	0.14	0.10	0.67	0.2	5	0.1	0.20	−462.97
250	3	11.61	0.14	0.10	0.75	0.2	5	0.1	0.22	−610.30
250	4	11.45	0.14	0.10	0.80	0.2	5	0.1	0.25	−758.57
250	5	11.34	0.14	0.10	0.83	0.2	5	0.1	0.28	−907.31
250	6	11.26	0.14	0.10	0.86	0.2	5	0.1	0.31	−1056.33
250	7	11.20	0.14	0.10	0.88	0.2	5	0.1	0.34	−1205.52
250	8	11.16	0.14	0.10	0.89	0.2	5	0.1	0.36	−1354.83
250	9	11.12	0.14	0.10	0.90	0.2	5	0.1	0.39	−1504.22
250	10	11.09	0.14	0.10	0.91	0.2	5	0.1	0.42	−1653.67

profitability coefficient $\beta = 0.14$ k_d* is equal to 0.14. The slope of the curve NPV(L) increases with investment profitability coefficient β for the same value of credit rate k_d.

We come to conclusion that for long-term projects (in perpetuity limit) for both cases for the equity values $k_0 = 20\%$ and $k_0 = 28\%$ it turns out that the cut off credit rate values k_d* are equal to investment profitability coefficient β, and does

Table 21.13 The dependence of the Net Present Value, NPV, on the leverage level L for the equity cost value $k_0 = 14\%$ and for debt capital costs $k_d = 0.1$; S = 250; tax on profit rate t = 0.2; investment profitability coefficient $\beta = 0.2$ and for project durations n = 3

S	L	WACC (%)	k_0	k_d	w_d	t	n	β	k_e	NPV
250	0	14.00	0.14	0.10	0.00	0.2	3	0.2	0.14	−157.14
250	1	12.51	0.14	0.10	0.50	0.2	3	0.2	0.17	−282.68
250	2	12.01	0.14	0.10	0.67	0.2	3	0.2	0.20	−413.66
250	3	11.76	0.14	0.10	0.75	0.2	3	0.2	0.23	−546.07
250	4	11.61	0.14	0.10	0.80	0.2	3	0.2	0.26	−679.06
250	5	11.51	0.14	0.10	0.83	0.2	3	0.2	0.29	−812.35
250	6	11.44	0.14	0.10	0.86	0.2	3	0.2	0.32	−945.80
250	7	11.39	0.14	0.10	0.88	0.2	3	0.2	0.35	−1079.36
250	8	11.35	0.14	0.10	0.89	0.2	3	0.2	0.38	−1212.99
250	9	11.31	0.14	0.10	0.90	0.2	3	0.2	0.41	−1346.67
250	10	11.28	0.14	0.10	0.91	0.2	3	0.2	0.44	−1480.38

Table 21.14 The dependence of the Net Present Value, NPV, on the leverage level L for the equity cost value $k_0 = 14\%$ and for debt capital costs $k_d = 0.1$; S = 250; tax on profit rate t = 0.2; investment profitability coefficient $\beta = 0.2$ and for project durations n = 5

S	L	WACC (%)	k_0	k_d	w_d	t	n	β	k_e	NPV
250	0	14.00	0.14	0.10	0.00	0.2	5	0.2	0.14	−112.68
250	1	12.41	0.14	0.10	0.50	0.2	5	0.2	0.17	−175.18
250	2	11.88	0.14	0.10	0.67	0.2	5	0.2	0.20	−246.02
250	3	11.61	0.14	0.10	0.75	0.2	5	0.2	0.22	−319.09
250	4	11.45	0.14	0.10	0.80	0.2	5	0.2	0.25	−393.09
250	5	11.34	0.14	0.10	0.83	0.2	5	0.2	0.28	−467.55
250	6	11.26	0.14	0.10	0.86	0.2	5	0.2	0.31	−542.29
250	7	11.20	0.14	0.10	0.88	0.2	5	0.2	0.34	−617.20
250	8	11.16	0.14	0.10	0.89	0.2	5	0.2	0.36	−692.22
250	9	11.12	0.14	0.10	0.90	0.2	5	0.2	0.39	−767.32
250	10	11.09	0.14	0.10	0.91	0.2	5	0.2	0.42	−842.47

not depend on the equity values k_0). This statement is not valid for the projects of arbitrary (finite) durations.

For arbitrary duration projects results are as folloing. The efficiency of investments strongly depends on project duration and increases with duration. One can see, that the slope of the curve NPV(L) at project duration n = 5 is always higher, than for project duration n = 3. The efficiency of investments increases with project duration and is less than for long-term (perpetuity) projects. Transition to increasing

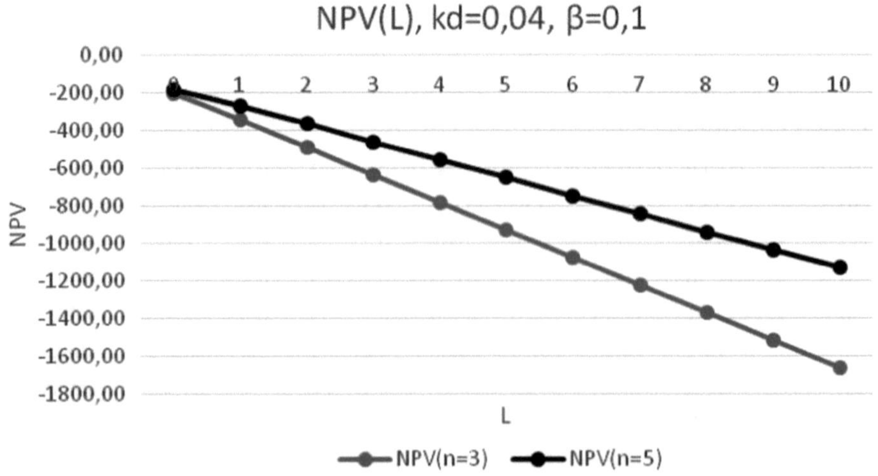

Fig. 21.13 The dependence of the Net Present Value, NPV, on the leverage level L for the equity cost value $k_0 = 14\%$ and for debt capital costs $k_d = 0.04$; $S = 250$; tax on profit rate $t = 0.2$; investment profitability coefficient $\beta = 0.1$ and for two project durations $n = 3$ and $n = 5$

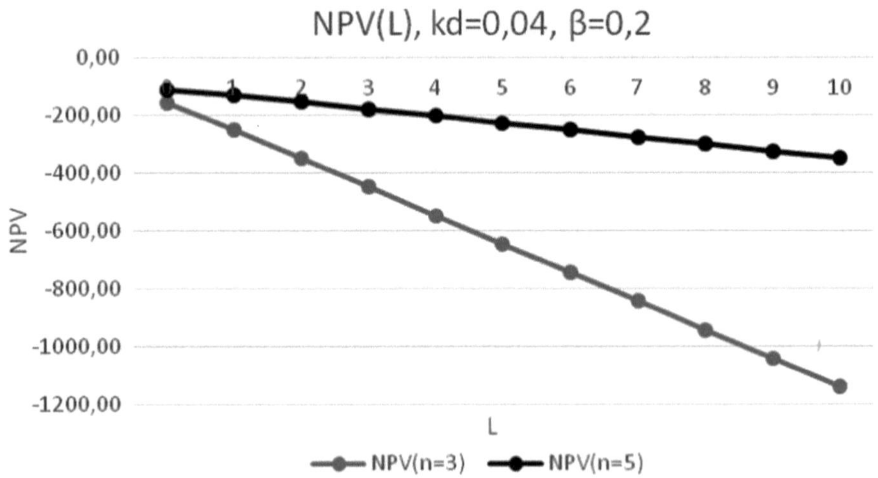

Fig. 21.14 The dependence of the Net Present Value, NPV, on the leverage level L for the equity cost value $k_0 = 14\%$ and for debt capital costs $k_d = 0.04$; $S = 250$; tax on profit rate $t = 0.2$; investment profitability coefficient $\beta = 0.2$ and for two project durations $n = 3$ and $n = 5$

NPV(L) behavior for finite duration projects requires much higher values of investment profitability coefficient β than in case of long-term (perpetuity) projects, where k_d* is approximately equal to β: for example, for equity cost $k_0 = 0.20$ and 5-years projects the cut off credit rate values k_d* for investment profitability coefficient β $= 0.325$ is equal to 0.14; for investment profitability coefficient $\beta = 0.345$ is equal

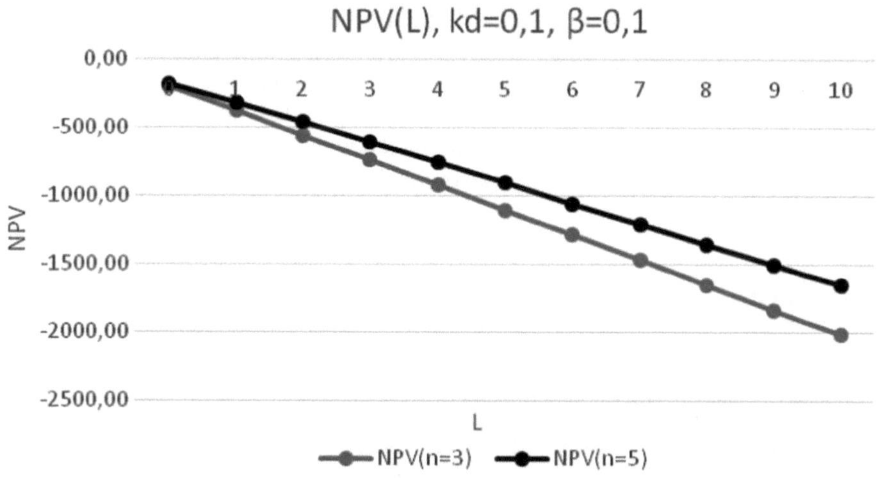

Fig. 21.15 The dependence of the Net Present Value, NPV on the leverage level L for the equity cost value $k_0 = 14\%$ and for debt capital costs $k_d = 0.1$; S = 250; tax on profit rate t = 0.2; investment profitability coefficient $\beta = 0.1$ and for two project durations n = 3 and n = 5

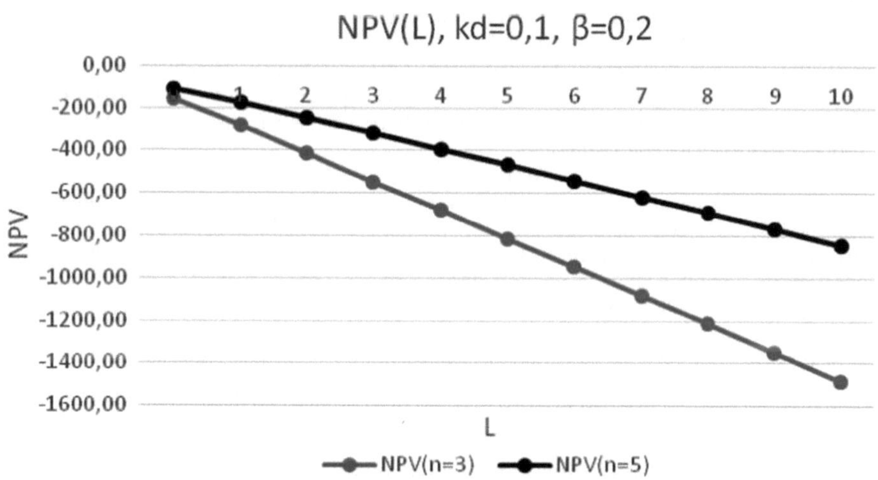

Fig. 21.16 The dependence of the Net Present Value, NPV, on the leverage level L for the equity cost value $k_0 = 14\%$ and for debt capital costs $k_d = 0.1$; S = 250; tax on profit rate t = 0.2; investment profitability coefficient $\beta = 0.2$ and for two project durations n = 3 and n = 5

to 0.16; for investment profitability coefficient $\beta = 0.365$ is equal to 0.18. Thus, for finite duration projects as well as for the long-term projects cut off credit rate values k_d* turn out to be proportional to investment profitability coefficients β, but investment profitability coefficients β, is approximately twice higher than k_d*.

We develop a method of determination of the cut off credit rate values k_d*, separating the range of increasing NPV(L) from range of decreasing NPV(L). We have found the cut off credit rate k_d* values within a wide range of values of equity costs k_0 and debt capital costs k_d under different project terms (long-term projects as well as projects of arbitrary duration) and different investment profitability coefficients β. Obtained results will help to the Central Bank keep its key rate at the level, which allow commercial banks keep their credit rates below the cut off credit rate values k_d* in order to create and maintain a favorable investment climate in the country.

References

Brusov PN, Filatova TV (2011) From Modigliani–Miller to general theory of capital cost and capital structure of the company. Financ Credit 435:2–8

Brusov PN, Filatova TV (2025a) Business valuation and company value: New qualitative approaches considering business and financial risks. Springer Nature Publishing, pp.1–654

Brusov PN, Filatova TV (2025b) Efficiency of investment projects: Modern investment models and their applications. Springer Nature Publishing, pp.1–843

Brusov P, Filatova T, Orehova N, Brusova A (2011a) Weighted average cost of capital in the theory of Modigliani–Miller, modified for a finite life-time company. Appl Financ Econ 21(11):815–824

Brusov P, Filatova T, Orehova N et al (2011b) From Modigliani–Miller to general theory of capital cost and capital structure of the company. Res J Econ Bus ICT 2:16–21

Brusov P, Filatova T, Orehova N et al (2011c) Influence of debt financing on the effectiveness of the investment project within the Modigliani–Miller theory. Res J Econ Bus ICT (UK) 2:11–15

Brusov P, Filatova T, Eskindarov M, Orehova N (2012a) Influence of debt financing on the effectiveness of the finite duration investment project. Appl Financ Econ 22(13):1043–1052

Brusov P, Filatova T, Eskindarov M, Orehova N (2012b) Hidden global causes of the global financial crisis. J Rev Global Econ 1:106–111

Brusov PN, Filatova TV, Kulik VL (2024) Capital asset pricing model (CAPM) 2.0: Account of business and financial risk. Finance: Theory and Practice. 28(2):128–142. https://doi.org/10.26794/2587-5671-2024-28-2-128-142

Brusov P, Filatova P, Orekhova N (2013a) Absence of an optimal capital structure in the famous tradeoff theory! J Rev Global Econ 2:94–116

Brusov P, Filatova T, Orehova N (2013b) A qualitatively new effect in corporative finance: abnormal dependence of cost of equity of company on leverage. J Rev Global Econ 2:183–193

Brusov P, Filatova P, Orekhova N (2014a) Mechanism of formation of the company optimal capital structure, different from suggested by trade off theory. Cogent Econ Financ 2:1–13. https://doi.org/10.1080/23322039.20946150

Brusov P, Filatova T, Orehova N (2014b) Inflation in Brusov–Filatova–Orekhova theory and in its perpetuity limit—Modigliani–Miller theory. J Rev Global Econ 3:175–185

Brusov P, Filatova T, Orehova N, Eskindarov M (2015) Modern corporate finance, investments and taxation, monograph, 1st edn. Springer, London, p 368

Brusov P, Filatova T, Orehova N, Kulk WI (2018a) New meaningful effects in modern capital structure theory. J Rev Global Econ 7:104–122

Brusov P, Filatova T, Orehova N, Kulk V (2018b) A "golden age" of the companies: conditions of its existence. J Rev Global Econ 7:88–103

Brusov P, Filatova T, Orehova N, Kulk V (2018c) Rating methodology: new look and new horizons. J Rev Global Econ 7:63–87

Brusov P, Filatova T, Orehova N, Kulk V (2018d) Rating: new approach. J Rev Global Econ 7:37–62

Brusova A (2011) A comparison of the three methods of estimation of weighted average cost of capital and equity cost of company. Financ Anal Prob Sol 34(76):36–42

Brusov PN, Filatova TV, Orekhova NP (2021) Ratings: Critical analysis and new approaches of quantitative and qualitative methodology. Springer Nature Publishing, pp.1–369

Brusov PN, Filatova TV, Orekhova NP (2022) Generalized Modigliani–Miller theory: Applications in corporate finance, investments, taxation and ratings. Springer Nature Publishing, pp.1–362

Brusov PN, Filatova TV, Orekhova NP (2023) The Brusov–Filatova–Orekhova theory of capital structure: Applications in corporate finance, investments, taxation and ratings. Springer Nature Publishing, pp.1–769

Filatova T, Orehova N, Brusova A (2008) Weighted average cost of capital in the theory of Modigliani–Miller, modified for a finite life-time company. Bull FU 48:68–77

Modigliani F, Miller M (1958) The cost of capital, corporate finance, and the theory of investment. Am Econ Rev 48:261–297

Modigliani F, Miller M (1963) Corporate income taxes and the cost of capital: a correction. Am Econ Rev 53:147–175

Modigliani F, Miller M (1966) Some estimates of the cost of capital to the electric utility industry 1954–1957. Am Econ Rev 56:333–391

Chapter 22
Cost of Equity, Taxes and Dividend Policy

22.1 Introduction

In this Chapter the impact of the tax burden on the company's dividend policy is analyzed.

As is well known, valuation of equity cost, which determines the amount of dividends, is an extremely complex task. It is possible to do this within one of the two main capital structure theories: either the Modigliani–Miller (MM) theory or the Brusov–Filatova–Orekhova (BFO) one. The first one is valid for perpetual companies only, while the second describes the companies of arbitrary ages. Until recently, both of these theories did not take into account some real conditions for the functioning of companies, such as the variable income of companies, the frequent payments of income tax, types of income tax payments (advance payments and payments at the end of reporting periods), etc. This was some gap in the study of the problem of the cost of equity. The challenge was to adapt both theories to these conditions and use the generalized Brusov–Filatova–Orekhova (BFO) and Modigliani–Miller (MM) theories in studying the problem of the cost of equity.

The correct dividend policy of the company, based on the correct assessment of the cost of equity, has both macroeconomic and microeconomic aspects.

From a macroeconomic point of view, it plays an important role in ensuring economic growth and economic efficiency, as well as the position in the financial and investment markets. At the macroeconomic level as well, an adequate dividend policy leads to increased investment and economic growth.

From a microeconomic point of view, the importance of a correct assessment of the cost of equity and the establishment of an adequate dividend policy of the company is determined by the following.

The rights of shareholders to receive adequate profit may be violated if the management of the company pursues an incorrect and inefficient dividend policy, due to the

P. Brusov and T. Filatova, *Taxes and Taxation*, Contributions to Finance and Accounting, https://doi.org/10.1007/978-3-032-11077-0_22

inability of management to correctly determine the amount of dividends (the economically justified amount of which is the cost of equity), or with a deliberate violation of the rights of shareholders in this sphere.

After the recent generalization of both theories, taking into account the real conditions of the functioning of the companies, it becomes possible to estimate the cost of equity in these conditions. Dependence of the cost of equity on the level of leverage for different ages of the company, different values of equity and debt costs, different frequencies of income tax payment, advance payments of income tax and payments at the end of periods, variable income of companies, etc. are being studied. The behavior and properties of the cost of equity are explored within the framework of the BFO theory. Several very important innovative effects have been discovered, which significantly change the company's dividend policy. Among them are the abnormal dependence of equity cost on leverage level at different growth rates of variable income, at different ages of the company, at different frequencies of income tax payment, at different debt costs etc. The developed methodology and results will help the company's management to develop an adequate and effective dividend policy.

A comprehensive analysis was carried out of one of the most striking and significant phenomena in corporate finance in general and in the capital structure in particular—the anomalous dependence of the cost of equity on the leverage level, L. The first qualitative theory of the capital structure—Modigliani–Miller theory (Modigliani and Miller 1958, 1963, 1966) had numerous limitations, the main ones being its perpetual nature and the absence of taxes: corporate and individual. Many scientists have tried to modify the Modigliani–Miller theory in different aspects (Hamada 1969; Miller 1977; Farber et al. 2006a; Fernandez 2006a; Berk and Marzo 2007a; Harris and Pringle 1985a; Baumol et al. 1982; Black 1986; Becker 2021; Berk and De Marzo 2007b; Brealey and Myers 1981; Brealey et al. 2014; Bhattacharya 1978; Myers 2001).

In 2008 the main limitation of the Modigliani–Miller theory—the eternity of companies—was removed by Filatova et al. (2008), and modern theories of the cost of capital and capital structure—Brusov–Filatova–Orekhova theory (BFO-theory) were created for companies of arbitrary age (BFO–1 theory) and for companies of arbitrary lifetime (BFO-2 theory) (Brusov et al. 2015, 2018a; Brusov and Filatova 2023). The well–known theory of the cost of capital and capital structure of Nobel laureates Modigliani and Miller has been replaced by Brusov–Filatova–Orekhova (BFO) theory (Brusov et al. 2021, 2022, 2023, 2024; Brusov and Filatova 2025a,b). The authors departed from the Modigliani–Miller assumption about the eternity (infinity of life) of companies and developed a quantitative theory for estimating the main parameters of the financial activity of companies of arbitrary age. The results of the modern BFO theory turn out to be quite different from the results of the Modigliani–Miller theory. They show that the latter, due to its perpetuity, underestimates the cost of raising capital (WACC and equity) and significantly overestimates the company value. Such an incorrect assessment of key performance indicators of companies' financial activities led to an underestimation of the associated risks and the impossibility or serious difficulties in making adequate management decisions, which was one of the latent causes of the 2008 global financial crisis, which began with the crisis in the MBS (mortgage–backed securities) market.

In the Modigliani–Miller theory, there is no time factor (time is equal to infinity), which does not allow us to investigate the dependence of the company's financial performance on the time factor. But the theories of Brusov–Filatova–Orekhova (BFO–theories) are created for companies of arbitrary age and allow studying the dependence of a company's financial performance on the time factor.

Over the past couple of years, two main theories of the capital structure—Brusov–Filatova–Orekhova and Modigliani–Miller—have been adapted to the established financial practice of the functioning of companies, taking into account the real conditions of their work (see Brusov and Filatova 2023 and references there). This made it possible to investigate the impact of frequent income tax payments p with advance income tax payments and payments at the end of reporting periods, as well as the impact of the company's variable income on its main financial results. In paper (Brusov and Filatova 2023), an analysis of all existing theories of the capital structure (with their advantages and disadvantages) was carried out in order to understand all aspects of the problem and make the right management decisions in practice. The role of the capital structure lies in the fact that the correct determination of the optimal capital structure allows the company's management to maximize the capitalization of the company and fulfill the long–term goal of the functioning of any company. In paper (Brusov and Filatova 2023), the state of the theory of the structure of capital and the cost of capital is considered from the middle of the last century, when the first quantitative theory was created, to the present. The two main theories of Modigliani–Miller (MM) and Brusov–Filatova–Orekhova (BFO) are discussed and analyzed, as well as their numerous modifications and generalizations. The Brusov–Filatova–Orekhova (BFO) theory, its methodology, and results are widely known (Brusov and Filatova 2023; Brusov et al. 2015, 2018b; Dimitropoulos 2014; Luiz and Cruz 2015; Barbi 2011; Franc-Dąbrowska et al. 2021; Angotti et al. 2018; Vergara-Novoa et al. 2018; Mundi et al. 2022; Sadiq et al. 2022; Becker 2022; El-Chaarani et al. 2022). Many authors [see, for example, Angotti et al. (2018), Vergara-Novoa et al. (2018) and Mundi et al. (2022)] use the BFO theory in practice.

In addition to the approach of Modigliani and Miller, there are alternative approaches: Harris and Pringle (1985b) and Miles and Ezzell (1980).

Below we discuss them.

The following notation will be used in the text below.

k_d, $w_d = \frac{D}{D+S}$—the debt capital cost and debt capital share, k_e, $w_e = \frac{S}{D+S}$—the equity capital cost and the equity capital share, and $L = D/S$—the value of financial leverage, D—the debt capital value, S—the equity capital value, k_0—the equity capital cost at zero leverage level, g—income growth rate, p—frequency of tax on income payments, $WACC$—the weighted average cost of capital, t—tax on profit, n—company age.

Alternate WACC Formula

An alternate formula for the *WACC* has been suggested (Berk and DeMarzo 2007b; Miles and Ezzell 1980; Farber et al. 2006b; Fernandez 2006b). It has the form below

$$WACC = k_0(1 - w_d t) - k_d t w_d + k_{TS} t w_d. \tag{22.1}$$

Here, k_0, k_d, and k_{TS} are the returns on the financially independent company, the debt, and the tax shield, respectively, t is the corporate tax rate, and w_d is the debt share.

Although Eq. (22.1) is quite general, additional conditions are needed for practical applicability. When the *WACC* remains constant over time, the value of a leveraged company can be found by discounting the unleveraged free cash flows using the *WACC*. In this case, specific formulas can be found in textbook (Black 1986).

In the Modigliani–Miller theory (Modigliani and Miller 1958, 1963, 1966), the debt value D is constant. V_0 is also constant, as the expected after–tax cash–flow of the financially independent company is fixed. By assumption, $k_{TS} = k_d$ and the tax shield value is $TS = tD$. Therefore, the company value V is a constant and the alternate *WACC* formula (22.1) simplifies the MM formula:

$$WACC = k_0(1 - w_d t). \tag{22.2}$$

The "classical" MM theory, suggesting that the returns on the debt k_d and the tax shield k_{TS} are equals (both these values have debt nature), is much more reasonable, so this is why we modify the "classical" MM theory, namely.

The Miles–Ezzell Model Versus the Modigliani–Miller Theory

Becker (Cooper and Nyborg 2018) discussed the differences between the Modigliani–Miller theory (Modigliani and Miller 1958, 1963, 1966) and the Miles–Ezzell model (Harris and Pringle 1985b), which deal with the stochasticity of free cash flows. The Modigliani–Miller theory considers a stationary process, while in the Miles–Ezzell model the process is stochastic. The author conducts a numerical experiment that allows you to determine the values and discount rates using a risk–neutral approach. He analyzes three formulas:

Modigliani–Miller theory (Modigliani and Miller 1958, 1963, 1966):

$$WACC = k_0(1 - w_d t); \tag{22.3}$$

Miles–Ezzell model (Miles and Ezzell 1980):

$$WACC = k_0 - w_d t k_f \frac{1 + k_0}{1 + k_f}; \tag{22.4}$$

Brusov et al. (2023a):

$$WACC = k_0 - w_d k_f t, \tag{22.5}$$

where k_f stands for the risk-free rate, which equals the required return of the debt holders.

The author shows that in the Miles–Ezzell model, all cash flows and the values depend on the path, in contrast to the Modigliani–Miller theory. Additionally, in the Miles–Ezzell model, all discount rates are time independent, with the exception of the discount rate used to discount tax shields, which depends on the duration of the cash flows. Conversely, in the Modigliani–Miller theory, all discount rates change over time except for the constant tax shield discount rate. This affects the applicability of the well–known formula for annuities and the development of models for estimating both finite and perpetual cash flows.

In this paper, Becker (Cooper and Nyborg 2018) raises the issue of paying the debt body together with the payment of interest on the debt. Regarding this issue, we would like to note that in both classical MM and BFO theories, the body of the debt is not paid. In the framework of the Modigliani–Miller theory, such an account is fundamentally impossible, while in the BFO theory it can be conducted and was conducted in the framework of the BFO–2 theory, where the amount of debt D decreases with time. This decrease in the value of debt D results in a decrease in the tax shield (see BFO-2 theory) (Brusov et al. 2018a, 2024; Miller 1985).

Dividend Policy Under Asymmetric Information

As we mentioned above, the economically justified amount of dividends is equal to the cost of equity. The task of calculating the cost of equity capital is one of the most difficult in financial management. Because of this problem, management decisions made by company managers are not always correct.

The rights of shareholders to receive adequate profits may be violated when the management of the company pursues an incorrect and ineffective dividend policy due to the inability of management to correctly determine the amount of dividends (the economically justified amount of which is the cost of equity capital), or with a deliberate violation of the rights of shareholders in this area.

The asymmetric information means that the company's managers know more than outside investors about the true state of the company's current earnings.

Miller and Rock (Hamada 1972) extended the standard financial model of dividend/investment/financing decisions of a company for conditions of asymmetric information. They showed that once stock trading along with asymmetric information is included in the model, Fisher's criterion for optimal investment becomes time–inconsistent: the market's belief that a company follows Fisher's rule creates incentives to violate the rule.

(Fisher's rule postulates that in the presence of efficient capital markets, a company's choice of investments is independent of the investment preferences of its owners, and therefore the company should be motivated only to maximize profits.)

Miller and Rock (Hamada 1972) showed that an informationally consistent signaling equilibrium exists under asymmetric information and stock trading, which restores the temporal consistency of investment policy but generally leads to lower levels of investment than the optimal achievable under perfect information and/or no trading. Contractual provisions that modify information asymmetry or the ability to profit from it could eliminate both temporary inconsistency and inefficiency in investment policies, but these contractual provisions are also likely to incur sunk costs.

In this study we do not use an econometric model, but rather a first principles approach. Both theories (MM and BFO) use this approach. However, there are empirical studies where scientists have considered the influence of various factors on the cost of equity capital using simpler models. One of them is as follows.

The paper (Brusov et al. 2022) examines the impact of environmental, social and governance (ESG) disclosures on the cost of equity capital in the food and beverage (F&B) sector.

This study analyses a sample of 171 internationally listed firms pertaining to the F&B sector and headquartered in North America, Western Europe and Asia Pacific (developed), forming an unbalanced panel of 1.316 observations, spanning the period 2010–2019. Authors run a fixed–effects panel regression model to test the relationship between ESG disclosure and the cost of equity capital. The authors' empirical outcomes suggest a significant negative relationship between ESG disclosure and the cost of equity capital. Authors find support for the notion that increased levels of ESG disclosure are linked to improved access to financial resources for firms.

The hypotheses of the current study are as follows (Raimo et al. 2021): (1) the actual operating conditions of companies affect the dependence of the cost of equity on debt financing and the company's dividend policy,(2) the abnormal dependence of the cost of equity on the company's debt financing can radically change the company's dividend policy. The presence and magnitude of the anomalous effect can be changed and controlled by changing such parameters as the cost of equity, k_e and debt capital, k_d, the frequency and method of paying income tax, the growth of the income rate, the age of the company, etc. The aims of this paper is to study the influence of the conditions of the real functioning of companies on the dependence of the cost of equity on debt financing, as well as on the anomalous effect: on its existence and management. The following research methods are used: the generalized Brusov–Filatova–Orekhova (BFO theory) and calculations by Microsoft Excel the equity cost depends on debt financing at different parameters, such as k_0 and k_d, the frequency and method of paying income tax, the growth of the income rate, the age of the company, etc. The anomalous effect affects the company's dividend policy and requires careful and detailed study. It's done here. The motivation of the study is to investigate one of the most striking effects in corporate finance—the anomalous dependence of the cost of equity on the company's debt financing. The significance of this study is determined by the importance of the anomalous effect that significantly affects the company's dividend policy. The limitation of the study is due to the fact that the case of a constant income growth rate is considered. In future publications, the case of a variable income growth rate will be considered. One more limitation of the consideration is related to the known limitations of the WACC approximation.

The structure of the paper is as follows:

We briefly discuss the literature review below. In Sect. 22.1 we will discuss the theoretical basis of our consideration and give the main formulas for *WACC* and k_d, which will be used to calculate *WACC* and k_e, and the influence of all considered factors on the dependence of equity cost k_e on the level of debt financing, *L*.

In Sect. 22.2 the influence of the following factors on the dependence of equity cost k_e on the level of debt financing, L is considered. In Sect. 22.2.1. Increase of tax on profit is considered; in Sect. 22.2.2. Variable income is considered; In Sect. 22.2.2.1. Influence of growth rate g is considered for tax on income payments at the ends of periods. In Sect. 22.2.2.2. Influence of growth rate g is considered with a comparison of results with advance income tax payments and payments at the end of periods. In Sect. 22.2.3. Frequent income tax payments is considered. In Sect. 22.2.3.1. Income tax payments at the ends of periods are considered. In Sect. 22.2.3.1. Frequent tax on income payments is considered with comparing the results for advance payments of tax on income and payments at the ends of periods. In Sect. 22.2.4. Simultaneous influence of the growth rate g and the frequency of income tax payment, p is considered. In Sect. 22.2.5. Influence of company age, n is considered. In Sect. 22.3 the explanations of the observed effects have been done. In Sect. 22.4 Conclusions are made.

22.2 Theoretical Basis

The Brusov–Filatova–Orekhova (BFO) theory and its perpetual limit—the Modigliani–Miller theory have recently been generalized to the established practice of the functioning of companies. This generalization took into account the real operating conditions of companies, such as variable income, frequent income tax payments, advance income tax payments, etc. This made it possible to investigate the impact of these conditions on its main financial performance (Brusov et al. 2018b). In this paper we use the generalized Brusov–Filatova–Orekhova (BFO) theory as well as the generalized Modigliani–Miller theory to study the influence of the conditions of the real functioning of companies on the dependence of the cost of equity on debt financing, as well as on the anomalous effect: on its existence and management.

Below we give a summary of the WACC formulas for BFO–theory as well as for MM-theory (Brusov et al. 2018b).

The classical BFO equation for *WACC*

$$\frac{1-(1+WACC)^{-n}}{WACC-g}=\frac{1-(1+k_0)^{-n}}{(k_0-g)\cdot\left(1-w_dt\left[1-(1+k_d)^{-n}\right]\right)} \tag{22.6}$$

and its limit for perpetuity companies (MM limit)

$$WACC=k_0\cdot(1-w_dt). \tag{22.7}$$

The formula for the equity cost comes from the definition of *WACC*

$$WACC=k_ew_e+k_dw_d(1-t), \tag{22.8}$$

accounting that

$$w_e = \frac{1}{1+L};\ w_d == \frac{L}{1+L} \tag{22.9}$$

and is as following

$$k_e = WACC(1+L) - Lk_d(1-t). \tag{22.10}$$

The *WACC* formulas for BFO–theory and for MM–theory under the conditions of the real functioning of companies are presented below (Brusov et al. 2018b).

22.2.1 Variable Income Case

Income Tax Payments at the Ends of Periods

$$\text{BFO}: \quad \frac{1-\left(\frac{1+g}{1+WACC}\right)^n}{WACC-g} = \frac{1-\left(\frac{1+g}{1+k_0}\right)^n}{(k_0-g)\cdot\left(1-w_d t\left[1-(1+k_d)^{-n}\right]\right)}, \tag{22.11}$$

$$\text{MM}: \quad WACC = (k_0-g)\cdot(1-w_d t)+g. \tag{22.12}$$

Advance Income Tax Payments

$$\text{BFO}: \quad \frac{1-\left(\frac{1+g}{1+WACC}\right)^n}{WACC-g} = \frac{1-\left(\frac{1+g}{1+k_0}\right)^n}{(k_0-g)\cdot\left(1-w_d t\left[1-(1+k_d)^{-n}\right]\cdot(1+k_d)\right)}. \tag{22.13}$$

$$\text{MM}: \quad WACC = (k_0-g)\cdot(1-w_d t\cdot(1+k_d))+g. \tag{22.14}$$

22.2.2 Frequent Income Tax Payments

Income Tax Payments at the Ends of Periods

$$\text{BFO}: \quad \frac{1-(1+WACC)^{-n}}{WACC} = \frac{1-(1+k_0)^{-n}}{k_0 \cdot \left(1 - \frac{k_d w_d t}{p} \frac{\left[1-(1+k_d)^{-n}\right]}{(1+k_d)^{1/p}-1}\right)}, \tag{22.15}$$

$$\text{MM}: \quad WACC = k_0 \cdot \left(1 - \frac{k_d w_d t}{p \cdot \left[(1+k_d)^{1/p} - 1\right]}\right). \tag{22.16}$$

Advance Income Tax Payments

$$\text{BFO}: \quad \frac{1-(1+WACC)^{-n}}{WACC} = \frac{1-(1+k_0)^{-n}}{k_0 \cdot \left(1 - \frac{k_d w_d t}{p} \frac{\left[1-(1+k_d)^{-n}\right]\cdot(1+k_d)^{1/p}}{(1+k_d)^{1/p}-1}\right)}, \tag{22.17}$$

$$\text{MM}: \quad WACC = k_0 \cdot \left(1 - \frac{k_d w_d t \cdot (1+k_d)^{1/p}}{p \cdot \left[(1+k_d)^{1/p} - 1\right]}\right). \tag{22.18}$$

22.2.3 *Simultaneous Accounting of Variable Income in Case of Frequent Income Tax Payments*

Income Tax Payments at the Ends of Periods

$$\text{BFO}: \quad \frac{1-\left(\frac{1+g}{1+WACC}\right)^n}{WACC-g} = \frac{1-\left(\frac{1+g}{1+k_0}\right)^n}{(k_0-g) \cdot \left(1 - \frac{k_d w_d t}{p} \frac{\left[1-(1+k_d)^{-n}\right]}{(1+k_d)^{1/p}-1}\right)}, \tag{22.19}$$

$$\text{MM}: \quad WACC - g = (k_0 - g) \cdot \left(1 - \frac{k_d w_d t}{p \cdot (1+k_d)^{1/p} - 1}\right). \tag{22.20}$$

Advance Income Tax Payments

$$\text{BFO}: \quad \frac{1-\left(\frac{1+g}{1+WACC}\right)^n}{WACC-g} = \frac{1-\left(\frac{1+g}{1+k_0}\right)^n}{(k_0-g)\cdot\left(1-\frac{k_d w_d t}{p}\frac{\left[1-(1+k_d)^{-n}\right]\cdot(1+k_d)^{1/p}}{\left[(1+k_d)^{1/p}-1\right]}\right)}, \quad (22.21)$$

$$\text{MM}: \quad WACC-g=(k_0-g)\cdot\left(1-\frac{k_d w_d t\cdot(1+k_d)^{1/p}}{p\cdot(1+k_d)^{1/p}-1}\right). \quad (22.22)$$

The general formula for equity cost, k_e, is as following

$$k_e = WACC(1+L) - Lk_d(1-t). \quad (22.23)$$

To study the dependence of the cost of equity capital, k_e, on various variables, it is first necessary to find the value of WACC and substitute it into formula (22.23).

22.3 Results and Discussion

Below we study the influence of the conditions of the real functioning of companies on the dependence of the cost of equity on debt financing, as well as the conditions for the existence of the "anomalous effect" and the possibility of controlling it in accordance with the program stated above.

Our consideration combines theoretical and numerical results: the latter are based on calculations in Microsoft Excel using some typical data on the cost of equity and debt capital of companies, as well as on the actual data of a particular company (see clause Sect. 22.3.4 and Figs. 22.30, 22.31, 22.32, 22.33, 22.34 and 22.35, where calculations were made for PJSC GAZP). The data are taken from company reports: profitability, leverage level, cost of debt, etc. Then the data is processed to obtain the necessary calculation parameters, the most important of which isk_0, the cost of equity at zero leverage level L.

22.3.1 Increase of Tax on Profit

Within the Modigliani–Miller theory formula for equity cost, k_e, has a view

$$k_e = k_0 + L(k_0 - k_d)(1 - t). \tag{22.24}$$

Using formula (22.19) we calculate the dependence of cost of equity, k_e, on leverage level, L at different tax on profit rates t.

It could be seen from Fig. 22.1, where the dependence of cost of equity, k_e, on leverage level, L at different tax on profit rates t is shown for the case $k_0 = 10\%$; $k_d = 8\%$ (line 1 corresponds to tax on profit rates $t = 0$; line 2 corresponds to tax on profit rates $t = 0.1$; line 3 corresponds to tax on profit rates $t = 0.2$; line 4 corresponds to tax on profit rates $t = 0.3$; line 5 corresponds to tax on profit rates $t = 0.4$; line 6 corresponds to tax on profit rates $t = 0.5$; line 7 corresponds to tax on profit rates $t = 0.6$; line 8 corresponds to tax on profit rates $t = 0.7$; line 9 corresponds to tax on profit rates line 10 corresponds to tax on profit rates $t = 0.9$; line 11 corresponds to tax on profit rates $t = 1$), that the slope k_e (L) decreases with t and becomes zero at $t = 1$. In this case (at $t = 1$) the line k_e (L) is horizontal. This behavior can be explained by the presence of a multiplier $(1 - T)$ (tax corrector).

The situation for the finite age company, described by the Brusov–Filatova–Orekhova (BFO) theory is completely different: there is an anomalous dependence of the cost of equity, k_e, on the level of leverage L: the cost of equity k_e decreases with the level of leverage L. This effect radically changes the principles of the company's dividend policy: shareholders receive smaller dividends with an increase in debt financing (which leads to financial difficulties and the risk of bankruptcy). In Fig. 22.2 the dependence of cost of equity k_e on leverage level L at different tax on profit rate t $(n = 5, k_0 = 10\%, k_d = 8\%)$ (1—$t = 0$; 2—$t = 0.2$; 3—t =0.4; 4—$t = 0.6$; 5—$T = 0.8$; 6—$t = 1$) is shown.

From Fig. 22.2 it can be seen that starting from certain values of the income tax rate (in this case, from $t^* = 40\%$), the cost of equity of a company with leverage does not increase, but decreases. Note, that$t$* value (as well as the presence or the absence of such an abnormal effect) depends on particular values of parameters n, k_0, k_d, and

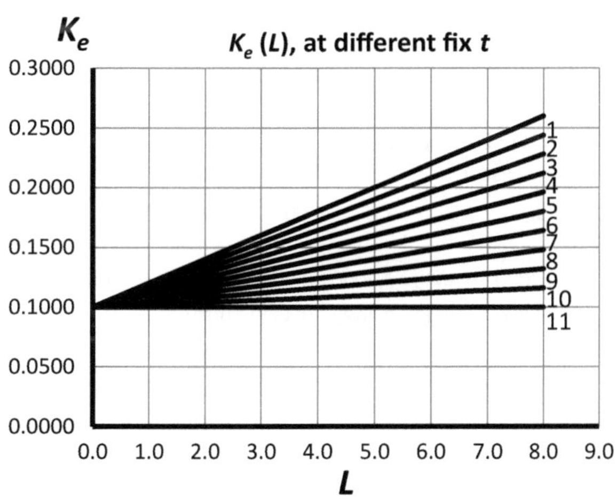

Fig. 22.1 Dependence of cost of equity on leverage level L at different tax on profit rates T

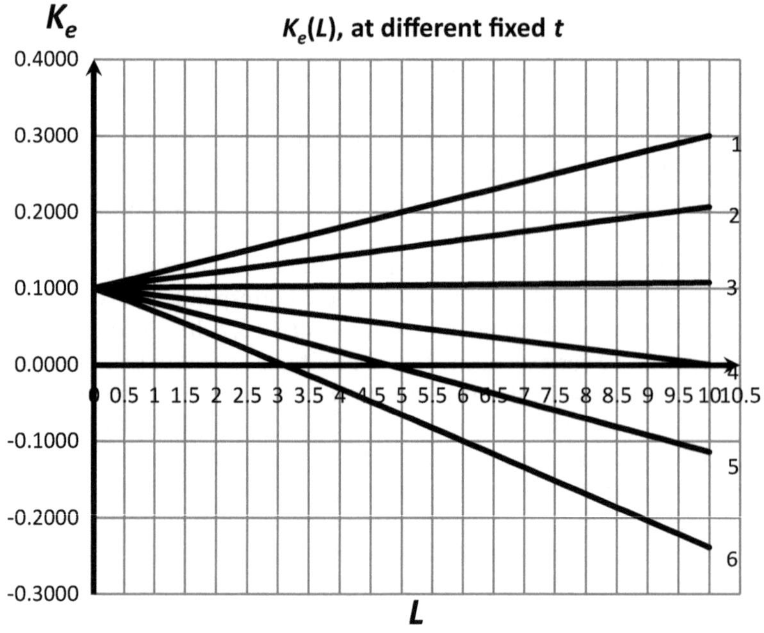

Fig. 22.2 Dependence of cost of equity k_e on leverage level L at different tax on profit rate T. *Source* Compiled by the authors

at other values of parameters n, k_0, k_d critical values of tax on profit rate t^* could be lower.

The anomalous effect could only take place for a finite–age company and is not observed in the eternal Modigliani–Miller limit.

This effect exists within the framework of the BFO theory NOT at all parameters values: below we give an example of the usual behavior similar to the Modigliani–Miller limit one (see Table 22.1 and Fig. 22.3).

Table 22.1 Dependence of cost of equity k_e on leverage level L at different fix tax on profit rates T for the case $n = 7$, $k_0 = 20\%$, $k_d = 10\%$

T/ L	0.0	1.0	2.0	3.0	4.0	5.0	6.0	7.0	8.0	9.0	10
0	0.2000	0.3000	0.4000	0.5000	0.6000	0.7000	0.8000	0.9000	1.0000	1.1000	1.2000
0.2	0.2000	0.2842	0.3682	0.4522	0.5362	0.6202	0.7042	0.7874	0.8713	0.9551	1.0389
0.4	0.2000	0.2677	0.3344	0.4008	0.4672	0.5335	0.5998	0.6661	0.7323	0.7986	0.8649
0.6	0.2000	0.2504	0.2984	0.3457	0.3928	0.4397	0.4865	0.5334	0.5802	0.6265	0.6731
0.8	0.2000	0.2323	0.2601	0.2861	0.3117	0.3369	0.3619	0.3867	0.4116	0.4364	0.4612
1	0.2000	0.2132	0.2185	0.2210	0.2223	0.2229	0.2231	0.2233	0.2231	0.2228	0.2224

Source Compiled by the authors

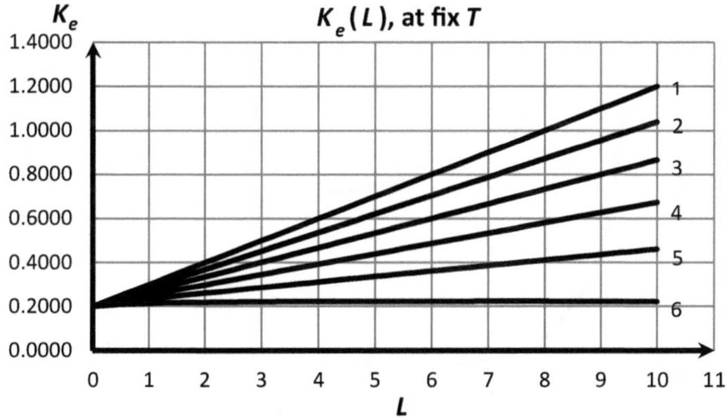

Fig. 22.3 Dependence of cost of equity k_e on leverage level L at different tax on profit rate T ($n = 7, k_0 = 20\%, k_d = 10\%$) (1—$T = 0$; 2—$T = 0.2$; 3—$T = 0.4$; 4—$T = 0.6$; 5—$T = 0.8$; 6—$T = 1$). *Source* Compiled by the authors

Let us calculate the dependence of the critical value of the income tax rate, t^*, on the age of the company, n. To do this, we must first calculate the *WACC* value over a set of parameters, including the age of the company, n, by solving the classical BFO Eq. (22.1). Then obtained value of *WACC* at a fixed n should be substituted into Eq. (22.18) and the right side should be equated to k_0.

$$k_0 = WACC(1 + L) - Lk_d(1 - t). \tag{22.25}$$

By solving this equation, one can obtain the critical value of the income tax rate t^* for a fixed n. At Fig. 22.4 the results of such calculations are shown: the dependence of the critical value of tax on profit rate $t*$ on the age of the company, n, under variation of the difference between k_0 and k_d ($\Delta k = k_0 - k_d = 2\%; 4\%; 6\%; 8\%$) (1—$k_d = 6\%, k_0 = 8\%$; 2—$k_d = 6\%, k_0 = 10\%$; 3—$k_d = 6\%, k_0 = 12\%$; 4—$k_d = 6\%, k_0 = 14\%$).

From the Fig. 22.4 it follows, that:

1. The critical value of tax on profit rate $t*$ increases with the difference $\Delta k = k_0 - k_d$,, therefore a small difference between the value of cost of equity (at $L = 0$) k_0 of the company and the credit rate k_d favor to existence of a new effect.
2. The critical value of tax on profit rate $t*$ decreases monotonically with the age of the company (only for 10-year in case of $\Delta k = k_0 - k_d = 2\%$ it has a minimum). Therefore the probability of the anomaly effect is higher for "adult" companies.
3. Recapitulating 1 and 2, one can note, that a small difference between the value of cost of equity (at $L = 0$) k_0 of the company and the credit rate k_d as well as old enough age of the company favor to existence of a new effect.

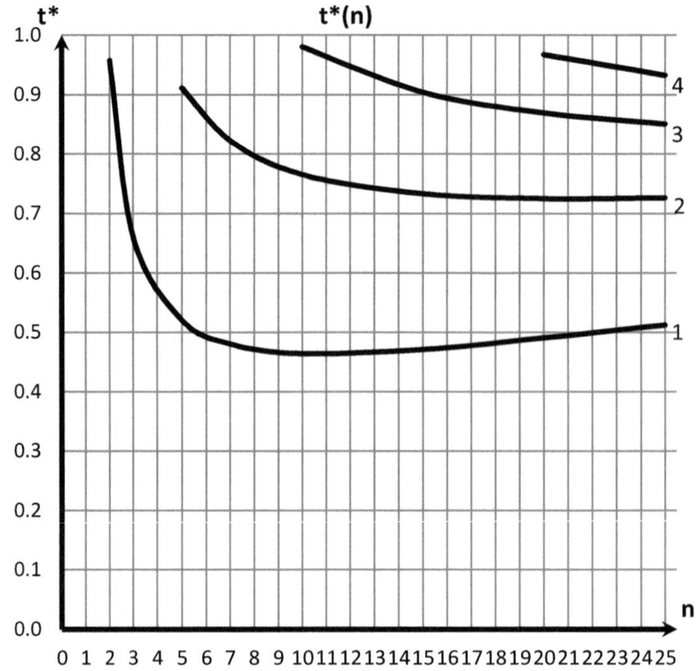

Fig. 22.4 The dependence of the critical value of tax on profit rate $t*$ on the age of the company

Below (Table 22.2) the dependence of the critical value of tax on profit rate $t*$ on the company age, n, under different values of k_0 and k_d at constant difference between them $\Delta k = k_0 - k_d = 2\%$ is studied.

In Fig. 22.5 the dependence of the critical value of tax on profit rate, $t*$, on the company age, n, is shown at different values of k_0 and k_d at constant difference between them $\Delta k = k_0 - k_d = 2\%$ (1—$k_0 = 8\%$; 2—$k_0 = 10\%$; 3—$k_0 = 12\%$; 4—$k_0 = 14\%$; 5—$k_0 = 16\%$; 6—$k_0 = 20\%$; 7—$k_0 = 24\%$).

The following conclusions could be made:

1. All curves are convex and the critical value of tax on profit rate t* reaches minimum, which value decreases with k_0.

   Min t* = 22.2% at $k_0 = 24\%$, min $t^* = 24.35\%$ at $k_0 = 20\%$, min $t^* = 28.1\%$ at $k_0 = 16\%$, min $t^* = 30.43\%$ at $k_0 = 14\%$, min $t^* = 33.92\%$ at $k_0 = 12\%$, min $t^* = 38.92\%$ at $k_0 = 10\%$, min $t^* = 46.4\%$ at $k_0 = 8\%$. Therefore the higher value of k_0 and the higher value of k_d at constant difference between them $\Delta k = k_0 - k_d = const$ favor for existence of a new effect.
2. The critical value of tax on profit rate $t*$ reach minimum at company age, decreasing with k_0: $n = 4.5$ years at $k_0 = 24\%$, $n = 5.5$ years at $k_0 = 16\%$, $n = 6.5$ years at $k_0 = 12\%$ and $n = 10.5$ years at $k_0 = 8\%$.
3. Thus, a parallel shift up of rates k_0 and k_d favor a for new effect, while company age, favorable a new effect, decreases with k_0.

Table 22.2 The dependence of the critical value of tax on profit rate $t*$ on the age of the company under different values of k_0 and k_d at constant difference between them $\Delta k = k_0 - k_d = 2\%$

$k_e(t)$\n	2	3	5	7	10	15	20	25
$k_d = 6\%$. $k_0 = 8\%$	0.9575	0.6600	0.5200	0.4800	0.4640	0.4710	0.4903	0.5121
$k_d = 8\%$. $k_0 = 10\%$	0.7313	0.5125	0.4140	0.3905	0.3892	0.4138	0.4453	0.4803
$k_d = 10\%$. $k_0 = 12\%$	0.6000	0.4280	0.3510	0.3392	0.3467	0.3840	0.4285	0.4733
$k_d = 12\%$. $k_0 = 14\%$	0.5125	0.3687	0.3110	0.3043	0.3218	0.3697	0.4239	0.4788
$k_d = 14\%$. $k_0 = 16\%$	0.4437	0.3266	0.2810	0.2821	0.3043	0.3636	0.4277	0.4904
$k_d = 18\%$. $k_0 = 20\%$	0.3625	0.2710	0.2435	0.2549	0.2895	0.3677	0.4468	0.5221
$k_d = 22\%$. $k_0 = 24\%$	0.3100	0.2370	0.2220	0.2400	0.2875	0.3818	0.4759	0.5588

Fig. 22.5 The dependence of the critical value of tax on profit rate $t*$ on the company age, n

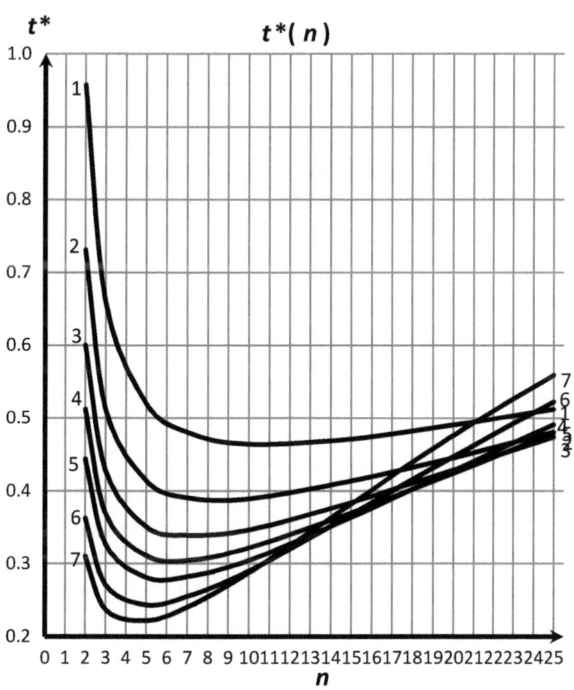

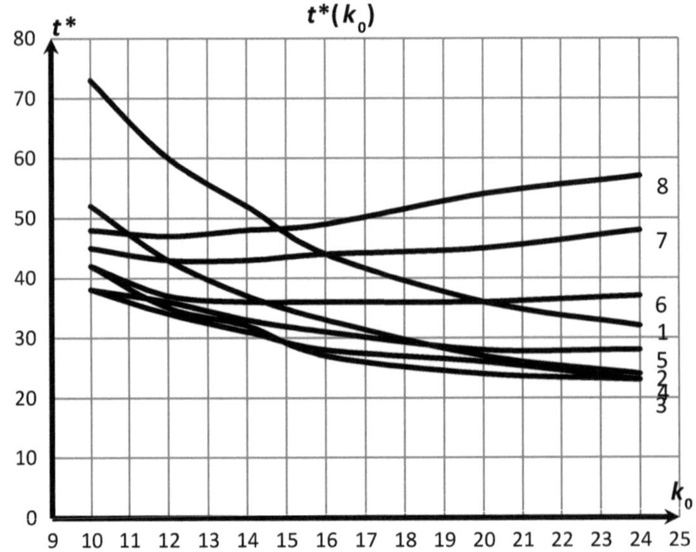

Fig. 22.6 The dependence of the critical value of tax on profit rate $t*$ on k_0 at constant difference between them $\Delta k = k_0 - k_d = 2\%$

The dependence of the critical value of tax on profit rate $t*$ on k_0(equity cost at zero leverage level, L) at constant difference between them $\Delta k = k_0 - k_d = 2\%$ is shown at Fig. 22.6, where (1—$n = 2$; 2—$n = 3$; 3—$n = 5$; 4—$n = 7$; 5—$n = 10$; 6—$n = 15$; 7—$n = 20$; 8—$n = 25$).

What is the practical value of the effect? Does it exist in real life, or is its discovery of purely theoretical interest? Since the new effect takes place at an income tax rate that is greater than a certain value of t^*, it is necessary to compare this value with the real income tax rates established in different countries. The biggest tax on profits of corporation rates is in USA—39.2%. In Japan it exceeds a little bit 38%. In France tax on profits of corporations varies from 33.3% for small and medium—sized companies, up to 36% for the major ones. In England tax on profits of corporations is in the range of 21% to 28%. In the Russian Federation tax on profits of corporations is installed in the amount of 20%.

In considered by us examples the value t^* strongly depends on the ratio between k_0, k_d, n and reaches a minimal value of 22.2%, and it is quite likely even lower values of $t*$ with other ratios between k_0, k_d, n.

In this way, we come to the conclusion that at some ratios between equity cost, debt cost and company age k_0, k_d, n discovered by us effect takes place at tax on profits of corporation rate established in most developed countries, that provides the practical value of the effect.

Its account is important in improving tax legislation and may change dividend policies of the company.

Opening the effect expands our view of the rules of the game in the economy.

If prior to that it was widely known that, with the rising of leverage, the cost of equity is always growing, that is associated with the decrease in financial sustainability of the companies, with an increase in the share of borrowing, when the shareholders require a higher rate of return on the share.

But now it becomes clear that this is not always the case, and the dependence of cost of equity on leverage depends on the ratio between the parameters k_0, k_d, n, and, ultimately, on the tax on profit rate.

This effect has never been known, therefore, it was not taken into account by controls tax legislation, but possibilities here are opening tremendously.

The effect is also important for the development of the dividend policy of the company.

It turns out that the rule adopted by shareholders since time immemorial to demand a higher rate of return per share when increasing the share of debt capital does not always work now. This will allow the company's management to pursue a more realistic dividend policy, limiting shareholders' appetites to an economically justified amount of dividends.

As we mentioned in Sect. 22.2, the Brusov–Filatova–Orekhova (BFO) theory and its eternal limit—the Modigliani–Miller theory have recently been generalized to the established practice of the functioning of companies, such as variable income, frequent income tax payments, advance payments on income tax, etc. Below, we use the generalized theory of Brusov–Filatova–Orekhova (BFO) to study the existence and behavior of an anomalous effect in a wide range of the financial parameters of the company. We start from the case of variable income.

22.3.2 Variable Income

Influence of Growth Rate G: Tax on Income Payments at the Ends of Periods

Below we study the influence of growth rate of income g in case of tax on income payments at the ends of periods.

Six Year Company

Figure 22.7 shows the dependence of equity cost, k_e, on leverage level, L, for six year company at $p = 1$; $k_0 = 0.16$; $k_d = 0.14$; $t = 0.2$; at different $g = -0.2$; -0.15; -0.1; -0.05; 0; 0.05; 0.1; 0.15; 0.2 with payments of tax on income at the end of periods.

From Fig. 22.7 it is seen, that with an increase in the rate of income growth g, the slope of the curve k_e (L) increases. The anomalous effect for six year company at k_0 $= 0.16$; $k_d = 0.14$ takes place at $g < -1$: the slope of the curve k_e (L) is negative.

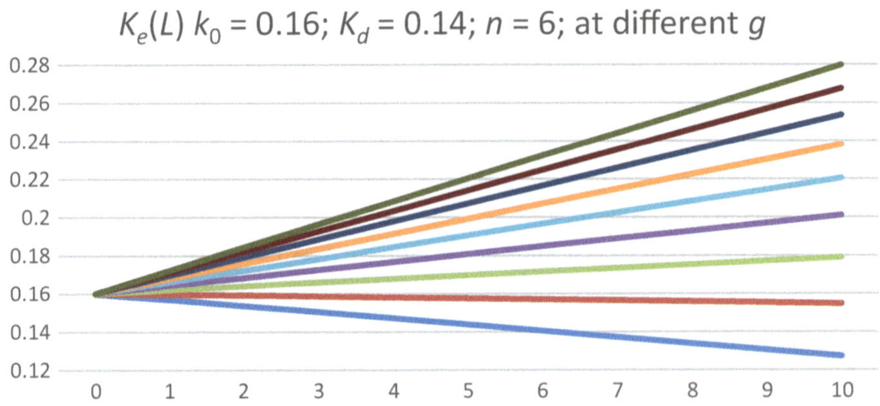

Fig. 22.7 The dependence of equity cost, K_e, on leverage level, L, at $p = 1$; $k_0 = 0.16$; $k_d = 0.14$; $t = 0.2$; $n = 6$ at different $g = -0.2$; -0.15; -0.1; -0.05; 0; 0.05; 0.1; 0.15; 0.2 (from the bottom to the top) with payments of tax on income at the end of periods

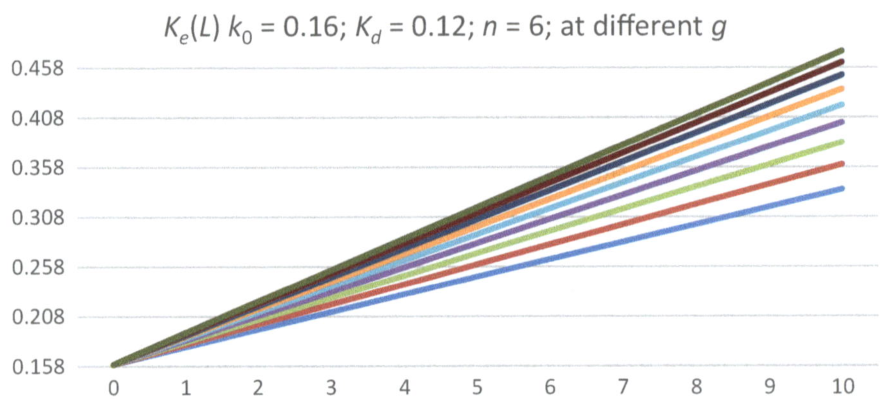

Fig. 22.8 The dependence of equity cost, k_e, on leverage level, L, at $p = 1$; $k_0 = 0.16$; $k_d = 0.12$; $t = 0.2$; $n = 6$ at different $g = -0.2$; -0.15; -0.1; -0.05; 0; 0.05; 0.1; 0.15; 0.2 (from the bottom to the top) with payments of tax on income at the end of periods

Figure 22.8 shows the dependence of equity cost, k_e, on leverage level, L, for six year company at $p = 1$; $k_0 = 0.16$; $k_d = 0.12$; $t = 0.2$; at different $g = -0.2$; -0.15; -0.1; -0.05; 0; 0.05; 0.1; 0.15; 0.2 with payments of tax on income at the end of periods.

From Fig. 22.8 it is seen, that, like previous case, with an increase in the rate of income growth g, the slope of the curve $k_e(L)$ increases. The anomalous effect for six year company at $k_0 = 0.16$; $k_d = 0.12$ is absent at all g values: the slope of the curve $k_e(L)$ is positive.

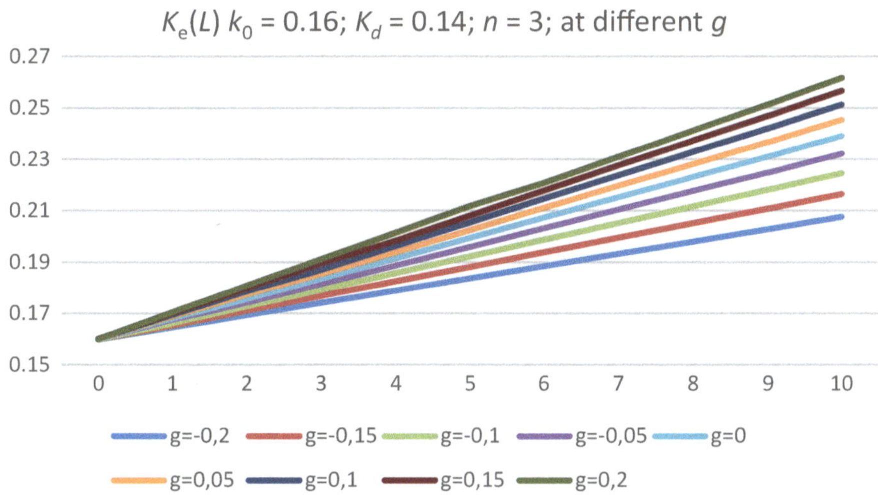

Fig. 22.9 The dependence of equity cost, k_e, on leverage level, L, at $p = 1$; $k_0 = 0.16$; $k_d = 0.14$; $t = 0.2$; $n = 3$ at different $g = -0.2; -0.15; -0.1; -0.05; 0; 0.05; 0.1; 0.15; 0.2$ (from the bottom to the top) with payments of tax on income at the end of periods

Three Year Company

Let us consider three year company.

From Fig. 22.9 it is seen, that, like previous case, with an increase in the rate of income growth g, the slope of the curve $k_e(L)$ increases. The anomalous effect for three year company at $k_0 = 0.16$; $k_d = 0.14$ is absent at all g values: the slope of the curve $k_e(L)$ is positive.

From Fig. 22.10 it is seen, that, like previous case, with an increase in the rate of income growth$g$, the slope of the curve $k_e(L)$ increases. The anomalous effect for three year company at $k_0 = 0.16$; $k_d = 0.12$ is absent at all g values: the slope of the curve $k_e(L)$ is positive. The width of the bundle of straight lines $k_e(L)$ narrows with decreasing k_d.

From Figs. 22.7, 22.8, 22.9, 22.10 and 22.11 we could conclude the following:

1. With an increase in the rate of income growth g, the slope of the curve $k_e(L)$ increases, since in this case shareholders can count on larger dividends.
2. The anomalous effect exists for a small difference between k_0 and k_d $(k_0 - k_d)$ and is absent for a larger value of this difference.

Influence of Growth Rate g: Comparison of Results with Advance Income Tax Payments and Payments at the End of Periods

Below we continue study the influence of growth rate g. We consider the case of advance income tax payments for 6 years and three year companies. The results for

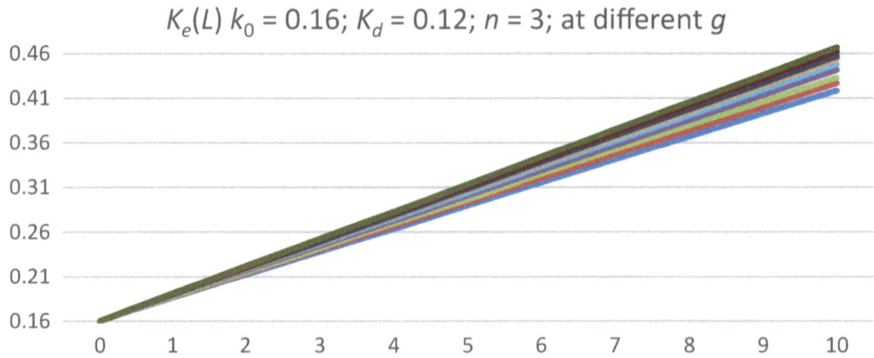

Fig. 22.10 The dependence of equity cost, k_e, on leverage level, L, at $p = 1$; $k_0 = 0.16$; $k_d = 0.12$; $t = 0.2$; $n = 3$ at different $g = -0.2; -0.15; -0.1; -0.05; 0; 0.05; 0.1; 0.15; 0.2$ (from the bottom to the top) with payments of tax on income at the end of periods

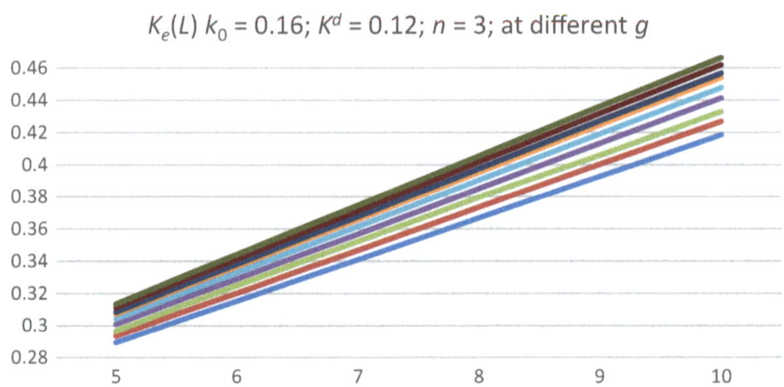

Fig. 22.11 The dependence of equity cost, k_e, on leverage level, L, at $p = 1$; $k_0 = 0.16$; $k_d = 0.12$; $t = 0.2$; $n = 3$ at Different $g = -0.2; -0.15; -0.1; -0.05; 0; 0.05; 0.1; 0.15; 0.2$ (from the bottom to the top) with payments of tax on income at the end of periods (lager scale)

advance income tax payments are shown at Figs. 22.12, 22.13, 22.14, 22.15 and 22.16.

Six year company

From Fig. 22.12 it is seen, that with an increase in the rate of income growth g, the slope of the curve $k_e(L)$ increases. The anomalous effect for six year company with advance payments of tax on income at $k_0 = 0.16$; $k_d = 0.14$ takes place at $g < 0$: the slope of the curve $k_e(L)$ is negative for all negative g.

From Fig. 22.13 it is seen, that with an increase in the rate of income growth g, the slope of the curve $k_e(L)$ increases. The anomalous effect for six year company with advance payments of tax on income at $k_0 = 0.16$; $k_d = 0.12$ is absent: the slope of the curve $k_e(L)$ is positive for all g values.

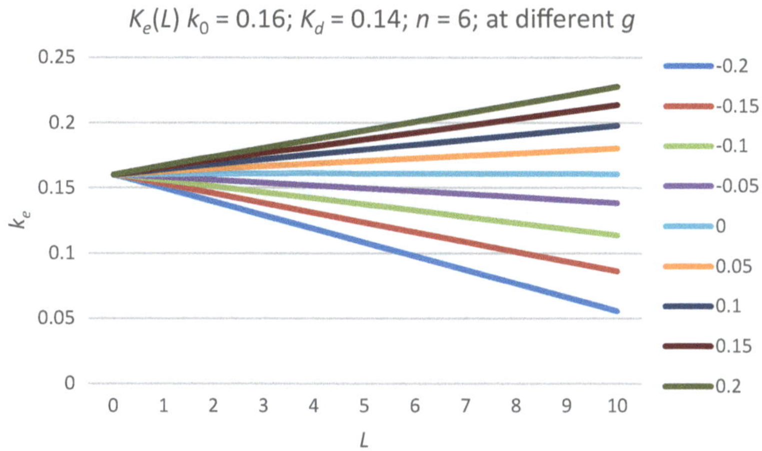

Fig. 22.12 The dependence of equity cost, k_e, on leverage level, L, at $p = 1$; $k_0 = 0.16$; $k_d = 0.14$; $t = 0.2$; $n = 6$ at different $g = -0.2; -0.15; -0.1; -0.05; 0; 0.05; 0.1; 0.15; 0.2$ (from the bottom to the top) with advance payments of tax on income

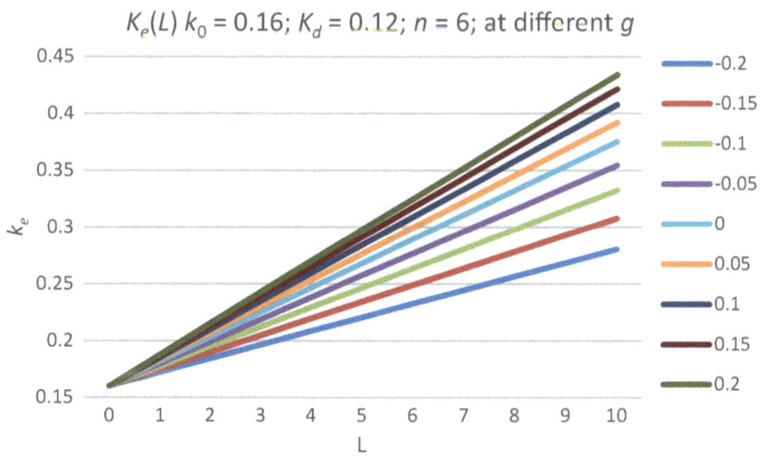

Fig. 22.13 The dependence of equity cost, k_e, on leverage level, L, at $p = 1$; $k_0 = 0.16$; $k_d = 0.12$; $t = 0.2$; $n = 6$ at different $g = -0.2; -0.15; -0.1; -0.05; 0; 0.05; 0.1; 0.15; 0.2$ (from the bottom to the top) with advance payments of tax on income

Three year company

Let us make calculation for three year company.

From Fig. 22.14 it is seen, that with an increase in the rate of income growth g, the slope of the curve $k_e(L)$ increases. The anomalous effect for three year company with advance payments of tax on income at $k_0 = 0.16$; $k_d = 0.14$ takes place at $g < -0.1$: the slope of the curve $k_e(L)$ is negative for $g < -0.1$. Note, that for six

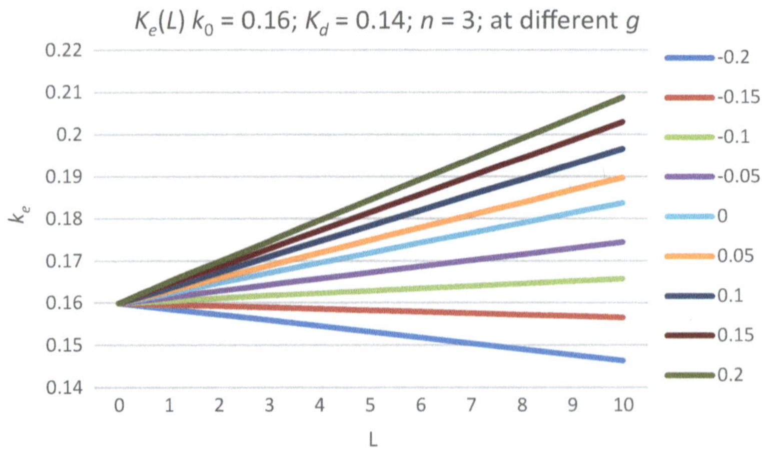

Fig. 22.14 The dependence of equity cost, k_e, on leverage level, L, at $p = 1$; $k_0 = 0.16$; $k_d = 0.14$; $t = 0.2$; $n = 3$ at different $g = -0.2; -0.15; -0.1; -0.05; 0; 0.05; 0.1; 0.15; 0.2$ (from the bottom to the top) with advance payments of tax on income

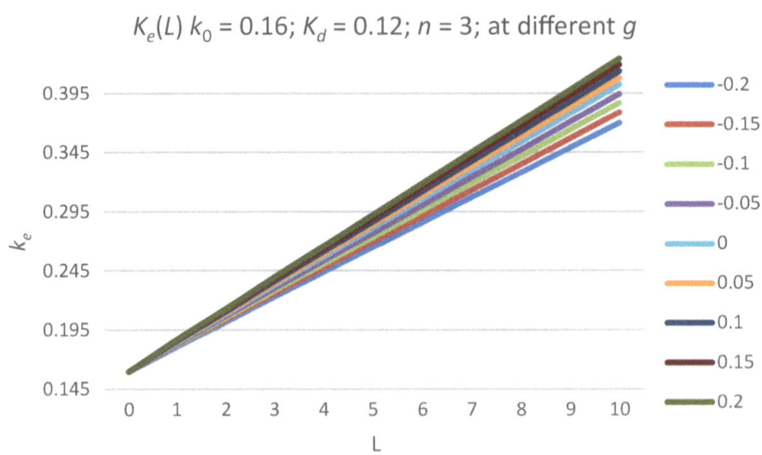

Fig. 22.15 The dependence of equity cost, k_e, on leverage level, L, at $p = 1$; $k_0 = 0.16$; $k_d = 0.12$; $t = 0.2$; $n = 3$ at different $g = -0.2; -0.15; -0.1; -0.05; 0; 0.05; 0.1; 0.15; 0.2$ (from the bottom to the top) with advance payments of tax on income

year company with advance payments of tax on income at $k_0 = 0.16$; $k_d = 0.14$ the anomalous effect takes place at bigger $g < 0$.

From Figs. 22.15 and 22.16 it is seen, that with an increase in the rate of income growth g, the slope of the curve $k_e(L)$ increases. The anomalous effect for three year company with advance payments of tax on income at $k_0 = 0.16$; $k_d = 0.12$ is absent:

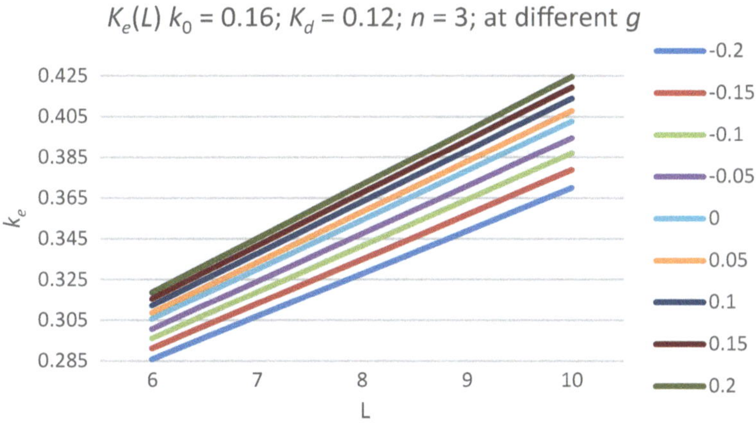

Fig. 22.16 The dependence of equity cost, k_e, on leverage level, L, at $p = 1$; $k_0 = 0.16$; $k_d = 0.12$; $t = 0.2$; $n = 3$ at different $g = -0.2$; -0.15; -0.1; -0.05; 0; 0.05; 0.1; 0.15; 0.2 (from the bottom to the top) with advance payments of tax on income

the slope of the curve $k_e(L)$ is positive for all g values. The width of the bundle of straight lines k_e narrows with decreasing k_d.

From Figs. 22.12, 22.13, 22.14, 22.15 and 22.16 the following conclusions follows:

1. With an increase in the rate of income growth g, the slope of the curve $k_e(L)$ increases, since in this case shareholders can count on larger dividends.
2. The anomalous effect exists for a small difference between k_0 and $k_d \Delta k = k_0 - k_d$ and is absent for a larger value of this difference.
3. The width of the bundle of straight lines k_e narrows with decreasing k_d.
4. Advance income tax payments are favorable for the existence of the anomalous effect.

The dependence of the existence of anomalous effect the $\Delta k = k_0 - k_d$, company age, n, and value of g^*, below which ($g < g^*$) this effect exists is shown in Table 22.1.

From the Table 22.3 it is seen that at company age $n = 6$ the effect exists at $\Delta k = 2\%$ only in both cases [for payments of tax on income at the ends (1) of periods as well as for advance payments of tax on income (2)] at that the g^*value increases under transition from (1) type of payments to (2) from -0.125 to zero. At company age $n = 3$ the effect exists at $\Delta k = 2\%$ only in the case of advance payments of tax on income at the $g^* = -0.125$.

Small value of Δk favorable to existence of effect, as well as bigger age of company and advance payments of tax on income.

Table 22.3 The dependence of the existence of anomalous effect on the Δk, company age, *n*, and value of g^*, below which ($g < g^*$) this effect exists

Company age	Δk	Payments of tax on income at the ends of periods		Advance payments of tax on income	
		Existence of effect	g^* value	Existence of effect	g^* value
$n = 6$	2%	+	−0.125	+	0
	4%	−		−	
	6%	−		−	
$n = 3$	2%	−		+	−0.125
	4%	−		−	
	6%	−		−	

Influence of Debt Cost k_d

Below, we examine the impact of the cost of debt k_d on the existence of an anomalous effect for advance income tax payments and income tax payments at the end of periods, both in the case of falling and rising profits.

–

It can be seen from Fig. 22.17 that the slope of the curve $k_e(L)$ decreases with the value of k_d for both cases of income tax payment [for payments at the end of periods (1) and also for advance payments (2)]. In this case, all curves (except curve at $k_d = 0.05$) related to case (1) have a greater slope compared to the curves related to case (2).

It can be seen Fig. 22.18 that the slope of the curve $k_e(L)$ decreases with the value of k_d for both cases of income tax payment [for payments at the end of periods (1) and also for advance payments (2)]. In this case, all curves (except curve at $k_d = 0.05$) related to case (1) have a greater slope compared to the curves related to case (2).

22.3.3 Frequent Income Tax Payments

Frequent Tax on Income Payments: Compare the Results for Advance Payments of Tax on Income and Payments at the Ends of Periods

Below we investigate the impact of frequent income tax payments on the existence and behavior of the anomalous effect for advance payments of tax on income and payments at the ends of periods for 3- and 6-year companies. For this, we calculate the dependence of equity cost, k_e, on leverage level, *L*, at different $p = 1; 2; 4; 6; 12;$

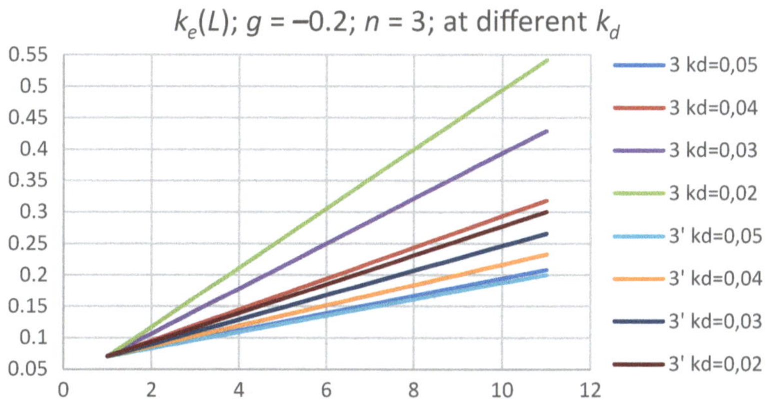

Fig. 22.17 The comparison of the dependences of equity cost, k_e, on leverage level, L, at $p = 1$; $k_0 = 0.07$; at different $k_d = 0.02; 0.03; 0.04; 0.05$; $t = 0.2$; $n = 3$ at negative $g = -0.2$ with advance payments of tax on income (3′) and payments of tax on income at the ends of periods (3)

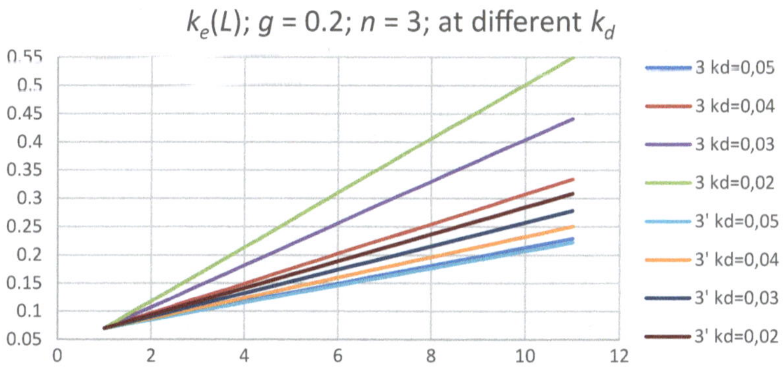

Fig. 22.18 The comparison of the dependences of equity cost, k_e, on leverage level, L, at $p = 1$; $k_0 = 0.07$; at different $k_d = 0.02; 0.03; 0.04; 0.05$; $t = 0.2$; $n = 3$ at positive $g = 0.2$ with advance payments of tax on income (3′) and payments of tax on income at the ends of periods (3)

$k_0 = 0.22$; at $k_d = 0.2$; $t = 0.2$; $n = 3$ with advance payments of tax on income (p') and payments of tax on income at the ends of periods (p). Results for 3 year company are shown in Table 22.4 and Fig. 22.19 and for six year company are shown in Table 22.5 and Fig. 22.20.

The slope $k_e(L)$ decreases with p when income tax is paid at the end of periods and becomes negative at $p > 4$ and higher for $n = 3$ and at $p > 2$ and higher for $n = 6$ (Fig. 22.20). For advance income tax payments, the slope $k_e(L)$, which is negative for any income tax frequency payments, increases (decreases modulo) with a frequency p, but never intersects with the curves $k_e(L)$ in case of income tax payment at the end of the periods. The anomalous effect disappears at $\Delta k = 4\%$ and above (see Fig. 22.21).

Table 22.4 The comparison of the dependences of equity cost, k_e, on leverage level, L, at different$p = 1; 2; 4; 6; 12$; $k_0 = 0.22$; at $k_d = 0.02$; $t = 0.2$; $n = 3$ with advance payments of tax on income (p') and payments of tax on income at the ends of periods (p)

L	0	1	2	3	4	5	6	7	8	9	10
$P1$	0.2202527	0.224593	0.228886	0.23312	0.237315	0.241494	0.245665	0.249829	0.25399	0.258148	0.262305
$P2$	0.2202527	0.221983	0.223697	0.225345	0.226963	0.228565	0.230162	0.231751	0.233333	0.234894	0.236496
$P4$	0.2202527	0.221029	0.220729	0.221286	0.221551	0.221801	0.222043	0.22228	0.222513	0.222744	0.222974
$P6$	0.2202527	0.220172	0.220075	0.219908	0.220674	0.220139	0.219594	0.219043	0.218488	0.217931	0.217371
$P12$	0.2202527	0.219711	0.219149	0.218517	0.217855	0.217179	0.216495	0.215805	0.215112	0.214416	0.213718
$P'1$	0.2199314	0.213774	0.207216	0.20056	0.193864	0.187147	0.180416	0.173609	0.166787	0.159962	0.153135
$P'2$	0.2199314	0.216589	0.212896	0.209117	0.205303	0.201472	0.19763	0.193783	0.189931	0.186075	0.182212
$P'4$	0.2199314	0.217965	0.21567	0.213294	0.210886	0.208461	0.206028	0.203588	0.201144	0.198697	0.196249
$P'6$	0.2199314	0.218419	0.216585	0.214672	0.212727	0.210766	0.208796	0.20682	0.204841	0.202858	0.200874
$P'12$	0.2199314	0.218871	0.217495	0.216041	0.214558	0.213058	0.211549	0.210035	0.208517	0.206996	0.205473

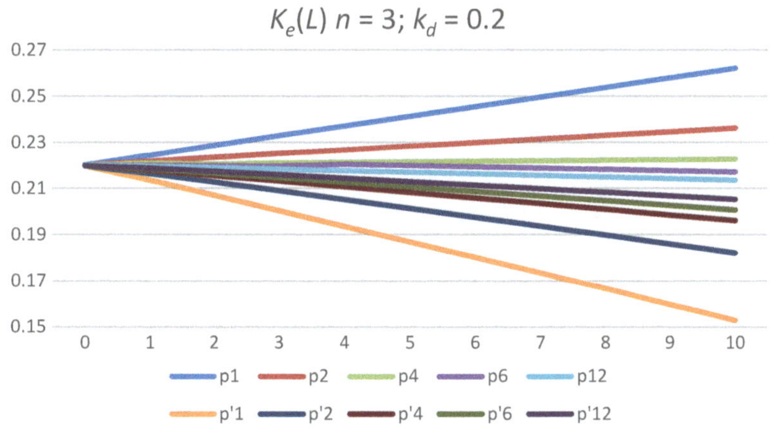

Fig. 22.19 The comparison of the dependences of equity cost, k_e, on leverage level, L, at different$p = 1; 2; 4; 6; 12$; $k_0 = 0.22$; at $k_d = 0.2$; $t = 0.2$; $n = 3$ with advance payments of tax on income (p') and payments of tax on income at the ends of periods (p)

The slope of $k_e(L)$ is positive for all p and both payment methods: this means that there is no anomalous effect. The slope $k_e(L)$ decreases with p when income tax is paid at the end of the period and increases when income tax advances are paid. The order of the curves $k_e(L)$ corresponding to these two methods of payment turns out to be mixed. This can lead to very interesting effects, providing new opportunities and the ability to manage the payment of income tax in accordance with tax laws (Fig. 22.21).

22.3.4 *Simultaneous Infliuence of the Growth Rate* g *and the Frequency of Income Tax Payment,* P

Tax Payments at the End of Periods

Below (see Figs. 22.22, 22.23), we examine the impact of growth rate g and income tax frequency payments, p on the existence of an anomalous effect for income tax payments at the end of periods, both in the case of falling and rising profits.

The slope $k_e(L)$ decreases with p and becomes negative at $p > 2$ ($p = 4; 6; 12$).

The slope $k_e(L)$ decreases with p and remains positive at all p.

The slope $k_e(L)$ decreases with p and remains positive at all p. Comparing to the case $g = 0$ the slope $k_e(L)$ is higher, this means, that the slope $k_e(L)$ growths with g (Fig. 22.24).

Table 22.5 The comparison of the dependences of equity cost, k_e, on leverage level, L, at different $p = 1; 2; 4; 6; 12$; $k_0 = 0.22$; at $k_d = 0.2$; $t = 0.2$; $n = 6$ with advance payments of tax on income (p') and payments of tax on income at the ends of periods (p)

P / L	0	1	2	3	4	5	6	7	8	9	10
$P1$	0.220001	0.223948	0.227332	0.230598	0.234363	0.237707	0.241035	0.244354	0.247667	0.250975	0.25428
$P2$	0.220001	0.221308	0.222079	0.222713	0.223284	0.223825	0.224352	0.224865	0.225367	0.225839	0.226362
$P4$	0.220001	0.219931	0.219315	0.218552	0.217729	0.216874	0.216737	0.215709	0.214677	0.213643	0.212606
$P6$	0.220001	0.219464	0.218373	0.217133	0.215831	0.214498	0.213147	0.211785	0.210415	0.209039	0.20766
$P12$	0.220001	0.218774	0.217249	0.215655	0.214025	0.21238	0.210725	0.209065	0.2074	0.205734	0.202836
$P'1$	0.219896	0.212774	0.20494	0.196401	0.188102	0.179762	0.1714	0.163023	0.154636	0.146243	0.137844
$P'2$	0.219896	0.215592	0.210457	0.205549	0.200371	0.195157	0.189921	0.184673	0.179415	0.174151	0.168883
$P'4$	0.219896	0.21697	0.213446	0.209762	0.20601	0.202225	0.19842	0.194603	0.190777	0.186946	0.18311
$P'6$	0.219896	0.217424	0.214366	0.21115	0.207869	0.204555	0.201221	0.197875	0.194521	0.191161	0.187798
$P'12$	0.219896	0.217876	0.215281	0.212531	0.209717	0.206871	0.204006	0.201128	0.198243	0.195353	0.192458

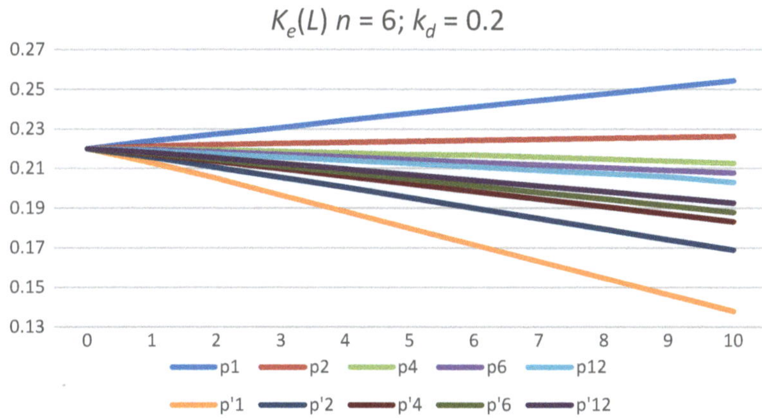

Fig. 22.20 The comparison of the dependences of equity cost, k_e, on leverage level, L, at different $p = 1; 2; 4; 6; 12$; $k_0 = 0.22$; at $k_d = 0.2$; $t = 0.2$; $n = 6$ with advance payments of tax on income (p') and payments of tax on income at the ends of periods (p)

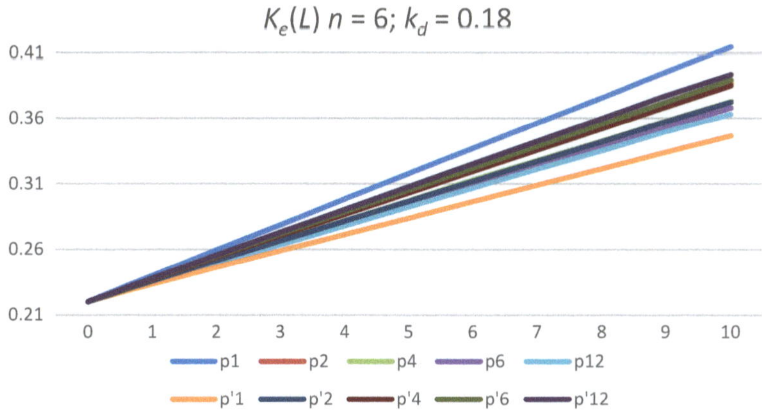

Fig. 22.21 The comparison of the dependences of equity cost, k_e, on leverage level, L, at different$p = 1; 2; 4; 6; 12$; $k_0 = 0.22$; at $k_d = 0.18$; $t = 0.2$; $n = 6$ with advance payments of tax on income (p') and payments of tax on income at the ends of periods (p)

Advance Tax Payments

Below, we examine the impact of the frequency of income tax payments on the existence of an anomalous effect for advance income tax payments, both in the case of falling and rising profits.

At negative growth rate g the slope $k_e(L)$ increases with frequency of payments of tax on profit, p, being negative at $p = 1$ and about zero.

At $p = 1$ the slope $k_e(L)$ increases with growth rate g, being negative at $g = -0.2$.

At $p = 2$ the slope $k_e(L)$ increases with growth rate g, being positive at all g.

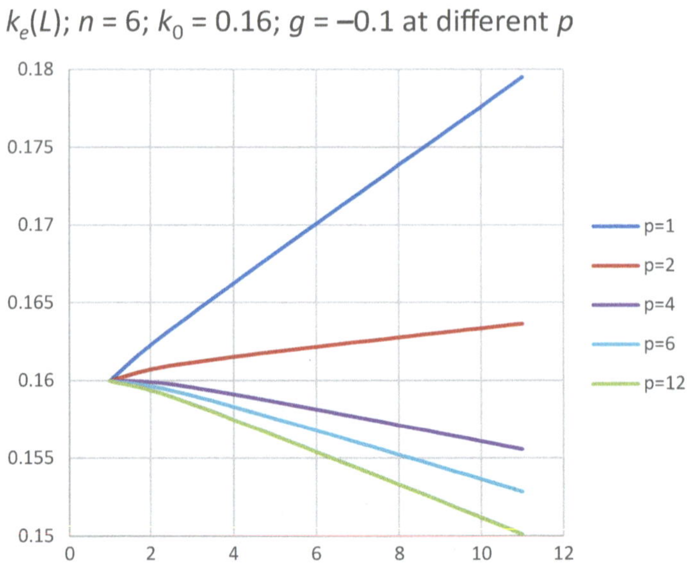

Fig. 22.22 The dependences of equity cost, k_e, on leverage level, L, at different $p = 1; 2; 4; 6; 12$; $k_0 = 0.16$; at $k_d = 0.14$; $t = 0.2$; $n = 6$, $g = -0.1$ with payments of tax on income at the ends of periods

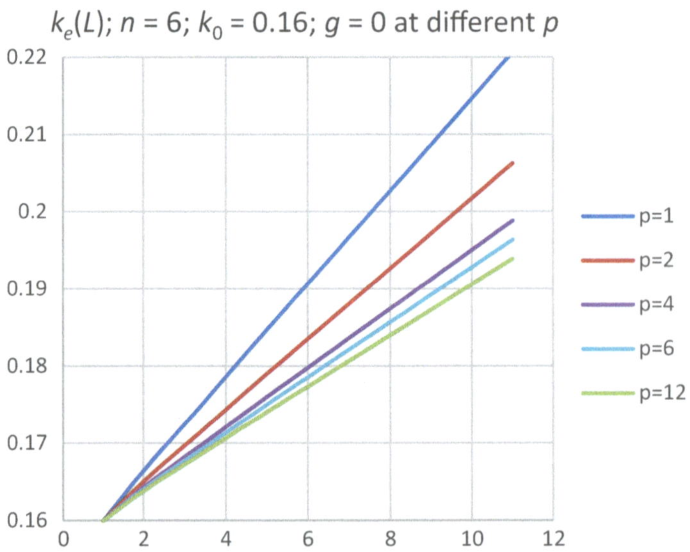

Fig. 22.23 The dependences of equity cost, k_e, on leverage level, L, at different$p = 1; 2; 4; 6; 12$; $k_0 = 0.16$; at $k_d = 0.14$; $t = 0.2$; $n = 6$, $g = 0$ with payments of tax on income at the ends of periods

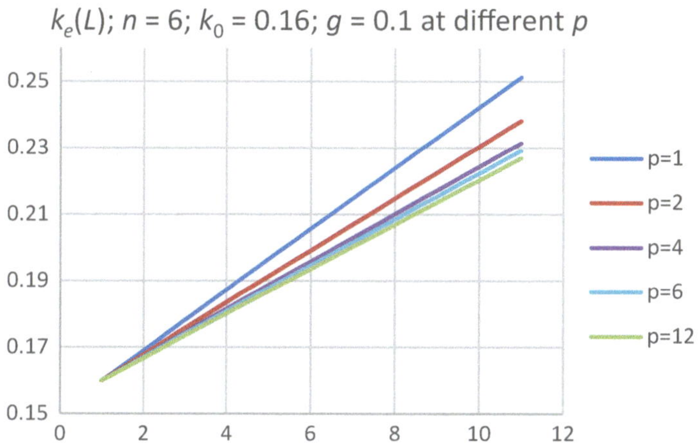

Fig. 22.24 The dependences of equity cost, k_e, on leverage level, L, at different$p = 1; 2; 4; 6; 12$; $k_0 = 0.16$; at $k_d = 0.14$; $t = 0.2$; $n = 6$, $g = 0.1$ with payments of tax on income at the ends of periods

At $p = 6$ the slope $k_e(L)$ increases with growth rate g, being positive at all g.

At $p = 12$ the slope $k_e(L)$ increases with growth rate g, being positive at all g. From Figs. 22.25, 22.26, 22.27, 22.28 and 22.29 it follows, that the slope of all curves $k_e(L)$ increase with frequency of advance payments of tax on income.

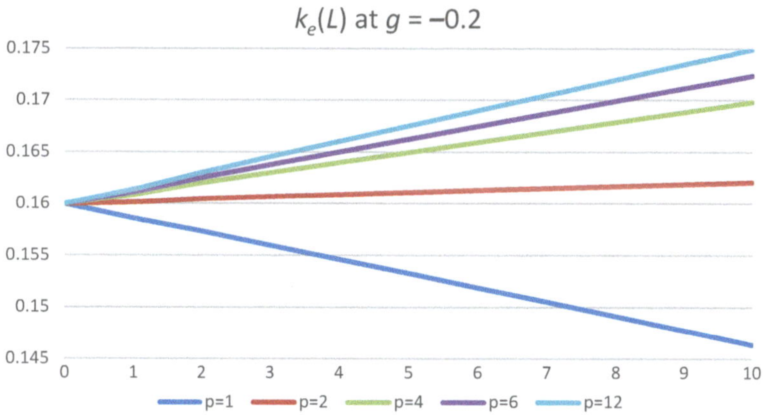

Fig. 22.25 The dependences of equity cost, k_e, on leverage level, L, at different $p = 1; 2; 4; 6; 12$; $k_0 = 0.16$; at $k_d = 0.14$; $t = 0.2$; $n = 6$, $g = -0.2$ with advance payments of tax on income

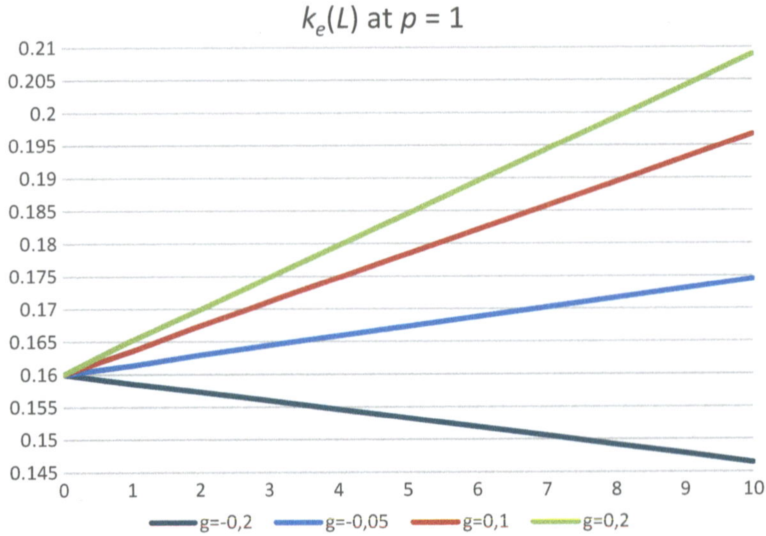

Fig. 22.26 The dependences of equity cost, k_e, on leverage level, L, at $p = 1$; $k_0 = 0.16$; at $k_d = 0.14$; $t = 0.2$; $n = 6$, at different $g = -0.2$;–0.05; 0.1; 0.2 with advance payments of tax on income

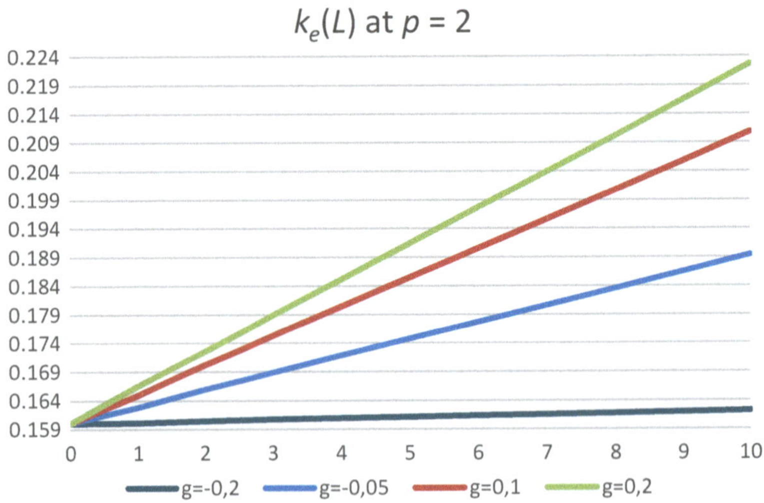

Fig. 22.27 The dependences of equity cost, k_e, on leverage level, L, at $p = 2$; $k_0 = 0.16$; at $k_d = 0.14$; $t = 0.2$; $n = 6$, at different $g = -0.2$;–0.05; 0.1; 0.2 with advance payments of tax on income

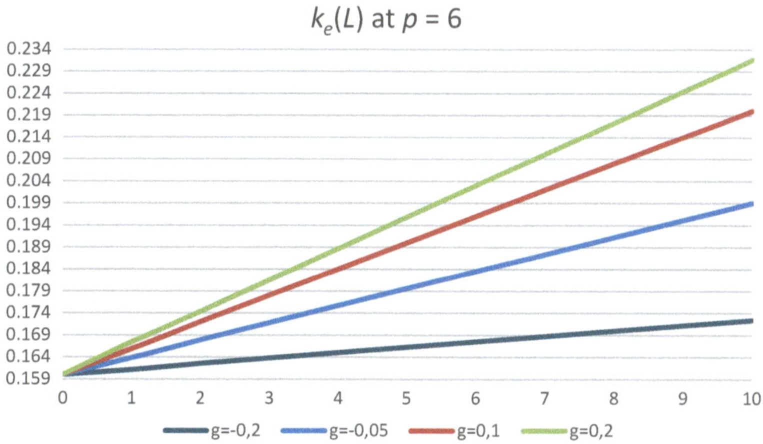

Fig. 22.28 The dependences of equity cost, k_e, on leverage level, L, at $p = 6$; $k_0 = 0.16$; at $k_d = 0.14$; $t = 0.2$; $n = 6$, at different $g = -0.2$;–0.05; 0.1; 0.2 with advance payments of tax on income

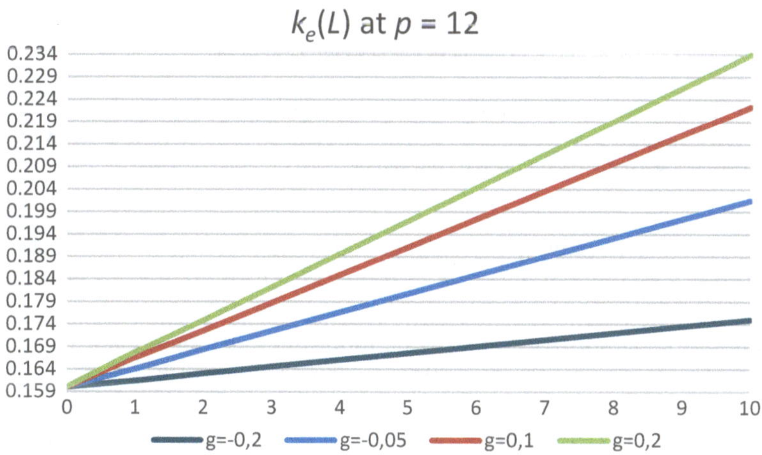

Fig. 22.29 The dependences of equity cost, k_e, on leverage level, L, at $p = 2$; $k_0 = 0.16$; at $k_d = 0.14$; $t = 0.2$; $n = 6$, at different $g = -0.2$;–0.05; 0.1; 0.2 with advance payments of tax on income

22.3.5 Impact of Company Age

The dependence of the cost of equity, k_e, on the level of leverage, L, at different ages of the company, n, was studied. It was shown that there are two kind of dependences of slope $k_e(L)$ on company age, n: monotonic decrease of tilt angle $k_e(L)$ with n (see Fig. 22.30) and seems random addiction of tilt angle $k_e(L)$ with n (see Fig. 22.31).

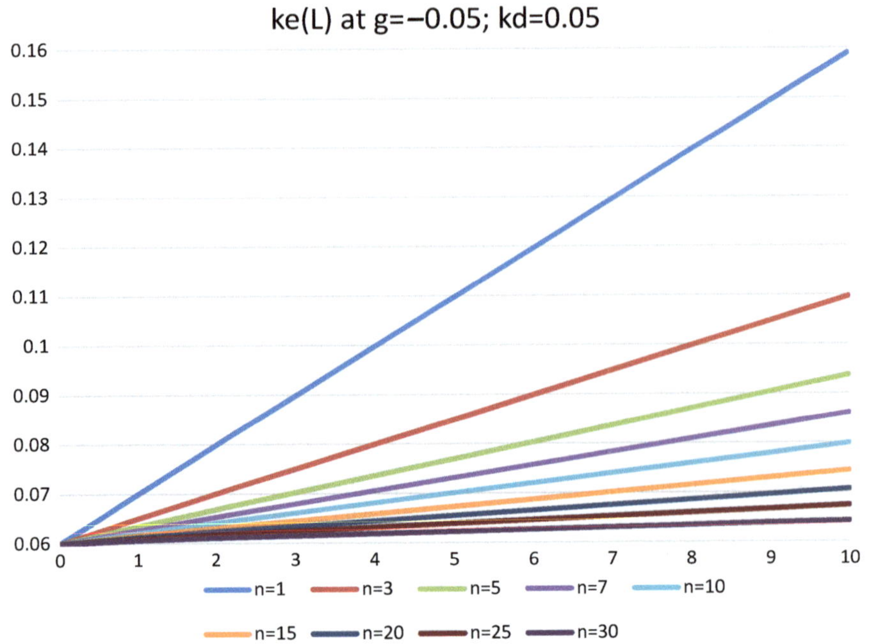

Fig. 22.30 The dependences of equity cost, k_e, on leverage level, L, at $p = 1$; $k_0 = 0.06$; at $k_d = 0.05$; $t = 0.2$; at negative $g = -0.5$ and at different company age n with payments of tax on income at the end of periods. *Source* Compiled by the authors

At Fig. 22.30 at negative $g = -0.05$ the following ordering of curves $k_e(L)$ takes place: $n = 1$; $n = 3$; $n = 5$; $n = 7$; $n = 10$; $n = 15$; $n = 2\ 0$; $n = 25$; $n = 30$. This ordering is monotonic.

At Fig. 22.31, at positive $g = 0.05$ the following ordering of curves $k_e(L)$ takes place $n = 1$; $n = 30$; $n = 25$; $n = 20$; $n = 15$; $n = 3$; $n = 10$; $n = 5$; $n = 7$. This ordering is not monotonous, but seemingly random.

The reason for the existence of two types of dependences of the slope $k_e(L)$ on the age of the enterprise, n: a monotonous decrease in the slope angle $k_e(L)$ with n and a seemingly random dependence of the slope angle $k_e(L)$ with n, is the absence or presence of the so–called "golden age" company effect (Brusov et al. 2018b).

The so–called "golden age" of the company effect is the situation, when the cost of capital raised (*WACC*) is below the perpetuity limit, and the company's value is higher. The absence or presence of the "golden age" company effect could explain the ordering of curves $k_e(L)$ [of slopes of curves $k_e(L)$] (see Figs. 22.32, 22.33 and 22.34):

- in case of the absence of the "golden age" company effect, the ordering of curves $k_e(L)$ is monotonic (Fig. 22.32).
- in case of the presence of the "golden age" company effect, the ordering of curves $k_e(L)$ is not monotonous (Fig. 22.33).

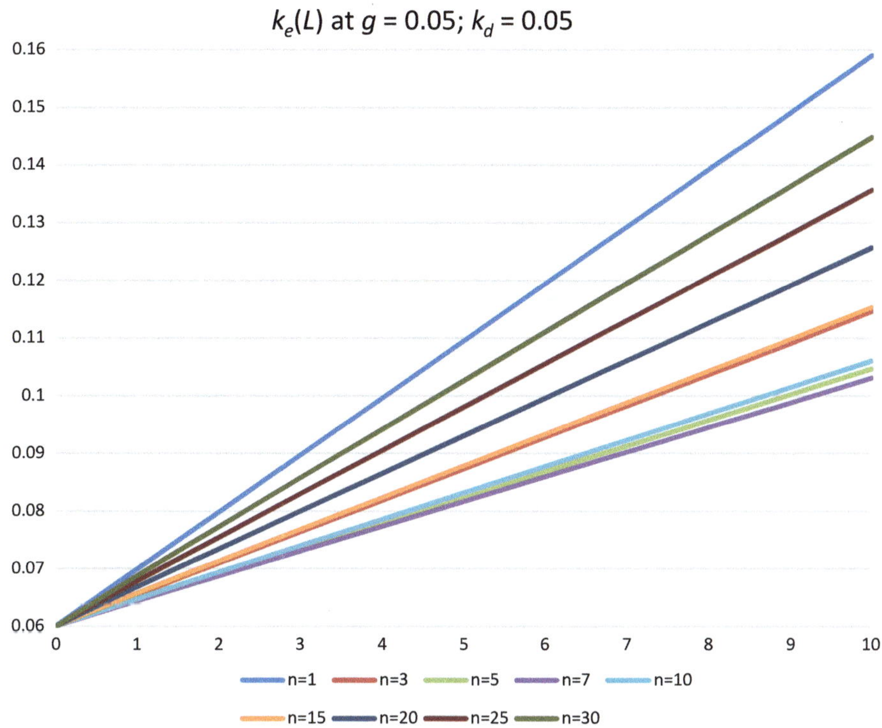

Fig. 22.31 The dependences of equity cost, k_e, on leverage level, L, at $p = 1$; $k_0 = 0.06$; $k_d = 0.05$; $t = 0.2$; at positive $g = 0.5$ and at different company age n with payments of tax on income at the end of periods

From Fig. 22.34 it is seen, that the main factor affecting the slope $k_e(L)$ (between the cost of debtk_d and the growth rate g) is the cost of debt k_d. From Fig. 22.34 it can be seen that the slope $k_e(L)$ decreases as the cost of debt k_d increases. We deliberately choose a leverage level, $L = 10$, where the difference between the cost of equity values is the largest, in order to make this difference more noticeable. Of the doublet of curves corresponding to the fixed cost of debt k_d, the upper curve refers to the larger growth rate g. Note, that the shape of the $k_e(n)$ curve is similar to the shape of the $WACC(n)$ curve.

22.3.6 *Simultaneously Impact of Company Age,* N, *and Growth Rate,* g

The conclusions from Fig. 22.35 are as following:

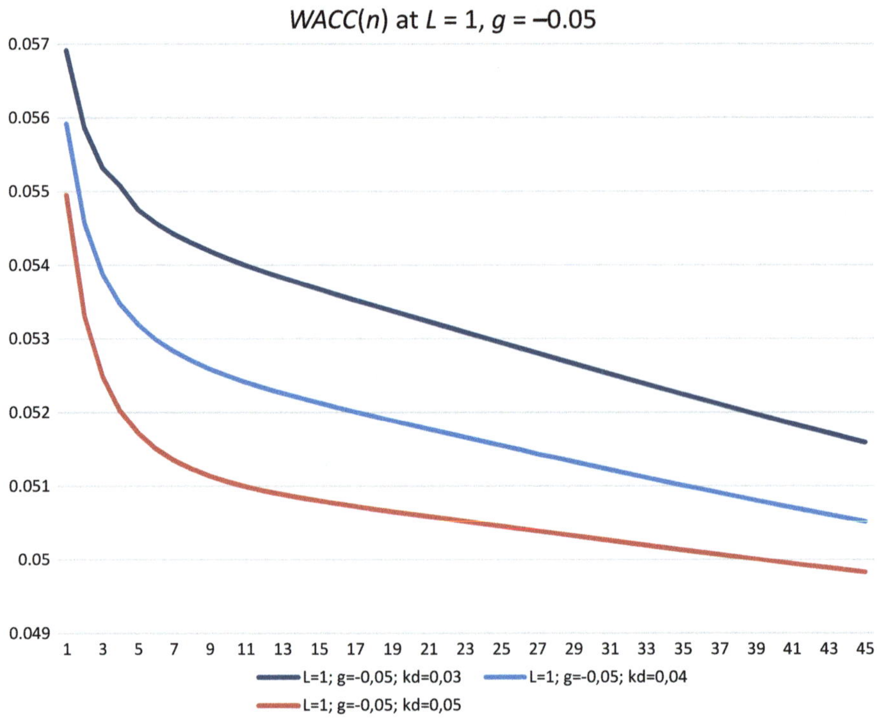

Fig. 22.32 The absence of the "golden age" company effect. The dependences of equity cost, k_e, on leverage level, L, at $p = 1$; $k_0 = 0.06$; $k_d = 0.03; 0.04; 0.05$; $t = 0.2$; at negative $g = -0.5$ and at different company age n with payments of tax on income at the end of periods

- The slope of curves, $k_e(L)$, decreases with company age, n, and increases with growth rate, g.
- The curves corresponding to different company ages mix at different growth rates g. This can lead to interesting effects and create new options for the company's dividend policy.

22.4 The Explanations of the Observed Effects

22.4.1 Increase of Ke with L

$k_e(L)$ rises with L, because as L increases, financial distress and the risk of bankruptcy increase, shareholders demand higher returns per share.

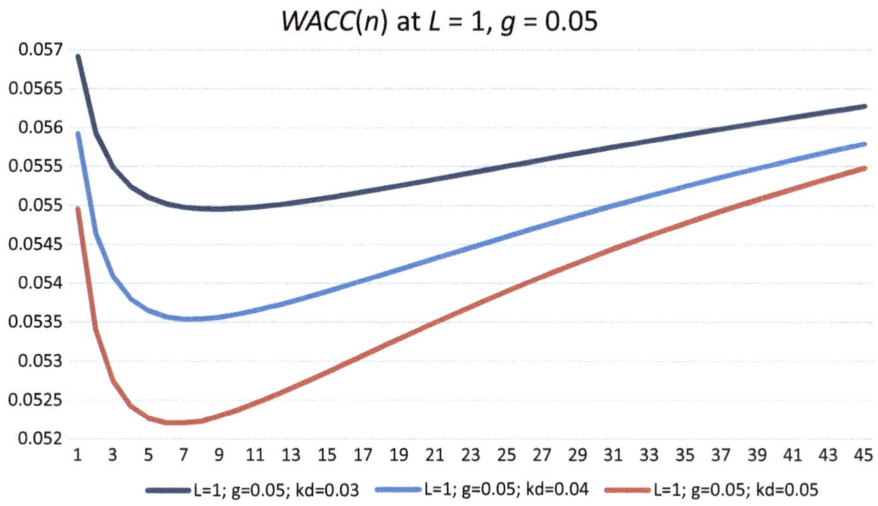

Fig. 22.33 The presence of the "golden age" company effect. The dependences of equity cost, k_e, on leverage level, L, at $p = 1$; $k_0 = 0.06$; $k_d = 0.03$; 0.04; 0.05; $t = 0.2$; at Positive $g = 0.05$ and at different company age n with payments of tax on income at the end of periods

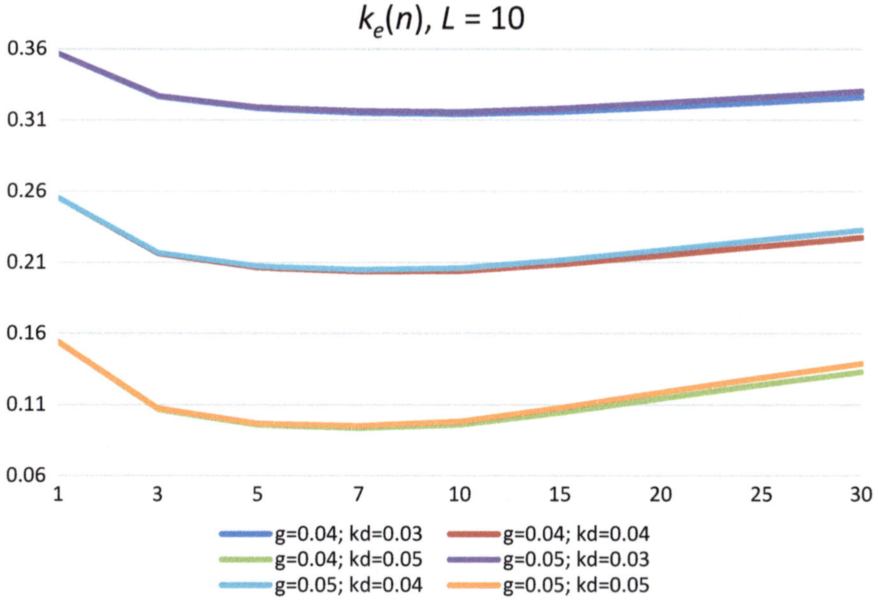

Fig. 22.34 The dependence of the cost of equity, k_e, on company age at different cost of debt k_d and growth rate g at leverage level $L = 10$ for advance payments of tax on income

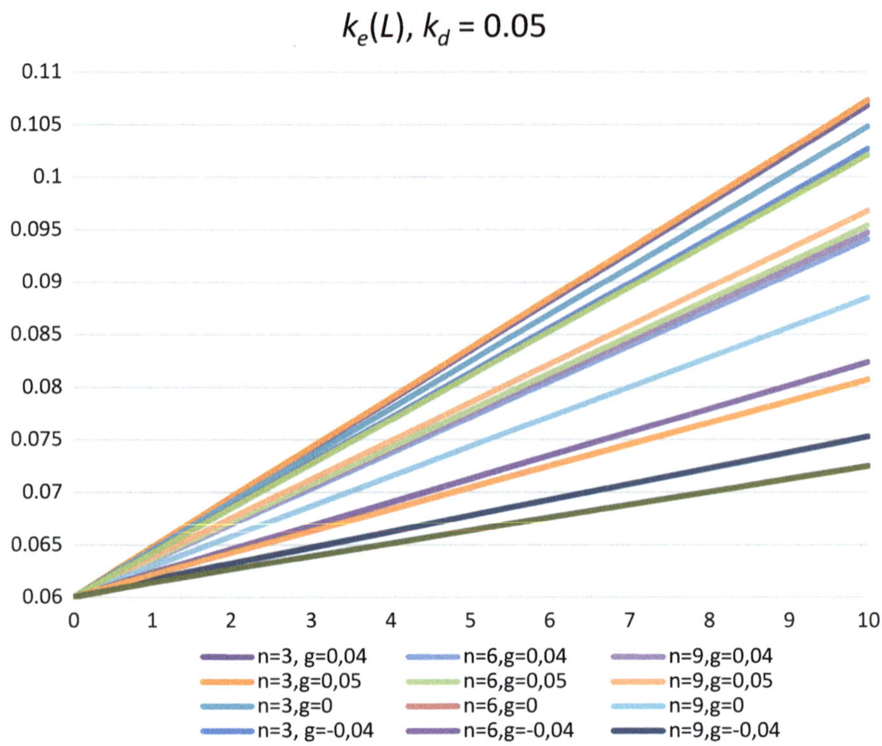

Fig. 22.35 The dependence of equity cost, k_e, on leverage level, L, at $p = 1$; $k_0 = 0.06$; $k_d = 0.05$; $t = 0.2$; at $g = -0.05$; -0.04; 0; 0.04; 0.05 and at different company age $n = 3$; 6; 9 with advance payments of tax on income

22.4.2 *Tax Rate Increases*

As taxes increase, the slope $k_e(L)$ decreases via tax corrector, which decreases with tax on profit rate.

22.4.3 *Influence of the Rate of Income Growth* g

With an increase in the rate of income growth g, the slope of the curve $k_e(L)$ increases, since in this case shareholders can count on larger dividends.

At $g < 0$ earnings per share decreases.

22.4.4 *Influence of the Frequency of Income Tax Payments*

For income tax payments at the ends of periods slope $k_e(L)$ decreases with p, thus earnings per share decreases (properties of ordinary annuity).

The increase in PV and FV of cash flows with the growth of p follows from their behavior in the ordinary p–term annuity with the growth of p. Both of them increase because an increase in p gives a percentage gain: their earlier accrual.

For advance income tax payments the slope $k_e(L)$ increases with p, thus earnings per share increases (properties of annuity due).

Advance income tax payments correspond to the case of p–term annuity due: the decrease in PV and FV of cash flows with increasing p follows from their behavior in the p–term annuity due with increasing p. They both decrease because an increase in p gives an interests decrease via charging interest on the smaller value of the annuity payment R/p instead of R.

22.5 Conclusions

The contribution of the current results to the theory is related to the use of generalized theories of capital structure (both BFO and MM) to estimate the cost of equity capital in real–life operating conditions of companies. A study was conducted of the dependence of the cost of equity on the level of leverage for different ages of the company, different values of the leverage level, of the cost of debt capital for different frequencies of payment of income tax, advance payments of income tax and payments at the end of periods, the company's variable income, etc. As a result, it becomes possible to estimate the cost of equity in these conditions. The behavior and properties of the cost of equity are explored within the framework of the BFO theory. Several very important innovative effects have been discovered, which significantly change the company's dividend policy. Among them are the abnormal dependence of equity cost on leverage level at different growth rates of variable income, at different ages of the company, at different frequencies of income tax payment, at different debt costs etc.

The developed approach can be applied to any country, you just need to use the tax rate for a specific company in a specific country. And the methods of paying income tax: advance payments or at the end of periods and with what frequency: annually, semi–annually, quarterly or monthly.

The following results have been obtained:

1. $k_e(L)$ rises with L, because as L increases, financial distress and the risk of bankruptcy increase, shareholders demand higher returns per share.
2. As taxes increase, the slope $k_e(L)$ decreases via tax corrector, which decreases with tax on profit rate.

3. With an increase in the rate of income growth g, the slope of the curve $k_e(L)$ increases, since in this case shareholders can count on larger dividends. At $g < 0$ earnings per share decreases.
4. For income tax payments at the ends of periods slope $k_e(L)$ decreases with the frequency of income tax payments p, thus earnings per share decreases (properties of ordinary annuity). The increase in PV and FV of cash flows with the growth of p follows from their behavior in the ordinary p–term annuity with the growth of p. Both of them increase because an increase in p gives a percentage gain: their earlier accrual.

   For advance income tax payments the slope $k_e(L)$ increases with p, thus earnings per share increases (properties of annuity due).
5. It was found two types of dependences of the slope $k_e(L)$ on the age of the enterprise, n: a monotonous decrease in the slope angle $k_e(L)$ with n and a seemingly random dependence of the slope angle $k_e(L)$ with n. The reason for the existence of is the absence or presence of the so–called "golden age" company effect (Brusov et al. 2018b).

The so-called "golden age" of the company effect is the situation, when the cost of capital raised (WACC) is below the perpetuity limit, and the company's value is higher. The absence or presence of the "golden age" company effect could explain the ordering of curves $k_e(L)$ [of slopes of curves $k_e(L)$] (see Figs. 22.32, 22.33, 22.34):

- in case of the absence of the "golden age" company effect the ordering of curves $k_e(L)$ is monotonic (Fig. 22.32);
- in case of the presence of the "golden age" company effect the ordering of curves $k_e(L)$ is not monotonous (Fig. 22.33).

The developed methodology and results will help the company's management to develop an adequate and effective dividend policy, taking into account the real conditions for the functioning of companies, such as variable income of companies, frequent income tax payments, types of income tax payments. (Advance payments and payments at the end of reporting periods), etc. This allows, when developing a dividend policy, the use of qualitatively new effects that we have discovered, such as the anomalous dependence of the cost of equity on the level of leverage at different growth rates of variable income, at different company ages (the "golden age" effect), at different frequencies of income tax payments, at different costs of debt, etc.

The limitation of the study is due to the fact that the case of a constant income growth rate is considered. In future publications, the case of a variable income growth rate will be considered. One more limitation of the consideration is related to the known limitations of the *WACC* approximation.

Concerning the direction of further research: the authors plan to take into account both business and financial risks when assessing the financial performance of companies, including the cost of equity.

22.5.1 Direction for Further Research

When studying the cost of equity capital within the framework of BFO and MM theory, we take into account only the financial risks associated with the use of debt financing. There is the Capital Asset Pricing Model (CAPM) that also looks at return on equity, but only considers business risks that relate to the investment in the portfolio rather than in the risk–free assets. In practice, companies use debt financing and operate at non–zero levels of leverage. This means that it is necessary to take into account the financial risk associated with the use of debt financing along with business. A new approach to CAPM has been developed recently (Fernandez 2006b) that takes into account both business and financial risk. The authors combine the theory of CAPM and the Modigliani–Miller (MM) theory. The first is based on portfolio analysis and accounting for business risks in relation to the market (or industry). The second one (the Modigliani–Miller (MM) theory) describes a specific company and takes into account the financial risks associated with the use of debt financing. The combination of these two different approaches makes it possible to take into account both types of risks: business and financial ones. The authors (Brusov et al. 2024; Miller 1985) combine these two approaches analytically, while Hamada (Hamada 1969; Brusov et al. 2023b) did it phenomenologically. Using the Modigliani–Miller (MM) theory (Modigliani and Miller 1958, 1963, 1966; Brusov and Filatova 2025a), it is shown that the Hamada's model, the first model, used for this purpose half a century ago, is incorrect. In addition to the renormalization of the beta–coefficient, obtained in the Hamada model, two additional terms are found: the renormalized risk–free return and the term dependent on the cost of debt k_d. A critical analysis of the Hamada model was carried out in Brusov et al. (2024) and Miller (1985). The vast majority of listing companies use debt financing and are leveraged, and the Hamada model is not applicable to them in contrast to a new approach applicable to leveraged companies. Two versions of CAPM (market or industry) have been considered. A recent application of the dividend theory to business valuation is described in Brusov and Filatova (2025b), Brusov and Filatova (2025c) and Brusov et al. (2025), where a new approach to business valuation was developed, including the monograph (Brusov and Filatova 2025c).

References

Angotti M, de Lacerda Moreira R, Hipólito Bernardes do Nascimento J, Neto de Almeida Bispo O (2018) Analysis of an equity investment strategy based on accounting and financial reports in Latin American markets. Reficont Rev Finanças Contabilidade Da Unimep 5:22–40

Barbi M (2011) On the risk-neutral value of debt tax shields. Appl Financ Econ 22:251–258

Brusov PN, Filatova TV (2025a) Business valuation and company value: New qualitative approaches considering business and financial risks. Springer Nature Publishing, pp.1–654

Brusov PN, Filatova TV (2025b) Efficiency of investment projects: Modern investment models and their applications. Springer Nature Publishing, pp.1–843

Brusov PN, Filatova TV, Kulik VL (2024) Capital asset pricing model (CAPM) 2.0: Account of business and financial risk. Finance: Theory and Practice. 28(2):128–142. https://doi.org/10.26794/2587-5671-2024-28-2-128-142

Brusov PN, Filatova TV, Orekhova NP (2021) Ratings: Critical analysis and new approaches of quantitative and qualitative methodology. Springer Nature Publishing, pp.1–369

Brusov PN, Filatova TV, Orekhova NP (2022) Generalized Modigliani–Miller theory: Applications in corporate finance, investments, taxation and ratings. Springer Nature Publishing, pp.1–362

Brusov PN, Filatova TV, Orekhova NP (2023) The Brusov–Filatova–Orekhova theory of capital structure: Applications in corporate finance, investments, taxation and ratings. Springer Nature Publishing, pp.1–7692

Baumol W, Panzar JG, Willig RD (1982) Contestable markets and the theory of industry structure. Harcourt College Publishers, New York

Becker DM (2021) The difference between Modigliani–Miller and Miles–Ezzell and its consequences for the valuation of annuities. Cogent Econ Financ 9:1

Becker DM (2022) Getting the valuation formulas right when it comes to annuities. Manag Financ 48:470

Berk J, De Marzo P (2007a) Corporate finance. Pearson-Addison Wesley, Boston

Berk J, De Marzo P (2007b) Corporate finance. Pearson-Addison Wesley, Boston

Bhattacharya S (1978) Project valuation with mean-reacting cash flows. J Financ 33:1317–1331

Black F (1986) Noise. J Financ 41:529–543

Brealey RA, Myers SC (1981) Principles of corporate finance, 1st edn. McGraw-Hill, New York

Brealey RA, Myers SC, Allen F (2014) Principles of corporate finance, 11th edn. McGraw-Hill, New York

Brusov P, Filatova T (2023) Capital structure theory: past, present, future. Mathematics 11(3):616. https://doi.org/10.3390/math11030616

Brusov P, Filatova T (2025a) Qualitatively new approach to business valuation and company value. Mathematics 13(1):80. https://doi.org/10.3390/math13010080

Brusov P, Filatova T (2025b) Business valuation and company value: new qualitative approaches considering business and financial risks. Springer, London, p 759

Brusov P, Filatova T (2025c) Business valuation and company value: new horizons. Theor Econ Lett 16(5):1

Brusov P, Filatova T, Orehova N, Kulik V (2015) The golden age of the company: (three colors of company's time). J Rev Glob Econ 4:21–42

Brusov P, Filatova T, Orehova N, Eskindarov M (2018a) Modern corporate finance, investments, taxation and ratings, 2nd edn. Springer, London, pp 1–571

Brusov P, Filatova T, Orehova N, Kulk V (2018b) A "golden age" of the companies: conditions of its existence. J Rev Global Econ 7:88–103

Brusov P, Filatova T, Orekhova N (2022) Generalized Modigliani–Miller theory: applications in corporate finance, investments, taxation and ratings. Springer, London, p 362. https://doi.org/10.1007/978-3-030-93893-2

Brusov P, Filatova T, Kulik V (2023a) Capital asset pricing model 2.0: account of business and financial risk. Preprints. https://doi.org/10.20944/preprints202310.0347.v1

Brusov P, Filatova T, Orekhova N (2023b) The Brusov–Filatova–Orekhova theory of capital structure: applications in corporate finance, investments, taxation and ratings. Springer, London, p 769

Brusov PN, Filatova TV, Kulik VL (2024) Capital asset pricing model (CAPM) 20: account of business and financial risk. Financ Theory Pract 28(2):128–142. https://doi.org/10.26794/2587-5671-2024-28-2-128-142

Brusov PN, Filatova TV, Kulik VL (2025) Cost of equity and dividend policy. Financ Theory Pract 29(3):229–260. https://doi.org/10.26794/2587-5671-2025-29-3-229-260

Cooper I, Nyborg KG (2018) Consistent valuation of project finance and LBO's using the flow-to-equity method. Eur Financ Manag 24:34–52

Dimitropoulos P (2014) Capital structure and corporate governance of soccer clubs: European evidence. Manag Res Rev 37:658–678

El-Chaarani H, Abraham R, Skaf Y (2022) The impact of corporate governance on the financial performance of the banking sector in the MENA (middle eastern and North African) region: an immunity test of banks for COVID-19. J Risk Financ Manag 15:82

Farber A, Gillet R, Szafarz AA (2006a) General formula for the WACC. Int J Bus 11:211–218

Farber A, Gillet R, Szafarz A (2006b) A general formula for the *WACC*. Int J Bus 11:211–218

Fernandez PA (2006a) General formula for the WACC: a comment. Int J Bus 11:219

Fernandez P (2006b) A general formula for the *WACC*: a comment. Int J Bus 11:219

Filatova T, Orehova N, Brusova A (2008) Weighted average cost of capital in the theory of Modigliani–Miller, modified for a finite life-time company. Vestnik Finansovogo Universiteta Bull Financ Univ 48:68–77

Franc-Dąbrowska J, Mądra-Sawicka M, Milewska A (2021) Energy sector risk and cost of capital assessment-companies and investors perspective. Energies 14:1613

Hamada R (1969) Portfolio analysis, market equilibrium, and corporate finance. J Financ 24:13–31

Hamada R (1972) The effect of the firm's capital structure on the systematic risk of common stocks. J Financ 1972:435–452

Harris R, Pringle J (1985a) Risk-adjusted discount rates-extension form the average-risk case. J Financ Res 8:237–244

Harris RS, Pringle JJ (1985b) Risk-adjusted discount rates-extensions from the average-risk case. J Financ Res 8:237–244

Luiz K, Cruz M (2015) The relevance of capital structure on firm performance: a multivariate analysis of publicly traded Brazilian companies. Rev Educação e Pesquisa Em Contabilidade (REPeC) Brasília 9:384–401

Miles JA, Ezzell JR (1980) The weighted average cost of capital, perfect capital markets, and project life: a clarification. J Financ Quant Anal 15:719–730

Miller M (1977) Debt and taxes. J Financ 32:261–275. https://doi.org/10.1111/j.1540-6261.1977.tb03267.x

Miller MH (1985) Kevin rock dividend policy under asymmetric information. J Financ 40(4):1031–1051. https://doi.org/10.1111/j.1540-6261.1985.tb02362.x

Modigliani F, Miller M (1958) The cost of capital, corporate finance, and the theory of investment. Am Econ Rev 48:261–297

Modigliani F, Miller M (1963) Corporate income taxes and the cost of capital: a correction. Am Econ Rev 53:147–175

Modigliani F, Miller M (1966) Some estimates of the cost of capital to the electric utility industry 1954–1957. Am Econ Rev 56:333–391

Mundi HS, Kaur P, Murty RLN (2022) A qualitative inquiry into the capital structure decisions of overconfident finance managers of family-owned businesses in India. Qual Res Financ Mark 14:357–379

Myers S (2001) Capital structure. J Econ Perspect 15:81–102

Raimo N, de Nuccio E, Giakoumelou A, Petruzzella F, Vitolla F (2021) Non-financial information and cost of equity capital: an empirical analysis in the food and beverage industry. Br Food J 123(1):49–65. https://doi.org/10.1108/BFJ-03-2020-0278

Sadiq M, Alajlani S, Hussain MS, Bashir F, Chupradit S (2022) Impact of credit, liquidity, and systematic risk on financial structure: comparative investigation from sustainable production. Environ Sci Pollut Res 29:20963–20975

Vergara-Novoa C, Sepúlveda-Rojas JP, Miguel DA, Nicolás R (2018) Cost of capital estimation for highway concessionaires in Chile. J Adv Transp 2018:2153536

Part VI
Conclusions

Chapter 23
Conclusions

The monograph is devoted to the description of innovative approach in the field of taxes and taxation has been developed, within the framework of the Brusov–Filatova–Orekhova (BFO) theory and in its perpetuity limit—Modigliani–Miller (MM) theory under taking into account the conditions of the actual functioning of companies (frequency and method of paying taxes advanced or at the ends of periods), variable income of the company, etc.) (Brusov et al. 2021, 2022, 2023, 2024; Brusov and Filatova 2025a, b).

The analysis examines the impact of the above conditions on the current value of taxes received, which could lead to improvements in tax legislation, as well as the impact of taxes under these conditions on the key financial indicators of the company and its investment projects.

Based on the results obtained, recommendations were developed for the Regulator on the amount, frequency and procedure for paying income tax, as well as the possibility of differentiating tax payments depending on the company's debt burden and other factors. Recommendations were also developed for companies on choosing the method and frequency of tax payment in accordance with tax legislation.

The impact of the tax burden on the company's dividend policy is analyzed. A number of innovative effects are identified that can significantly affect the tax policy of regulators and management decisions of the company's management, in particular in the area of dividend policy.

The structure of monograph is as following:

In **Part I** the impact of taxes at both the microeconomic and macroeconomic levels is discussed. Historical background is provided and the functions of taxes are described in detail.

Part II is devoted to study of the quantitative impact of taxes on the main financial indicators of companies (microeconomic level) and the development of recommendations for the regulator on taxation issues (macroeconomic level) requires the use of modern theories of capital structure: Brusov–Filatova–Orekhova (BFO) and Modigliani–Miller (MM) ones. In this part two these main theories are discussed

P. Brusov and T. Filatova, *Taxes and Taxation*, Contributions to Finance and Accounting, https://doi.org/10.1007/978-3-032-11077-0_23

and analyzed, as well as their numerous modifications and generalizations. Also discussed is the latest stage in the development of the theory of capital structure, which began a couple of years ago and is associated with the adaptation of two main theories of capital structure (Brusov–Filatova–Orekhova and Modigliani–Miller) to the established practice of the functioning of companies. This generalization takes into account the real working conditions of companies.

Taxes have a significant impact on investment efficiency. In **Part III** we describe modern investment models, created by the authors of this monograph from first principles, and well tested in the real economy. Within the framework of these models, we examine the impact of taxes on investment efficiency and study various investment problems, such as the impact of debt financing, leverage, taxation, project duration, financing method and some other parameters on investment efficiency and other problems. In Chapter 14 we look at investment models with debt repayment at the end of the project and their application, and in Chapter 15 we look at investment models with uniform debt repayment and their application.

In **Part IV**, we continue to explore the impact of taxes on investment efficiency. We describe innovative investment models with frequent payments of income tax and interest on debt with payments at the end of the period and advanced ones. Chapter 16 describes investment models with frequent payments of income tax and interest on debt at the end of periods. Chapter 17 describes investment models with advance frequent payments of income tax and interest on debt. The results of two these models are completely different.

PART V is devoted to the description of qualitatively new effects that we discovered in the influence of taxes on investments. In Chapter 18 a problem whether it is possible to increase taxing and conserve a good investment climate in the country is studied.

In Chapter 19 an abnormal influence of growth of tax on profit rate on the efficiency of the investment has been discovered and the answer on the question "Whether it is possible to increase of the investment efficiency, increasing tax on profit rate?" has been done.

In Chapter 20 Optimizing the investment structure of the telecommunication sector company is studied.

In Chapter 21 The Role of the Central Bank and Commercial Banks in Creating and Maintaining of a Favorable Investment Climate in the Country is investigated.

Chapter 22 examines the impact of taxation on the cost of equity and dividend policy of a company.

In **Part VI** Conclusions are made.

References

Brusov PN, Filatova TV, Orekhova NP (2021) Ratings: Critical analysis and new approaches of quantitative and qualitative methodology. Springer Nature Publishing, pp.1–369

Brusov PN, Filatova TV, Kulik VL (2024) Capital asset pricing model (CAPM) 2.0: Account of business and financial risk. Finance: Theory and practice 28(2):128–142. https://doi.org/10.26794/2587-5671-2024-28-2-128-142

Brusov PN, Filatova TV (2025a) Business valuation and company value: New qualitative approaches considering business and financial risks. Springer Nature Publishing, pp.1–654

Brusov PN, Filatova TV (2025b) Efficiency of investment projects: Modern investment models and their applications. Springer Nature Publishing. pp.1–843

Brusov PN, Filatova TV, Orekhova NP (2022) Generalized Modigliani–Miller theory: Applications in corporate finance, investments, taxation and ratings. Springer Nature Publishing, pp.1–362

Brusov PN, Filatova TV, Orekhova NP (2023) The Brusov–Filatova–Orekhova theory of capital structure: Applications in corporate finance, investments, taxation and ratings. Springer Nature Publishing. pp.1–769

MIX
Papier aus verantwortungsvollen Quellen
Paper from responsible sources
FSC® C105338

If you have any concerns about our products,
you can contact us on
ProductSafety@springernature.com

In case Publisher is established outside the EU,
the EU authorized representative is:
Springer Nature Customer Service Center GmbH
Europaplatz 3, 69115 Heidelberg, Germany

Printed by Libri Plureos GmbH
in Hamburg, Germany